Chinese Law
v.
Common Law
中国法与普通法比较

Bilingual Book/双语书籍

Dr. Vivek Jain / 简唯唯珂
Dr. Shouzhi AN / 安寿志

Chinese Law v. Common Law

The authors of chapters in the book have made every effort to give proper recognition to various scholars and their publishers for their ideas by noting proper references and ensuring credit is always given. If any acknowledgements for their contributions have been inadvertently missed in this book, those omissions brought to the editor's attention will be rectified in future editions or reprints and we apologise in advance for any such inadvertent omission(s).

The views, thoughts, and opinions expressed in this book belong solely to the authors and not their employers or contractors or their colleagues/friends/relatives. The book is an honest scholarly attempt to understand laws and does not in any way setting across any political or geopolitical statement(s) of any kind whatsoever.

First Edition: 22 April 2025

ISBN 979-8-89777-933-8

Preface

序言

During the last few years, China has indeed become an economic superpower. No one can be surpr -ised with this achievement, as one of the authors (being not native of China) had seen the potential in the invisible part of China's culture way back in 1999.

在过去几年来，中国确实已成为一个经济大国。没有人会对这一成就感到惊讶，早在 1999 年，本书合著作者中的一位（外国人）就看到了中国非物质文化中的那一部分潜力。

No one can ignore China in the 21st century. That being the case, one must properly understand the invisible factors and contexts surrounding China. *The legal system is the mirror image of any society,* and the comparative law analysis carried out in this book can assist lawyers, judges, professors and teachers, arbitrators, political scientists, students of common law from China, students of Chinese law from countries outside of China to find reasons behind the reasons and to get answers in this book. We hope this book serves the purpose for its readers.

没人可以忽视 21 世纪的中国。在这种情况下，我们必须适当得理解围绕中国的无形事实和背景。法律制度是任一社会的镜像，本书的比较法分析可以帮助律师、法官、教授和老师、仲裁员、政治学家、来自中国的普通法学生、来自中国以外国家的中国法学生找到原因背后的原因，并在本书中得到答案。我们希望这本书对读者有帮助。

These *reasons behind the reasons* for law are often ignored by practising lawyers, judges and laymen. We had to go deeper into the invisible factors and contexts. This book is a project to assist readers to understand the invisible factors and contexts behind law by carrying out comparative analysis of all aspects of Chinese law with the Common Law. It was a huge project, but we hope readers will like the analysis in this book.

这些法律*原因背后的原因*往往被执业律师、法官和非专业人士所忽视。我们必须深入研究那些看不见的因素和背景。本书旨在通过对中国法与普通法的比较分析，帮助读者理解法律背后的无形因素和语境。这是一个大工程，我们希望读者会喜欢本书中的分析。

The journey of the book started with English version and part of research was carried out in his PhD project of one of the authors. Any book about China and Chinese law must be in the native language. Therefore, the author of the English version looked around to collaborate with a learned Chinese lawyer. This bilingual book that is not only the translated version of the book but also updated version meant for readers around the world, in particular, from China and tremendous hard work and updates were carried out by Dr. An Shouzhi over many months.

本书的旅程从英文版开始，部分研究是在其中一位作者的博士项目中进行的。任何关于中国和中国法的书都必须是用母语书写。因此，本书英文版的作者寻找与一位博学的中国律师合作。本书不仅是该书的翻译版本，而是面向全世界特别是中国读者的更新版本，这是安寿志博士数月来辛勤工作和更新的结果。

We felt the comparative analysis of *invisible factors and contexts* is essential to understanding the codes, statutes, case precedents and *law in action in China and how it compares with Common Law*. In fact, as the icing on the cake, we feel that analysis as put forward in the book will make readers well informed as it has made us better lawyers & negotiators. We hope it does the same for readers of this book, who might be professionals in any field.

我们认为，对*无形因素和语境*的比较分析对于理解中国的法典、成文法、判例、现行法以及其与普通法的比较非常重要。事实上，作为锦上添花，本书中的分析使读者了解情况，并成为更好的律师和谈判者。我们希望这对任何领域的专业人士读者也同样有用。

The importance of book lies in the fact that many transnational arbitration and litigation involves elements of common law, civil law, Chinese law, people from all jurisdictions and we hope the book will provide assistance in this respect.

这本书的重要性在于，许多跨国仲裁和诉讼都涉及到普通法、成文法和中国法，以及来自各个司法管辖区的相关人士。我们希望本书在这一领域可以协助大家。

The law is stated as available to me on 31 March 2025.

本书中提及的法律截至 2025 年 3 月 31 日。

Dr. (Capt.) Vivek Jain

简唯唯珂博士（船长）

Dr. An, Shouzhi

安寿志博士

About the Author – Dr., Capt. Vivek Jain

关于作者：简唯唯珂博士（船长）

Dr, Capt. Vivek Jain is a Master Mariner (UK), Barrister (England & Wales) and has a doctorate in international law from prestigious University in China (China University of Political Science and Law). His special forte is in embarking upon difficult contemporary topics, at times comparative or interdisciplinary in nature encompassing law, nautical science, philosophy and management. His earlier published five books are testament to this aspect. He himself regularly deals with topics of Public and Private International Law, Maritime Law, Commercial Law, Arbitration Law, Law of Sea, Nautical science, compliance and last but not the least subtle cultural and geo-political aspects in his practice as Director (Marine Services) based in Singapore. He would like to be called a "*problem solver*" by his clients.

简唯唯珂博士是一名船长（英国），大律师（英格兰和威尔士），拥有中国政法大学的国际法博士学位。他的特长是着手研究困难的当代话题，时常是比较的或跨学科的性质，包括法律、航海科学、哲学和管理。简博士早期出版的五本书足以证明了这一点。简博士担任驻新加坡的海事服务总监，经常处理国际公法和国际私法、海商法、商法、仲裁法、海洋法、航海科学、合规以及并非最不微妙的文化和地缘政治方面的问题。客户尊称简博士为"问题解决者"。

He handles and pursues commercial and maritime international arbitrations and maritime claims in various international forums. One of the major requirements in his role is management of clients. He has also been appointed as arbitrator on various commercial and maritime disputes and has been a committee member of many arbitration institutions for several years including Far East Committee member of LMAA (UK), advisor to Silk Road Arbitration Council (Xiamen, China), panel member at EDAC (Turkey), panel member at BDAC (Brunei). He has worked as a maritime lawyer for many years in London, Shanghai, Hong Kong and Singapore in law firms and insurance companies. He has also worked for a few years as a Senior Lecturer at a University in the UK teaching Maritime and Commercial Law to graduate and postgraduate students.

简唯唯珂博士在世界各地处理商业和海事国际仲裁以及海事索赔。他职责的主要之一是客户管理。他还被任命为各种商业和海事纠纷的仲裁员，多年来一直是许多仲裁机构的委员会成员，包括伦敦海事仲裁协会（英国）远东委员会成员、海丝国际仲裁促进中心的咨询专家（厦门）、土耳其能源争议仲裁中心（EDAC）在册仲裁员、文莱达鲁萨兰国际仲裁中心（BDAC）在册仲裁员。他曾在伦敦、上海、香港和新加坡的律师事务所和保险公司担任海事律师多年，还曾在英国一所大学担任高级讲师若干年，为研究生讲授海商法和商法。

He had sailed on different types of merchant vessels for number of years and completed his Master Mariner Certificate of Competency (unlimited) from the UK with an award. He was awarded Robert Galloway award for highest marks in Class2/1 CoC exams. He was among the few selected to become an On-Scene Commander through a Course by Singapore Maritime and Port Authority in 2001.

简唯唯珂博士曾在不同类型的商船上工作多年，并获得英国颁发的船长合格证书（无限制）。他在一类和二类适任证书考试中获得最高分，被授予 Robert Galloway 奖。在2001 年，他成为被新加坡海事管理局指定的极少数通过考核的现场指挥官。

Over the years, he has pursued an LLB (Hons.) and LLM (Maritime Law) with merit from the University of London, BVC (Very Competent) (London), MBA (Norway), PGC in Compliance (Singapore), PGCE (Singapore) and B.Sc. (N. Sc.) (India) by way of First Class with Distinction from a very selective and prestigious T.S. Rajendra, College of

Nautical Science, India. He was selected to be in cover page with many alumni such as Nobel Prize winners, Mandela and Gandhi on 150-year anniversary of University of London in 2008.
过去多年来，简唯唯珂博士以优异的成绩获得伦敦大学的法学学士（荣誉）和法学硕士（海商法），BVC 课程（非常胜任）（伦敦），MBA（挪威），PGC 合规（新加坡）、教育学研究生证书（新加坡）和理科学士（印度），并获得印度航海学院一等荣誉学士学位。在 2008 年伦敦大学建校 150 周年校庆上，简唯唯珂与诺贝尔奖得主、曼德拉、甘地等众多校友一起被选为封面人物。

He has recently authored/co-authored/edited a few books – (1) authored *Common Law v Chinese Law* (Notion Press, 2019), (2) Co-authored a book, *Comparative Interim Measures – Interim Remedies (England & Wales) v Preservation Measures (China)* (Routledge, 2022), (3) edited and authored a book on *Imprints of History, Religions and Revolutions on law – Perspectives from Prominent Jurisdictions* (Notion Press, 2022) involving top lawyers and jurists, (4) edited and authored a book on *Maritime Skills on Vessels and Shore* (Notion Press, 2023) and (5) edited and authored a book on *The Role of Indian Ocean for Global Peace – Interdisciplinary Issues* (Notion Press, 2023).
简唯唯珂博士撰写、合著和编撰的著作：1、《普通法与中国法》，Notion 出版社，2019；2、《临时措施比较——英格兰和威尔士临时救济与中国保全措施》，Routledge 出版社，2022；3、《历史、宗教和革命对法律的印记——基于领先司法管辖区的视角》，Notion 出版社，2022；4、《船舶和离岸海事技能》，Notion 出版社，2023 年；5、《印度洋对全球和平的角色——跨学科问题》，Notion 出版社，2023 年。

About the Co-author - Dr. An, Shouzhi

关于合著作者：安寿志博士

Dr. An, Shouzhi, Doctor of Laws in International Law from Wuhan University, Master of Law in European Union Law from Stockholm University, Master of Law in Maritime Law from Dalian Maritime University, founding partner of Anjie Broad Law Firm Xiamen Office, Chair of Maritime Silk Road Chamber of International Arbitration Promotion (MSRCIAP), Visiting Scholar at Columbia University in the New York City, Visiting Research Associate at the University of Hong Kong, Standing Director of the Sports Law Research Association of the Law Society of China, Consulting Expert on civil and administrative cases of the Supreme People's Procuratorate of China, Editor-in-Chief of Modern Law Research(USA).
安寿志博士，武汉大学国际法博士，瑞典斯德哥尔摩大学欧盟法硕士，大连海事大学海商法硕士，北京安杰世泽（厦门）律师事务所创始合伙人，海丝国际仲裁促进中心理事长、厦门市第十二批引进高层次“双百计划”领军人才，中国司法部“全国千名涉外律师人才”，中国法学会“全国优秀首席法律咨询专家”，美国哥伦比亚大学访问学者，香港大学访问副研究员，中国法学会体育法学研究会常务理事，最高人民检察院民事和行政案件咨询专家、美国《Modern Law Research》刊物主编。

Dr. An is a licensed lawyer in China, a Registered Foreign Lawyer in Hong Kong and a registered of foreign lawyer before Singapore International Commercial Court, Advisory Member of the Court of Arbitration for Sport Shanghai Hearing Center, Member of Representative Arbitrators' Council of the Singapore Chamber of Maritime Arbitration, Deputy Director of the Arbitrators Appointment Committee of the China Commission of Arbitration for Sport, Member of the International Arbitration Professional Committee of Chongqing Arbitration Commission. He has extensive experience as counsel or arbitrator in more than hundreds arbitration cases under HKIAC, ICC, SIAC, CIETAC, LMAA,

GAFTA, CAS and the United Nations UNCITRAL Arbitration Rules and has seats at AALCO, CAS, CCAS, CIETAC, CMAC, CQAC, HKIAC, LCIA, LMAA, RAC, SCC, SCIA, SCMA, SHIAC, SIAC, XMAC, mediator for investment disputes under the CEPA Investment Agreement between Mainland China and Hong Kong SAR.
安博士具有中国执业律师、香港注册外地律师、新加坡国际商事法庭全权注册外国律师资格，担任国际体育仲裁院上海听证中心咨询专家委员会委员，新加坡海事仲裁院仲裁员代表委员会委员、中国体育仲裁委员会仲裁员聘任委员会副主任委员、重庆仲裁委员会国际仲裁专业委员会委员。具有超过上百宗仲裁案中担任仲裁员或代理律师的经验，担任伦敦国际仲裁院、香港国际仲裁中心、新加坡国际仲裁中心、国际体育仲裁院、俄罗斯仲裁中心、亚非法协香港区域仲裁中心、瑞典斯德哥尔摩商会仲裁院、伦敦海事仲裁协会、新加坡海事仲裁院、香港海事仲裁协会、中国国际经济贸易仲裁委员会、中国海事仲裁委员会、中国体育仲裁委员会、上海国际仲裁中心、深圳国际仲裁院、重庆仲裁委员会、厦门仲裁委员会等仲裁员、内地和香港政府《CEPA 投资协议》投资争端调解员。

2015-2016 Interned at the United Nations Office of Legal Affairs and Visiting Scholar at Columbia University, United States of America, working on the project "International Energy Security and Cooperation under the Belt and Road Initiative: Policies, Projects and Challenges". Awarded by Asia Law Review as Top Shipping Lawyers in Asia Pacific, Legal 500 as Leading Individual of International Arbitration, Shipping, LEGALBAND as Top 15 Innovative Lawyers in China, Legal 500 as Arbitration Powerlist China; China Business Law Journal as A-List Elite Chinese Business Visionaries, and so on.
2015-2016 年在联合国法律事务厅实习工作，哥伦比亚大学访问学者，从事"一带一路倡议下国际能源安全与合作：政策，项目和挑战"研究。Asialaw Reivew 评为"亚太地区一流航运律师"，Legal 500 评为"国际仲裁、航运"代表性人物，入选 LEGALBAND 风云榜：中国大陆地区创新律师 15 强，The Legal 500 首届 Arbitration Powerlist China 榜单，《商法》The A-List 法律精英：中国业务睿见领袖等。

Acknowledgments

致谢

Vivek Jain wishes to thank his better-half Lifei Yang Jain for preparing various tables/diagrams in the book and discussing various aspects of Chinese culture and philosophy when he wanted to go deeper into many aspects. She also assisted in going deeper into the meaning of some Chinese words for his research. He also wishes to thank CUPL, Beijing that provided wonderful environment for him to discuss candidly many aspects of Chinese philosophy and law. In addition, he wishes to thank many professors, barristers, and solicitors from the common law system with who he had either worked or had scholarly debates. Similarly, he wishes to thank his fellow learned and very reputed Chinese lawyer to agree to collaborate on this project. He also wishes to thank many Chinese lawyers, his Chinese law professors, Chinese clients over many years to have allowed him to learn from discussions and experience.

简唯唯珂感谢他的妻子杨琍斐为本书制作了各种表格和图表,并在作者需要深入了解许多中国文化和哲学方面时一起探论，同时协助深入研究一些中文词的含义。简博士还要感谢中国政法大学提供了一个非常好的环境，让作者能够坦诚地讨论中国哲学和中国法律的方方面面。此外，感谢许多与他曾共事和学术讨论的普通法教授、大律师和事务律师们。同样，感谢学识渊博、声誉卓著的中国律师安寿志博士同意在本项目上合作，以及感谢同许多中国律师、中国法教授、中国客户多年来的讨论和经验学习。

An, Shouzhi wishes to thank Dr., Capt. Vivek Jain for his sincere invitation and collaboration in this book project. Based on the author's study and visiting scholar life and observations in Stockholm University, Columbia University in the New York City and the University of Hong Kong, as well as years of experience in international law and international arbitration, and foreign-related legal services, the author is well aware of the role of common law in international commercial and maritime dispute resolution, and the significance of China in the process of modernization and internationalization and of the construction of prominent place of international commercial and maritime dispute resolution. Thanks colleagues from Anjie Broad Law Firm Xiamen Office and Maritime Silk Road Chamber of International Arbitration Promotion, especially Ms. Chen Linghan, Mr. Li Jilong (lawyer), Mr. Wang Pengxin (lawyer), Mr. Zhan Shudi, Mr. You Zihao and Mr. He Chuyang for their discussion and assistance. It is those busy work that has made this book available faster.

安寿志籍此感谢海丝国际仲裁促进中心咨询专家简唯唯珂博士对本书项目的诚挚邀请和合作，基于作者在瑞典斯德哥尔摩大学、美国哥伦比亚大学和香港大学的留学和访学经历和观察，以及多年来对国际法、国际仲裁以及涉外法律服务的经验，作者深知普通法在国际商事海事争议解决中的作用，以及对中国在现代化和国际化进程中对于国际商事海事争议解决优选地建设的借鉴作用。感谢安杰世泽律师事务所以及海丝国际仲裁促进中心的同事们，特别是陈凌涵女士、李纪龙律师、王鹏鑫律师、詹书迪先生、尤梓豪先生、何楚阳先生的讨论和帮助，正是大家在忙碌工作之余的付出让本书得以更快面世。

TABLE OF CONTENT
目录

Chapter 1 - Introduction

第一章 - 介绍

1.1 Global Undercurrents and China's rise

全球暗涌与中国崛起

As international trade has become more globalized over the last few decades, another important parallel development has also taken place: the People's Republic of China ("PRC") has emerged as an economic powerhouse. A sizable amount of global trade in goods and services either originates in the PRC or is destined for the PRC. Nowadays, therefore, International Trade includes numerous connections and networks with the PRC, centered around trade in goods and services. These developments have had a profound impact, comparable to the changes that occurred in the late nineteenth century,[1] when the Qing dynasty was coerced into opening up the economy to western powers. This opening up led to demands by the Qing elites to gradually introduce changes in then-existing laws.

在过去数十年间，国际贸易日益全球化。与此同时，另一重大发展也呈现在世人面前：中华人民共和国崛起成为经济强国。如今，规模可观的全球商品和服务贸易量，要么源自中国，要么流向中国。可以说，当前国际贸易以商品和服务贸易为核心，涵盖了众多与中国相关的联系与网络。这些发展影响深远，堪比十九世纪晚期清朝被迫向西方强国开放经济时所产生的变化。彼时，这一开放促使清朝精英逐步在当时的法律中引入变革。

Dynasties **朝代**	**Year** **年份**	**Comments** **注释**
Xia Dynasty 夏朝	2300-1800 BCE	
Shang Dynasty 商朝	1600 – 1045 BCE	1800-1200 BCE, according to a few other historians. 少数史学家认为是公元前 1800-1200 年。

[1] Refer to Table 1 - Ancient Chinese History.
参照表 1 - 中国古代史。

Western Zhou 西周	1046 – 771 BCE	1122-255 BCE, Combined Western and Eastern according to a few historians. It covered the central plains of present PRC. 公元前 1122-255 年，少数史学家认为是东西的结合。它覆盖了现在中国的中部平原地区。
Zheng Kingdom 郑国	806-375 BCE	
Kingdom of Lu 鲁国	722 -481 BCE	Around the present-day Shandong province. 在现山东省一带。
Jin 晋朝	772-468 BCE	Vassal state of Zhou. 周的属国。
Eastern Zhou 东周	771 – 221 BCE	Spring and Autumn Period (c. 771-476 BCE) & the Warring States Period (c.476-221 BCE). 春秋时期（约公元前 771-476 年）和战国时期（约公元前 476-221 年）。
Qin Dynasty 秦朝	221-205 BCE	Famous for reuniting various provinces in a big land mass, into what is now called China. 因将各省统一在一块大地上而闻名，这块大地就是现在所称的中国。
Han Dynasty 汉朝	206 BCE - 220 CE	
Three Kingdoms 三国	220-280 CE	
Jin Dynasty 晋朝	265-420 CE	
Northern & Southern Dynasties 南北朝	420-589 CE	
Sui Dynasty 隋朝	581-618 CE	

Tang Dynasty 唐朝	681-906 CE	
Song Dynasty 宋朝	960-1279 CE	
Yuan Dynasty 元朝	1206-1367 CE	
Ming Dynasty 明朝	1368-1644 CE	
Qing Dynasty 清朝	1644-1911 CE	Last Dynasty before Imperial system was abolished. 废除帝制前的最后一个朝代。

Table 1 – Ancient Chinese Dynasties

表 1 - 中国古代各朝

In a somewhat similar way, the profound economic prosperity that has occurred in the PRC in the past has created a demand for a thorough analysis of current laws to enable future legal reforms to reach specific outcomes to continue this momentum of economic growth in the PRC.

与此类似，过去中国经济的蓬勃发展也要求对现行法律进行全面分析，使未来的法律改革能够取得具体成果，以延续中国的经济增长势头。

In order to appreciate just how profound these economic changes have been to the PRC, it is necessary to look back at the history of its economy since the early 20th century. At the end of the 1940s, the Chinese economy was nearly bankrupt. Still greater economic suffering came about as a result of the Great Leap Forward (1958-60) and the Cultural Revolution (1966-76).[2] The decades of economic suffering were followed by market reforms in 1978, and from that time until 2008, real GDP growth in the PRC was at an annual rate of almost 10%.[3] This economic growth was nearly double that of India and even higher than that of newly industrialised economies in the Asia-Pacific region, such as South Korea and Singapore. This

为了解过去经济变革对中国的深远影响，有必要回顾中国自二十世纪初以来的经济发展历程。二十世纪四十年代末，中国经济几近崩溃。“大跃进”（1958-60 年）和“文化大革命”（1966-76 年）给经济带来了更大的苦难。在数十载的经济苦难之后，1978 年进行了市场改革。从那时起至 2008 年，中国实际 GDP 年增长率近 10%。这一经济增速几乎是印度的两倍，甚至高于亚太地区如韩国和新加坡之类的新兴工业化经济体。中国如此惊人

[2] Rongxing Guo, *An Introduction to the Chinese Economy: The Driving Forces Behind Modern Day China* (Singapore: John Wiley & Sons, 2010), 11.
郭嵘兴,《中国经济导论：现代中国的驱动力》，新加坡：John Wiley & Sons, 2010, 第11页。

[3] Ibid.

striking economic growth has to be seen in the context of the PRC's land mass, which is much bigger than that of most of these other countries.[4]

的经济增长成就，需结合广袤的国土面积来看待，毕竟其面积远超其他大多数国家。

The impressive rate of economic growth was supported by an increase in consumption of commodities, as the reserves of these commodities available in the PRC are lower on a per capita basis.[5] The growth in consumption led to the growth, at an unprecedented level never seen before in human history, of numerous PRC-related commodity transactions, contracts, and finalised business deals.

由于中国的人均商品储备量较低，商品消费的增长支撑了令人瞩目的经济增速。消费的增长导致与中国有关的大量商品交易、合同和最终商业交易的增长，达到了人类历史上前所未有的水平。

It has also transformed the PRC's agriculture-based society into an industrial society in a very short span of time.[6] The PRC's Human Development Index ("HDI") in some provinces/cities such as Shanghai, Beijing and Tianjin is comparable to that in advanced economies, and currently the PRC's overall HDI itself is in the category of middle-income countries.[7] However, the unprecedented economic development observed in the PRC is not matched by an equivalent political development; this has led to a massive drop in accountability and control of corruption, most notably from 2002-2007.[8]

它还在很短的时间内将中国以农业为基础的社会转型为工业社会。中国部分省市（如上海、北京和天津）的人类发展指数（"HDI"）可与发达经济体媲美，目前中国的整体人类发展指数本身已跻身中等收入国家行列。然而，中国经济的空前发展导致了问责制和腐败控制的大幅下降，尤其是在 2002-2007 年期间。

The economic development discussed above was supported by a high saving rate and a large supply of labour, keeping the rate of return on investment profitable.[9] The PRC's economic growth was supported by the intensifying undercurrents of globalisation, as a result of which the PRC gained massively through access to Foreign Direct Investment ("FDI"), technology, modern management techniques, demand for its manufactured goods, and increased efficiency due to the competition in the globalised market. This rapid economic growth was accompanied by rising income levels at the start of reforms to foster increased competition, due to the official policy of "getting some people rich first." A discussion of rapid

高储蓄率和大量劳动力供应支撑了上述经济发展，使投资回报率保持在有利可图的水平。中国的经济增长得到了全球化流动的支持，在全球化的市场竞争中，中国通过获得外商直接投资（"FDI"）、技术、现代管理技术、对制成品的需求和效率的提高而获得了巨大的利益。在经济快速增长的同时，由于官方实行"让一部分人先富起来"的政策，在改革之初收入水平不断提高，促进了竞争。在讨论经济快速增长和经济理念时，不能

[4] Ibid., 111.
[5] Ibid., 35–37.
[6] Ibid., 61.
[7] Ibid., 63.
[8] Ibid., 104–5.
[9] Ibid., 113.

economic growth and economic philosophy cannot be complete without mention of PRC's core leader Deng Xiaoping, who said:

不提到中国的核心领导人邓小平，他曾说过：

> To take the road to socialism is to realize common prosperity step by step. Our plan is as follows: where conditions permit, some areas may develop faster than others; those that develop faster can help promote the progress of those that lag behind, until all become prosperous. If the rich keep getting richer and the poor poorer, polarization will emerge. The socialist system [emphasis added] must and can avoid polarization. One way is for the areas that become prosperous first to support the poor areas by paying more taxes or turning in more profits to the state. Of course, this should not be done too soon. At present, we don't want to dampen the vitality of the developed areas or encourage the practice of having everyone "eat from the same big pot." We should study when to raise this question and how to settle it.[10]

> "走社会主义道路，就是要逐步实现共同富裕。共同富裕的构想是这样提出的：一部分地区有条件先发展起来，一部分地区发展慢点，先发展起来的地区带动后发展的地区，最终达到共同富裕。如果富人越来越富，穷人越来越穷，两极分化就会出现。社会主义制度就应该而且能够避免两极分化。解决的办法之一，就是先富起来的地区多交点利税，支持贫困地区的发展。当然，太早这样办也不行，现在不能剥削发达地区的活力，也不能鼓励吃'大锅饭'。什么时候突出地提出和解决这个问题，要研究。"

The PRC, as a socialist nation founded in 1949, remained a closed economy for a number of years, as it preferred to limit itself to trading with other socialist states. This was similar to the *Hanjin policy* of the Qing Dynasty (1644-1911) banning particular kinds of maritime voyages.[11] However, due to the economic woes suffered during the Cultural revolution, the PRC abandoned this closed economic policy and initiated market reforms. As early as 1979 it implemented a law concerning *Joint Ventures with Chinese and Foreign Investment*; also in 1979 it granted a few provinces such as Guangdong the authority to initiate flexible measures to advance commerce, called *xian zou yi bu.*[12] In 1984, a further fourteen coastal cities were allowed to form Special Economic Zones; later, Economic Development Zones were created to

作为 1949 年成立的社会主义国家，中国曾多年一直是一个封闭的经济体，因为它倾向于只与其他社会主义国家进行贸易。这类似于清朝（1644-1911 年）禁止特定种类海上航行的"汉人政策"。然而，由于"文化大革命"期间的经济困境，中国放弃了这种封闭的经济政策，开始了市场改革。早在 1979 年，中国就实施了《中外合资经营企业法》；1979 年，中国还授权广东等少数省份采取灵活措施促进商业发展，即"先走一步"。1984 年，又有 14 个沿海城市获准成立经济特区；后来又成立了经济开发

[10] Deng Xiaoping in 1992 as quoted in Guo, *Introduction to the Chinese Economy*, 110.
邓小平1992年讲话引自郭,《中国经济概论》，第110页。

[11] Guo, *Introduction to the Chinese Economy*, 130–131.
郭,《中国经济导论：现代中国的驱动力》，第130-131页。

[12] Ibid., 134.

enhance economic development.

区，以促进经济发展。

The gradual movement of the PRC towards a market economy gained momentum and impetus when it joined the World Trade Organisation ("WTO") on December 11, 2001.[13] From the point of view of legal reforms, the PRC abolished laws that were deemed inconsistent with the then-existing WTO regulations. Market reforms, meanwhile, followed the four-stage process of decentralisation followed by centralisation (*shou*), which was followed by rigidity and again followed by decentralisation (*fang*) as a result of political compromises made at the level of the top leadership of the PRC.[14]

2001 年 12 月 11 日，中国加入了世界贸易组织（“世贸组织”），这为中国逐步走向市场经济增添了动力和活力。从法律改革的角度来看，中国废除了被认为与当时的世贸组织规定不一致的法律。与此同时，中国最高领导层的政治智慧，市场改革经历了先分权后集权（“收”）、再先僵化后分权（“放”）的四个阶段。

Even though the PRC's economic growth is unprecedented, it has to be seen from a global perspective as its GDP per capita is still considerably less than that of the US and other developed countries, which signifies that there remain challenges that need to be overcome. The analysis or comparison of law has to be seen within this context as well. Income disparity exists between rural and urban areas and the gap ratio in per capita income in these two areas has increased in the last few years, rising to nearly 3.5 in 2008.[15] Based on the above quote from Deng, and to reduce the income disparities between provinces, the "western region Development Strategy" (*xibu da kaifa*) was introduced to raise the prosperity level of the PRC's western regions.

尽管中国的经济增长是史无前例的，但必须从全球的角度来看待，因为中国的人均国内生产总值仍然大大低于美国和其他发达国家，这表明中国仍然面临着需要克服的挑战。对法律的分析或比较也必须在这一背景下进行。城乡之间存在收入差距，这两个地区的人均收入差距比在过去几年中有所上升，2008 年上升到近 3.5。根据邓小平的上述论述，为了缩小各省之间的收入差距，中国提出了“西部大开发战略”，以提高中国西部地区的繁荣水平。

In the authors' view, the rate of legal development is affected by the level of prosperity and income disparity, and this factor should not be overlooked in any comparison between the legal systems. The understanding of the country through its legal system can be achieved by understanding this context. Income disparity has a direct effect on the less privileged, and also on

笔者认为，法律发展的速度受到繁荣程度和收入差距的影响，在进行任何法律制度比较时都不应忽视这一因素。了解了这一背景，才能通过法律制度了解国家。收入差距直接影响

13 For many experts, the making of the PRC as a market economy is still a work in progress due to the domination of state enterprises in the PRC's economy. It is also a major bone of contention in the current trade war between the two largest economies of the world, that is, the US and the PRC.
在许多专家看来，由于国有企业在中国经济中的主导地位，中国的市场经济建设仍在进行之中。这也是当前世界上最大的两个经济体，即美国和中国之间贸易战的主要争论焦点。

14 Guo, *Introduction to the Chinese Economy*, 163.
郭，《中国经济导论：现代中国的驱动力》，第163页。

15 Ibid., 119.

the ability of new or developing corporations to access the investments with a higher rate of return. Another equally important factor affecting them is a general lack of credit liquidity in the system. All such factors directly affect the legal system as it will have the effect of reducing access to justice and thereby affecting litigants' ability to seek remedies in court against powerful business corporations.

到弱势群体，也影响到新兴或发展中企业获得高回报率投资的能力。另一个同样重要的影响因素是整个系统普遍缺乏信贷流动性。所有这些因素都会直接影响法律制度，因为它们会减少诉诸司法的机会，从而影响诉讼当事人对强大的商业公司通过法庭寻求救济的能力。

It is no secret that even though there is a body of PRC laws to govern commerce, the experience at ground level can differ widely. It is apparent from the experiences of many businessmen that there is some discrepancy in terms of enforcement of these central regulations as exhibited by central, provincial and local officials in the PRC.[16] This issue, in the authors' own experience, is evident in many provincial courts in the PRC, which are at a considerable distance from Beijing.

众所周知，尽管中国有一整套法律法规来规范商业活动，但在实际操作中却存在很大差异。从许多商人的经验来看，中国的中央、省级和地方官员在执行这些中央法规时有时有一些差异。根据笔者的亲身经历，这个问题在中国许多省级法院都很明显，因为这些法院与北京相距甚远。

In the authors' view, this type of economic development, which is unprecedented in human history, has also led to enormous changes in society. To sustain such unprecedented economic growth, the level of economic growth brought about through increased exports, imports, business and commercial transactions has to be maintained to avoid catastrophic social unrest. This has necessitated immense changes in the PRC legal system in the past; for example, new laws have been introduced with the intention of improving the PRC legal system at provincial level (*sheng*), autonomous body level (zi zhi qu), municipalities controlled by the central government in Beijing (*zhixiashi*), and in the special administrative regions of Hong Kong and Macao.

笔者认为，这种人类历史上前所未有的经济发展也导致了社会的巨大变化。为了维持这种前所未有的经济增长，必须保持通过增加出口、进口、商业和商业交易带来的经济增长水平，以避免灾难性的社会动荡。这就要求中华人民共和国的法律制度在过去发生巨大变化，例如，在省、自治区、直辖市以及香港和澳门特别行政区，都出台了旨在完善中国法律制度的新法律。

[16] Ibid., 117.

1.2 Role of Legal Systems in Business Disputes

法律体系在商事争议中的作用

As economic growth accelerates in any country, it boosts commerce and all-round development within its frontiers. This increase in commerce & trade leads to even further investments (domestic & foreign direct investment), contracts, trade, and movements of people; as a result, augmented transactions are carried out by that country's own citizens and organisations. These transactions transpire within domestic trade as well as international trade through export or import of goods and services from other countries.

国家经济增速加快，其境内的商业和全面发展也会随之增长。商贸增长会带来更多的投资（国内外直接投资）、合同、贸易和人员流动；因此，该国公民和组织会进行更多交易。这些交易既包括国内贸易，也包括通过从其他国家出口或者进口商品和服务进行的国际贸易。

However, if disputes occur during these transactions, and the parties involved cannot resolve their differences amicably, they will have to turn to the courts in a particular jurisdiction. This jurisdiction could have been selected by the parties in their contracts, or it could be the jurisdiction which is closely related to the dispute. In developed countries with fully developed legal systems, the courts are the source of economic development as they are not only involved in resolving the commercial disputes of stakeholders in its economy, but also assist in restraining legislative and bureaucratic excesses.[17]

然而，倘若交易期间产生争议，而有关各方又无法友善地化解分歧，则须求助于特定司法管辖区的法院。该司法管辖区可能是双方在合同中选定，也可能是与争议密切相关的司法管辖区。在法律体系完善的发达国家，法院是经济发展的源泉，因为法院不仅参与解决经济体中利益相关者的商业纠纷解决，还协助限制立法和官僚主义的过度行为。

However, the courts in many East Asian countries, which have been experiencing breakneck economic growth for a while, are not given high status, and as a result are considered as secondary to the legislature. In some cases, the judiciary is not fully independent. The claimants in any civil litigation will endeavour to establish the validity of their claims, and thereafter will try to succeed in their claims, or to reach an outcome as close as possible to what they are demanding from the defendants. The defendant will try to avoid any of the two outcomes that the claimants are hoping

但在许多长期遭遇经济发展瓶颈的东亚国家，法院地位偏低，因此被视为立法机构的次要机构。在某些情况下，司法机构并非完全独立。在任何民事诉讼中，原告都会尽力确定其诉讼请求的有效性，并在此基础上努力使其诉讼请求获得成功，或取得与其向被告提出的要求尽可能接近的结果。被告会试图通过民事司法系统体系规避原告所希望的两种结果中的任何一种。

[17]John Gillespie, "Rethinking the Role of Judicial Independence in Socialist-Transforming East Asia," *I.C.L.Q.* 56, no. 4 (2007): 838. 约翰·吉莱斯皮，"反思司法独立在东亚社会主义转型中的作用"，《国际刑法杂志》，I.C.L.Q.56，第4期，2007，第838页。

for by using the civil justice system.[18]

At the same time, there are stakeholders in the civil courts, and in the businesses that may be affected by the filing of a case by the claimants. These other stakeholders in the courts are the judges and even the states where these courts are located. The aim of the judges is to reach a just resolution to the dispute before them; the states' purpose, however, will be similar in most scenarios, as both the executive and legislative branch of any country will expect the civil courts that are manned by an independent judiciary to resolve commercial disputes in such a way as to enhance trade between the parties.

同时，民事法庭和企业中也有利益相关者，他们可能会受到原告提起诉讼的影响。法院的其他利益相关者是法官，甚至是法院所在国家。法官的目的是公正地解决所审理的争议；而国家的目的在大多数情况下是相似的，因为任何国家的行政和立法部门都希望由独立司法机构管理的民事法庭能够以促进相关方贸易的方式解决商事争议。

Any potential commercial or business disputes in commerce and trade are hurdles to enhancing trade and increasing the Gross Domestic Product ("GDP") of any country,; it is in the interests of the state that citizens, foreign investors and traders, businessmen and business organisations, all have trust in its civil courts.

商事和贸易中任何潜在的商业或业务纠纷都是促进贸易和提高国家国内生产总值（“GDP”）的障碍，因此，公民、外国投资者和贸易商、企业家和商业组织都信任国家的民事法庭，这符合国家的利益。

The trust of these stakeholders, who carry out commercial activities, is the vital factor to sustain and enhance the economic activities that ultimately benefit citizens through increased GDP per person, which will raise their standard of living, improve their quality of life and even encourage sustainable development. For example, England & Wales, a common law jurisdiction, has been a popular destination for resolving commercial, maritime and corporate disputes for over one hundred fifty year, even where the parties or the subject matter of the disputes have no connection whatsoever with England & Wales. Wales has a unified justice system with England, and all laws of England in commercial matters and civil procedure are applicable in Wales. England & Wales are also the most popular centers for resolving disputes through arbitration. The authors will refer to the courts of England & Wales following common law as

这些开展商业活动的利益相关方的信任是巩固和增强经济活动的重要因素，而这些经济活动最终会通过增加人均国内生产总值使公民受益，提高生活水平、改善生活质量、甚至于鼓励可持续发展。例如，英格兰和威尔士作为一个普通法司法管辖区，一百五十多年来一直是解决商事、海事和公司争议的热门目的地，即使当事人或争议标的与英格兰和威尔士毫无联系。威尔士与英格兰司法系统统一，并且英格兰在商事和民事诉讼程序方面的所有法律均适用于威尔士。英格兰和威尔士也是最受欢迎的通过仲裁解决争议的中心。笔者将把遵循普通法的英格兰和威尔士法院称为“英格兰法院”。

[18] J.A. Jolowicz, "Civil Litigation: What is it For?" *Camb. L.J.* 67, no. 3 (2008): 67.
J.A. 乔洛维茨，“民事诉讼：为了什么？”，《剑桥法律杂志》 67，第三期，2008，第67页。

'English Courts'.

Initially, the popularity of English courts in the Commonwealth was because Great Britain was the major imperial power of the world for over two centuries. However, the major factor for the popularity of English courts in recent years is that its legal system is readily accepted by litigants around the world due to its ability to evolve and impart justice in commercial disputes. Most importantly, in general, English judges feel confident to employ their discretionary power within the common law system. In the authors' view, these English judges are also empowered to a certain extent due to their training in a common law system.

起初，英格兰法院之所以在英联邦广受欢迎，是因英国在两个多世纪的时间里一直是世界上主要的帝国主义强国。然而，近年来英格兰法院受欢迎的主要原因是其法律体系能够在商事纠纷中不断发展并伸张正义，因此很容易被世界各地的诉讼当事人所接受。最重要的是，英格兰法官通常有信心在普通法体系内运用他们的自由裁量权。在笔者看来，由于在普通法体系中接受的培训，这些英格兰法官也在一定程度上获得了权力。

On the other hand, the PRC has become an economic superpower only in the twenty-first century. Therefore, commercial stakeholders, both domestic and foreign, have an interest in the legal system and philosophy of PRC not only to resolve disputes, but also to provide necessary assurances that their hard-earned money will be protected without bias, if anything were to go wrong. Furthermore, the expectations of these stakeholders for the PRC courts would be in relation to the remedies available through these PRC courts.

在另一方面，中国在二十一世纪才成为经济强国。因此，国内外的商业利益相关者都对中国的法律体系和理念感兴趣，这不仅是为了解决争议，也是为了放心，确保他们辛苦挣来的钱在出现任何问题时都能受到公正的保护。此外，这些利益相关者对中国法院的期望会与中国法院提供的补救措施有关。

These stakeholders will expect that these remedies are well founded in its civil procedural law and will assist them in time of need. Therefore, a comparison of the two jurisdictions is appropriate in the contemporary context. Because businessmen and commercial interests from the PRC are investing abroad or involved in big-ticket projects, this book will provide a timely and relevant comparison of the two legal systems & philosophies.

这些利益相关方会期望这些救济措施在其民事诉讼法中有充分的依据，并能在他们需要的时候为他们提供帮助。因此，在当代背景下对这两个司法管辖区进行比较是合适的。由于来自中国的企业家和商业利益集团正在海外投资或参与大型项目，本书将对两种法律体系和理念提供适时的相关比较。

An important question that could be asked by the readers is whether the jurisdiction of England & Wales, a common law jurisdiction can really be compared with the jurisdiction of PRC. A few of the reasons to argue against such comparison could be the rapid advent of PRC as an economic superpower

读者可能会提出的一个重要问题是，英格兰和威尔士作为一个普通法司法管辖区，其司法管辖权是否确实可以与中国的司法管辖权相比较。反对这种比较的几个理由可能是，中国作为一个

and a completely different system from England & Wales. A justification for the comparison of a Western legal system with the jurisdiction of the rising economic superpower such as the PRC has been suggested by Eberle.[19] In particular, Eberle has praised old civilisations such as the PRC for their rules and norms that could assist even scholars trained in advanced common law legal system such as England & Wales:

经济超级大国的迅速崛起以及其与英格兰和威尔士拥有完全不同的制度体系。埃伯勒（Eberle）提出了将西方法律体系与正在崛起的经济超级大国（如中国）的司法体系进行比较的理由。埃伯勒尤其赞扬了中国等古老文明的规则和规范，这些规则和规范甚至可以帮助在那些在英格兰和威尔士等先进的普通法法律体系中接受培训的学者：

> Evaluation of older cultures in place before the rise of legal systems can yield important information about the basic elements and structure of modern societies. Looking at ourselves through these mirrors could reveal important ideas, norms, rules or principles, forcing a reevaluation that may improve the social order or, alternatively, lead us to confirm the tenets of our own legal system.[20]

> 对法律体系兴起之前的古老文化进行评估，可以获得有关现代社会基本要素和结构的重要信息。透过这些镜子来反观我们自身，可以揭示重要的思想、规范、规则或原则，迫使我们进行有益于改善社会秩序的再评估，抑或引导我们确认自身法律体系中的信条。

As a means to show the comparative difference between the philosophies, let us start by highlighting the difference of philosophy in Civil Procedure Law of both the systems. These differences have a profound effect on the way the disputes are litigated in the respective courts. For example, *Civil Procedure Rules 1998* (hereinafter "CPR")[21] of England & Wales, in particular CPR r.1.1 (1) states *inter alia* that:

为了说明两种理念之间的比较差异，让我们首先强调两种体系的民事诉讼法在理念上的差异。这些差异对各自法院审理争议的方式有着深远的影响。例如，英格兰和威尔士《1998 年民事诉讼程序规则》（以下简称“CPR”），CPR 第 1.1(1) 条具体规定：

> These Rules are a new procedural code with the *overriding objective* of enabling the court to deal with cases justly and at proportionate cost [emphasis added].

> 这些规则是一部新的程序法典，其首要目标是使法院能够公正地处理案件，并以相称的成本处理案件。

---

[19] Edward J. Eberle, "The Method and Role of Comparative Law," *Wash. U. Global Stud. L. Rev.* 8, no. 3 (2009): 454.
爱德华 J. 埃伯勒, “比较法的研究方法和作用”，《华盛顿大学全球研究法律评论》，第3期，2009，第454页。

[20] Ibid., 454–55.

[21] *Civil Procedure Rules 1998*, No. 3132 (L.17)*, as amended by Civil Procedure (Amendment No. 3) Rules 2016,* No. 788 (L.11) that came into force on October, 3, 2016. *CPR 1998.* CPR is regularly amended, and the authors have taken into account all the amendments until this date. The old Civil Procedural Rules before CPR will be hereinafter called as *pre-CPR.*
1998年《民事诉讼程序规则》（第3132（L.17）号），经2016年10月3日生效的2016年《民事诉讼程序（第3号修正案）规则》（第788（L.11）号）修订。CPR 1998. CPR 定期修订，笔者已考虑到截至目前的所有修订。CPR之前的旧民事诉讼程序规则以下简称为pre-CPR。

Similarly, Article 2 of *Civil Procedural Law 1991* (hereinafter '*CPL 1991*') of the People's Republic of China (hereinafter 'PRC') provides *inter alia* very similar objectives as *CPR 2023*:[22]

同样，中国 1991 年《中华人民共和国民事诉讼法》（以下简称“1991 年《民事诉讼法》”）第 2 条也规定了与 2023 年《中华人民共和国民事诉讼法》非常相似的目标。

> …
>
> apply the law correctly, try civil cases promptly; and the law, [to] *maintain the social and economic order*; and to guarantee the smooth progress of the *socialist* construct [sic] [emphasis added].
>
> …

> …
>
> 正确适用法律，及时审理民事案件，确认民事权利义务关系，制裁民事违法行为，保护当事人的合法权益，教育公民自觉遵守法律，维护社会秩序、经济秩序，保障社会主义建设事业顺利进行。
>
> …

The reader can clearly appreciate that the judges in the PRC have to consider the public interests in private disputes between the parties as can be seen from the above. PRC judges have to take into account issues such as social and economic order, and in that sense function as guarantors of socialist society of PRC. This is surely a huge burden for the PRC judges as compared to the English or any common-law judges in respect of litigation of ordinary civil and commercial disputes. In addition, the authors will highlight that such burdens are also not defined precisely in the relevant statutes in the PRC Code.

从上文可以清楚地看出，中国法官在处理当事人之间的私人纠纷时必须考虑公共利益。其必须考虑到社会和经济秩序等问题，并在这个意义上充当中国社会主义社会的保障者。与英国或任何普通法国家的法官相比，中国法官在处理普通民商事纠纷诉讼时，这无疑是一个巨大的负担。此外，笔者要强调的是，《中华人民共和国民法典》中的相关法规也没有对这些负担作出准确的界定。

It may moreover mean that a somewhat deal of leeway is given to the PRC judges, when they are litigating private civil and commercial law disputes. The litigants, who are financially stronger, can usually employ their financial might in the commercial/civil litigation in any jurisdiction, unless the courts are equipped with the proper case management power or have power to order mediation or assist in mediation themselves. For example, in order to assist the judges in the English Courts, discretionary power is provided for them through the development and evolution of law

此外，这可能意味着中国法官在审理私人民商法纠纷时有一些可能的回旋余地。在任何司法管辖区，除非法院拥有适当的案件管理权，或有权下令调解或自行协助调解，否则财力雄厚的诉讼当事人通常可以在商业/民事诉讼中运用其财力。例如，为了协助英格兰法院的法官，通过英格兰和威尔士普通法体系中的案例先例来发展和演变法律，或通过起草新的程序法典及随后的解释、意

[22] *Civil Procedure Law 1991 (as Amended in 2023)*, Order 44 of President of PRC on April, 9, 1991.
1991年民事诉讼法（2023年修订），1991年4月9日中华人民共和国主席令第44 号。

through case precedents in the common law system in England & Wales, or through the drafting of new procedural codes & subsequent interpretations, opinions or replies to ensure the objectives of civil procedure are met.

见或答复来确保实现民事诉讼程序的目标，从而为法官提供自由裁量权。

Another issue that will have a deep impact on how cases are progressed through civil litigation in the courts is whether judges are entitled to find the truth in any case, or their focus is just on resolving the dispute before them, as per the overriding objectives and to achieve procedural fairness. Administrative reasons, legal philosophies, and jurisprudence behind the civil procedural system are some of the factors affecting how the cases are progressed from their first contact with the legal system.

另一个将对法院民事诉讼案件的进展产生深刻影响的问题是，法官是否有权查明任何案件的真相，或者他们的重点是否只是按照首要目标解决他们面前的争端，并实现程序公正。民事诉讼制度背后的行政原因、法律理念和法理是影响案件从第一次接触法律制度开始就如何进展的一些因素。

These philosophies will have a profound effect upon the outcome for any case, and it is quite possible that the same case can be lost in one jurisdiction but can be won easily in another. The success or failure will all depend on the jurisprudence and philosophy behind the procedural systems. These factors will affect the judges' discretionary powers in granting the relevant remedies in commercial or civil litigation and so forth.

这些理念对任何案件的结果都会产生深远的影响，很有可能同一个案件在一个司法管辖区败诉，但在另一个司法管辖区却能轻松胜诉。成败完全取决于程序制度背后的法理和理念。这些因素都会影响法官在商事或民事诉讼等方面给予相关补救的自由裁量权。

The approach in England & Wales is to ensure that civil procedural rules encourage settlement as a first resort, thus avoiding these cases progressing all the way to costly civil trials before the courts.[23] The above factors are ordinarily not appreciated by laymen, traders and so forth.

英格兰和威尔士的做法是，确保民事诉讼规则鼓励将和解作为第一手段，从而避免这些案件一直发展到法院进行代价高昂的民事审判。上述因素通常不为外行、商人等所理解。

This approach of English courts will avoid the tying up of judicial resources of the courts in deciding mere questions of fact, as opposed to the more important matter of deciding questions of law. The issues of questions of law are, in fact, essential for development of laws that could benefit societies with the common law systems. This philosophical approach

英格兰法院的这种做法，可以避免法院的司法资源被牵涉在纯粹就事实问题作出裁决，而非更重要的就法律问题作出裁决。事实上，法律问题对于制定有利于普通法系社会的法律至关重要。这种哲学方法是导致发展各种补救措施

[23] Lord Woolf, *Access to Justice: Final Report to the Lord Chancellor on the Civil Justice System in England and Wales* (London: HMSO, 1996).
伍尔夫勋爵，《诉诸司法》： Woolf 勋爵，《诉诸司法：向大法官提交的关于英格兰和威尔士民事司法系统的最终报告》（伦敦：HMSO，1996 年）。

is one of the factors that led to the development of various remedies as a substitute for litigation in the common-law courts, such as freezing injunctions or interim injunctions during litigation. This approach is essential in times of breakneck technological advances, digital connections, and globalisation, all of which affect commercial transactions and communications.

以替代普通法法院诉讼的因素之一，如诉讼期间的冻结令或临时禁令。在技术飞速发展、数字连接和全球化的时代，这种方法至关重要，因为所有这些都会影响商业交易和通信。

The jurisprudential theories dominating the legal and administrative thought processes of these jurisdictions will also affect how such remedies, if any, are granted in commercial disputes that reach the courts in any jurisdiction. Factors such as jurisprudence, legal philosophy, legal history, culture, evolution of law, substantive law and civil procedural law, and methods of judicial activities are the **invisible factors and contexts** that are responsible for differences or similarities between the two jurisdictions' practice. **The focus of the book is on understanding these invisible factors and contexts in which the law is made, interpreted, and then applied in the courts.** Each of the invisible factors and contexts for both common law and PRC law will be examined in separate chapters in this book. The authors have tried to ensure that each of these invisible factors and contexts can be read as a stand-alone chapter.

在这些司法管辖区的法律和行政思维过程中占主导地位的法学理论也会影响到在任何司法管辖区的法院受理的商业纠纷中如何给予此类救济（如有）。法理学、法律哲学、法律历史、文化、法律演变、实体法和民事诉讼法以及司法活动方法等因素是造成两个司法管辖区实践异同的**无形因素和背景。本书的重点在于理解这些无形的因素和背景，在这些因素和背景下，法律得以制定、解释，然后在法庭上得以适用。**普通法和中国法律的每一种隐形因素和背景都将在本书的不同章节中进行研究。笔者努力确保每个隐形因素和背景都可以作为独立的章节来阅读。

The two jurisdictions, that is the common law system of England & Wales and PRC law, have different terminology for similar remedies or court processes. In any comparative analysis, the real challenge lies in comparing the relevant laws from the perspective of these invisible factors and contexts. Otherwise, merely comparing exercise of laws and codes will remain a superficial exercise. Even when comparing the remedies in commercial and/or civil litigation, there is a need to have the invisible factors and contexts in mind. It is appropriate at this juncture to quote Rable at length:

两个司法管辖区，即英格兰和威尔士的普通法体系和中华人民共和国的法律，对类似的救济措施或法院程序使用了不同的术语。在任何比较分析中，真正的挑战在于从这些隐形因素和背景的角度对相关法律进行比较。否则，仅仅比较法律和法典的执行情况仍然是肤浅的。即使在比较商业和/或民事诉讼中的救济措施时，也需要考虑到这些看不见的因素和背景。因此有必要引用雷布尔所述：

> [T]he student of the problem must encompass the law of the whole world, past and present, and everything that

> 研究这个问题的学生必须了解全世界过去和现在的法律，以及影响法

affects the law, such as geography, climate and race, developments and events shaping the course of country's history — war, revolution, colonisation, subjugation — religion and ethics, the ambition and creativity of individuals, the needs of production and consumption, the interests of groups, parties and classes. Ideas of every kind have their effect, for it is not just feudalism, liberalism and socialism which produce different types of law; legal institutions once adopted may have logical consequences; and not least important is the striving for a political or legal ideal. Everything in the social, economic and legal fields interacts. The law of every developed people is in constant motion, and the whole kaleidoscopic picture is one which no one has ever clearly seen.[24]

律的一切因素，如地理、气候和种族，影响国家历史进程的发展和事件——战争、革命、殖民化、征服，宗教和伦理，个人的抱负和创造力，生产和消费的需求，团体、党派和阶级的利益。各种思想都会产生影响，因为不仅仅是封建主义、自由主义和社会主义会产生不同类型的法律；法律制度一旦被采用，就会产生合乎逻辑的后果；而最重要的是，人们会努力追求一种政治或法律理想。社会、经济和法律领域的一切都相互影响。每个发达民族的法律都在不断运动，而整个万花筒般的图景从未有人清晰地看到过。

The granting of remedies in courts, from the initial stage when the applications are made by the claimant, to the stage when any orders granted are to be enforced, is always dependent, in any jurisdiction, on the administrative setup and framework of a legal system, including its administrative aspects. These factors cannot be overlooked.

在任何司法管辖区，从原告提出申请的最初阶段，到执行所下达的任何命令的阶段，法院给予救济总是取决于法律制度的行政设置和框架，包括其行政方面。这些因素不容忽视。

[24]Ernest Rable was quoted in Hein Kotz, "Comparative Law in Germany Today," *Revue Internationale de Droit Compare* 51, no. 4 (1999): 756.
欧内斯·特雷布尔在海恩·科茨"当今德国的比较法 "一文中被引述，《国际比较法杂志》第 51 卷第 4 期（1999 年）："德国的比较法"，4，1999，第 756 页。

1.2.1 Administration of Disputes in Market economy

市场经济中的争议管理

'Market economy' in any country refers to an economic system where economic decisions as to investments, distribution and price of goods and services are steered only on the basis of transactions and dealings of citizens and business, and there is no planned state intervention. Civil dispute resolution and how parties are assisted by this system are an important part of any market economy, as they are instrumental in reducing transaction costs. It is important that civil litigation is considered as part of the service sector of the economy, especially with the increasing clout of the PRC in global economic spheres.[25]

在任何国家，“市场经济”都是指一种经济体系，其中有关商品和服务的投资、分配及定价的经济决策仅以公众与企业的买卖交易为基础，国家不进行计划干预。民事纠纷的解决以及当事人如何在这一制度中获得帮助，因有助于降低交易成本，已是市场经济的重要组成部分。尤为重要的是，民事诉讼被视为经济体中服务部门的一部分，特别是在中国在全球经济领域的影响力与日俱增之际。

A legal system with a proper framework to manage the expectations of commercial interests will ensure that many of these cases are resolved satisfactorily; this can even improve the local economy. The vital factor is the perception of fairness, and in a market economy, any negative view cannot be swept under the carpet. A good legal system will assist in disposal of commercial disputes without full civil trials or without determination by the courts, and thus assist in achieving the aim of legislators in any country.

一个具备适当框架来管理商业利益期望的法律体系将确保众多此类案件得到妥善解决；甚至可以改善当地经济。其中至关重要的因素是人们对公平的看法，而在市场经济中，任何负面看法都不可忽视。良好的法律制度将有助于在无需全面民事审判或不经法院裁决的情况下化解商业纠纷，进而有益于达成国家立法者的目标。

The following quote from a 2013 OECD Report describes succinctly the importance of the civil justice system:

以下引用的2013年经合组织的一份报告，简明扼要地说明了民事司法系统的重要性：

> Judicial systems serve important purposes in up-holding [sic] social values but also in determining economic performance. Well-functioning judiciaries guarantee security of property rights and enforcement of contracts. Security of property rights strengthens incentives to save and invest, by protecting returns

> 司法系统不仅在维护社会价值观方面发挥着重要作用，对决定经济表现来说亦是关键。运作良好的司法机构保障安全的财产权和合同执行。财产权的保障通过保护储蓄和

[25] Peter Middleton, *Review of Civil Justice and Legal Aid*, Report to the Lord Chancellor (London: Lord Chancellor's Department, 1997), Ch 1, where he wrote in the article that "Justice- by which I mean the satisfactory resolution of disputes - is part of the service sector of the economy."
彼得米·德尔顿，民事司法和法律援助审查，提交大法官的报告（伦敦：大法官办公室，1997），第一章，他在文章中写道：“司法——我指的是令人满意地解决争端——是经济服务部门的一部分”。

from these activities. A good enforcement of contracts stimulates agents to enter into economic relationships, by dissuading opportunistic behaviour and reducing transaction costs. This has a positive impact on growth through various channels: it promotes competition, fosters specialisation in more innovative industries, contributes to the development of financial and credit markets and facilitates firm growth [emphasis added].[26]

投资活动的收益，加强了对这些活动的激励。良好的合同执行，通过阻止机会主义行为和降低交易成本，刺激代理人建立经济关系。这将通过多种渠道对经济增长产生积极影响：促进竞争，推动创新型产业的专业化发展，促进金融和信贷市场的发展，促进企业成长。

This is also an appropriate time to introduce Rawls' concept of *formal justice*,[27] which states that there is a need to impart consistent, impartial administration of procedural rules where the decision makers (the judges) do not exercise their own personal discretion that is available to any one of them at the personal level. The sheer size of the PRC means that it will have to overcome the challenge of applying the rules uniformly and consistently, and it is the authors' view that it will need to bring in the concept of formal justice within the legal framework.

这也是引入罗尔斯的*形式正义*概念的恰当时机，该概念指出，有必要在决策者（法官）不行使任何其在个人层面上享有的个人自由裁量权的情况下，对程序规则进行一致、公正的管理。中国的庞大规模意味着它必须克服统一一致地适用规则的挑战，且笔者认为其需在法律框架内引入形式正义的概念。

This brings the authors to the principle of rule of law, namely the formal rules and procedures, the formal application of which will control the exercise of human discretion. In such a system, Dicey's concept of the primacy of rules over all institutions is established, with the aim to curb the arbitrary power of officials.[28] This requirement of formal justice is important, in spite of the achievement of having almost all procedural codes and substantive law established in the span of just a few years, as stated by the ex-chairman of the Standing Committee of NPC, Mr. Wu Bangguo, who stated that a socialist legal system with Chinese characteristics was established in China in 2011.

这使笔者想到了法治原则，即正式的规则和程序，正式适用这些规则和程序将控制人的自由裁量权的行使。在这样的制度中，狄西提出的"规则高于一切制度"的概念得以确立，其目的在于遏制官员的专断权力。正如全国人大常委会前委员长吴邦国先生所说，中国在2011年建立了中国特色社会主义法律体系。尽管在短短几年时间内就实现了几乎所有程序法和实体法的确立，但这种形式正义的要求是非常重要的。

---

[26]OECD, *What Makes Civil Justice Effective*, OECD Economic Department Policy Notes, No. 18 June 2013 (2013), 2, 1–12.www.oecd.org/eco/growth/civil%20Justice%20Policy%20note.pdf.
经合组织，《什么使民事司法有效》，经合组织经济部政策说明，2013年6月第18期（2013 年），2，1-12. www.oecd.org/eco/growth/civil%20Justice%20Policy%20note.pdf。

[27]Refer, Chapter 5, § 5.3.1 & Chapter 6, § 6.2 for the concept of Rawls' formal justice in context of discretionary powers of the decision-makers.
关于罗尔斯形式正义的概念，请参阅第5章第5.3.1节和第6章第6.2节中有关决策者自由裁量权的内容。

[28]Ibid. Dicey is discussed in the same section of Chapter 3.
见上引，第3章的同一章节对狄西进行了讨论。

2011 was the year when the PRC established a good system of PRC Codes to cover various aspects of trade and society. In the history of a civilisation and relative to other countries' legal systems, the PRC's codes are new and recently established. This has to be appreciated by the readers of the book from the start, as do the challenges that the implementation of any law brings to the PRC.

2011 年，中国建立了完善的法典体系，涵盖了贸易和社会的各个方面。在文明史上，相对于其他国家的法律体系，中国的法典是新近制定的。本书的读者必须从一开始就认识到这一点，以及任何法律的实施给中国带来的挑战。

1.3 Background to the Book

本书背景

When there are commercial and civil disputes and all attempts to resolve those disputes have failed, in that scenario, civil litigation before the courts is the most important medium to resolve the disputes. This will hold true, as long as there are no mandatory arbitration and/or other alternative dispute resolution clauses in the contracts governing that dispute. However, civil litigation is principally an adversarial process, where the final judgments after a civil trial ultimately settle the respective position of the parties to the commercial dispute. In the authors' view, this statement is true not only for the common law systems such as England & Wales, but also for jurisdictions like the PRC that follow the civil law system. In order to understand the differences between the two systems, it is important to focus on the contemporary philosophies and then link them subtly to the invisible factors and contexts.

当商事和民事纠纷通过其他所有方式均无法得到解决时，民事诉讼是解决纠纷的最为重要的手段。只要纠纷相关的合同中未设有强制的仲裁条款和/或其他替代性纠纷解决方式条款，此论断依然成立。然而，民事诉讼在原则上是一个对立的过程，通过民事审判后的终审判决来最终解决商业纠纷当事人各自的立场。在笔者看来，这种说法不仅适用于英格兰和威尔士等普通法系国家，也适用于中国等大陆法系国家。要理解这两种制度之间的差异，就必须关注当代哲学，然后将其与无形的因素和背景巧妙地联系起来。

Therefore, the authors will discuss the practical example of civil dispute between parties, and how the respective courts in both the jurisdictions approach the issues currently; the purpose of this is to understand the differences in the current philosophy and what has led to this thought process. **By taking civil dispute as a background, the authors hope to help the readers to understand the similarities and differences between the two systems.**

因此，笔者将探讨民事诉讼的实际案例，以及两司法管辖区中的法庭当前如何审视这些问题；其目的在于明晰当代哲学中的差异，并探寻导致这一思维流程的缘由。**以民事诉讼为背景，笔者希望帮助读者了解两个体系间的异同。**

Civil procedures have evolved in both the common law systems and the civil law systems to ensure fairness to both parties; however, these formal civil procedures have costs implications for the parties to commercial disputes. In addition, civil procedures can result in complexities, tactical moves and even obstructions by one of the parties to the commercial dispute, exploiting the civil procedural rules by the parties concerned. England & Wales follow a common law system, whereas the PRC follows a civil law system. The jurisprudence affecting both these civil procedural systems is

民事诉讼程序在普通法系和大陆法系中都有发展，以确保对双方当事人的公平；但是，这些正式的民事诉讼程序对商事争议的当事人有成本影响。此外，民事诉讼程序还可能导致商业纠纷中的一方当事人利用民事诉讼程序规则进行复杂化、策略性行动甚至阻挠。英格兰和威尔士采用普通法系，而中国采用大陆法系。尽管就争议各方而言，大陆法系的大部分客体与普通法系相似，但影

a bit different, even though it is a fact that most of the objectives of the civil law systems, as far as the parties to disputes are concerned, are similar to the common law systems.

响这两种民事诉讼制度的法理却略有不同。

Civil litigation, in general, is all about 'winning the case', and sometimes the parties are baffled by the need for formal civil procedures that are costly and are, in fact, the principal reason for delay as observed by the parties to commercial disputes. In addition, at times the civil and commercial cases are won just on tactical procedural moves rather than arguments on relevant substantive law. Effective civil/commercial lawyers in any jurisdiction will usually utilise the civil procedural rules effectively and aptly; in particular, they will not hesitate to issue many tactical interim applications to the court.

一般来说，民事诉讼都是为了"打赢官司"，有时当事人对正式民事诉讼程序的必要性感到困惑，因为这些程序费用高昂，而且事实上是商事纠纷当事人观察到的冗长的主要原因。此外，有时民事和商事案件的胜诉仅仅是因为在程序上采取了策略，而不是对相关实体法的争论。在任何司法管辖区，有效的民商事律师通常都会有效和恰当地利用民事诉讼规则；特别是他们会毫不犹豫地向法院提出许多战术性临时申请。

Recently, in England & Wales, as a result of the Woolf Reforms in April 1999, civil procedures went through drastic changes to reduce legal costs and delays by the introduction of case management powers for the courts. As a result of this power, courts can set timetables, by demanding more cooperation between the parties and increasing focus on *overriding objective*. Even though the procedural rules have, in fact, developed over the centuries in England & Wales, the new *CPR 1998* was meant to break with the past. In order to accomplish that, the English courts have resisted the use of old cases to interpret the fresh rules from *CPR 1998*, except where the form and intention of written rules in the new *CPR 1998* are the same as in the old cases pursuant to *City and County Properties Ltd v Kamali*.[29]

最近，在英格兰和威尔士，由于1999年4月的伍尔夫改革，民事诉讼程序发生了巨大变化，法院引入了案件管理权，以减少法律费用和延误。由于有了这项权力，法院可以通过要求当事人之间更多的合作和更加关注首要目标来设定时间表。尽管诉讼程序规则在英格兰和威尔士事实上已经发展了几个世纪，但新的CPR 1998意在与过去决裂。为了实现这一目标，英格兰国法院抵制使用旧案例来解释CPR 1998中的新规则，除非根据市郡物业有限公司诉卡马利案，新的CPR 1998中书面规则的形式和意图与旧案例相同。

The most important change in the *CPR 1998* was the setting out of the overriding objective in Part 1 of *CPR 1998* to ensure fairness between the parties to litigation; cases are dealt with expeditiously; costs are saved; and the courts' resources are safeguarded. In *CPR 1998* r. 1.4 active case management powers were given to the courts. In spite of

CPR 1998最重要的变化是在第1部分规定了首要目标，即确保诉讼各方之间的公平；案件得到迅速处理；节省费用；以及法院的资源得到保障。CPR 1998第1.4条赋予法院积极的案件管理权力。尽管有这些重要的新增条文，以及法官在案件管理方面的权利，但优秀的诉讼

[29] [2007] 1 WLR 1219.

these remarkable additions and the judges' power over case management, an effective litigator would never lose sight of the fact that the client's objectives are the prime factor, which cannot be put on the back burner. In addition, the lawyers have obligations pursuant to the Solicitors' professional code of conduct to identify clients' clear objectives. In England & Wales, which is a common law system, judges do not have the power to seek evidence in order to establish the truth but have to determine the case based on the best case presented by the lawyers acting on behalf of the parties.

律师绝不会忽略当事人的目标才是首要因素，不能将之置于次要位置。此外，根据《律师职业行为守则》，律师有义务确定客户的明确目标。英格兰和威尔士实行的是普通法制度，法官无权为查明真相而寻求证据，只能根据代表当事人的律师所提出的最佳理由对案件作出裁决。

In any legal system, these are the stages in any civil litigation:

在任何法律体系中，这些都是民事诉讼的各个阶段：

- Pre-action stage where issues are identified and information is collated, to decide how the case is to be framed; the right court is chosen in which to commence the action; and a strategy is developed for applying for any pre-action interim orders;
- Issuance of a claim form at a tactical time chosen by the lawyer through which a relevant court is notified; followed by the service of the claim form and exchange of statements of claim by the parties, defence and any counterclaims;
- Court's powers to allocate the case and manage the case;
- Interim applications such as disclosure of evidence, attachment of assets, interim or behavior injunctions and so forth;
- Trial;
- Judgment and assessment of costs.

- 诉前，确定问题并整理信息，以决定如何立案；选择合适的法院开始诉讼；以及制定申请任何诉讼前临时命令的策略；
- 在律师选择的策略时间内提交索赔表，并通过该时间通知相关法院；随后送达索赔表，并交换各方的索赔声明、辩护和任何反诉；
- 法院有权分配案件和管理案件；
- 临时申请，如证据披露、资产扣押、临时或行为禁令等；
- 庭审；
- 审判和费用评估。

In any litigation, there are numerous interim applications. Even though the main purpose for the development of *CPR 1998* was to ensure fairness for all parties, in the last few decades, the commercial burdens and the money involved have ensured that astute lawyers are using these civil procedure rules as a tool to fit the individual case. Accordingly, numerous interim applications are made in the courts. Interim applications can be made any time during the civil process. A large percentage of cases do not reach the stage of out-and-out civil trials as one of the parties to the commercial dispute would have used the route of an interim application to its advantage or there some sort of settlement has been put in place.

在任何诉讼中，都会有大量的临时申请。尽管制定 CPR 1998 的主要目的是为了确保各方的公平，但在过去几十年中，所涉及的商业负担和金钱确保了精明的律师将这些民事诉讼程序规则作为适合个别案件的工具。因此，法院收到了许多临时申请。临时申请可以在民事诉讼过程中的任何时候提出。由于商业纠纷的一方当事人已经利用临时申请这一途径取得了优势，或者已经达成了某种和解，因此很大一部分案件都没有进入正式的民事审判阶段。

Scholars have highlighted that Comparative law is a special branch of jurisprudence,[30] and therefore, this branch of law has been used less often in comparison to the procedural laws between the two jurisdictions. Comparative law though has been employed in research about issues pertaining to private international law, forum shopping and so forth.

学者们强调，比较法是法理学的一个特殊分支，因此，与两个司法管辖区之间的程序法相比，这一法律分支较少使用。不过，比较法已被用于有关国际私法、择地诉讼等问题的研究。

In this book, the authors have eschewed the assumptions based on views usually advocated by western practitioners and academics. The main reason for adopting this approach is that many western experts' views are largely based on the fact that they have failed to comprehend fully the cultural aspects of law. Western scholars have viewed PRC law as lacking 'formal-rational rules' as understood by them.[31] The two very common misunderstandings and assumptions that are prevalent amongst western scholars are that there is absence of law in East Asia or law is not that developed in East Asia as compared to the western common law system or

在本书中，笔者摒弃了通常由西方从业者和学者所倡导的基于观点的假设。采用这种方法的主要原因是，许多西方专家的观点在很大程度上是基于他们未能充分理解法律的文化层面这一事实。西方学者认为中国法律缺乏他们所理解的“形式理性规则”。西方学者普遍存在两种非常常见的误解和假设，即东亚没有法律，或者与西方普通法体系甚至大陆法系相比，东亚的法律并不发达。因此，本书重点关注规则背后的法律传统和隐形因素，摒弃了这些预存的

30 M. Martinek, "Rechtsverglechung Als Akademische Disziplin in Deutschland," *Ritsumeikan Law Review (International Edition)* 17 (2000): 84. This aspect as suggested by Martinek was discussed in Peter Gottwald, "Comparative Civil Procedure," *Ritsumeikan L. Rev.* 22 (2005): 23.
M·马丁内克,“比较法作为一门学科在德国的发展情况”, *Ritsumeikan Law Review*（国际版）17 (2000): 84. 彼得·戈特瓦尔德在“比较民事诉讼程序”中讨论了马丁内克提出的这一方面。 *Ritsumeikan L. Rev.* 22 (2005): 23。

31 Teemu Ruskola, "The East Asian Legal Tradition," in *The Cambridge Companion to Comparative Law*, in *The Cambridge Companion to Comparative Law*, ed. M. Bussani and U. Mattei (Cambridge; New York: Cambridge University Press, 2012), 261.
泰穆·卢斯科拉，“东亚法律传统”，载《剑桥比较法指南》，M. Bussani和U. Mattei 编辑，剑桥；纽约：剑桥大学出版社，2012 年，第261页。

even civil law system.[32] The book therefore focuses on the legal traditions and invisible factors behind the rules, to eschew such ready-made assumptions.

假设。

The only limitation in pursuing this project is whether the two jurisdictions can be compared, as Scott has elaborated in his paper associated with the Comparative law lectures. In the eighteenth to early twentieth centuries, as a big colonial power, England was the center of International trade. Meanwhile in this decade and for the foreseeable future, the PRC as a current economic superpower will remain a major exporter and importer of goods and services.

正如斯科特在其与比较法讲座相关的论文中所阐述的那样，开展此项目的唯一限制在于能否对两个司法管辖区进行比较。在十八世纪到二十世纪初，作为殖民大国，英国是国际贸易的中心。与此同时，在本十年以及可预见的未来，中国作为当前的经济超级大国，仍将是货物和服务的主要出口国和进口国。

As discussed earlier, this will involve commercial people/merchants having trust in the PRC courts and a clear understanding of how the PRC civil procedural law can protect their assets, businesses and commercial interests, when they carry out commercial transactions with PRC connections. In parallel, there is another development that is evolving, where cash rich organisations and enterprises from the PRC are expanding abroad in other countries, and therefore, have to grapple with other jurisdictions' laws, or understand the contexts and invisible factors in these jurisdictions. The PRC's investors in these other countries are facing similar issues as foreign investors are currently facing in the PRC, arising due to a lack of understanding of foreign laws and the cultural framework in which these foreign laws operate. This raises the importance of such Comparative law analysis.

如前文所述，这将涉及商业人士/商人对中国法院的信任，以及在进行与中国有关的商业交易时，清楚了解中国民事诉讼法如何保护其资产、业务和商业利益。与此同时，还有另一种情况正在发生变化，即现金富裕的中国机构和企业正在其他国家进行海外扩张，因此，他们不得不应对其他司法管辖区的法律，或了解这些司法管辖区的背景和隐形因素。中国投资者在这些其他国家面临的问题与外国投资者目前在中国面临的问题类似，都是由于缺乏对外国法律和这些外国法律运作的文化框架的了解而产生的。这就提高了此类比较法分析的重要性。

[32] Ruskola, "The East Asian Legal Tradition," 261。卢斯科拉，"东亚法律传统"，第261页。

1.4 Comparative Law — Definition, Meaning and Various Approaches

比较法 — 定义，含义和多种方式

This book involves the comparison of the legal systems in the two quite distinct jurisdictions, focusing on the contexts and invisible factors underpinning issues within these jurisdictions. In order to carry out a systematic scientific study, it is important to first analyse the concept of Comparative law.

本书对两个截然不同的司法管辖区的法律体系进行了比较，重点研究了这些司法管辖区内问题的背景和隐形因素。为了进行系统的科学研究，首先必须分析比较法的概念。

G. Swanson has highlighted, with reference to comparative research, that any scientific thinking devoid of comparison is unthinkable and cannot be classed even as scientific research or thought.[33] In simple terms, Comparative law is the comparison of the different legal systems of the world. Many jurists have avoided any kind of definition of Comparative law or of comparative methodology as they feel that it is a very complex area of study that cannot be condensed into a brief definition or an abridged version of study.[34]

G. 斯旺森在谈到比较研究时强调，任何缺乏比较的科学思维都是不可想象的，甚至不能被归类为科学研究或思维。简单地说，比较法就是对世界上不同的法律体系进行比较。许多法学家都避免对比较法或比较方法论下任何定义，因为他们认为这是一个非常复杂的研究领域，无法浓缩成一个简短的定义或研究节选。

Comparative law, however, is described in an influential book on Comparative law as the comparison of law with the extra dimension of internationalism.[35] For example, for an English common-law lawyer, just to study and research a few elements of PRC law, or to compare superficially the codes or statutes, will not be considered research into Comparative

然而，在一本颇具影响力的比较法著作中，比较法被描述为具有国际主义额外维度的法律比较。例如，对于一名英国普通法律师来说，仅仅学习和研究中国法律的一些内容，或对法典或成文法进行肤浅的比较，并不能被视为对比较法的研究。斯科特在他的文章中翻译

---

33 G. Swanson, "Framework for Comparative Research: Anthropology and the Theory of Action," in *Comparative Methods in Sociology: Essays on Trends and Applications*, ed. Vallier Ivan and Aptter. David E. (Berkeley: University of California Press, 1971), 141–202.
G·斯旺森,"比较研究框架：人类学与行动理论"，载《社会学中的比较方法： 趋势与应用论文集》，瓦利埃·伊万和Aptter. 大卫 E.，伯克利：加州大学出版社，1971，第141–202页。

34 Scott, "The Comparative Method of Legal Research," 1. The article was accessed on 21 April 2016. Scott used the Latin adage '*Omnis definition periculosa est*' to highlight the patent truism that it is not easy for any jurist to discuss the definition of concepts like Comparative law or comparative methodology; however, there is a contrasting adage, '*tot hominess, quot sententiae*', which reveals the simple truth that academics are brave enough to provide a definition of some kind for any concepts including Comparative law.
斯科特，"法律研究的比较方法"，1。该文章的访问日期为2016年4月21日。斯科特用拉丁谚语 "Omnis definition periculosa est "来强调一个不争的事实，即任何法学家都不容易讨论比较法或比较方法论等概念的定义；然而，有一句与之相对的谚语 "tot hominess, quot sententiae "却揭示了一个简单的事实，即学术界勇于为包括比较法在内的任何概念提供某种定义。

35 Konrad Zweigert, Hein Kotz, and Tony Weir, trans., *An Introduction to Comparative Law: Volume I: The Framework*, 2nd Revised ed. (Oxford: Clarendon Press, 1987), 2.
康拉德·茨威格特，海恩·科茨, and Tony Weir, trans.，《比较法导论：第一卷：框架》，第二次修订版，牛津：克拉伦登出版社，1987年。

Law.[36] Scott in his article has translated a definition of the comparative method as provided by the famous jurist Venter:

了著名法学家文特尔对比较法的定义：

> The comparative method [of legal research] is that unique, systematic, jurisprudential method, which we apply to gain new knowledge about the legal systems in respect of which we apply it, by taking cognisance of the similarities and differences of those legal systems [emphasis added].[37]

> 比较法[法学研究]是一种独特的、系统的法学方法，我们采用这种方法是通过了解我们所采用的法律制度的异同，获得有关这些法律制度的新知识[着重部分由笔者标明]。

Comparative law is quite distinct from Private International Law, but they do interact with each other.[38] Disciplines such as Private International Law, Public International Law, and Transactional Law consist of a body of positive legal rules, but Comparative law is a 'method of studying law and stock of academic knowledge.'[39] Many issues in Private International Law are resolved by using Comparative law rather than using national tests. Article 38(1)(c) of *Statute of the International Court of Justice 1945* ('ICJ') laid down the guidelines for 'general principles of law recognized by civilised nations'; a decision as to how many countries need that common general principle of law enshrined in ICJ's articles can be resolved in a way by Comparative law.[40]

比较法与国际私法截然不同，但两者确实相互影响。国际私法、国际公法和交易法等学科由一系列实在法规则组成，但比较法是一种"研究法律的方法和学术知识的储备"。国际私法中的许多问题都是通过比较法而非国家检验来解决的。《1945 年国际法院规约》（"国际法院"）第 38(1)(c)条规定了"文明国家承认的一般法律原则"的准则；至于有多少国家需要国际法院条款中所载的共同一般法律原则，可以通过比较法的方式来解决。

Legal historians have also compared the law over a period of time, and their systematic approach could be classed as similar to scholars comparing laws existent at a particular time.[41] Zweigert and Kotz have discussed Genzmer's ideas in the context of legal historians and Comparative law, saying that experts:

法律史学家也对一段时间内的法律进行比较，他们的系统方法可归类为类似于学者对特定时间内存在的法律进行比较。茨威格特和科茨从法律史学家和比较法的角度讨论了根茨默的观点，认为专家们：

---

[36] Ibid., 6. Authors were of the view that merely studying another country's law is not Comparative law。见前引6，作者们认为，仅仅研究另一个国家的法律并不是比较法。

[37] Scott, "The Comparative Method of Legal Research," 1–2, where he translated the quote was taken from Venter, *F et al Regsnavorsing - Metode en Publikasie Juta* (1990), 206-244.
斯科特，"法律研究的比较方法"，1-2，其中他翻译的引文摘自 Venter, F et al Regsnavorsing - 方法和受众 (1990), 206-244。

[38] Zweigert, Kotz, and Weir, *Introduction to Comparative Law*, 6。茨威格特，科茨 and Weir，比较法入门，6。

[39] Mathias Reimann, "Comparative Law and Neighbouring Disciplines," in *The Cambridge Companion to Comparative Law*, ed. Mauro Bussani and Ugo Mattei, Cambridge Companions to Law (Cambridge; New York: Cambridge University Press, 2012), 14.
Mathias Reimann，"比较法和邻近学科"，载于《剑桥比较法指南》，Mauro Bussani and Ugo Mattei,《剑桥比较法指南》，剑桥；纽约：剑桥大学出版社，2012 年，第14页。

[40] See also, Zweigert, Kotz, and Weir, *Introduction to Comparative Law*, 8。见茨威格特，科茨，和威尔，比较法入门，第8页。

[41] It succinctly described the approach of legal historians in Zweigert, Kotz, and Weir, *Introduction to Comparative Law*, 8.
它简明扼要地描述了茨威格特、科茨和威尔在《比较法导论》中所采用的法律史学家的方法，第8页。

...no longer believe that legal history unrolls independently, but see law and history as fully interfused and try to illuminate the extra-legal context and hidden stimuli of legal development. Legal history is therefore not simply self-serving, but contributes to a critical evaluation of the policy of law which is, after all, the principal aim of pure comparative law [emphasis added].[42]

...不再认为法律史是独立展开的，而是认为法律和历史是完全相互融合的，并试图阐明法律之外的背景和法律发展的促进因素。因此，法律史不仅仅是为自己服务，而是有助于对法律政策进行批判性评估，毕竟这才是纯粹比较法的主要目的[着重部分由笔者标明]。

In addition, according to Zweigert and Kotz, Comparative law can be classified as '*vertical comparative law*' when practised by legal historians, and '*horizontal comparative law*' when comparing the modern systems of law in different countries.[43]

此外，根据茨威格特和科茨的观点，比较法在法律史学家的实践中可分为"纵向比较法"，在比较不同国家的现代法律体系时为"横向比较法"。

Legal Ethnologists, on the other hand, study the history of law to understand the evolution of civilisation. There are many theories propounded by Legal Ethnologists, but they do not focus on studying the evolution of law in societies that are not touched by modern civilisation.[44] These studies could have shed light on the evolution of modern societies as well. This area of law too could make an important contribution in studying Comparative law.[45]

法律民族学家则通过研究法律史来了解文明的演变。法律民族学家提出了许多理论，但他们并不专注于研究现代文明未触及的社会中法律的演变。这些研究也可以阐明现代社会的演变。这一法律领域也可为比较法研究做出重要贡献。

In the authors' view, the above studies could even be useful in analysing methodologies in all areas of substantive law such as contract, tort and so forth, and relevant civil procedures that have been developed over the years to resolve civil disputes germane to these various substantive laws. These aspects will form part of the context in this book and will be discussed in the subsequent Chapters. For example, if the authors were to analyse injunctions, the analysis would not be complete without a discussion of the

笔者认为，上述研究甚至有助于分析合同法、侵权法等实体法所有领域的方法，以及多年来为解决与这些实体法相关的民事纠纷而制定的相关民事诉讼程序。这些方面将构成本书背景的一部分，并将在后续章节中讨论。例如，如果笔者要分析强制令，那么如果不讨论几百年前衡平法中衡平法救济的演变及

[42] Genzmer E., "Verhaltnis von Rechtsgeschichte und Rechtvergleichung," *ARSP 41* (1954/55): 334. It was quoted in Zweigert, Kotz, and Weir, *Introduction to Comparative Law*, 9.
热兹默 E.,"法律史与比较法之间的关系"ARSP 41 (1954/55): 334. 转引自茨威格特，科茨，和威尔，比较法入门, 9.

[43] Zweigert, Kotz, and Weir, *Introduction to Comparative Law*, 9。茨威格特，科茨，和威尔，《比较法入门》，9。

[44] Adam, "Ethonologische Rechtsforschung," in *Lehrbuch der Volkerkunde*, ed. Adam and Trimborn (1958), 192.
Adam, "伦理法律研究"，载《民俗学教科书》. Adam and Trimborn (1958), 192。

[45] Zweigert, Kotz, and Weir, *Introduction to Comparative Law*, 10。茨威格特，科茨和威尔，《比较法入门》，第10页。

evolution of equitable remedies in laws of equity and their interaction with common law courts a few hundred years previously. Similarly, if one were to analyse the procedural remedy in the PRC, the analysis would have to take into account the lack of civil procedure for many centuries, and the very recent evolution of such remedies in the 1990s.

其与普通法法院的互动，分析就不完整。同样，如果要分析中国的程序救济，就必须考虑到中国许多世纪以来都没有民事诉讼程序，而此类救济是在 20 世纪 90 年代才发展起来的。

Modern comparative scholars believe that there are many more disciplines that Comparative law seems to be related to in practice, such as disciplines of transnational law, legal anthropology and economic analysis of law. Transnational law is also related to this branch, as suggested by Jessup's definition of transnational law "all law which regulates actions or events that transcends national frontiers."[46]

现代比较学者认为，比较法在实践中似乎与之相关的学科还有很多，如跨国法、法律人类学和法律经济分析等学科。正如杰瑟普对跨国法的定义"所有规范超越国界的行为或事件的法律"所表明的那样，跨国法也与这一分支相关。

1.4.1 Aims & Objectives of Comparative Law with respect to the Book

与本书相关的比较法目的与目标

From the perspective of this book, with the advent of globalisation, businessmen are trading more across the nations. Common people are travelling more and are therefore exposed to laws of other nations. Even businessmen trading across frontiers are forced to resolve their disputes in unfamiliar jurisdictions. Commercial lawyers have to give advice to such businessmen from other nations/jurisdictions, who are only familiar with their own legal system. Comparative law touches all aspects of laws in the modern globalised world, and it is particularly important for commercial lawyers. Both the PRC and England & Wales are influential players in the global economy due to high GDP, advanced technical capabilities, and strong military powers.

从本书的角度来看，随着全球化的到来，商人们在各国间进行的贸易越来越多。普通人的旅行越来越多，因此也会接触到其他国家的法律。即使是跨国贸易的商人也不得不在陌生的司法管辖区解决纠纷。商业律师必须为这些来自其他国家/司法管辖区但只熟悉其本国的法律制度的商人提供建议。比较法涉及现代全球化世界中法律的方方面面，对商业律师尤为重要。中国和英格兰与威尔士都是全球经济中具有影响力的国家，因为其拥有较高的国内生产总值、先进的技术能力和强大的军事实力。

---

[46]P. Jessup, *Transnational Law* (New Haven: Yale University Press, 1956), 2。
P. 杰瑟普，《跨国法》，纽黑文：耶鲁大学出版社，1956 年），第2页。

Laws across the nations are not uniform, and there is no law than can be aptly called a common law of mankind.[47] This problem is compounded by the fact that most lawyers in almost all jurisdictions are not exposed to Comparative law at an early stage. According to Zweigert and Kotz, "legal studies only become scientific when they rise above the actual rules of any national system, as it happens in legal philosophy, legal history, the sociology of law, and comparative law."[48] This succinctly describes the importance of comparative law. In addition, Zweigert and Kotz have defined the main purpose of Comparative law as being:

各国的法律并不统一，没有一部法律可以被恰当地称为人类共同法。几乎所有司法管辖区的大多数律师在早期阶段都没有接触过比较法，这使得问题更加复杂。茨威格特和科茨认为，“只有当法律研究超越任何国家制度的实际规则时，法律研究才会变得科学，就像在法律哲学、法律史、法律社会学和比较法中发生的那样”。这简明扼要地描述了比较法的重要性。此外，茨威格特和科茨将比较法的主要目的定义为：

> ...practical, namely reform and improvement of the law [emphasis added] at home, rather than theoretical, philosophical, or speculative; but a part was played also by natural curiosity about other peoples' law and by the impartial feeling that perhaps those others had something to offer — a contrast with the haughty concentration of legal scholars on their own newly codified systems.[49]

> ......实用的，即改革和完善本国的法律[着重部分由笔者标明]，而不是理论的、哲学的或投机性的；但对其他民族法律的天然好奇心和或许其他民族的法律也有可取之处的公正感觉，也起到了一定的作用——这与法律学者傲慢地专注于自己新编纂的体系截然不同。

The above quote is certainly relevant to this book, as we arecomparing English common law with PRC law.

因我们正在比较英格兰普通法和中国法，所以上述引文自然与本书有关。

It seems to be the case that Comparative law cannot help to find all the answers due to internal debate within the field. However, one issue is crystal clear: Comparative law is one branch of Jurisprudence that can assist the authors in the interpretation of existing laws and analysis of invisible factors & contexts in both the PRC and England &

由于该领域内部的争论，比较法似乎对找到所有答案没有助益。然而，有一个问题是非常明确的：比较法是法理学的一个分支，可以帮助笔者解释现行法律，分析中国和英格兰及威尔士的隐形因素和背景。比较法还有助于了解本国司法管辖区的法律并提出改革建议，

---

[47] Lambert ideally wished for law of humanity as "*droit, commun de l'humanite*" in "Conception Generale et Definition de la Science Due Droit Compare, Proces-Verbaux Des Seances et Documents, Congress International de Droit Compare I," *Congress International de Droit Compare I* (1905): 26.
兰伯特在《一般概念与应有法律科学的定义比较》中将人道法理想化为“权利，人类社群”，国际比较法学大会第1册: 26.

[48] Zweigert, Kotz, and Weir, *Introduction to Comparative Law*, 4.
茨威格特、科茨和威尔,《比较法导论》，4。

[49] Ibid., 53.

Wales.[50] Comparative law can also assist in understanding the laws within one's home jurisdiction and developing proposals for reforms, and even can be a means and guide for unification and harmonisation of law, including the development of model codes.[51]

甚至可以成为统一和协调法律的手段和指南，包括制定示范法典。

This book will avoid the trap of exhibiting mere curiosity, or of limiting the research to the purely philosophical level. In the authors' view, the objective should be to provide a practical guide that can be used to resolve real issues for commercial lawyers in the globalised world, where the PRC is the economic powerhouse, and London is still one of the leading financial centers around the world.

本书将避免走马观花、或将研究局限于纯哲学层面的陷阱。笔者认为，本书应致力于为解决全球化世界中商业律师面临的切实问题提供实用指南。中国是经济强国，而伦敦仍是全球领先的金融中心之一。

1.4.2 Methodology of Comparative Law — Warnings to be kept in mind from the beginning

比较法方法——从最初就应牢记的告诫

There are inherent risks in pursuing Comparative law methodology, and the authors will keep those in mind from the beginning. Palmer has also mentioned that Comparative law needs to prove that it is cost-effective when resolving day to day problems.[52] In the authors' view, a realist way of doing a comparative process may involve just focusing on textual comparisons,[53] and/or in words of Palmer, "...simple juxtapositions of material without elaboration or comment, -- all of these could have legitimacy and value in practical forms of legal research."[54]

采用比较法方法存在固有风险，笔者将从一开始就牢记这些风险。帕尔默还提到，比较法需要证明它在解决日常问题时具有成本效益。笔者认为，现实主义的比较方法可能只是侧重于文本比较，和/或用帕尔默的话说，"……简单地将材料并列起来，不加阐述或评论，——所有这些在实际形式的法律研究中都可能具有合法性和价值"。

---

[50]It is a branch of jurisprudence and as discussed also in Gottwald, "Comparative Civil Procedure," 23. The authors of this book chose to introduce the readers to comparative law in the Chapter 1 itself to appreciate the phenomenon of comparing the two legal systems.
比较法是法理学的一个分支，在Gottwald的"比较民事诉讼程序"一文中也有论述。笔者选择在第 1 章中向读者介绍比较法，以了解两种法律体系的比较现象。

[51]J.A. Jolowicz, "On the Comparison of Procedures," in *Law and Justice in Multistate World: Essays in Honour of Arther T. Von Mehren*, ed. James Nafziger and Symeon Symeonides (New York: Transnational Publishers, 2002), 721.
J.A. 乔洛维茨, "关于程序的比较," 载于法律与司法,多州世界： 纪念阿瑟-T-冯-梅赫伦, ed.詹姆斯-纳夫齐格 和西米恩-西米恩尼德斯 (纽约: 跨国出版社, 2002), 721。

[52] V.V. Palmer, "From Lerotholi to Lando: Some Examples of Comparative Law Methodology," *Global Jurist Frontiers* 4, no. 2 (2004): 3.
V.V. 帕尔默, "从 Lerotholi 到 Lando：比较法方法论的一些实例," 全球法学家前沿，4, no. 2，2004，第3页。

[53] See also, Palmer was of the same view in Palmer, "Comparative Law Methodology," 4.
另见，帕尔默在帕尔默,"比较法方法论"一文中的相同观点，第4页。

[54] Palmer, "Comparative Law Methodology," 4。 帕尔默, "比较法方法论"，第4页。

However, Comparative law for *law in practice and in action* is crucial for its utility to lawyers and stakeholders with an interest in the area, and the realist mode of comparison will not capture the essence of a law without also having knowledge of when the law came into existence, sources of law and above all its social context. To capture this essence, a high cognitive bar is expected from the author.[55] Palmer even suggested, "... it [comparative law process] *always* requires total immersion and deep preparation [emphasis added] in specific foreign languages and cultures before being attempted: the foreign system should always be seen with the inside and in socio-cultural context [emphasis added]."[56]

然而，*法律实践和行动中*的比较法对于律师和对该领域感兴趣的利益相关者的实用性至关重要，若不了解法律产生的时间、法律渊源，尤其是其社会背景，现实主义比较模式将无法抓住法律的本质。要抓住这一本质，对笔者的认知要求很高。帕尔默甚至建议："......它（比较法过程）总是需要在尝试之前完全沉浸在特定的外国语言和文化中，并做好深入的准备[着重号由笔者后加]：应始终从内部和社会文化背景来看待外国体系[着重号由笔者后加]"。

The *limit of what the book, the authors* and the readers can manage needs to be appreciated from the start in light of the PRC's phenomenal economic growth in the last few decades. Each year in the PRC, the changes in terms of urbanisation, prosperity levels, rising levels of migration, etc., are unprecedented and probably unimaginable in other societies and jurisdictions. This also affects the role of commercial law & commercial/ civil litigation in the fast-changing PRC; therefore, even a snapshot of such rapid change is difficult for any local Chinese researcher/lawyer in the PRC, let alone for a foreign researcher such as the authors embarking upon a Comparative law study by comparing the PRC legal system with the common law system. It will be important for the readers to to understand the need to analyse the *sub-context* behind the law, and to ensure that factors such as culture, language, socio-cultural context are clearly understood.[57]

鉴于中国过去几十年惊人的经济增长，从一开始就需要认识到*本书、笔者和读者所能把握的限度*。中国每年在城市化、繁荣程度、移民水平上升等方面的变化都是前所未有的，这也许是其他社会和司法管辖区难以想象的。在瞬息万变的中国，这也影响了商法和商事/民事诉讼所扮演的角色；因此，对于任何在中国当地的研究人员/律师来说，即使是对这种快速变化的缩影也是困难的，更不用说像笔者这样通过比较中国法律体系和普通法体系来开展比较法研究的外国研究人员了。重要的是，读者需要理解对法律背后的*次语境*进行分析的必要性，并确保清楚地了解文化、语言、社会文化背景等因素。

---

[55] Ibid.

[56] Ibid., 5. The author of this book has spent a considerable number of years in the PRC. He attempted to immerse himself in the culture and tried to maintain an objective view of the things around him. The author has avoided the trap of either just appeasing the hosts by praising everything or being overly critical of things after seeing them from the prism of west or a different kind of system. This approach helped the author to maintain an objective view that assisted in the research.
本书作者在中国度过了相当长的岁月。他努力使自己沉浸在中国文化中，并试图保持对周围事物的客观看法。作者避免了这样的陷阱，即一味地赞美东道主，或者从西方或另一种制度的棱镜下看待事物后对其进行过度批评。这种做法有助于作者保持客观的观点，从而有助于研究工作。

[57] Janet E. Ainsworth, "Categories and Culture: On the 'Rectification of Names' in Comparative Law," *Cornell L. Rev.* 82, no. 1 (1996): 19–42. http://scholarship.law.cornell.edu/clr/vol82/iss1/3. In addition, the theories of post-modern critiques have highlighted that criticism of comparative law is unfair as even within England, the law researchers will not be able to know the entire context. In relation to the PRC, the knowledge of any sub-context is in fact impossible due to the size and constant changes within the PRC.

However, there is a counter argument from post-modern critics that the criticism of Comparative law is unfair, and that even within a researcher's own jurisdiction, they are unable to comprehend completely the socio-cultural concepts that underpin the legal concepts and subsequent law, which have evolved in that jurisdiction. Accordingly, scholars have argued that even lawyers who only practise law within their own jurisdictions, should also free themselves from the 'limitations and distortions of their legal culture.'[58]

然而，也有后现代批评家提出反驳，认为对比较法的批评是不公平的，即使是在研究者自己的管辖范围内，他们也无法完全理解作为该管辖范围内法律概念和后续法律基础的社会文化概念。因此，学者们认为，即使是只在自己管辖范围内从事法律工作的律师，也应该摆脱'其法律文化的限制和扭曲'。

Ainsworth has succinctly described the dangers for researchers, if they were to rely on legal terminology taken from their own jurisdiction and then try to understand the same concept in a similar way in another jurisdiction. According to Ainsworth, "the very concepts and categories with which the scholar organizes this purportedly universal legal framework are freighted with culturally contingent normative baggage."[59] The authors have tried his best to avoid such pitfalls in this book, but the readers should accept some errors in this difficult and complicated task.

安斯沃斯简明扼要地描述了研究人员的危险，如果他们依赖本国司法管辖区的法律术语，然后试图在另一个司法管辖区以类似的方式理解相同的概念。根据安斯沃斯的说法，"学者用来组织这个据称具有普遍性的法律框架的概念和范畴本身，就带有文化上偶然的规范性包袱"。笔者在本书中尽力避免这些陷阱，但读者应该接受在这项艰巨而复杂的任务中出现的一些错误。

珍妮特E.安斯沃斯，"分类和文化：论比较法中的'正名'," Cornell L. Rev. 82, no. 1 (1996): 19–42. http://scholarship.law.cornell.edu/clr/vol82/iss1/3. 此外，后现代批评理论强调，对比较法的批评是不公平的，因为即使在英国，法律研究者也无法了解整个背景。就中国而言，由于中国幅员辽阔且不断变化，事实上不可能了解任何子语境。

[58] James Gordley, "Comparative Legal Research: Its Function in the Development of Harmonized Law," *Am. J. Comp. L.* 43, no. 4 (1995): 555–68, as cited in Palmer, "Comparative Law Methodology," 15.
詹姆斯-戈德利，"比较法研究： 比较法研究：它在制定统一法律中的作用," Am. J. Comp. L. 43, no. 4 (1995): 555–68，转引自Palmer，"比较法方法论"，第15页。

[59] Ainsworth, "Categories and Culture," quoted in Palmer, "Comparative Law Methodology," 17, n53.
安斯沃斯，"分类和文化"，引自帕尔默，"比较法"，17，n53。

1.4.3 Comparative Law Methodology — Most Suited for the Book

比较法方法——最适合本书的方法

The methodology is based upon the classification of the legal systems and the six to eight families into which jurisdictions can be divided:[60] according to Church and Edwards, there are six groupings for the purposes of Comparative law — *Romanic-Germanic family*, which comprises civil law countries such as France and Germany; *Common law family* such as England & Wales, USA, India, Australia; *Socialist legal family* such as China, Russia, many of which are also Civil Law countries; Religious-philosophical laws such as *Islamic* or *Hindu Law*, *African customary law*; *Mixed legal system* such as the combination of Common law and Civil law such as Quebec in Canada or Louisiana in the USA.[61]

该方法基于法律体系的分类以及可将司法管辖区划分为六至八个系的方法：根据丘奇和爱德华兹的观点，比较法可分为六类——*罗马-日耳曼法系*，包括民法系国家，如法国和德国；*普通法系*，如英格兰和威尔士、美国、印度、澳大利亚；*社会主义法系*，如中国、俄罗斯，其中许多国家也是民法系国家；宗教-哲学法，如*伊斯兰法或印度教法*、*非洲习惯法*；*混合法系*，如普通法与民法的结合，如加拿大的魁北克或美国的路易斯安那。

Church & Edwards[62] succinctly described the comparison at a *'micro level'*, where two jurisdictions within the same system of family are compared. On the other hand, political or legal philosophers can also compare two or more different systems at a *'macro level'*.

丘奇和爱德华兹简明地描述了"*微观层面*"的比较，即对同一家族体系中的两个司法管辖区进行比较。另一方面，政治或法律哲学家也可在"*宏观层面*"对两个或多个不同体系比较。

This book will involve looking at invisible factors and contexts including cases, statutes, codes from each jurisdiction, in particular, from the PRC and England & Wales at the micro level, but will also look at issues from the macro level to fully understand the issues- similarities

本书将涉及研究隐形因素和背景，包括各司法管辖区的案例、法规、法典，特别是中国和英格兰及威尔士的微观层面，但也将研究宏观层面的问题，以充分了解这些问题——异同、差距、对

---

60 Scott, "The Comparative Method of Legal Research," 4. Cf Pier Giuseppe Monateri, "Methods in Comparative Law: An Intellectual Overview," in *Methods of Comparative Law* (Cheltenham, U.K.; Northampton, MA, USA: Edward Elgar Pub., 2012), 18, where, Monateri, described the division of legal systems needs to be "seen for what they really are: biased, non-neutral political projects of governance supported by the use of the academic discipline of Comparative Law."
斯科特，"法律研究的比较方法，" 4. Cf 皮埃尔-朱塞佩-莫纳泰利，"比较法方法： 知识概述，"载于《比较法方法》（切尔滕纳姆，英国；北安普顿，美国马萨诸塞州：爱德华埃尔加出版社，2012），18，其中莫纳泰利认为，法律体系的划分需要"看清它们的真实面目：在比较法学术学科的支持下，有偏见的、非中立的政治治理项目"。

61 Refer to Figure 1- Families of Legal Systems. 参见图 1--法律体系树状图。

62 Scott, "The Comparative Method of Legal Research," 5, where he discussed a concept from Church and Edwards, "Comparative Law/Comparative Method," 1270.
斯科特，"法律研究的比较方法"， 5，他讨论了Church和Edwards的一个概念，即"比较法/比较方法"，第1270页。

and differences, gaps, protection of local businessmen in their jurisdictions. This will take into account the socio-economic aspects that underpin the relevant laws, codes, guidance, and practice directions at the macro level, including any debates that have taken place.

其司法管辖区内本地商人的保护。这将考虑到在宏观层面支撑相关法律、法规、指南和实践指南的社会经济方面，包括已经进行的任何辩论。

In order to compare the laws in the two separate jurisdictions, there is a need to deconstruct the laws, premises and justifications, as sometimes, many rules or laws in a particular jurisdiction are socially irrelevant and are just followed by practitioners and commercial men of that jurisdiction.[63]

为了对两个不同司法管辖区的法律进行比较，有必要对法律、前提和理由进行解构，因为有时特定司法管辖区的许多规则或法律与社会无关，只是该司法管辖区的从业者和商业人士遵循的规则或法

[63] Monateri, "Intellectual Overview of Comparative Law," 23. However, this approach of Comparative law clashes with that of the norm and rule approach of jurisprudents from positivist school of thought.
莫纳泰利，"比较法的知识性概述"， 23。然而，比较法的这种方法与实证主义学派法学家的规范和规则方法相冲突。

Figure 1: Families of Legal Systems
Jain Model – incorporating Chinese Legal System

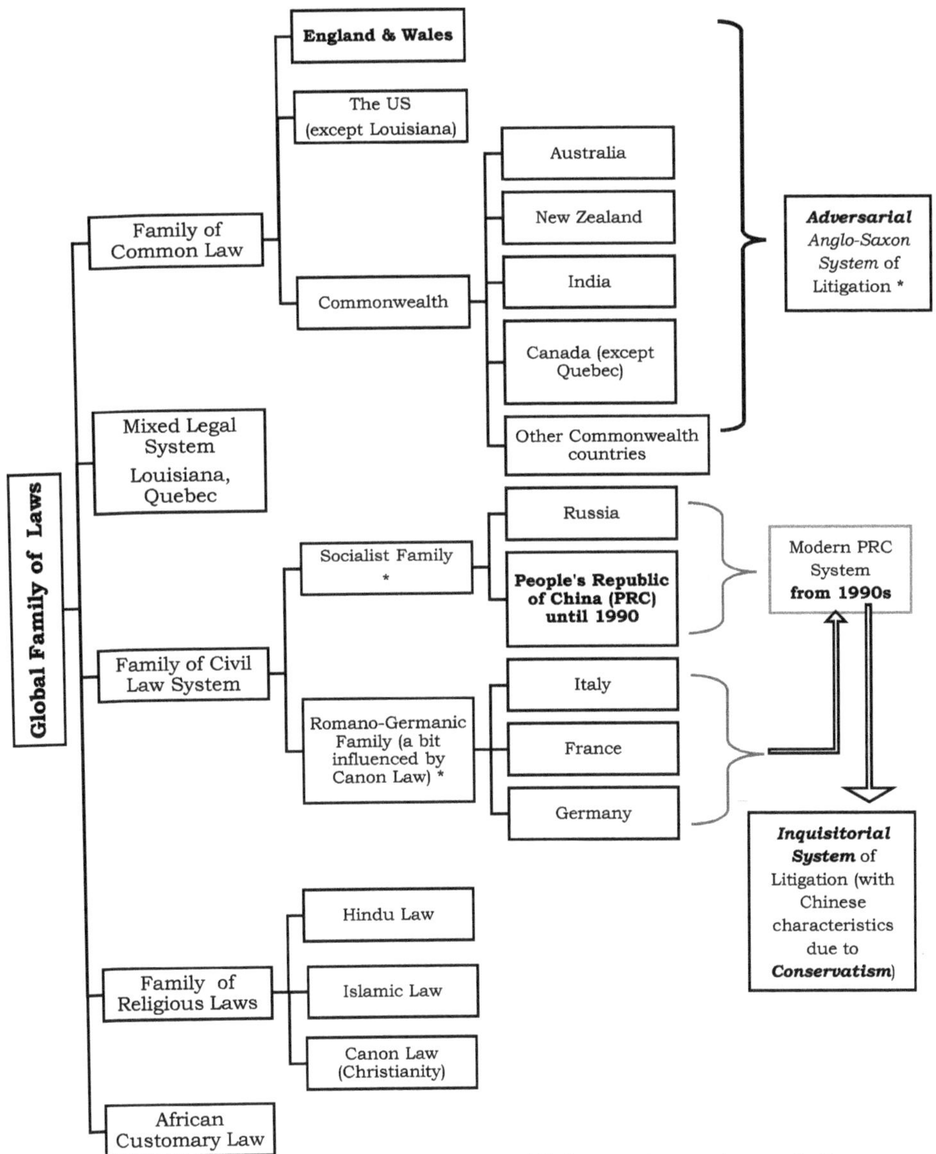

*Civil procedure systems of Romano-Germanic & Anglo-Saxon are together called *systems liberaux*. Socialist civil procedure system is different from Systems liberaux.

图 1：法律体系树状图

JAIN典范 - 融入中国法律体系

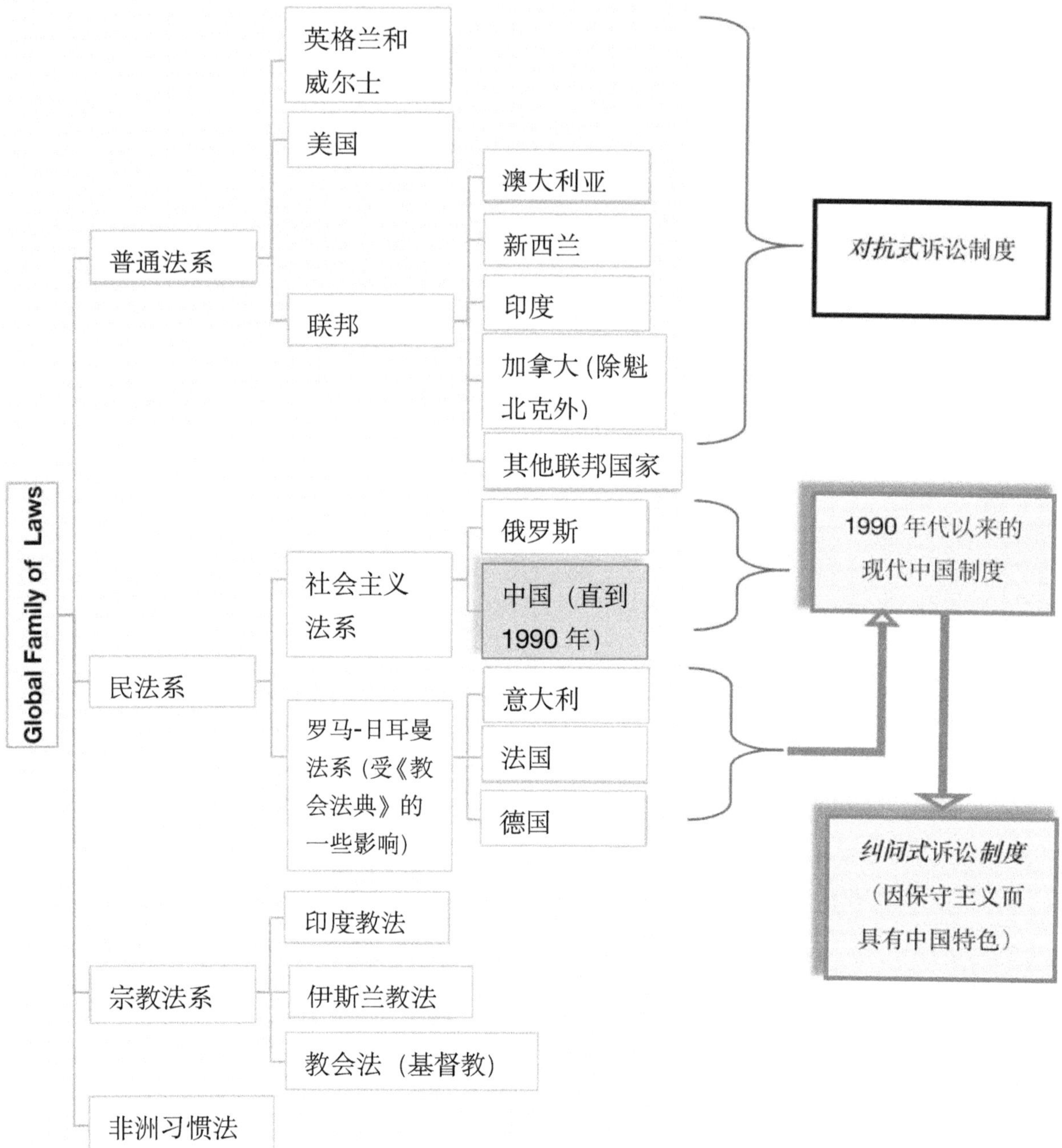

Konrad and Kotz's *Functionality Method* takes into account the problems of the society/commercial men and these problems are stated in the *functional terms*.[64] The proposition in the functionality method is that every society in every jurisdiction faces essentially the same questions due to universal values in all legal systems;[65] they may even face equivalent problems, though the methods to resolve those problems might be different.[66]

康拉德和科茨的"*功能性方法*"考虑到了社会/商业人士的问题，并用*功能性术语*来表述这些问题。功能性方法的命题是，由于所有法律体系中的普遍价值，每个司法管辖区的每个社会都面临着基本相同的问题；它们甚至可能面临着相同的问题，尽管解决这些问题的方法可能不同。

It is important to appreciate that even though rules can serve their purpose, it cannot be said with certainty that the purpose can be achieved by following the rules.[67] In addition, each legal system faces different problems due to invisible factors such as legal history and legal philosophy. In many jurisdictions, many rules may serve the purpose, and the purpose itself may not be limited to the application of rules, but they might be useful in maintaining overall legal order.[68] This methodology requires the authors not only to study the *rules*, but also to try to understand the *concepts* behind the rules that have a specific *purpose* in a particular jurisdiction.[69]

重要的是要认识到，即使规则可以达到目的，也不能肯定地说遵守规则就能达到目的。此外，由于法律历史和法律哲学等隐形因素，每个法律体系都面临不同的问题。在许多司法管辖区，许多规则可能都是为了达到目的，而目的本身可能并不局限于规则的适用，但它们可能对维护整体法律秩序有用。这种方法要求笔者不仅要研究规则，还要努力理解这些规则背后的概念，这些概念在特定的司法管辖区具有特定的目的。

In contrast to the Functional method, *the Contextual method* of Comparative law tries to find the reasons behind the law and ordinarily involves various fields of law. It is generally a difficult approach and will invariably broaden the scope of the research area. In this method, the authors will have to go beyond the pure legal devices.[70] The approach will focus on finding the *'why'* behind the laws, but there is an issue with such an approach as such research can continue

与功能法相比，比较法的语境法试图找到法律背后的原因，通常涉及法律的各个领域。这通常是一种困难的方法，而且会在无形中扩大研究领域的范围。在这种方法中，笔者必须超越纯粹的法律手段。这种方法的重点是找到法律背后的"原因"，但这种方法存在一个问题，即这种研究可能会永久持续下去。

[64] Zweigert, Kotz, and Weir, *Introduction to Comparative Law*, 31. See also, James Gordley, "The Functional Method," in *Methods of Comparative Law*, ed. Monateri. Pier G., Research Handbooks in Comparative Law. (Cheltenham, U.K.; Northampton, MA: Edward Elgar Pub., 2012), 117. See also, Ralf Michaels, "The Functional Method of Comparative Law," in *The Oxford Handbook of Comparative Law*, ed. Mathias Reimann and Reinhard Zimmermann (Oxford: Oxford University Press, 2008), 339–82.
茨威格特，科茨和威尔，比较法入门，第31页。另见James Gordley，"实用方法"，载《比较法方法》，莫纳泰利·皮尔G.，《比较法研究手册》，切尔滕纳姆，英国；北安普顿，马萨诸塞州：爱德华埃尔加出版社，2012，第117页。另见拉尔夫·迈克尔斯，"比较法的功能方法"，载《牛津比较法手册》，马蒂亚斯·莱曼和莱因哈特·齐默尔曼，牛津大学出版社，2008，第339–382页。

[65] 戈德利, "实用方法," 118。

[66] Ibid., 117.

[67] Ibid., 114.

[68] Ibid., 111.

[69] Ibid.

[70] Ibid., 35, 38.

perpetually.[71]

Palmer has differentiated between '*methods*' and '*techniques*' in the context of comparative methodology.[72] Pursuant to this method any Comparative law scholar should consider the interactions of the laws of a particular jurisdiction with the philosophy, culture, language, and nuances in the same jurisdiction.[73] This is referred to as an *organic* method,[74] where every important element of law or doctrine is looked at through the prism of culture in detail; thus, an attempt is made to capture 'its essence as a unique manifestation of the community.'[75]

帕尔默对比较方法论中的"*方法*"和"*技术*"进行了区分。根据这种方法，任何比较法学者都应考虑特定司法管辖区的法律与同一司法管辖区的哲学、文化、语言和细微差别之间的相互作用。这种方法被称为"*有机方法*"，即通过文化棱镜详细审视法律或学说的每一个重要元素，从而试图抓住"其作为社会独特表现形式的本质"。

Another method is the '*factual method*' where each jurisdiction will find a solution based on the facts of the case, rather than the terminology.[76] Palmer divided the rules into three levels — *Operative Rules, Descriptive Formants,* and *Metalegal Formants.* In Operative Rules, the judges will resolve conflicts based on judicial doctrine(s), and whether any exception has been created in finding solutions for specific types of problems. In Descriptive Formants, however reasons will be cited on the basis of procedural rules, constitutional doctrines fit within the scheme of legal arguments based on law, equity and so forth. Lastly, in Metalegal Formants, these are the *reasons for the other reasons* such as economic policy issues, other policy issues,

另一种方法是"*事实法*"，即每个司法管辖区根据案件事实而不是术语来找到解决方案。帕尔默将规则分为三个层次——执行规则、描述性形式和金属形式。在"执行规则"中，法官将根据司法理论解决冲突，以及在寻找特定类型问题的解决方案时是否存在例外情况。而在描述性表式中，则会根据程序规则、宪法理论以及基于法律、衡平法等的法律论证方案引用理由。最后，在大法律共振峰（Metalegal Formants）中，这些是其他原因的原因，如经济政策问题、其他政策问题、历史演变、法理学

[71] Antonios Emmanuel Plastas, "Functional and the Dysfunctional in the Comparative Method of Law" (December 2008), 4.
安东尼奥斯·埃马纽埃尔·普拉斯塔斯，"比较法中的功能性和非功能性"，2008年12月，第4页。

[72] Palmer, "Comparative Law Methodology," 2。帕尔默，"比较法方法论"，第2页。

[73] Eberle, "Methods of Comparative Law," 458. In this article, Eberle highlighted the concept of cultural immersion required of a researcher and as highlighted by comparativist Vivian Grosswald Curran in Vivian Grosswald Curran, "Cultural Immersion, Difference and Categories in U.S. Comparative Law," *Am. J. Comp. L.* 46, no. 1 (1998): 43–92. http://www.jstor.org/stable/841076. Vivian highlighted that a comparativist needs to free themselves of "cognitive lock-in".
艾伯勒，"比较法方法"，第 458页。在这篇文章中，Eberle 着重强调了研究人员所需的文化沉浸概念，比较法学家Vivian Grosswald Curran在 Vivian Grosswald Curran，"美国比较法中的文化沉浸、差异和类别"，Am. J. Comp. L. 46, no. 1 (1998): 43–92. http://www.jstor.org/stable/841076. Vivian强调，比较主义者需要摆脱"认知锁定"。

[74] Palmer, "Comparative Law Methodology," 7。帕尔默，"比较法方法论"，第7页。

[75] Ibid. Palmer, "Comparative Law Methodology," 7。见上引。

[76] An example used to understand the factual approach in methodology in Palmer, "Comparative Law Methodology," 18. The example used was that of the concept of pure economic tort losses that are usually unrecoverable in most common law jurisdictions; if this is applied to the facts of a case, then the question posed to the civil law jurisdiction should not be whether such pure economic losses could be recovered in that civil law jurisdiction. The civil law jurisdiction traditionally has no concept of pure economic loss.
帕尔默《比较法方法论》第 18 页中所使用的例子是纯经济侵权损失的概念，在大多数普通法司法管辖区，这种损失通常是无法赔偿的；如果将这一概念应用于案件事实，那么向大陆法系司法管辖区提出的问题就不应该是这种纯经济损失是否可以在该大陆法系司法管辖区得到赔偿。大陆法系法域传统上没有纯经济损失的概念。

historical evolution, jurisprudential reasons, contemporary social values and so forth. The authors will attempt to find such *reasons for reasons* in both the jurisdictions.

原因、当代社会价值观等。笔者将试图在这两个法域中找到这些原因的原因。

Hosten's comparative method prompts the authors to go through various *reference points*.[77] For example in England & Wales's jurisprudence, the focus is on *property rights*, while in jurisdictions such as the PRC, the focus or the reference point is *state ownership and society*; similarly the focus in many countries in Africa is on *community values*. Hosten underscores the importance of reference points, saying that "this aspect of a comparative study of laws enables jurists and statesman alike to better understand foreign attitudes to law and not mistake them for bad faith".[78] Reitz has also stressed on the same methodology, referring to the reference points as '*data points.*'

霍斯顿的比较法促使笔者通过各种*参照点*进行比较。例如，在英格兰和威尔士的判例中，重点是财产权，而在中国等司法管辖区，重点或参照点是国家所有权和社会；同样，非洲许多国家的重点是*社区价值观*。霍斯顿强调了参照点的重要性，他说："法律比较研究的这一方面使法学家和政治家都能更好地理解外国对法律的态度，而不会误认为它们是恶意的"。瑞茨也强调了同样的方法，将参考点称为"数据点"。

McEvoy's categories of Comparative law, as applied to this analysis in book, will involve, the following — (1) External I (Homogenous), where the authors will include both *horizontal* and *synchronic comparisons* along with *diachronic comparisons* that include the historical development of the horizontal laws that are being compared; (2) External II (Heterogeneous), where the authors have to consider v*ertical, synchronic* and *diachronic comparison* from various disciplines such as history, legal philosophy and so forth; (3) Internal (Homogenous) Comparative law will entail that a researcher includes *horizontal synchronic comparison* of procedural law along with the relevant substantive law with *diachronic comparisons*; and (4) Purposive categories such as harmonisation, Anti-systemisation, Cognitive explanation and Polyphonisation.[79]

麦克沃伊的比较法分类适用于本书的分析，将涉及以下内容-- (1) 外部 I（同质），笔者将进行*横向比较*、*同步比较*和*非同步比较*，其中包括所比较的横向法律的历史发展；(2) 外部 II（异质），笔者必须考虑来自不同学科（如历史、法律哲学等）的*纵向*、*同步*和*非同步比较*；(3) 内部（同质）比较法要求研究者包括程序法的*横向同步比较*以及相关实体法的*非同步比较*；(4) 目的性类别，如协调、反系统化、认知解释和复调。

---

77 WJ Hosten, "Romeinse Reg, Regsgeskeidenis en Regsvergelyking" (1962), 30.
WJ 霍斯顿，"罗马政府、政府机构和政府官员"，1962，第30页。

78 Scott, "The Comparative Method of Legal Research," 2. WJ Hosten, "Romeinse Reg, Regsgeskeidenis en Regsvergelyking" (1962), cited and translated by Scott, "The Comparative Method of Legal Research," 2. See also, Eberle, "Methods of Comparative Law," 457, where it was discussed that a comparativist should "shed built-in, native bias".
斯科特，"法律研究的比较方法"，第2页。WJ Hosten，"罗马政府、政府机构和政府官员"，1962，斯科特引用并翻译，"法律研究的比较方法"，第2页。另见Eberle，"比较法方法"，每457页，其中讨论了比较主义者应"摆脱固有的、本土的偏见"。

79 Sebastian McEvoy, "Descriptive and Purposive Categories of Comparative Law," in *Methods of Comparative Law*, ed. Pier G. Monateri (Cheltenham, U.K.; Northampton, MA: Edward Elgar Publishing, 2012), 148–52.
塞巴斯蒂安·麦科沃伊，"比较法的描述性和目的性类别"，载《比较法方法》，皮尔·G·莫纳泰利，切尔滕纳姆，英国：北安普顿，马塞诸塞州：爱德华埃尔加出版社，2012年，第148–152页。

The authors also need to avoid cultural biases referred to as 'cognitive lock-in',[80] and avoid patronising views as to what 'should' happen instead of uncovering the law and practice. This advice has been kept in mind throughout the book. In addition, the authors have adopted the best routes from the above comparative methodologies to guide the readers in this book.

笔者还需要避免被称为"认知锁定"的文化偏见，避免以偏概全地认为"应该"发生什么，而不是揭示法律和实践。本书始终贯穿这一建议。此外，笔者还采用了上述比较方法中的最佳路径来指导本书的读者。

1.5 The Practice and Procedure of Comparing Laws and Systems

比较法律和制度的实践与程序

During the last stage of Qing dynasty,[81] the civil law model of law as adopted, for example, in countries such as France or Germany. One of the reasons to adopt civil law traditions was the desire to preserve the legal traditions of ancient China. These traditions when adopted emphasised the primacy of central authority, thereby preventing judges from having flexibility and thus curbing their exercise of discretionary power. In addition, it was about keeping up with the tradition of the existing system's propensity for legal generalisation.

清朝末期，法国或德国等国采用大陆法系的法律模式。采用民法传统的原因之一是希望保留中国古代的法律传统。这些传统强调中央权威的至高无上，使法官无法灵活行事，从而限制他们的自由裁量权。此外，这也是为了保持现行制度倾向于法律泛化的传统。

Furthermore, by then, Japan had already adopted the German civil code; therefore scholars from the Qing Dynasty could easily use their knowledge in the neighbouring country because of these similarities.[82] Similarly, in the authors' view, there is always a need in any legal system to compare prevailing and popular legal systems; using various methodologies for comparisons will allow the development of legal reforms in order to reach desired outcomes that can

此外，当时日本已经采用了德国民法典；因此，清朝学者可以很容易地将他们的知识用于邻国，因为这些知识具有相似性。同样，笔者认为，任何法律体系都有必要对现行法律体系和流行法律体系进行比较；使用多种方法进行比较将有助于法律改革的发展，从而达如愿以偿地促进贸易和商业交易。

---

80 Curran, "Cultural Immersion"。库兰，"文化浸润"。

81 Refer to Table 1 of the book。参考本书表 1。

82 Chen Lei, "Contextualizing Legal Transplant: China and Hong Kong," in *Methods of Comparative Law*, ed. Pier G. Monateri (Cheltenham, U.K.; Northampton, MA: Edward Elgar Pub., 2012), 196–97.
陈磊，"法律移植的语境化：中国和香港特别行政区"，载《比较法方法》，Pier G. Monateri，切尔滕纳姆，英国；北安普顿，马塞诸塞州：爱德华埃尔加出版社，2012年，第196–197页。

stimulate trade and commercial transactions.

Merchants and businessmen in other countries are often told daunting stories by foreign lawyers and media about the legal and civil procedural system in the PRC; thus by word of mouth, transaction costs are increased for all parties. A few of the stories may be true, but in the authors' view, no system is perfect. Anyone with an interest in the PRC, be they foreign lawyers, businessmen or research scholars, should have some awareness of the PRC legal system. However, the authors are writing from the position of having personally encountered the justice system in the PRC.

外国律师和媒体经常向其他国家的商人和商人讲述关于中国法律和民事诉讼制度令人生畏的故事；因此，通过口口相传，各方的交易成本都增加了。其中一些故事可能是真实的，但笔者认为，任何制度都不可能十全十美。任何对中国感兴趣的人，无论是外国律师、商人还是学者，都应对中国的法律制度有一定的了解。不过，笔者是站在亲身经历过中国司法制度的立场上写作的。

As with any justice system, the PRC's system is not perfect. However, the authors have observed a noticeable keenness and genuine desire on the part of judges, legal academicians and local PRC lawyers to improve the legal system. This, in the authors' view, is a good foundation for any legal system to blossom. This is in sharp contrast to many common law jurisdictions, where the centuries-old tradition of uninterrupted development has led to an element of haughtiness and superiority creeping in. These unwanted elements are detrimental to the smooth evolution of law.

与任何司法系统一样，中国的司法系统也并非完美无缺。然而，笔者注意到，法官、法学学者和中国本地律师对完善法律制度有着明显的热忱和真诚的愿望。笔者认为，这是任何法律制度开花结果的良好基础。这与许多普通法司法管辖区形成了鲜明对比，在这些司法管辖区，数百年来不间断的发展传统导致了傲慢和优越感的悄然滋生。这些不良因素不利于法律的顺利发展。

According to Plastas, the purpose of Comparative law studies is not only that they provide 'valid comparison but they serve some purpose.'[83] In the context of pure academic research, the purpose of Comparative law research is to gain 'knowledge'.[84] Plastas has described the process of comparison, and states that its purpose is law reforms in legislatures, while Zweigert, Kotz & Weir highlight that the aim of practising lawyers may be to obtain better legal solutions, which might be available in other jurisdictions. The current comparison will consider the astonishingly rapid development of the PRC's economy in the last two decades,

普拉斯塔斯认为，比较法研究的目的不仅在于提供“有效的比较，还在于服务于某种目的”。就纯学术研究而言，比较法研究的目的是获取“知识”。普拉斯塔斯描述了比较的过程，并指出其目的是立法机构的法律改革，而茨威格特、科茨和威尔则强调，执业律师的目的可能是获得更好的法律解决方案，而这些解决方案可能在其他司法管辖区可用。本次比较将考虑中国经济在过去二十年中惊人的快速发展，以及自二十世

83 Antonios Emmanuel Plastas, "Functional and the Dysfunctional in the Comparative Method of Law" (December 2008), 6.
安东尼奥斯·埃马纽埃尔·普拉斯塔斯，“比较法中的功能性和非功能性”，2008年12月，第6页。

84 Konrad Zweigert and K. Kotz, trans., Tony Weir, *An Introduction to Comparative Law*, 3rd revised ed. (Oxford: Clarendon Press, 1998), 15. Kotz and Zweigert have described the purpose of Comparative law as a means to harvest and garner knowledge.
康拉德·茨威格特和K·科茨翻译，Tony Weir著：比较法入门，第3版，牛津：克拉伦登出版社，1998年，第15页。科茨和茨威格特将比较法的目的描述为收获和获取知识的一种手段。

and other issues that have become important for stakeholders since the 1980s.

纪八十年代以来对利益相关者变得重要的其他问题。

This comparison of common law v. Chinese law will become even more important in the coming years as there will be more cross-border transactions, and gradually corporations and businessmen, local and from around the world, will come to rely more on the PRC courts to protect their commercial interests. The question will further gain prominence due to the PRC's big-ticket projects like the '*Belt and Road Initiative*' and other similar international projects. The remedies available in the PRC legal system to protect the interests of the parties are essential for ensuring sustained economic growth in those jurisdictions, and for ensuring that businessmen and corporations, both local and foreign, continue to have faith in the PRC's legal system.

普通法与中国法的比较在未来几年将愈发重要，因为将有更多的跨境交易，本地和来自世界各地的公司和商人将逐渐更依赖中国法院来保护他们的商业利益。随着中国如"一带一路"倡议和其他类似的大型国际项目展开，这一问题将进一步凸显。中国法律体系中可用来保护当事人利益的救济措施对于确保这些司法管辖区的持续经济增长以及确保本地和外国商人和公司继续对中国法律体系抱有信心来说至关重要。

This book has been written for purely practical purposes, for example, to ensure that commerce can flourish, and that scholars, businessmen & those in commerce can supplement their knowledge about PRC laws, have realistic expectations, and understand how the local courts in the PRC can assist them.[85] A similar aim was also discussed by Scott, echoing Church and Edwards; he asserted that the purpose of Comparative law is to assist people in commerce learn about foreign laws and how these laws can affect them.[86] Scott gave further examples of many Comparative law institutes that are in existence in France and Germany to assist regional businessmen and corporations.[87]

本书的写作目的纯粹是为了能学以致用，例如，确保商业繁荣，让学者、商人和从事商业活动的人能够增进有关中国法律的知识，实事求是，并了解中国当地法院如何为他们提供帮助。斯科特也讨论了类似的目的，与丘奇和爱德华兹如出一辙；他断言，比较法的目的是帮助商人了解外国法律及这些法律会如何影响他们。斯科特进一步举例说明了法国和德国现有的许多旨在为地区商人和公司提供帮助的比较法研究所。

The authors hope that the readers will gain a good overview of the PRC legal system and the invisible factors affecting it. This will assist them to compare it against their own

笔者希望读者们能对中国的法律制度及影响该制度的隐形因素有一个全面的了解。这有助于他们将自己的经验与

[85] It is the authors' view that this is even more relevant during the times of apprehensions about trade under WTO, ongoing trade war between US & China starting from 2018 and so forth.
笔者认为，在人们对世贸组织下的贸易感到忧虑，2018 年起中美贸易战持续不断等情况下，这一点显得更为重要。

[86] J Church and A.B. Edwards, "Comparative Law/Comparative Method," in *Introduction to South African Law and Legal Theory*, WJ Hosten, et al. (Durban: Butterworths, 1995), 1264. Church and Edwards was discussed by T.J. Scott, "The Comparative Method of Legal Research," 3, http://italeem.iium.edu.my/2014.
J·丘奇和A·B·爱德华兹，"比较法/比较方法"，载《南非法律和法律理论入门》，WJ 霍斯顿，德班：巴特沃斯出版社，1995年，第1264页。T·J·斯科特在"法律研究的比较方法"一文中讨论了丘奇和爱德华兹，3，http://italeem.iium.edu.my/2014。

[87] Scott, "The Comparative Method of Legal Research," 2。斯科特，"法律研究的比较方法"，第 2页。

experience with the most common legal system of England and Wales, which follows the common law system.

英格兰和威尔士最常见的法律制度（遵循普通法制度）进行比较。

CHAPTER 2 — HISTORICAL ORIGINS OF SUBSTANTIVE AND PROCEDURAL LAW – COMMON LAW v. CHINESE LAW

第二章 实体法与程序法的历史渊源——普通法与中国法

2. Introduction to Chapter Two

第二章导言

In order to understand laws in any jurisdiction, it is important to consider the historical evolution of the substantive and procedural law. Without taking into account the origins, it is very difficult to understand the context of the laws and to speculate how a judge in a foreign jurisdiction will think. These are important *invisible factors* and provide *one of the contexts*, which businessmen and/or foreign lawyers need to appreciate before working with legal experts in a foreign jurisdiction. The authors here discusses the historical origins of substantive and civil procedural law for both the common law of England & Wales and PRC law.

为了理解任何司法管辖区的法律，重要的是要考虑实体法和程序法的历史演变。如果不考虑起源，就很难理解法律的背景，也很难推测外国司法管辖区的法官会如何思考。这些都是重要的无形因素，提供了商人和/或外国律师在与外国司法管辖区的法律专家合作之前需要了解的背景之一。本文探讨了普通法系和中华人民共和国法系实体法和民事诉讼法的历史渊源。

The authors provide the readers with a comparison of the two jurisdictions in relation to historical evolution at the end of this Chapter. However, it is important that readers try to reach their own conclusions as to the comparison of the evolution of substantive and procedural law in both the jurisdictions.

在本章的最后，作者为读者提供了两个司法管辖区在历史演变方面的比较。然而，重要的是，读者在比较两个司法管辖区的实体法和程序法的演变时，尽量得出自己的结论。

2.1 Historical Origins of Substantive Law and Civil Procedural Law in England & Wales

英格兰和威尔士实体法和民事诉讼法的历史渊源

In this book, historical analysis of the evolution of substantive law and civil procedure law provides context and is an essential invisible factor in understanding the relevant issues in each of the jurisdictions. The area covered by these factors is colossal; however, the authors will try to convey the ideas succinctly to allow readers to comprehend the issues clearly.

在本书中，对实体法和民事诉讼法演变的历史分析为理解每个司法管辖区的相关问题提供了背景，是一个必不可少的无形因素。这些因素所涵盖的领域是巨大的；然而，作者将尽量简洁地传达思想，让读者清楚地理解问题。

Figure 2: Historical Origins of Common Law and Civil Procedural Law in England & Wales

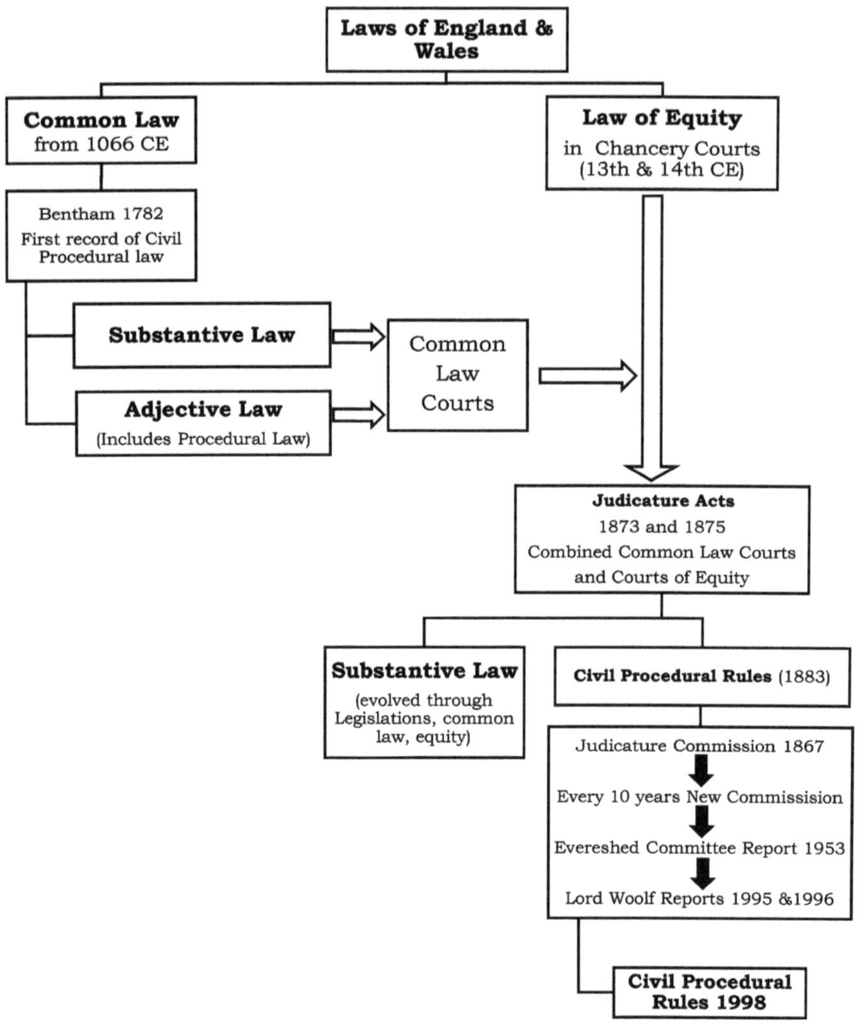

图 2：英格兰和威尔士普通法和民事诉讼法的历史渊源

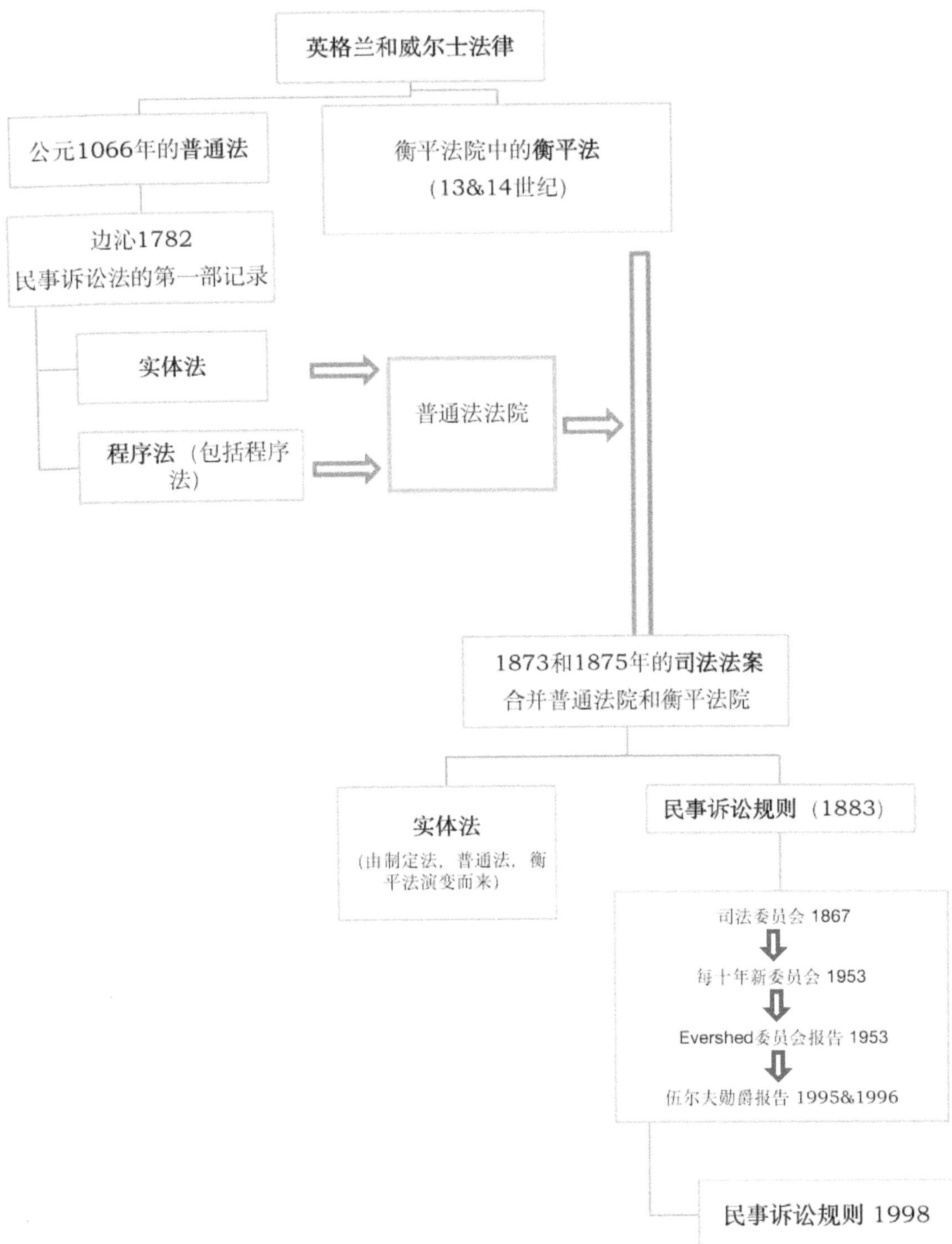

2.1.1 Common Law & Equity - Substantive Law v. Civil Procedure Law

普通法与衡平法-实体法与民事诉讼法

For many centuries in England, civil cases were litigated either in the common-law courts or the courts of equity. Each of these courts had different kinds of relief, and different procedural reliefs were granted to the litigants.

几个世纪以来，英国的民事案件不是在普通法法庭提起诉讼，就是在衡平法法庭提起。每个法院都有不同种类的救济，给予诉讼当事人的程序性救济也不同。

2.1.1.1 Common Law

普通法

There is a long history of substantive law in common law. For example, according to history, common law originated in 1066 CE, meaning that this body of law is nearly a thousand years old. However, according to Risinger, the earliest record of procedural law in England & Wales (with the division of laws into either substantive or procedural law) can only be traced to the eighteenth century:

实体法在普通法中有着悠久的历史。例如，根据历史，普通法起源于公元 1066 年，这意味着这一法律体系已有近千年的历史。然而，根据 Risinger 的说法，英格兰和威尔士最早的程序法记录（将法律分为实体法和程序法）只能追溯到 18 世纪：

The dichotomy was fathered by Jeremy Bentham in a 1782 work entitled Of Laws in General, sub norm [emphasis in original] the distinction between substantive law and adjective law. Bentham there makes clear that he believes he is drawing a near distinction in the descriptive organization and analysis of the concept of law, and an examination of the leading pre-Bentham sources on English legal theory supports his claim.[Michael D. Risinger, "'Substance' and 'Procedure' Revisited: With Some Afterthoughts on the Constitutional Problems of 'Irrebuttable Presumptions'," UCLA L. Rev. 30, no. 2 (1982): 191 (footnotes omitted), and quoted in Thomas O. Main, "The Procedural Foundation of Substantive Law," Wash. U. L. Rev. 87, no. 4 (2009): 4. http://ssrn/abstract=1113916. However, in the same article,

这种二分法是由杰里米·边沁在 1782 年的著作《论一般法律，次规范（原文强调）》中提出的实体法和程序法的区别。边沁在书中明确表示，他相信他在对法律概念的描述性组织和分析中描绘了一种近似的区别，对边沁之前英国法律理论的主要来源的考察支持了他的主张。[Michael D. Risinger，“重新审视“实质”和“程序”：对“不可辩驳的推定”的宪法问题的一些反思”，UCLA L. Rev. 30, no。2(1982)：191（脚注省略），引自 Thomas O. Main，“实体法的程序基础”，华盛顿。《美国法典》第 87 号。4(2009)：4。http://ssrn/abstract=1113916。然而，在同一篇文章中，瑞辛格在脚注 3 中提到了许多作

Risinger has mentioned in footnote 3, many ancient books by authors such M. Bacon, A New Abridgment of the Law (5th ed, 1798), and N. Blackstone, Commentaries on Laws of England (1765) that seemed to have no distinction between procedural and substantive law.]

者的古书，如M.培根的《法律新删节》(1798年第5版）和N.布莱克斯通的《英国法律评论》（1765年），这些书似乎没有区分程序法和实体法。]

In the earlier years of the development of procedural law, it seems there was a difference between '*adjective law*' and '*procedural law*'. Risinger mentioned that procedural law was 'only a part, though a major part, of adjective law'.[88]

在程序法发展早期，“程序法（作者注：关于法律诉讼手续和程序的法律））”和“程序法”似乎是有区别的。瑞辛格提到，程序法“只是程序法的一部分，尽管是主要的一部分”。

Later, it became common knowledge which of the adjective laws would be helpful to litigants, and thus the way in which the law would protect the rights of the litigants would be specified. In spite of the debate as to whether procedural law ever existed in a separate form before this development, this particular format has been used to bring actions in court for a long time, to pursue the claims or rights of the claimants.

之后,它成为常识的形容词将有助于当事人的法律,因此,法律会保护当事人的权利会被指定。尽管关于在这一发展之前程序法是否曾以一种单独形式存在的争论，但这种特殊形式长期以来一直被用于在法庭上提起诉讼，以追求索赔人的要求或权利。

There were also separate forms for different causes of action. Common-law courts in England & Wales had experience in writs, forms, and pleadings for centuries.[89] It is important to note that in those years, common-law lawyers thought about the substantive law through these forms.

不同的诉因也有不同的诉讼形式。几个世纪以来,英格兰和威尔士的普通法法院在令状、表格和诉状方面都有经验。值得注意的是，在那些年，普通法律师是通过这些形式来思考实体法的。

There would have been no remedy available through the courts for a civil dispute, if a form of a writ already fixed was not available.[90] In a few areas, where the substantive law was just evolving, such as in law of tort, lawyers used the forms and procedures to evaluate the merits of a case. Sir Henry Maine has said, "Substantive law has at first the look of being gradually secreted in the interstices of procedure."[91]

就没有补救措施可以通过法院民事纠纷,如果命令的形式已经固定并不是可用的。在一些实体法刚刚发展的领域，例如侵权法，律师使用表格和程序来评估案件的是非曲直。亨利·缅因爵士曾说过：“实体法初看起来像是逐渐隐藏在程序的间隙中。

---

[88] Risinger, "Substance and Procedure Revisited," n 11 at 191, where Risinger discussed Bentham's discussion on adjective law.
里辛格，“重新审视实质与程序”，第11期，第191页，里辛格讨论了边沁关于程序法的讨论。

[89] Thomas O. Main, "Traditional Equity and Contemporary Procedure," *Wash. L. Rev.* 78, no. 2 (2003): 454.
托马斯·O·梅因，《传统衡平法与当代程序》，*Wash. L.* 第78卷，第2期，2003，第454页。

[90] Rhee and Verkerk, "Civil Procedure," 3。李和沃克，《民事程序》，第3页。

[91] Henry S. Maine, *Dissertations on Early Law and Custom* (Delhi: B. R. Pub Corporation, 1985), 389 and as quoted in Main, "Procedural Foundation of Substantive Law," 7.

2.1.1.2 Law of Equity

衡平法

Historically, and even today, the law of equity is famous for allowing for the exercise of judges' discretion, and its emphasis on fairness.[92] In jurisprudential terms, the term 'equity' means "power to do justice in a particular case by exercising discretion to mitigate the rigidity of strict legal rules."[93] Bray has discussed the special characteristics of equity, namely that it involves "case-specific judgment, moral reasoning, discretion, or anti-opportunism."[94] It seems that this distinction slowly is blurring the lines between common law and the law of equity.[95] According to Bray, in law of equity, there are three categories of equitable remedies:[96]

从历史上看，甚至在今天，衡平法以允许法官行使自由裁量权和强调公平而闻名。在法学术语中，"衡平法"一词是指"在特定案件中行使自由裁量权以减轻严格法律规则的刚性的权力"。布雷讨论了衡平法的特殊特征，即它涉及"个案判断、道德推理、自由裁量权或反机会主义"。布雷认为，在衡平法中，衡平法救济有三类：

- First category: injunctions, constructive trusts, accounting for profits and specific performance;
- Second category: equitable remedies such as contempt of power;
- Third category: equitable remedies such as defenses and equitable justifiability requirements.

- 第一类：禁制令、推定信托、利润核算和具体履行；
- 第二类：藐视权力等衡平法救济；
- 第三类：衡平法救济，如抗辩和衡平法合理要求。

The English courts of Equity, called Court of Chancery procedures, were based on the Romano-canonical European

英国衡平法院，称为衡平法院程序，是以罗马-规范的欧洲大陆法律模式为基

亨利·S·缅因，《早期法律与习俗论文集》，德里：B.R. Pub Corporation，1985年，第389页，引自Main，"实体法的程序基础"，第7页。

[92] Samuel L. Bray, "The System of Equitable Remedies," *UCLA L. Rev.* 63, no. 3 (2016): 532.
塞缪尔·L·布雷，《衡平法救济制度》，UCLA L.，第63卷，第3期，2016，第532页。

[93] Kevin C. Kennedy, "Equitable Remedies and Principled Discretion: The Michigan Experience," *U. Det. Mercy L. Rev.* 74, no. 4 (1997): 609.
凯文·C·肯尼迪，《公平救济和原则性自由裁量权：密歇根的经验》，《美国高等法院》第74卷，第74期，4，1997年，第609页。

[94] Bray, "Equitable Remedies," 536。布雷，《衡平法救济》，第536页。

[95] Ibid., 532.

[96] Ibid., 533–34.

continental model of law, and no common-law method of writs was applicable in such courts.[Rhee and Verkerk, "Civil Procedure," 3.] The Romano-canonical model was itself based on Roman as well as medieval laws, namely " the law of northern Italian cities and papal decretals."[Ibid.] Equitable remedies were developed in this Court of Chancery. In the thirteenth and fourteenth centuries, the Chancery Court, which started as the administrative department, slowly took over the judicial role to resolve disputes.

础的，没有普通法令状方法适用于这些法院。[Rhee 和 Verkerk，"民事诉讼，" 3。] 罗马正典模式本身是基于罗马和中世纪的法律，即"意大利北部城市的法律和教皇的法令"[同上]。衡平法院所发展了衡平法救济。在 13 世纪和 14 世纪，衡平法院，最初作为行政部门，慢慢地接管了解决纠纷的司法角色。

The Chancery Court gradually developed its own procedure; at the turn of the sixteenth century, common-law lawyers began to be chosen as Chancellor instead of bishops, who had up till then been heading these courts.[97] Bit by bit, principles of equity started to develop in the Chancery courts. In the early nineteenth century, the court of equity was dissolved, but the principles of equity remained in the English legal system. This step is often talked of in terms of fusion of law & equity in England & Wales, or merger in the United States.[98] The fusion of common law and equity courts was finally accomplished in *Judicature Acts of 1873 – 1875* in England.[99]

衡平法院逐渐发展了自己的程序；在 16 世纪初，普通法律师开始被选为大法官，而不是主教，在此之前一直是主教领导这些法庭。渐渐地，衡平法原则开始在衡平法院里发展起来。19 世纪初，衡平法院被解散，但衡平法原则仍留在英国法律体系中。在英格兰和威尔士法律与衡平法的融合或在美国的合并中，这一步骤经常被谈论。英国普通法与衡平法的融合最终在 1873 - 1875 年的《司法法案》中完成。

When claimants made claims pursuant to equity, there were no forms, no special way of arguing a cause of action. The main yardsticks to decide the cases were the judge's discretion, fairness, and good conscience. These criteria do not match with the formal procedural requirements that were the hallmark of the common-law courts. In the Court of equity, there were no procedural requirements such as pleadings or forms, and the focus, in particular, was on the substantive law to determine the relief in equity.

当索赔人根据衡平法提出索赔时，没有形式，没有特殊的方式来争论诉因。判决案件的主要标准是法官的自由裁量权、公正性和良知。这些标准不符合作为普通法法院标志的正式程序要求。在衡平法院，不存在诉状或表格等程序性要求，尤其侧重于确定衡平法救济的实体法。

97 Bray, "Equitable Remedies," 537。布雷，《衡平法救济》，第537页。

98 Ibid.

99 See *Supreme Court of Judicature Act 1873* ,36 & 37 Vict, c 66 and *Supreme Court of Judicature Act 1875*, 38 & 39 Vict, c 77.
参见1873年最高司法法院法，第36和37条，第66条和1875年最高司法法院法，第38和39条，第77条。

2.1.1.3 Evolution of Common Court of Common Law and Equity

普通法庭中普通法与衡平法的演变

The common courts that were developed in the twelfth century were largely procedural as to evidence and proof, but matters of facts were left for the jury selected from the community.[100] As the system of case precedents had not yet evolved during that time, it still represented a unified application of law.[101] In fact, in these earlier centuries, the substantive law was created in courts on arguments based on hypothetical facts.[102] The judges in these earlier times, while making law, were thinking in procedural terms rather than substantive terms.[103]

12 世纪发展起来的普通法庭在证据和证明方面主要是程序性的，而事实问题则留给从社会中选出的陪审团。由于当时判例制度尚未形成，它仍然代表着法律的统一适用。事实上，在早期的几个世纪里，实体法是在法庭上基于假设事实的争论而创立的。这些早期的法官在制定法律时，考虑的是程序问题而不是实体问题。

As seen in the above section, even though there were no procedural rules in courts of equity, these courts started making a few rules to assist the litigants. On the other hand, the common-law courts started to adopt the good practices of the courts of equity by simplifying the process for resolving civil disputes. Gradually, over the years, the differences between these two courts were limited to procedure or mode of trial.

如上节所述，尽管衡平法院没有程序规则，但这些法院开始制定一些规则来帮助当事人。另一方面，普通法法院开始采用衡平法院的良好做法，简化解决民事纠纷的程序。多年来，这两个法院之间的差异逐渐局限于程序或审判方式。

In the end, both the courts — Courts of common law and Courts of equity – were merged.[104] Across the Atlantic, the US was establishing a new court system modelled on the common law system but comprised of the dual system of state and federal courts. There were statutes that were drafted by US Congress that distinguished the substantive law from procedural law. These US courts in later years were to have a profound effect on civil procedure law in

最后，两个法院-普通法法院和衡平法法院-被合并。在大西洋彼岸，美国正在建立一种以普通法体系为蓝本的新法院体系，但由州法院和联邦法院的双重体系组成。美国国会起草的成文法区分了实体法和程序法。这些美国法庭在后来的岁月里对英国的民事诉讼法产生了深远的影响。因此，借鉴类似普通法制度的良好

[100]Gerald J. Postema, "Classical Common Law Jurisprudence (Part I)," *Oxford U. of Commw. L.J.* 2, no. 2 (2002): 160.
杰拉尔德·波斯特马，古典普通法法理学（第一部分），*Oxford U. of Commw.L.J.* 2，第2期，2002年，第160页。

[101] Ibid.

[102] Ibid., 162.

[103] Ibid.

[104] Main, "Equity and Contemporary Procedure," 464。
缅因，"衡平法与当代程序"，第464页。

England. Therefore, the development of common law was enhanced by adopting good practices in similar common law systems.

做法，促进了普通法的发展。

As codification was gaining momentum in England & Wales, procedural laws and substantive law were slowly drifting apart, and common aspects between the two laws were slowly decreasing. As substantive law and procedural law were developing distinct identities, scholars slowly started to consider civil procedural law as inferior to substantive law. Even after many years of discussion by scholars, this tag of procedural law being inferior to substantive law has remained.

随着英格兰和威尔士的法典化势头渐强，程序法与实体法逐渐渐行渐远，两者之间的共同点也逐渐减少。随着实体法与程序法逐渐形成鲜明的同一性，学者们逐渐开始认为民事诉讼法不如实体法。即使经过学者们多年的讨论，程序法不如实体法的标签仍然存在。

However, the definition of and divide between substantive law and procedural law have never been that clear. We can see from the examples below that it is difficult to state with certainty, whether something is procedural or substantive in nature:

然而，实体法和程序法的定义和区分却一直不那么明确。从下面的例子中我们可以看出，很难肯定地说明某件事是程序性的还是实质性的：

- Issue of Time bar in context of claims - does this issue fall under substantive law, or does it come under procedural law?

诉请背景下的时间限制问题-这个问题属于实体法，还是属于程序法？

- Issue of case law in relation to issuing and service of claim forms - whether such issues fall under substantive law, or procedural law?

有关发出及送达索偿表格的判例法问题-这些问题是属于实体法还是程序法范畴？

- Issue of interim remedies, both pre-trial and post-trial - whether such issues are under substantive law or under procedural law?

审前和审后临时补救办法的问题--这些问题是属于实体法还是程序法？

- Issue of statutes dealing with Evidence and Burden of Proof - are they a matter of substantive law or procedural law?

关于证据和举证责任的成文法问题——它们是实体法问题还是程序法问题？

The answers to the above questions are not clearly identifiable, nor can they be separated easily into substantive or procedural law.

上述问题的答案并不明确，也不能轻易区分为实体法或程序法。

In simple words, civil procedure law is a body of law that the English courts follow to adjudicate the litigation before them. It traditionally starts with the issuance of a claim form, its service on the opponents, pleadings such as Statement of Claim & Defence Submissions, various interim applications in courts & orders, legal aid and so forth. The main aim of any civil procedure, as in the common-law grounded US legal system, is based on the 'liberal ethos',[105] where the main purpose of any civil procedure is to ensure easy access to the justice system and to adjudicate disputes based on merit.[106]

简而言之，民事诉讼法是英国法院在审理诉讼时所遵循的法律体系。传统上，诉讼程序首先是发出诉讼表格、向对手送达诉讼表格、诉状（如起诉状及答辩状）、向法庭提出的各种临时申请及命令、法律援助等。任何民事诉讼程序的主要目的，就像以普通法为基础的美国法律体系一样，都是基于“自由主义精神”，其中任何民事诉讼程序的主要目的都是确保容易进入司法系统，并根据价值裁决纠纷。

Civil Procedure law, as discussed earlier, is a body of law that is not completely isolated from the various substantive laws. This body of law is usually drafted in all jurisdictions to facilitate the resolution of disputes in the courts, where substantive law(s) such as law of contract, tort, agency and so on are applicable to the matter of dispute. When the litigants knock on the doors of the courts that are established by the Constitution of any country, then these courts represent the overall system that is present in that jurisdiction. This system is the combined product of the constitution, legal system, legal philosophy, legal culture, legal education and so forth of that jurisdiction; therefore, one selected element within a system cannot just be looked at in isolation. These are the invisible factors and contexts that the stakeholders cannot ignore.

如前所述，民事诉讼法是一个不完全脱离各种实体法的法律体系。这一法律体系通常是在所有司法管辖区起草的，以便在法庭上解决争议，其中实体法，如合同法、侵权法、代理法等适用于争议事项。当诉讼当事人敲开根据任何国家宪法设立的法院的大门时，这些法院就代表了该司法管辖区的整体制度。这一制度是该司法管辖区的宪法、法律制度、法律哲学、法律文化、法律教育等因素综合作用的产物；因此，不能孤立地看待系统中的一个选定元素。这些是利益相关者不能忽视的无形因素和背景。

---

105 Benjamin A. Spencer, "The Restrictive Ethos in Civil Procedure," *Geo. Wash. L. Rev.* 78, no. 2 (2010): 101. Benjamin used the term 'liberal ethos' to describe the Federal civil procedure under 1938 rules.
本杰明·A·斯宾塞：《民事诉讼中的限制性精神》，*Geo. Wash. L.*，第78卷，第2期，2010年，第101页。本杰明用“自由主义精神”一词来描述1938年规则下的联邦民事诉讼程序。

106 Spencer, "Restrictive Ethos of Civil Procedure," 101. See also Main, "Procedural Foundation of Substantive Law," 5.
斯宾塞，《民事诉讼的限制性精神》，第101页。参见缅因，“实体法的程序基础”，第4页。

2.1.1.4 Origins of the Current English Procedural System

现代英国诉讼制度的起源

When parties have a civil dispute, one of the oldest ways to resolve the dispute was by means of violence. However, as societies advanced up the ladder of sophistication, as businesses prospered and nations started to trade with each other, civil dispute resolution systems for and within the society began to be developed. Legal historians have also confirmed that civil litigation procedures in advanced societies replaced the rough justice of self -help, revenge, counter-reprisal and vendetta.[107]

当当事人发生民事纠纷时，最古老的解决纠纷的方法之一就是暴力。然而，随着社会的发展，随着商业的繁荣和国家之间的贸易往来，社会内部和社会内部的民事纠纷解决机制开始发展起来。法律历史学家也证实，在发达社会，民事诉讼程序取代了自助、报复、反报复和仇杀等粗暴的司法程序。

Along similar lines, Coutre described civil litigation as 'civilisation's substitute for vengeance'.[108] In a way, the civil procedural system replaced violence as the common means to resolve civil disputes. Consistency of decisions in the courts along with the way the system can make parties feel about the legal system, especially the weaker parties, are hallmarks of advanced societies. These markers will in turn ensure the legitimacy of the civil courts and in the broader context will ensure the application of the rule of law within a society.

类似地，Coutre 将民事诉讼描述为"文明的复仇替代品"。在某种程度上，民事诉讼制度取代了暴力，成为解决民事纠纷的常用手段。法院判决的一致性，以及司法体系能让各方（尤其是弱势方）对法律体系产生感觉的方式，是先进社会的标志。这些标志将反过来确保民事法庭的合法性，并在更广泛的背景下确保法治在社会中的适用。

There were demands for swift justice after the adoption of the *Magna Carta* in AD 1215. However, over the years, in both the common law and the court of equity, litigants began to experience excessive delays. In the nineteenth century, even the novelist Charles Dickens highlighted the ills of the civil litigation system in England.[109] It was also

公元 1215 年《大宪章》通过后，人们要求迅速伸张正义。然而，多年来，无论是在普通法法院还是衡平法法院，诉讼当事人都开始经历过度的拖延。在 19 世纪，就连小说家查尔斯·狄更斯也强调了英国民事诉讼制度的弊病。当时的法学家在许多讲座中也强调了这一点。

---

107 See F. Pollock and F. Maitland, *The History of English Law Before the Time of Edward I, Volume 1 & 2* (Cambridge: Cambridge University Press, 1988).
见F·波洛克和F·梅特兰，《爱德华一世之前的英国法律史》，第一卷和第二卷，剑桥：剑桥大学出版社，1988年。

108 E.J. Couture, "The Nature of Judicial Process," *Tul. L. Rev.* 25, no. 1 (1950–51): 7.
E·J·科图雷，《司法程序的本质》，*Tul. L. Rev.* 第25卷，第1期，1950–51，第7页。

109 C. Dickens, *Bleak House* (Harmondsworth: Penguin, 1996). It was discussed in Anthony Clarke, "The Woolf Reforms: A Singular Event or an Ongoing Process," and in *The Civil Procedure Ten Years On*, ed. Deirdre Dwyer (Oxford: Oxford University Press, 2009), 33–49.
C·狄更斯，《荒凉山庄》，哈蒙兹沃斯：企鹅出版社，1996年。这在安东尼·克拉克的《伍尔夫改革：一个单一事件或一个持续的过程》和迪尔德丽·德怀尔主编的《民事诉讼十年》，牛津：牛津大学出版社，2009年，第33-49页中有所讨论。

highlighted in many lectures by jurists of the time.[110]

In the early twentieth century, due to the advent of *Judicature Acts of 1873 and 1875*,[111] the Chancery Courts and the common-law courts together became a Supreme Court. In addition, the new rules of the Supreme Court ('RSC') came into existence pursuant to *Supreme Court of Judicature Act 1875*. These rules themselves were replaced later by RSC 1883. Though these new rules brought in more litigants to access the civil courts, leading to more reliance upon the litigation system, over the years again, the civil courts found themselves in a state of crisis.[112]

20 世纪初，由于 1873 年和 1875 年《司法法案》的出台，衡平法法院和普通法法院一起组成了最高法院。此外，根据 1875 年《最高法院司法法》，最高法院（RSC）的新规则应运而生。这些规则后来被 RSC 1883 所取代。虽然这些新规则使更多的诉讼当事人进入民事法院，导致对诉讼制度的更多依赖，但多年来，民事法院再次发现自己处于危机状态。

There were thus two crises - one in the eighteenth and nineteenth centuries, and another in the late twentieth century. To deal with the first crisis, two commissions were appointed - first in 1828, and then again in 1850 with the appointment of the second common law commission. Both these commissions attempted to bring in reforms to cut expenses and delays in courts by making the civil process faster and less cumbersome. This was done by simplifying the civil procedures. The Chancery Court was given power of common-law courts and was reformed as well. However, these structural and procedural simplifications could not resolve the ongoing crisis.

因此，出现了两次危机——一次发生在 18、19 世纪，另一次发生在 20 世纪后期。为了应对第一次危机，任命了两个委员会，第一次是在 1828 年，第二次是在 1850 年，任命了第二个普通法委员会。这两个委员会都试图进行改革，通过加快民事诉讼程序，减少繁琐的程序，以减少费用和法庭延误。这是通过简化民事程序来实现的。衡平法院被赋予普通法院的权力，并进行了改革。然而，这些结构和程序上的简化并不能解决目前的危机。

The *Judicature Commission* was appointed in 1867. This Commission argued to replace all courts by 'one single omnipresent Supreme Court',[113] meaning that just one

司法委员会于 1867 年成立。该委员会主张用"一个无所不在的最高法院"取代所有的法院，这意味着只需要一个

[110] W. B. Odgers, "Changes in Procedure and in the Law of Evidence," in *A Century of Law Reform: Twelve Lectures on the Changes in the Law of England During the Nineteenth Century* (London: The Macmillan Company, 1901), 212. In this article, Odger said "Sadly hampered in the year 1800 by cumbrous procedure and pedantic technicalities which caused the suitors expense, delay, vexation and disgust. It took years for a merchant to recover a debt due to him... [and even then] ... half the actions were decided not on their real merits, but on questions of forms and pleadings."
W·B·Odgers，W·B·欧哲斯，"程序和证据法的变化"，载《一个世纪的法律改革：关于 19 世纪英国法律变化的十二场讲座》（伦敦：麦克米伦公司，1901 年），第 212 页。在这篇文章中，Odger 说："在 1800 年，繁琐的程序和迂腐的技术导致了追求者的花费，拖延，烦恼和厌恶。一个商人花了好几年才收回欠他的债。[即使那样]…一半的案件不是根据案情的真伪来决定的，而是根据形式和诉状来决定的"。

[111] See *Supreme Court of Judicature Act* 1873, 36 & 37 Vict, c 66 and *Supreme Court of Judicature Act 1875*, 38 & 39 Vict, c 77.
参见1873年最高司法法院法，第36和37条，第66条和1875年最高司法法院法，第38和39条，第77条。

[112] C. Glasser, "Solving the Litigation Crisis," *The Litigator* (1994): 14. This article was discussed recently by Anthony Clarke in Clarke, "Woolf Reforms- Singular Event?" 39.
C·格拉瑟，"解决诉讼危机"，《诉讼律师》，1994年，第14页。这篇文章最近由安东尼·克拉克在克拉克《伍尔夫改革——奇异事件？》，第39页。

[113] Clarke, "Woolf Reforms- Singular Event?" 39。克拉克《伍尔夫改革——奇异事件？》，第39页。

system of procedure would be needed. That was a big simplification in itself as all procedure was to be found in just one *White Book* as edited by Thomas Snow in later years.[114] It is important to note that similar reforms, where the common law and equity merged, were introduced in the United States by David Dudley Field through the 1848 Code of Procedure of the State of New York.[115] Therefore, the necessary and relevant reforms in the common law grounded US legal system came even before those in the English Legal System, which was the founder of the common law legal system.

程序系统。这本身就是一个很大的简化，因为所有的程序都可以在后来由托马斯·斯诺编辑的一本白皮书中找到。值得注意的是，美国的大卫·达德利·菲尔德（David Dudley Field）通过 1848 年《纽约州程序法典》(Code of Procedure of New York）引入了类似的改革，将普通法与衡平法合并。因此，以美国法系为基础的普通法系的必要和相关的改革，甚至比普通法系的奠基人英国法系的改革还要早。

Thereafter, every ten years, new Procedural Reform Committees or Commissions[116] were appointed in England & Wales. All the Reports generated by such Committees and Commissions attempted to reduce cost and complexity, except for the Peel Committee Report in 1932. All such reports relied on the structural and procedural reforms within the court system in England & Wales. However, a fresh approach was recommended in the Evershed Committee Report.[117]

此后，每十年在英格兰和威尔士任命新的程序改革委员会或委员会。除了 1932 年的皮尔委员会报告外，这些委员会的所有报告都试图降低成本和复杂性。所有这些报告都依赖于英格兰和威尔士法院系统的结构和程序改革。然而，Evershed 委员会报告建议采用一种新的方法。

For the first time, there was discussion about the need for new features of case management using sanctions and summons for directions to limit legal costs, and issues to control costs for ordinary litigants. Some other minor recommendations were introduced in relation to the use of relevant documentary evidence instead of oral evidence. The most important of such reports was by Lord Woolf in 1995 and 1996.[118] It replaced RSC, which were already 124 years

会议首次讨论了需要采用制裁和传唤指示的案件管理新特点来限制法律费用，以及控制普通诉讼当事人费用的问题。关于使用有关的书面证据而不是口头证据，提出了其他一些次要建议。这类报告中最重要的是伍尔夫勋爵在 1995 年和 1996 年的报告。它取代了 1999 年已有 124 年历史的皇家莎士比亚剧团。

---

114 Earlier there were multiple procedures such as Daniell's Chancery Practice, Stephen's Pleading in Civil Actions, Tidd's Practice, a guide to common law process, or Chitty's Precedents in Pleading; all these were converted into just one civil procedure book called the White Book.

115 Rhee and Verkerk, "Civil Procedure," 3，李和沃克，《民事程序》，第3页。

116 For e.g., in 1908 Gorell Committee, in 1913 St Aldwyn Committee, in 1922 Swift Committee, in 1932 Hanworth Committee and Peel Commission, in 1947 Evershed Commission, in 1968 Win Committee, in 1979 Cantley Committee, in 1988 Civil Justice Review Report followed by Heilbron/Hodge in 1994 and Middleton's views in 1997.
例如，1908年的Gorell委员会，1913年的St Aldwyn委员会，1922年的Swift委员会，1932年的Hanworth委员会和Peel委员会，1947年的Evershed委员会，1968年的Win委员会，1979年的Cantley委员会，1988年的民事司法审查报告，随后是1994年的Heilbron/Hodge和1997年的Middleton的观点。

117 Lord Evershed, *Committee on Supreme Court Practice and Procedure, Final Report*, Cmd 8878 (1953). It was discussed in Clarke, "Woolf Reforms - Singular Event?" 40.
埃弗谢德勋爵，最高法院惯例和程序委员会，最后报告，Cmd 8878（1953）．克拉克在《伍尔夫改革——奇异事件？》"第40页。

118 See Lord Woolf, *Acces s to Justice: Interim Report to the Lord Chancellor on the Civil Justice System in England and Wales* (London: HMSO, 1995) See also Lord Woolf, *Access to Justice: Final Report to the Lord Chancellor on the Civil Justice System in England and Wales* (London: HMSO, 1996). These reports highlighted the need for results in the court to be just, fairness of the courts towards litigants,

old in 1999. In addition, it also replaced County Court Rules. County Courts are the lowest court in the hierarchy of the Court System in England & Wales. The details of the court systems in England and Wales will be discussed in Chapter Four of this book.

此外，它还取代了县法院规则。郡法院是英格兰和威尔士法院系统等级制度中最低的法院。英格兰和威尔士法院制度的细节将在本书的第四章中讨论。

The *Woolf Reforms 1999* simplified procedural rules were simplified, and the use of old case precedents in civil procedure was done away with.[119] Rules were simplified in brand new Civil Procedural Rules (hereinafter 'CPR').[120] These are regularly updated and amended based on the experience of the courts. It is the authors' view a similar approach might be needed in many other common-law jurisdictions such as India, where delay in courts is legendary.

1999 年伍尔夫改革简化了程序规则，废除了民事诉讼中的旧判例。新的《民事诉讼规则》（以下简称《民事诉讼规则》）对规则进行了简化。根据法院的经验，定期更新和修订这些准则。作者认为，在许多其他普通法司法管辖区（如印度），可能需要采取类似的方法，在这些司法管辖区，法庭延误是众所周知的。

It is crucial to note that the first reforms introduced in England in the eighteenth and nineteenth centuries to deal with the crisis in the civil litigation system failed because the rules became more technical. In addition, the culture and mindset of litigation as practiced by the judges and lawyers of the times did not change. This resulted in the failure of the first set of reforms that were implemented to bring about improvements in the way civil litigation was conducted in the courts.

值得注意的是，18 世纪和 19 世纪英国为应对民事诉讼制度危机而进行的第一次改革失败了，因为规则变得更加技术性。此外，当时法官和律师实践的诉讼文化和思维并没有改变。这导致了第一批改革的失败，这些改革旨在改善法院审理民事诉讼的方式。

According to Clarke, the Woolf forms brought about changes in litigation culture in the following ways:

克拉克认为，伍尔夫形式在以下几个方面带来了诉讼文化的变化：

- By introduction of active case management that took the control of progress of claims from the hands of the parties (mainly their lawyers) and

采用积极的案件管理办法，从当事人（主要是他们的律师）手中收回对索偿进度的控制，并将其交回法院；

appropriate procedures at a reasonable cost, the need to deal with cases with reasonable speed, the need to be understandable to those who use it, to be responsive to those who use it, to be responsive to the needs of litigants, to provide as much certainty as possible, and to ensure courts are effectively resourced and organized. See also Deirdre Dwyer, ed., *The Civil Procedure Rules Ten Years On* (Oxford; New York: Oxford University Press, 2009), 2–3.
参见伍尔夫勋爵，《诉诸司法：向大法官提交的关于英格兰和威尔士民事司法制度的临时报告》（伦敦：英国移民局，1995年）。另见伍尔夫勋爵，《诉诸司法：向大法官提交的关于英格兰和威尔士民事司法制度的最终报告》（伦敦：英国移民局，1996年）。这些报告强调，法院的结果必须公正，法院对诉讼人公平，以合理的费用进行适当的程序，必须以合理的速度处理案件，必须让使用它的人理解，对使用它的人作出反应，对诉讼人的需要作出反应，提供尽可能多的确定性，并确保法院得到有效的资源和组织。另见Deirdre Dwyer主编，《民事诉讼规则十年》，牛津；纽约：牛津大学出版社，2009年，第2-3页。

[119] The philosophy behind the new Rules is discussed a bit more in Chapter 4, §4.2.1。新规则背后的理念在第4章第4.2.1节中有更多的讨论。

[120] *Civil Procedural Rules 1998, SI 1998/3132 (as amended until August 2016)*. 1998年民事诉讼规则，SI 1998/3132（修订至2016年8月）。

put it back in the hands of the Courts;[121]

- By introducing the overriding objective and secondary objectives;[122]

通过介绍首要目标和次要目标；

- By imposing duty on the litigants and their representatives to assist the courts in furthering the overriding objectives.[123]

通过规定诉讼当事人及其代表有责任协助法院推进最重要的目标。

Under the new *CPR 1999*, new judges are more active as compared to judges in the years before the reforms set in. Rhee and Verkerk are of the view that this development in England in 1998 was influenced by the early twentieth century Austrian reformer Klein, who also advocated active judges in contrast to passive judges. The Klein model was adopted by many countries in continental Europe such as Germany and France.[124]

根据新的《1999年刑事司法改革条例》，新法官比改革前几年的法官更加活跃。Rhee和Verkerk认为，1998年英国的这种发展受到了20世纪初奥地利改革家克莱因的影响，克莱因也提倡主动法官，而不是被动法官。克莱因模式被德国、法国等欧洲大陆的许多国家所采用。

2.1.2 Historical Origins of Substantive Law and Civil Procedural Law in PRC

中国实体法与民事诉讼法的历史渊源

It is essential to first discuss the subtle difference between the substantive and procedural Law of the PRC. Thereafter, the author will discuss the historical origins of procedural law in traditional PRC and recent developments in the current PRC Civil Procedure Law (‘*CPL 1991, latest amended in 2023).*

首先有必要讨论中华人民共和国实体法与程序法之间的微妙区别。之后，作者将讨论传统中华人民共和国程序法的历史渊源以及现行中华人民共和国民事诉讼法（CPL 1991，2023年最新修订）的最新发展。

121 Jack I.H. Jacob, *The Fabric of English Justice*, Hamlyn Lecture Series (London: Sweet & Maxwell, 1987), 7.
杰克·I·H·雅各布：《英国司法的结构》，哈姆林系列讲座，伦敦：Sweet & Maxwell出版社，1987年，第7页。

122 For more discussion on this topic, refer Chapter 4, §4.2.1.1. The importance of overriding objective was cited in A. Zuckerman, *Zuckerman on Civil Procedure: Principles of Practice*, 2nd ed. (London: Sweet and Maxwell, 2006), 3.
关于这个主题的更多讨论，请参阅第4章，§4.2.1.1。A. Zuckerman, Zuckerman on Civil Procedure: Principles of Practice，第2版，London: Sweet and Maxwell，2006。A·扎克曼，《民事诉讼：实践原则》中引用了压倒一切目标的重要性，第2版，伦敦：Sweet and Maxwell出版社，2006年，第3页。

123 See CPR r.1.1(3); In this rule, the hope of previous Commissions' was converted into an obligation on the parties, as discussed in Clarke, "Woolf Reforms- Singular Event?" 45.
见CPR r.1.1(3)；在这条规则中，以前委员会的希望被转化为各方的义务，正如克拉克在《伍尔夫改革-单一事件？》，第45页。

124 Rhee and Verkerk, "Civil Procedure," 4.
李和沃克，《民事程序》，第4页。

2.1.2.1 History of Substantive Law v. Civil Procedural Law in PRC

中国实体法与民事诉讼法的历史

Throughout Chinese legal history, the main focus was on penal Codes and the importance of family relationships.[125] However, surprisingly, within the context of the family relationship, details of inheritance, property and commerce in society are not as detailed as one would have expected in a civilized society.[126] Whatever rules were present in ancient China, such as for land use, regulation of debt and market transactions, were primarily concerned with maintenance of good order,[127] rather than with encouragement of commerce for wealth creation. Another reason cited by Chinese legal historians for the sparseness of rules was the Confucian concept of 'nourishing the people' (*yang min*) based on the concept of sharing of resources to keep the populace 'fed, housed and employed'.[128]

纵观中国的法律历史，主要的焦点是刑法和家庭关系的重要性。然而，令人惊讶的是，在家庭关系的背景下，社会中继承、财产和商业的细节并不像人们在文明社会中所期望的那样详细。无论古代中国有什么规则，比如土地使用、债务管理和市场交易，主要都是为了维护良好的秩序，而不是为了鼓励商业创造财富。中国法律史学家列举的另一个原因是儒家"养民"的概念，该概念基于共享资源的概念，以保证民众"吃、住、就业"。

Possibly the lack of civil litigation within ancient Chinese society was also the result of Confucian thought about 'self-cultivation', which encouraged individuals to reflect on their conduct, and such reflection was treated as a mitigating factor.[129] Further, the Confucian school of thought led to distrust of lawyers and valuing education,[130] and in the authors' view, stunted the growth of civil litigation over the centuries. There are extreme examples from its history, in which 'litigation tricksters' or 'pettifoggers' (*sung kun*) found promoting litigation were subjected to severe punishments.

中国古代社会缺乏民事诉讼可能也是儒家"修身"思想的结果，儒家思想鼓励个人反思自己的行为，这种反思被视为一种缓解因素。此外，儒家思想导致了对律师的不信任和对教育的重视，在作者看来，这阻碍了几个世纪以来民事诉讼的发展。历史上有一些极端的例子，其中"诉讼骗子"或"诉讼骗子"（宋坤）被发现促进诉讼受到严厉的惩罚。

---

125 Refer to Table VIII on Chinese Dynasties in Chapter 1。
参见第一章关于中国历代的表八。

126 Geoffrey MacCormack, *The Spirit of Traditional Chinese Law*, The Spirit of the Laws (Athens; London: University of Georgia Press, 1996), 8.
杰弗里·麦考马克：《中国传统法律精神》，《法律精神》，雅典；伦敦：佐治亚大学出版社，1996年，第8页。

127 Ibid.

128 Ibid., 9.

129 Ibid., 9–11.

130 Ibid., 10–11.

A very similar concept to that of human rights, which has gained prominence in western jurisprudence in the last few decades, was available in ancient China; termed '*jen*', this concept was prized by neo-Confucians,[131] especially after the Song dynasty.[132] It was founded on the Confucian teaching that a ruler, in whose hands were placed all legislative powers, has to be benevolent and humane. However, the authors' view is that this concept of '*jen*' was very particular to Chinese society and in reality, cannot be compared with the current school of thought pertaining to human rights as available in western societies.

一个与人权概念非常相似的概念，在过去几十年里在西方法理学中获得了突出地位，在古代中国也可以找到；这个概念被称为"仁"，受到新儒家的推崇，尤其是在宋朝之后。它是建立在儒家学说的基础上的，即一个统治者必须仁慈和人道，他掌握着所有的立法权。然而，作者的观点是，这种"仁"的概念是中国社会所特有的，在现实中，不能与西方社会当前有关人权的思想流派相提并论。

131 Ibid., 9.
132 Refer to Chapter 1, Table VIII。参见第一章，表八。

Figure 3: Historical Origins of Substantive and Civil Procedural Law in PRC

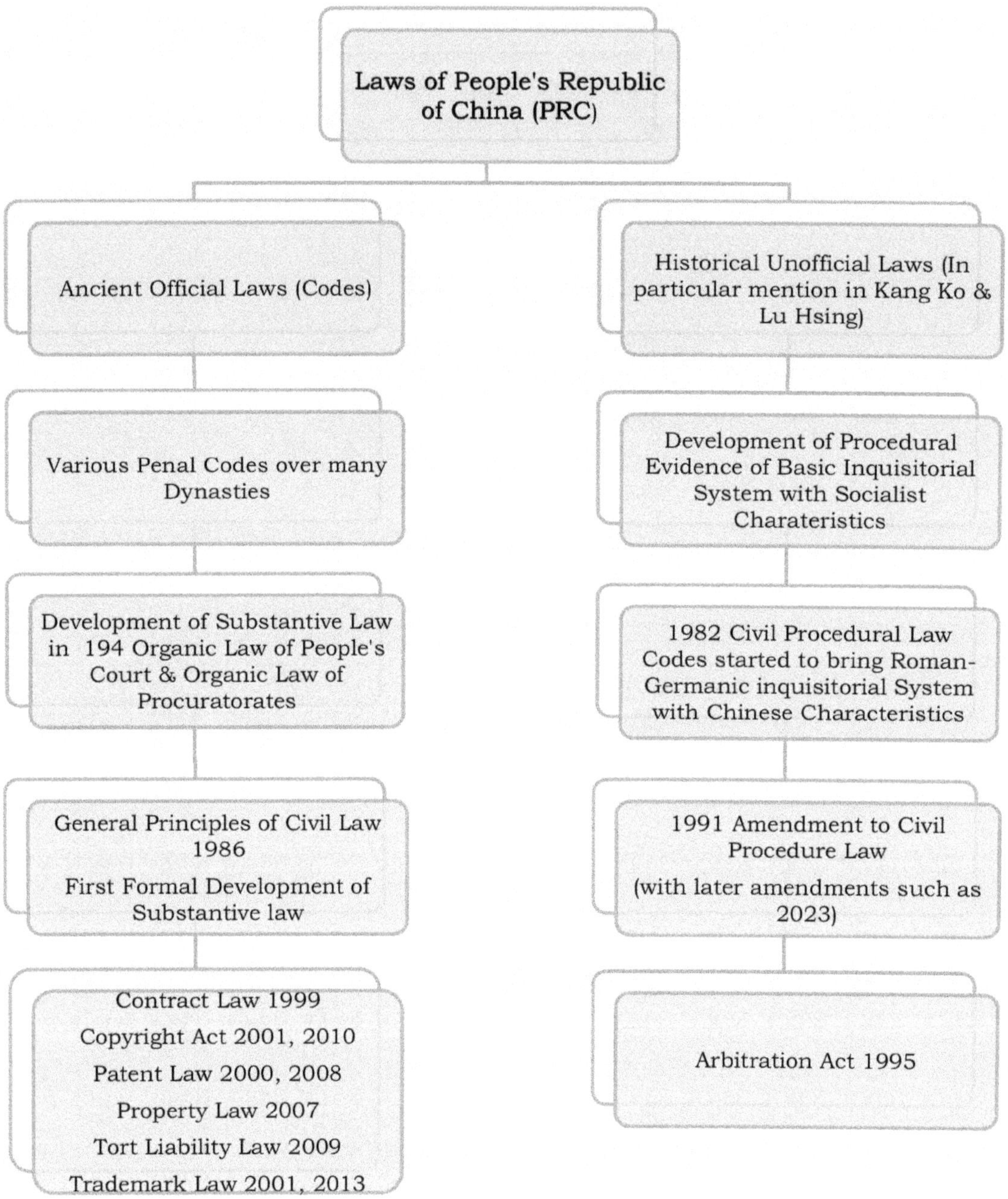

图 3：中国实体法和民事诉讼法的历史渊源

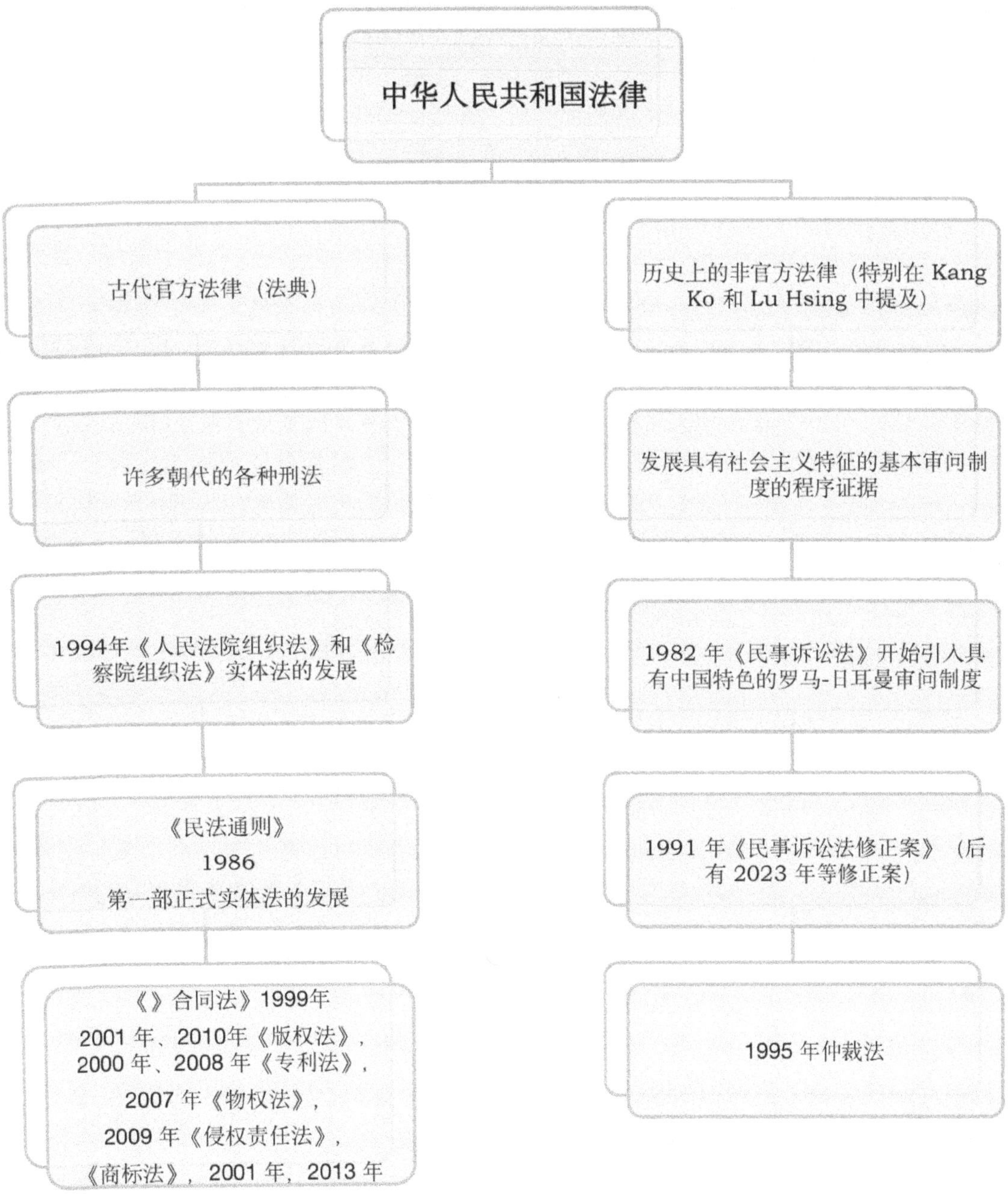

Chinese legal history and jurisprudence are famous for constructing a narrative that harmonious society should prevail over any conflict, and therefore, society needs to avoid any kind of litigation.[133] Tang dynasty Code not only discouraged, but actually put a prohibition on litigation. Wu, reflecting a complete change in attitude in the PRC in relation to litigation, said, "The prosperity of law and the development of legal spirit are all based on litigation. With no litigation, there will be no truth and justice."[134] In the authors' view, this current thought process of scholars such as Wu is a significant departure from ancient thought processes and should not be treated lightly.

中国法制史和法理学以构建和谐社会战胜冲突的叙事而闻名，因此，社会需要避免任何形式的诉讼。唐代法典不仅不鼓励诉讼，实际上还禁止诉讼。他说："法律的繁荣和法律精神的发展都是以诉讼为基础的。没有诉讼，就会有公平和正义。"在笔者看来，像吴这样的学者目前的思维过程与古代的思维过程有很大的不同，不能掉以轻心。

Historically, unlike the ancient Chinese Penal Codes (mostly for criminal offences) that were available during most dynasties, it has been very difficult for foreign historians even to decipher the historical administrative legal system and its principles that governed ancient China. This may be because there could have been a lack of human interest in any non-criminal laws; however, such legal principles are available sometimes from varied sources, including customary rules that can be assumed culturally or are occasionally discussed.[135]

从历史上看，与大多数朝代都有的中国古代刑法典（主要针对刑事犯罪）不同，外国历史学家甚至很难解读古代中国的历史行政法律体系及其原则。这可能是因为人类对任何非刑事法律都可能缺乏兴趣；然而，这些法律原则有时可以从各种来源获得，包括可以在文化上假定或偶尔讨论的习惯规则。

Fortunately, after the fall of the Qing dynasty, there was an attempt to compile those principles that were not readily available in most provinces, and findings were even published later by Kroker.[136] Two things were clear: first, that there was a system of delegation to manage the huge land mass of ancient China; and second, at the same time, there was an extensive and well-established system of supervision. Specially commissioned imperial investigators

幸运的是，清朝灭亡后，有人试图编纂这些在大多数省份都不容易获得的原则，Kroker后来甚至发表了这些发现。有两件事是明确的：第一，古代中国有一种委派制度来管理巨大的土地；第二，与此同时，有一个广泛而完善的监督体系。专门委任的皇家调查员接受了监督、审查等角色的培训。这一制度也遵循和

---

133 Book of Changes, for "ten evils" provided by the Codes of Tang Dynasty and as discussed in Jing-Xiong Wu, *A Study of Legal Philosophy* (Shanghai: Shanghai Law Translation & Edition Press, 1933), 15; and cited and discussed in Qinhua He, "The Birth and Growth of Modern Jurisprudence in China," *Frontiers of Law in China* 1, no. 4 (2006): 508.
《易经》，对《唐法典》规定的"十恶"及吴敬雄所述，《法哲学研究》，上海：上海法律译版出版社，1933，第15页；何勤华：《现代法学在中国的诞生与成长》，载《中国法学前沿》第1期，第2期。4，2006，第508页。

134 Wu, *A Study of Legal Philosophy*, 24 as quoted and discussed in He, "Birth and Growth of Modern Jurisprudence," 508.
吴：《法哲学研究》第24页，引用并讨论于何《现代法学的诞生与成长》，第508页。

135 MacCormack, *Spirit of Traditional Chinese Law*, 19–20. 麦科马克，《中国传统法律精神》，第19-20页。

136 MacCormack, *Spirit of Traditional Chinese Law*, 21, cited in an endnote on page 215, Kroker "rechtsgewohnheiten in der Provinz Shantung nach *Ming Shang shih hsi kuan tiao ch'a pao kao lu*" that was published in *Monumenta Serica* 14 (1949-55), 215-302.
《中国传统法的精神》，第21页，引用于第215页的尾注。克洛克《rechtsgewohnheiten in der Provinz山东nach Ming Shang shih hsi kuan tiao cha pao kao lu》，载《历史古迹》第14期，1949-1955，第215-302页。

were trained for the role of supervisor, censor and so on. The system followed and adopted legalist jurisprudential thought as well.[137]

采纳了法家法理学思想。

Most of the private or civil law in ancient Chinese legal history was contained in something equivalent to an *unofficial law*. The Emperor and his officials in various provinces adopted a 'hands-off' attitude.[138] The likely reason for this could be that many of the civil laws were actually included in the penal codes, as they assisted the authorities in maintaining law & order; for example, rules on debt or recovery or borrowing or pledging of property and even sales of goods were included in these penal codes (instead of having a separate civil code).

中国古代法制史上的私法或民法大多包含在某种相当于非正式法的东西中。皇帝和各省的官员采取了"不干涉"的态度。可能的原因是，许多民法实际上包含在刑法中，因为它们有助于当局维持法律和秩序；例如，关于债务或追回、借款或财产质押甚至货物销售的规则都列入这些刑法（而不是单独的民法典）。

Another reason can be found in the prevailing philosophy and thought processes in ancient China, which maintained that the populace should remain well-fed and clothed, and should have a share in the available resources. The hands-off attitude could also be due to concern for maintaining the harmony of society as a whole by avoiding civil litigation. Magistrates were discouraged from intervening due to their responsibility for maintaining order efficiently. Magistrates were also prevented from acting as arbiters in civil disputes.

另一个原因可以在古代中国盛行的哲学和思想过程中找到，它认为民众应该保持温饱，并且应该分享可用的资源。这种不干涉的态度也可能是由于担心通过避免民事诉讼来维持整个社会的和谐。由于治安官有责任有效地维持秩序，因此他们不愿干预。地方法官也被禁止在民事纠纷中担任仲裁者。

However, there were contradictions: on one hand, there was a desire to maintain harmony, peace and order in ancient Chinese society, but on other hand, there seemed to be no available mechanisms for resolving civil disputes. However, in the Ming and Qing dynasties, older and more influential people were appointed through the perfectures to prevent and settle disputes. There is evidence in legal history that magistrates' help was indeed asked for in order to resolve such civil disputes, and these magistrates would then refer the matter back to the elders in the villages.

然而，矛盾是存在的：一方面，中国古代社会有维护和谐、和平与秩序的愿望，但另一方面，似乎没有解决民间纠纷的有效机制。然而，在明清时期，更年长和更有影响力的人通过完美来防止和解决争端。法律史上有证据表明，为了解决这类民事纠纷，确实需要地方法官的帮助，然后这些地方法官会把问题提交给村里的长老。

However, the civil court system available in the west at around that time, during the development of the common

然而，在普通法系或大陆法系的发展过程中，西方的民事法院制度并没有

137 MacCormack, *Spirit of Traditional Chinese Law*, 21。麦科马克，《中国传统法律精神》，第21页。

138 Ibid., 23.

law system or the continental civil law system, was not established in ancient China. As discussed in preceding paragraphs, the legal profession was not so developed in ancient China, and lawyers were in fact looked down upon and in some cases were even punished.[139]

在中国古代建立起来。正如前面几段所讨论的，中国古代的法律职业并没有那么发达，律师实际上是被看不起的，在某些情况下甚至受到惩罚。

Lawyers in most jurisdictions play an important part in developing the legal system; this tradition in the authors' view seems to be missing in ancient China. In contrast, one of the old books, *Ming shang shih hsi kuan tiao ch'a pao kao lu*, which means 'Reports on Investigation of Civil and Commercial Customs' had compiled lists of various customs used to deal with issues of that time. In this book, legal customs were arranged by province, under three main headings: "real rights and obligations, personal rights and obligations and rights and obligations arising from marriage, adoption or inheritance."[140] However, further investigation of these customs indicates that not much thought went into important issues such as the relationship of those customs with the statutory law of that time. Further, a significant question asked by legal historians is whether it was completely an '*unofficial law*'?[141]

在大多数司法管辖区，律师在法律制度的发展中发挥着重要作用；在作者看来，这一传统在古代中国似乎缺失了。相比之下，《明商事海关调查报告》(《明商事海关调查报告》）汇编了当时处理各种问题的海关清单。在这本书中，法律习俗按省份排列，分为三个主要标题：“物权和义务，个人权利和义务，婚姻，收养或继承产生的权利和义务。”然而，对这些习俗的进一步考察表明，对这些习俗与当时成文法的关系等重要问题的思考并不多。此外，法律史学家提出一个重要问题，它是否完全是一部“非官方法律”？

However, procedural justice in ancient China could be found as early as during the Zhao period through *Kang ko*, or a few centuries later in *Lu hsing*, which was the procedural manual for a ruler to order punishments. The processes were inquisitorial, and the magistrates would investigate the circumstances to find relevant facts.[142]

然而，中国古代的程序正义早在赵朝时期就通过《纲令》，或几个世纪后的《律行》（统治者命令惩罚的程序手册）中得到了体现。审判过程是询问式的，地方法官将调查情况以找出相关事实。

In contrast, in modern PRC, regulations were promulgated on 3 September, 1953, identifying principles for trials and systems, including open trial, circuit justice and jury system. These regulations also required the Procuratorate's involvement in civil litigation. Most socialist legal systems have a Procuratorate body to investigate and prosecute such issues. The regulations that were promulgated at all levels by the Central People's Government Committee were

而现代中华人民共和国则于1953年9月3日颁布了《条例》，明确了审判原则和制度，包括公开审判、巡回审判和陪审制度。这些规定还要求检察院参与民事诉讼。大多数社会主义法制国家都设有检察院来调查和起诉这类问题。中央人民政府委员会在各级颁布了《人民法院组织暂行条例》、《最高人民检察

[139] Ibid., 25–26.
[140] Ibid., 26.
[141] Ibid.
[142] Ibid., 27–31.

Interim Organic Regulation of People's Courts, Interim Organic Regulation of the Supreme People's Procuratorate and Organic General Principles of People's Procuratorate.[143]

院组织暂行条例》和《人民检察院组织总则》。

Subsequently, in 1954, the PRC promulgated the *First Constitution* together with *Organic Law of People's Courts and Organic Law of People's Procuratorate*s, which further developed principles and systems concerning civil litigation and established trial organization, basic trial principles and systems of civil litigation.[144]

1954 年，中华人民共和国第一部《宪法》和《人民法院组织法》、《人民检察院组织法》相继颁布，进一步完善了民事诉讼的原则和制度，确立了民事诉讼的审判组织、审判基本原则和制度。

In October 1956, the Supreme People's Court (highest hierarchical PRC Court) summarized civil trial experience since the founding of the PRC and delivered a summary of the experiences associated with Civil Case Handling Procedure by various courts at various levels in the PRC. This *Summary* assisted in correcting mistakes in trial practices and thereby assisted in enhancing judicial efficiency.[145] The Summary was composed of seven parts: receiving cases, pre-trials, trial, adjudication, appeal, retrial, enforcement. In 1957, the Supreme Court changed the Summary into Provisions, and enacted the Procedure of Hearing Civil Cases (draft), which included eighty-four provisions.

1956 年 10 月，最高人民法院（中华人民共和国最高法院）总结了中华人民共和国成立以来的民事审判经验，并发表了《中华人民共和国各级法院民事案件处理程序的经验总结》。这一摘要有助于纠正审判实践中的错误，从而有助于提高司法效率。摘要由七个部分组成：受理案件、预审、审判、裁决、上诉、再审、执行。1957 年，最高法院将《摘要》改为《规定》，制定了《民事案件审理程序（草案）》，共 84 条规定。

Thereafter, in 1963, the national civil trial working meeting, the first of its kind, highlighted the principles of civil trial, which were to "investigate and study, resolve on site and *prioritize mediation* [emphasis added]."[146]

此后，在 1963 年召开的第一次全国民事审判工作会议上，明确提出了"调查研究、现场解决、调解优先"的民事审判原则。

The introduction of the above principle in 1964 has been acknowledged as having a great impact on the development of civil procedure law in the PRC.[147] The establishment of

上述原则于 1964 年的引入，被公认为对中国民事诉讼法的发展产生了重大影响。这些原则的确立对中国随后几年

143 Jianfeng Pan, "Scientific Reforms of Civil Trial Procedure System in China - Reflection on the Civil Procedure and Its Relationship," *Tribune of Political Science and Law*, no. 5 (2012): 99–113.
潘剑锋："中国民事审判程序制度的科学改革——关于民事诉讼及其关系的思考"，《政法论坛》，第5期，2012，第99-113页。

144 Jianfeng Pan, "On the Revision of Civil Procedure Law (2012)," *China Law* 5 (2012): 65-71. See also, Weijian Tang, "The Evolution of Civil Procedure System of China," *Frontiers L. China* 7, no. 2 (2012): 192–93.
潘剑锋："论民事诉讼法的修改（2012）"，《中国法学》第5期，2012，第65-71页。另见唐卫建：《中国民事诉讼制度的演变》，《中国前沿》第7卷，第2期，2012，第192-193页。

145 Pan, "Revision of PRC's CPL"。潘，《中华人民共和国民事诉讼法修订》。

146 Ibid.

147 Ibid.

these principles has had a profound impact on the PRC's civil trial activities in subsequent years.

的民事审判活动产生了深远的影响。

However, the rapid pace of law reforms was halted in 1966, that is, from the start of the Cultural Revolution[148]; this also meant that the development of civil procedure law in the PRC was finally halted.[149] In February 1979, SPC issued the "*Supreme Court's Regulation Regarding the Institution of the Procedure of Civil Cases*."

然而，快速的法律改革步伐在 1966 年停止了，也就是说，从文化大革命开始；这也意味着中华人民共和国民事诉讼法的发展最终停止。1979 年 2 月，最高人民法院发布《最高人民法院关于设立民事诉讼程序的规定》。

In recent years, the need for procedural law has arisen as a result of the rapid opening up of the PRC's economy. Before, any Civil Procedure Code could be enacted or put in place, it was necessary for the PRC to lay down some basic principles for different areas of civil law relating to substantive law matters such as contracts, business enterprises, land, intellectual property, marriage and succession. This resulted in the landmark General Provision of Civil Law (*Minfa tongze*) in 1986, which also marked the acceptance of Continental European traditions.[150] It should be appreciated that these were the first major Codes for substantive laws such as contract and property issues.

近年来，由于中国经济的快速开放，对程序法的需求出现了。在制定或实施任何《民事诉讼法》之前，中华人民共和国有必要为涉及合同、商业企业、土地、知识产权、婚姻和继承等实体法问题的不同民法领域制定一些基本原则。这导致了 1986 年具有里程碑意义的《民法通则》，这也标志着对欧洲大陆传统的接受。应当认识到，这些是诸如合同和财产问题等实体法的第一批主要法典。

2.1.2.2 Origins of the PRC's current Civil Procedural System

中华人民共和国现行民事诉讼制度的起源

The PRC's current Civil Procedure System was introduced on a trial basis in 1982, and culminated in *Civil Procedure*

中华人民共和国现行民事诉讼制度于 1982 年试行，并在 1991 年《民事诉讼法》中达到高潮。如果我们只比较现行有效的法律，那么这个民事诉讼法

[148] Chairman Mao, the supreme leader of the PRC, the leader of the communist revolution in 1949, in his last years in power (1966-76), fearing the Soviet Union's influence on the PRC and the dilution of the Communist revolution by those not believing in the principles of communism, started this great upheaval in the PRC. It was an era of constant changes in economic policies and affected the PRC as a whole in many ways.
毛主席，中华人民共和国的最高领导人，1949 年共产主义革命的领导人，在他执政的最后几年（1966-1976），担心苏联对中华人民共和国的影响，以及那些不相信共产主义原则的人对共产主义革命的稀释，在中华人民共和国开始了这场巨大的动荡。这是一个经济政策不断变化的时代，在许多方面影响了整个中华人民共和国。

[149] Tang, "Evolution of CPL in PRC," 193。唐，"中华人民共和国民事诉讼法的演变"，第193页。

[150] Albert H.Y. Chen, "The Developing Chinese Law and the Civil Law Tradition," *China Rev.* (1996): 31. <http://www.jstor.org/stable/23453139>.
陈海英：《中国法律的发展与大陆法系传统》，《中国法学》1996年第31期。http://www.jstor.org/stable/23453139。

Law 1991 in its current form.[151] If we were to only compare the current law in force, then this Civil Procedure Law ('CPL') is older than the current CPR applicable in England & Wales. However, the history of Civil Procedure System in England & Wales is relatively much older. There have been regular amendments to it over the years, compared to the PRC's Civil Procedure Law.[152]

（"CPL"）比现行适用于英格兰和威尔士的 CPR 更早。然而，英格兰和威尔士的民事诉讼制度的历史相对要古老得多，与之相比，中国《中华人民共和国民事诉讼法》多年来一直在进行定期修订。

CPL 1991 went from 205 articles in the 1982 version of *CPL* to 270 articles in its 1991 version. In 1991 the *CPL* for the first time introduced special provisions applicable to civil cases involving foreign cases, as more and more countries were investing in and doing business with the PRC. Additionally, the Supreme People's Court of PRC has issued the following pertinent guidelines, among many others that will be referred to throughout this chapter, that have the force of law:[153]

《中华人民共和国民事诉讼法》1991 从 1982 年版的 205 条增加到 1991 年版的 270 条。1991 年，随着越来越多的国家在中国投资和经商，《中华人民共和国民事诉讼法》首次对涉外民事案件作出了特别规定。此外，中华人民共和国最高人民法院还发布了以下相关指导意见，以及本章将提及的许多其他具有法律效力的指导意见：

- Judicial Committee of the Supreme People's Court on July 14, 1992, issued guidelines in relation to the application of *Civil Procedure Act, Fa Fa [1992] No. 22.*[154]

  最高人民法院审判委员会于1992年7月14日发布了《关于适用民事诉讼法的指导意见》（法发[1992]22号）。

- *Interpretation of the Supreme People's Court on the Application of The Civil Procedure Law of the People's Republic of China Fa Shi [2015] No.5*, January 30, 2015.[155]

  最高人民法院关于适用<中华人民共和国民事诉讼法>的解释[2015]5号，2015年1月30日。

---

151 Adopted at the Fourth Session of the Seventh National People's Congress on April 9, 1991 and promulgated by *Order No. 44 of the President of the People's Republic of China on April 9, 1991.*
1991年4月9日第七届全国人民代表大会第四次会议通过1991年4月9日中华人民共和国主席令第44号公布。

152 Amended for the first time according to the "*Decision on Amending the 'Civil Procedure Law of the People's Republic of China'*" as adopted at the 30th Session of the Standing Committee of the 10th National People's Congress on *28, October, 2007* (came into effect on 1, April,2008), and amended for the second time according to the "*Decision on Amending the 'Civil Procedure Law of the People's Republic of China'*" as adopted at the 28th Session of the Standing Committee of the 11th National People's Congress on *31 August 2012* (came into effect on 1, January, 2013).
根据2007年10月28日第十届全国人民代表大会常务委员会第三十次会议《关于修改<中华人民共和国民事诉讼法>的决定》（自2008年4月1日起施行）第一次修正。根据2012年8月31日第十一届全国人民代表大会常务委员会第二十八次会议《关于修改<中华人民共和国民事诉讼法>的决定》（2013年1月1日起施行）第二次修正。

153 *Provisions of the Supreme People's Court on the Work of Judicial Interpretations 2007*, Art. 5.《最高人民法院司法解释工作规定》2007年第5条。

154 See Adopted at the 528th meeting of the Judicial Committee of the Supreme People's Court on July 14, *1992, Fa Fa [1992] No. 22.*
见1992年7月14日最高人民法院审判委员会第528次会议法发[1992]22号通过。

155 See Adopted at the 1636th session of the Judicial Committee of the Supreme People's Court on December 18, 2014, basically the *Interpretation of Application of Civil Procedure Law of PRC.*

- *Circular of the Supreme People's Court on the Issuance of the Document Samples for the Certain Rules for Evidence in Civil Procedures, Fa Fa [2003] No. 2,* September 1, *2003.*

  最高人民法院关于印发《民事诉讼若干证据规则文件样本》的通知，发法[2003]2号，2003年9月1日。

- *Guiding Opinions of the Supreme People's Court on Several Issues Concerning Trial of Cases on Disputes over Civil and Commercial Contracts in the Current Situation, Fa Fa [2009] No. 40*, July 7, 2009.

  《最高人民法院关于当前形势下审理民商事合同纠纷案件若干问题的指导意见》，法发[2009]40号，2009年7月7日。

- *Provisions of the Supreme People's Court on Several Issues concerning the Hearing of Cases by Circuit Courts, Fa Shi [2015]* No.3, January 28, 2015.

  《最高人民法院关于巡回法院审理案件若干问题的规定》，载法始[2015]第3号，2015年1月28日。

- On April 15, the Supreme People's Court released the *Opinions on the Implementation of the People's Courts of the Reform concerning the Case-filing Registration System (the "Opinions"), stipulating that regarding case filings, the current review system shall be changed into a registration system as of May 1, 2015.*

  4月15日，最高人民法院发布《关于人民法院实施立案登记制度改革的意见》（以下简称《意见》），规定自2015年5月1日起，将立案审查制度改为立案登记制度。

- *Circular of the Supreme People's Court on Promulgation of the Amended Regulations on Causes of Action in Civil Cases, Fa [2011] No.42*, February 18, 2011.

  最高人民法院关于公布修改后的《民事诉讼事由条例》的通知，发[2011]42号，2011年2月18日。

In the authors' view, The *CPL 1991* is a major achievement for the PRC, which historically did not have any procedural rules in the context of civil litigation;[156] furthermore,

笔者认为，1991年《中华人民共和国民事诉讼法》是中国历史上没有民事诉讼程序规则的重大成就；此外，义坤认为，

见2014年12月18日最高人民法院审判委员会第1636次会议通过的《中华人民共和国民事诉讼法基本适用解释》。

[156] Chen Weizuo, *Chinese Civil Procedure and the Conflict of Laws*, Tsinghua Chinese Law Series. (Beijing: Tsinghua University Press, 2011), 4.
陈卫佐，《中国民事诉讼与法律冲突》，清华法学丛书，北京：清华大学出版社，2011，第4页。

according to Yikun, the PRC traditionally lacked the culture of rule of law.[157] However the PRC has, in the recent past, adopted the *Criminal Procedure Code on July 1, 1979*, *Administrative Litigation Law* of April 4, *1989*, *Organic Rules for People's Mediation Committees of 1989* and *Measures of Handling Disputes among the people of 1990.* Lately, the *Law on Arbitration of March 31, 1995* was also promulgated. These are major achievements when seen from the prism that as late as 1979, there was no difference between the substantive law and procedural law in traditional Chinese law.[158] It is an even bigger achievement that in a small span of time, many new substantive laws have been promulgated and made effective in the PRC.

中华人民共和国传统上缺乏法治文化。然而，在最近的过去，中国通过了1979年7月1日的《刑事诉讼法》、1989年4月4日的《行政诉讼法》、1989年的《人民调解委员会组织规则》和1990年的《人民纠纷处理办法》。最近，1995年3月31日的《仲裁法》也颁布了。这些都是重大的成就，从这个角度来看，直到1979年，中国传统法律中还没有实体法和程序法的区别。更大的成就是，在很短的时间内，中国颁布了许多新的实体法并使之生效。

Without keeping the above in mind, any businessmen and/or foreign lawyers will approach the PRC with unrealistic hopes and expectations. The authors' view is that one should avoid looking at the PRC legal system from the prism of western historical experience of civil litigation and/or from a similar experience in other common law jurisdictions and/or continental civil law systems. Rather, readers must appreciate that civil litigation in the PRC is of relatively recent origin as compared to common law systems and continental civil law systems.

如果不牢记以上几点，任何商人和/或外国律师都会带着不切实际的希望和期望来中国。作者的观点是，人们应该避免从西方民事诉讼的历史经验和/或其他普通法系和/或大陆法系的类似经验的棱镜来看待中国的法律制度。相反，读者必须认识到，与普通法系和大陆法系相比，中国民事诉讼的起源相对较晚。

Currently, in the PRC, the classification of law into procedural and substantive laws is similar to that in England & Wales. In the PRC, procedural law exists to enforce rights created by substantive laws such as contract or tort. Zhu Yikun has rightly said, *"Substantive law is concerned with what, while procedural law is concerned with how."*[159]

目前，在中国，法律分为程序法和实体法的分类与英格兰和威尔士类似。在中国，程序法的存在是为了执行实体法（如合同法或侵权法）所创造的权利。朱一坤说得好："实体法关心的是什么，程序法关心的是怎样。"

157 Yikun Zhu, *China's Procedural Law* (Beijing: Law Press China, 2003), 1. It was also discussed in Weizuo, *Chinese Civil Procedure and the Conflict of Laws*, 3.
朱义坤：《中国诉讼法》，北京：中国法律出版社，2003，第1页。《中国民事诉讼与法律冲突》第3期也有论述。

158 Weizuo, *Chinese Civil Procedure and the Conflict of Laws*, 4。卫佐，《中国民事诉讼与法律冲突》，第4页。

159 Yikun Zhu, *Concise Chinese Law* (Beijing: Law Press, 2007)。朱义坤：《中国简法》，北京：法律出版社，2007年。

2.1.3 Comparison of Historical Evolution of Substantive and Procedural Law

实体法与程序法历史演进之比较

Common Law has been in existence in England & Wales from around the middle of the eleventh century and has developed a large body of substantive law in these years.[160] This body of law was also enhanced by law of equity, which itself was later merged with the common law courts.[161] This body was further developed by the reasoning of judges in other common law jurisdictions such as the US, Australia, India and so forth. Common-law courts further developed adjective law, that included procedural law to assist litigants, but these procedures over the years had the tendency to become too formal. Such excessive formalities require separate forms for different causes of actions and accordingly the understanding of substantive law was through these forms.

普通法在英格兰和威尔士大约从 11 世纪中叶开始存在，并在这些年中发展了大量的实体法。这一法律体系也因衡平法而得到加强，衡平法本身后来与普通法法庭合并。美国、澳大利亚、印度等其他普通法司法管辖区法官的推理进一步发展了这一机构。普通法法院进一步发展了程序法，其中包括程序法来协助诉讼当事人，但这些程序多年来有变得过于正式的趋势。这种过分的手续要求对不同的诉因采取不同的形式，因此对实体法的理解就是通过这些形式。

On the other hand, the civil procedures lacked any formality in the courts of equity. In such courts, the focus was on moral reasoning and/or case-specific judgment and/or discretion of the judges and/or anti-opportunitism and/or good conscience.[162] The civil procedure system in a way developed after the advent of the *Magna Carta* in 1215 CE. However, as discussed above, it developed as a part of an adjective law, but slowly began to produce its own body of rules. However, too many rules were added in these courts over the years, resulting in the litigants facing increased complexity.

另一方面，衡平法院的民事诉讼程序缺乏程序性。在这种法院，重点是道德推理和/或具体案件的判决和/或法官的自由裁量权和/或反机会主义和/或良心。民事诉讼制度在某种程度上是在 1215 年《大宪章》问世后发展起来的。然而，正如上面所讨论的，它作为程序法的一部分发展，但慢慢地开始产生自己的规则体系。然而，多年来，这些法院增加了太多的规则，导致诉讼当事人面临的复杂性增加。

The complexities faced by litigants were even commented upon by some of the novelists of the eighteenth and nineteenth centuries in England. Legal costs and delays in the civil courts were increasing, which was quite contrary to the requirements of access to justice for civil litigants. After

诉讼当事人所面临的复杂性甚至被一些十八、十九世纪的英国小说家评论过。民事法庭的法律费用和延误正在增加，这与民事诉讼人诉诸司法的要求完全相反。经过一个世纪的许多委员会和

---

160 Refer, Chapter 2, § 2.1.1.1.
161 Refer, Chapter 2, § 2.1.1.2.
162 Refer, Chapter 2, § 2.1.1.2, and in particular, Bray's analysis on equitable remedies。
参见第2章第2.1.1.2节，特别是布雷对衡平法救济的分析。

a century of many Commissions and Committees, the *Woolf Reforms of 1999* were bought in and introduced, *inter alia*:

委员会，1999 年的伍尔夫改革被采纳并引入，除其他外：

- active case management that was quite similar to what judges are used to doing in the PRC;

  主动的案件管理，这与中国法官习惯做的事情非常相似；

- introduction of overriding objectives of civil procedure that provides the judges with enough flexibility; and

  引入民事诉讼的首要目标，为法官提供足够的灵活性；和

- imposition of penalties on the litigants for their conduct in order to further these overriding objectives.[163]

  对诉讼当事人的行为施加惩罚，以促进这些压倒一切的目标。

The other important feature than cannot be overlooked is that even though the civil procedure system in both common law and the PRC is about resolving private disputes; they still serve the public purpose of avoiding conflicts due to civil disputes. In addition, most civil disputes are not publicly funded.

另一个不容忽视的重要特征是，尽管普通法系和中国大陆的民事诉讼制度都是关于解决私人纠纷的；它们仍然服务于公共目的，以避免因民事纠纷而引起的冲突。此外，大多数民事纠纷都不是由政府资助的。

On the other hand, even though ancient China was economically an advanced civilisation, the dominant focus was on penal codes, and any civil law that was needed for society was developed out of concern for maintaining public order.[164] Many reasons have been cited for this monumental neglect, foremost being the Confucian concept of '*Yang Min*', where the focus is on the sharing of resources between the people. Another reason cited was the ideology of '*sung kun*' bringing in distrust of litigation and lawyers, who were even considered as tricksters. Though there are examples of an ancient Chinese version of human rights in the form of '*jen*,' that required rulers to be kind and humane, it did not assist in bringing in the concept of access to justice for civil disputes.

另一方面，尽管古代中国在经济上是一个先进的文明，但主要的焦点是刑法，任何社会所需的民法都是出于维护公共秩序的考虑而制定的。造成这种严重忽视的原因有很多，最主要的原因是儒家的"杨民"观念，其重点是人与人之间的资源共享。另一个原因是，"崇根"思想使人们对诉讼和律师产生不信任，甚至认为律师是骗子。虽然古代中国也有以"仁"的形式描述人权的例子，要求统治者仁慈和人道，但它并没有帮助引入民事纠纷诉诸司法的概念。

All the above reasons cited for lack of civil procedure law were actually there to ensure a harmonious society by

上述种种民事诉讼法缺失的原因，实际上都是为了通过禁止诉讼来保障和

---

163 Refer, Chapter 2, § 2.1.2。参见第2章第2.1.2节。

164 Refer, Chapter 2, § 2.2.1。参见第2章第2.1.2节。

prohibiting litigation.[165] However, in the authors' view, the route taken came at the expense of the development of a body of substantive and procedural law, and basically denied access to justice; it actually let to suppression of the truth in civil cases. In addition, most of the ancient traditional laws were included as part of the *unofficial law*, and in civil cases, the administration would try to avoid any kind of involvement. The Ming and Qing dynasties commenced a *dispute resolution system* across ancient China that was to be *managed by seniors or elderly persons,* and there were no civil courts or procedures along the lines of *'Kang Ko'* or *'Lu hsing'*, which were the procedural manuals applying to penal codes.

谐社会。然而，发件人认为，所采取的路线是以牺牲一套实体法和程序法的发展为代价的，而且基本上剥夺了诉诸司法的机会；它实际上导致了对民事案件真相的压制。此外，大多数古代传统法律都是作为非正式法律的一部分被纳入的，在民事案件中，尽量避免任何形式的介入。明清两朝在中国古代开始了一种由老年人管理的纠纷解决制度，没有类似于"康科"或"路行"的民事法庭或程序，这是适用于刑法的程序手册。

It was not until 1954, with the promulgation of the *Organic Law*, that the trial system and principles of civil litigation were established. However, this development too was halted during the Cultural Revolution (1966-76). The first body of substantive law in the field of civil law (*Minfa tongze*) came about only in 1986, following which the *Civil Procedure Law* was introduced in 1991.[166]

直到 1954 年，随着《组织法》的颁布，民事诉讼审判制度和原则才得以确立。然而，这一发展也在文化大革命（1966-76）期间停止了。民法领域的第一部实体法（民法通则）于 1986 年才出现，随后于1991年出台了《民事诉讼法》。

Given the above, in the authors' view, it is still too early in the PRC for a body of considerable procedural law that could assist litigants to have spread in the local courts. In addition, it was only in 2012 that *CPL 1991* was amended, and this body has yet to blossom in the PRC. However, even though the PRC has relatively new rules, in the authors' view, this may actually confer on the PRC some procedural advantages, as the complexities that have been added in England & Wales through numerous case precedents can be avoided.

综上所述，作者认为，中国在地方法院建立一套完备的程序法体系以协助诉讼当事人还为时过早。此外，直到 2012 年，《民事诉讼法》1991 才进行了修订，该机构尚未在中国开花结果。然而，即使中华人民共和国有相对较新的规则，在作者看来，这实际上可能赋予中华人民共和国一些程序上的优势，因为可以避免在英格兰和威尔士通过大量案例先例增加的复杂性。

Foremost, PRC rules are not burdened by the set of rules that has been appended over the years, adding to complexity for the litigants. However, the reasons for inclusion of principles in courts in PRC, namely that public interest should always be maintained, have historical linkages. Historically, the focus, from ancient China to the current PRC, has always

最重要的是，中国的规则不受多年来附加的一套规则的负担，这增加了诉讼当事人的复杂性。然而，中国法院纳入原则的原因，即应始终维护公共利益，具有历史联系。历史上看，从古代中国到现在的中华人民共和国，重点一直是

[165] Pursuant to Tang Code during Tang Dynasty (681-906 CE)。根据唐朝（公元681-906年）的《唐律》。
[166] Ibid.

been on the maintenance of public order. However, whether this point is needed in Commercial Law or civil disputes is another question.

维护公共秩序。然而，在商法或民事纠纷中是否需要这一点则是另一个问题。

Substantive law in England & Wales as compared to the PRC has developed over centuries with debates in courts or advocates' arguments in the courts or discussed in Parliament. On the other hand, the origin of substantive law as civil law code in the PRC is just a few years old. As the economy has developed in the PRC, it has become clear that the body of substantive law such as law of contract, agency, tort, commercial law, restitution and so forth is not adequate to cater to new causes of actions, new economic activities, training of judges in the new substantive law and so forth. However, there is a great push from the top echelons of the political class of the PRC to improve the state of affairs in this respect.

与中国相比，英格兰和威尔士的实体法已经发展了几个世纪，在法庭上辩论或在法庭上辩论或在议会讨论。另一方面，实体法作为民法典在中国的起源只有几年的历史。随着中国经济的发展，合同法、代理法、侵权法、商法、赔偿法等实体法已不足以适应新的诉因、新的经济活动、新的实体法对法官的培训等问题。然而，中国高层政治阶层大力推动改善这方面的状况。

However, in the authors' view, it is easier to draft the laws, still easier to circulate them; the most difficult task is the training of judges, especially given the vast continental size of the PRC. It can be said that manufacturing hardware is easy, but the real challenge lies in developing the software for the hardware. This is the real challenge for the PRC.

然而，在笔者看来，起草法律更容易，传播法律更容易；最困难的任务是培训法官，特别是考虑到中国幅员辽阔。可以说，制造硬件很容易，但真正的挑战在于为硬件开发软件。这是中国面临的真正挑战。

2.1.4 Comparative Relationship between Substantive Law and Procedural Law

实体法与程序法的比较关系

The relationship between substantive law and procedural law needs to be understood, before we can go further. It could be argued that procedural law exists because of substantive law. However, substantive law in the form of the best codes or legislations will be of no benefit without the support of good civil procedure rules.[167] The aims of

实体法和程序法之间的关系需要理解，然后我们才能进一步探讨。可以说，程序法因实体法而存在。然而，如果没有良好的民事诉讼规则的支持，以最好的法典或立法形式出现的实体法将毫无用处。程序法的目的依赖于实体法与程序法的

167 W J Habscheid, "The Fundamental Principles of the Law of Civil Procedure," *Comp. & Int'l L.J. S. Afr.* 17, no. 1 (1984): 4.www.jstor.org/stable/23246919.
W·J·哈布沙伊德，《中华人民共和国民事诉讼法基本原则》，载《中华人民共和国民事诉讼法》第17期。1，1984 年， 第4页。www.jstor.org/stable/23246919。

procedural law rely on the relationship between substantive and procedural laws. There are, however, jurisdictions where the legal philosophy's aim is to focus on the aims of substantive law and remove procedural hurdles, for example, in Germany pursuant to the old civil procedure code.[168]

关系。然而，有些司法管辖区的法律哲学的目的是集中于实体法的目的和消除程序障碍，例如，在德国，根据旧的民事诉讼法。

There are three broad theories in the context of the relationship of substantive law to procedural law:[169]

在实体法与程序法关系的背景下，有三种广泛的理论：

- The aim of civil procedural law is procedural and therefore, does not rest on substantive law;
- The aim of civil procedural law should emphasise and concentrate on the realisation of substantive law;
- The aim of civil procedural law should be on the realisation of individual rights, and on a broader level should be the maintenance of social harmony and rule of law.

民事诉讼法的目的是程序性的，因此不以实体法为基础；

民事诉讼法的宗旨应强调并注重实体法的实现；

民事诉讼法的目标应该是实现个人权利，在更广泛的层面上应该是维护社会和谐与法治。

At one extreme, a few scholars assert that the aim of civil procedural law should be to provide the requisite authority for judgment (*res judicata*), though other scholars are of the view that it may be the consequence of the civil procedure, but this cannot be the sole aim of the civil procedure.[170] A few scholars are of the view that the main aim of civil procedure should be formulating a judgment to end a dispute.[171] However, procedural law cannot be separated from substantive law. Habscheid said, "*The civil process is consequently a procedure in which the pre-existing substantive law is concretised in each decided case, or possibly settled* [emphasis in original]."[172] Without doubt, civil procedural law also protects the "objective private law."[173]

在一个极端，一些学者断言，民事诉讼法的目的应该是为判决提供必要的权威（既判权），尽管其他学者认为，这可能是民事诉讼的结果，但这不能是民事诉讼的唯一目的。少数学者认为，民事诉讼的主要目的应是作出判决以结束纠纷。但是，程序法与实体法是分不开的。哈布沙伊德说："因此，民事诉讼程序是一个程序，在这个程序中，预先存在的实体法在每一个已判决的案件中具体化，或者可能得到解决。"毫无疑问，民事诉讼法也保护"客观私法"。

[168] Ibid., 5.
[169] Ibid., 6.
[170] Ibid.
[171] Ibid., 7.
[172] Ibid., 9.
[173] Ibid., 13.

From the perspective of the English law, lots of substantive laws in the areas of contract, tort and restitution are developed after litigation has commenced in the courts. In fact, in common law systems, it is essential for disputes to go through the process in courts all the way up to the trials, and then for judgments to be passed for these substantive laws to develop.

从英国法律的角度来看，许多合同、侵权和赔偿等领域的实体法都是在诉讼开始后才发展起来的。事实上，在普通法体系中，纠纷必须经过法庭的审理，然后通过判决，才能使这些实体法得以发展。

Legal scholars are of the view that the aim of protecting *individual's rights* will lead to the adversarial system, and the importance of *protecting public interest* will lead to the inquisitorial system.[174] However, there are many disputes where both private and stakeholders' interests are at stake; in such a scenario, which system will be most appropriate is difficult to predict.

法律学者认为，保护个人权利的目的会导致对抗性制度，保护公共利益的重要性会导致讯问制度。然而，在许多纠纷中，私人和利益相关者的利益都受到了威胁；在这种情况下，很难预测哪个系统是最合适的。

Civil procedural laws in most countries have developed independently of substantive law, but there are jurisdictions such as England & Wales, where in the past, precise forms were required to be filled for a specific cause of action. Therefore, the procedures were overly dependent on substantive law.[175] However, although civil procedural law has developed independently of substantive law in most other jurisdictions, the civil procedural law still complements the substantive law.[176] However, the procedural laws cannot develop properly without keeping the substantive laws in mind.

大多数国家的民事诉讼法都是独立于实体法而发展起来的，但在英格兰和威尔士等司法管辖区，过去需要为特定的诉因填写精确的表格。因此，程序过于依赖实体法。然而，尽管在大多数其他司法管辖区，民事诉讼法是独立于实体法而发展起来的，但民事诉讼法仍然是实体法的补充。但是，程序法的正常发展离不开实体法的保护。

The principle of *procedural justice* in the context of ensuring equality for all litigants before the courts, and the emphasis on the need for just and equitable judgement, has developed over the years in the field of civil procedural law independently of the substantive law. It includes *inter alia* the following issues:[177]

多年来，在独立于实体法的民事诉讼法领域，在确保所有诉讼当事人在法庭上平等的背景下，程序正义原则以及强调公正和公平判决的必要性已经发展起来。除其他外，它包括下列问题：

- Functional independence of the judges,

法官的职能独立性，不需要行政部门

[174] Ibid., 11. Refer also, Chapter 1, Figure 1 for families of legal systems and resulting in adversarial system and inquisitorial systems. 见上引，11。也请参阅第1章，图1中关于家庭的法律制度，以及由此产生的对抗制度和讯问制度。

[175] Ibid., 14.

[176] Ibid., 15.

[177] Ibid., 15–30.

who require no interference from the executive;

的干预；

- Personal independence of the judges, so that they can have tenured positions; and a legal procedure for their removal (if required);

法官的个人独立性，使他们可以拥有终身职位；以及将其移除的法律程序（如果需要）；

- Powers available through the courts to uphold the dignity and prevent the contempt of court; for example, in England & Wales such powers are supreme over other fundamental rights such as freedom of press, expression or speech;[178]

通过法院维护尊严和防止藐视法庭罪的权力；例如，在英格兰和威尔士，这种权力高于出版、表达或言论自由等其他基本权利；

- Allocation of a judges to the cases (in socialist systems, the judges can be replaced easily by superior courts);

分配一名法官审理案件（在社会主义制度下，法官很容易被上级法院取代）；

- Impartiality of the judges, including the recusal process to ensure impartiality and bias. It could be voluntary such as in England & Wales, or it could be written in the procedural codes;

法官的公正性，包括回避程序，以确保公正性和偏见。它可以像英格兰和威尔士那样是自愿的，也可以写在程序法典中；

- Issues of Access to justice such as form of pleadings, pre-trial and trial procedures, availability of legal aid to prevent the harshness of costs, and right to notice allowing a defendant to argue his case. Additionally, right to be heard available to litigants and parties affected by the litigation, where the judges and courts follow a fair procedure;

诉诸司法的问题，如诉状的形式、审前和审判程序、为防止费用过高而提供的法律援助，以及允许被告为其案件辩护的通知权。此外，在法官和法院遵循公平程序的情况下，诉讼当事人和受诉讼影响的当事方享有发表意见的权利；

- Authority of the judges to determine a case, whereby parties alone can decide

法官裁决案件的权力，当事人可以自行决定需要采取什么行动来解决争

[178] See *Morris and Others v The Crown Office* [1970] 2 QB 114, where the issues around contempt of court were clarified.
参见莫里斯等人诉皇家办公室[1970]2 QB 114，其中澄清了有关藐视法庭罪的问题。

what actions are required to settle the dispute; but in many socialist countries and countries following civil law system, judges have been given power to investigate the facts, or to interfere actively. This happens in the PRC, where a public body such as *Procuratorate* has supervisory powers. Procuratorates has oversight over judges and judgments; this is unique to the PRC legal system. It is an organ of the PRC system, just like the People's Court and the government. It exists as an independent body to uphold the Communist party system and its leadership and also has its roots in *Marxism and conservatism*.[179] It is also important to appreciate that there is no concept of separation of power in the PRC. The judiciary is not independent in the PRC when seen through the prism of western concepts of independence. In England & Wales, there is usually much less interference in determining the facts, unless the parties have requested the courts specifically. This shows clearly the subtle differences between the common law and the inquisitorial system in relation to collation of evidence and investigation into the cases;

端；但在许多社会主义国家和大陆法系国家，法官被赋予调查事实或积极干预的权力。这种情况发生在中国，检察院等公共机构拥有监督权力。检察院对法官和判决进行监督；这是中国法律制度所独有的。它是中华人民共和国的一个机关，就像人民法院和政府一样。它作为维护共产党制度及其领导的独立机构而存在，其根源也在于马克思主义和保守主义。同样重要的是要认识到，在中华人民共和国没有权力分立的概念。从西方独立概念的角度来看，中国的司法并不独立。在英格兰和威尔士，除非当事人特别向法院提出请求，否则对确定事实的干预通常要少得多。这清楚地显示了普通法与讯问制度在证据整理和案件调查方面的细微差别；

- Public nature of trials, including the need for oral or written arguments.

审判的公共性，包括口头或书面辩论的必要性。

For the sake of completeness, after discussing the interrelationship between substantive and procedural law, it is important to appreciate that in commercial cases, procedural rules, including rules of evidence and standards

为了完整起见，在讨论了实体法和程序法之间的相互关系之后，必须认识到，在商事案件中，程序规则，包括证据规则和证明标准，可以根据法庭法，但有关的实体法可以由合同各方选择，或者可以采

[179] Refer to Chapter 3, §3.6 & §3.7. 参见第 3 章，§3.6 和§3.7。

of proof, may be according to the *lex fori*,[180] but the relevant substantive law may be as selected by the parties to the contract or a different substantive law may govern disputes over rights and obligations.

用不同的实体法管辖权利和义务纠纷。

2.1.5 Comparative Analysis of Overview of Differences between Civil Procedure systems

民事诉讼制度差异概论之比较分析

The authors are conscious of warnings from Chase and Varano, who said "There are as many differences among the civil law countries as there are between the English and the US model of procedure (which diverged especially after the virtual abolition of the jury in England [in civil litigation], and still further after the sweeping reform of the Civil Procedure Rules of 1998)."[181] Jolowicz highlighted the differences between the procedural systems more realistically when he said:

作者意识到蔡斯和瓦拉诺的警告，他们说"大陆法系国家之间的差异就像英美诉讼模式之间的差异一样多（尤其是在英国（民事诉讼）实际上废除陪审团制度之后，在 1998 年民事诉讼规则的全面改革之后，分歧就更大了）。" Jolowicz 更现实地强调了程序系统之间的差异，他说：

> ...a pure adversarial procedure is no more capable of existing in the real world than a purely inquisitorial one ...the most that can be said is that some systems are more adversarial —or more inquisitorial —than others.[182]

> 在现实世界中，纯粹的对抗程序并不比纯粹的调查程序更有可能存在……最多可以说的是，一些系统比其他系统更具对抗性，或者更具探究性。

---

[180] C.H. Van Rhee and R. Verkerk, "Civil Procedure," in *Elgar Encyclopedia of Comparative Law*, ed. J.M. Smits (Cheltenham: Edward Elgar Publishing, 2006), 121.
C·H·范李和 R·沃克，《民事诉讼程序》，载《埃尔加比较法百科全书》，J·M·Smits 主编，切尔滕纳姆：爱德华·埃尔加出版社，2006，第 121 页。

[181] Oscar G. Chase and Vincenzo Varano, "Comparative Civil Justice," in *The Cambridge Companion to Comparative Law*, ed. M. Bussani and U. Mattei (Cambridge; New York: Cambridge University Press, 2012), 213. See also, Neil Andrews, "Fundamental Principles of Civil Procedure: Order Out of Chaos," in *Civil Litigation in a Globalising World*, ed. X.E. Kramer and Rhee, H (The Hague: T.M.C. Asser Press, 2012), 22, 387.
奥斯卡·G. Chase和文森佐·瓦瑞诺，"比较民事司法"，载《剑桥比较法指南》，M·Bussani和U·马泰主编，剑桥；纽约：剑桥大学出版社，2012，第213页。另见尼尔·安德鲁斯，"民事诉讼的基本原则：混沌中的秩序"，载《全球化世界中的民事诉讼》，X·E·Kramer和Rhee·H编，海牙：T.M.C. Asser出版社，2012，22，第387页。

[182] J.A. Jolowicz, "Adversarial and Inquisitorial Models of Civil Procedure," *I.C.L.Q.* 52, no. 2 (2003): 281. See also, Chase and Varano, "Comparative Civil Justice," 222, where Jolowicz was quoted.
J·A·乔洛维兹，《民事诉讼的对抗性和调查性模式》，《美国最高法院判例汇编》，第52期。2，2003年，每 281页。另见蔡斯和瓦拉诺，《比较民事司法》222页，其中引用了乔洛维茨的话。

In this book, historical analysis of the evolution of substantive law and civil procedure law provides context and is an essential invisible factor in understanding the relevant issues in each of the jurisdictions. The area covered by these factors is colossal; however, the authors will try to convey the ideas succinctly to allow readers to comprehend the issues clearly.

在本书中，对实体法和民事诉讼法演变的历史分析为理解每个司法管辖区的相关问题提供了背景，是一个必不可少的无形因素。这些因素所涵盖的领域是巨大的；然而，作者将尽量简洁地传达思想，让读者清楚地理解问题。

Oscar suggested that the civil process is a reflection of political, social, and legal reality in any jurisdiction, and any change in the political or moral or social side will be reflected during the operations of civil procedure in any jurisdiction.[183] In order to discuss comparative civil procedures, it is important to appreciate from the start the *cultural* dimensions of civil procedure as local practices even within a jurisdiction will affect the practice of procedural law in the courts. This factor is even more noticeable in the PRC due to its geographical size, as the practice of law in the local courts may vary from one province to another and the practice may vary even within various cities or villages within a province. The local courts, while applying the Civil Procedure Code that is applicable for the whole of the PRC, may also apply very local practices within the working of the courts.

Oscar认为，民事诉讼程序是任何司法管辖区的政治、社会和法律现实的反映，任何政治、道德或社会方面的变化都会在任何司法管辖区的民事诉讼程序运行过程中得到反映。为了讨论比较民事诉讼程序，重要的是要从一开始就认识到民事诉讼程序的文化层面，因为即使在一个管辖范围内的地方做法也会影响法院程序法的实践。由于中国的地理面积，这一因素在中国更为明显，因为地方法院的法律实践可能因省而异，甚至在一个省的不同城市或村庄也可能有所不同。地方法院在适用适用于全中华人民共和国的《民事诉讼法》的同时，也可以在法院的工作中采用非常具有地方特色的做法。

It is very difficult to document culture, but it is a representation of collective personality for a group of people within a boundary.[184] Chase discussed the work of the Dutch socialist and organisational theorist Hofstede, who found that organisations are culturally bound; Chase includes the legal process as part of that culture.[185]

记录文化是非常困难的，但它是在一个边界内的一群人的集体个性的表现。蔡斯讨论了荷兰社会主义者和组织理论家霍夫斯泰德（Hofstede）的研究成果，后者发现组织是受文化约束的；大通将法律程序作为这种文化的一部分。

At this stage, it is important to appreciate that the PRC has

在这个阶段，重要的是要认识到，

183 Oscar G. Chase, "Some Observations on the Cultural Dimension in Civil Procedure Reform," *Am. J. Comp. Law* 45, no. 4 (1997): 862. Oscar said while discussing the views of famous proceduralists Piero Calamandrei and Chiovenda.
奥斯卡·G·蔡司"民事诉讼制度改革中的文化维度观察"，第3期。J. Comp. Law 45，no.4，1997，第862页。奥斯卡在讨论著名程序主义者皮耶罗·卡拉安德烈和基奥文达的观点时说。

184 Oscar G. Chase, "Some Observations on the Cultural Dimension in Civil Procedure Reform," 863.
奥斯卡·G·Chase，《论民事诉讼制度改革中的文化维度》，第863页。

185 Oscar G. Chase, "Some Observations on the Cultural Dimension in Civil Procedure Reform," 864–5. Hofstede's findings were published in a book in 1980 called *Cultural Consequences*; these findings were extended by Oscar in the context of legal processes.
奥斯卡·G·蔡司，《论民事诉讼制度改革中的文化维度》，第864 - 65期。霍夫斯泰德的研究结果发表在1980年的《文化后果》一书中；奥斯卡在法律程序的背景下扩展了这些发现。

adopted the inquisitorial *system* as part of its civil procedure system, where a judge can investigate the facts. This system is different from the *common law adversarial system*. In common-law courts, judges will decide on the basis of the case that is presented to them by each party to the dispute. From 1949 onwards, the PRC's civil law system was modelled after the Socialist legal system; however after the 1990s, with more relevant substantive law being drafted along with amendments to Civil Procedure Law containing codes, the PRC has slowly started to adopt the Romanic-Germanic model.[186] It involves more formality, notarization, powers to judge to investigate facts and so forth.

中国已经采用了讯问制度作为其民事诉讼制度的一部分，法官可以调查事实。这一制度不同于普通法的对抗性制度。在普通法法庭，法官将根据争议各方提交的案件作出裁决。1949 年以来，中华人民共和国的大陆法系以社会主义法系为蓝本；然而，在 20 世纪 90 年代之后，随着更多相关的实体法的起草以及包含法典的民事诉讼法修正案的起草，中国已经慢慢开始采用罗马-日耳曼模式。它涉及到更多的手续、公证、判断和调查事实的权力等等。

The authors will discuss the difference between the philosophies of civil litigation in common law and in the PRC in Chapter 4, the judges' power and discretionary power within this system in Chapter 5 and 6 respectively, and in the end will compare both the civil procedures of the common law and the PRC in context of judicial activities in Chapter 7.

作者将在第 4 章讨论普通法系和中国民事诉讼理念的差异，在第 5 章和第 6 章分别讨论该制度下法官的权力和自由裁量权，最后在第 7 章比较普通法系和中国在司法活动背景下的民事诉讼程序。

[186] Refer Chapter 2, § 2.2.1 & § 2.2.2。参考第 2 章，§2.2.1 和§2.2.2。

Chapter 3 - JURISPRUDENCE AND LEGAL SYSTEM – COMMON LAW v. CHINESE LAW

第三章 - 司法系统-普通法与中国法

3.1 Jurisprudence Influencing the Judges in England & Wales and PRC

影响英格兰和威尔士及中国法官的法理学

In this book, historical analysis of the evolution of substantive law and civil procedure law provides context and is an essential invisible factor in understanding the relevant issues in each of the jurisdictions. The area covered by these factors is colossal; however, the authors will try to convey the ideas succinctly to allow readers to comprehend the issues clearly.

在本书中，对实体法和民事诉讼法演变的历史分析为理解每个司法管辖区的相关问题提供了背景，是一个必不可少的无形因素。这些因素所涵盖的领域是巨大的；然而，作者将尽量简洁地传达思想，让读者清楚地理解问题。

In Chapter one, the authors analyzed the need to evaluate the Internal Law, as any lawyer or researcher needs to analyze the invisible factors that influence the judges' judicial activities in any jurisdiction. It influences judges and stakeholders at a foundational level, even to the extent of influencing thought processes, such as asking relevant questions in the courtrooms. The authors will start with the jurisprudential thoughts of Northrop:

在第一章中，笔者分析了评估《内部法》的必要性，因为任何律师或研究人员都需要分析影响任何司法管辖区法官司法活动的无形因素。它在基础层面上影响着法官和利益相关者，甚至影响到思维过程，如在法庭上提出相关问题。笔者将从诺斯罗普的法理学思想谈起：

> In Law, as in other things, we shall find that the only difference between a person "without philosophy" and someone with a philosophy is that the latter knows what his philosophy is, and is, therefore, more able to make clear and justify the premises that are implicit in his statement of the facts of his experience and his judgment about

> 在法律领域，正如其他领域一样，我们会发现"没有哲学"的人与有哲学的人之间的唯一区别在于后者知道自己的哲学是什么，因此更能清楚地说明和证明他在陈述自己的经验事实和对这些事实的判断时所隐含的前提。

those facts.[187]

The above definition is from the perspective of philosophy; however, the authors will now discuss the concept of jurisprudence in the context of judicial activities. Postema has described jurisprudence in the context of the judges' legal reasoning and their ability in this context as follows:

上述定义是从哲学的角度出发的；然而，笔者现在要讨论的是司法活动背景下的法理学概念。波斯特马从法官的法律推理及其能力的角度对法理学进行了如下描述：

> This learned capacity for reflective judgment-*juris*prudence [emphasis in original], we might call it is a social capacity: the ability to reason from a body of shared experiences with normative significance to solutions for new practical problems.[188]

> 我们可以将这种反思性判断的学习能力--法理学[着重号为原文所加]--称为一种社会能力：从具有规范意义的共享经验中推理出新的实际问题解决方案的能力。

Jurisprudence in any jurisdiction is not the law of the particular subject area, but the law in general. In the authors' view, even at the primary level of origins of humans, there is an essential jurisprudence that governs the actions, thinking and activities of all humans. However, a particular kind of thinking has assisted in the development of the legal system in each jurisdiction. This section of this Chapter will attempt to go into detail about the jurisdiction of England & Wales and the PRC, in the context of jurisprudence. Each and every judicial activity is part of jurisprudence.

任何司法管辖区的法理学都不是特定主题领域的法律，而是一般法律。笔者认为，即使在人类起源的初级层面，也有一种基本的法理学支配着全人类的行动、思维和活动。然而，一种特殊的思维方式帮助了各司法管辖区法律制度的发展。本章的这一部分将试图从法理学的角度详细介绍英格兰和威尔士以及中华人民共和国的司法制度。每一项司法活动都是法理学的一部分。

Written jurisprudence attempts to unravel the unconscious way the judges, lawyers or even populace think, and attempts to clarify it in words.[189] *Legal theorists* are the scholars who ask the basic questions about the law, duties, obligations and

书面法理学试图揭示法官、律师甚至民众无意识的思维方式，并试图用文字将其阐明。*法学理论家*是提出有关法律、责任、义务和治理等基本问题的学

[187] F. S. C. Northrop, *The Complexity of Legal and Ethical Experience: Studies in the Method of Normative Subjects*, 1st ed. (Boston: Little, Brown, 1959), 6. This quote was also discussed in James Penner, David Schiff, and Richard Nobles, "Approaches to Jurisprudence, Legal Theory, and the Philosophy of Law," in *Introduction to Jurisprudence and Legal Theory: Commentary and Materials*, Anne Barron, et al. (London: Butterworths, 2002), 4.

F. S. C. 诺斯罗普, 法律和伦理经验的复杂性： 规范主体方法研究，第一版。(Boston: Little, Brown, 1959), 6. 这句话也被詹姆斯-彭纳、戴维-希夫和理查德-诺布尔斯在法理学和法律理论导论： 评注与材料，安妮-巴伦，et al. (London: Butterworths, 2002), 4. "法理学、法律理论和法律哲学的研究方法"中讨论

[188] Gerald J. Postema, "Classical Common Law Jurisprudence (Part II)," *Oxford U. of Commw. L.J.* 3, no. 1 (2003): 9。杰拉尔德·J·波斯特马，"经典普通法法理学（第二部分）" Oxford U. of Commw. L.J. 3, no. 1，2003，第 9 页。

[189] Penner, Schiff, and Nobles, "Approaches to Jurisprudence," 4。彭纳、希夫和诺布尔斯，"法理学的方法"，第 4 页。

governance, while *philosophers of law* have a narrower focus on one aspect of the law, such as nature of authority or obligation or freedom, etc. Philosophers of law share this aspect with other philosophers, such as political or economic philosophers. However, *jurisprudents* connect the various philosophies with the *practice of law and judicial activities*.

者，而*法学哲学家*则更狭隘地关注法律的某一方面，如权力或义务或自由的性质等。在这方面，法学哲学家与其他哲学家（如政治或经济哲学家）有共同之处。不过，*法学家*将各种哲学与*法律实践和司法活动*联系起来。

This Chapter will also connect with the previous Chapter in relation to the origins of the legal system in both common law and PRC jurisdictions. A word of warning: the invisible factors involved here are extensive, and the authors have had to condense them to a single chapter. It is advised to study this area in greater detail through books on Jurisprudence, after grappling with the basic concepts used for comparative analysis in this Chapter.

本章还将就普通法和中华人民共和国司法管辖区的法律制度起源与前一章进行衔接。需要提醒的是：本章涉及的隐形因素非常广泛，笔者不得不将其浓缩在一章中。建议在掌握本章用于比较分析的基本概念之后，通过法理学书籍对这一领域进行更详细的研究。

3.2 Western Jurisprudence (in particular, England & Wales)

西方法理学（特别是英格兰和威尔士）

Jurisprudence can mean the critical analysis of a case in a particular court in a particular jurisdiction; for others it may mean law in general; and it can also mean the study of legal philosophy.[190] Jurisprudence as a subject in itself will not attempt to study a particular law. Instead, it will attempt to analyze the law at a broader level.[191] It may at a very specific level mean "what is implicit in a lawyer's understanding of law that forms the background assumptions or beliefs he or she has."[192] The authors will proceed with the study of legal philosophies that are most appropriate to the

法理学可以指对某一司法管辖区的某一法院的案件进行批判性分析；对其他人来说，法理学可以指一般法律；法理学也可以指法律哲学研究。法理学作为一门学科，本身并不试图研究特定的法律。相反，它试图在更广泛的层面上分析法律。在一个非常具体的层面上，它可能是指“律师对法律的理解中隐含的、构成其背景假设或信念的东西”。

190 Thomas Lundmark, *Charting the Divide between Common and Civil Law* (New York; Oxford: Oxford University Press, 2012), 89–90。托马斯-伦德马克，普通法与民法的分界线（纽约；牛津：牛津大学出版社，2012），89-90 页。

191 Penner, Schiff, and Nobles, "Approaches to Jurisprudence," 3。彭纳、希夫和诺布尔斯，“法理学的方法”，第 3 页。

192 Anne Barron, et al., *Introduction to Jurisprudence and Legal Theory: Commentary and Materials* (London: Butterworths, 2002), 4。安妮·巴伦等人，法理学和法律理论导论：评注和材料。伦敦：巴特沃斯出版社，2002，第 4 页。

subject matter of this book. These legal theories will be discussed more in context with the practice of law in both common law and civil law jurisdictions such as France and Germany.

笔者将着手研究最适合本书主题的法律哲学。这些法律理论将更多地结合普通法系和大陆法系司法管辖区（如法国和德国）的法律实践进行讨论。

For the sake of completeness, it is important to highlight that pure philosophers of law are different from jurisprudents as they don't concentrate on the practice of law or even consider that philosophy of law is necessary for everyday lawyers working in the legal system in any jurisdiction.[193] In this Chapter, the authors will analyze first the legal philosophies, and thereafter how these philosophies are linked to the practice of law in the relevant jurisdictions.

为完整起见，有必要强调的是，纯粹的法哲学家不同于法理学家，因为他们并不专注于法律实践，甚至不认为法律哲学对于在任何司法管辖区的法律体系中工作的日常律师是必要的。在本章中，笔者将首先分析法律哲学，然后分析这些哲学如何与相关司法管辖区的法律实践相联系。

The authors will discuss the background to Classical English jurisprudence, before examining different types of legal philosophies, and jurisprudents' thought processes about law.

笔者将讨论英国古典法理学的背景，然后研究不同类型的法律哲学，以及法学家对法律的思考过程。

[193] Ibid., 5.

Figure 4: Jurisprudence Influencing Judges in England & Wales - JAIN Analysis

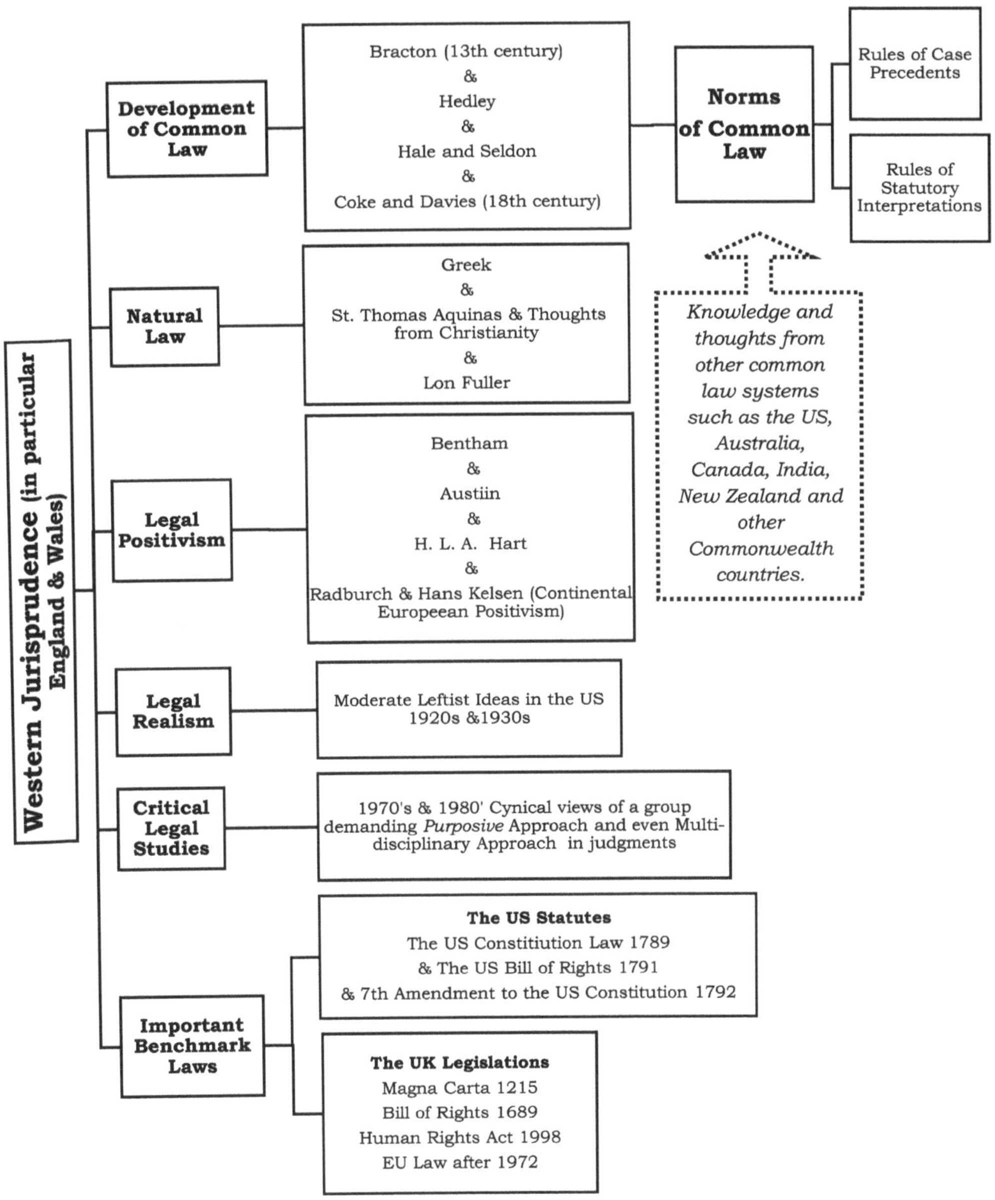

图 4：影响英格兰和威尔士法官的法理学
JAIN式解析

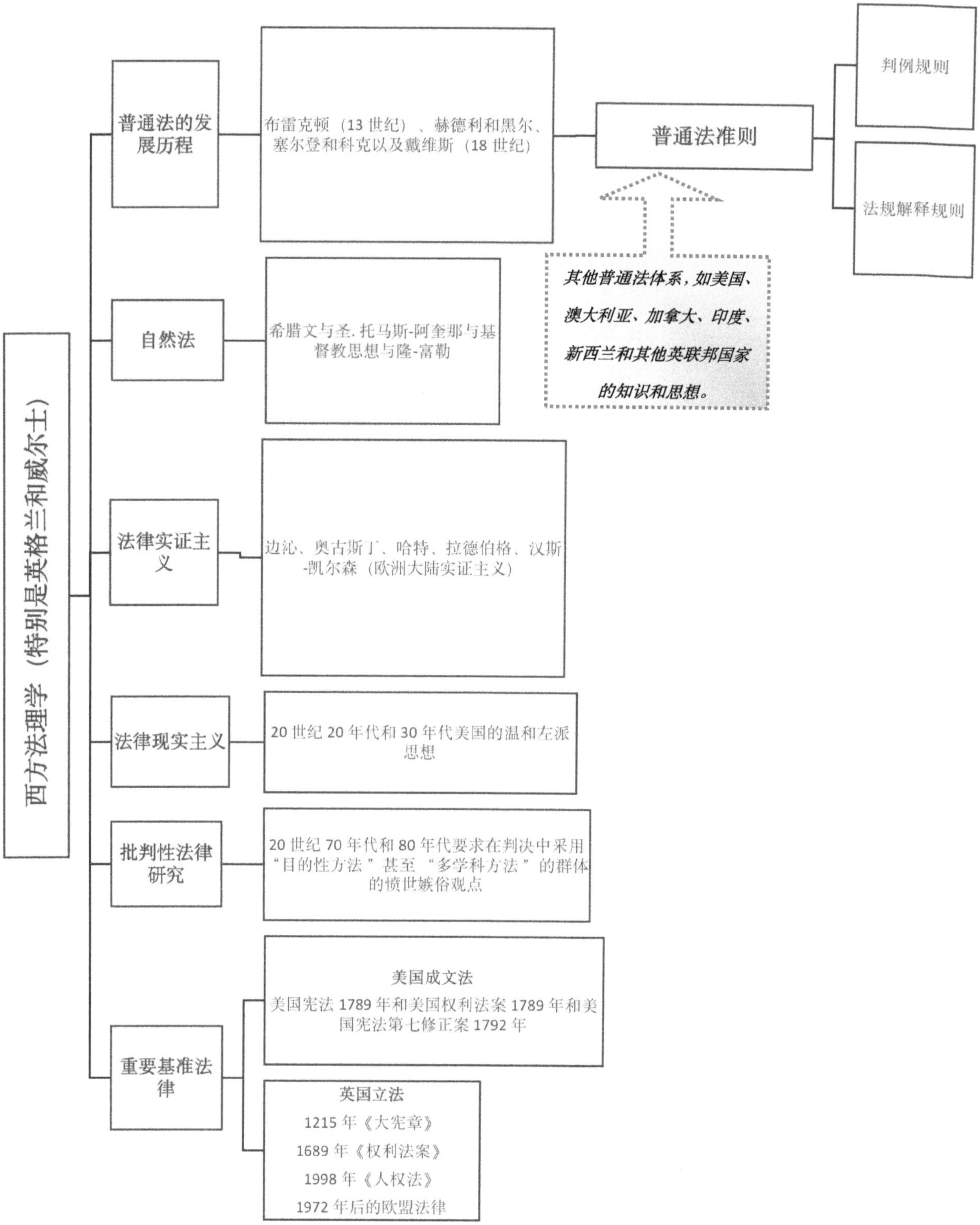

3.2.1 Background to Classical English Jurisprudence

英国古典法理学的背景

Henry II, the twelfth century English king, created a system whereby laws and customs for the whole of England were administered by a centralized court system.[194] A permanent court was established at Westminster, and justices would travel from there around the country, in this way harmonising the different laws of local areas within England.[195] By the thirteenth century, Bracton was able to compile the laws and customs of England. Regional and local customs were instrumental in the development of a law common throughout England.[196] This led to the emergence of common customs in the whole of England.

十二世纪的英国国王亨利二世创建了一个由中央法院系统管理整个英格兰的法律和惯例的系统。在威斯敏斯特设立了一个常设法院，法官们从那里出发，周游全国，从而协调了英格兰各地不同的法律。到 13 世纪，布雷克顿已经能够汇编英格兰的法律和习俗。地区和地方惯例在英国共同法律的发展过程中发挥了重要作用。这导致了全英格兰共同惯例的出现。

It developed as an oral tradition, but slowly records began to be kept; for example, case decisions that were made, were cited later in other cases, and thus started to act as *case precedents*. This led to the development of year books containing judgments and pleadings. In other words, *the law in action* was recorded by those yearbooks containing pleadings, arguments and decisions of courts.[197] The arguments developed in the judges' reasoning in their judgments were given prominence, as compared to the actual decisions, which could be fact-sensitive. The legal arguments before the court based on hypothetical facts seemed to create the laws that would eventually decide the matter on the actual facts about the case.[198] The role of the jury developed,

它是作为口头传统发展起来的，但慢慢地开始有了记录；例如，做出的案件判决后来在其他案件中被引用，从而开始成为案件先例。这导致了包含判决书和诉状的年鉴的发展。换言之，载有诉状、论据和法院判决的年鉴记录了法律的实施情况。与实际判决相比，法官在判决推理中形成的论点更为重要，因为实际判决可能对事实敏感。法庭上基于假设事实的法律论证似乎创造了法律，最终将根据案件的实际事实做出裁决。陪审团的作用得到了发展，而律师的作用最初只是在法官的指导下向陪审

194 Gerald J. Postema, "Classical Common Law Jurisprudence (Part I)," *Oxford U. of Commw. L.J.* 2, no. 2 (2002): 157.

杰拉尔德·J·波斯特马，"经典普通法法理学（第一部分）"，Oxford U. of Commw. L.J. 2, no. 2，2002，第 157 页。

195 Ibid., 158.

196 Ibid., 159.

197 Ibid., 161.

198 Ibid., 162.

and the role of lawyers, in the beginning, was merely to interpret and to explain the story containing facts to the jury under the guidance of the judges.

团解释和说明包含事实的故事。

Legislations would often correct the anomalies and would fill the gaps in decisions emanating from the common law courts, thus starting the relationship between the legal system and legislature. The courts would develop legal rules out of the legislation that fit with the common-law reasoning in the cases. The common law system slowly became an institution in itself by the seventeenth century. Therefore, the common law was "body or practices and patterns of practical thinking,"[199] that has been developed over years by customs, its application through reasons and through experience of the courts and stakeholders. The common law arose out of the customs (local or merchants) shared assumptions, though some scholars in the past distinguished common law from customs and traditions.[200] Legal theories were developed around common law as a product of customs, or normative force of customs that were part of the common law or as a product of rules that were recorded.[201]

立法往往会纠正不正常的现象，填补普通法法院判决中的空白，从而开启了法律系统与立法机构之间的关系。法院会根据立法制定符合普通法案件推理的法律规则。到 17 世纪，普通法体系本身慢慢成为一种制度。因此，普通法是“实践思维的主体或惯例和模式”，是多年来由习俗、法院和利益相关者的适用理由和经验形成的。普通法产生于惯例（地方或商人）的共同假设，尽管过去有些学者将普通法与习俗和传统区分开来。法律理论是围绕普通法发展起来的，普通法是惯例的产物，或作为普通法一部分的惯例的规范力，或作为记录在案的规则的产物。

A few scholars, such as Coke and Davies in the eighteenth century, argued the common law was made up of customs which were affected by conquerors such as Romans, and that these customs had not changed since then. The other reason that they cited for its wide acceptance was that it was antique in nature, and was therefore accepted by the populace.[202] Other scholars argued that the real issue was the effect of natural law on the common law, and not that the common law had its origins in past customs. The authors will discuss the theory of natural law in a later part of this Chapter. However, no scholars deny the common law is made up of rules, norms, doctrines and customs, and has slowly become

少数学者，如 18 世纪的古柯和戴维斯，认为普通法是由受罗马人等征服者影响的惯例构成的，这些惯例自那时起就没有改变过。他们提出的普通法被广泛接受的另一原因是，普通法渊源古老，因此为民众所接受。另一些学者则认为，真正的问题是自然法对普通法的影响，而不是普通法起源于过去的习俗。笔者将在本章后半部分讨论自然法理论。然而，没有学者否认普通法是由规则、规范、学说和惯例组成的，并且经过几个世纪的发展，慢慢变得非常技术化。

199 Ibid.
200 Ibid

201 Ibid.

202 Ibid., 169–71.

very technical in nature over centuries of development.

St German in the sixteenth century argued that the *maxims* that were only known to the courts and the learned professionals can actually be distinguished from the general customs.[203] Maxims are the specialised rules and principles that govern the working of judicial activities, but are "congruent with the ordinary customs of people."[204] Thomas Hedley in the seventeenth century was of the view that though common law was not synonymous with customs, its source could be traced back to customs.[205] Thus, there were enormous debates amongst scholars about the philosophical origins of the common law.

十六世纪的圣德曼认为，只有法院和博学的专业人士才知道的格言实际上可以与一般惯例区分开来。格言是指导司法活动的专门规则和原则，但"与人们的一般习惯相一致"。十七世纪的托马斯·赫德利认为，尽管普通法并非习俗的同义词，但其渊源可以追溯到习俗。因此，学者们对普通法的哲学渊源展开了激烈的辩论。

Seldon in the seventeenth century had a view quite different from Hedley; he commented that the common law was affected by many cultures as a result of successive invasions of England, and accordingly common law has its own distinctive features. In any event, according to Seldon, the source of the common law could be traced all the way to the fundamental nature of humans that had remained unchanged even after many interpretations and adjustments of law.[206] According to the scholars of this school of thought, even the legislated laws had left imprints in the common law, even if they had been amended or repealed over time. Hale suggested validity of *a* norm, rather than the rules that are followed by the populace, is crucial to the existence of common law.[207] Therefore, for scholars such as Seldon, the source of rules was not important, but what was important was incorporation of such rules over the years.[208]

十七世纪的塞尔登与赫德利的观点截然不同；他评论说，普通法因他国相继入侵而受到多种文化的影响，因此普通法有其自身的独特之处。塞尔登认为，无论如何，普通法的渊源可以一直追溯到人类的基本本性，即使经过多次法律解释和调整，人类的基本本性仍然没有改变。该学派的学者认为，即使是立法的法律也在普通法中留下了印记，即使这些法律随着时间的推移而被修改或废除。黑尔认为，规范的有效性，而不是民众遵循的规则，是普通法存在的关键。因此，对于塞尔顿等学者来说，规则的来源并不重要，重要的是这些规则多年来的融合。

---

203 Ibid., 172.
204 Ibid.
205 Ibid.
206 Ibid., 173.
207 Ibid., 174.
208 Ibid.

It was gradually accepted by many scholars that common *reasons* have a great role to play in the common law.[209] However, the source of reasons cannot be natural law, as it can be too general in nature. These reasons must be rooted in the experience and reasons of the judges.[210] Hale argued the essential feature of these reasons was "consistency and its constancy".[211] Hale was of the view that natural law was not the source of rules in common law, but it assisted in ensuring that the populace followed the common law.[212] Over time, rules of interpretation and rules in context as to how the judges were required to fill the gaps in common law came into existence. Hale was of the view that with any such rules, it was not the discretion exercised by the judges, but rather the process by which they found the solutions within cases, that was critical. Judges' reasons are ordinarily called artificial reasons by jurists as they bear no resemblance to any one thread of philosophy. However, the judges' reasons are pragmatic and practical, and have many unique qualities. A few such qualities as postulated by Postema are as follows:[213]

普通理由在普通法中发挥着巨大的作用，这一点逐渐被许多学者所接受。但是，理由的来源不能是自然法，因为自然法的性质可能过于笼统。这些理由必须植根于法官的经验和推理。黑尔认为，这些理由的基本特征是"一致性及其恒定性"。黑尔认为，自然法不是普通法规则的来源，但它有助于确保民众遵守普通法。随时间推移，关于法官如何填补普通法空白的解释规则和上下文规则应运而生。黑尔认为，对于任何此类规则，关键不在于法官行使的自由裁量权，而在于他们在案件中找到解决方案的过程。法官的理由通常被法学家称为人为理由，因为它们与任何一种哲学思想都不相似。然而，法官的理由是务实的、实际的，具有许多独特的品质。波斯特马提出的几个特质如下：

- *Practical* and common-law reasoning by which the judges in the courts tend to solve the real particular and specific problems before the courts by going deeper into the issues of law and facts;

*实用性*和普通法推理，法院法官往往通过深入研究法律和事实问题来解决法院面临的真正特殊和具体的问题；

- *Contextual* as the common-law judges have learned legal skills over many years by immersing themselves in the legal profession. The reasons of such common-law judges are mostly analogical,

普通法系法官通过多年沉浸于法律职业中学习法律技能，具有一定的*背景*。这些普通法法官的理由大多是类比性的，即利用他们作为普通法法院法官的身份所拥有的一切资

[209] Ibid.

[210] Postema, "Classical Common Law Jurisprudence - II," 2。波斯特马，"经典普通法法理学-2"，第 2 页。

[211] Postema, "Classical Common Law Jurisprudence - I," 178。波斯特马，"经典普通法法理学-1"，第 178 页。

[212] Ibid.

[213] Postema, "Classical Common Law Jurisprudence - II," 3–8。波斯特马，"经典普通法法理学-2"，第 3-8 页。

where difference and similarities are found using all resources that are available to them in their capacity as judges in the common law courts;

源来发现差异和相似之处；

♦ *Public mission,* where common-law lawyers and judges' skills such as public reasoning, deliberation, judgement and oratory are essential elements to solve even cases with particular and specific facts;

公共使命，普通法律师和法官的技能，如公共推理、商议、判断和演说，是解决具有特殊和具体事实的案件的基本要素；

♦ *Non-systematic* as common-law lawyers and judges are trained to utilise all available means to provide justice as long as their reasons are locally congruent with the other parts of law in their own jurisdiction, as compared to the need to have global congruence. The common law can appear chaotic to continental civil law lawyers, and sometimes even to early common-law lawyers. As a result, many lawyers who are trained outside of common law jurisdictions are usually puzzled by the multitude of resources and lack of a list of ready-made doctrines to solve problems. A few common-law lawyers, like the scholar Bacon in the seventeenth century, tried to find relevant doctrines on similar lines, but found it impossible to list all the doctrines that can impact specific cases. This is also an area where many clever PRC lawyers or students from the PRC studying in the common law system have struggled with or not appreciated the uniqueness of the common law system. The most general issue has been trying to understand the common law system through the prism of the PRC system or civil law system;

非系统性，因为普通法系的律师和法官接受的培训是利用一切可用的手段伸张正义，只要他们的理由与本辖区的其他法律部分在当地是一致的，而不是需要全球一致。在大陆法律师看来，普通法可能是混乱的，有时甚至在早期普通法律师看来也是如此。因此，许多在普通法法域之外接受过培训的律师通常会对众多的资源和缺乏解决问题的现成理论清单感到困惑。少数普通法系律师，如十七世纪的学者培根，试图按照类似的思路寻找相关学说，但发现不可能列出所有能够影响具体案件的学说。这也是许多聪明的中国律师或在普通法体系中学习的中国学生苦苦思索或不理解普通法体系独特性的地方。最普遍的问题是试图通过中华人民共和国法系或大陆法系的棱镜来理解普通法系；

♦ *Discoursive* as legal reasons are developed during oral arguments and debates in the court rooms. The skills of oral advocacy are very important for the common law's development, as

在法庭的口头辩论和辩论中，法律推理得以形成。口头辩护技巧对普通法的发展非常重要，因为在公众面前辩论法律论点可以提高法院的合法性。笔者认为，这一点至关重

legal arguments are debated in front of the public to increase the legitimacy of the courts. In the author's view, this is crucial, especially when there are gaps in legislation, and common law is being developed in the courts by these legal arguments to resolve a particular problem;

要，尤其是当立法存在漏洞时，普通法就是通过这些法律论证在法庭上发展起来的，以解决特定问题；

- ♦ *Common reasons* that come out in the open courts through arguments from various stakeholders, rather than discovery of reasons by philosophers. These reasons are congruent, compatible and consistent with the law as a whole in a common law jurisdiction and accordingly will become part of the shared experience that is acceptable to the populace living in that common law jurisdiction, such as England & Wales.

通过各利益相关者的争论而在公开法庭上出现的共同推理。这些推理与普通法司法管辖区的整体法律是一致的、相容的和连贯的，因此将成为生活在该普通法司法管辖区（如英格兰和威尔士）的民众所接受的共同经验的一部分。

For the common-law judges and lawyers, the moral acceptability of reasons is not a requirement, as long as there is a coherence of reasons, and pragmatic solutions to problems in the disputes are available. Any case law itself is not supposed to bind future cases, but illustrates the common law's underlying principles, or a view that it is a "...practised framework of practical reasoning and this practised framework constitutes a form of social ordering."[214]

对于普通法法官和律师而言，只要理由推理一致，并能务实地解决争议中的问题，理由在道德上的可接受性并非必要条件。任何判例法本身都不应该约束未来的案件，而是说明普通法的基本原则，或者说是一种观点，即普通法是"……实用推理的实践框架，这种实践框架构成了一种社会秩序"。

n common law, legal reasoning from past cases provides a benchmark for future reasoning, and gives judges a framework to keep in mind for the case at hand. In common law, technically speaking, even statutes legislated in Parliament need to be incorporated into practice by judges in order to become part of the common law. In addition, in later years, more and more rules have been devised by the judges based on interpretation of the statutes in the courts. This has also become part of the common law.

在普通法中，过去案例中的法律推理为未来的推理提供了基准，并为法官提供了一个框架，使其在处理当前案件时牢记于心。在普通法中，从技术上讲，即使是议会立法的法规，也需要法官将其纳入实践，才能成为普通法的一部分。此外，近年来，法官根据法院对成文法的解释制定了越来越多的规则。这也成为普通法的一部分。

[214] Ibid., 14.

3.2.2 Natural Law – Greeks, St. Thomas Aquinas to Lon Fuller

自然法——希腊人，从圣托马斯·阿奎那，再到隆·富勒

The authors have discussed the issues of customs, rules and so forth in the common law in the previous section. One such issue was the effect of natural law, from the time of the origins of humans, on the development of common law. The focus of such theories is not on the creator of the law, but rather on their acceptance by the populace. If an immoral or unethical law is accepted by the populace, it is likely out of fear, and that is tantamount to a threat. According to such theories, *morality* is an important consideration in the content of the law. Under this legal philosophy, any law devoid of morality is mere pronouncements.[215] Justice is the ultimate aim of any law under this legal philosophy or under similar philosophies. These concepts are ancient in origin, and it can be traced in western jurisprudence to the formation of the Greek cities, and specifically to Plato.[216]

笔者在上一节讨论了普通法中的习惯、规则等问题。其中一个问题是人类起源时期的自然法对普通法发展的影响。此类理论的重点不在于法律的创造者，而在于其是否被民众所接受。如果一项不道德或不伦理的法律被民众接受，很可能是出于恐惧，而这无异于一种威胁。依据此理论，*道德*是法律内容的一个关键考量要素。在这种法律哲学下，任何缺乏道德的法律都只是宣示。根据这种法律哲学或类似的哲学，正义是任何法律的最终目标。这些理念源远流长，在西方法学中可以追溯到希腊城市的形成，特别是到柏拉图时期。

With the formation of empires, such as the Greek or Roman empires, it was realized that the community law or a particular custom from the conqueror's land, cannot be held supreme in conquered lands. There must therefore be something universal, a 'common legal order' that was superior, called *jus naturale*, along with secondary customs, such as those that facilitate trade, called *jus gentium*.[217] In the thirteenth century, St. Thomas Aquinas combined Christianity with natural law and distinguished such natural

在希腊、罗马等帝国逐步形成的过程中，人们意识到，征服者所在国的共同体法律或特定惯例无法在被征服的土地上确立起至高无上的地位。因此，必须有一种普遍性的东西，一种具有优越性的“共同法律秩序”，称为自然法，以及次要的惯例，如促进贸易的习俗，称为万民法。13 世纪，圣托马斯·阿奎那将基督教与自然法结合起来，并将自然法与人为法区分开来。阿奎那认为，

215 Lundmark, *Divide between Common and Civil Law*, 94。伦德马克，《普通法与民法之分》，第 94 页。

216 Plato thought of law as the embodiment of justice, beauty and ethics. In addition, Plato gave prominence to these theories even above customs or conventions. For details, see Richards Nobles and David Schiff, "The Evolution of Natural Law," in *Introduction to Jurisprudence and Legal Theory: Commentary and Materials*, by Anne Barron, et al. (London: Butterworths, 2002), 39.

柏拉图认为法律是正义、美和道德的体现。此外，柏拉图还将这些理论置于习俗或惯例之上。详见理查兹·诺布尔斯和戴维·希夫合著：《自然法的演变》，载《法理学和法律理论导论》：安·巴伦等著，评论与材料。伦敦：巴特沃斯出版社，2002，第 39 页。

217 Richards Nobles and David Schiff, "Natural Law," 41。理查兹·诺布尔斯和戴维·希夫，“自然法”，第 41 页。

law from human-made law. Morality is a science that needs to be learned by most, according to Aquinas.

道德是一门需要大多数人学习的科学。

Such theories presume that even though humans are not perfect, they have a sense of justice, a sort of inbuilt compass based on morality. According to scholars in this field, if in any country there are no declarations as to human rights as a result of not signing any International Conventions or local legislations, it does not necessarily mean the populace does not have such rights. It merely means that such rights are denied by the institutions. Thomas Jefferson wrote in the US Declaration of Independence that "We hold these truths to be self-evident, that all men are created equal, that they are endowed by their Creator with certain unalienable rights that among these are Life, Liberty and the pursuit of Happiness."[218] It appears that by using word 'Creator' in the previous statement, Jefferson, a lawyer, would seem to believe in such philosophies. Common law jurisdictions, however, are more in favor of the legal philosophy of natural law.

该理论主张，纵使人无完人，然而皆具正义感，拥有一副建基于道德之上的内在圭臬。该领域的学者认为，如果任何国家由于没有签署任何国际公约或地方立法而没有人权宣言，这并不一定意味着民众没有这种权利。这仅仅意味着这些权利被体制所剥夺。托马斯·杰斐逊在《美国独立宣言》中写道："我们认为这些真理是不言而喻的，人人生而平等，造物主赋予他们某些不可剥夺的权利，其中包括生命、自由和追求幸福的权利"。杰斐逊作为一名律师，在前面的陈述中使用了"造物主"一词，似乎相信这些哲学。然而，普通法司法管辖区更倾向于自然法的法律哲学。

A very important sub-set of the theories in this section was propounded by Lon Fuller. His natural law theories were based upon the concept that a social contract exists between the government and the populace that is governed.[219] He concentrated on procedural aspects of any law, saying for example that there is a need for laws to be understood, and they can only be understood by governance of rules.[220] The rules will allow for the laws to be published enabling the governed to understand and thereafter show 'fidelity' to those laws. This philosophy was also an attempt to distinguish them from theories of Legal Positivism (to be discussed later in this Chapter) because it still draws

这部分理论中一个非常重要的子集是由伦·富勒提出的。他的自然法理论基于这样一个概念，即政府与被统治的民众之间存在社会契约。他专注于任何法律的程序方面，举例说，法律需要被理解，而只有通过规则治理才能理解法律。规则将使法律得以公布，从而使被统治者能够理解并"忠实"于这些法律。这一哲学思想也是将其与法律实证主义理论（将在本章后面讨论）区分开来的一种尝试，因为它仍然提请人们注意法

---

[218] Preamble of United States Declaration of Independence, 4, July, 1776。美国独立宣言序言，1776年7月4日。

[219] Richards Nobles and David Schiff, "Natural Law," 44。理查兹·诺布尔斯和戴维·希夫合著的《自然法的演变》，第44页。

[220] Richards Nobles and David Schiff, "Natural Law," 44. It was also discussed in Lon L. Fuller, *The Law in Quest of Itself*(Boston, Mass.: Beacon Press, 1940), 33–42。理查兹·诺布尔斯和戴维·希夫合著的《自然法的演变》，第44页。它也在伦·富勒的探索自身的法律．波士顿，麻省：灯塔出版社，1940，第33-42页。

attention to elements of ethics and content of the law. Nonetheless this school of thought is more relevant to the practice of law.[221] Fuller succinctly described the difference between "*what law is*" as described by the jurisprudents of the positivist school of thought, and *"what law ought to be."*[222]

律的伦理要素和内容。尽管如此，这一思想流派与法律实践更为相关。富勒简明扼要地描述了实证主义学派法学家所描述的“*法律是什么*”与“*法律应是什么*”之间的区别。

3.2.3 Legal Positivism – Bentham, Austin, H L A Hart, Radburch, Kelson

法律实证主义——边沁、奥斯汀、哈特、拉德伯奇、凯尔森

Positivists believe there must be a creator (man-made) of some rules or *customary rules* that are given legal sanctity. Such rules are clear and usually described in detail to prevent as much as possible the intrusion of subjectivity and unnecessary exercise of discretion. Such rules are created by a 'sovereign' and are habitually followed by the populace. These aspects of the rules were interpreted by the analytical branch of positivism as the difference between real and mystical matters.[223] Bentham argued that English Law was not the product of natural law,[224] and he criticised other lawyers arguing otherwise. However, rules or laws will have to be interpreted by judges at a later stage, and therefore, the jurisprudents of natural theories have pointed this out as a shortcoming.[225] There is a need for some institution to

实证主义者认为，某些规则或*习惯规则*必须有一个创造者（人为的），并被赋予法律的神圣性。这些规则是明确的，通常有详细的说明，以尽可能防止主观性的侵入和不必要的自由裁量权的行使。这些规则由“主权”制定，并由民众习惯性地予以遵守。实证主义的分析流派将规则的这些方面阐释为现实问题与神秘问题的分野。边沁认为英国法律不是自然法的产物，他批评了其他持相反观点的律师。然而，规则或法律必须由法官在稍后阶段进行解释，因此，自然理论法学家指出这是一个缺陷。有必要通过某种制度来建议将某一特定习

221 Refer §3.2.1 & §3.2.3。参见 3.2.1 和 3.2.3 节。

222 Fuller, *The Law in Quest of Itself*, 5–11。富勒，探索自身的法律，第 5-11 页。

223 See the discussion on Bentham's analytical jurisprudence in Richard Nobles and David Schiff, "Debating with Natural Law; the Emergence of the Legal Positivism," in *Introduction to Jurisprudence and Legal Theory: Commentary and Materials*, Anne Barron, et al. (London: Butterworths, 2002), 92.

见理查兹-诺布尔斯和戴维-希夫对边沁的分析法学的讨论，“与自然法辩论：法律实证主义的兴起"，载《法理学与法律理论导论》：评注与材料》，安妮-巴伦等（伦敦：巴特沃斯出版社，2002 年），第 92 页。

224 Richard Nobles and David Schiff, "Legal Positivism," 93–94。理查兹·诺布尔斯和戴维·希夫，“法律实证主义”，第 93-94 页。

225 Fuller, *The Law in Quest of Itself*, 5–11。富勒，探索自身的法律，第 5-11 页。

suggest that a particular custom is to be treated as a law; only then will all the populace and business organisations consider that particular custom as a law within that jurisdiction.

俗视为法律；只有这样，所有民众和商业组织才会将该特定习俗视为该司法管辖区内的法律。

John Austin, a famous positivist, has explained that a law needs a creator, and once the law has been created, it will require a declaration. Austin's scheme of things includes the science of making good laws. An element of coercion in the form of sanctions is also necessary. Rules that have been created are *formally valid*; whether at a later stage the stakeholders *like* such rules is not important or even relevant in this school of thought. In this authors' view, however, this top-down approach will not work where the government is elected by the people and there is a vibrant democracy. The requirement for formal validity, with rules needing to be declared as law, was criticised by Ronald Dworkin, who refers to it as a 'pedigree thesis" of positivism.[226]

著名的实证主义者约翰·奥斯汀解释道，法律需要一个创制者，而法律一旦被创制出来，就需要一个宣言。奥斯汀的计划包括一门关于制定良善法律的科学。制裁形式的强制因素也是必要的。已经制定的规则在形式上是有效的；在以后的阶段，利益相关者是否喜欢这些规则在这一学派中并不重要，甚至无关紧要。然而，笔者认为，在政府由人民选举产生、民主机制蓬勃运转的地区，这种自上而下的方法是行不通的。罗纳德·德沃金批评了形式有效性的要求，并将其称为实证主义的"血统论"。

The famous twentieth-century jurisprudent H L A Hart has classed as '*primary rules*' laws such as criminal law, that governs the behaviour of the populace or the powers of the population to make contracts; and as *'secondary rules'*, laws such as constitutional law or contract law that assists in identification of the primary rules, and acts as a guide to interpret them.[227] The legal rules lead to obligations, and authority comes from a set of recognised criteria such as statutes or judicial precedents. According to Hart, the secondary rules can be classed as *rules of recognition*,[228]

二十世纪著名法学家哈特将规范民众行为或民众订立契约的权力的法律（如刑法）归类为"*主要规则*"；将协助确定主要规则并作为解释主要规则指南的法律（如宪法或合同法）归类为"*次要规则*"。法律规则导致义务，而权威则来自一套公认的标准，如法规或司法判例。根据哈特的观点，次要规则可分为*识别规则和裁决规则*，前者是识别一个体系或考虑特定主要规则是否有效所

[226] Lundmark provides a succinct discussion of Positivism in *Divide between Common and Civil Law*, 92.

伦德马克在《普通法与民法之分》一书中对实证主义进行了简洁的论述，第 92 页。

[227] H.L.A. Hart, *The Concept of Law*, 2nd ed. (Oxford: Oxford University Press, 1994), 79, for further discussion on 'primary rules' and 'secondary rules'. See also, Nicola Lacey, "Modern Positivism: H L A Hart and Analytical Jurisprudence," in *Introduction to Jurisprudence and Legal Theory: Commentary and Materials*, by Anne Barron, et al. (London: Butterworths, 2002), 157.

H·L·A·哈特，法律的概念，第二版，牛津：牛津大学出版社，1994，第 79 页，进一步讨论"主要规则"和"次要规则"。另见尼古拉·莱西，"现代实证主义：哈特与分析法理学"，载《法理学与法律理论导论： 评注和材料》，安妮·巴伦等著，伦敦：巴特沃斯出版社，2002 年，第 157 页。

[228] Hart, *The Concept of Law*, 105–10。哈特，法律的概念，第 105-110 页。

which are necessary in order to identify a system or to consider whether a particular primary rule is valid or not; and *rules of adjudication*, that are used to interpret and apply such rules.[229] A legal system can only be understood as an entity once it has the above set of rules in place.

必需的，后者则用于解释和适用这些规则。一个法律体系只有具备了上述规则，才能被理解为一个实体。

However, apart from the *'external aspects'* of these rules, there are also the '*internal aspects*' that are used akin to reasons or as a benchmark for behaviour of the populace in relation to the external law. In the words of Hart a "...wide range of normative language is used...."[230] to describe the internal rules, in contrast to external behaviour, of the populace. "There is no contradiction in saying that people accept certain rules but experience no such feelings of compulsion."

然而，除了这些规则的 *"外在方面"*，还有 *"内在方面"*，这些"内在方面"被用作与外在法律相关的民众行为的理由或基准。用哈特的话说，"...广泛的规范性语言被用于..."描述民众的内部规则，与外部行为形成对比。"称人们接受某些规则，但却没有这种强迫感，这并不矛盾"。

Thus, while Austin's theory sees the law as the command of a sovereign, Hart's ideas and system of rules are more suited for democracies, secular and pluralistic societies. Hart agreed that any power associated with a sovereign cannot be unlimited, and in view of that, he discussed bills of rights and constitutional laws that bind the sovereign.[231] Hart explained the difference between the rules that are sanction-oriented and the rules that can empower the populace to conduct their day-to-day business, such as contract or family laws.[232]

因此，奥斯汀的理论将法律视为君主的命令，而哈特的思想和规则体系则更适合民主、世俗和多元社会。哈特同意，任何与君主相关的权力都不可能是无限的，有鉴于此，他讨论了对君主具有约束力的权利法案和宪法法律。哈特解释了以制裁为导向的规则与能够授权民众处理日常事务的规则（如合同法或家庭法）之间的区别。

Very fundamentally, Hart believed that the populace follows the law not just because they are worried about any sanctions

从根本上说，哈特认为民众遵守法律不仅仅是因为他们担心不遵守法律会

229 There is a detailed discussion of Hart's classification of secondary rules in Lacey, "Modern Positivism," 164–65.

莱西：《现代实证主义》第 164-165 页中详细讨论了哈特对次要规则的分类。

230 Hart, *The Concept of Law*, 56–57。哈特，法律的概念，第 56-57 页。

231 Ibid., 68.

232 Hart, *The Concept of Law*, 84. Further discussion on the same issues can be seen in the analysis of Hart's jurisprudence in Lacey, "Modern Positivism," 161–62.

哈特，法律的概念，84。关于同样问题的进一步讨论，可参见莱西对哈特判例的分析，"现代实证主义"，第 161-162 页。

consequent on *not* following the law, but also because the laws serve as a benchmark that can be seen as providing a reason for their actions. Further, Hart was of the view that officials also need to have such an attitude towards their own legal system's rules, thereby bringing a form of democracy within the rule-based system.[233]

受到制裁，还因为法律是一个基准，可以被视为他们行动的理由。此外，哈特还认为，官员也需要对自己法律体系的规则持这种态度，从而在以规则为基础的体系中实现某种形式的民主。

Hart was an analytical positivist; however, he did not negate the use of natural law to fill the gaps in law during adjudication. Hart acknowledged that judges had to exercise their discretionary power during the process of adjudication in the courts, and he further conceded that there were elements of natural law in most law. However, Hart was clear that natural law did not guide the judges or populace.

哈特是一位分析实证主义者，但他并不否认在裁决过程中使用自然法来填补法律空白。哈特承认法官在法庭裁决过程中必须行使自由裁量权，他还承认大多数法律中都有自然法的元素。然而，哈特明确指出，自然法并不能指导法官或民众。

While the authors have discussed the school of positivism that developed in common law jurisdictions, there was also a parallel development of this concept in civil law jurisdictions. This was also quite influential in the development of jurisprudential thought. The authors will also discuss two jurisprudents from the civil law jurisdictions found in continental Europe — Hans Kelsen and Radbruch – who share a similar school of thought. The populace can adhere to these rules out of respect for the institution that is the creator of such rules, and/ or respect for the laws, and/or out of custom, and/or out of pure submission to the authorities. However, the main reasons are irrelevant.

虽然笔者讨论了在普通法司法管辖区发展起来的实证主义学派，但这一概念在大陆法系司法管辖区也有平行发展。这对法理学思想的发展也有相当大的影响。笔者还将讨论欧洲大陆大陆法系的两位法理学家——汉斯·凯尔森和拉德布鲁赫——他们拥有类似的思想流派。民众遵守这些规则可能是出于对制定这些规则的机构的尊重，也可能是出于对法律的尊重，和/或出于习俗，和/或出于对当局的纯粹服从。然而，主要原因无关紧要。

Hans Kelsen, a positivist in the continental European tradition, commented in the context of law that "any desired content can be the law."[234] Pursuant to this school of thought, it is immaterial whether the contents of the rules are good or bad or capricious, immoral, unethical, racist or

欧洲大陆传统的实证主义者汉斯·凯尔森在谈到法律时评论说，"任何想要的内容都可以成为法律"。根据这一学派的观点，规则的内容是好是坏或任性、不道德、不伦理、种族主义或

[233] Hart, *The Concept of Law*, 116. For further discussion on the same issues, see Lacey, "Modern Positivism," 166.

哈特，法律的概念，116。关于同样问题的进一步讨论，可参见莱西对哈特判例的分析，"现代实证主义"，第 166 页。

[234] Lundmark, *Divide between Common and Civil Law*, 92。伦德马克，《普通法与民法之分》，第 92 页。

vulgar and so forth, as all these factors are irrelevant to its validity. During the years of enlightment in Europe, law was more like a science and as a result, any consideration of morality or human rights was considered part of political thinking.

庸俗等等都无关紧要，因为所有这些因素都与规则的有效性无关。在欧洲的启蒙运动时期，法律更像是一门科学，因此，对道德或人权的任何考虑都被视为政治思想的一部分。

While it was common to view the law from the angle of morality or human rights, these issues themselves could be seen as quite separate matters and were very subjective in nature. This is popularly called the 'separation thesis' within the theory of positivism.[235] Kelsen's main idea was to search for the fundamental character of law, and according to him, it was to be found in what the law was rather than what the law ought to have been.[236]

虽然从道德或人权的角度来看待法律是很常见的，但这些问题本身可以被视为完全不同的问题，而且具有很强的主观性。这就是实证主义理论中流行的“分离论”。凯尔森的主要思想是寻找法律的基本特征，根据他的观点，法律的基本特征在于法律是什么，而不是法律本应是什么。

Kelsen notably seemed to distinguish societal foundations from foundations of law. Kelson firmly believed in keeping politics or morality out of the concept of law and was a proponent of the *pure theory of law*. A particular act passing through a chain of legal norms can be provided with a *legal normative meaning*; norms give meaning to an act. This school of thought suggests that behaviour resulting in that act is due to the fact that the behaviour was "commanded or permitted or authorised."[237] Norms are also related to other norms in a hierarchical chain and are necessary to validate the relatively lower norms.

凯尔森似乎将社会基础与法律基础区分开来。凯尔森坚信，政治或道德不应被纳入法律概念，他是纯粹法律理论的支持者。通过法律规范链的特定行为可以获得法律规范意义；规范赋予行为以意义。该学派主张，导致该行为的行为是由于该行为是“被命令、允许或授权的”。规范与其他规范之间也存在着等级关系，规范是确认相对较低规范的必要条件。

However, Kelsen agreed that in this chain of legal norms, the highest norm, for example, the US Constitution, will be an exception, and accordingly it will not require another superior legal norm for it to be classed as valid. This is an

然而，凯尔森同意，在这一法律规范链中，最高规范，例如美国宪法，将是一个例外，因此，它不需要另一个更高的法律规范才能被归类为有效。这是法律规范链中所允许的例外情况。此外，

235 Ibid., 93.

236 David Schiff, "Modern Positivism: Kelsen's Pure Theory of Law," in *Introduction to Jurisprudence and Legal Theory: Commentary and Materials*, Anne Barron, et al. (London: Butterworths, 2002), 191.
戴维·希夫，“现代实证主义：凯尔森的纯粹法学理论”，载《法理学和法律理论导论》： 评注和材料，安妮·巴伦等著，伦敦：巴特沃斯出版社，2002 年，第 191 页。

237 Lacey, "Modern Positivism," 195。莱西：《现代实证主义》，第 195 页。

exception which is allowed in this chain of legal norms. Additionally, such norms together form a legal system, and as a result they demonstrate the systematic nature of norms within a legal system. These norms are followed by the populace. These norms need to be understood from a particular point of view and not necessarily from the point of view of morality. Kelson also highlighted the concept of *coercion* in this positivist theory based on norms.[238]

这些规范共同构成了一个法律体系，因此它们展示了法律体系中规范的系统性。这些规范为民众所遵循。这些规范需要从特定的角度来理解，而不一定要从道德的角度来理解。凯尔森还在这种基于规范的实证主义理论中强调了强制的概念。

However, continental legal philosophers such as Radbruch were very vocal in suggesting that not all laws declared by institutions should be seen as formally valid and therefore suitable to be called law. In his view, such laws can be ignored by judges.[239] Radbruch suggested that issues of morality and ethics cannot be separated from the issue of validity of law. In Radburch's view, the declaration of such law, when missing vital ingredients of morality and ethics, renders it unsuitable to be classed as law.

然而，拉德布鲁赫等大陆法系哲学家却极力主张，并非所有由机构宣布的法律都应被视为形式上有效，因而适合被称为法律。在他看来，法官可以忽略这些法律。拉德布鲁赫认为，道德和伦理问题不能与法律的有效性问题分开。拉德布鲁赫认为，如果缺乏道德和伦理的重要内容，那么宣布这种法律就不适合将其归类为法律。

3.2.4 Legal Realism (1920s & 1930s onwards) and Critical Legal Studies (1970s and 1980s)

法律现实主义（20 世纪 20 年代和 30 年代以后）和批判性法律研究（20 世纪 70 年代和 80 年代）

In the common law jurisdiction of the US, the school of thought of Legal Realism (also called '*socio-legal*' studies),[240] had gained so much popularity in 1920s and

在美国的普通法司法管辖区，法律现实主义学派（也称为“社会法律”研究）在 20 世纪 20 年代和 30 年代大受欢

[238] Ibid., 196.

[239] Lundmark, *Divide between Common and Civil Law*, 93。伦德马克，《普通法与民法之分》，第 93 页。

[240] Hugh Collins, "Law as Politics: Progressive American Perspectives," in *Introduction to Jurisprudence and Legal Theory: Commentary and Materials*, Anne Barron, et al. (London: Butterworths, 2002), 281.

1930s that it even affected other common law jurisdictions such as England & Wales. In the US, legislations and cases have to conform to the *US Constitution Law 1789*, especially the *Bill of Rights 1791*, which includes the principles of liberty, equality, and freedom of speech; these principles result in political or social issues such as privacy, that are ultimately resolved by the courts.

迎，甚至影响到英格兰和威尔士等其他普通法司法管辖区。在美国，立法和案件必须符合 1789 年《美国宪法》，特别是 1791 年《权利法案》，其中包括自由、平等和言论自由原则；这些原则导致的政治或社会问题，如隐私问题，最终由法院解决。

The US Courts were applying the general principles enshrined in the framework of the *US Constitution 1789*, and therefore, were exercising broader discretion, and in that way, were going much further than the formal processes that were envisaged in the first place. Thus the US Courts themselves raised the issue of the legitimacy of judicial decisions, as well as questions about the judicial reasons coming out of the courts.[241] It raised fears that US judges, who were not elected through a democratic process by citizens of the US, were putting across their own subjective political affiliations in their judgments, on the pretext that their judgments conformed with the *Bill of Rights 1791* enshrined in the US constitution.

美国法院适用的是 1789 年《美国宪法》框架中的一般原则，因此行使的是更广泛的自由裁量权，这样就比最初设想的正式程序走得更远。因此，美国法院本身提出了司法判决的合法性问题，以及对法院提出的司法理由的质疑。这使人们担心，并非由美国公民通过民主程序选举产生的美国法官，会以其判决符合美国宪法所载的 1791 年《权利法案》为借口，在判决中加入自己的主观政治倾向。

This school of thought was developed by the moderate leftist parties in the USA, who challenged the established rules and even institutions of the US. This naturally provoked fierce reaction from the other side of the fence.[242] According to believers of this philosophy, the protection of private rights, privacy and similar concepts obstructs social welfare policies. Therefore, the developers and followers of this school of thought believe that the law is actually used in practice as an instrument of the government and this was the primary reason for the development of this school of thought.[243]

这一学派源于美国的温和左派政党，他们向美国的既定规则甚至制度发起挑战。此举自然而然引起了另一方的激烈回应。这种思想的信奉者认为，保护私权、隐私和类似概念会阻碍社会福利政策。因此，该学派的发展者和追随者认为，法律在实践中实际上被用作政府的工具，这是该学派发展的主要原因。

休·柯林斯，“法律即政治：美国进步观点”，载《法理学和法律理论导论： 评注和材料》，安妮·巴伦等，伦敦：巴特沃斯出版社，2002 年，第 281 页。

[241] Ibid., 279.

[242] Ibid., 280.

[243] Ibid., 281.

Some scholars who can be considered '*rules sceptic*' and '*facts sceptic*', feel that the law and society is in constant flux, and they therefore look at the process of adjudication.[244] According to scholars from this school of thought, no rules could be drafted in such detail as to cover all aspects and issues from the start. The scholars therefore recommended including inter-disciplinary approaches to the law and suggested that subjects such as sociology and economics should also be considered for the study of law. Scholars of this school of thought believed in '*law in action*' and analysed the law as practised in court rooms.

一些可被视为“*规则怀疑论* ”和“*事实怀疑论者*”的学者认为，法律和社会是不断变化的，因此他们关注裁决的过程。该学派的学者认为，任何规则都不可能起草得如此详细，从一开始就涵盖所有方面和问题。因此，学者们建议将跨学科方法纳入法律，并建议在研究法律时也应考虑社会学和经济学等学科。该学派的学者相信“*行动中的法律*”，并分析了在法庭上实践的法律。

The believers in this school of thought advocated the progressive interpretation of statutes and case laws in court rooms. This would have to include arguments about justice and morality to ensure that judges adapt to the rapid changes experienced in society.[245] According to these scholars, law and politics cannot be separated, and they were therefore more interested in what they called '*law in action*'.[246]

这一学派的信徒主张在法庭上对法规和判例法进行渐进式解释。这必须包括对正义和道德的论证，以确保法官适应社会的快速变化。这些学者认为，法律与政治不可分割，因此他们对所谓的“*行动中的法律*”更感兴趣。

Even though Hart, the famous English jurisprudent,[247] agreed that any judiciary can encounter and fill gaps during the application of law by inclusion of natural law principles, he disagreed with the notion that there are gaps that need to be actively filled. According to Hart, the judges are constrained by "rule-governed operations over the vast, central areas of the law".[248] It is here that the 'rule sceptic' scholars in the common law argue that the main reasons

尽管英国著名法学家哈特同意任何司法机构在适用法律的过程中都可能遇到并通过纳入自然法原则来填补空白，但他不同意需要积极填补空白的观点。哈特认为，法官受制于“在广阔的法律中心领域的规则运作”。正是在此，普通法中的“规则怀疑论 ”学者认为，法官在判决中给出的主要理由实际上是他们自己基于主观政治倾向的合理解释。

---

[244] Thomas Lundmark, *Charting the Divide Between Common and Civil Law* (New York; Oxford: Oxford University Press, 2012), 96. The legal realism of this aspect is further discussed in Collins, "American Perspectives," 281.

托马斯·伦德马克，普通法与民法的分界线，纽约；牛津：牛津大学出版社，2012 年，第 96 页。柯林斯，“美国视角”，第 281 页进一步讨论了这方面的法律现实主义。

[245] Lundmark, *Divide between Common and Civil Law*, 96. See also, for further discussion, Karl Llewellyn, "Some Realism About Realism-Responding to Dean Pound," *Harv. L. Rev.* 44, no. 8 (1931): 1222.

伦德马克，普通法与民法之分，第 96 页。另见进一步讨论，卡尔·卢埃林，“关于现实主义的一些现实主义--回应迪安·庞德”，哈佛法律评论 44, no. 8，1931，第 1222 页。

[246] Collins, "American Perspectives," 281。柯林斯，“美国的视角”，第 281 页。

[247] Refer above §3.2.3。参见上文 3.2.3 节。

[248] Hart, *The Concept of Law*, 154。哈特，法律的概念，第 154 页。

given by judges in their judgments are actually their own rationalisations based on their subjective political affiliations. Therefore, to analyse the judgments, according to realists, researchers have to go deeper into the political opinions of the judges to dissect their own subjectivity and political affiliations.

因此，现实主义者认为，要分析判决，研究者必须深入法官的政治观点，剖析法官自身的主观性和政治倾向。

The authors' view is that even Supreme Court judges are approved by politicians based on such affiliations, and therefore, this subjectivity is not something secret. This argument has been taken further forward by the 'fact sceptics', who suggested that even facts were rationalised by the judges and interpreted subjectively to arrive at their judgments.[249] This has been frequently discussed by lawyers in almost every jurisdiction; for example, many state that there is a need for the judges to be selected from wider sections of society, as the judges themselves are required to have the ability to relate to the disputes that come to the courts.

笔者认为，即使是最高法院的法官也是由政治家基于这种关系批准的，因此，这种主观性并不是什么秘密。事实怀疑论者"进一步推进了这一论点，他们认为即使是事实也会被法官合理化，并通过主观解释得出判决。几乎所有司法管辖区的律师都经常讨论这一问题；例如，许多律师指出，有必要从更广泛的社会阶层中选拔法官，因为法官本身需要具备与诉至法院的争议相联系的能力。

The realist scholars favoured a '*purposive approach*' to law, which can guide judges and courts using research in 'policy science' that has its roots firmly founded in social sciences.[250] This argument has actually in a way been adopted by judges in England & Wales as 'purposive interpretation of statutes'. It means that now, the interpretation of statutes in England & Wales is based on this inter-disciplinary approach, and the legal reasons in any judgment clearly reflect this approach.

现实主义学者倾向于对法律采取“目的论方法”，这种方法可以利用扎根于社会科学的 “政策科学 ”研究来指导法官和法院。这一论点实际上在某种程度上已被英格兰和威尔士的法官采纳为 “成文法的目的性解释”。这意味着，现在英格兰和威尔士的法规解释是基于这种跨学科的方法，任何判决中的法律理由都清楚地反映了这种方法。

Realists in relation to the philosophy of natural law argued that morality is usually fixed by the dominant groups within a society, and there was actually no fundamental and universal moral truth. It appears they have borrowed this

与自然法哲学有关的现实主义者认为，道德通常是由社会中的主流群体固定下来的，实际上并不存在根本的、普遍的道德真理。他们似乎借用了“实用

249 An example was cited where the description of event in Court of Appeal was judged in a particular way in the Court of Appeal but was reversed on appeal in House of Lords which described in a different way to arrive at different judgement. For details, see Collins, "American Perspectives," 283.

有人举例说，上诉法院对事件的描述以特定方式作出判决，但在上议院上诉时被推翻，上议院以不同方式进行描述，作出不同判决。详见柯林斯，"美国的视角，"第 283 页。

250 Collins, "American Perspectives", 284。柯林斯，“美国的视角”，第 284 页。

argument from the 'pragmatic' school of thought.[251]

主义”学派的这一论点。

Natural Law scholars were worried at the thought of realists rejecting the concept of morality and undermining the legal system, and they were basically appalled by the realists' notion that the legal system exists to meet social ends. The natural law scholars were worried that this approach by realist scholars might open the doors for totalitarian systems, where legal systems are used without any constraints.

自然法学者对现实主义者摒弃道德概念、破坏法律制度的想法感到担忧，他们基本上对现实主义者认为法律制度的存在是为满足社会目的的观念震惊。自然法学者担心，现实主义学者的这种做法可能会为极权主义制度敞开大门，在这种制度下法律制度不受任何约束。

The jurisdiction of England & Wales, though affected by the currents of the realist school flowing across the Atlantic Ocean, was in fact not willing to examine the political orientation of its judges. However, it did incrementally adopt the purposive approach in relation to the interpretation of statutes in the subsequent years. At the same time, a few studies on political orientation have been done in the recent past, and results are not very different from the US' studies on the same subject.[252] The application of *Human Rights Act 1998* has recently increased the opportunity for judges in England & Wales to display their political orientations.[253]

英格兰和威尔士的司法管辖区虽然受到大西洋彼岸现实主义学派潮流的影响，但事实上并不愿意研究其法官的政治倾向。然而，在随后的几年中，它确实逐渐在法规解释方面采用了目的论方法。与此同时，近年亦有少数有关政治取向的研究，结果与美国的同期研究相差不大。《1998 年人权法》近期的实施增加了英格兰和威尔士法官展示其政治倾向的机会。

At the other extreme end are the scholars of Critical Legal Studies (1970s and 1980s), who attempted to demonstrate that legal reasoning in most judgments was just a hoax, and many principles in the context of interpretation of statues, reasoning provided in common law judgments, and even the basic principles used in these judgments, were actually

另一个极端是批判性法律研究（20 世纪 70 年代和 80 年代）的学者，他们试图证明大多数判决中的法律推理只是一个骗局，在成文法解释、普通法判决中提供的推理，甚至这些判决中使用的基本原则中，许多原则实际上是相互矛盾的。他们试图通过攻击法律制度来实现社会

[251] Discussion on pragmatism was cited in Collins, "American Perspectives," 284, Pragmatism as a school of though was developed by scholars such as John Dewey and William James

柯林斯在《美国视角》第 284 页中引用了关于实用主义的讨论，实用主义作为一个学派，是由约翰·杜威和威廉·詹姆斯等学者发展起来的。

[252] For more detail see J.A.G. Griffith, *The Politics of the Judiciary*, 5th ed. (London: Harper Collins, 1997), 337. See also the discussion in Collins, "American Perspectives," 285–6.

详见 J·A·G·格里菲斯，司法政治，第 5 版，伦敦：哈珀·柯林斯出版社，1997 年，第 337 页。另见柯林斯的讨论，“美国视角”，第 285-286 页。

[253] A further discussion on application of *Human Rights Act 1998* is carried out in §7.2.1.7 & §7.2.1.7.1.

第 7.2.1.7 节和第 7.2.1.7.1 节进一步讨论了《1998 年人权法》的适用问题。

contradictory.[254] They attempted to bring about social change by attacking the legal system. However, judges and lawyers across the Atlantic Ocean reacted furiously even at the suggestion that they were 'making sense out of nonsense' in the context of common law. Many legal professionals were furious that their commitment to the profession in their lives was questioned in such a manner.[255]

变革。然而，大西洋彼岸的法官和律师们甚至对他们在普通法中“无中生有”的说法做出了愤怒的反应。许多法律专业人士对自己毕生的职业承诺受到如此质疑而感到义愤填膺。

3.3 Jurisprudence in context of Practice by Judges and Lawyers in English Courts

从英国法院法官和律师的实践看法理学

In the previous section, the authors have discussed various theories in jurisprudence that have been developed over the last few centuries. They have observed that currently in England & Wales, judges use policy reasons in their judgments to justify a stand taken in cases. The main arguments that have been raised over the years are in relation to the use of policy reasons by the judges. These arguments were raised by scholars as according to them, these judges are not even elected by the populace, and therefore they should leave the setting out of policy to legislatures. A recent study comparing the English jurisdiction to other jurisdictions confirmed that the English jurisdiction is gradually focusing more on interdisciplinary areas such as economics, sociology and so forth in legal practice.[256]

在上一节中，笔者讨论了过去几个世纪发展起来的各种法理学理论。笔者注意到，目前在英格兰和威尔士，法官在判决中使用政策理由来证明其在案件中所采取的立场是正确的。多年来提出的主要论点与法官使用政策理由有关。这些论点是由学者提出的，因为根据他们的观点，这些法官甚至不是由民众选举产生的，因此他们应将政策的制定留给立法机构。最近一项将英国司法管辖区与其他司法管辖区进行比较的研究证实，英国司法管辖区在法律实践中逐渐更加注重经济学、社会学等跨学科领域。

For centuries, legal scholars accepted that it was due to the concept of consent that the relevant parties, including

几个世纪以来，法律学者们一直认

254 Collins, “American Perspectives,” 318–20。柯林斯，“美国的视角”，第 381-420 页。

255 See the defence of common law in D Howarth, “Making Sense out of Nonsense,” in *Jurisprudence: Cambridge Essays*, ed. Hyman Gross and Ross Harrison (Oxford: Clarendon Press, 1992), 29–53 and as discussed in Collins, “American Perspectives,” 323.

见 D·豪沃斯的《普通法辩护，从胡言乱语中找出道理》，载《法理学》：海曼·格罗斯和罗斯·哈里森合编的《剑桥论文集》，牛津：克拉伦登出版社，1992 年，第 29-53 页。

256 Lundmark, *Divide between Common and Civil Law*, 110。伦德马克，普通法与民法之分，第 110 页。

monarchs, had agreed to be bound by the Constitution or Acts of Parliament.[257] Consent is developed by long usage of the common law and this could be classed as the normative foundation of common law. In the authors' view, a few snapshots from English legal history such as the *Bill of Rights 1689*, as discussed later, can suitably demonstrate these foundations.

为，包括君主在内的有关各方同意接受宪法或议会法案的约束是由于“同意”这一概念。同意是在普通法的长期使用中发展起来的，这可以被归类为普通法的规范基础。笔者认为，英国法律史上的几个缩影，如稍后讨论的1689年《权利法案》，可以适当地证明这些基础。

It is impossible to understand even English civil & criminal procedural law without citing and appreciating the *Bill of Rights,*[258] which was instituted in the year 1689. It limited the power of the monarchs. In the United Kingdom, the *Bill of Rights 1689* was accompanied by the famous declarations *Magna Carta 1215*, *Petition of Right* 1628,[259] and *Habeas Corpus Act 1679*.[260] The purpose of all these ancient laws was to curtail the arbitrary powers of the state in various areas that directly affect the populace. There is a need to know and appreciate this basic foundation of English law, and the mere mention of declarations or statutes will not fulfil that purpose.

若不援引并理解 1689 年制定的《权利法案》，便难以真正领会英国的民事和刑事诉讼法。这部法案对君主权力起到了限制作用。在英国，与1689年《权利法案》同时颁布的还有著名的1215年《大宪章》、1628年《权利请愿书》和1679年《人身保护法》。所有这些古老法律的目的都是为了限制国家在直接影响民众的各个领域的专制权力。我们有必要了解和认识英国法律的这一基本基础，而仅仅提及宣言或者法规并不能达到这一目的。

Lord Denning, a famous jurist, described the *Magna Carta 1215* as "the greatest constitutional document of all times — the foundation of the freedom of the individual against the arbitrary authority of the despot."[261] After nearly 850 years, the *Magna Carta* is still an important symbol of liberty in the western world and India, and most lawyers need to understand its significance even to appreciate procedural rules. The *Magna Carta* limited arbitrary powers to illegally imprison a subject, or to impose arbitrary taxes, and ensured swift justice; most importantly all the principles enshrined in

著名法学家丹宁勋爵将 1215 年的《大宪章》描述为“有史以来最伟大的宪法文件--个人自由对抗专制者专横权力的基础”。时隔近 850 年，《大宪章》在西方世界和印度仍然是自由的重要象征，大多数律师甚至需要了解其意义，才能理解程序规则。《大宪章》限制了非法监禁臣民或任意征税的专横权力，并确保迅速伸张正义；最重要的是，其

---

[257] Postema, “Classical Common Law Jurisprudence - II,” 23–4。波斯特马，“古典普通法法理学– II”，第 23-24 页。

[258] *1 William and Mary Sess 2 c 2*。1 威廉玛丽 Sess 2 c 2。

[259] *3 Car 1 c 1.*

[260] 31 Cha. 2. 2.

[261] Danny Danziger and John Gillingham, *1215: The Year of Magna Carta* (New York: Simon & Schuster, 2004), 268.

丹尼·丹齐格和约翰·吉利安姆，1215：《大宪章之年》，纽约：西蒙与舒斯特出版社，2004 年，第 268 页。

it are in the context of common men. In the authors' view, its significance is under appreciated in the younger generation.

中所载的所有原则都是以普通人为背景的。在笔者看来，年轻一代对于《大宪章》的重要意义缺乏足够深刻的认识。

Therefore, even the hard-core lawyers specializing in commercial law or intellectual property law, who are interested in contract and commercial laws, cannot afford to lose sight of this powerful document that has formed the core of jurisprudence and even percolates through the civil procedure rules in the form of words such as 'just', 'fairness', 'equality of arms,' and so forth.

因此，即使是对合同法和商法感兴趣的专攻商法或知识产权法的资深律师，也不能轻视这份极具影响力的文件。它构成了法理学的核心，甚至以"公正"、"公平"、"权利平等"等词语的形式渗透到民事诉讼规则中。

3.4 Classical Chinese Jurisprudence

中国古典法理学

It is important to appreciate that due to the PRC's long history and its position as a civilisation state like India, the study of its jurisprudence needs to be divided into different periods: classical Chinese Jurisprudence, jurisprudence in later centuries until the end of the Qing Dynasty, and modern jurisprudence in the later years. The authors will try to discuss each of these briefly within the confines of this chapter. However, readers are advised to study specialised texts if they want to study any particular jurisprudence in detail.

重要的是要认识到，由于中华人民共和国历史源远流长，和印度一样都是文明古国。基于此，对其法学的研究应当划分成不同时期，分别为中国古典法理学、清末之前的法理学，以及稍后的现代法理学。笔者将尝试在本章的范围内逐一简要论述。不过，如果读者想详细研究任何一种法理学，建议研读专业书籍。

Classic Chinese Jurisprudence will be analysed in the context of ancient history, when many kingdoms were spread around in the geographical area of the present PRC. The authors will refer to Table 1 in Chapter 1 in this book for the detailed and relevant chronology of the ancient history of China. The authors here inserts a warning that a few of the dates in the Table are not exact, as they seem to vary slightly in different legal history articles.

中国古典法理学将会置于古代历史背景中展开剖析。在那个时期，在如今中华人民共和国所处的地理区域内，分布着众多王国。笔者将参考本书第一章中的表 1，以了解中国古代历史的详细相关年表。笔者在此提醒，表中的几个时间并不准确，因为在不同的法制史文献中似乎略有不同。

The Western Zhou Kingdom (1046–771 BCE) in ancient China established their royal authority over peripheral kingdoms through heavy reliance upon lineage affiliations and kinship hierarchies.[262] In ancient China, in order to maintain cohesion affected by demands from other kingdoms for more autonomy, an institution called ba, or hegemony system, was designed to re-establish inter kingdom cohesion. [3] However, gradually, Zhou rulers were weakened, and there were societal changes. Accordingly, there was a demand for different kinds of institutions that included written scripts, new ceremonies and rites. This was the advent of written codes and along with these codes, a period of debate commenced. As a result of such debates, various jurisprudential thoughts occupied the intellectual space.

中国古代的西周王国（公元前 1046 年至公元前 771 年）通过严重依赖世系隶属关系和亲属等级制度，建立了对周边王国的王权。在中国古代，由于其他王国要求更多的自治权，为了保持凝聚力，一种被称为“霸”的制度被设计出来，以重建王国间的凝聚力。然而，周朝统治者逐渐被削弱，社会也发生了变化。因此，人们需要不同类型的制度，包括书面文字、新的仪式和礼仪。这就是成文法典的出现，而伴随着这些法典的出现，一个辩论时期也开始了。由于这些辩论，各种法学思想占据了思想空间。

[262] In particular, ruler Wu of the Western Zhou dynasty overthrew the Shang dynasty (1600–1045 BCE)。尤其是西周统治者武王推翻了商朝（公元前 1600-1045 年）。

[263] Ernest Caldwell, “Social Change and Written Law in Early Chinese Legal Thought,” *L. and History Rev.* 32, no. 1 (2014): 7.

欧内斯特·考德威尔，“中国早期法律思想中的社会变迁与成文法”，载《法史研究》第 32 卷第 1 期，2014 年，第 7 页。

Figure 5: Jurisprudence Influencing Judges in PRC - JAIN Analysis

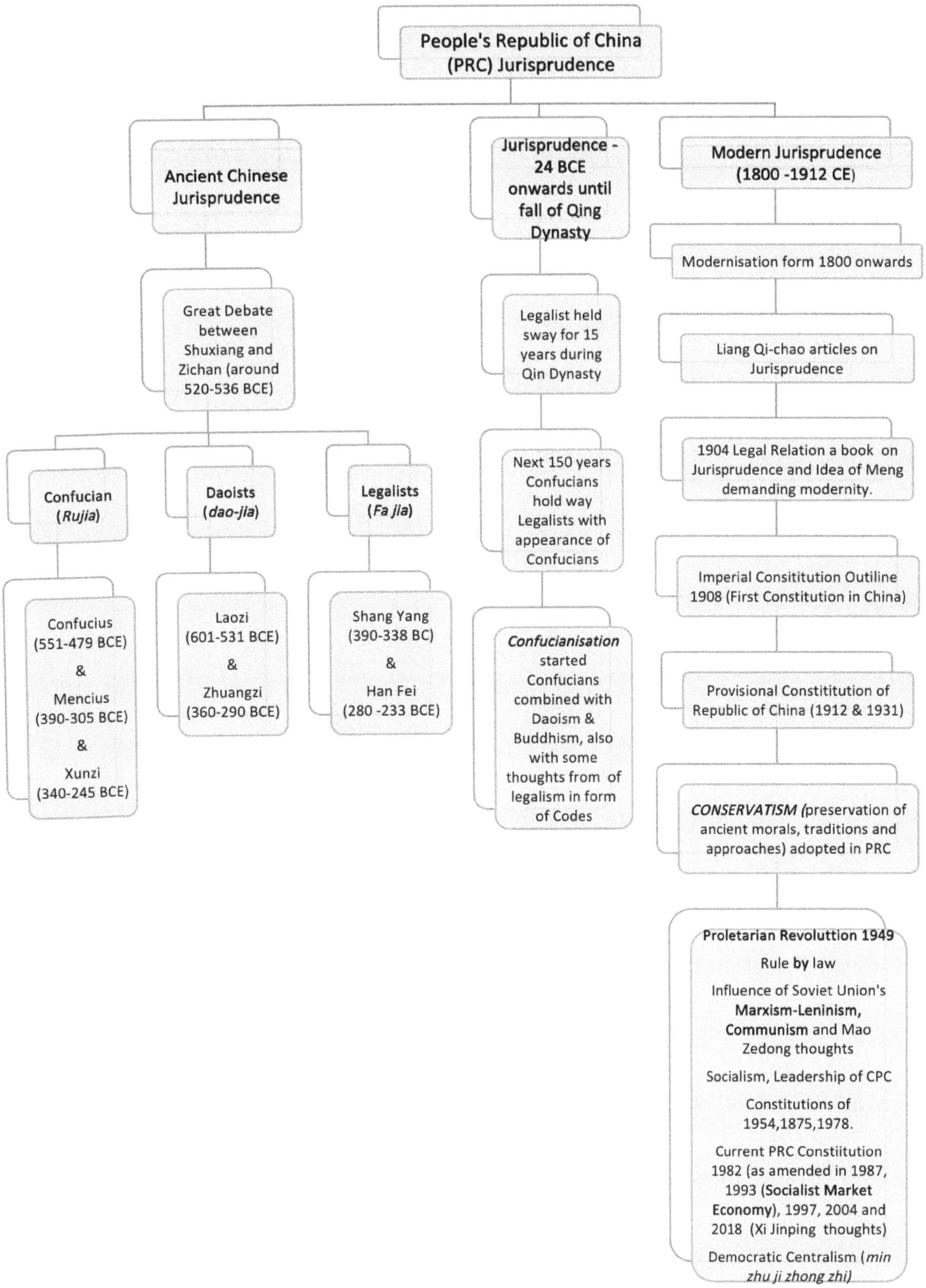

图 5：影响中国法官的法理学 - JAIN解析

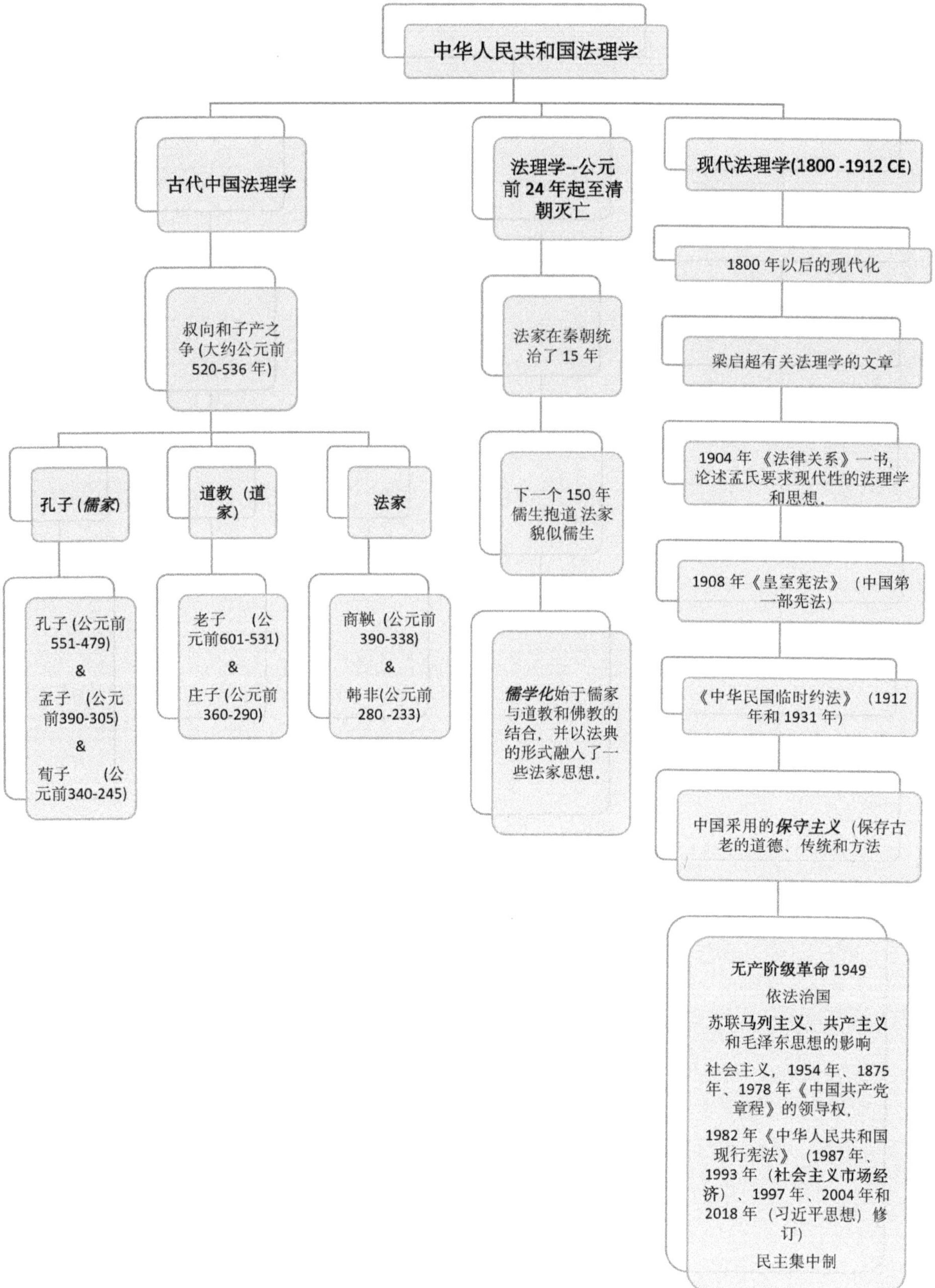

3.4.1 Background to Classical Chinese Jurisprudence

中国古典法理学的背景

Before discussing Classical Chinese jurisprudence, it is important to appreciate that its main concepts will be different, as compared with the western concepts or modern concepts that are available in Jurisprudence.[264] In addition, it will again be erroneous to divide ancient Classical Legal Jurisprudence into modern sub-divisions of law.[265] It is important to highlight the words of Zeng and Ma before looking at classical Chinese jurisprudence:

在探讨中国古典法理学之前，我们务必要认识到，相较于西方法理学概念以及现代法理学概念，中国古典法理学的核心概念有所差异。此外，将古代古典法理学划分为现代法理学的分支也是错误的。在研究中国古典法理学之前，有必要强调一下曾、马二人的话：

> In traditional Chinese law, "*fa*" usually refers to an institutional dimension, especially after Qin and Han dynasties, whereas *li*, especially *li yi* (moral basis for rites and ceremonies), is where the value and spirit of traditional Chinese law can be found [emphasis added].[266]

> 在中国传统法律中"法"通常指制度层面，尤其是秦汉以后；而"礼"，尤其是"礼义"（礼仪的道德基础），则是中国传统法律的价值和精神所在[着重号后加]。

There were already established social and political norms – '*li*' (the rites), which were the social norms and behaviour for the aristocrats, and '*fa*' (the law), which was for the commoners and slaves, and governed anti-social behaviour in ancient China. For example, same aspects in relation to the above can be analysed across several dynasties, in particular, during Xia (2300-1800 BCE), Shang (1800-1200 BCE) and Zhou (1122- 255 BCE) dynasties.[267]

中国古代已经有了既定的社会和政治规范——"礼"是贵族的社会规范和行为准则，而"法"则是平民和奴隶的社会规范和行为准则，对反社会行为进行约束。例如，在多个朝代，特别是夏朝（公元前 2300-1800 年）、商朝（公元前 1800-1200 年）和周朝（公元前 1122-255 年），都可以对上述方面进行分析。

264 Xianyi Zeng and Xiaohong Ma, "A Dialectic Study of the Structure and Basic Concept of Traditional Chinese Law and an Analysis of the Relationship between Li (Ceremony) and Fa (Law)," *Frontiers of Law in China* 1, no. 1 (2006): 35。曾宪义、马小红，《中国传统法的结构与基本概念辩正——兼论古代礼与法的关系》，《中国法学前沿》第 1 期，2006 年，第 35 页。

265 Ibid., 52.

266 Ibid., 34.

267 Wejen Chang, "Classical Chinese Jurisprudence and Development of Chinese Legal System" (2009–10), 210.

张伟仁，《中国古典法理学与中国法律制度的发展》（2009-10 年），第 210 页。

As the economy picked up in ancient China, there was a need for the relationships between the ruler and commoners, as well as the relationship of the commoners with the aristocrats, to be managed. There was a need for rules to be drafted clearly for commoners, so that they could comprehend them easily. This resulted in a statue with criminal law provisions being installed by the provincial chief, Zichan, in 536 BCE.[268]

随着中国古代经济的发展，需要处理好统治者与平民之间的关系，以及平民与贵族之间的关系。有必要为平民起草明确的规则，使他们易于理解。因此，公元前 536 年，子产设立了一个包含刑法条款的雕像。

Shuxiang, a prominent statesman of the state of Jin, argued that if the rules were too clear and specific, then people might find loopholes, and might even think that these were the only rules that were to be obeyed.[269] The populace therefore in theory could commit crimes that were not even written in the edicts, possibly leading to an increase in the number of cases, and corruption in the judiciary. According to Shuxiang, crime can be controlled by setting an example for people to follow from the top, leading the people to be orderly and peaceful. However, Zichan argued that he could only control the present bad state of crime in the area of Zeng;[270] he agreed in principle with Shuxiang's view, seeing it as ideal for long-term improvement in the law and order situation in his Kingdom. However, he was short of the talent needed to implement the ideals proposed by Shuxiang.

晋国著名政治家叔向认为，如果规定过于明确和具体，人们就会发现漏洞，甚至会认为只有这些规定才是必须遵守的。因此，从理论上讲，民众可能会犯下诏令中根本没有写明的罪行，这可能会导致案件数量增加和司法腐败。叔向认为，可以通过从上至下树立榜样，引导民众遵守秩序、安分守己来控制犯罪。然而，子产认为，他只能控制曾国地区目前的恶劣犯罪状况；他原则上同意叔向的观点，认为这是长期改善曾国治安状况的理想办法。然而，他缺乏实现叔向提出的理想所需的人才。

Shuxiang preferred to practice *xi xian-wang yi-shi yi zhi bu wei xing-pi.*, where those in authority would give direction

叔向倾向于实行“昔先王议事以制，不为刑辟”，即当权者在不使用任何诏

[268] Ibid., 211.

[269] Wejen Chang, "Classical Chinese Jurisprudence and Development of Chinese Legal System," *Tsinghua China L. Rev.* 2, no. 2 (2010): 211.

张伟仁，“中国古典法理学与中国法律制度的发展”，《清华中国法学评论》第 2 期（2010 年），第 211 页。

[270] James Legge, trans., *The Ch'un Ts'ew with the Tso Cheun in 5 the Chinese 609,* Taiwan (1883) (Oxford: Clarendon Press, 1971), 610, as discussed in Wejen Chang, "Classical Chinese Jurisprudence and Development of Chinese Legal System," 211.

詹姆斯·莱格译，《钱穆与曹全碑》，1883，牛津：克拉伦登出版社，1971 年，第 610 页。张伟仁《中国古典法理学与中国法律制度的发展》中有论述。

without making use of any kind of edict or rule.[271] A few scholars have highlighted that Shuxiang's main aim in his school of thought was to maintain the status quo of aristocratic power.[272] It also highlights "the traditional tension in ancient China between **rule-by-man and rule-by-law** [emphasis added] notions of political legitimacy."[273]

书或规则的情况下发出指示。一些学者强调，叔向学派的主要目的是维持贵族权力的现状。这也凸显了"中国古代在政治合法性的**人治与法治**[着重号后加]观念之间的传统紧张关系"。

However, over the years, other rulers seemed to prefer Zichan's view and even in Shuxiang's kingdom of Jin, rules were made and instituted. Shuxiang was not there anymore to argue against the practice. However, in 513 BCE, Confucius argued on similar lines as Shuxiang and was of the view that people would now only follow the rules instead of respecting the authority. This was the start of jurisprudential theories in ancient China. The authors have looked at this acknowledgment of the need to manage societal change. In addition, this issue has been acknowledged by legal historians studying from the point of history.[274]

然而，随着时间的推移，其他统治者似乎更倾向于子产的观点，甚至在叔向的晋国也制定和确立了规则。叔向不再反对这种做法。然而，公元前 513 年，孔子提出了与叔向类似的观点，认为人们现在只会遵守规则，而不会尊重权威。这是中国古代法哲学理论的开端。笔者研究了这种对管理社会变革的必要性的认识。此外，从历史角度研究这一问题的法律史学家也承认这一点。

These basic ideas were turned into two important jurisprudential themes of Classical Chinese jurisprudence – one, the arguments of Zichan, known as *Fajia,* the legalist branch of jurisprudence; and the other, the approach of Shuxiang, supported by Confucius' views, which formed a branch called the Confucian branch of jurisprudence, or *Rujia.*[275]

这些基本思想被转化为中国古典法理学的两个重要法学主题--一个是子产的论点，被称为法家，即法学的法家分支；另一个是叔向的方法，得到孔子观点的支持，形成了一个分支，被称为儒家法学，即儒家法学。

---

271 See Caldwell, "Early Chinese Legal Thought," 15. See also, James Legge, trans., *Thet Ch'un Ts'ew with the Tso Cheun in 5 the Chinese 609,* Taiwan (1883) (Oxford: Clarendon Press, 1971), as discussed in Wejen Chang, "Classical Chinese Jurisprudence," 210.

参见考德威尔，"早期中国法律思想"，第 15 页。另见詹姆斯·莱格译，《春秋左氏传》，1883，牛津：克拉伦登出版社，1971 年，张伟仁《中国古典法理学》第 210 页对此有论述。

272 Caldwell, "Early Chinese Legal Thought," 16。考德威尔，《中国早期法律思想》，第 16 页。

273 Ibid.

274 Ibid., 17.

275 Wejen Chang, "Classical Chinese Jurisprudence and Development of Chinese Legal System," 212.

Although the thought processes in the two branches are different, there is a common thread, namely the belief that humans can resolve issues themselves. However, a third branch of jurisprudence was also being established in ancient China, which criticised institutions, rules, and regulations, and advocated a simple form of life following the way of nature; this branch was called *Daojia* or Daoists.[276]

虽然这两个分支的思维过程不同，但有一个共同点，即相信人类可以自己解决问题。然而，中国古代还出现了法学的第三个分支，它批判制度、规则和条例，主张遵循自然之道的简单生活形式，这个分支被称为道家或道教徒。

3.4.1.1 Confucians (Rujia) – Confucius, Mencius & Xunzi

儒家--孔子、孟子和荀子

Confucian jurisprudential thought was initiated by Confucius but was further developed by many scholars in later centuries. The key features under this stream of jurisprudence as developed by important scholars are discussed below.

儒家法学思想由孔子开创，后世许多学者对其进行了进一步发展。下文将讨论重要学者所发展的这一法学流派的主要特征。

3.4.1.1.1 Confucius

孔子

This was the start of classical theories; Confucius was the first to propound certain theories in detail.[277] Primarily, he looked at the rules of behaviour (*li*) and the principles behind

这是古典理论的开端；孔子是第一个详细阐述某些理论的人。他主要研究行为准则（礼）及其背后的原则（儒）。

张伟仁：《中国古典法理学与中国法律制度的发展》，第 212 页。

276 Ibid.

277 *Shu-jing, The Book of Historical Documents,* (a collection of proclamations of rulers), *Shi-jing (i# The Book of Poetry,* a selection of verses from folk songs), and *Yi-jing,* (The Book of Changes*)* all observed a set of rules of refined behaviour known as *li* (the rites) and studied the principles behind them (*ru*) (as cited in Wejen Chang, "Classical Chinese Jurisprudence and Development of Chinese Legal System," 212.)。

《书经》、《诗经》和《易经》都遵守一套被称为"礼"的高雅行为准则，并研究其背后的原则（儒）（引自张伟仁，"中国古典法理学与中国法律制度的发展"，第 212 页。

them *(ru*). Two other scholars and philosophers, Mencius and Xunzi, who were from the period before the Qin dynasty (221-205 BCE), then further enhanced and diffused the teachings of Confucius. Instead of focusing on heavens (*tian*), Confucius focused more on earthly affairs and believed humans could regulate their own affairs.

秦朝（公元前 221-205 年）之前的另外两位学者和哲学家孟子和荀子进一步完善和传播了孔子的学说。孔子不以天为中心，而是更多地关注人间事务，认为人类可以管理自己的事务。

Confucius recommended two principles – a positive one that recommended humans to help each other to reach their goals and another negative principle that recommended humans to avoid doing things that they did not want others to do to them.[278] This was Confucius' way of explaining that man is capable of reason and compassion, and this led to the formation of the rules of social interaction as follows:

孔子提出了两个原则：一个是积极原则，建议人类相互帮助以实现自己的目标；另一个是消极原则，建议人类避免做自己不希望别人对自己做的事情。孔子用这种方式来说明人是有理性和同情心的，并由此形成了如下的社会交往规则：

> In *Lun-yu* (*The Analects)* they appeared in four groups: *de (*moral principles), *li* (the rites), *zheng* (government decrees), and *xing* (penal laws). Among the moral principles, the primary one was *ren* (humaneness). Basically, *ren* denoted that people should treat fellow human beings with empathy, care and respect. From this principle Confucius derived more specific moral rules, including *xiao (*filial piety), *ti* (brotherly love), *zhong* (loyalty), *xin* (faithfulness), *qian-rang* (modesty and yielding), *gong-jing (*humility and respect), *hui (*kindness and generosity), *shu* (understanding and forgiving), yi *(*rectitude and justice) and *zhi (*straightforwardness, honesty, truthfulness, uprightness) [emphasis in original].[279]

> 在《论语》中，它们分为四组："德"（道德原则）、"礼"（礼仪）、"政"（政府法令）和"刑"（刑法）。在道德原则中，最主要的原则是"仁"（人道）。从根本上说，"仁"是指人们应该以同情、关心和尊重的态度对待他人。从这一原则出发，孔子引申出更多具体的道德规范，包括孝（孝道）、悌（兄弟和睦）、忠（忠心）、信（信义）、谦让（谦逊、礼让）、恭敬（谦虚恭敬）、惠（仁慈宽厚）、恕（理解宽容）、义（正直正义）和直（直率、诚实、真实、正直）[着重号为原文所加]。

One of the important aspects of Confucius' approach to jurisprudence was *li*, behaviour by which humans restrain

孔子法学思想的一个重要方面是"礼"，即人类约束自己的行为。一个

[278]Wejen Chang, "Classical Chinese Jurisprudence and Development of Chinese Legal System," 213.

张伟仁：《中国古典法理学与中国法律制度的发展》，第 213 页。

[279] Wejen Chang, "Classical Chinese Jurisprudence and Development of Chinese Legal System," 214. Also the Chinese characters have been removed from the quote.

张伟仁：《中国古典法理学与中国法律制度的发展》，第 214 页。此外，引文中的汉字已被删除。

themselves. Adoption of such behavior by a society can create a *harmonious* society and *li* was therefore considered very important. Confucius did not discuss government decrees and laws in detail as his preference was for modifying human behaviour. According to Confucius, humans might know that some acts can lead to punishment, but this in itself will not change their behaviour or make them aim for higher standards. Among all his principles, he reserved the top rank for the notion of moral principles of humaneness.

社会采用这种行为可以创造一个和谐的社会，因此"礼"被认为是非常重要的。孔子没有详细讨论政府法令和法律，因为他更倾向于修改人类行为。孔子认为，人类可能知道某些行为会导致惩罚，但这本身并不会改变他们的行为，也不会使他们追求更高的标准。在他的所有原则中，他将"人道"这一道德原则放在首位。

Penal laws, according to Confucius, had a systemic issue – they were drafted by people lacking in wisdom, or they were arbitrary in nature. He suggested that the right people had to be selected to draft penal laws, and the ultimate authority should always be vested in the king or the feudal lord. According to him, the king or the feudal lord must also follow the rules of behaviour. According to Confucius, the only way people will respect the king or law is through the concept of moral authority and not because of penal laws or codes, which Confucius thought were inferior in his ranking system.[280] Pursuant to this school of thought, the most effective form of education was not preaching but "teaching by example" (*shen-jiao*).[281]

孔子认为，刑法有一个系统性的问题——由缺乏智慧的人起草，或者具有任意性。他建议，必须选择合适的人来起草刑法，而最终的权力应始终属于国王或封建主。他认为，国王或封建主也必须遵守行为规则。孔子认为，人们尊重国王或法律的唯一途径是通过道德权威的概念，而不是因为刑法或法典，孔子认为刑法或法典在他的等级制度中处于劣势。根据这一学派，最有效的教育形式不是说教，而是"身教"。

Scholars agreed with an adage in *Yi-jing* that litigation always ends in disaster *(song-ze zhong-xiong*) and should be avoided in society.[282] According to Confucius, punishments were needed, but in fact, this very act of punishment signified the failure of society. According to him, 'rightness' or 'justice' was not an absolute concept; it could have different meanings in different contexts, but the moral duty of humans is always supreme.[283] In addition, a relationship between a ruler and his subjects is based on mutual benefit.

学者们同意《易经》中的一句格言，即诉讼总是以灾难（讼则终凶）告终，社会应避免诉讼。孔子认为，惩罚是必要的，但事实上，这种惩罚行为本身就意味着社会的失败。他认为，"正确"或"正义"并不是一个绝对的概念，在不同的语境中会有不同的含义，但人类的道德责任始终是至高无上的。此外，统治者与臣民之间的关系建立在互利的基础上。

---

280 Caldwell, "Early Chinese Legal Thought," 20。考德威尔，《中国早期法律思想》，第 20 页。

281 Wejen Chang, "Classical Chinese Jurisprudence and Development of Chinese Legal System," 217. 张伟仁《中国古典法理学与中国法律制度的发展》，第 217 页。

282 Ibid.

283 Ibid., 219.

In summary, according to him, the state through a ruler should use both persuasion and coercion to enforce the moral values that need to be inculcated in the people.[284]

总之，他认为，国家应通过统治者使用说服和强制两种手段，向人民灌输道德价值观。

3.4.1.1.2 Mencius

孟子

Mencius (390-305 BCE), who was a believer in the Confucian branch of jurisprudence, in his work *Mengzi* discussed that all humans share the following qualities:

孟子（公元前 390 年至公元前 305 年）是儒家法学分支的信奉者，他在著作《孟子》中论述了人类共有的以下品质：

- Heart of compassion *(ce-yin zhi xin)* leads to humanness;
- Heart of shame (*xiu-e zhi xin*) leads to rightness;
- Heart of right and wrong *(shi-fei zhi xin)* leads to wisdom;
- Heart of humility (*ci-rang zhi xin*) leads to the concept of propriety.[285]

- 恻隐之心通向人性；
- 羞恶之心通向正确；
- 是非之心通向智慧；
- 辞让之心通向礼仪观念。

According to Confucius, it was impossible for people to be unable to distinguish right from wrong; this apparent inability was because of the influence of evil forces. Mencius, however, was of the view that a few people cannot distinguish between right and wrong. Mencius suggested there were four groups of norms, as noted by Chang: "for self-cultivation, personal interactions, government action and

孔子认为，人不可能不辨是非，这种表面上的不辨是非是因为受到了邪恶势力的影响。孟子则认为，少数人不能明辨是非。孟子认为有四类规范，正如张伟仁所言："修身、个人交往、政府行为以及个人与当局之间的关系；在每一类规范中，他看到了不同等级的规

[284] Geoffrey MacCormack, *The Spirit of Traditional Chinese Law*, The Spirit of the Laws (Athens; London: University of Georgia Press, 1996), 7.

杰弗里·麦克科马克，《中国传统法律的精神，法律的精神》，雅典；伦敦：佐治亚大学出版社，1996 年，第 7 页。

[285] Wejen Chang, "Classical Chinese Jurisprudence and Development of Chinese Legal System," 221–22.

张伟仁：《中国古典法理学与中国法律制度的发展》，第 221-222 页。

the relationship between the individual and the authorities; and in each group he saw the norms in different ranks."[286]

范”。

Mencius did not discuss the origins of law and its enforcement; presumably it does not come from the hearts of the ordinary people. However, he did refer to *ren-zheng*,[287] which meant the benevolent policies of the government. These policies aimed to provide education so that people could learn from the good things; they could then make a decent living, and profits could be shared. Mencius highlighted the need for division of labour in society and a need for good government officials.

孟子没有讨论法律及其执行的起源，想必它并非来自普通百姓的内心。不过，他提到了“仁政”，即政府的仁政。这些政策的目的是提供教育，使人们能够从好的事物中学习；然后他们可以过上体面的生活，利润可以分享。孟子强调社会需要分工，需要好的政府官员。

These views were rejected by many people due to their own experiences with bad rulers and local leaders.[288] However Mencius was of the view that good rulers were required to implement rules, and as long as there was legitimacy in the selection of the successors of such rulers, the system was credible. According to him, the people were the most important, followed by the state and then the rulers, who were the least important in terms of ranking within a society. Chang clarifies this point in relation to Mencius' statement about ranking within society:

这些观点遭到了许多人的反对，因为他们亲身经历过不好的统治者和地方领袖。然而，孟子认为，好的统治者是实施规则的必要条件，只要这些统治者的继任者的选择具有合法性，这个制度就是可信的。根据他的观点，人民是最重要的，其次是国家，然后是统治者。张氏结合孟子关于社会等级的论述阐明了这一点：

> the people were the most important, the "altars of the gods of earth and grain" (*she-ji*, the state) was the next, the ruler the least. Therefore when a ruler was cruel and abusive, the people were justified to revolt and exterminate him, and, in Mencius's view, executing a tyrant (*zhu yi-fu*) was different from murdering an ordinary ruler, it was not regicide.

> 民为贵，社稷次之，君为轻。孟子认为，诛一夫（zhu yi-fu）不同于弑君，它不是弑君。（《孟子·尽心上》）[着重号为原文所加]。

[286] Wejen Chang, "Classical Chinese Jurisprudence," 223。张伟仁：《中国古典法理学与中国法律制度的发展》，第 223 页。

[287] Konrad Zweigert, Hein Kotz, and Tony Weir, trans., *An Introduction to Comparative Law: Volume I: The Framework*, 2nd Revised ed. (Oxford: Clarendon Press, 1987), 224.

康拉德·茨威格特、海因·科茨和托尼·威尔译注，比较法导论：第一卷：框架，第二次修订版，牛津：克拉伦登出版社，1987 年，第 224 页。

[288] Xu Xing, an agriculture leader, alleged that a good ruler should live just like his subjects as discussed in Wejen Chang, "Classical Chinese Jurisprudence and Development of Chinese Legal System," 225.

农业领袖徐兴声称，一个好的统治者应该像他的臣民一样生活，这在张伟仁的《中国古典法理学与中国法律制度的发展》中有论述，第 225 页。

(*shi-jun*) [emphasis in original]. [289]

Mencius did not give a lot of attention to the law/codes, or its development; in fact to the authors, it appears that they ignored it, even in comparison to Confucius.

孟子并不十分重视法律/法典或其发展；事实上，在笔者看来，即使与孔子相比，孟子似乎也忽视了法律/法典。

3.4.1.1.3 Xunzi

荀子

The last classical jurisprudent in the Confucian school of thought was Xunzi (340-245 BCE), before the advent of Qin dynasty (that unified many provinces of ancient China). His legal jurisprudence was based on reason. According to him, humans liked living in groups, and had fairly similar needs leading to common likes and dislikes. With limited resources, however, humans were competing with each other and therefore, in general, human nature was bad, *'e,'*[290] or the humans could get be swayed by their bad nature. Therefore, norms were needed to regulate humans. Mencius thought norms could be found in their hearts, but Xunzi disagreed with that view. He suggested that such norms had originated from learned people such as sages, but ordinary people would not be capable of coming up with such norms.

儒家学派的最后一位经典法学家是荀子（公元前 340-245 年），当时秦朝尚未建立（秦朝统一了中国古代的许多省份）。他的法学以理性为基础。根据他的观点，人类喜欢群居，需求相当相似，从而产生共同的好恶。然而，在资源有限的情况下，人类相互竞争，因此，总的来说，人性是坏的、“恶”的，或者说，人类会被他们的坏本性所左右。因此，需要规范来约束人类。孟子认为规范可以在人的心中找到，但荀子不同意这种观点。他认为，这种规范源于圣人等有学问的人，普通人不可能想出这种规范。

Xunzi was of the view that there were two principles which could lead any person – compassion *(ren)* and righteousness (*yi*). Additionally, Xunzi suggested that in order to achieve these two principles, the sages in ancient lands created rites (*li*), music (*yu*) for noble persons, and law (*la*) for the commoners.[291] He was of the view that there must have been reasons for the ancient dynasties such as Zhou or Xia to have

荀子认为，有两个原则可以引导任何人--“仁”和“义”。此外，荀子还提出，为了实现这两个原则，古代圣人为贵族创造了礼、乐，为平民创造了法。他认为，周、夏等古代王朝建立制度和详细的程序来执行这些原则，肯定是有

[289] Wejen Chang, "Classical Chinese Jurisprudence and Development of Chinese Legal System," 228. In the quote the authors have removed the Chinese characters.

张伟仁：《中国古典法理学与中国法律制度的发展》，第 228 页。此外，引文中的汉字已被删除。

[290] Wejen Chang, "Classical Chinese Jurisprudence and Development of Chinese Legal System," 230.

张伟仁：《中国古典法理学与中国法律制度的发展》，第 230 页。

[291] Ibid., 231.

established institutions (*zhi*) and detailed procedures (*ming*) for the enforcement of those principles.[292]

原因的。

Xunzi was of the view that such institutions and procedures were artificial and believed that humans were impressionable. He believed, therefore, that humans could be taught compassion. According to him, moral principles deserved to be ranked higher as compared to other principles. He would rank the laws made by previous rulers more highly in comparison to the laws made by the later rulers. Although he believed that rites should be placed at a lower level as compared to morals, he still felt that rites can be taught to people. Importantly, Xunzi discussed the problem of social equality in greater depth than Confucius and Mencius. According to him, individuals who were trying to learn and to move up the social ladder should be rewarded accordingly. Xunzi seemed to have been encouraging social mobility within ancient China, rather than preserving the aristocrat's power and rank within society.

荀子认为这些制度和程序都是人为的，并认为人是易受影响的。因此，他认为可以教导人们学会同情。他认为，道德原则应高于其他原则。他将前任统治者制定的法律与后任统治者制定的法律相比较，认为前任统治者制定的法律更重要。虽然他认为 "礼" 的地位低于 "德"，但他仍然认为 "礼 " 是可以教化人的。重要的是，荀子比孔子和孟子更深入地讨论了社会平等问题。他认为，对于努力学习和向上爬的人，应该给予相应的奖励。荀子似乎一直在鼓励古代中国的社会流动，而不是维护贵族在社会中的权力和地位。

He maintained that 'where there is law it should be followed' (*you fa zhe yi fa xing*)'.[293] However, laws were below the rank of norms as he felt that human behaviour was too varied and complicated for laws to be able to cover all contingencies; furthermore, they were not sufficient to manage all aspects of human behaviour.[294] According to him, the laws on their own were also not sufficient to motivate people to follow them. Additionally, in the authors' view, Xunzi seems to have suggested a solution similar to the doctrine of precedent in common law: where there was no applicable law, the judges should place the case in a category of similar cases, drawing an analogy (*yi leiju*) and deliberating (*yi*) on an appropriate solution.[295]

他认为"有法者以法行"。 然而，法律的地位低于规范，因为他认为人类的行为过于多样和复杂，法律无法涵盖所有的突发事件；此外，法律也不足以管理人类行为的方方面面。 他认为，法律本身也不足以促使人们遵守法律。此外，在笔者看来，荀子似乎还提出了一种类似于普通法中先例理论的解决方案：在没有适用法律的情况下，法官应将案件归入类似案件的类别，进行类比（以类聚）并商议（议）适当的解决方案。

Xunzi believed deliberation (*yi*) was needed when handling

[292] Ibid.

[293] Ibid., 233.

[294] Ibid., 234.

[295] Ibid., 235.

cases, and the relevant person should not only know the law from the texts (*shu*), but also should know the intention (*yi*) behind it. Xunzi described the intention as 'the spirit of law' (*yi*); he had also put forward interesting questions as to the purpose of all laws.[296] In summary, according to him, a good ruler with good conduct could establish a set of concrete rules for good conduct, while the rites and laws could be strengthened to make them more efficient and harmonious. Xunzi's ultimate objective was for human society to be 'greatly transformed and absolutely unified' (*da hua zhi yi*).[297] He could, in fact, be considered as the bridge between pure Confucians and Legalists in Chinese jurisprudential theory.

荀子认为办案需要"斟酌"（议），相关人员不仅要指导法律文本（知书），还要知道法律的目的（意）。荀子将"意"描述为"法的精神"（义）；他还就所有法律的目的提出了有趣的问题。总之，荀子认为，一个品行端正的统治者可以建立一套具体的行为规范，而礼法则可以得到加强，使之更加有效、和谐。荀子的终极目标是使人类社会"大化至一"（《大化至一》）。事实上，他可以被视为中国法理学理论中纯粹儒家与法家之间的桥梁。

3.4.1.2 Daoists (dao-jia) – Laozi, Zhuangzi

道家—老子，庄子

Confucians propounded theories based on society and recommended societal solutions, especially for rulers to follow. However, Laozi and Zhuangzi disagreed with those solutions and were very pessimistic about the state of affairs during their time. These two scholars were therefore perceived as great expounders of 'the Way' (*dao*) and were later labelled as the founders of the 'Daoist school' (*dao-jia*). These theories were built on a healthy cynicism about the authorities, a critical view of the man-made rules that governed the populace, and belief that the common folk's conscience could make them stand up to the authorities. They could be said to have brought in the concept of equality among all men before the authorities.

儒家提出了基于社会的理论，并建议社会解决方案，尤其是统治者应遵循的解决方案。然而，老子和庄子不同意这些解决方案，对他们所处时代的状况非常悲观。因此，这两位学者被视为"道"的伟大阐释者，后来被称为"道家"学派的创始人。这些理论建立在对当局的健康嘲讽、对统治民众的人为规则的批判以及相信普通民众的良知可以使他们反抗当局的基础之上。可以说，他们带来了当局面前人人平等的观念。

[296] Ibid.

[297] Ibid., 236.

3.4.1.2.1 Laozi

老子

Laozi was a contemporary of Confucius and alleged that there was a set of rules, which operated constantly and affected everything. He explained by giving the example of the rain, which would naturally stop after a while. He explained that, similarly, physical laws also governed human behaviour. According to him, there was a natural, universal valid law, *the way*, and the way was 'natural' (*zi-ran*).[298] Laozi was of the view that harmony with the universe was affected by unlimited desires, and especially by the teachings of so-called learned men called sages. According to him, such teachings were artificial and thus imperfect, and therefore caused more problems.[299] According to him, when morality failed, the rulers would end up making laws to protect the special interests.[300]

老子是孔子的同时代人，他认为有一套规则在不断运行，并影响着一切。他举例说，雨下一段时间后就会自然停止。他解释说，同样，物理规律也支配着人类的行为。他认为，有一种自然的、普遍有效的规律，即“道”，而“道”就是“自然”。老子认为，与宇宙的和谐受到无限欲望的影响，尤其是受到所谓圣人的学说的影响。他认为，这些教义是人为的，因此是不完美的，因而会造成更多的问题。他认为，当道德失效时，统治者最终会制定法律来保护特殊利益。

In summary, he advocated discarding morality and laws and exterminating the false 'sages' (*jue-sheng*). His view on governance seems to be against authority, but there were contradictions as noted by scholars of Chinese jurisprudence, and at times he appeared to be advocating governance by extreme authoritarianism.[301] In the authors' view, the most controversial aspect of his philosophy was the view that a sage or authority should take care of the common population like well-cared-for infants, and this well-cared-for population

总之，他主张抛弃道德和法律，消灭虚伪的“圣人”（绝圣）。他的治理观似乎反对权威，但正如中国法理学学者所指出的那样，其中存在矛盾，有时他似乎主张以极端专制的方式治理国家。笔者认为，他的哲学中最有争议的一点是，圣人或权威应该像照顾婴儿一样照顾普通民众，而这种照顾好的民众应该没有知识和欲望（无知无欲）。

---

298 Ibid., 241.

299 Ibid., 242.

300 In the authors' view, this is remarkable as these views were expressed a few thousand years ago. And yet the practice exists in most current systems, where lobbying of legislators by interest groups is common practice. It affects the drafting laws, which works to protect such special interest groups.

笔者认为，这一点很了不起，因为这些观点是在几千年前提出的。然而，这种做法却存在于大多数现行制度中，利益集团对立法者进行游说是常见的做法。这影响了法律的起草，从而起到了保护这些特殊利益集团的作用。

301 Wejen Chang, "Classical Chinese Jurisprudence and Development of Chinese Legal System," 245.

张伟仁：《中国古典法理学与中国法律制度的发展》，第 245 页。

should be devoid of knowledge and desire *(wu-zhi wu-yu)*.[302]

3.4.1.2.2 Zhuangzi

庄子

Unlike Laozi, Zhuangzi (360-290 BCE) was of the view that there could be many, indeed infinite *ways* and the sages should attempt to guide people by any means, including deceit.[303] The rules that people followed naturally were better than any morals suggested by any sage or philosopher. Interestingly, even though this was a few thousand years ago, he referred to the possibility of technological inventions leading to strife and competition; he felt that tough laws and rules would be needed and therefore, should have been drafted. He was of the view that with the increase in talk of morality from sages, there would be a corresponding increase in issues of law and order.

与老子不同，庄子（公元前 360-290 年）认为可以有很多方法，甚至是无穷无尽的方法，圣人应尝试用包括欺骗在内的任何方法来引导人们。人们自然遵循的规则比任何圣人或哲学家提出的道德都要好。有趣的是，尽管这是几千年前的事情，他还是提到了技术发明可能导致的纷争和竞争；他认为需要制定严厉的法律和规则，因此应该起草这些法律和规则。他认为，随着圣人谈论道德的增多，法律和秩序问题也会相应增多。

Zhuangzi's views on the relationship between the ruler and his subjects were based on the idea that the ruler should remain aloof, which he referred to as *hang ru biao-zhi, min ru ye-lu*. What this meant was that ruler and subjects should have as little as possible to do with each other; this could be

庄子对君臣关系的看法是建立在“君不语”又称“行如标枝，民如野鹿”的基础上的。这意味着统治者和臣民之间应尽可能少地产生关联；这可以通过相互回避来实现。他似乎不信任当局，重视自由。他的建议是，平民百姓无论

[302] Ibid., 244.

[303] Ibid., 246.

achieved by avoiding each other.[304] It seems to be the case that he distrusted the authorities and valued freedom. His advice was that the common people should not become 'upside-down people' (*daozhi zhi min*) at any cost as freedom was the most valuable commodity.[305]

如何都不应成为“倒置之民”，因为自由是最宝贵的东西。

3.4.1.3 Legalists (Fa-Jia) – Shang Yang, Han Fei

法家 —— 商鞅，韩非子

Even in ancient China, it has been observed that there were incidents of ministers protecting *xiangwei* or *bianshu* or *Mozi* in order to protect the compilations of written laws, or using iron pillars to communicate the law to the populace within the state.[306] Therefore, it can be seen that it was customary to have some form of written edicts or policies emanating from the rulers.

即使在中国古代，也曾出现过大臣为保护成文法集而保护襄卫、扁鹊或墨子，或用铁柱向国内民众传达法律的事件。由此可见，统治者制定某种形式的成文法令或政策是一种习惯。

Legalists placed a great deal of emphasis on law, which slowly gained prominence just before the Qin Dynasty (221-206 BCE), which unified China nearly two thousand years ago. Shang Yang (390-338 BCE) and Han Fei (280-233 BCE), produced two substantial works – *Shangjun shu* and *Han Feizi* respectively. During their time, both Confucian and Daoist schools of thought were popular. It was a period of turmoil, known as 'a time of great strife' (*da-zheng zhi shi*), also termed as the warring period, from 467-221 BCE.[307]

法家非常重视法律，在秦朝（公元前221-206年）统一中国近两千年之前，法律逐渐受到重视。商鞅（公元前390-338年）和韩非子（公元前280-233年）分别创作了两部重要著作--《商君书》和《韩非子》。在他们的时代，儒家和道家思想都很流行。公元前467-221年是一个动荡时期，被称为“大争之世”，也称战国时期。

---

304 Ibid., 248.

305 Ibid., 249.

306 Caldwell, "Early Chinese Legal Thought," 23–24。

考德威尔：《中国早期法律思想》，第23-24页。

307 Wejen Chang, "Classical Chinese Jurisprudence and Development of Chinese Legal System," 250.

张伟仁：《中国古典法理学与中国法律制度的发展》，第250页。

After 221 BCE, the State of Qin defeated all of its rivals and created a unified country that was made up of many regions and provinces, very similar to the present-day PRC. During the Warring Period, strict rules were required; they would come from the top that is the ruler or Emperor. These rules were drafted for the subjects and contained no discussion of morals or rites. In any event, these morals were impractical, given the great strife which occurred during the Warring Period. It was also a time when different schools of thought had their own followers such as Daoists and Confucians. Many rulers of the region aspired to establish something similar but were thoroughly confused as to which one of the schools of thought was more relevant for the times.

公元前 221 年后，秦国打败了所有对手，建立了一个由许多地区和省份组成的统一国家，与今天的中华人民共和国非常相似。战国时期需要严格的规则；这些规则来自最高层，即统治者或皇帝。这些规则是为臣民起草的，不涉及道德或礼仪。无论如何，鉴于战国时期发生的巨大纷争，这些道德是不切实际的。战国时期，道家和儒家等不同学派都有自己的追随者。该地区的许多统治者都希望建立类似的思想体系，但却对哪一学派更适合当时的时代感到困惑。

3.4.1.3.1 Han Fei
韩非子

Han Fei (280-233 BCE) felt that the Confucians' views were ideal, as loving all and maintaining harmony within society were good concepts, but according to him, these concepts were not practical under the circumstances of his time. *Compassion and benevolence* (*ci-ren, guo zhi mu ye*), the two qualities favoured by all the philosophers, were actually harming the cause of rulers as they were proving to be too lenient in punishing criminals or were too lavish in bestowing benefits on underlings. In addition, as a result of being influenced by the concepts of compassion and benevolence, these rulers were acting like common men, and as a result were losing the respect and awe of their subjects. He was of the view that these qualities could bring about disaster for the rulers, and consequently the states would suffer.

韩非子（公元前 280-233 年）认为儒家的观点是理想的，因为博爱和维护社会和谐是很好的理念，但他认为这些理念在当时的环境下并不实用。所有哲学家都推崇的“慈”和仁”（“慈仁，过之母也”），实际上却损害了统治者的事业，因为事实证明他们在惩罚罪犯时过于宽大，或在给予下属好处时过于奢侈。此外，由于受到怜悯和仁慈观念的影响，这些统治者表现得像普通人一样，结果失去了臣民的尊重和敬畏。他认为，这些品质会给统治者带来灾难，从而使国家遭受损失。

Han Fei was of the view that humans by nature are wicked and are competing for scarce resources. Therefore, punishment and reward were important tools for rulers who had to manage people who were perhaps not very clever. For Han Fei, law was a coercive device, similar to a timber

韩非子认为，人的本性是邪恶的，是对稀缺资源的争夺。因此，惩罚和奖赏是统治者的重要工具，因为他们必须管理可能并不十分聪明的人。在韩非子

straightening machine (*bang-qing*), or a hammer and an anvil (*zhui-duan*); the system of punishment and reward functioned as 'two handles' (*er-bing*) for the rulers to control the common people, as they were not intelligent enough to appreciate what was important to the state as a whole.[308] He recommended heavy punishment even for minor offences, as it caused to people to fear. This fear according to him had prevented them from committing even minor crimes. In his eyes, all sections of society were required to be punished before the law, but his views on whether the rulers were also answerable to the laws were not apparent in his jurisprudence.

看来，法律是一种强制手段，类似于木材矫直机（榜檠）或锤子和铁砧（椎锻）；惩罚和奖励制度是统治者控制平民的两种手段（二柄），因为他们没有足够的智慧来理解什么对整个国家是重要的。他建议即使是轻微的罪行也要严惩不贷，因为这会引起人们的恐惧。他认为，这种恐惧使人们甚至不敢犯下轻罪。在他看来，社会各阶层都必须在法律面前受到惩罚，但他对统治者是否也要对法律负责的看法在他的判例中并不明显。

According to him, the role of the rulers was to guide people away from the self-destruction. Therefore, the persona of the rulers was very important for Han Fei.[309] He was of the view that if the ruler were the upholder of laws, they needed to be of strong character, and then the likelihood of their states being strong was higher. Additionally, he felt that power cannot reside in two places.[310] It is arguable whether he placed the authority in the upholder of law (an institution), or the person who was actually the upholder of law as an individual. Han Fei advocated that the rulers should lead through a method of *wuwei*, translated as 'the ruler should do nothing or take no action'.[311]

他认为，统治者的作用是引导人们远离自我毁灭。因此，统治者的人格对韩非子非常重要。他认为，如果统治者是法律的维护者，那么他们就需要有强大的人格，这样国家强大的可能性就会更大。此外，他还认为权力不能掌握在两个地方。究竟是把权力放在法律的维护者（机构）身上，还是放在作为法律维护者的个人身上，这一点值得商榷。韩非子主张统治者应通过“无为”的方法进行领导，“无为 ”的意思是 “统治者无为或不行动”。

Han Fei did not believe in embracing diversity, but rather wanted to establish unity and stability in the state through law or order (*fa*), strategic method (*shu*), and position/power of the ruler (*shi*).[312] Han Fei's views are very persuasive

韩非子不相信包容多样性，而是希望通过法律或秩序（法）、战略方法（术）以及统治者的地位/权力（势）来建立国家的统一和稳定。即使在当前的中华人民共和国，韩非子的观点也很有说服力。

---

308 Ibid., 255.

309 Arabella Lyon, "Rhetorical Authority in Athenian Democracy and the Chinese Legalism of Han Fei," *Philosophy & Rhetoric* 41, no. 1 (2008): 58.

阿拉贝拉·里昂，“雅典民主制中的修辞权威与韩非子的中国法家思想”，《哲学与修辞学》第 41 期，2008 年，第 58 页。

310 Ibid., 59.

311 Ibid., 62.

312 Ibid., 56.

even in the current PRC.[313]

3.4.1.3.2 Shang Yang

商鞅

Shang Yang (390-338 BCE), who came earlier than Han Fei, nonetheless had similar views about compassion and benevolence being recipes for disaster. He condemned kindness and benevolence as 'the mother of transgressions' (*ci-ren, guo zhi mu ye*) and rites and music as 'the symptoms of excess and license' (*liyue, yin-yi zhi zheng ye*); he also disapproved of various other moral principles such as filial piety, brotherly love, sincerity, faithfulness, and so on. He condemned the Confucian classics that highlighted the virtues as "Six Parasites" *(liu-shi)*.[314] Shang Yang was also not kind to the advocates of Confucian schools of thought, calling them 'insects' (*ming te qu zhu*).[315] He worked from the belief that people were always looking for personal gains in the form of fame and profit (*ming li*).

商鞅（公元前 390-338 年）比韩非子来得更早，但他也有类似的观点，认为仁慈和仁爱是灾难的根源。他谴责仁慈和仁爱是“过失之母”（慈仁，过之母也），礼乐是“过度和放纵的表征”（礼乐，淫佚之征也）；他还不赞成其他各种道德原则，如孝、悌、诚、信等。他把强调美德的儒家经典斥为“六虱”。商鞅对儒家学派的倡导者也不客气，称他们为于国有害的“螟螣蚼蠋”。他认为人们总是在追求名望和利益（名利）。

He wanted efficiency within the state to be the hallmark of any state that aspires to become prosperous. Accordingly, he wanted the rulers to reward people involved in agriculture and military service. Additionally, he wanted all doors to other professions to be closed by the imposition of taxes and prohibitions. He recommended doing that by promulgating laws and thereafter by the strict enforcement of those laws within the states.

他希望国家内部的效率成为任何渴望繁荣的国家的标志。因此，他希望统治者奖励从事农业和军事服务的人。此外，他还希望通过征税和禁令来关闭通往其他职业的所有大门。他建议通过颁布法律，然后在各州严格执行这些法律来实现这一目标。

In order to enforce those laws, even petty crimes or deviations would have to be punished, with the goal that this would prevent any crimes in the future due to the fear of the

为了执行这些法律，即使是轻微的犯罪或偏差也必须受到惩罚，目的是今后因法律震慑而防止犯罪。他将此称为“以刑去刑”。他认为，所有部门都要

---

313 Ibid., 57.

314 Wejen Chang, "Classical Chinese Jurisprudence and Development of Chinese Legal System," 253–54.

张伟仁：《中国古典法理学与中国法律制度的发展》，第 253-254 页。

315 Ibid., 254.

law. He referred to this as 'using punishments to eliminate punishment' (*yi xing qu xing*).[316] According to him, all sections were answerable to the law; however, he also felt that the ruler and his heirs were not answerable. He and other legalists suggested that rulers needed to be a 'brilliant master' (*ming-zhu*), a 'sage' (*sheng-ren*), a '*sagacious lord*' (*sheng-zhu*), or a 'bright ruler' (*ming-jun*).[317]

对法律负责；但他也认为统治者及其继承人不需要负责。他和其他法家认为，统治者必须是"明主"、"圣人"、"圣主"或"明君"。

3.4.1.4 Comparison of Classical Chinese Jurisprudence

中国古典法理学的比较

Legalist views were very similar to Daoist thinking, with ruthless implementation of the laws for the common people, and the belief that there was no need for respect for the common people. Unlike Confucians, the rules of the legalists were more quickly implemented and were uniform. Confucians' views were more suitable for achieving long-term peace, and this was perhaps not applicable in a society that was changing rapidly during the Warring Period. In addition, Confucians' ranking of rites and norms were seen as having the potential to create confusion among the masses.

法家的观点与道家思想十分相似，对平民百姓无情地执行法律，认为不需要尊重平民百姓。与儒家不同的是，法家的规则执行得更快，也更统一。儒家的观点更适合实现长治久安，这在战国时期瞬息万变的社会中或许并不适用。此外，儒家的礼仪和规范等级被认为有可能在群众中造成混乱。

In Daoist philosophy, a Daoist sage has an absolute understanding about the world; and the ruler in the template of the Legalist traditions had the absolute authority as an upholder of laws.[318] Concentration of power in the hands of a ruler who was above the law was good for stability and success in the short-term. In the long run, however, the problems that the concentration of power in one person could create within a society were manifold – and the Confucians foresaw this. Drafters of law, according to the legalist

在道家哲学中，道家圣人对世界有绝对的理解；而法家传统模板中的统治者作为法律的维护者，具有绝对的权威。权力集中在一个凌驾于法律之上的统治者手中，在短期内有利于稳定和成功。但从长远来看，权力集中在一个人身上可能会给社会带来多方面的问题--儒家预见到了这一点。法家学者认为，法律的起草者必须非常聪明，具备一个人无

[316] Ibid., 255.

[317] Ibid., 260.

[318] Lyon, "Chinese Legalism and Athenian Democracy," 63。

里昂，"中国的法家思想与雅典民主"，第 63 页。

scholars, had to be very clever, with multiple skills that a single person could not have all at the same time.

法同时具备的多种技能。

For Confucians, the ruler could be a wise and educated person. Legalists, however, expected rulers to be clever people born with the skills to draft the most intelligent laws. Legalists believed if they were not able to find such a clever man as a ruler then it would lead to the drafting of arbitrary rules, and the arbitrary enforcement of these rules would then lead to break down of the state. It seems clear that the legalist solution was just a quick-fix solution and completely neglected the long-term approach of Confucians.[319]

对于儒家来说，统治者可以是一个有智慧、有教养的人。而法家则希望统治者是天生的聪明人，有能力起草最明智的法律。法家认为，如果找不到这样的聪明人作为统治者，就会导致任意制定规则，而任意执行这些规则又会导致国家崩溃。很显然，法家的解决方案只是一种急功近利的解决方案，完全忽视了儒家的长远考虑。

One thing that was noticeable in the legalist tradition was that self-interest and distrust among stakeholders within a society was assumed; therefore, debate and reasoning were not valued because it was assumed that people were scheming and self-interested. Their arguments were therefore distrusted.[320] In the authors' view, these concepts have had profound effects on the thinking of drafters and stakeholders in the legal system even 2000 years later.

法家传统中值得注意的一点是，假定社会中的利益相关者之间存在私利和不信任，因此不重视辩论和推理，因为假定人们都是诡计多端、自私自利的。因此，人们不信任他们的论点。笔者认为，即使在两千年之后，这些观念对法律体系中起草者和利益相关者的思维方式仍有深远影响。

Furthermore, it is to be noted that the retreat from virtue-based Confucian governance towards laws that even the general populace could understand would have had a profound societal change. This move meant a change from laws being the province of governing rulers and noble families, to a position where even ordinary people could know the origins of law. However, the written laws in the legalist template could just have been a way to perpetuate the power and control of the competing nobles in ancient China.[321] There was another function of the drafted laws, that is, to communicate authority and thereby convey the

此外，需要指出的是，从以德治国的儒家治理向普通民众也能理解的法律的退缩，将产生深刻的社会变化。此举意味着法律从统治者和贵族家族的专利，转变为普通人也能了解法律起源的地位。然而，法家模板中的成文法可能只是中国古代贵族竞争中延续权力和控制的一种方式。草拟的法律还有另一个功能，即传达权威，从而传达统治者的政策决定。

319 Wejen Chang, "Classical Chinese Jurisprudence and Development of Chinese Legal System," 261.
张伟仁：《中国古典法理学与中国法律制度的发展》，第 261 页。

320 Lyon, "Chinese Legalism and Athenian Democracy," 66。里昂，"中国的法家思想与雅典民主"，第 66 页。

321 Caldwell, "Early Chinese Legal Thought," 26。考德威尔：《中国早期法律思想》，第 26 页。

policy decisions of rulers.[322]

3.5 History of Chinese Jurisprudence over Later Years/Centuries

中国历代法学史

The legalists won the war of thoughts, when the unifier of all regions of ancient China, the Qin, seemingly in ruthless Daoist traditions, removed traces of Confucian thought and scholarship. However, this success was short-lived, lasting only fifteen years before the arrival of the Han dynasty (260-24 BCE). The Han dynasty followed Zhuangzi by not taking active part in the sphere of disputes (*hang ru biao-zhi, min ru ye-lu*); it also enacted many laws in the form of penal codes.

法家赢得了思想战争的胜利，当时中国古代所有地区的统一者--秦国--似乎以无情的道家传统清除了儒家思想和学术的痕迹。然而，这种成功是短暂的，在汉朝（公元前 260-24 年）到来之前只持续了 15 年。汉朝效仿《庄子》，不积极参与争端领域（行如标枝，民如野鹿），还以刑法的形式颁布了许多法律。

However, in the next 150 years after the fall of this dynasty, Confucians made a slow return to mainstream political and legal thought, even though the legalists remained in power. One reason for the return of the Confucians was that they had rules to prevent the excesses experienced by the populace in the previous dynasties and the Warring period. In later years, many legalists survived but they appeared to emulate the Confucians (*yang-ru yin-fa*).[323] Initial attempts by Confucians in the subsequent years to dilute the harshness of the criminal code drafted by legalists were unsuccessful, but gradually, over the years, the process of

然而，在这个王朝灭亡后的 150 年里，尽管法家仍然掌权，但儒家思想慢慢回归到政治和法律思想的主流。儒家回归的一个原因是，他们制定了一些规则，以防止前朝和战国时期民众的过激行为。后来，许多法家留存下来，但他们似乎在效仿儒家（阳儒阴法）。后来，儒家最初试图淡化法家起草的刑法的严酷性，但没有成功，但随着时间的推移，“儒家化”的过程逐渐开始。

322 Ibid., 27.

323 Wejen Chang, “Classical Chinese Jurisprudence and Development of Chinese Legal System,” 263.

张伟仁：《中国古典法理学与中国法律制度的发展》，第 263 页。

'Confucianization' started.[324]

This Confucianization brought with it the dilution of penalties for offences. It also attempted to create more trust within society with the following steps–

儒家化带来了对罪行刑罚的淡化。它还试图通过以下步骤在社会中建立更多信任—

- removing the duty to report others;

取消举报他人的义务;

- commencing the development of procedural law;

开始制定程序法;

- allowing the use of evidence to some extent;

允许在一定程度上使用证据;

-commencing the system of punishment according to the level of crime, and so on.

开始实行罪刑法定制度，等等。

Confucianization also brought in the concept that laws are never complete, and that principles of morality are therefore needed to interpret them. In addition, the application of laws was slowly eased to avoid harshness, thus bringing the concept of compassion into society.

儒家化还带来了一个概念，即法律永远不会是完整的，因此需要道德原则来解释法律。此外，法律的适用也慢慢变得宽松，避免苛刻，从而将"仁爱"的概念带入社会。

Slowly, the effects of Confucianization had an effect on the common people, allowing them to avoid the authorities. It also assisted in the formation of local government and informal civil codes, which co-existed with the formal code. There were seeds of change and subsequent improvements in the idea of a harmonious society, but Confucianization within Chinese society also led to a decline in legal training in comparison with the time when legalists were dominant.

慢慢地，"儒家化"对普通民众产生了影响，使他们能够避开当局。这也有助于地方政府和非正式民法典的形成，它们与正式法典并存。和谐社会的理念有了变革的种子，并在随后得到了改善，但中国社会的儒家化也导致法律培训与法家占主导地位的时代相比有所下降。

Drafters of law were sarcastically called 'petty clerks' (*dao-bi-li*), and those who provided legal services to private individuals were called litigation tricksters (*song-gun*). Even the civil examination system that commenced during the Tang dynasty (618-906 CE) focused more on Confucian

起草法律的人被讽刺地称为"刀笔吏"，为私人提供法律服务的人被称为"讼棍"。即使是始于唐朝（公元 618-906 年）的文官考试制度，也更注重儒家思想而非法律知识。慢慢地，接受过法律培训

[324] Ibid.

ideas rather than knowledge about laws. Slowly, judicial assistants trained in law did emerge, but they were still much lower in the ranks, unless they had passed the civil service exams.

的司法助理人员确实出现了，但他们的级别仍然很低，除非他们通过了文官考试。

Fixed laws tend to provide only one solution, that is, only one party is correct and the other party is wrong. This motivated the populace to develop close-knit communities that could find their own solutions to disputes without resorting to the use of laws. This resulted in the development of a system of community mediation in ancient China that is still followed centuries later in many parts of modern PRC.

固定的法律条文往往只能提供一种解决方案，即只有一方是正确的，另一方是错误的。这就促使民众发展紧密联系的社区，在不诉诸法律的情况下找到解决争端的办法。这种内生性的纠纷解决需求，推动了中国古代社区调解制度的诞生与发展。几百年后，现代中国的许多地区仍在沿用这一制度。

During the same time, there was a movement towards Daoism being followed as a religion, in conjunction with ancient Chinese beliefs that there was an interaction of god and spirits with humans, with rewards for good deeds. It also coincided with the arrival of Buddhism from present day India/Nepal into various regions of ancient China. Buddhism became popular with the common people, especially the concept that justice will eventually be done, if not in their current lives, then in their after-life.

在同一时期，道教作为一种宗教受到追捧，这与中国古代神灵与人类互动、善有善报的信仰是一致的。与此同时，佛教也从今天的印度/尼泊尔传入古代中国的各个地区。佛教开始受到普通民众的欢迎，尤其是“正义终将得到伸张”的观念，即使不是在今生，也会在来世得到伸张。

There was no concept of ‘rights’ in any of the classical models of Chinese jurisprudence, but a concept of share (*fen*) in the resources for an individual’s effort developed in ancient China.[325] Additionally, the Confucian view that one should avoid doing anything that they don’t want others to do to them, and that one should assist others in achieving their objectives, was the nearest that ancient Chinese jurisprudence came to the concept of human rights.[326]

中国古典法理学模式中没有“权利”的概念，但在中国古代形成了个人努力所获资源的份额（分）概念。此外，儒家认为一个人应该避免做任何他不希望别人对他做的事，并且应该帮助别人实现他们的目标，这是中国古代法学最接近人权概念的地方。

Traditionally, ancient Chinese Society was also lacking in respect for the laws. Many articles suggest that the lack of procedural laws was one of the many reasons for this, not to

传统上，中国古代社会也缺乏对法律的尊重。许多文章认为，缺乏程序法是造成这种情况的众多原因之一，更不用说缺

325 Ibid., 269.

326 Ibid.

mention the lack of culture of debate, which was actually abhorred in ancient China.

乏辩论文化，而辩论在中国古代实际上是被深恶痛绝的。

It is important to note that in order to understand modern PRC jurisprudence, it is also necessary to look beyond the dichotomy between Confucians and Legalists, and therefore there is also a need to analyse the earlier drafted codes from the viewpoint of the socio-political role the same codes had played in various dynasties.[327] It is important to highlight the words of Caldwell in the context of Chinese Legal history:

值得注意的是，要理解中国现代法理学，还必须超越儒家与法家的对立，因此还需要从同一法典在不同朝代所发挥的社会政治作用的角度来分析早期起草的法典。 在中国法律史的背景下，强调考德威尔的话很重要：

The early Chinese, therefore, seem to espouse a positive belief that by writing down laws and making them publically [sic] known, they can provide a visible, written standard of conduct for all levels of society.[328]

因此，早期中国人似乎信奉一种积极的信念，即通过写下法律并将其公之于众，他们可以为社会各阶层提供一个清晰可辨、以文字形式呈现的行为规范。

327 Caldwell, "Early Chinese Legal Thought," 28。考德威尔：《中国早期法律思想》，第 28 页。

328 Ibid., 30.

3.6 Jurisprudence and Legal History in the Modern Chinese/PRC Legal System

现代中国/中华人民共和国法律体系中的法理学和法律史

Classical Chinese jurisprudence has formed the basis of modern jurisprudence, but in a real sense, the advent of modern Chinese jurisprudence started after the economy was opened up.[329]

中国古典法理学构成了近代法学的基础，但从真正意义上讲，中国近代法学的出现始于经济开放之后。

However, the actual process of modernisation started around one hundred and fifty years before that. In the last Qing dynasty, the Chinese legal system interacted with the western legal system through the work of missionaries, such as Prussian missionary Gutzlaff (1803-1851), who established the *Monthly Digest of Oriental and Occidental Studies* in Guangzhou in August, 1833; and the American missionary Yong John Allen (1836-1907), who began a journal originally named *New Church News*, 1868, which was later changed to *International News* in September, 1874.

然而，现代化的实际进程大约始于一百五十年之前。在清朝末年，中国的法律体系通过传教士的工作与西方法律体系产生了互动，如普鲁士传教士郭士立（1803-1851 年）于 1833 年 8 月在广州创办了《东西洋考每月统记传》；美国传教士林乐知（1836-1907 年）创办了一份刊物，原名《教会新报》，1868 年创刊，后于 1874 年 9 月更名为《万国公报》。

The latter Journal discussed concepts such as separation of powers, or how laws were legislated in the US Congress, including jurisprudential studies.[330] After that, a project involving the revision of the existing laws by the Qing government in 1901 brought a lot of western ideas into China. This task was also assisted by scholars from abroad, as well as Chinese students who returned to China after studying law in foreign countries such as the US and various European countries.

后者讨论了三权分立或美国国会如何立法等概念，包括法理学研究。 此后，清政府在 1901 年开展的一项修订现行法律的计划将大量西方思想带入中国。这项任务也得到了国外学者以及在美国和欧洲各国等外国学习法律后回国的中国留学生的协助。

A prominent scholar, Liang Qi-chao, published a famous series of long articles on jurisprudence, such as *China should*

著名学者梁启超于 1896 年发表了一系列著名的法理学长篇文章，如《论中国

[329] Qinhua He, "The Birth and Growth of Modern Jurisprudence in China," *Frontiers of Law in China* 1, no. 4 (2006): 487.

何勤华，"中国现代法理学的诞生与发展"，《中国法学前沿》1，No. 4，2006，第 487 页。

[330] Ibid.

Pursue the Study Of Law in 1896.[331] From the late Qing dynasty to 1949, China saw the publication of approximately 424 works on jurisprudence[332] Many scholars emerged from this development in Chinese jurisprudence.[333]

宜讲求法律之学》。从晚清到 1949 年，中国共出版了约 424 部法学著作。在中国法理学的这一发展过程中，涌现出了许多学者。

A real need to bring the Chinese legal system in line with the International legal system arose, when there was an abuse of the extra-territorial system of justice delivered by the United States and other foreign powers, who managed to gain the right from the Qing Dynasty to govern their own citizens according to their own laws, in China. Various treaties with the western imperial powers coerced the then Emperor Guangxu to reform the existing legal system, as this was the condition set by the foreign powers for relinquishing the extra-territorial right to adjudicate the crimes of their nationals according to their own country's laws in China.[334] Shen Jiaben was tasked by the Emperor Guangxu to bring about the necessary reforms within the existing legal system.[335]

美国和其他外国列强设法从清王朝那里获得了在中国根据自己的法律管理本国公民的权利，他们滥用域外司法制度，这就产生了使中国法律制度与国际法律制度接轨的现实需要。与西方帝国主义列强签订的各种条约胁迫当时的光绪皇帝改革现有的法律制度，因为这是列强放弃在中国根据本国法律判决其国民罪行的治外法权的条件。 沈家本受光绪皇帝委托，对现有法律制度进行必要的改革。

A book on jurisprudence, *Legal Relations*, for the first time in Chinese legal history talked of rights in 1904, and was

1904 年，一本法理学著作在中国法律史上首次谈及权利，甚至被北京大学用

331 Ibid., 488.

332 It is based on *General Catalogue of Law Books in China* (compiled by the library of China University of Political Science and Law, China University of Political Science and Law Press, 1991), *General Catalogue of Kuomintang Government* - Law (compiled by the National Library, and published by Catalogue and Bibliography Press, 1990), and that collected from the National Library, Library of Peking University, Shanghai Library and Library of Shanghai Academy of Social Sciences, as cited in He, "Birth and Growth of Modern Jurisprudence," 490.

《中国法律图书总目》（中国政法大学图书馆编著，中国政法大学出版社 1991 年版）、《国民党政府法律总目》（国家图书馆编著，目录书目出版社 1990 年版），以及国家图书馆、北京大学图书馆、上海图书馆、上海社会科学院图书馆的馆藏资料。转引于何：《现代法理学的诞生与成长》，第 490 页。

333 Scholars such as Liang Qi-chao, Yan Fu, Xiong Yuan-han, Meng Sen, Wang Chuan-bi, Wu Jing-xiong, Qiu Han-ping, Ruan Yi-cheng, Zhang Ruo-yuan, Mei Ru-ao etc as cited in He, "Birth and Growth of Modern Jurisprudence," 495–6.

334 See Article 12 of the *Treaty of Commerce and Navigation Renewed between China and Britain (also called Mackay Treaty), September, 5, 1902,* that provided that "China having expressed a strong desire to reform her judicial system and to bring it into accord with that of the Western nations, Great Britain agrees to give every assistance to such reform, and she will also be prepared to relinquish her extra-territorial rights when she is satisfied that the state of the Chinese laws, the arrangement for their administration, and other considerations warrant her in so doing." Cf. Shiming Zhang, "Re-Examination of Abolishing Consular Jurisdiction," *Frontiers L. China* 10, no. 2 (2015): 344–45.

参见 1902 年 9 月 5 日《中英续议通商行船条约》第 12 款规定："中国深欲整顿本国律例，以期与各西国律例改同一律，英国允愿尽力协助，以成此举，一俟查悉中国律例情形及其审断办法及一切相关事宜皆臻妥善，英国即允弃其治外法权。"参见张世明：《再探领事管辖权废除》，《中国边疆学》第 10 卷，2015 年第 2 期，第 344-345 页。

335 Decree for Law Reform, March 11, 1902.

even used by Peking University to guide officials.[336] Liang, a legalist, wanted the assistance of new legislations to develop a strong state and in his papers discussed the reasons behind the failure of earlier legalists in previous dynasties. He cited the main reasons as being opposition to legalists, and the fact that law affairs were actually managed by low-ranking officials.[337]

来指导官员。 梁启超是一位法学家，他希望借助新的立法来发展强大的国家，并在其论文中讨论了前朝法家失败的原因。他认为主要原因是法家遭到反对，以及法律事务实际上由低级官员管理。

Another scholar, Meng believed that the law should not be the product of history, but instead should represent the current place, time, and social aspirations; he represented the *idealistic school* of thought.[338] Wu Jing-Xiong rejected the excessive focus on morality, which suppresses creativity and tries to artificially produce a harmonious society.[339] Meng encouraged litigation in society to bring out the truth and even went on to say, "true peace comes from litigation."[340]

另一位姓孟的学者认为，法律不应是历史的产物，而应代表当前的地点、时间和社会愿望；他代表了理想主义学派。吴经熊反对过分注重道德，压制创造力，试图人为地制造一个和谐社会。孟姓学者鼓励社会通过诉讼来揭示真理，甚至说“真正的和平来自诉讼”。

After various discussions on western jurisprudential ideas, the Qing government finally and formally adopted the *Imperial Constitution Outline 1908*,[341] which could be called the first Constitution ever in China. It was to represent the meaning of *xian fa*. Thereafter, subsequent to the Wuhan uprising, the *Provisional Constitution of Republic of China (Zhōnghuá Mínguó línshí yuēfǎ) 1912* and then in 1931, the *Provisional Constitution of Titulary Period of Republic of China 1931* were promulgated.

经过对西方法学思想的各种讨论，清政府最终正式通过了《钦定宪法大纲》（1908 年），这可谓是中国有史以来的第一部宪法。它代表了“宪法”的含义。此后，在武汉起义之后，1912 年颁布了《中华民国临时约法》，1931 年又颁布了《中华民国临时约法》（1931）。

In the middle period of the Kuomintang government, major concepts that were available in Western jurisprudence, such

国民党政府中期，西方法学中的主要概念，如权利与义务、市民社会的诉讼效

---

336 He, "Birth and Growth of Modern Jurisprudence," 496.

337 Qi Chao Liang, *The Collection of Yin Bing Shi, Vol. 5* (Shanghai: Shanghai China Bookstore, 1936), 43, and as discussed in He, "Birth and Growth of Modern Jurisprudence," 498.

338 Sen Meng, *New Introduction to Jurisprudence* (Shanghai: Shanghai Commercial Press,1911),23, as was discussed in He, "Birth and Growth of Modern Jurisprudence," 503.

339 Jiang-Xiong Wu, *A Study of Legal Philosophy* (Shanghai: Shanghai Law Translation & Edition Press, 1933), 15, as was discussed in He, "Birth and Growth of Modern Jurisprudence," 508.

340 Jing-Xiong Wu, *A Study of Legal Philosophy* (Shanghai: Shanghai Law Translation & Edition Press, 1933), 26, and quoted in He, "Birth and Growth of Modern Jurisprudence," 508.

341 Qinding Xianfa Dagang 1908.

as rights and obligations, efficiency of litigation in the civil society, separation of powers, rule of law, international law, and so forth had arrived in China. Discussions among the then Chinese scholars later developed into the definition of law, essence of law, role of law, functions of law, forms of law, and so forth. Nonetheless, even after the development of scholarly debates and translation of western jurisprudence ideas, it was observed by the scholars that there was still disconnect between the theory and practice of law.[342]

率、三权分立、法治、国际法等已经传入中国。当时的中国学者对法的定义、法的本质、法的作用、法的功能、法的形式等问题进行了讨论。然而，即使在学术讨论和西方法学思想的翻译发展之后，学者们也发现法学理论与实践之间仍然存在脱节。

During the proletarian revolution, the Soviet Union's philosophy of Marxism and Communism was dominant. It led to the *First Common Programme of the Chinese People's Political Consultative Congress*, which was promulgated in 1949 and officially adopted in 1954. It contained both the essential principles of Constitution guided by *Marxism – Leninism*, and the thoughts of Mao Zedong.[343] It mainly reflected the will of the dominant class. It was moderated by different classes based on their changing relationships.[344] It was marked by Lenin's own ideas:

在无产阶级革命时期，苏联的马克思主义和共产主义哲学占主导地位。1949年颁布的《中国人民政治协商会议共同纲领》于1954年正式通过。它既包含了以马列主义为指导的宪法的基本原则，也包含了毛泽东思想。它主要反映了占统治地位的阶级的意志。不同阶级根据其不断变化的关系对宪法进行了修改。它打上了列宁自己思想的烙印：

The crux of constitution lies in: all basic laws of the state and laws relating to the power of election of the representative institutions and to the competence of the latter to express a contrast of all forces in class struggle.[345]

宪法的关键在于：国家的一切基本法律以及与代议机构的选举权和代议机构在阶级斗争中表达各种力量对比的权限有关的法律。

---

342 He, "Birth and Growth of Modern Jurisprudence," 512。何，《现代法理学的诞生与发展》，第512页。

343 Guobin Zhu, "Constitution Law and State Structure," in *Chinese Law*, ed. Wang Guiguo and John Mo (The Hague, London, Boston: Kluwer Law International, 1999), 25. See also, Albert H.Y. Chen, "The Developing Chinese Law and the Civil Law Tradition," *China Rev.* (1996): 30. http://www.jstor.org/stable/23453139.

朱国斌，"宪法法律与国家结构"，《中国法律》，王贵国、莫约翰主编，海牙、伦敦、波士顿：克鲁瓦法律国际出版社，1999年，第25页，海牙，伦敦，波士顿：威科国际法律，1999，另见阿尔伯特·陈，《发展中的中国法律与民法传统》，《中国评论》（1996年）：30。http://www.jstor.org/stable/23453139。

344 Guobin Zhu, "Constitution Law and State Structure," 25. See also, Jialin Wu, *Xian Fa Xue ('Constitutional Law')* (Beijing: The Press of Central Radio and TV University, 1985).

朱国斌，"宪法法律与国家结构"，25。另见吴家麟，《宪法学》，北京：中央广播电视大学出版社，1985年。

345 Jialin Wu, *Xian Fa Xue ('Constitutional Law')* (Beijing: The Press of Central Radio and TV University, 1985), 36, and as discussed in Guobin Zhu, "Constitution Law and State Structure," 25.

吴家麟，《宪法学》，北京：中央广播电视大学出版社，1985年，第36页；朱国斌，《宪法与国家结构》，第25页。

Marx's model of law was based on ideas in relation to the need for structural reforms that can make the working class's struggle successful. Law according to Marx has symbolic and practical dimensions.[346] The new thought of Mao Zedong followed Confucianism to an extent, but feudalistic thoughts within it were filtered out to help achieve the Communist utopian society. Confucian thought about loyalty to family was converted to loyalty to the Chinese Communist Party ('CPC') and the state. In the Maoist school of thought, any written law was eschewed in favor of general principles, resulting in there being no written laws in the 1970s. Elements of Legalism were also borrowed in the Maoist school of thought, particularly the idea that the state can only determine what is right and what is wrong with the exclusion of religion-related morality.

马克思的法律模式是建立在与结构改革的必要性有关的思想基础之上的，这种改革能够使工人阶级的斗争取得成功。马克思认为，法律具有象征性和实践性。毛泽东的新思想在一定程度上沿袭了儒家思想，但其中的封建思想被过滤掉，以帮助实现共产主义乌托邦社会。儒家忠于家庭的思想被转换为忠于中国共产党和国家。在毛泽东思想学派中，任何成文法都被摒弃，代之以一般原则，这导致在 20 世纪 70 年代没有成文法。毛泽东思想学派还借鉴了法家思想的元素，特别是认为国家只能决定什么是对的，什么是错的，而不能决定与宗教有关的道德。

The four Constitutions were adopted in 1954, 1975, 1978 and 1982 along with 1949 Common Programme. The *1954 Constitution* emphasised the concept of 'the socialist legality'.[347] The *1975 Constitution* was less focused on law, but instead preferred to focus on the class struggle.

四部宪法分别于 1954 年、1975 年、1978 年和 1982 年与 1949 年《共同纲领》一起获得通过。1954 年宪法强调了"社会主义合法性 "的概念。 1975 年《宪法》不太注重法律，而是倾向于关注阶级斗争。

In 1978, it was affirmed that the *proletarian revolution* for class struggle had succeeded in China, and thereafter a new Constitution was promulgated. Finally, a new Constitution was promulgated in 1982; this Constitution is still in use in the PRC, and has four principles as set out in its Preamble:

1978 年，阶级斗争的无产阶级革命在中国取得了成功，此后颁布了新宪法。最后，1982 年颁布了新宪法；这部宪法目前仍在中华人民共和国使用，其序言中规定了四项原则：

- The socialist road;

社会主义道路；

- The people's democratic dictatorship;

人民民主专政；

[346] Robert Reiner, "Classical Social Theory and Law," in *Introduction to Jurisprudence and Legal Theory: Commentary and Materials*, in *Jurisprudence and Legal Theory: Commentary and Materials*, Anne Barron, et al. (London: Butterworths, 2002), 246.

罗伯特·莱纳：《古典社会理论与法律》，载《法理学与法律理论导论： 评注和材料》，载《法理学和法律理论： 评注与材料》，安妮·巴伦等，伦敦：巴特沃斯出版社，2002 年，第 246 页。

[347] See the discussion on this concept in Guobin Zhu, "Constitution Law and State Structure," 30.

朱国斌，"宪法法律与国家结构"，第 30 页中关于此概念的讨论。

- The leadership of the CPC; and

中国共产党的领导；以及

- The guidance of Marxism - Leninism and Maoist thought.[348]

马克思主义--列宁主义和毛泽东思想的指导。

It was the first time in Chinese history that the rulers were also to be governed by the Constitution, as the Constitution was declared supreme.[349] The Constitution of 1982 has been amended in 1987, 1993 and 1997, 2004 and most recently in 2018. This is the Constitution that is applicable currently in the PRC.

这是中国历史上第一次宣布宪法至高无上，统治者也要以宪法为准绳。1982 年《宪法》先后于 1987 年、1993 年和 1997 年、2004 年以及最近的 2018 年进行了修订。这就是目前适用于中华人民共和国的宪法。

However, the disconnect between the theory and practice of real jurisprudence, and its purpose in modern China continued until the *Third Plenary Session of the Eleventh Central Committee of the Communist Party of China* ('CPC').[350]The route of making amendments to Constitution is usually taken to allow for policy changes as determined by the CPC. The 1993 amendment to *PRC Constitution 1982* introduced the concept of '*socialist market economy*'.

然而，真正的法理学理论与实践的脱节及其在现代中国的目的一直持续到中国共产党第十一届中央委员会（"中国共产党"）第三次全体会议。对宪法进行修改的途径通常是允许中国共产党确定的政策变化。1993 年对 1982 年《中华人民共和国宪法》修正案提出了"社会主义市场经济"的概念。

According to the ranking from top to bottom, the major legislative documents are – Constitution of the PRC (as amended), basic laws such as civil law by National People's Congress (hereinafter 'NPC'), laws, resolutions and decisions by NPC Standing Committee, Administrative laws and regulations and normative documents made by State Council, and local rules and regulations of Local People's

按照从上到下的顺序，主要的立法文件有：《中华人民共和国宪法》（修正案），全国人民代表大会（以下简称"全国人大"）制定的民法等基本法律，全国人大常委会制定的法律、决议和决定，国务院制定的行政法规和规范性文件，省级地方人大和地方人民政府制定的地方性法规

348 Guobin Zhu, "Constitution Law and State Structure," 31; the principles were restated in General programme of the Constitution of CPC 1997.

朱国斌，"宪法法律与国家结构"，第 31 页；1997 年《中国共产党章程》总纲重申了这些原则。

349 See *Constitution of PRC 1982*, Art. 5。见 1982 年《中华人民共和国宪法》第 5 条。

350 He, "Birth and Growth of Modern Jurisprudence," 512; this session was held from 18 to 22 December 1978 and is famous for 'reform and opening' policy of China; more attention was paid to the economy and the push to make 'China a strong powerful socialist country.'

何，《现代法理学的诞生与发展》，第 512 页；这届会议于 1978 年 12 月 18 日至 22 日举行，因中国的"改革开放"政策而闻名；会议更加关注经济，并推动"中国成为强大的社会主义国家"。

Congress & Local Peoples Government at the provincial level. The rapid development of the economy has, however, led to supervisory issues over the local rules and regulations.[351]

和规章。然而，经济的快速发展导致了对地方性法规和规章的监督问题。

3.7 Jurisprudence in context of Practice by Judges and Lawyers in Modern China

现代中国法官和律师实践背景下的法理学

Jerome Cohen, as far back as 1980, wrote:

杰罗姆·科恩早在 1980 年就写道

> ... both in basic assumptions and in institutions and practices, judicial administration in contemporary China displays some striking resemblances to its predecessor under the Chinese empire.[352]

> ...无论是在基本假设上，还是在制度和实践上，当代中国的司法行政都与其中华帝国时期的前身有一些惊人的相似之处。

The above statement is not surprising given that the seventh century Tang Code was similar to the twentieth century Qing Code in respect of the penal codes.[353] The influence of the many ancient jurisprudential theories is still there on the current legal system, and can still be observed by legal researchers, and therefore in the authors' view, Cohen's statement is correct. This is the right time to bring in the words of scholars from the Qing Dynasty, Wang Kuo-Wei and Ching-I Tu, who discussed the concept of *conservatism*:

鉴于七世纪的《唐律疏议》与二十世纪的《大清律例》在刑法方面相似，上述说法并不令人惊讶。 古代诸多法学理论对现行法律制度的影响依然存在，法学研究者依然可以观察到，因此笔者认为科恩的说法是正确的。在此，我们不妨引述清代学者王国维和涂经诒对保守主义概念的论述：

[T]he essence of conservatism is "preservation of the ancient

保守主义的本质是"维护人类古老的

[351] Guobin Zhu, "Constitution Law and State Structure," 47。朱国斌，"宪法法律与国家结构"，第 47 页。

[352] Jerome Cohen, ed., *Essays in China's Legal Tradition* (Princeton: Princeton University Press, 1980), 4, as quoted in Roderick O'Brien, "The Survival of Traditional Chinese Law in the People's Republic of China," *Hong Kong L. J.* 40, no. 1 (2010): 165.

杰罗姆·科恩编，《中国法律传统论文集》，普林斯顿：普林斯顿大学出版社，1980 年，第 4 页，引自罗德里克·奥布莱恩，《中国传统法律在中华人民共和国的生存》，《香港法学杂志》第 40 期，第 1 号，2010 年，第 165 页。

[353] MacCormack, *Spirit of Traditional Chinese Law*, 3。麦考马克，《中国传统法律的精神》，第 3 页。

moral traditions of humanity." A conservative has a great respect for the wisdom of his ancestors and is somehow dubious of sweeping change. He regards society as "a spiritual reality, possessing an eternal life, but a delicate constitution: it cannot be scrapped and recast as if it were a machine." Most important is the conservative's belief that a civilized society "requires order" and the "tradition and sound prejudice can provide checks upon man's anarchic impulse," especially in a revolutionary age.[354]

道德传统”。保守主义者非常尊重祖先的智慧，对大刀阔斧的变革持怀疑态度。他认为社会是“一种精神现实，拥有永恒的生命，但又是一种微妙的构成：它不能像机器一样被废弃和重铸”。最重要的是，保守主义者认为，文明社会“需要秩序”，“传统和合理的偏见可以遏制人的无政府主义冲动”，尤其是在革命时代。

Conservatism has had a profound effect upon the development of law in the PRC, even on the procedural aspects, and its effects are still relevant. For the sake of completeness, even though the above were major jurisprudential thoughts, it is important to appreciate at this stage that between the period of the Han dynasty in 206 BCE until the fall of the Qing dynasty in 1911, the dominant doctrines about morals were from Confucian thought. However, there were some emperors and dynasties which were also swayed by Buddhist and Daoist schools of thought and some elements of these are also reflected in current legal practice.

保守主义对中国法律的发展产生了深远的影响，甚至在程序方面也是如此，其影响至今仍有现实意义。为完整起见，尽管上述是主要的法学思想，但在现阶段，我们必须认识到，自公元前 206 年汉朝至 1911 年清朝灭亡期间，关于道德的主流学说来自儒家思想。不过，也有一些皇帝和朝代受到佛教和道教思想的影响，其中的一些内容也反映在当前的法律实践中。

After the proletarian revolution that culminated in 1949, the PRC followed the concept of '*rule by law*', where the Communist party of China through institutions ruled the populace by rule by law, instead of '*rule of law*'.[355] In the Confucian model also the purpose of law was to control the masses, and it appears that this tradition had continued after

在 1949 年无产阶级革命达到高潮后，中华人民共和国遵循 “依法治国”的理念，中国共产党通过机构以法治而非“法治”来统治民众。在儒家模式中，法律的目的也是为了控制大众，这一传统似乎在 1949 年革命后得以延续。这一特点影响了所有形式的法律机构。然而，笔者

---

[354] Ching-I Tu, "Conservatism in a Constructive Forum: The Case of Wang Kuowei (1877–1927)," *Monumenta Serica 28* (1969): 188, as quoted in MacCormack, *Spirit of Traditional Chinese Law*, 32.

涂静怡，“建设性论坛中的保守主义：王国维（1877-1927 年）案例"，Serica 纪念册 28（1969 年）：188，引自麦考马克，《中国传统法律的精神》，第 32 页。

[355] O'Brien, "Survival of Traditional Chinese Law," N.7 on 166, where he distinguished the meaning as "Jurists distinguish between rule by law, and rule of law. The essence of the distinction is that in the former case, the ruler rules by means of law, but is not subject to the law, while in the latter the ruler is subject to the law. At best, China presently has a system of rule by law. However, in English, the terminology carries many assumptions. In order to avoid these, I have chosen to use the neutral term "ruling according to law".

奥布莱恩，“中国传统法律的生存"，第 7 节，第 166 页，他将其含义区分为"法学家将法治与法治区分开来。区别的实质在于，前者是统治者以法律为手段进行统治，但不受制于法律，而后者则是统治者受制于法律。充其量，中国目前实行的是依法治国制度。然而，在英语中，这一术语带有许多假设。为了避免这些，我选择使用“依法治国”这一中性词。

the 1949 revolution.[356] This feature has affected all forms of legal institutions. However, it appears that with more senior officials being convicted for corruption in the last few years (2012 onwards), this implies, according to the author, a slow movement towards *rule of law*. In addition, jurists have been debating whether China has been following 'rule by ethics'. The *socialist legality* model of Chinese law which followed after 1949 slowly started moving into the realms of the *Romano-Germanic* family of law in the 1990s with various procedure codes that were promulgated.[357]

认为，随着过去几年（2012 年起）越来越多的高级官员因腐败而被定罪，这似乎意味着走向法治的步伐正在放缓。此外，法学家们一直在争论中国是否一直在遵循“以德治国”。1949 年后中国法律的社会主义法制模式在20世纪90年代随着各种程序法典的颁布而开始慢慢进入罗马-日耳曼法系的领域。

In 2000, scholars viewed the governing philosophy as '*rule by ethics*'; this was actually socialism in ethical form. However, it appears that 'rule by ethics' disappeared by 2003 in official circles, remaining only in academic discussion.[358]

2000 年，学者们将其执政理念视为“以德治国”，这实际上是伦理形式的社会主义。然而，到 2003 年，“以德治国 ”似乎在官方圈子中消失了，只停留在学术讨论中。

Another similarity to Confucians in the current system is that in the initial years of the PRC, few laws were published by the authorities. However, this has changed in recent years. The PRC's accession to the World Trade Organization ("WTO") brought about profound changes in many published legislations in order to satisfy external and domestic stakeholders.[359] However, in practice, at local levels, many officials and official machinery are still in the Confucian mode and still believe that more dissipation of law and knowledge means more demands from the populace and could cause social unrest.[360] It is the authors' view that the motive for drafting and publishing many legislations was more due to international stakeholders in the PRC's

现行制度与儒家的另一个相似之处是，在中华人民共和国成立之初，当局很少公布法律。然而，近年来这种情况发生了变化。中国加入世界贸易组织（“WTO”）后，为满足国内外利益相关者的要求，许多已公布的法律都发生了深刻变化。 但实际上，在地方层面，许多官员和官方机构仍停留在儒家模式中，仍然认为法律和知识的更多散失意味着民众的更多要求，并可能引发社会动荡。笔者认为，许多立法的起草和发布动机更多是出于中国经济和社会中的国际利益相关者。

356 Roderick O'Brien, "Survival of Traditional Chinese Law in the People's Republic of China," *40 Hong Kong L.J.165* (2010): 167. See also, Ann D. Jordan, "Lost in Translation: Two Legal Cultures, Common Law Judiciary and the Basic Law of Hong Kong Special Administrative Region," *Cornell Int'l L. J.* 30, no. 2 (1997): 338.

罗德里克·奥布莱恩，“中国传统法律在中华人民共和国的生存”，40， 香港法律评论 165 (2010)： 167。另见安·乔丹，“翻译中的迷失：两种法律文化、普通法司法机构和香港特别行政区基本法”，康奈尔康奈尔国际法杂志 30， no. 2， 1997， 第 338 页。

357 Albert H.Y. Chen, "Developing PRC's Civil Tradition," 30。阿尔伯特·陈，“发展的中华人民共和国的民间传统”，第 30 页。

358 O'Brien, "Survival of Traditional Chinese Law," 167。奥布莱恩 ，“中国传统法律的生存"，第 167 页。

359 Ibid., 169.

360 Ibid., 170.

economy and society.

The bureaucrats are again all too powerful in the PRC today; in this way, it is very similar to the traditional Chinese system which relied on the administrative system with penal laws to manage the administration through powerful bureaucrats.[361] The PRC bureaucratic system is similar to such systems anywhere in the world, in which the bureaucracy prefers to manage problems rather than solve them. This means availability of only general guidelines in the absence of concise laws or may be the availability of multiple laws on same topic, will only assist bureaucracy to become all powerful in PRC. This will affect the practice of governance and even the practice of law in the PRC.[362] In the authors' view, it may be one of the reasons why there is a gulf between theory and the actual practice of law in the PRC. This particular feature is one of the major reasons for the consternation noticed in external stakeholders.

在今天的中国，官僚的权力又是如此之大，这与中国的传统制度非常相似，中国的传统制度是通过强大的官僚，依靠带有刑法的行政制度来管理行政。中国的官僚体制与世界上任何地方的官僚体制都很相似，官僚机构更愿意管理问题而不是解决问题。这意味着，在没有简明法律的情况下，只有一般性的指导原则，或者可能存在关于同一主题的多部法律，这只会帮助中国的官僚机构变得无所不能。这将影响中国的治理实践，甚至法律实践。笔者认为，这可能是中国法律的理论与实践之间存在鸿沟的原因之一。这一特点也是外部利益相关者感到不安的主要原因之一。

The traditional magistracy in ancient China used to operate both as the investigator and as the judge. Additionally, there was no requirement in ancient Chinese society for the magistrate to be perceived as impartial and distant when compared with the adversarial system of common law. Zhu is of the view that the *inquisitorial system* was also followed in the modern PRC's courts due to traditional Chinese practices, and not due to the classification of the legal system into civil or common law system as one might have expected.[363]

中国古代传统的地方官既是调查员又是法官。此外，与普通法的对抗制相比，中国古代社会并不要求地方官被视为公正和疏远。朱光潜认为，近代中国法院也沿用审问制，是中国传统习俗使然，而非人们想象的将法律制度划分为大陆法系或普通法系。

From the above discussion, it seems that in the current practice of law in the PRC, there are many elements from traditional jurisprudence that are still applicable to modern jurisprudence and practice. However, there are views within

从以上讨论来看，在中华人民共和国目前的法律实践中，传统法学中的许多内容似乎仍然适用于现代法理学和实践。不过，学术界也有观点认为，习惯法并未完全纳入中华人民共和国的法律体系。 不

[361] Ibid., 171.
[362] Ibid.

[363] Yikun Zhu, *Concise Chinese Law* (Beijing: Law Press, 2007), 3, and as discussed in O'Brien, "Survival of Traditional Chinese Law," 172.

朱翊坤，《简明中国法》，北京：法律出版社，2007 年，第 3 页，以及奥布莱恩《中国传统法律的生存》第 172 页中的论述。

the academic community that the customary laws were not incorporated fully into the PRC system.[364] Nonetheless, a few scholars would disagree with the notion that, in practice, more laws, clarifications and certainty need to be incorporated into the current legal system.

过，也有少数学者不同意这样的观点，即在实践中，需要将更多的法律、澄清和确定性纳入现行法律体系。

With the advent of the Internet, apps like Wechat, and mobile technology, it is very difficult to keep any policy, rules or local regulations away from the populace. The demands of the populace will only increase in the coming months and years, and in the authors' view, the PRC's legal system, in practice, should be prepared for this eventuality. This is particularly true in the practice of adjudication of civil disputes between persons or businesses, especially when they might have cross-border elements.

随着互联网、微信等应用程序和移动技术的出现，任何政策、规则或地方法规都很难远离民众。在未来的岁月里，民众的要求只会越来越多，笔者认为，中华人民共和国的法律体系在实践中应当为这种可能的情况做好准备。这一点在审理个人或企业之间的民事纠纷时尤为明显，尤其是当纠纷可能涉及跨境因素时。

Additionally, the PRC has demonstrated a desire to learn from and be influenced by foreign systems; for example, tax laws from the US and industrial property laws from Germany have influenced corresponding laws in the PRC. However, the PRC has still resisted the phenomenon of wholesale copying and transplantation.[365] The major changes introduced in the legal system were due to PRC's accession to World Trade Organisation ("WTO"), and the PRC's planned transition towards the socialist market economy. These changes brought profound changes in Commercial law and set the basic foundations of Civil law in the PRC. They also brought a profound understanding of the essence of law from the point of view of Marxist ideology. It was described in China Grand Encyclopedia (1984) as:

此外，中国也表现出了向外国制度学习并受其影响的愿望；例如，美国的税法和德国的工业产权法都对中国的相应法律产生了影响。然而，中国仍然抵制全盘照搬和移植的现象。 中国加入世界贸易组织（"WTO"）以及中国有计划地向社会主义市场经济过渡，给中国的法律制度带来了重大变化。这些变革给商法带来了深刻变化，并为中华人民共和国民法奠定了基础。它们还从马克思主义意识形态的角度深刻地理解了法律的本质。《中国大百科全书》（1984 年）将其描述为：

[364] Jianfu Chen, "Civil Codification and Foreign Influence in China - Towards China's Own Civil Code," *Culture, Law and Order: Chinese and Western Traditions, Macao Ricci Institute* (2004): 221, and as discussed in O'Brien, "Survival of Traditional Chinese Law," 172.

陈建福：《中国的民法典编纂与外国影响--走向中国自己的民法典》，《文化、法律与秩序》，澳门利玛窦学院（2004 年）：《中国与西方的传统》： 文化、法律与秩序：中西传统》，澳门利玛窦学院（2004 年）：第 221 页，以及奥布莱恩的讨论，"中国传统法律的生存"，第 172 页。

[365] Wang Guiguo, "The Legal System of China," in *Chinese Law*, ed. Wang Guiguo and John Mo (The Hague, London, Boston: Kluwer Law International, 1999), 3.

王贵国：《中国的法律制度》，载《中国法学》主编。王贵国和约翰·莫，海牙，伦敦，波士顿：克鲁瓦法律国际，1999，第 3 页。

[T]otal sum of the codes of behaviour enacted or approved by the State to be implemented with the guarantee of the State's power of enforcement in accordance with interest and will of the ruling class.[366]

国家根据统治阶级的利益和意志，在国家强制力的保证下，制定或者批准实施的行为规范的总和。

Nonetheless, in the later years, PRC scholars changed the meaning of essence of law by adding qualifications:

然而，在后来一些年，中国学者改变了法的本质的含义，增加了限定条件：

[T]he nature of law is a reflection of the will of the ruling class, whose contents are decided by material conditions of the society.... while making the law the ruling class must take into account the endurance and strength of the ruled or the non-ruling class.[367]

法律的本质是统治阶级意志的反映，其内容由社会的物质条件决定....，统治阶级在制定法律时必须考虑被统治者或非统治阶级的承受力和力量。

However, from the 1990's the stamp of continental European tradition has been clearly visible in PRC law, and in the authors' view, has surely affected jurisprudence. The scholars Ping and Jian summarize the point succinctly:

然而，从 20 世纪 90 年代开始，欧洲大陆传统的印记在中华人民共和国法律中清晰可见，在笔者看来，这肯定会对法理学产生影响。学者平和建简明扼要地概括了这一点：

As two stages in the history of the development of Chinese law, the law of the Kuomintang period and the present law of the People's Republic of China have a necessary historical and cultural connection. This is an objective manifestation of the national character and continuity of Chinese legal development in the contemporary age.

作为中国法律发展史上的两个阶段，国民党时期的法律与现在的中华人民共和国法律有着必然的历史文化联系。这是当代中国法律发展的民族性和连续性的客观体现。

It is true that for long periods after 1949, particularly in the 1960s, Chinese legislative work and the legal system could not undergo normal development. But since the 1980s, the legislative work and legal system of contemporary China have been able to develop rapidly and to perfect themselves step by step, even though there have existed many

诚然，1949 年以后，特别是 20 世纪 60 年代，中国的立法工作和法制建设在相当长的时期内未能得到正常发展。但自 20 世纪 80 年代以来，当代中国的立法工作和法律体系得以迅速发展，并逐步完善，尽管在这一过程中还存在许多不足。可以预见，未来中国法制的快速进步

366 Ibid., 5.

367 Zongling Shen, ed., *Jurisprudence (Fa Li Xue)*, 3rd ed. (Taipei: Beijing Univeristy Press, 2009), 28, as quoted in Guiguo, "Legal System," 5–6.

沈宗灵主编，《法理学》，第三版，台北：北京大学出版社，2009 年，第 28 页，转引自桂冠，《法律制度》，第 5-6 页。

deficiencies in this process. It may now be predicted that the rapid progress of the Chinese legal system in future is an irreversible trend of history. And in this process, the characteristics of the Civil Law tradition [emphasis added] will continue to stamp themselves upon the Chinese legal system.[368]

是不可逆转的历史潮流。而在这一过程中，大陆法系传统的特点[着重号后加]将继续在中国法律体系中烙下自己的印记。

3.8 Various Comparisons

各种比较

The authors will carry out various comparisons between the two jurisdictions in following paragraphs.

笔者将在下文中对这两个司法管辖区进行各种比较。

3.8.1 Comparison of Jurisprudence – Common Law v PRC

判例比较--普通法与中国法

Ancient Chinese classic thinkers Zichan and Shuxiang put forward two classic arguments around 536 BCE:

公元前 536 年左右，中国古代经典思想家子产和叔向提出了两个经典论点：

- Laws need to be publicized for the people to have clear instructions to follow;

  法律需要公之于众，让民众有明确的指示可循；

- Laws along without social norms will not be able to bring lasting change in the populace.

  仅有法律而没有社会规范，将无法给民众带来持久的变化。

---

368 Ping Jiang and Jian Mi, "The Civil Law Tradition and Contemporary Chinese Law [Part II]. (Lun Minfa Chuantong Yu Dangdai Zhangguo Falii (Xia))," *The Tribune of Political Science and Law (Zhengfa Luntan)*, no. 3 (1993): 7, as quoted in Albert H.Y. Chen, "Developing PRC's Civil Tradition," 53.

江平、米健，《民法传统与当代中国法律[下]．(伦民法传通于当代章诰（夏）》，《政法论坛报》，第 3 期，1993 年；"民法传统与当代中国法律[第二部分]"，3 (1993): 7，引自阿尔伯特·陈，"发展中华人民共和国的公民传统"，第 53 页。

These arguments were later fleshed out in detail by later Chinese thinkers a few thousand years ago and settled into two groups: *Fajia* (the Legalists, who believed in the former argument), and *Rujia* (the second argument, followed by the Confucians) respectively. The first thread of rules, as discussed earlier,[369] is not very different from what common law jurisprudent Lon Fuller said in 1940 about the need for making public the procedural aspects of jurisprudence to allow the public to understand. The second argument later divided broadly into two groups under the questions '*what law is*' and '*what law ought to be?*'. These were called *positivism* and *natural law* respectively in western jurisprudence.[370]

几千年前，中国后来的思想家们对这些论点进行了详细的阐释，并将其分为两派：法家（信奉前一种论点的法家）和儒家（信奉后一种论点的儒家）。如前所述，规则的第一条主线与普通法法理学家伦·富勒在 1940 年所说的需要公开法理学的程序性内容以便让公众理解并无太大区别。第二个论点后来在“法律是什么”和“法律应该是什么”的问题下大致分为两派。西方法学界分别称之为实证主义和自然法。

There was a third group of jurisprudents, who argued in ancient China that any norms or laws or man-made rules or man-made institutions were the real cause of misery for the people and advocated a simpler way of life more in conformity with the way of nature, or *dao* (the Way). They were called *Daojia* or Daoists.[371] In modern times, in western jurisprudence, realists in the USA (of the 1920s and 1930s) and from the CLS movement of the 1970s and 1980s had similar views about the institutions and judges in the US, and advocated the *purposive approach* to the law.[372] Xunzi also raised questions about the purposive approach to the law.

中国古代还有第三类法学家，他们认为任何规范、法律或人为的规则或人为的制度都是造成人民痛苦的真正原因，并主张一种更符合自然之道或道的更简单的生活方式。他们被称为道家或道教徒。近代，在西方法学界，美国（20 世纪 20 年代和 30 年代）的现实主义者以及 20 世纪 70 年代和 80 年代"批判法学运动"(Critical Law Studies Movement，简称“CLS 运动”)运动中的现实主义者对美国的制度和法官持有类似的观点，并主张对法律采取目的论的方法。荀子也对法律的目的性方法提出了质疑。

The written law of Zichan also had the undesired effect of shaking the foundations of the aristocratic pillars of ancient

子产成文法还产生了一个不良后果，即动摇了中国古代社会贵族支柱的根基，

369 Refer, Chapter 3, §3.4.1 and §3.4.1.1。参见第 3 章第 3.4.1 节和第 3.4.1.1 节。

370 Refer, Chapter 3, §3.2.1 and §3.2.2 & §3.2.3。

参见第 3 章第 3.2.1 节和第 3.2.2/3.2.3 节。

371 Refer, Chapter 3, §3.4.1.2。

参见第 3 章第 3.4.1.2 节。

372 Refer, Chapter 3, §3.2.4 for Legal Realism and Critical Legal Studies。

参见第 3 章第 3.2.4 节“法律现实主义与批判性法律研究”。

Chinese society, who for centuries had maintained a monopoly over legal authority. It altered the perception of the populace toward authority and brought in benchmarks in judgment. Written laws such as this were preferred only during times of chaos and social disorder. As a positivist Austin, many centuries later, was no different; he focused on making good laws and stated that the coercion of sanction was necessary. The positivist point of view of civil law tradition, as propounded by Kelson, states that any custom will need validation by the authority or through a higher norm (ending at the highest). Hart described these norms as *secondary rules* that are needed to identify the primary rules.

数百年来他们一直垄断着法律权威。它改变了民众对权威的看法，并带来了判断的基准。这样的成文法只有在混乱和社会无序的时期才会受到青睐。作为实证主义者，许多世纪后的奥斯丁也不例外；他专注于制定良好的法律，并指出强制制裁是必要的。凯尔森提出的民法传统实证主义观点认为，任何习惯都需要权威机构或通过更高的规范（以最高规范结束）来验证。哈特将这些规范描述为确定主要规则所需的次要规则。

The focus of Confucians was on regulating human behaviour by principles that lead to a good society. It was generally thought that litigation (*song*), that by nature is adversarial, can only bring catastrophe (*song-ze zhong-xiong*). This in turn removed the focus from civil litigation, and turned it to finding solutions based on compassion, good social interactions and norms that were always higher than the written law. The focus of Confucian though on the need for authorities to cultivate themselves (*xiu-ji*) and ensure impeccable conduct by improving themselves (*zhengqi-shen*) means that high standards of conduct, integrity, fairness were demanded of authorities when dealing with subjects, though again the focus was not on the law but on good human behaviour.

儒家的重点是用原则规范人类行为，从而建立一个良好的社会。人们普遍认为，本质上具有对抗性的诉讼只能带来灾难（讼则终凶）。这反过来又使人们不再关注民事诉讼，而是将注意力转向基于同情、良好的社会互动以及始终高于成文法的规范来寻找解决方案。儒家虽然强调当局需要修己，并通过完善自身（正其身）来确保行为无懈可击，但这意味着当局在处理与臣民的关系时，需要有高标准的行为、诚信和公平，尽管重点同样不是法律，而是良好的人类行为。

Mencius, on the other hand, did refer to *ren-zheng* and the importance of educating the populace and human nature, but he did not emphasise the development of law. According to the author, Xunzi was the first Confucian to have come out with a theory on the development of law, albeit only for the commoners, with moral principles occupying the highest rank. This can be arguably compared with ancient Greek jurisprudence, with its focus on universal morality in the form of *jus naturale*, and its belief that people were capable of having a sense of justice based on this natural law.

另一方面，孟子确实提到了“仁政”以及教化民众和人性的重要性，但他并不强调法律的发展。笔者认为，荀子是第一个提出法律发展理论的儒家，尽管只是针对平民，而道德原则占据最高地位。这可以与古希腊法学相提并论，古希腊法学注重以自然法为形式的普遍道德，并相信人们能够在自然法的基础上具有正义感。

Xunzi suggested a solution similar to the doctrine of

荀子提出了一种类似于普通法中先

precedents in the common law, whereby the judges could place the case in a category of similar cases, drawing an analogy (*yi leiju*) and deliberating (*yi*) on an appropriate solution. It was a remarkable view considering it was formed nearly 2400 years ago. Xunzi was a bridge between the pure Confucians and the Legalists in Chinese jurisprudential theory, as he stressed the importance of morals, but also developed a legal theory about the legal system and laws. Xunzi even raised questions about the purposive approach to the law. Hart also, in spite of being a positivist, stressed the *internal aspects to the law* which are used by the authorities and populace to accept the external rules that are there to govern them, in spite of the fact they are not compelled to follow them.

例学说的解决方案，即法官可以将案件归入类似案件的类别，进行类比并商议适当的解决方案。考虑到这一观点形成于近2400年前，它是一个了不起的观点。荀子是中国法学理论中纯粹儒家和法家之间的桥梁，因为他强调道德的重要性，同时也发展了关于法律制度和法律的法学理论。荀子甚至对法律的目的论方法提出了质疑。尽管哈特是实证主义者，但他也强调法律的内在性，即当局和民众接受外在规则的作用，尽管他们并不被迫遵守这些规则。

However, this is different from the hardcore Confucian view where the behaviour (*li*) of the populace is targeted, but it was governed by moral principles. In English jurisprudence, moral principles would be used only to fill the gap in the legislations and there is usually no role for them.

然而，这与儒家的核心观点不同，儒家的观点针对的是民众的行为（礼），但它受道德原则的支配。在英国法学中，道德原则只是用来填补立法空白的，通常没有任何作用。

Daoists, on the other hand, had some similarity with the US' CLS movement of the 1970s and 80s. However, Daoists believed in authoritarianism, which put forward the belief that the common population should be deliberately deprived of knowledge. The followers of CLS and the Realist movement from the US seem to bring about a subtle purposive approach in secondary rules as proposed by Hart. According to these schools of thought, this purposive approach was to be followed by the judges during the interpretation of the legislations.

另一方面，道家与美国上世纪七八十年代的CLS运动有一些相似之处。不过，道家信奉专制主义，认为应该故意剥夺普通民众的知识。来自美国的CLS运动和现实主义运动的追随者似乎带来了哈特提出的次要规则中的微妙的目的性方法。根据这些学派的观点，法官在解释立法时应遵循这种目的性方法。

In summary, English jurisprudence has focused more on technicalities of secondary rules, of norms to validate the primary rules; morals have no place in the laws, though they can be used at times to fill in gaps in the law. In principle, populations following the common law jurisprudence were not coerced to follow any rule but should have an internal desire to respect the rules to maintain order. This summary is still valid in the current practice of English Law.

总之，英国法学更注重次要规则的技术性，即验证主要规则的规范；道德在法律中没有地位，尽管有时可以用来填补法律空白。原则上，遵循西方普通法法理的民众不会被强迫遵守任何规则，但应该有尊重规则以维护秩序的内在愿望。这一总结在当前的英国法实践中仍然有效。

However, classical jurisprudence in ancient China predominantly was in the Legalist frame but with a Confucian touch. Even though there were many Codes, the stress on behaviour, vesting of all authority in the Emperor (*shi*), the domination of morality, and dislike for litigation prevailed, and persuasion & coercion were both used. However, in history, when the legalists, or legalists cloaked as Confucians, (*yang-ru yin-fa*) were dominant in most dynasties, the political elites would reject reason or deliberations because of their distrust of scheming, self-interested people. However, *compassion and benevolence* (*ci-ren, guo zhi mu ye*) had an important place. It also led to there being no concept of 'rights' in any of the ancient Chinese schools of jurisprudence, but a concept of having a share (*fen*) in resources for individual effort developed over time in ancient China.

然而，中国古代的古典法理学主要属于法家范畴，但带有儒家色彩。尽管有许多法典，但强调行为、一切权力归于皇帝（士）、道德占主导地位、不喜欢诉讼以及说服和强制并用的思想占主导地位。然而，在历史上，当法家或披着儒家外衣的法家（"阳儒阴法"）在大多数朝代占据统治地位时，政治精英们会因为不信任心怀鬼胎、自私自利的人而拒绝理性或商议。然而，"恻隐"和"仁"却占有重要地位。这也导致中国古代的法学流派中没有"权利"的概念，但中国古代逐渐形成了一种个人努力获得资源份额的概念。

The reference point is society rather than individuals' rights, as deduced from classical Chinese jurisprudence, in contrast to the excessive focus on individual rights in the English jurisdiction.[373] This led to a system of deliberations and debates in the English system and jurisprudence, while in ancient China, devotion to authority and strictly following the drafted codes became the norm; in the authors' experience this is followed even today in the PRC courts.

从中国古典法理学中推导出的参照点是社会而非个人权利，这与英国司法中过分注重个人权利形成了鲜明对比。这导致了英国司法制度和判例中的审议和辩论制度，而在中国古代，忠于权威和严格遵守起草的法典成为规范；根据笔者的经验，即使在今天的中国法院中也是如此。

At the level of practice by the judges in the courts in any jurisdiction, there are constant instances of the judges trying to find rules in the form of statutes, legislations, and case law, and subsequently exercising their *discretion*. But there are also regular instances in difficult cases, where no appropriate law is available. In those scenarios, the judges then proceed to apply general principles utilising the history of application of law in a similar set of circumstances. Many scholars describe the steps in relation to the application of

在任何司法管辖区法院的法官实践层面上，经常会出现法官试图从成文法、立法和判例法中寻找规则，然后行使自由裁量权的情况。但是，在没有适当法律可用的疑难案件中，也经常会出现这种情况。在这种情况下，法官就会利用法律在类似情况下的适用历史来适用一般原则。许多学者描述了法官适用法律和填补空白的步骤，似乎这些法官在摒弃既定规

[373] Refer, Chapter 1, § 1.4.3 for Hosten's reference points in context to know the clear reference points for comparative law in different cultures.

请参阅第 1 章第 1.4.3 节，了解霍斯腾在上下文中的参照点，以了解不同文化中比较法的明确参照点。

law and filling in of the gaps by the judges as if these judges were rejecting the established rules.[374] Surprisingly, some of the principles that the judges employ to alter the established rules of the positivist model are actually based on justice, morality or natural law and so forth in the same way Xunzi and Hart suggested.

则。令人惊讶的是，法官改变实证主义模式的既定规则所采用的一些原则实际上是基于正义、道德或自然法等，这与荀子和哈特的观点如出一辙。

These steps of the judges create problems for positivists (in England & Wales) and legalists (in the PRC), whose focus exclusively is on the concept of '*what the law is?*', and it is painful for them to see that the judges are actually applying these principles at an adjudication level. The positivists and legalists are further shocked by the judges overturning the law established by valid norms pursuant to the positivists' jurisprudence.[375] Some positivists such as Hart could not ignore this fact in the practice of law in courts, where the judges' discretion is used regularly such as in the field of interim applications.

法官的这些步骤给实证主义者（在英格兰和威尔士）和法律主义者（在中国）带来了问题，因为他们只关注"法律是什么？"法官根据实证主义者的法理学推翻了有效规范所确立的法律，这更让实证主义者和法理学者感到震惊。哈特等一些实证主义者无法忽视法院在法律实践中的这一事实，在法院中，法官的自由裁量权经常被使用，例如在临时申请领域。

Hart argued that judicial practice is based on *judicial customary practice* that has been accepted by the law over the years. The guidelines established by the judges in various cases assist the courts in knowing the issues that affect the stakeholders, but in the PRC only the highest court can issue the guidelines, though there are instances of the local courts' guidance as well in the PRC. In the authors' view, in commercial law and business, where speed is the key, more power being made available to the judges may be the key in any jurisdiction.

哈特认为，司法实践的基础是多年来为法律所接受的司法习惯做法。法官在不同案件中制定的指导原则有助于法院了解影响利益相关者的问题，但在中国，只有最高法院才能发布指导原则，尽管在中国也有地方法院提供指导的情况。笔者认为，在商法和商业领域，速度是关键，因此向法官提供更多权力可能是任何司法管辖区的关键。

The focus of Confucians was on regulating human behaviour by principles and discarding litigation (*song*) to avoid catastrophe (*song-ze zhong-xiong*); because of this, the Confucians abhorred civil litigation. This had a profound effect in practice for receiving legal remedies in the PRC, as

儒家的重点是以原则规范人的行为，摒弃诉讼（讼）以避免灾难（讼则终凶）；正因为如此，儒家对民事诉讼深恶痛绝。这对中国接受法律救济的实践产生了深远影响，因为首要的重点仍然是在同情、

[374] Ronald Dworkin, *Taking Rights Seriously* (London: Duckworth, 1977), 37. Dworkin was discussed in detail in James Penner, "Law and Adjudication: Dworkin's Critique of Positivism," in *Introduction to Jurisprudence and Legal Theory: Commentary and Materials*, by Anne Barron, et al. (London: Butterworths, 2002), 346–51.

罗纳德·德沃金，《认真对待权利》，伦敦：达克沃斯，1977 年，第 37 页。德沃金在詹姆斯·彭纳的《法律与裁决：德沃金对实证主义的批判》中被详细讨论，载《法理学与法律理论导论》：安妮·巴伦等著，《评论与材料》，伦敦：巴特沃斯出版社，2002 年，第 346-351 页。

[375] Penner, "Law and Adjudication," 346–50。彭纳：《法律与裁决》，第 346-350 页。

the overriding focus remains on finding solutions based on compassion, good social interactions and public interests. In the authors' view it seems these norms, if we were to look from the point of view of English Jurisprudence, appears to be always higher than the written law. The external stakeholders with businesss interest can be puzzled by the application of such norms in PRC.

良好的社会互动和公共利益的基础上寻求解决方案。笔者认为，如果从英国判例的角度来看，这些规范似乎总是高于成文法。有商业利益的外部利益相关者可能会对这些规范在中国的适用感到困惑。

The Supreme People's Court's of China (SPC's) guidance and *CPL 1991 (as amended in 2012)*, in the authors' view, are drafted on the lines of cultivating the judges and authorities (*xiu-ji*) and also affecting the behaviour (*li*) of the populace. The populace, and the judges have little room to exercise their own discretion for the cases before them. On the other hand, in England & Wales, Hart's theory of internal aspects to the law is used in the practice of law, so that the populace and more importantly the judges have to mandatorily follow the case precedents, laws as a reason or a benchmark, leaving the door wide open for the judges to exercise discretion during the cases. The effect of this philosophy can be widely seen from the way in which procedural remedies in the English Courts have evolved, because the judges have exercised wide discretion.

笔者认为，中国最高人民法院的指导意见和1991年民事诉讼法(2023年修订)是按照培养法官和当局（修己）以及影响民众行为（礼）的思路起草的。民众和法官对所审理的案件几乎没有行使自由裁量权的余地。另一方面，在英格兰和威尔士，哈特的法律内部理论被用于法律实践，因此民众，更重要的是法官，必须强制遵循案例先例、法律作为理由或基准，为法官在案件中行使自由裁量权敞开大门。从英国法院程序补救措施的演变过程中，我们可以广泛地看到这一理念的影响，因为法官行使了广泛的自由裁量权。

Many remedies in English & Welsh courts have been developed using the arguments submitted to the judges by commercial lawyers, and it assisted greatly in ensuring that balance of interests among the parties is maintained not only when the orders are granted, but also for the necessary duration due to the effects of the orders. In the authors' view, debate is required between the parties and even to challenge the judges in the PRC, especially in commercial law, as the stakeholders are working every day in that environment; therefore, in the authors' view, it will not be catastrophic (*song-se zhong -xiong*) for the PRC legal system.

英国和威尔士法院的许多救济措施都是根据商业律师向法官提交的论据制定的，这极大地帮助确保了各方利益的平衡，不仅在命令被批准时如此，在命令生效后的必要期限内也是如此。笔者认为，在中国，尤其是在商法领域，当事人之间需要辩论，甚至需要挑战法官，因为利益相关者每天都在这种环境中工作；因此，笔者认为，这不会给中国的法律制度带来灾难。

The authors are mindful of the fact that debates are allowed in the PRC courts, but excessive reverence for the hierarchical authorities is not conducive for such open debates and can stymie the development of law in PRC. From 1986 onward,

笔者注意到，中国法院允许辩论，但过分尊崇等级权威不利于这种公开辩论，会阻碍中国法律的发展。从 1986 年起，民法总则、实体法在各个法律领域的发展

there has been a development of general principles of civil law, development of substantive law in various areas of law, and *CPL 1991*, thereby bringing in the legalist approach (*Faji*a). This has assisted the stakeholders, both local and external to be made aware of what the law is.

以及 1991 年《民事诉讼法》的制定，从而带来了法家方法（法家）。这有助于当地和外部的利益相关者了解法律是什么。

However, in the authors' view and experience, the challenge lies in ensuring that court orders are respected not only because the populace has to follow it, but because it is in the interests of society and the development of trade and commerce, along the lines of Hart's internal aspects of the law. The continental size of the PRC is a major hurdle in ensuring uniformity throughout the legal system in all provinces. Uniformity is, in the authors' view, what is needed to sustain the momentum of the astronomical growth of the PRC's economy, and to build the trust of stakeholders with commercial interests in the PRC courts. In commercial matters, especially international trade, this is also a matter of ensuring comity of nations is maintained, as most commercial courts throughout the world would tend to follow the path of reciprocity of availability of remedies in other jurisdictions.

然而，根据笔者的观点和经验，所面临的挑战在于如何确保法院命令得到遵守，这不仅是因为民众必须遵守，而且还因为这符合社会利益和贸易与商业的发展，这与哈特的法律内在方面是一致的。中华人民共和国幅员辽阔，这是确保各省法律制度统一的一大障碍。笔者认为，统一性是保持中华人民共和国经济天文数字增长势头的必要条件，也是建立商业利益相关者对中华人民共和国法院的信任的必要条件。在商业事务中，尤其是国际贸易中，这也是一个确保维护国际礼让的问题，因为世界上大多数商业法院都倾向于遵循其他司法管辖区提供救济的互惠原则。

This aspect will be further analysed in the context of general legal thought for the practice of law at an *adjudication level* and the issue of exercise of judge's discretion in the adjudication process. If the judges can alter the established rule, then no law can be considered safe at the level of practice of law in the courts, and this holds relevance in the context of the practice of civil litigation before the courts. Some limitations on the judge's discretionary power in English Courts and to some extent PRC courts are the rules that have been developed within the areas of deference to legislation, doctrine of precedent, courts' customs. This will have to be analysed from the jurisprudential aspect in forthcoming Chapters. These are other invisible factors that need comparing between common law and PRC law.

我们将结合裁决层面法律实践的一般法律思想以及法官在裁决过程中行使自由裁量权的问题进一步分析这一方面。如果法官可以改变既定规则，那么在法院的法律实践层面，任何法律都不能被认为是安全的，这与法院的民事诉讼实践相关。英国法院对法官自由裁量权的一些限制，以及在一定程度上对中国法院自由裁量权的限制，是在服从立法、先例理论、法院习惯等领域内形成的规则。在接下来的章节中，我们将从法理学的角度对此进行分析。这些都是普通法和中国法律之间需要比较的其他隐形因素。

3.8.2 Comparison of Current Jurisprudence and its influence

现行判例及其影响的比较

As discussed above in §3,8.1, the focus on developing principles of justice that led to the development of procedural justice came out of the above jurisprudential processes. These thought processes also led to declarations such as the *Magna Carta 1215, Petition of Right 1628*, *Habeas Corpus Act 1679,* and these set in motion further development of rights for individuals in the English common law legal system. *Procedural justice* was an extension of the above concepts as enshrined in the above Acts such as concepts of fairness, justice, equality of arms. These concepts are common to both common law and PRC legal system.

如上文第 3.8.1 节所述，上述法学进程注重制定正义原则，从而导致了程序正义的发展。这些思考过程也导致了一些宣言的产生，如 1215 年的《大宪章》、1628 年的《权利请愿书》、1679 年的《人身保护法》，这些都推动了英国普通法法律体系中个人权利的进一步发展。程序正义是上述法案中所载概念的延伸，如公平、正义、权利平等等概念。这些概念在普通法系和中华人民共和国法律体系中都是通用的。

The jurisprudential theories of Hart in England & Wales and the influence of realist movements are still valid in the current legal system in the same way they were valid a few hundred years ago. These days the concepts of morality or policy reasons are often alluded to by judges to fill in the gaps in the law, following the purposive approach. The law in practice in the common law system is also taking on ideas from other disciplines regularly. In England & Wales, the focus on the adversarial system to protect with all might the individuals' rights led to development of concepts along these lines, as well as principles within civil procedures such as judicial independence, access to justice and so forth. However, issues over the years in the English common law are becoming more complex due to intricate principles that are emerging out of the judgments. In addition, it has led to debates about whether the civil litigation system has been hijacked by adversarial lawyers and affected due to systemic procedural inefficiencies and so forth.

英格兰和威尔士哈特的法理学理论以及现实主义运动的影响在当前的法律体系中仍然有效，与几百年前的有效方式相同。如今，法官们经常引用道德或政策理由的概念来填补法律空白，遵循目的论的方法。普通法体系中的法律实践也经常吸收其他学科的理念。在英格兰和威尔士，对抗制的重点是全力保护个人权利，这导致了相关概念的发展，以及民事诉讼程序中的原则，如司法独立、诉诸司法等。然而，由于判决中出现了错综复杂的原则，多年来英国普通法中的问题变得越来越复杂。此外，这也引发了关于民事诉讼制度是否已被对抗式律师所劫持、是否因系统性程序效率低下而受到影响等问题的争论。

On the other hand, thousands of years of legal jurisprudence in ancient China have not led to the development of litigation culture, or led to culture of debates & deliberation, or allowed the current courts to focus strongly on individuals' rights. Through the concept of *conservatism*, old traditions are preserved even to this day to ensure order and have deeply affected even current jurisprudence in the PRC. There are striking resemblances in the current legal system to the ancient power structure where the *rule by law* was favoured over *rule of law*; where the focus was on authorities, who were presumed to be brilliant masters (*ming-zhu*); where the

另一方面，中国古代几千年的法学并没有导致诉讼文化的发展，也没有导致辩论和审议文化的发展，更没有让现在的法院强烈关注个人权利。通过保守主义的理念，古老的传统被保留至今，以确保秩序，甚至深深影响了中国当前的法学。现行法律制度与古代的权力结构有着惊人的相似之处，在古代，依法治国优于以法治国；权力机构被认为是高明的主人（明主）；以儒家观念为蓝本的德治是重点；成文法是社会行为的

focus was on virtue-based governance modeled on Confucian concepts; where the written law was to serve as a common benchmark for conduct for society; where the focus was on morals, concepts such as teaching by example (*shen-jio*), behaviour training and so forth. These influences from ancient jurisprudence carried from the past into the present were also affected by the proletarian revolution, import of western ideas during Qing Dynasty, effect of socialism according to Marxism - Leninism and Mao Zedong's thoughts, resulting in the requirement for devotion to the CPC and the state, where religion was separated from the concept of morality. These concepts are preserved in Article 5 of *Constitution of PRC 1982*.[376]

共同基准；道德、言传身教、行为训练等观念是重点。这些从古至今的古代法学影响也受到了无产阶级革命、清朝西方思想的传入、马克思主义-列宁主义和毛泽东思想的社会主义影响，导致了对中国共产党和国家的奉献要求，宗教与道德观念分离。1982 年《中华人民共和国宪法》第 5 条保留了这些概念。

Law is not supposed to be a means to control the masses, and this had a profound effect on development of civil litigation and civil law until *CPL 1991* was promulgated in the PRC. It also affected concepts such as judicial independence, judicial neutrality, supervisory systems such as that of procuratorates, administrative supervisory powers and so forth.

法律不应该成为控制大众的手段，这对民事诉讼和民事法律的发展产生了深远的影响，直到 1991 年《民事诉讼法》在中国颁布。它还影响了司法独立、司法中立、检察院等监督制度、行政监督权等观念。

The above concepts and rules, though ideal for resolving the usual civil disputes in the PRC, are not adequate and flexible in the context of the advent of the socialist market economy after the 1993 amendment to *Constitution of PRC 1982*, as economic stakeholders are independent and autonomous and they require rule of law.[377] The need for market-friendly PRC courts has been further increased by the PRC's accession to WTO. It affects the issue of procedural injustice in any aspect of civil litigation as a result of lack of social

上述概念和规则虽然是解决中国一般民事纠纷的理想选择，但在 1993 年 1982 年《中华人民共和国宪法》修订后社会主义市场经济到来的背景下，这些概念和规则并不充分和灵活，因为经济利益相关者是独立自主的，他们需要法治。 中国加入世贸组织后，对市场友好型中国法院的需求进一步增加。由于缺乏社会公正，这影响到民事诉讼任何方

[376] Article 5 of *PRC Constitution 1982* provides: "The state upholds the uniformity and dignity of the socialist legal system. No law or administrative or local rules and regulations shall contravene the constitution. All state organs, the armed forces, all political parties and public organizations and all enterprises and undertakings must abide by the Constitution and the law. All acts in violation of the Constitution and the law must be investigated. No organization or individual may enjoy the privilege of being above the Constitution and the law."
1982 年《中华人民共和国宪法》第 5 条规定"国家维护社会主义法制的统一和尊严。任何法律、行政法规和地方性法规、规章都不得同宪法相抵触。一切国家机关、武装力量、各政党和各社会团体、各企业事业组织都必须遵守宪法和法律。一切违反宪法和法律的行为都必须受到追究。任何组织和个人都不得享有凌驾于宪法和法律之上的特权".

[377] Huang Lie, "Rule of Law in China: Ideal and Reality," in *Constitutionalism and China*, in *Constitutionalism and China*, Buuyun Li (Beijing: Law Press, 2006), 189.

黄烈，《中国的法治：理想与现实》，载《宪政与中国》，李步云译，北京：法律出版社，2006 年，第 189 页。

justice.[378] Many laws are enforced by administrative organs that are prone to arbitrariness and at times recklessness, and also raise the issues of impartial administration of justice along with principles of *judicial independence* and *judicial neutrality*.[379] These are the issues that are least needed in commercial litigation by the stakeholders.

面的程序不公正问题。 许多法律是由行政机关执行的，这些行政机关很容易恣意妄为，有时甚至不计后果，这也提出了司法独立和司法中立原则下的公正司法问题。 这些都是利益相关者在商业诉讼中最不需要解决的问题。

The stakeholders require many remedies for the PRC courts, and a few of these remedies require exercise of discretion of the judges. But discretion does not mean arbitrariness, as experienced by stakeholders in the local PRC courts. On the other hand, in the common law system of England & Wales, access to justice is affected due to the escalating costs of solicitors and barristers, courts fees, and other costs. These systemic issues have over the years become serious issues for most common law jurisdictions and as discussed earlier, these legal systems seem at times to have been hijacked by vested interests.

利益相关者要求中国法院采取许多补救措施，其中一些补救措施需要法官行使自由裁量权。但自由裁量权并不意味着任意妄为，正如利益相关者在中国本地法院所经历的那样。另一方面，在英格兰和威尔士的普通法体系中，由于律师和大律师的费用、法庭费用和其他费用不断上涨，影响了诉诸司法的机会。多年来，这些系统性问题已成为大多数普通法司法管辖区的严重问题，而且如前文所述，这些法律制度有时似乎被既得利益所强行控制。

3.8.3 Comparison of Origins of current Legal System and Philosophical Development

现行法律制度的起源与哲学发展的比较

In the common law system, a framework for the legal system originated around the twelfth century, leading to the development of local customs; records were also compiled. The legal reasoning provided by the judges in their judgments was important for the development of law. This was accompanied by developments such as jury trials, and legislations enacted to fill the gaps that remained after

在普通法体系中，法律制度的框架起源于 12 世纪左右，这导致了地方习俗的发展；同时还编纂了记录。法官在判决中提供的法律推理对法律的发展非常重要。与此同时，陪审团审判和为填补判决后的空白而制定的法律也得到了发展。因此，新兴的普通法由与法院司

[378] Ibid., 179.

[379] Ibid., 183–84.

judgments. The emergent common law was thus made up of rules, doctrines, customs, norms and, later, maxims that were relevant to the working of judicial activities in the courts.

法活动有关的规则、理论、习惯、规范以及后来的格言组成。

The emerging common law was also affected by natural law or the influence of foreign culture, but the most important thing for its sustainability as a whole was the *rules, doctrines, customs,* and *norms that were incorporated regularly in the future cases* in the courts. Their future use was also based on reasons that were consistent, constant, practical, contextual, and congruent with other parts of law. Additionally, these rules, doctrines, customs, norms and so forth were made after considerable debate & deliberation.

新兴普通法也受到自然法或外国文化的影响，但对其整体可持续性而言，最重要的是规则、学说、习惯和规范，这些规则、学说、习惯和规范被定期纳入法院未来的案件中。这些规则、学说、习惯和规范今后的使用也是基于一致、恒定、实用、语境以及与其他法律部分相一致的理由。此外，这些规则、学说、习惯、规范等都是经过大量辩论和审议后制定的。

Eventually, common reasons came out of debates and oral arguments during trials in the common law system, which were coherent and not necessarily governed by the rules of morality. This brings into focus the issue of *culture of training of lawyers, the judges, and the legal clerks;* the soft aspects of training had to keep up with the development of law. In summary, there was an internal aspect of law that developed where the populace will respect the law, but this respect from the populace was not out of compulsion or coercion from the authorities.

最终，普通法体系里辩论环节以及审判过程中的言辞论辩，催生出了共通的理据。这些理由是连贯的，不一定受道德规则的约束。这使律师、法官和书记员的培训文化问题成为焦点；培训的软性层面必须跟上法律的发展。总之，法律的发展有其内在的一面，即民众会尊重法律，但民众的这种尊重并不是出于当局的强制或胁迫。

Traditionally, the effect of the Confucian mode was that there were formal codes to govern the populace, but there also existed informal codes in society. There was also hardly any training in law, and even drafters of law were called ‘petty clerks’ (*dao-bi-li*). This was even repeated in the civil examinations which started during the Tang Dynasty (AD 618 – 906).

传统上，儒家模式的效果是有正式的法典来管理民众，但社会上也存在非正式的法典。此外，几乎没有任何法律培训，甚至起草法律的人也被称为“刀笔吏”。这种情况甚至在唐朝（公元618-906年）开始的民间考试中重演。

The focus of the thoughts and jurisprudence in ancient China was more on sharing the resources (*fen*) and there was no specific focus on individual rights. Traditionally, respect

中国古代的思想和法学更注重资源共享，并没有特别关注个人权利。中国社会传统上缺乏对法律的尊重。法律的

towards the law was missing in Chinese society.[380] The only focus of law was limited to penal codes. However, with the arrival of western thought during the Qing dynasty and the arrival of imperial powers and the drafting of commercial treaties with them, there was compulsion to reform the legal system of China.

重点仅限于刑法。然而，随着清朝西方思想的传入、帝国列强的到来以及与他们签订的商业条约，中国的法律制度不得不进行改革。

The resulting interaction of Chinese scholars with western scholars also acted as a catalyst to reform the legal system during the Qing dynasty. In the middle period of the Kuomintang government after the fall of the Qing dynasty, many principles from western jurisprudence arrived on Chinese shores.

由此产生的中国学者与西方学者的交流也成为清朝法律制度改革的催化剂。清朝灭亡后的国民党政府中期，西方法学的许多原则传入中国。

Nevertheless, there was disconnect between theory and practice, and to certain extent it is still felt by many. The focus on training of lawyers and judges is a relatively new phenomenon in the PRC. In addition, bureaucrats, who were traditionally powerful in ancient China, were again all too powerful. This phenomenon was not very different to the traditional Chinese system's emphasis on an efficient administrative system managing the penal laws. The PRC also adopted the *inquisitorial system*, which is still followed in the modern PRC's courts, more due to principles of conservatism. The requirements for additional formalities such as *notarisation* or *legalisation* of evidence and other documents stems from the historical development of law in the PRC, but it definitely affects access to justice in relation to urgent applications.

尽管如此，理论与实践之间仍然存在脱节，而且在某种程度上，许多人仍然感觉到这种脱节。在中国，注重律师和法官的培训是一个相对较新的现象。此外，在中国古代历来权倾朝野的官僚也再次大行其道。这种现象与中国传统制度强调由高效的行政系统管理刑法并无太大区别。中国还采用了审问制，现代中国的法院仍然沿用审问制，这更多是出于保守主义的原则。对证据和其他文件进行公证或认证等额外手续的要求源于中国法律的历史发展，但这无疑影响了与紧急申请有关的司法救助。

380 See *Interpretations of the Supreme People's Court on Several Issues concerning the Application of Law in the Trial of Criminal Cases of Refusing to Enforce Judgments or Rulings*, *Fa Shi* [2015] No.16 promulgated on 20 July, 2015 and effective from 22 July 2015. Surprisingly, this kind of provision took so many years to be promulgated. It is akin to contempt of court proceedings in England & Wales. Any preservation order will gain strength with the application of the stated provisions.

参见《最高人民法院关于审理拒不执行判决、裁定刑事案件适用法律若干问题的解释》，法释[2015]16 号，2015 年 7 月 20 日公布，2015 年 7 月 22 日起施行。令人诧异的是，这样的规定竟然颁布了这么多年。这类似于英格兰和威尔士的藐视法庭诉讼。任何保全令都将随着所述条款的适用而变得更加有力。

General principles of Civil law were finally introduced in the PRC in preparation for accession to WTO in 1986. In addition, the recent growth in the economy combined with the new focus on law means it will still take some time before the full legal system blossoms, especially in respect of training of lawyers and judges in continental-size PRC.

中国在1986年准备加入世界贸易组织时最终引入了民法的一般原则。此外，近期的经济增长加上对法律的新关注，意味着法律制度的全面开花还需要一些时间，特别是在中国大陆规模的律师和法官培训方面。

In summary, the legal system in the PRC is relatively new as compared to England & Wales, but it has picked up the pace in the last three decades by incorporating customs from ancient China and a few thoughts & influences from the Western legal systems. PRC law has managed to absorb foreign influences, while maintaining strict Chinese characteristics. However, whether these characteristics are adequate with the rise of the PRC as an economic superpower is not easy to answer.

总之，与英格兰和威尔士相比，中国的法律制度相对较新，但在过去的三十年中，它吸收了中国古代的习俗以及西方法律制度的一些思想和影响，从而加快了发展步伐。中国法律既吸收了外来影响，又保持了严格的中国特色。然而，随着中华人民共和国作为经济超级大国的崛起，这些特色是否足够，并不容易回答。

The authors' view is that the PRC might have to give up a few special Chinese characteristics in the realm of commercial law and civil procedure as more foreign & external stakeholders will come to rely on the PRC's legal system in the near future. This need for reforms will further increase with the PRC's '*Belt and Road Initiative*' and as the PRC continues to increase its share in global exports and imports.

笔者认为，随着越来越多的外国和外部利益相关者在不久的将来开始依赖中国的法律制度，中国可能不得不在商法和民事诉讼领域放弃一些特殊的中国特色。随着中国"一带一路"倡议的提出以及中国在全球进出口中所占份额的不断扩大，改革的必要性将进一步增强。

From the 1990's, the PRC's legal system has shown the influence of continental Romano-Germanic civil traditions in contrast to the common law adversarial system. This aspect definitely has its own unique effects on PRC's procedural law. These effects are compounded by the availability of modest substantive law in PRC, along with the limited avenues of judicial and legal training in many provinces of the PRC. Most of the substantive law in the PRC was drafted as recently as the 1990s.

自20世纪90年代以来，中国的法律体系一直受到罗马-日耳曼大陆民事传统的影响，与普通法对抗制形成鲜明对比。这无疑对中国的诉讼法产生了独特的影响。中国实体法存在一定局限性，与此同时，国内众多省份的司法实践机会和法律培训途径也相对有限，这诸多因素交织，致使上述影响变得更为错综复杂。需指出的是，中国大部分实体法都是在20世纪90年代拟定而成的。

Chapter 4 - LEGAL PHILOSOPHY OF CIVIL LITIGATION – COMMON LAW v. CHINESE LAW

第四章 - 民事诉讼的法哲学--普通法与中国法

4.1 Basic Introduction to Civil Litigation — England & Wales and PRC

民事诉讼基本介绍--英格兰和威尔士及中国

In this Chapter the authors will discuss briefly the structures of the courts in England & Wales as well as in the PRC. The basic steps of civil litigation in both jurisdictions will also be discussed. The authors will introduce the relevant terminology used in both jurisdictions as well. In the later part of the Chapter, the legal philosophy behind civil litigation in both jurisdictions is discussed and then compared using comparative analysis.

The distinction between the civil law involving general tort, contract, agency, civil disputes or similar cases and commercial law involving bigger disputes about projects, company laws and so forth in both jurisdictions is also discussed. It is important to appreciate the comparative analysis in this Chapter to fully fathom the analysis going forward in Chapters 5, 6 and 7.

在本章中，作者将简要讨论英格兰和威尔士以及中国的法院结构。还将讨论两个司法管辖区民事诉讼的基本步骤。作者还将介绍两个司法管辖区使用的相关术语。在本章的后半部分，作者将讨论两个司法管辖区民事诉讼背后的法律理念，然后通过比较分析进行比较。此外，还讨论了两个司法管辖区涉及一般侵权、合同或类似案件的民事法律与涉及项目、公司法等较大争议的商业法律之间的区别。理解本章的比较分析对于全面理解第 5、6、7 章的分析非常重要。

4.1.1 Court Structure in England & Wales

英格兰和威尔士的法院结构

Briefly, the Court structure and related terminologies in England and Wales are as follows:[381]

简言之，英格兰和威尔士的法院结构和相关术语如下：

- *The UK Supreme Court* – This is the highest court, and it hears appeals on points of law in cases of major public importance. In this Court, the judgments are given by Justices of the Supreme Court. The Supreme Court hears appeals from the Court of Appeal and in exceptional circumstances can hear appeals from the High Court. These appeals are normally heard by five Justices (formerly Lords of Appeal in Ordinary, or Law Lords), but there can be as many as nine such Justices.

- 英国最高法院——这是最高级别的法院，负责审理重大公共案件中有关法律问题的上诉。该法院由最高法院法官做出判决。最高法院受理来自上诉法院的上诉，在特殊情况下也可受理来自高等法院的上诉。这些上诉通常由五名大法官（前普通上诉法院大法官或法律大法官）审理，但也可能有多达九名这样的大法官。

- *The Civil Division of* Court *of Appeal* – It hears appeals on points of law in civil cases from all the courts. The Civil Division of the Court of Appeal hears appeals from all Divisions of the High Court and, in some instances from the County Courts and certain tribunals. The judgments are given by the Lord Chief Justice, Heads of this division, and Court of Appeal judges. The Civil Division is presided over by the Master of the Rolls. Bringing an appeal is subject to obtaining '*permission*', which may be granted by the court below or, more usually, by the Court of Appeal itself. Applications for permission to appeal are commonly determined by a single Lord Justice, and full appeals are heard by two or three judges. The Civil Division of the Court of Appeal also deals with family cases.

上诉法院民事庭——审理来自所有法院的民事案件法律要点上诉。上诉法院民事庭审理来自高等法院各庭的上诉，有时也审理来自郡法院和某些法庭的上诉。判决由首席大法官、民事庭庭长和上诉法院法官作出。民事庭由首席法官主持。提起上诉必须获得“许可”，“许可”可能由下级法院授予，更常见的是由上诉法院本身授予。上诉许可申请通常由一名大法官裁定，正式上诉由两名或三名法官审理。上诉法院民事庭也处理家庭案件。

381 The authors have prepared a basic Court system in a flowchart in Chapter 4, §4.1.1。作者在第 4 章第 4.1.1 节的流程图中编制了一个基本的法院系统。

- *The High Court* – It hears complex or important civil cases and appeals from the County courts. High Court judges use the title in office of *Justice.* The head office of the High Court is in London. The High Court consists of three divisions:

高等法院——高等法院审理复杂或重要的民事案件以及来自郡法院的上诉案件。高等法院法官使用 "大法官 "这一职称。高等法院总部设在伦敦。高等法院由三个庭组成：

- *Queen's Bench Division ('QBD')* – where all commercial, common-law cases of contract and tort & similar cases, and judicial review applications are dealt with.

-王座庭（QBD）--处理所有商业、普通法合同和侵权及类似案件，以及司法审查申请。

- *Family Division* – where matrimonial cases are dealt with.

- 家事庭 - 处理婚姻案件。

- *Chancery Division ('Ch D')* – all matters of insolvency, intellectual property, trusts, probate, deeds, company law, mortgages, and land-related issues are handled in this court. As discussed in Chapter 2, it was originally the Court of Equity before it was merged with common-law courts between1872-75.

-大法官法庭（"Ch D"）--所有与破产、知识产权、信托、遗嘱认证、契约、公司法、抵押以及土地相关的事务均由该法庭处理。如第 2 章所述，它最初是衡平法院，1872-1875 年间与普通法法院合并。

- There are *specialist courts* as well within the High Court such as Admiralty, Technology & Construction courts, Patent Court.

-高等法院内还设有专门法院，如海事法院、技术与建筑法院、专利法院。

- *County Courts* hear a wide range of civil actions, including small claims and family cases. They are located around each district in England & Wales. There are also Magistrates Courts, but they have limited jurisdiction in civil matters. *District judges* are full-time judges who deal with the majority of cases before the county courts of England and Wales.

- 郡法院审理范围广泛的民事诉讼，包括小额索赔和家事案件。郡法院分布在英格兰和威尔士的各个地区。英格兰和威尔士也有治安法院，但它们对民事案件的管辖权有限。地区法官是全职法官，负责处理英格兰和威尔士郡法院审理的大部分案件。

- *The Enforcement of Judgments Offices* enforces civil judgments. For the sake of completeness, it should be mentioned that there are a number of other tribunals

- 判决执行办公室负责执行民事判决。为完整起见，应当提及的是，在法院结构之外，还有一些其他法庭（例如，学

outside of this court structure (for example, School Exclusion Panels, Employment Tribunals) which are equally important within the legal system – their supporting legislations explain their individual appeal routes.

校排斥问题小组、就业法庭），它们在法律体系中同样重要--它们的辅助立法解释了各自的上诉途径。

Most civil cases are tried in courts that do not have a system of jury trial. The only exceptions are for cases involving libel and slander trials. In all the above courts, very briefly, the judges hear these cases on their own, deciding them by first finding relevant facts, then applying the relevant law to those facts – and there may be considerable arguments about what that law actually is – and finally giving reasoned judgments. The judges also decide on all matters of procedure which may arise during a hearing. The reasons cited by the judges in the cases are important for the development of common law as discussed in Chapter 3 of this book.

大多数民事案件都是在没有陪审团审判制度的法院审理的。唯一的例外是涉及诽谤和中伤的案件。简而言之，在上述所有法院中，法官自行审理这些案件，首先查明相关事实，然后将相关法律适用于这些事实--可能会对该法律的实际内容存在大量争论--最后做出合理判决。法官还就审理过程中可能出现的所有程序问题做出裁决。正如本书第 3 章所讨论的，法官在案件中引用的理由对于普通法的发展非常重要。

After their judgments, the judges then go on to decide the fees of any lawyers, court fees to be paid out by the parties involved, fees of expert witnesses, allowances that may be allowed to the litigants who have acted in person (without lawyers), earnings that have been lost by the litigants, and travelling & other expenses incurred by the parties and their witnesses. The general rule in relation to legal costs is that the unsuccessful party will have to pay the successful party's costs, but the judges have a wide discretion to depart from this rule under the *Civil Procedure Rules 1998*.

在做出判决后，法官将继续决定律师费、当事人支付的法庭费用、专家证人费、亲自出庭（无律师在场）的诉讼当事人可能获得的津贴、诉讼当事人损失的收入，以及当事人及其证人产生的差旅费和其他费用。有关法律费用的一般规则是，败诉方必须支付胜诉方的费用，但根据《1998 年民事诉讼规则》，法官有很大的自由裁量权来偏离这一规则。

Figure 6: Structures of Courts in England & Wales

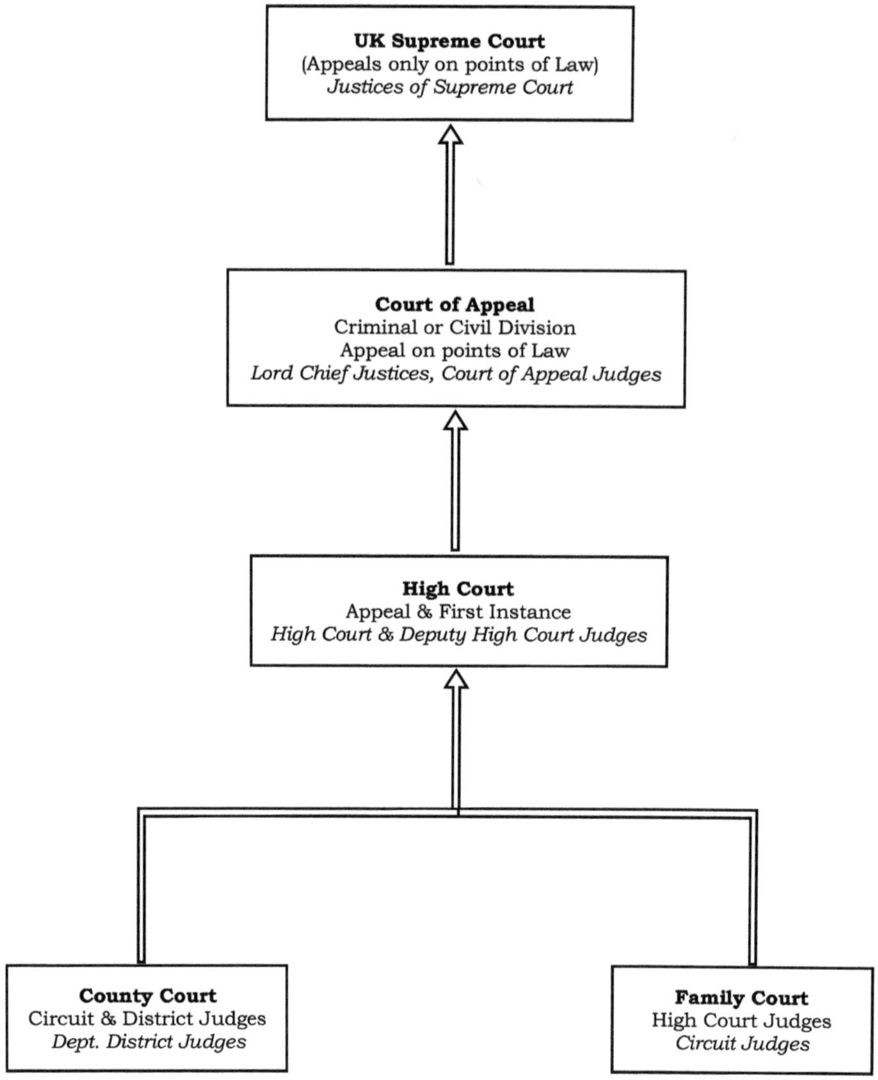

图 6：英格兰和威尔士的法院结构

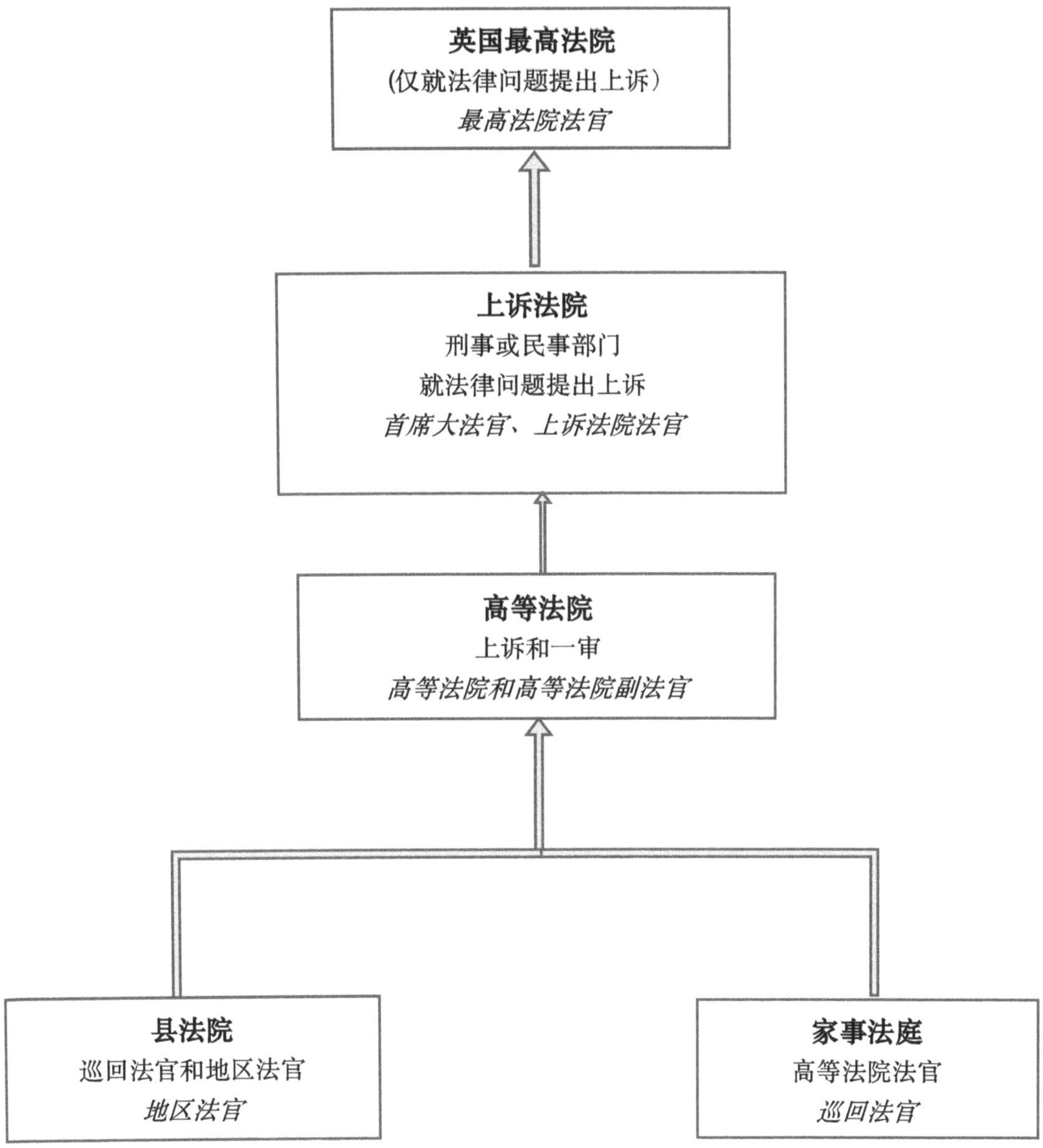

4.1.2 Procedural Steps in Civil Litigation in England & Wales

英格兰和威尔士民事诉讼的程序步骤

The authors had also briefly discussed procedural steps in any civil litigation in Chapter 1. In more detail, the various procedural steps in civil litigation in England & Wales are as follows:[382]

笔者在第 1 章中也简要讨论了任何民事诉讼的程序步骤。更详细地说，英格兰和威尔士民事诉讼的各个程序步骤如下：

- A claimant formally notifies the appropriate court (depending on nature and value of claim) by '*issuing*' a claim form;

原告通过"签发"请求表格正式通知相关法院（取决于请求的性质和价值）；

- A defendant receives a notification of the claim through '*service*' of a copy of the claim form; service of the claim form must be made within the first four months of issue;

被告通过"送达"请求表副本收到请求通知；请求表必须在签发后的头四个月内送达；

- *Aacknowledgement* of the service of the claim form is filed with the court by the Defendant;

被告向法院提交请求表送达回执；

-The Claimant provides sufficient details of the claim, normally in *Particulars of claim*. This is followed by a *Defence and Counterclaim* from the Defendant; thereafter the Claimant can file a *Reply and Defence to the Counter Claim*;

原告通常在"请求细节"中提供请求的充分细节。随后，被告会提出抗辩和反诉；之后，原告可以对反诉提出*答辩和抗辩*；

- Additional party(ies) can be jointed to the main parties by an additional CPR *Part 20 procedure*;

其余当事方可通过 CPR 第 20 部分的附加程序 加入主要当事方；

[382] Susan Blake, *A Practical Approach to Effective Litigation*, 8th ed. (Oxford: Oxford University Press, 2015), 107–29. See also, in detail, *Civil Procedural Rules 1998, SI 1998/3132 (as Amended until August 2016)*. See also, "Civil Procedure: White Book Volume 1 & 2" (2015). See also, "Civil Procedure: White Book Volume 1 & 2" (2016). Refer also, Chapter 4, §4.1.2, where the authors have prepared a basic steps in civil litigation in England & Wales.

Susan Blake, A Practical Approach to Effective Litigation, 8th ed. (Oxford: Oxford University Press, 2015), 107-29。另详见《1998 年民事诉讼程序规则》，SI 1998/3132（修订至 2016 年 8 月）。另见《民事诉讼程序》：白皮书第 1 卷和第 2 卷"（2015 年）。另见《民事诉讼程序：白皮书第 1 卷和第 2 卷》（2015 年）。另见《民事诉讼程序：白皮书第 1 卷和第 2 卷》（2016 年）。另参见第 4 章第 4.1.2 节，作者在该节中编写了英格兰和威尔士民事诉讼的基本步骤。

- *Case management questionnaires* are filed by the parties to the civil litigation;

案件管理调查表由民事诉讼各方提交；

- *Case Management Conference* is held, where Case Management and allocation of the case are done by a Judge according to the complexity of the case;

举行案件管理会议，由法官根据案件的复杂程度进行案件管理和分配；

- *Disclosure of evidence* (including what is not favourable) by each party;[383]

各方披露证据（包括不利证据）；

- *Exchange of Witness Statements and Expert Reports*;

交换证人陈述和专家报告；

- *Trial* of the case;

案件审理；

- *Judgment* including *Cost orders*; and

包括费用令在内的判决；以及

- Appeal

上诉

Interim applications can be made any time by any party in the civil litigation. In the usual course of things, interim applications are made at the Case Management Conference, unless there are urgent issues or tactical applications before the courts are needed.

民事诉讼中的任何一方均可随时提出*临时申请*。在通常情况下，临时申请是在案件管理会议上提出的，除非有紧急问题或需要向法院提出策略性申请。

383 This is the step that is considered as most controversial by PRC lawyers about the common law system. PRC lawyers or even parties from the PRC fail to understand why they must disclose evidence that is unfavourable to them when they are running a case in the common law system, such as in many shipping law cases that have English jurisdiction clause.
这是中国律师对普通法体系争议最大的一步。中国律师甚至是来自中国的当事人都不理解，为什么在普通法体系下打官司，例如在很多有英国司法管辖权条款的航运法案件中，必须披露对自己不利的证据。

Figure 7: Steps for Civil Litigation Pursuant to CPR 1998 (England & Wales)

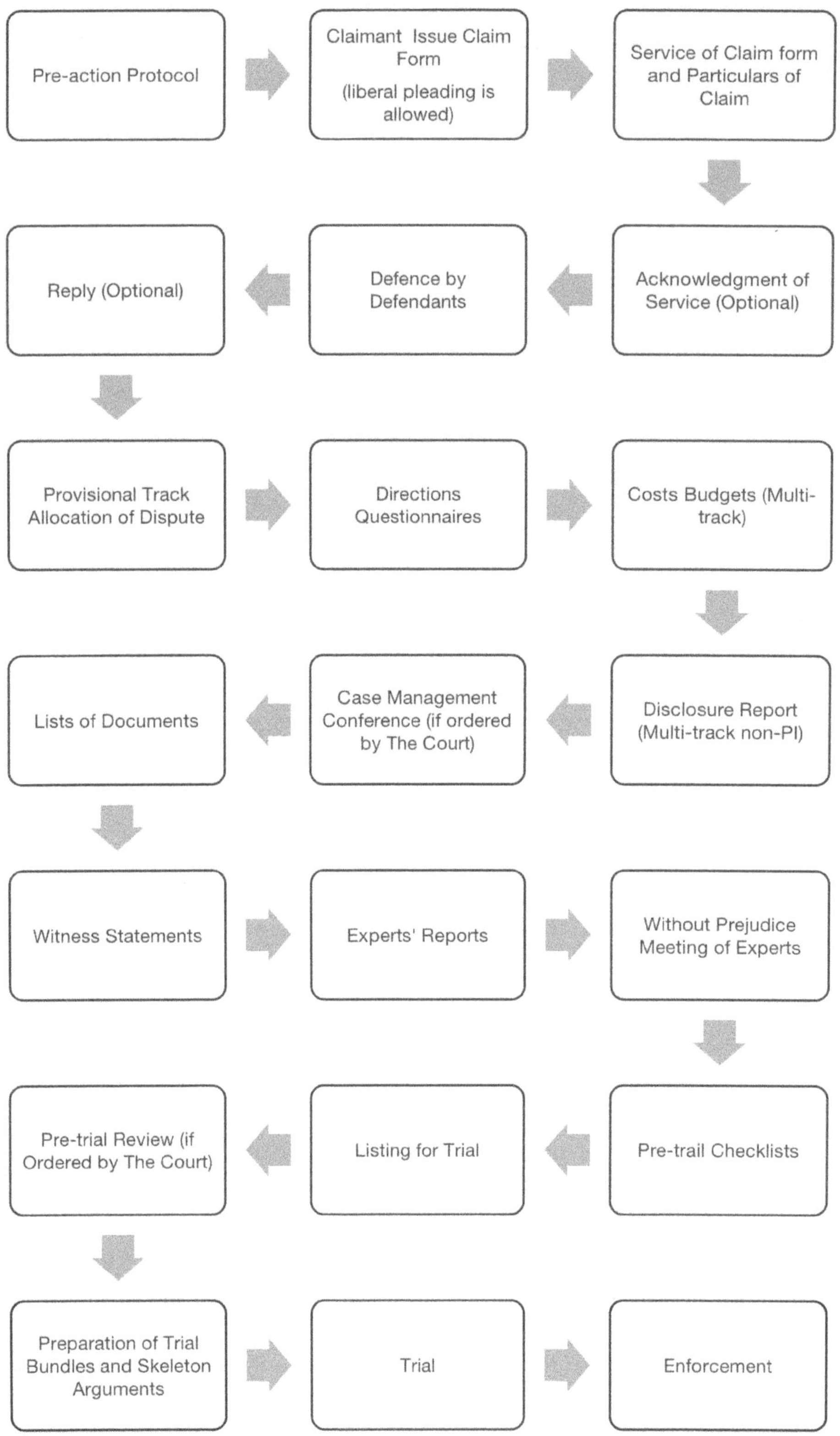

图 7：根据《1998 年民事诉讼程序法》进行民事诉讼的步骤（英格兰和威尔士）

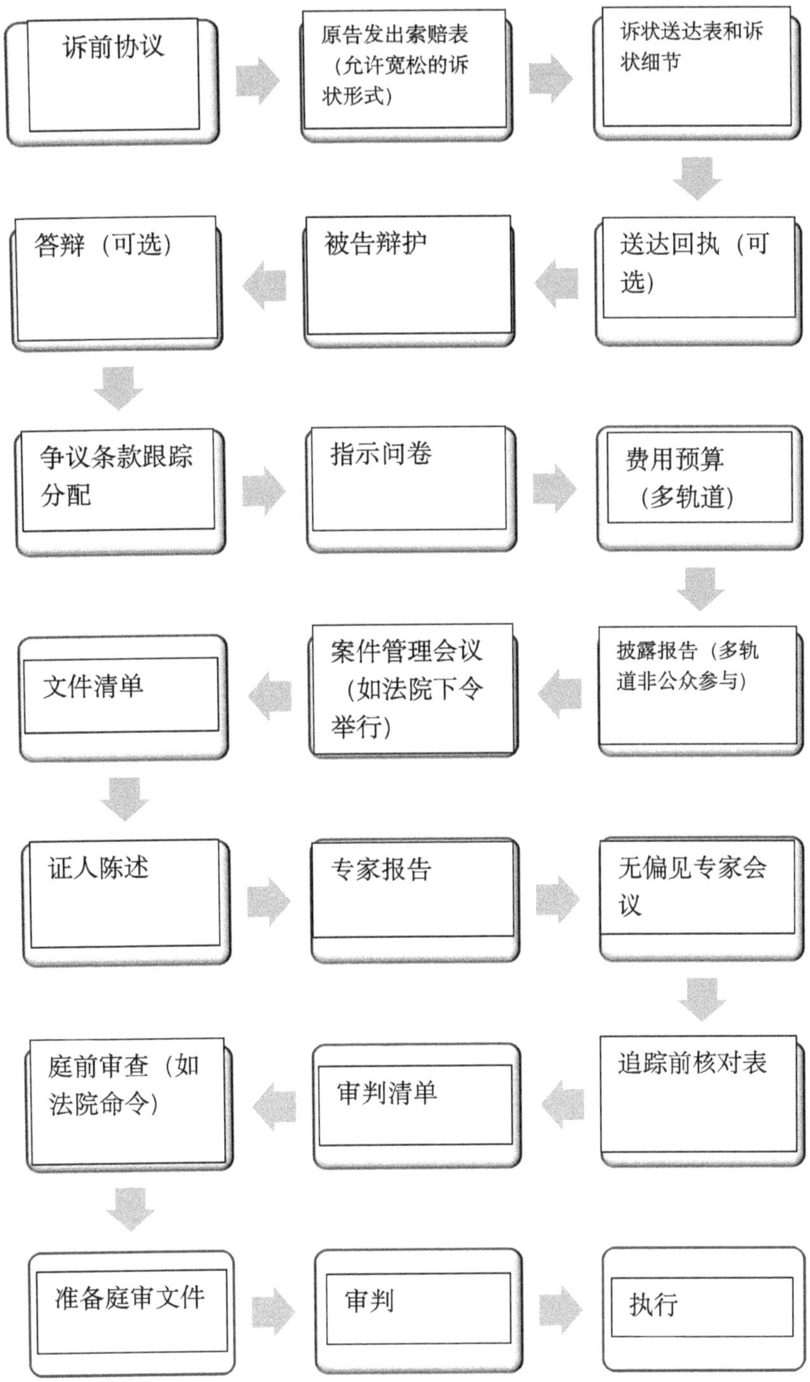

4.1.3 Court Structure in PRC

中国的法院结构

The authors had also briefly discussed procedural steps in any civil litigation in Chapter 1. In more detail, the various procedural steps in civil litigation in England & Wales are as follows:[384]

笔者在第 1 章中也简要讨论了任何民事诉讼的程序步骤。更详细地说，英格兰和威尔士民事诉讼的各个程序步骤如下：

- A claimant formally notifies the appropriate court (depending on nature and value of claim) by '*issuing*' a claim form;

原告通过"签发"请求表格正式通知相关法院（取决于请求的性质和价值）；

- A defendant receives a notification of the claim through '*service*' of a copy of the claim form; service of the claim form must be made within the first four months of issue;

被告通过"送达"请求表副本收到请求通知；请求表必须在签发后的头四个月内送达；

- *Aacknowledgement* of the service of the claim form is filed with the court by the Defendant;

被告向法院提交请求表送达回执；

-The Claimant provides sufficient details of the claim, normally in *Particulars of claim*. This is followed by a *Defence and Counterclaim* from the Defendant; thereafter the Claimant can file a *Reply and Defence to the Counter Claim*;

原告通常在"请求细节"中提供请求的充分细节。随后，被告会提出抗辩和反诉；之后，原告可以对反诉提出*答辩和抗辩*；

- Additional party(ies) can be jointed to the main parties by an additional CPR *Part 20 procedure*;

其余当事方可通过 CPR 第 20 部分的附加程序 加入主要当事方；

---

[384] Susan Blake, *A Practical Approach to Effective Litigation*, 8th ed. (Oxford: Oxford University Press, 2015), 107–29. See also, in detail, *Civil Procedural Rules 1998, SI 1998/3132 (as Amended until August 2016)*. See also, "Civil Procedure: White Book Volume 1 & 2" (2015). See also, "Civil Procedure: White Book Volume 1 & 2" (2016). Refer also, Chapter 4, §4.1.2, where the authors have prepared a basic steps in civil litigation in England & Wales.

Susan Blake, A Practical Approach to Effective Litigation, 8th ed. (Oxford: Oxford University Press, 2015), 107-29。另详见《1998 年民事诉讼程序规则》，SI 1998/3132（修订至 2016 年 8 月）。另见《民事诉讼程序》：白皮书第 1 卷和第 2 卷"（2015 年）。另见《民事诉讼程序：白皮书第 1 卷和第 2 卷》（2015 年）。另见《民事诉讼程序：白皮书第 1 卷和第 2 卷》（2016 年）。另参见第 4 章第 4.1.2 节，作者在该节中编写了英格兰和威尔士民事诉讼的基本步骤。

- *Case management questionnaires* are filed by the parties to the civil litigation;

案件管理调查表由民事诉讼各方提交；

- *Case Management Conference* is held, where Case Management and allocation of the case are done by a Judge according to the complexity of the case;

举行案件管理会议，由法官根据案件的复杂程度进行案件管理和分配；

- *Disclosure of evidence* (including what is not favourable) by each party;[385]

各方披露证据（包括不利证据）；

- *Exchange of Witness Statements and Expert Reports*;

交换证人陈述和专家报告；

- *Trial* of the case;

案件审理；

- *Judgment* including *Cost orders*; and

包括费用令在内的判决；以及

- Appeal

上诉

Interim applications can be made any time by any party in the civil litigation. In the usual course of things, interim applications are made at the Case Management Conference, unless there are urgent issues or tactical applications before the courts are needed.

民事诉讼中的任何一方均可随时提出*临时申请*。在通常情况下，临时申请是在案件管理会议上提出的，除非有紧急问题或需要向法院提出策略性申请。

There are many aspects of civil litigation in any jurisdiction. In this section, the basic court structure and procedural steps in civil litigation in the PRC will be briefly discussed.

任何司法管辖区的民事诉讼都涉及多方面。本节将简要讨论中国民事诉讼的基本法院结构和程序。

The structure of the PRC's Court system is characterised by

中华人民共和国法院系统的结构特点是四级两审：

[385] This is the step that is considered as most controversial by PRC lawyers about the common law system. PRC lawyers or even parties from the PRC fail to understand why they must disclose evidence that is unfavourable to them when they are running a case in the common law system, such as in many shipping law cases that have English jurisdiction clause.
这是中国律师对普通法体系争议最大的一步。中国律师甚至是来自中国的当事人都不理解，为什么在普通法体系下打官司，例如在很多有英国司法管辖权条款的航运法案件中，必须披露对自己不利的证据。

four levels and two instances of trial:[386]

- National Supreme People's Court based in Beijing, including Circuit Courts in the various provinces;[387]

设在北京的国家最高人民法院，包括各省的巡回法院；

- High People's Courts at the provincial level;

省级高级人民法院；

- Intermediate People's Courts (at prefecture level), usually in the capitals of provinces in the PRC;

中级人民法院（地级），通常设在中国各省省会；

- Basic People's Courts at country level, including People's Tribunals;

基层人民法院，包括人民法庭；

- There are also special courts such as Military Courts, Maritime Courts, Forest Courts and Railway Courts.[388]

此外，还有军事法院、海事法院、森林法院和铁路法院等特别法院。

The PRC follows the principle of *two instances*: as the first instance, the trial is carried out, and any subsequent appeal from the first instance takes place in the Intermediate People's Court and the High People's Court. The case may also be transferred from the lower court to the higher courts. The jurisdictions of the courts are decided both hierarchically and geographically. Intermediate People's Courts have jurisdiction as the courts of first instance over cases involving foreign elements.[389] Civil cases of first instance are tried in Basic People's Courts by a collegial bench consisting of both judges and assessors, or of

中国遵循两审终审的原则：一审进行审判，一审后的上诉由中级人民法院和高级人民法院进行。案件也可由下级法院移交上级法院。法院的管辖权按级别和地域划分。中级人民法院对涉外案件拥有一审管辖权。基层人民法院由法官和陪审员组成的合议庭或仅由法官组成的合议庭审理一审民事案件。陪审员享有与法官相同的权利和义务。

---

[386] See Art. 2 of *Organic Law of People's Courts of PRC 1979* (as amended in 1983 & 2018). Refer to flowchart highlighting the court structure in PRC, another flow chart to highlight the status of courts within the PRC as they have to report to National People's Congress and the last flow charter related to Procuratorate system in the PRC that is the supervisory system.

见 *1979 年《中华人民共和国人民法院组织法》（1983 年和 2018 年修订）*第 2 条。参见中国法院结构流程图，另一个流程图强调了中国法院的地位，因为它们必须向全国人民代表大会报告，最后一个流程章程涉及中国的检察院系统，即监督系统。

[387] Circuit courts are a crucial step in China's judicial reform. They are meant to facilitate the filing of inter-provincial cases and prevent local-government intervention, thus freeing Beijing headquarters from complex cases and policy issues in relation to the judicial system.

巡回法庭是中国司法改革的关键一步。巡回法庭旨在为跨省案件的立案提供便利，防止地方政府的干预，从而将北京总部从与司法系统有关的复杂案件和政策问题中解脱出来。

[388] Arts. 2 and 18 of *Organic Law of People's Court of PRC 1979 (as amended in 1983 & 2018)*。1979 年*《中华人民共和国人民法院组织法》（1983 年和 2018 年修订）*第 2 条和第 18 条。

[389] See Art. 19 of *CPL 1991 (as amended in 2023)*。见 1991 年《中华人民共和国民事诉讼法》（2023 年修订）第 19 条。

judges alone. Assessors have the same rights and obligation as judges. Civil cases to which summary procedure is applied shall be tried by a single judge.[390]

适用简易程序的民事案件由一名法官审理。

In the PRC, the Procuratorate system works in a similar way to the Court system, and it has similar hierarchies to the PRC court system. The Procuratorate supervises the functioning of the courts, in particular, trials in criminal and civil courts at all levels of the courts within the legal system. This organ within the Constitution of the PRC even has investigative powers within the legal system. It also has another role within the PRC system, that is to ensure public interests are maintained.

在中国，检察院系统的工作方式与法院系统类似，其等级也与中国法院系统类似。检察院监督法院的运作，特别是法律系统内各级法院的刑事和民事审判。根据《中华人民共和国宪法》，该机关甚至在法律系统中拥有调查权。它在中华人民共和国体制内还有另一个作用，即确保公共利益得到维护。

390 See Art. 40 of *CPL 1991 (as amended in 2023)*。见 1991 年《中华人民共和国民事诉讼法》（2023 年修订）第 40 条。

Figure 8: Relationship of Courts with Legislature and Governing body: Highlighting no separation of power

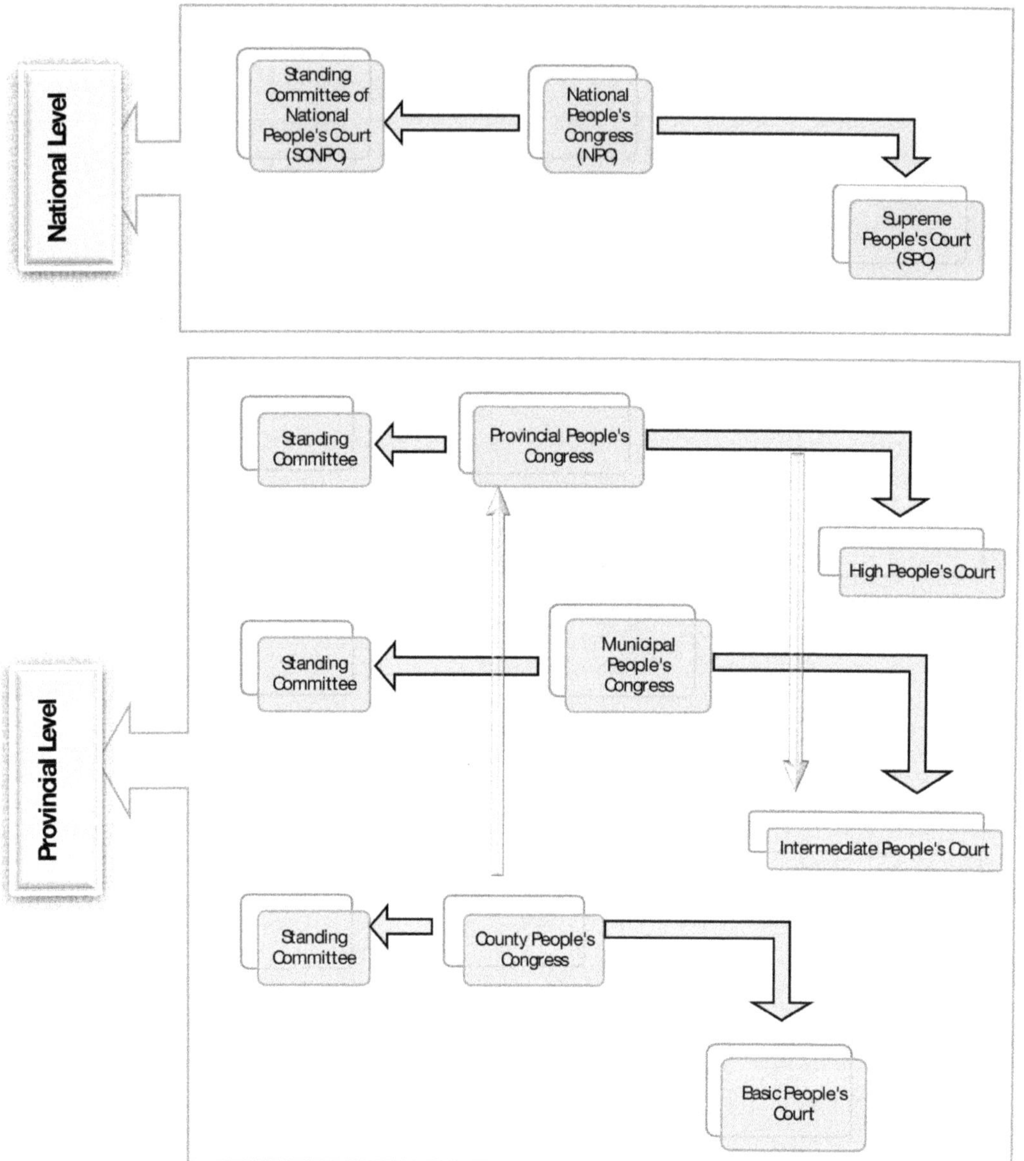

图 8：法院与立法机构和管理机构的关系：凸显权力不分割

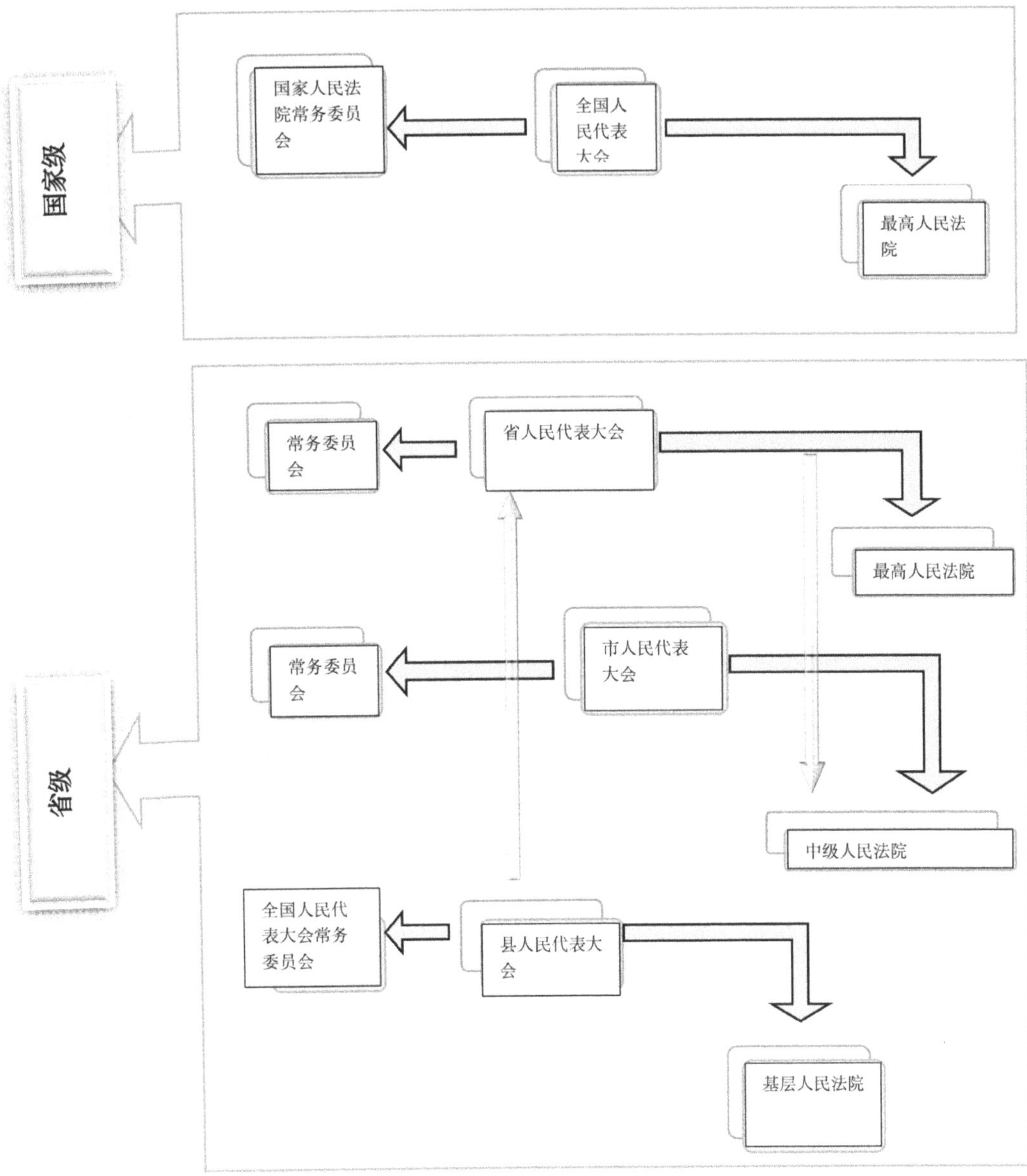

Figure 9: Structures of Courts in People's Republic of China's (PRC)

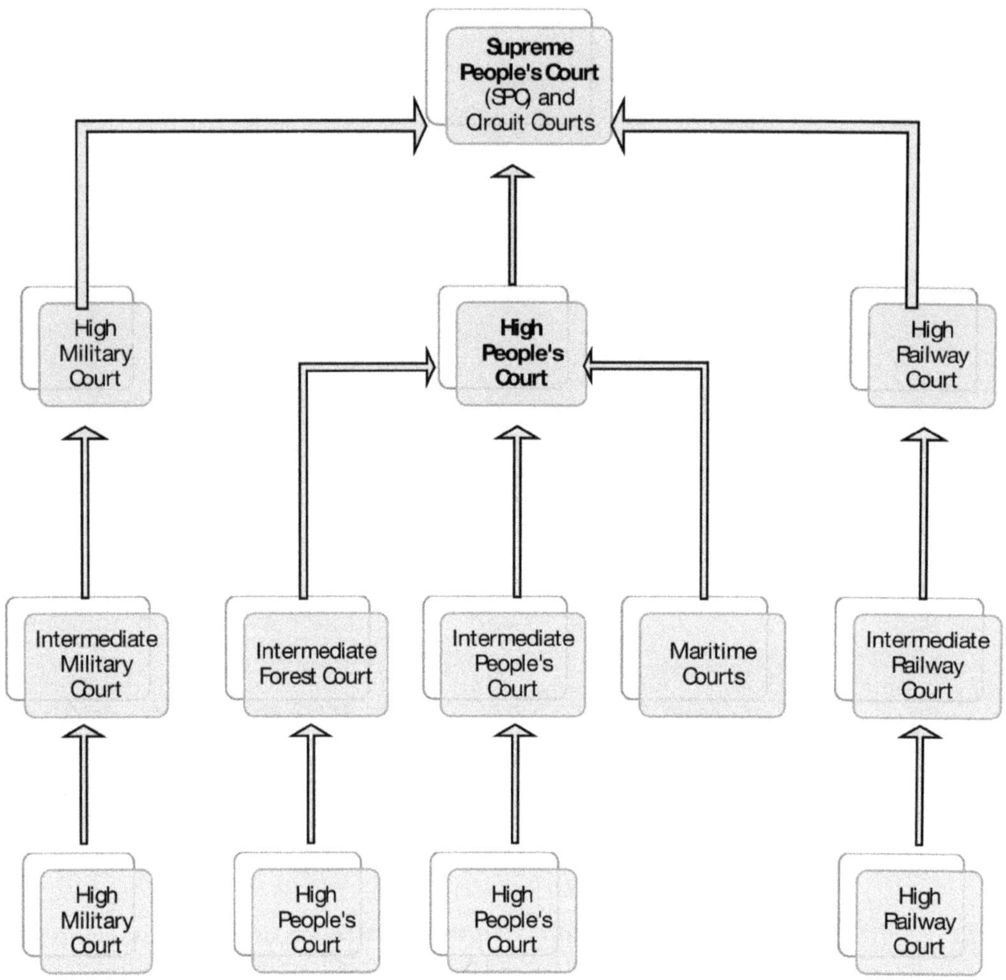

图 9：中华人民共和国（PRC）的法院结构

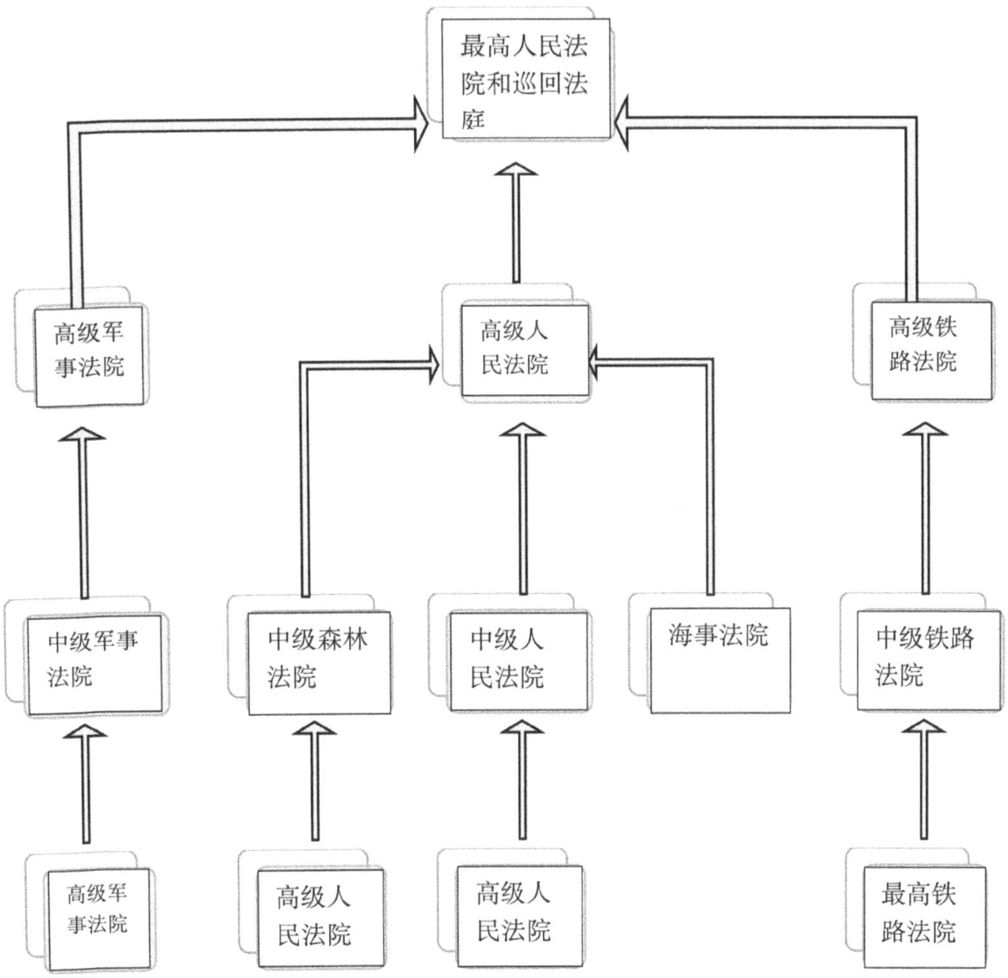

Figure 10: Procuratorates System (Supervisory System) in PRC: Supervises Courts and Decisions

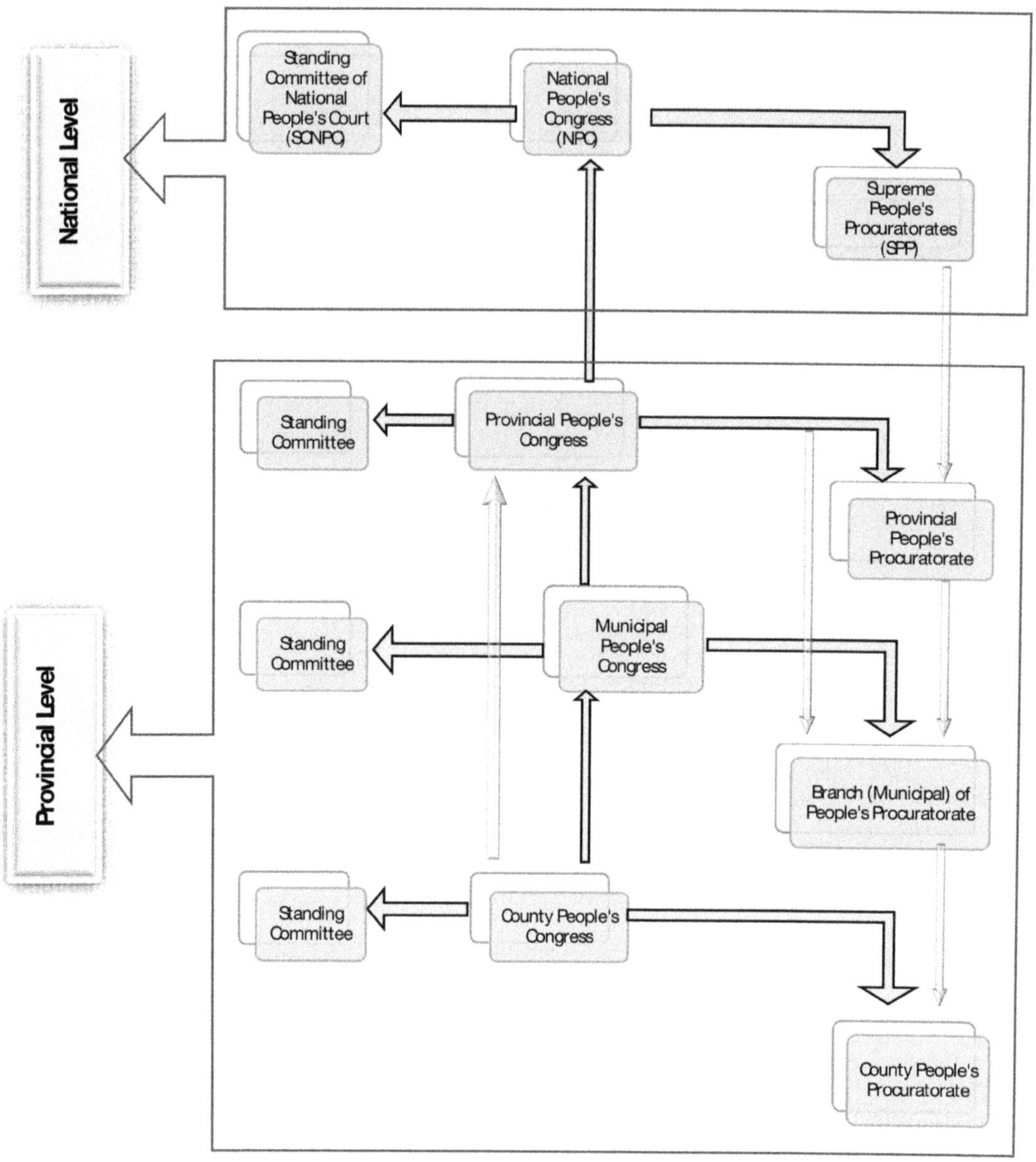

图 10：中国的检察院系统（监督系统）：监督法院和裁决

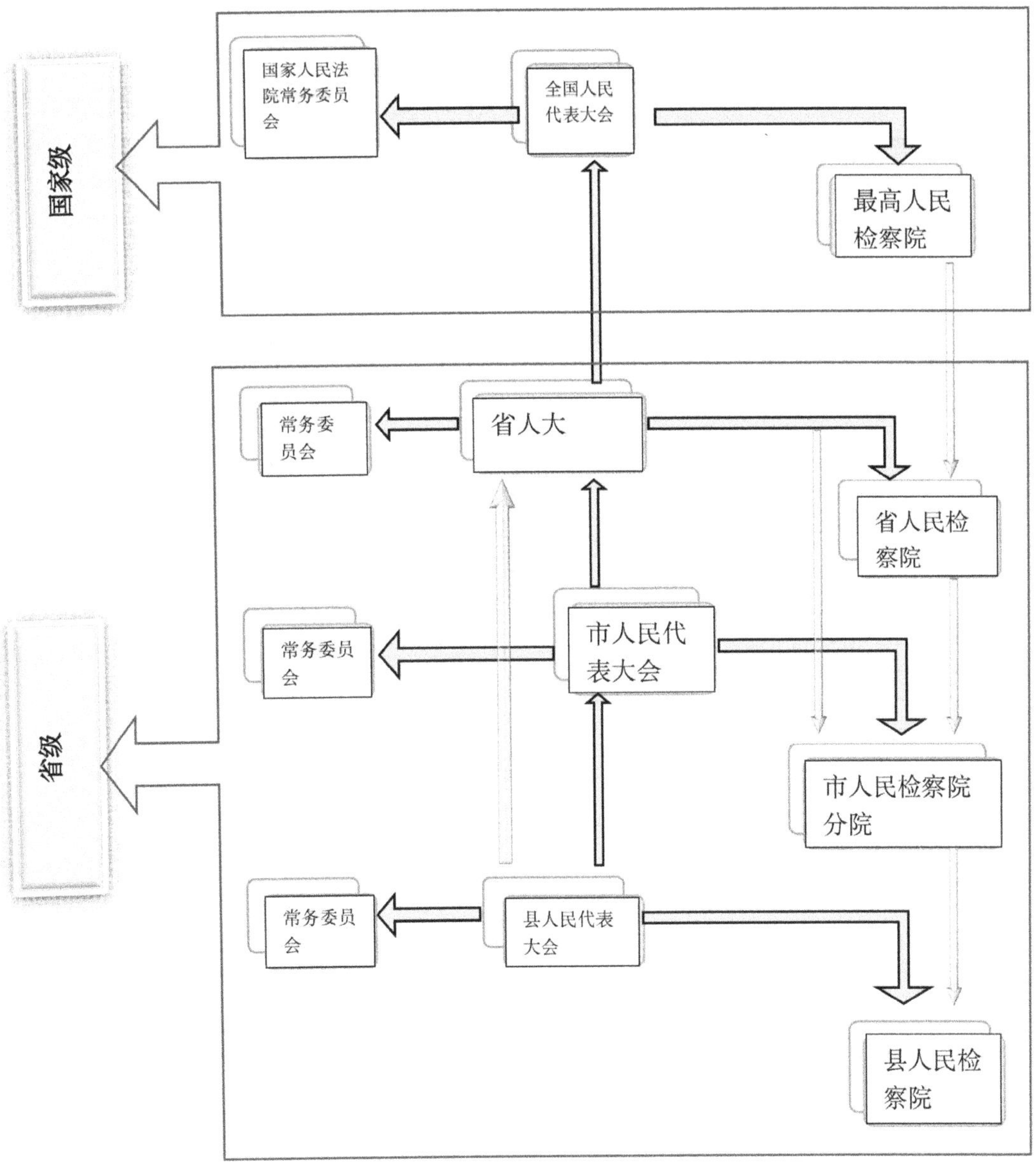

4.1.4 Procedural Steps in Civil Litigation in PRC

中国民事诉讼的程序步骤

An overview of procedural steps in civil litigation in PRC courts is important in the common law versus PRC debate. The important procedural steps in the PRC's civil litigation process are as follows:[391]

在普通法与中国法的辩论中，对中国法院民事诉讼的程序步骤进行概述非常重要。中国民事诉讼中的重要程序步骤如下：

- Filing and accepting lawsuits with *Motion of complaint* and satisfying all the requirements of CPL.[392] It has been observed by many stakeholders that many times the claimants could not pass the hurdle of satisfying the court officials of his case, and his applications are not accepted. This aspect is discussed in relation to the standard of proof in context of evidence that is required by the court officials even at this stage of the process. Such evidence must accompany the application;

提交和受理附有诉状动议的诉讼，并满足CPL的所有要求许多利益相关者注意到，很多时候原告无法通过让法院官员对其案件满意的关卡，因此其申请未被受理。这一方面的讨论涉及到举证标准，即即使在程序的现阶段，法院官员也要求提供证据。这些证据必须与申请一并提交；

- *Mediation* should be attempted by the parties before the case is passed through the courts;[393]

在案件提交法院之前，当事方应尝试进行调解；

- Pre-trial preparation with the claim passed to the defendant in five days. Defendant has fifteen days to present the defence satisfying the conditions of the courts;[394]

庭前准备，五天内将诉讼请求转交给被告。被告可在 15 天内提出符合法庭条件的辩护；

- Courts inform the parties about their rights and obligations going forward;[395]

法院告知各方后续权利和义务；

---

[391] See The flow chart in this section of the book, where all the procedural steps in the civil litigation can be seen for easy reference.

参见本书本节中的流程图，民事诉讼的所有程序步骤都可以在这里看到，以方便参考。

[392] See Arts. 122, 123, 124 of *CPL 1991(as amended in 2023)*。参见 1991《中华人民共和国民事诉讼法》（2023 年修订）第 122、123 和 124 条。

[393] See Art. 125 of *CPL 1991(as amended in 2023)*。参见 1991 年《中华人民共和国民事诉讼法》（2023 年修订）第 125 条。

[394] See Art. 126 of *CPL 1991(as amended in 2023)*。1991 年《中华人民共和国民事诉讼法》（2023 年修订）第 126 条。

[395] See Art. 127 of *CPL 1991(as amended in 2023)*。1991 年《中华人民共和国民事诉讼法》（2023 年修订）第 127 条。

- Argument as to the jurisdiction (if any) is dealt with, and collegiate bench is established. Thereafter, the parties are informed within three days of its constitution;[396]

处理关于管辖权（如有）的争论，并成立合议庭。此后，在合议庭成立三天内通知各方；

- Investigation by the courts as to the dispute by entrusting an adjudicating person at the courts or other courts in another jurisdiction within the PRC;[397]

委托中国境内其他司法管辖区的法院或其他法院的审判人员对争议进行调查；

- Courts can decide the process relevant to the dispute – (1) Where the parties concerned have no dispute and the requirements of the procedure for hastening debt recovery are met; such procedure may be initiated by the court ; (2) Where mediation may be conducted before trial, mediation shall be conducted in a timely manner to solve the dispute; (3) The summary procedures or ordinary procedures may be applied according to the specific conditions of the case; and (4) Where a court session is needed, the focus on the dispute may be clarified through requiring the parties concerned to swap evidence or by other means;[398]

法院可以决定与争议相关的程序 -- (1) 当事人无争议且符合债务催收程序要求的，可由法院启动该程序；(2) 可先调解后开庭的，应及时调解解决争议；(3) 可根据案件具体情况适用简易程序或普通程序； (4) 需要开庭审理的，可通过要求当事人调换证据或其他方式明确争议焦点；

- Summary procedure can be decided by the courts according to the facts of the case;[399]

简易程序可由法院据案情决定；

- Trial is conducted in open courts, including opening statements, exchange of evidence and experts' reports, adducing new evidence, and cross-examination, including debate between the litigants;[400]

审判在公开法庭进行，包括开庭陈述、交换证据和专家报告、提出新证据和交叉质证，包括诉讼双方之间的辩论；

---

396 See Arts. 128 & 129 of *CPL 1991(as Amended in 2023)*。1991 年《中华人民共和国民事诉讼法》（2023 年修订）第 127、128 条。

397 See Arts. 130, 131 & 132 of *CPL 1991 (as amended in 2023)*。1991 年《中华人民共和国民事诉讼法》（2023 年修订）第 130、131 和 132 条。

398 See Art. 136 of *CPL 1991 (as amended in 2023)*。1991 年《中华人民共和国民事诉讼法》（2023 年修订）第 136 条。

399 See Art. 160 of *CPL 1991 (as amended in 2023)*。1991 年《中华人民共和国民事诉讼法》（2023 年修订）第 160 条。

400 See Arts. 139, 140, 141 of *CPL 1991 (as amended in 2023)*。见 1991 年《中华人民共和国民事诉讼法》（2023 年修订）第 139、140 和 141 条。

- Mediation can be tried again if the parties agree before the judgment;[401]

如果双方在判决前达成一致，可以再次尝试调解；

- Judgment is usually given within six months of case filing date;[402]

判决通常在立案之日起六个月内做出；

- Motion of appeal by any party to the litigation, if any, within fifteen days after the judgment;[403]

诉讼任何一方在判决后 15 天内提出上诉请求（如有）；

[401]See Art. 145 of *CPL 1991(as amended in 2023).*

参见 1991 年《中华人民共和国民事诉讼法》（2023 年修订）第 145 条。

[402]See Art. 152 of *CPL (as amended in 2023).*

见 1991 年《中华人民共和国民事诉讼法》（2023 年修订）第 152 条。

[403]See Art. 171of *CPL 1991(as amended in 2023).*

参见 1991 年《中华人民共和国民事诉讼法》（2023 年修订）第 171 条。

Figure 11: Civil Litigation Steps Pursuant to CPL 1991 in People's Republic of China (PRC) (as amended in 2023)

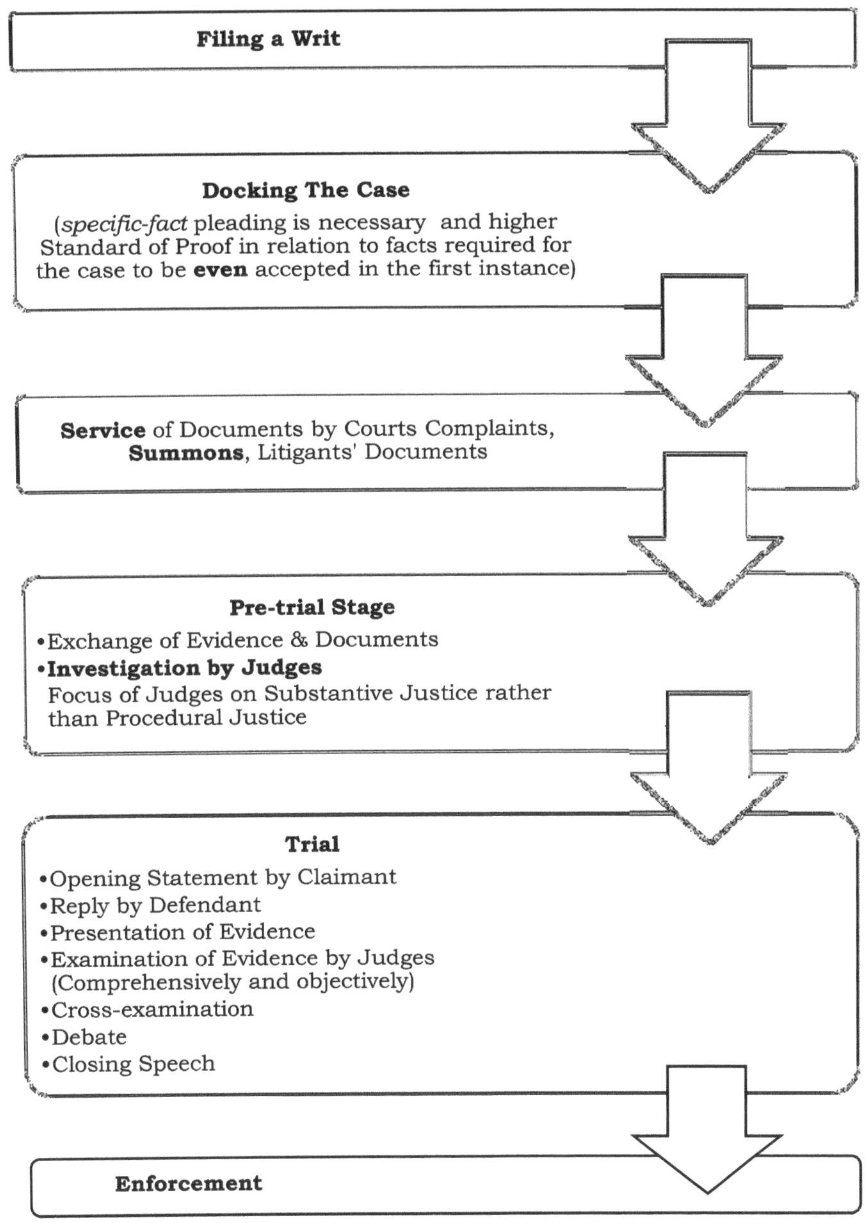

图11：中华人民共和国根据CPL1991(2023年修订）进行民事诉讼的步骤

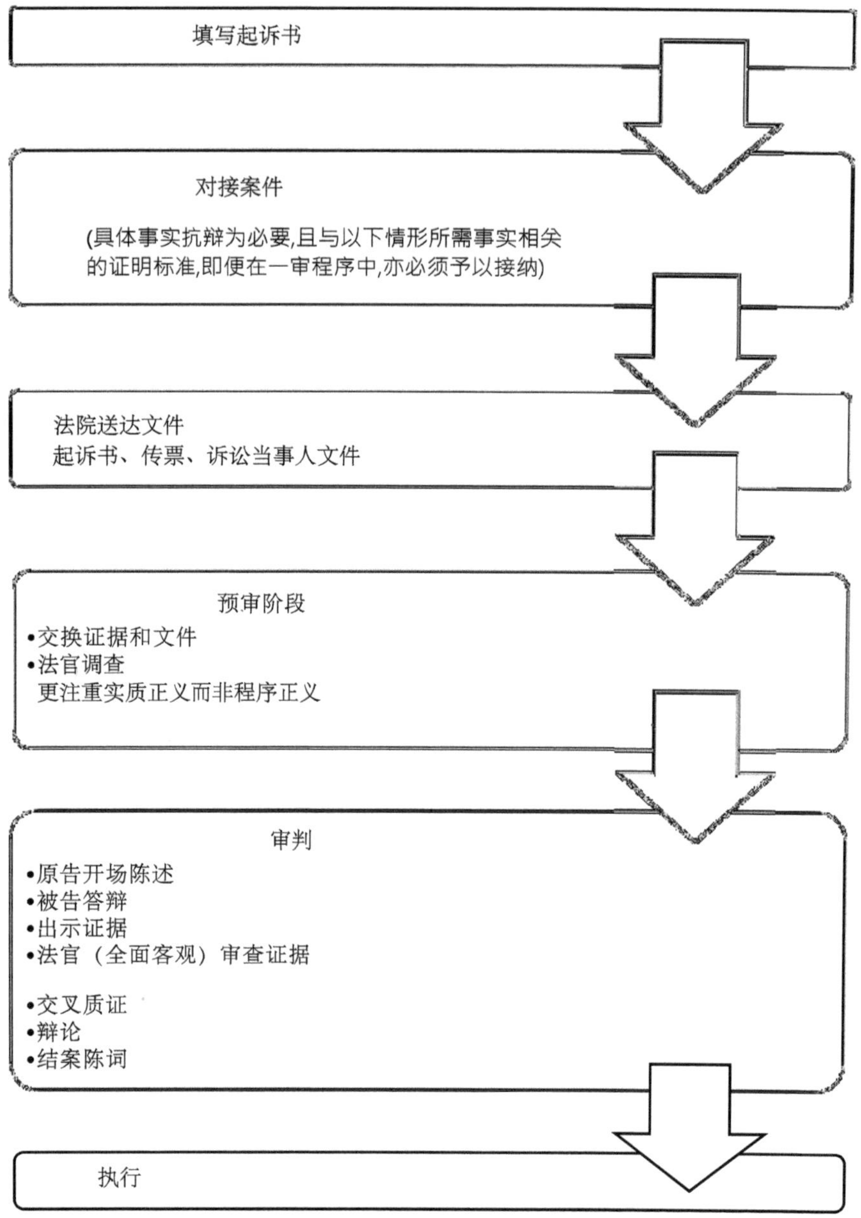

4.2 Legal Philosophy of Civil Litigation Influencing the Judges

影响法官的民事诉讼法律理念

The authors have discussed earlier in this book that the civil litigation system is an alternative to the self-help system that often led to violence in the past.[404] However, participation in civil litigation is also voluntary, which means parties are not compelled to come to the legal system to seek help to resolve their dispute. Civil Litigation has a close relationship with the substantive law in any legal system but has also developed many principles independently of the substantive law.[405]

作者在本书前文已经论述过，民事诉讼制度是过去经常导致暴力的自助制度的替代制度 然而，参与民事诉讼也是自愿的，这意味着当事人不会被迫来到法律体系寻求帮助以解决纠纷。在任何法律体系中，民事诉讼都与实体法有着密切的关系，但也形成了许多独立于实体法的原则。

Civil Litigation serves a public purpose even though private disputes are resolved through it. Many third parties such as family of an injured person, and/or local or central government, and/or other stakeholders in commercial disputes and so forth have stakes in such litigation in courts. In most jurisdictions it is not a dispute resolution center that is fully publicly funded. However, civil litigation definitely has a public purpose, as stated by the Chief Justice of New South Wales, Australia, another common law jurisdiction similar to England & Wales:

尽管通过民事诉讼可以解决私人纠纷，但民事诉讼仍具有公共目的。许多第三方，如伤者家属、和/或地方或中央政府、和/或商业纠纷中的其他利益相关者等，都与法院的此类诉讼有利害关系。在大多数司法管辖区，法院并不是一个完全由政府资助的纠纷解决中心。然而，正如澳大利亚新南威尔士州（另一个与英格兰和威尔士相似的普通法司法管辖区）首席法官所言，民事诉讼肯定具有公共目的：

The enforcement of legal rights and obligations, the articulation and development of the law, the resolution of private disputes by a public affirmation of who is right and who is wrong, the denunciation of conduct in both criminal and civil trials, the deterrence of conduct by public process with public outcomes — these are all public purposes served by the courts, [emphasis added] even in the resolution of private disputes. An economist might call them 'externalities'. They constitute, collectively, a

法律权利和义务的执行、法律的阐述和发展、通过公开确认谁是谁非来解决私人纠纷、在刑事和民事审判中谴责行为、通过结果公开的公共程序威慑行为--这些都是法院的公共目的，[着重部分由作者标明]即使在解决私人纠纷时也是如此。经济学家可以称之为 "外部因素"。

[404] Refer, Chapter 2, §2.1.2, Origins of English Procedural System.
参见第 2 章第 2.1.2 节，英国程序制度的起源。
[405] Refer, Chapter 2, §2.4, Comparative Relationship between Substantive & Procedural Law.
参见第 2 章第 2.4 节，实体法与程序法之间的比较关系。

core function of government.[406]

Habscheid also said:

哈布舍伊德还说：

Since the state embodies the social system, procedural law reflects the ethical, ideological and political ideas which characterise a society. In consequence, the law of civil procedure must not be considered in isolation, but rather as an integral part of the ideas and conceptions which are expressed in the constitutional order.[407]

由于国家体现了社会制度，程序法反映了作为社会特征的伦理、意识形态和政治观念。因此，不能孤立地看待民事诉讼法，而应将其视为宪法秩序所表达的思想和观念的组成部分。

Therefore, when anyone studies any issue in civil litigation, every aspect of the legal system, its jurisprudence, associated political thoughts, its stage of economic development and so on must be analysed. Civil procedure systems have been divided into two major types in the comparative studies –Romano-Germanic & Anglo-Saxon systems (together called *systemes liberaux*), and socialist systems.[408]

因此，任何人在研究民事诉讼中的任何问题时，都必须对法律制度、法理、相关政治思想、经济发展阶段等各个方面进行分析 。在比较研究中，民事诉讼制度被分为两大类--罗马-日耳曼和盎格鲁-撒克逊制度（合称自由制度）以及社会主义制度。

In socialist systems of civil procedure systems, an individual that is a subject of litigation is a member of a society and of a class. Therefore, all legal philosophy will rotate around this concept. This has a considerable bearing on the role of the courts and their approach during litigation in courts. An inquisitorial regime is common in socialist systems. In western legal systems, the concept of procedural rights is inherent in an individual and not conferred on the litigant; this is an important distinction from socialist systems.[409] As a result, the legal philosophy in western systems, even in civil systems such as in Germany, is more in tune with the adversarial concept (*principe de contradiction*), and there is no room for outside third-party

在社会主义民事诉讼制度中，作为诉讼主体的个人是社会和阶级的成员。因此所有的法律哲学都将围绕这一概念展开。这对法院的作用及法院在诉讼过程中的做法有相当大影响。纠问式制度在社会主义制度中很常见。在西方法律制度中，诉讼权利的概念是个人固有的，而不是赋予诉讼当事人的；这是与社会主义制度的一个重要区别。因此西方制度中的法律理念，即使是在德国这样的民事制度中，也更符合对抗制概念（矛盾原则），没有外部第三方干预的余地，也没有

[406] J. Spigelman, “Judicial Accountability and Performance Indicators,” *Civil Justice Quarterly* 21 (2002): 26. www.http://ssrn.com /abstract=1802176 as J. A. Jolowicz, “Civil Litigation: What is It For?” in *The Civil Procedure Ten Years On*, ed. Deirdre Dwyer (Oxford: Oxford University Press, 2009), 60.

[407]WJ Habscheid, “The Fundamental Principles of the Law of Civil Procedure,” *Comp. & Int’l L.J. S. Afr.* 17, no. 1 (1984): 2. www.jstor.org/stable/23246919.

[408]Habscheid, “Fundamental Principles of Civil Procedure,” 2. Habscheid has clearly distinguished the civil litigation process in western liberal democracies from socialist systems.

Habscheid, "Fundamental Principles of Civil Procedure," 2。Habscheid 将西方自由民主国家的民事诉讼程序与社会主义制度的民事诉讼程序作了明确区分。

[409]Habscheid, “Fundamental Principles of Civil Procedure,” 3.

interference,[410] or any retrial without the request of the litigants.

任何未经诉讼当事人请求的重审。

It is important to appreciate from the start what is considered as a matter that can be considered as 'civil' and can be brought to the civil courts. In England & Wales, anything that is not governed by the criminal law is a civil matter and civil procedure rules will apply.[411] On the other hand in most continental countries, the deciding factor is the difference between private and public law.[412]

重要的是要从一开始就了解什么是可被视为 "民事 "并可提交民事法庭的事项。在英格兰和威尔士，不受刑法管辖的任何事项都属于民事事项，适用民事诉讼规则。 另一方面，在大多数大陆国家，决定因素是私法和公法之间的区别。

Legal philosophy of the civil courts has been influenced by political thought such as the *Seventh Amendment to the US Constitution 1792* that allows for the litigant's right to jury trial, or codification of principles in continental civil procedures,[413] International conventions such as Article 6 of *European Court of Human Rights 1998*, c 42 that provides for the right to a fair and public hearing, and, similarly, Article 14(1) of the *International Convention on Civil and Political rights of the United Nations 1966*.[414]

民事法庭的法律理念受到政治思想的影响，如 1792 年《美国宪法》第七修正案允许诉讼当事人享有陪审团审判的权利，或大陆民事诉讼程序原则的编纂， 国际公约，如 1998 年欧洲人权法院第 6 条第 42 款规定了公平和公开审理的权利，以及类似的 1966 年联合国《公民权利和政治权利国际公约》第 14(1)条。

4.2.1 Legal Philosophy of English Civil Courts

英国民事法院的法律理念

It is often said in the English courts that the best judge to resolve the matter is an 'uninformed judge'. This means that the judge's decision is based entirely on the pleadings, evidence and

英国法院常说，解决问题的最佳法官是"不知情的法官"。这意味着法官的裁决完全基于诉状、证据和诉

410Ibid., 3–4.
同上，3-4 页。
411See dicta of Lord Goff in *Re State of Norway's Application (Nos 1 and 2) [1991]* 1 AC 723, where he clarified that all commercial matters can be considered as part of proceedings in civil matters. See also, *Evidence (Proceedings in other Jurisdictions) Act 1975*, c 34.
見 Goff 勳爵在 Re State of Norway's Application (Nos 1 and 2) [1991] 1 AC 723 一案中的判詞，他在該案中澄清，所有商業事宜均可視為民事訴訟程序的一部分。另见 1975 年证据（其他司法管辖区的诉讼）法，c 34。
412C.H.Van Rhee and R. Verkerk, "Civil Procedure," in *Elgar Encyclopedia of Comparative Law*, ed. J.M. Smits (Cheltenham: Edward Elgar Publishing, 2006), 120.
413See Principes Directeurs du proces in the first Chapter of *French Code of Civil Procedure 2007*.
参见 2007 年《法国民事诉讼法》第一章中的 "程序指导原则"。
414Rhee and Verkerk, "Civil Procedure," 4–5.
Rhee 和 Verkerk，"民事诉讼程序"，4-5。

arguments by the litigants or parties. It is common knowledge that pleadings are based on issues as decided by the parties themselves, which are formulated into those pleadings and presented to the civil courts. It means that the court's role (or judge's role in the common law system) is not to find the truth, but to decide upon the basis of what is in front of him, that is, pleadings, evidence and arguments.

讼当事人或当事方的论点。众所周知，诉状是基于当事人自己决定的问题，这些问题被写入诉状并提交给民事法庭。这意味着法院的作用（或普通法体系中法官的作用）不是查明真相，而是根据他面前的东西，即书状、证据和论据作出裁决。

In the case of *Air Canada v Secretary of State for Trade (No 2)*[415], where an International airline had a dispute with the Secretary of State for Trade that concerned landing charges at Heathrow Airport in London, the case went all the way up to the House of Lords. A few other airlines also decided to be included as the parties in the same case. This very interesting case came before the High Court; Bingham J at the High Court, in order to find the truth, wanted to see particular documents that were with the defendants. The claimants (airlines) could not state with certainty whether such disclosure would be useful or would damage their case. The Court of Appeal and House of Lords disagreed with Bingham J. on important facets of jurisprudential issues on which the English civil procedure is founded.

在加拿大航空公司诉贸易大臣案（第 2 号）中，一家国际航空公司与贸易大臣就伦敦希思罗机场的着陆费发生争议，案件一直闹到上议院。其他几家航空公司也决定将其列为同一案件的当事方。高等法院的宾汉姆法官为了查明真相，要求查看被告持有的特定文件。原告（航空公司）无法确定披露这些文件是有用还是会损害他们的案件。上诉法院和上议院在英国民事诉讼程序所依据的法理学问题的重要方面与宾汉姆法官意见不一。

Two statements from the House of Lords, need to be analysed deeply in order to understand the jurisprudential issue. Lord Edmund Davies bluntly said:

我们需要对上议院的两个声明进行深入分析，以了解法理问题。埃德蒙-戴维斯勋爵直言不讳地说：

to urge that, on principle, justice is most likely to be done if free access is had to all relevant documents is pointless, for it carries no weight in our adversarial system of law [emphasis added].[416]

原则上，如能够自由查阅所有相关文件，正义就最有可能得到伸张，但这种主张毫无意义，因为它在我们的对抗制法律体系中没有任何分量[着重部分由作者标明]。

Lord Wilberforce explained the jurisprudential position or English law in the same case as follows:

威尔伯福斯勋爵在同一案件中对英国法律的判例立场作了如下解释：

Yet if the decision has been in accordance with the available evidence and with the law, justice will have been fairly done. It

然而，如果裁决符合现有证据和法律，那么正义就得到了公正的伸张。

[415] 2 AC 394 (HL).
[416] Ibid., 441 (Lord Edmund Davies).
同上，441（埃德蒙-戴维斯勋爵）。

is in aid of justice in this sense that discovery may be ordered, and it is so ordered upon the application of one of the parties who must make out his case for it. If he is not able to do so, that is the end of the matter. There is no independent power in the court to say that, nevertheless, it would like to inspect the documents with a view to possible production for its own assistance [emphasis added].[417]

从这个意义上讲，正是为了维护正义，才可以下令进行证据开示，而且是在一方当事人提出申请的情况下下令进行开示的。如果他不能这样做，事情也就到此为止了。法院没有独立的权力说，尽管如此，它还是希望检查文件，以便在可能的情况下出示文件，为自己提供帮助[着重部分作者标明]。

However, within the community of judges in England & Wales, this analysis is controversial. The argued that no party would ever come to the courts if the judges' role were not to find the truth of matter using procedures. Sir John Donaldson MR argued this point vehemently:

然而，在英格兰和威尔士的法官群体中，这一分析是有争议的。其认为如果法官职责不是利用程序查明事实真相，就不会有当事人来到法院。唐纳森爵士激烈地争辩了这一点：

Litigation is not a war or even a game. It is designed to do real justice between opposing parties and if the court does not have *all* the relevant information [emphasis added and italics in original], it cannot achieve this object.[418]

诉讼不是战争，甚至不是游戏。诉讼的目的是在对立双方之间实现真正的公正，如果法院不掌握*所有*相关信息[着重部分由作者标明，斜体为原文所加]，就无法实现这一目标。

Another judge, Denning LJ, in the High Court said the judges' objective in the courts is "above all to find out the truth [emphasis added] and to do justice according to law."[419] However, with the advent of the new *CPR 1998*, relatively more written evidence is now available to the judges; the old idea of the uninformed judge has slowly been replaced by judges who have a wealth of information, well in advance of a civil trial. Therefore, the old issues that existed pre-*CPR 1998* do not exist anymore with new *CPR 1998* and its case management principles.

另一位法官丹宁在高等法院说，法官在法庭上的目标"首先是查明真相[着重号后加]并依法伸张正义"。然而，随着 1998 年新《民事诉讼程序法》的出台，法官现在可以获得相对较多的书面证据；过去那种不了解情况的法官的观念已慢慢被在民事审判之前就掌握大量信息的法官所取代。因此，随着新的《1998 年民事诉讼程序法》及其案件管理原则的出台，之前存在的老问题已不复存在。

Old issues which are no longer relevant with the new *CPR 1998* are: a) whether judges in the English courts should adjourn the

《1998 年民事诉讼程序法》已不再适用的老问题是：a) 英国法院的法官是否应将案件审理延期以寻求更

---

[417]Ibid., 438 (Lord Wilberforce)。同上，第 438 页（威尔伯福斯勋爵）。

[418]See *Davies v Eli Lilly & Co* [1987] 1 WLR 428,431(Sir John Donaldson MR)。见 Davies 诉 Eli Lilly & Co [1987] 1 WLR 428、431（约翰-唐纳森爵士）。

[419]See *Jones v National Coal Board [1957]* 2 QB 55, 63 (Denning LJ)。见 Jones 诉国家煤炭委员会 [1957] 2 QB 55、63（Denning LJ）。

case hearing for more evidence, or b) whether, according to jurisprudence, in principle, the judges really have power to adjourn the hearing to seek more evidence, or c) whether it is too late for the judges to adjourn due to the need for additional evidence in the middle of the hearing.[420]

多证据，或 b) 根据法理，原则上法官是否真的有权将审理延期以寻求更多证据，或 c) 法官在审理中途因需要更多证据而延期是否为时已晚。

Therefore, the question that could be asked by the authors are whether, in the English procedural law, the English judges are under an obligation to find the truth in any case before him and whether this standpoint in English jurisprudence has finally arrived on the lines of continental civil law traditions? Jolowicz,[421] in order to answer this question, compared English civil procedure with French jurisprudence as a result of an amendment to the then-existing French civil procedural system in 1972 that provided:

因此，笔者可以提出的问题是，在英国诉讼法中，英国法官是否有义务在其审理的任何案件中查明真相，英国判例中的这一观点是否最终与大陆民法传统接轨？为了回答这个问题，约洛维茨将英国的民事诉讼程序与法国的判例进行了比较，因为 1972 年对当时存在的法国民事诉讼制度进行了修订，规定：

Everyone is bound to co-operate with the administration of justice with a view to revelation of truth.[422]

每个人都有义务配合司法工作，以揭示真相。

According to Jolowicz, the position in the English civil procedure is still different from the French law, and the case of *Air Canada* still retains jurisprudential authority in the courts. The main principle that still remains is in relation to the resolution of disputes, as emphasized in Sir Peter Middleton's report:

约洛维茨认为，英国民事诉讼程序的立场仍然不同于法国法律，加拿大航空公司案在法院仍然具有判例权威。正如彼得-米德尔顿爵士的报告所强调的那样，主要原则仍然与解决争端有关：

Justice — by which I mean the satisfactory resolution of disputes — is part of the service sector of the economy.[423]

司法—我指的是令人满意地解决争端—是经济服务部门的一部分。

In order to understand the application and practice before the courts, the administrative purpose of civil procedure needs to be analysed closely. According to Lord Woolf, it is important to note that the goal of the civil procedure system is to ensure that

为理解法院的适用和实践，需仔细分析民事诉讼程序的行政目的。伍尔夫勋爵认为，需要注意的是，民事诉讼制度的目标是确保通过过滤的案

[420]J. A. Jolowicz, "Civil Litigation - Purpose?" 56。 J.A. 约洛维茨，"民事诉讼--目的？"第 56 页。
[421]J.A. Jolowicz, "Civil Litigation: What is it For?" *Camb. L.J.* 67, no. 3 (2008): 56–58.
J.A. 约洛维茨，"民事诉讼：What is it For?" Camb.Camb.L.J. 67, no.3 (2008):56-58.
[422]See *Code de procedure civile 1806*, art 11, al 1.
见《1806 年民事诉讼法》第 11 条第 1 款。
[423]Peter Middleton, *Review of Civil Justice and Legal Aid*, Report to the Lord Chancellor (London: Lord Chancellor's Department, 1997), Chapter 1.

fewer cases should pass through the filter, so that full-fledged civil trials can be avoided in most cases; he said, "My approach to civil justice is that disputes should, whenever possible, be resolved without litigation."[424] However, Fiss puts forward a dissenting opinion from across the Atlantic, which is very much against the policy of encouraging settlement:

件数量减少，从而在大多数情况下避免全面的民事审判；他说“我对民事司法的态度是，只要有可能，纠纷就应该在没有诉讼的情况下得到解决。”然而菲斯从大西洋彼岸提出了不同意见，他非常反对鼓励和解的政策：

[T]hat settlement as generic practice is preferable to judgment… should be treated instead as a highly problematic technique for streamlining dockets.... Like plea bargaining, settlement is a capitulation to the conditions of mass society and should be neither encouraged nor praised.[425]

和解作为通用做法比判决更可取......应被视为简化诉讼程序的一种极有问题的技术.....。与辩诉交易一样，和解是对大众社会条件的屈服，既不应鼓励也不应赞扬。

The authors' view is that Fiss's statement, though true from the point of view of jurisprudence of a pure adversarial process, does not take into account the administrative burden that is required to manage the huge case load of such civil disputes at the executive level of any state. At times, the clients' objectives are in fact fulfilled by mechanisms available at the courts that ensure settlements, rather than encouraging the parties to be adversarial and request civil trials at the courts.

笔者认为，菲斯的说法虽从纯对抗程序的法理角度来看是正确的，但没有考虑到任何国家的行政部门在管理此类民事纠纷的大量案件时所需要的行政负担。有时，当事人的目标实际上是通过法院现有的确保和解的机制来实现的，而不是鼓励当事人采取对抗的方式，要求法院进行民事审判。

With the advent of new *CPR 1998*, the case management powers of the courts have been considerably increased; it is the authors' view that it is no longer the case of the 'uninformed judge' in civil law cases. If the powers that are available to the courts are used effectively by the judges, then it will be the case of very informed judge.

随着新的《1998 年民事诉讼程序法》的出台，法院的案件管理权限大大增加；笔者认为，在民法案件中不再存在 "法官不知情 "的情况。如果法官能够有效地利用法院所拥有的权力，那么就会成为非常知情的法官。

A number of legal philosophers, then, argue not only that the fairness of the process is desirable, but also that the civil process should ensure that the decisions are arrived at by the courts after using all tools available to the judges, pursuant to civil procedural code. These include tools available to the judges to

因此，一些法律哲学家认为，不仅程序的公正性是可取的，而且民事诉讼程序应确保法院在根据民事诉讼法使用法官可用的所有工具后做出裁决。这些工具包括法官可用来查明争

[424] Lord Woolf, *Access to Justice: Final Report to the Lord Chancellor on the Civil Justice System in England and Wales* (London: HMSO, 1996), 107. This Report was discussed in J. A. Jolowicz, "Civil Litigation - Purpose?" 58.
Lord Woolf, Access to Justice：Woolf 勋爵，《诉诸司法：向大法官提交的关于英格兰和威尔士民事司法系统的最终报告》（伦敦：HMSO，1996 年），第 107 页。J. A. Jolowicz, "Civil Litigation - Purpose?" 一文对该报告进行了讨论。58.

[425] Owen M. Fiss, "'Against Settlement'," *Yale L.J.* 93, no. 6 (1984): 1073–92.
Owen M. Fiss，"'反对和解'"，《耶鲁法学》第 93 卷第 6 期（1984 年）：1073-92.

find the truth in disputes. Therefore, in this context, it is argued by the scholars that judgments should not be confused with settlements or amicable solutions reached through Alternative Dispute Resolution mechanisms.

端真相的工具。因此，在此背景下，学者们认为判决不应与通过替代性争议解决机制达成的和解或友好解决方案相混淆。

Judges should no longer rely only on the *Statements of the parties*;[426] and further, no judges should believe that such statements of parties are gospel truth in the context of the cases put forward by them. Without any doubt, in any litigation, one of the parties must be saying the truth or must be relying on the result of *cross-examination*.[427] Jolowicz discussed Wigmore's statement[428] that cross-examination is the greatest ever legal engine invented for the discovery of truth, from which various inferences could be drawn.

法官不应再仅仅依赖当事人的陈述；此外，没有法官应当认为，在当事人所提出的案件情境中，他们的此类陈述就是绝对真理。毫无疑问，在任何诉讼中，必有一方当事人所述为真，或者必须依靠交叉询问的结果。乔洛维茨探讨了威格莫尔的观点，即交叉询问是有史以来为发现真相而发明的最伟大的法律工具，由此可以得出各种推论。

In the authors' experience, no matter how competent and skillful a lawyer is when cross-examining a witness, there are seldom any witnesses who will readily agree that they have breached a contract or have been a participant in conduct that could be penalized in the law. Ultimately, the result will be based on inferences, guesswork and speculation. However, it is the authors' view that the new case management powers under the new *CPR 1998* have given ample ammunition to the judges to at least try to find the truth, while maintaining the adversarial nature of litigation in English courts.

根笔者的经验，无论律师在盘问证人时多么称职，技巧多么娴熟，都很少有证人会轻易承认自己违反了合同或参与了可能受到法律制裁的行为。最终的结果将建立在推论、猜测和推测的基础上。然而，笔者认为新《1998 年民事诉讼程序法》所规定的新的案件管理权力为法官提供了充足的弹药，使他们至少可以尝试查明真相，同时保持英国法院诉讼的对抗性。

---

[426]See *Ex p Lloyd (1822) Mont 70*, where Lord Eldon was reported to have said '[T]ruth is best discovered by powerful statements on both sides of the questions.'
见 Ex p Lloyd (1822) Mont 70，据报道，埃尔登勋爵曾说过 "对问题正反两面的有力陈述最能发现真理。

[427]John Henry Wigmore, *A Treatise on the Anglo-American System of Evidence in Trials at Common Law - V3* (Whitefish: Literary Licensing, 2012), 1367.
约翰-亨利-维格摩尔，《英美普通法审判证据制度论》-V3（白鱼：文学许可，2012 年），第 1367 页。

[428]J.A. Jolowicz, "Civil Litigation," 508. Jolowicz discussed Wigmore in context of cross-examination.
J.A. Jolowicz，"民事诉讼"，508。Jolowicz 从盘问的角度讨论 Wigmore 一案。

4.2.1.1 Overriding Objectives and Secondary objectives of English Civil Procedural Code《英国民事诉讼法》的首要目标和次要目标

It is important to introduce and highlight in full the first rule, *CPR 1998* r. 1.1 that provides as follows:

有必要介绍并强调第一条规则，即 1998年《民事诉讼规则》第1.1 条，其规定如下：

(1) These Rules are a new procedural code with the **overriding objective** [emphasis added] of enabling the court to deal with cases justly and at proportionate cost.

(1) 本《规则》是一部新的程序法典，其**首要目标**[黑体后加]是使法院能够公正地处理案件，并以相称的成本处理案件。

(2) Dealing with a <u>case justly and at proportionate cost</u> [emphasis added] includes, so far as is practicable –

(2) 在切实可行的范围内，<u>以公正和费用相称的方式</u>处理案件[着重部分由 作者标明]，包括

(a) ensuring that the parties are on an equal footing;

(a) 确保各方地位平等；

(b) saving expense;

(b) 节约开支；

(c) dealing with the case in ways which are proportionate –

(c) 以相称的方式处理案件

(i) to the amount of money involved;
(ii) to the importance of the case;
(iii) to the complexity of the issues; and
(iv) to the financial position of each party;

(i) 所涉金额；
(ii) 案件的重要性；
(iii) 问题的复杂性；以及
(iv) 各方的财务状况；

(d) ensuring that it is dealt with expeditiously and fairly;

(d) 确保问题得到迅速、公正处理；

(e) allotting to it an appropriate share of the court's resources, while taking into account the need to allot resources to other cases; and

(e) 虑及需将资源分配给其他案件的情况下，将法院资源的适当份额分配给该案；以及

(f) enforcing compliance with rules, practice directions and orders.

(f) 规则、程序指示和命令强制遵守。

The *CPR 1998* r. 1.1(1) is referred to as the *primary* objectives of *CPR 1998*, while *CPR 1998* r. 1.1(2) is referred to as the *secondary* objectives of Civil Procedure Rules of England &Wales.

1998 年《民事诉讼规则》第 1.1(1)条被称为其首要目标，而《1998 年民事诉讼程序规则》第 1.1(2)条被称为《英格兰及威尔士民事诉讼程序规则》的次要目标。

The most important terminology from *CPR 1998* r. 1.1(1) are the words as '*overriding objective*'. The meaning of the word 'overriding', according to the Oxford English Dictionary, is 'able to overtake or supersede another authority, or taking precedence over all other subjects, or considerations, or predominant and primary'. In many legislations, before the advent of the new *CPR 1998*, the concepts of a few statutes having an 'overriding' effect was only understood by legal stakeholders.[429]

1998 年《民事诉讼规则》第 1.1 (1) 条中最重要的术语是"首要目标"一词。据《牛津英语词典》，"overriding"一词含义是"能超越或取代另一权威，或在所有其他事项、考量因素中占据优先地位，或者具有主导性和首要性"。在 1998 年新《民事诉讼规则》出台之前，在许多立法中，只有法律相关利益方才能理解少数具有 "优先" 效力的法规概念。

However, the moot question that is asked by legal scholars has been whether this overriding objective can trump anything else. To answer this question, the evolution of the new *CPR 1998*, a part of which was discussed in Chapter 2 of this book, needs to be discussed in detail.[430] However, from the jurisprudential point of view, it is important to trace the arguments in legal philosophy leading up to the new civil procedural code. In the various Lord Woolf Reform Reports, different meanings were

然而，法律学者提出的一个悬而未决的问题是，这一首要目标是否可以压倒其他任何目标。要回答这个问题，需详细讨论 1998 年新《民事诉讼规则》的演变过程，本书第 2 章讨论了其中一部分。不过从法理学角度来看，有必要追溯一下新民诉法出台前的法律哲学争论。《伍尔夫勋爵改革报告》中，"首要目标"这一概念被赋

[429]A few examples such as s 70(1)(g) *Land Registration Act 1925 (repealed)* c 21 ,15 and 16 Geo 5, whereby certain interests in registered land can override the entry on the register & s 1 *(repealed)* of the *Employment Act 1989*, c 19, which can have similar effects. Even within the new *Civil Procedural Rules r. 35.3* titled 'experts', an expert has an overriding duty to the court, where the expert's duty to court will override any duty even to his own client, who has appointed the expert; s 42 of *Access to Justice Act 1999*, c 22, where advocates have duties to act with complete independence in court when exercising rights of audience were also discussed in Deirdre Dwyer, "What is the Meaning of CPR r 1.1(1)," in *The Civil Procedure Rules Ten Years On*, Deirdre Dwyer (Oxford: Oxford University Press, 2009), 72.
有几个例子，如 1925 年《土地注册法》（已废除）c 21、15 和 16 Geo 5 第 70(1)(g)条，根据该条，注册土地中的某些权益可以优先于注册簿上的条目；1989 年《就业法》c 19 第 1 条（已废除）也有类似的效力。即使在题为 "专家 "的新《民事诉讼程序规则》第 35.3 条中，专家也对法院负有优先责任，专家对法院的责任甚至高于对其委托人（委托人已指定专家）的任何责任；《1999 年诉诸司法法》第 22 卷第 42 条规定，辩护人在行使出庭权时有责任在法庭上完全独立行事，Deirdre Dwyer 的 "What is the Meaning of CPR r 1.1(1)," in The Civil Procedure Rules Ten Years On, Deirdre Dwyer (Oxford: Oxford University Press, 2009), 72.
[430]Refer, Chapter 2, §2.1.2, where the origins of New English Procedure Code were discussed in detail.
参见第 2 章第 2.1.2 节，其中详细讨论了《新英语诉讼法》的起源。

provided for this concept of '*overriding objective*'. In the *Interim Report*,[431] the overriding objective was itself called '*general objective*', and even in the *Final Report*,[432] leading up the Civil Procedure Code, it came under the heading of '*overall objective*'.

予了不同含义。在《中期报告》中，"首要目标"本身被称为"一般目标"，甚至在《最后报告》中，"首要目标"也被置于"总体目标"标题之下，从而导致《民事诉讼法》的出台。

Therefore, while it seems that the judges and the courts could utilize the concept of overriding objective to trump other rules, in fact, the meaning of the concept of 'overriding objective' is in fact much broader. This concept of overriding objective encompasses the concept that lawyers and judges should also keep the overriding objectives in mind when analysing the other rules of new *CPR 1998*.

因此，尽管表面上法官和法院似乎可以利用 "首要目标" 这一概念凌驾于其他规则之上，但实际上，"首要目标" 概念的含义要宽泛得多。这一 "首要目标" 概念涵盖了这样一层意思：律师和法官在分析 1998 年新《民事诉讼规则》的其他规则时，也应将首要目标牢记于心。

It was further stated, that the judges should not rely on the cases concerning civil procedure as a matter of precedence, but instead should use these cases to ensure that there is consistency in application of the new Civil Procedure Code.[433] This is known as the *purposive approach* and even Lord Woolf's Final Report, which was prepared before the Civil Procedural Rules came into existence, seems to be suggest that this is the best approach. In the Report, the idea of '*purposive construction*'[434] was highlighted:

报告进一步指出，法官不应将有关民事诉讼程序的案例作为先例，而应利用这些案例来确保新的《民事诉讼法》在适用上的一致性，这就是所谓的 "*目的性方法*"，甚至伍尔夫勋爵在《民事诉讼程序规则》出台之前编写的《最后报告》似乎也认为这是最好的方法。在该报告中，"有目的解释"的观点得到了强调：

Although the rules can offer detailed directions for the technical steps to be taken, the effectiveness of those steps depends upon the spirit in which they are carried out. That in turn depends on an understanding of the fundamental purpose of the rules and of the underlying system of procedure... Rule 1 ... provides a compass to guide courts and litigants and legal advisers as to

虽然规则可以为所要采取的技术步骤提供详细的指示，但这些步骤的有效性取决于执行这些步骤的精神。而这又取决于对规则的基本宗旨和基本程序制度的理解....。规则第 1 条...提供了一个指南针，为法院、诉讼当

431 Lord Woolf, *Acss t o Justice: Interim Report to the Lord Chancellor on the Civil Justice System in England and Wales* (London: HMSO, 1995).
伍尔夫勋爵，《诉诸司法》：向大法官提交的关于英格兰和威尔士民事司法系统的中期报告（伦敦：HMSO，1995 年）。

432 Lord Woolf, *Access to Justice: Final Report to the Lord Chancellor on the Civil Justice System in England and Wales.*
伍尔夫勋爵，《诉诸司法》：伍尔夫勋爵，《诉诸司法：向大法官提交的关于英格兰和威尔士民事司法系统的最终报告》。

433 Dwyer, "Overriding Objective," 73.

434 Refer Chapter 3, §3.1.1.4, where scholars of Legal Realism school of thought pursuant to which there was a demand for purposive construction during judicial activities.
参见第 3 章第 3.1.1.4 节，法律现实主义学派的学者认为，司法活动中需要进行目的性解释

their general course.[435]

事人和法律顾问提供了一般指导。

However, in a case,[436] where the default judgment was given against a party that was not the correct defendant and subsequently the civil court justified this decision on the basis that it could not be set aside due to the operation of the concept of overriding objective to prevent escalating costs. The judge in this case was not willing to allow the procedural errors to be corrected. This justification by the civil court was severely criticised by lawyers, academics and judges. Even a few other jurisdictions that usually follow the English courts also rejected the overriding approach of the English courts in this particular case; for example, Hong Kong (part of the PRC but operating under the banner of 'one country two systems') had similar concerns about such a powerful tool being put in the hands of inexperienced judges.[437]

然而，某案中缺席判决是针对并非正确被告一方做出的，随后民事法庭为这一判决辩解，理由是由于防止诉讼费用攀升的首要目标这一概念的实施该判决不能被撤销。本案法官不愿意让程序错误得到纠正。民事法庭的这一理由受到了律师、学者和法官的严厉批评。甚至一些通常追随英国法院的其他司法管辖区也拒绝接受英国法院在这一特定案件中的凌驾性做法；例如，香港（中华人民共和国的一部分，但在"一国两制"的旗帜下运作）对于将如此强大的工具交到缺乏经验的法官手中也有类似的担忧。

In the authors' view, the fact that the authorities gave such a powerful tool to English judges means that they believe in their competence and training, and in fact empowered them by doing so. This can be contrasted with the PRC system where, far from empowering judges, there is a supervision system to keep an eye on judges, in the form of the Procuratorate System

.

笔者认为当局为英国法官提供如此强大的工具，意味着他们相信法官的能力和训练，并通过这样做事实上赋予了他们权力。这一点可与中国的制度形成对比，在中国不但没有赋予法官权力，反而有一个以检察院制度为形式的监督制度对法官进行监督。

It is important to note that there are jurisdictions such as the US, where a similar purposive approach was used in their own *Federal Rules of Civil Procedure 1938*;[438] later, a similar

值得注意的是，在美国等司法管辖区，1938 年的《联邦民事诉讼规则》也采用了类似的目的解释法；之后，

---

[435]Lord Woolf, *Access to Justice: Final Report to the Lord Chancellor on the Civil Justice System in England and Wales*, n2 [20.10]. Quoted in Dwyer, "Overriding Objective," 70.
伍尔夫勋爵，《诉诸司法：向大法官提交的关于英格兰和威尔士民事司法系统的最后报告，n2 [20.10]。引自 Dwyer，"首要目标"，第 70 页。

[436]See *Law v St Margarets Insurance Ltd [2001] EWCA Civ 30, 18 January 2001.*
见 Law 诉 St Margarets Insurance Ltd [2001] EWCA Civ 30，2001 年 1 月 18 日。

[437]Civil Justice Reform (Hong Kong), *Final Report of the Working Party on Civil Justice Reform* (Hong Kong, 2004). http://www.civiljustice.gov.hk/eng/archives_fr.html> as cited in Dwyer, "Overriding Objective," 71.
民事司法制度改革（香港），《民事司法制度改革工作小组最后报告》（香港 2004 年）。http://www.civiljustice.gov.hk/eng/archives_fr.html> 转引自 Dwyer，"首要目标"，71。

[438]See *r.* 1 of *Federal Rules of Civil Procedure 1938 (US)* provides that "These rules govern the procedure in all civil actions and proceedings in the United States district courts...They should be construed and administered to secure the just, speedy, and inexpensive determination of every action and proceeding." See also, s 2 of *Supreme Court Rules 1987 (Australia)* that was superseded by *Supreme Court Civil Rules 2006.* See also, Dwyer, "Overriding Objective," 70.

approach was followed in South Australia via section 2 of the Supreme Court Rules 1987. In fact, they were the pioneers in the purposive approach to the interpretation of the civil procedure rules. However, it is important to note that civil law jurisdictions such as the *German Zivilprozessordnung 1877* and French *Nouveau Code De Procedure Civile 1975*, both of which are famous for introducing the case management approach, did not take the similar approach based on the concept of overriding objectives, as was done in common law jurisdictions.

南澳大利亚州通过 1987 年《最高法院规则》第 2 条也采用了类似的方法。事实上，他们是采用目的性方法解释民事诉讼规则的先驱。然而，须注意的是，大陆法系司法管辖区，如德国的《1877 年民事诉讼法典》和法国的《1975 年新民事诉讼法典》，都以引入案件管理方法而著称，但它们并没有像普通法系司法管辖区那样采取类似的基于首要目标概念的方法。

4.2.1.2 Quasi-Public nature of English Civil Procedure Code

英国《民事诉讼法》的准公共性质

Many traditional jurisprudential philosophers, who are firm believers in the traditional adversarial system of English Law, are generally not pleased that there is a quasi-public[439] aspect to disputes, even if the cases are between private parties. This is in complete contrast with civil law jurisdictions, in particular the PRC jurisdiction as discussed in Chapter 1, where judges must consider public purpose to civil litigation involving private commercial disputes according to the PRC Code.[440]

许多传统法学哲学家坚信英国法的传统对抗制，他们通常不乐见纠纷存在准公共方法，即使案件是私人当事方间的纠纷。这与大陆法系司法管辖区形成鲜明对比，尤其是第一章讨论的中国司法管辖区，根据《中华人民共和国法典》，法官须考虑涉及私人商业纠纷的民事诉讼的公共目的。

To demonstrate the quasi-public nature of disputes, it is necessary to discuss a particular case from English Law.[441] In this case, the dispute was between one of the Councils in London (Bromley London Borough Council (“LBC”)) and the overall London Administrative Council (“LAC”). The LAC had decided to reduce the fares for the local buses and trains by 25%, but that reduction had to be paid for by various Local Councils in London. One such local Council, LBC, rejected the

为说明争端的准公共性质，有必要讨论英国法中的一个具体案例。该案中，纠纷发生在伦敦的一个议会（布罗姆利伦敦市议会）和整个伦敦行政理事会间。伦敦行政委员会决定将当地公共汽车和火车的票价降低 25%，但降低的票价须由伦敦各地方议会支付。其中一个地方议会 LBC 拒绝这一

见 1938 年《联邦民事诉讼程序规则》（美国）第 1 条规定："本规则适用于美国地区法院所有民事诉讼和诉讼程序......本规则的解释和执行应确保每项诉讼和诉讼程序得到公正、迅速和廉价的裁决。另见被 2006 年《最高法院民事规则》取代的 1987 年《最高法院规则》（澳大利亚）第 2 条。另见 Dwyer，"首要目标"，第 70 页。

439 A term used in J.A. Jolowicz, “Civil Litigation.”
J.A. Jolowicz "民事诉讼 "中使用的术语。

440 Refer, Chapter 1, §1.2。参见第 1 章第 1.2 。

441 See *Bromley LBC v Greater London Council [1983] 1 AC 768*。见 Bromley LBC 诉 Greater London Council [1983] 1 AC 768。

proposal, and sued the LAC (on behalf of the Bromley residents) on the grounds that everyone who lived in Bromley would have to pay for the fare reduction through increased taxes. Even though the case was between the two parties, there were many stakeholders, for example, the local taxpayers living within the tax jurisdiction of Bromley and all commuters using the local trains and buses within London.

提议，并（代表布罗姆利居民）起诉LAC，理由是居住在布罗姆利的所有人都须通过增加税收来支付票价下调的费用。尽管案件是双方间的，但利益相关者众多，例如居住在布罗姆利税收管辖区的当地纳税人及在伦敦使用当地火车和公共汽车的所有乘客。

In the above case, the tax payers of Bromley prevailed over the LAC, and as a result any tax increase arising out of fare reduction was ruled as unlawful. This means that the LAC will have to consult all local Councils in future before taking any similar decisions.

在上述案例中，布罗姆利的纳税人战胜了地方行政委员会，因此，因降低票价而增加的税款被裁定为不合法。这意味着法咨委今后在作出任何类似决定前，都须征求所有地方议会。

In such cases, as discussed above, there are instances of repercussions and conflicts of interest. In many jurisdictions such as France, these types of cases will not even be considered as a part of civil litigation procedure but will rather be the part of *administrative jurisdiction.* Similarly, there are other cases that are in the field of law of tort which also have many stakeholders. This itself will generate lots of conflicts of interest.

在这种情况下，如上文所述，会出现反响和利益冲突。在许多司法管辖区，如法国，这类案件甚至不被视为民事诉讼程序的一部分，而是属于行政管辖的一部分。同样，还有一些侵权法领域案件也有许多利益相关者。这本身就会产生很多利益冲突。

Therefore, in the authors' view, the increased efficiency in case management after the advent of *CPR 1998* means that disputes between parties are being resolved; but the courts will always be mindful of public interests even in private disputes.

因此，笔者认为，在 1998 年《民事诉讼规则》问世后，案件管理的效率有所提高，这意味着当事人之间的争议正在得到解决；但即使在私人争议中，法院也会始终牢记公共利益。

4.2.2 Legal Philosophy of the PRC Civil Court

中华人民共和国民事法院的法律理念

In the English civil procedural system, along with most continental civil procedural systems founded on western jurisprudence, there is an emphasis on ensuring *procedural rights*.[442] However, in the PRC system there is an emphasis on securing *substantive justice*.[443] In the modern PRC Civil courts, ancient Chinese traditions have been combined with new ideas to draft a modern civil procedural law that sits pretty well within the ideas of *democratic centralism* (*min zhu ji zhong zhi*) and socialism, which is one of the fundamental principles of the Constitution of the PRC. Huo is of the view that the modern PRC civil procedure law, which is relatively new, adheres to the following principles:[444]

在英国民事诉讼制度中，以及大多数建立在西方法理学基础上的大陆民事诉讼制度中，都强调确保程序权利。然而，在中国的制度中，强调的是确保实体正义。在现代中国民事法院中，中国古代传统与新思想相结合，起草了一部现代民事诉讼法，该法与民主集中制和社会主义的思想相当契合，而民主集中制和社会主义是《中华人民共和国宪法》的基本原则之一。霍认为，相对较新的中华人民共和国现代民事诉讼法坚持了以下原则：

- Principle of Right to debate;

辩论权原则；

- Principle of right of action and various procedures in accordance with litigation theory;

诉讼权原则和诉讼理论中的各种程序；

- Principle of maintaining a balance between procedural justice and substantive truth using theory of evidence;

利用证据理论，在程序公正与实质真实之间保持平衡的原则；

- Principle of the role of binding arbitration, mediation and adjudication and related adjudication theories and their combination with Judgment;

有约束力的仲裁、调停和裁决的作用原则以及相关的裁决理论及其与判决的结合；

- Principle of supervision and retrial theory.

监督原则和重审理论。

For the first principle, the starting point is Article 12 of the *CPL 1991 (as amended in 2023)* that provides:

第一项原则的出发点是 1991 年《民事诉讼法》（经 2023 年修订）第 12 条，该条规定

442 Kristie Thomas, "Dynamism in China's Civil Procedure Law: Civil Justice with Chinese Characteristics," in *The Dynamism of Civil Procedure – Global Trends and Developments*, ed. C. Picker and G. Seidman (London: Springer, 2015), 2.

443 Margaret Y.K. Woo and Mary E. Gallagher, eds., *Chinese Justice: Civil Dispute Resolution in Contemporary China* (Cambridge: Cambridge University Press, 2011), 13. Woo has discussed that populations with experience with the courts have relatively more negative experience with the legal system. In addition, *distribution of justice* was preferred over *procedural justice*.
Margaret Y.K. Woo and Mary E. Gallagher, eds：中国司法：当代中国的民事纠纷解决》（剑桥：剑桥大学出版社，2011 年），第 13 页。Woo 曾讨论过，与法院打过交道的人群对法律体系的负面体验相对较多。此外，司法分配比程序正义更受青睐。

444 Haihong Huo, "Chinese Expression or Theory of Civil Procedure Law," *Legal System and Social Development*, no. 4 (2013): 3–9.
霍海红，"民事诉讼法的中国表达或理论"，《法制与社会发展》，2013 年第 4 期，第 3-9 页。

When adjudicating civil cases by the people's court, the parties shall have the right to engage in argument [emphasis added].[445]

人民法院审理民事案件，当事人有权进行辩论[着重号后加]。

According to Chai and Chang,[446] the principle of right to debate is essential in litigation, to ensure the parties' positions can be preserved by debating both orally and in the written form. The right to debate is also part of the democratic rights provided to its citizens. Even though in Article 12 of *CPL* 2023 the right to debate is not specifically guaranteed, courts will ensure that litigants are provided the opportunity for right to debate.[447] If any civil procedure court deprives a litigant of such a right, then there are provisions for retrial in the *CPL*.[448]

根据柴发邦和常怡的观点，辩论权原则在诉讼中至关重要，可以通过口头和书面形式的辩论确保各方立场得以维护。辩论权也是公民民主权利的一部分。尽管 2023 年《民事诉讼法》第 12 条并未明确保障辩论权，但法院将确保诉讼当事人有权进行辩论。如果任何民事诉讼法院剥夺了诉讼当事人的这一权利，那么《民事诉讼法》中有重审的规定。

The principle of right to debate provided in the PRC system is a non-binding debate system, so that courts are not constrained by the facts presented by the parties, but the courts can choose to actively investigate. This system of debate is different from the continental civil law systems, where the principle of debate is binding in nature.[449] However, over the years, there have been demands from scholars such as Jiang Wei to adopt some of the principles of the continental civil law system. In the authors' view, the demand is appropriate as the judges' power to investigate on their own pursuant to *CPL* gives too much discretionary power to the judges. The discretionary power of judges is further discussed in Chapter 6.[450]

中国法律制度中规定的辩论权原则是一种非约束性的辩论制度，因此法院不受当事人陈述事实的约束，但法院可以选择主动调查。这种辩论制度不同于大陆法系，大陆法系的辩论原则具有约束性。但多年来，也有学者如姜伟等要求采纳大陆法系的一些原则。笔者认为，这一要求是恰当的，因为根据中国《民事诉讼法》，法官的自行调查权赋予了法官过多的自由裁量权。第 6 章将进一步讨论法官自由裁量权。

The second principle of civil procedure in *CPL* is the *right to action*, which is based on the Soviet Union's binary theory right

中国《民事诉讼法》中的第二项民事诉讼原则是诉权，它借鉴了苏联的二元诉权理论，即以程序权利和实

[445]See Art. 12 of *CPL 1991 (as amended in 2023)*。见 1991 年《中华人民共和国民事诉讼法》第 12 条（2023 年修订）。

[446]Yi Chang, Chief Editor, *The Civil Procedure Law* (Beijing: China University of Law and Political Science and Law Press, 1996), 69–70. Fabang Chai, *New Civil Procedure* (Beijing: Law Press, 1992), 96–97. Both Chai and Chang were cited in Huo, "Chinese Expression in CPL".
常怡 主编，《民事诉讼法》（北京：中国政法大学出版社，1996 年），69-70 页。柴发邦，《新民事诉讼法》（北京：法律出版社，1992 年），96-97 页。Huo, "Chinese Expression in CPL" [《民事诉讼法中的中国表达》]中引用了柴和常的观点。

[447]Huo, "Chinese Expression in CPL"。Huo，"CPL 中的英文表达"。

[448]See Art. 211 (9) of *CPL 2023*。见 2023 年《中华人民共和国民事诉讼法》第 211 条第 9 款。

[449]Weiping Zhang, "Restatement of China's Principles of Debate in Civil Litigation," *Legal Research* (1996), as cited in Huo, "Chinese Expression in CPL".
张卫平：《中国民事诉讼辩论原则重述》，《法学研究》（1996 年），转引自霍：《中外法学中的中国表达》。

[450]Refer, Chapter 6, §6.3.3 in context of PRC judges' discretionary power.
请参阅第 6 章第 6.3.3 节中有关中华人民共和国法官自由裁量权的内容。

of action, which is based on procedural right and substantive right.[451] In theory, the courts should not prevent the right of action as long as the procedural requirements specified in *CPL* are clearly satisfied.

体权利为基础的诉权。从理论上讲，只要明确满足《民事诉讼法》中规定的程序要求，法院就不应阻止诉权。

However, in practice, there have been occasions where the judges have refused to accept cases on the grounds that adequate evidence and facts are not presented with the applications. In many instances, PRC judges have failed to distinguish between procedural rights, & the substantive rights that are essential at the judgment stage of the matter, and not when the matter is just at the initial right of action stage. In the authors' view, this is also the result of inconsistent training of judges, and difficulty in maintaining consistency in all courts due to the continental size of the PRC. It could be argued that since the public interest is so important in PRC law, the authorities can filter out problematic applications from litigants at this early stage. This is a major issue that certainly needs rectification, in particular for foreign stakeholders in the PRC economy.

然而，在实践中，法官有时会以申请中未提供充分证据和事实为由拒绝受理案件。在许多情况下，中国法官未能区分程序性权利和实体性权利，而实体性权利在案件的判决阶段是至关重要的，而不是在案件刚进入最初的诉讼权利阶段。作者认为，这也是法官培训不一致的结果，而且由于中国幅员辽阔，很难在所有法院保持一致。可以说，由于公共利益在中国法律中非常重要，当局可以在这一早期阶段过滤掉诉讼当事人提出的有问题的申请。这是一个肯定需要纠正的重大问题，尤其是对中国经济中的外国利益相关者而言。

There is recognition amongst PRC scholars that the right of action in civil courts is related to various other issues such as human rights, constitutional rights and so forth.[452] Another issue that is relevant in the above context is the test of standards of proof in relation to the evidence that has to be filed with the claim forms. In addition, it is argued that the principle of right of action should exist alongside the abuse of such right of action by frivolous litigation wasting judicial resources.[453] *CPL 1991* has preserved the right to litigate for litigants.[454] However, in the authors' experience, *CPL 1991* still requires a considerable amount of detail in the pleadings from litigants, before a court will even accept a case; the standard of proof at this stage is also a bit higher. Therefore, in the authors' view, while in common law systems such as in the US or in England

中国学者承认，在民事法庭的诉讼权与人权、宪法权利等其他各种问题有关。与上述情况相关的另一个问题是与索赔表中必须提交的证据有关的举证标准的检验。此外，有观点认为，诉讼权原则应与滥用诉讼权、浪费司法资源的琐屑诉讼并存 1991 年《民事诉讼法》保留了诉讼当事人的诉讼权。然而，根据笔者的经验，1991 年民事诉讼法仍然要求诉讼当事人在诉状中提供相当多的细节，然后法院才会受理案件；这一阶段的举证标准也更高一些。因此，笔者认为，在美国或英格兰和威尔士等普通法体系中，允许以宽松的诉状来启动索赔，

[451]Huo, "Chinese Expression in CPL"。Huo，"CPL 中的中文表达"。

[452]Ibid.

[453]Ming Shao, "Abuse of Civil Litigation Law and Regulation," *Tribune of Political Science and Law*, no. 6 (2011): 175–80. Shao's views were discussed in Huo, "Chinese Expression in CPL".
邵明：《民事诉讼法律法规的滥用》，《政法论坛》，第 6 期（2011 年）：175-80。邵明的观点在霍建国的《中国表达在民事诉讼法中的应用》一文中有所论述。

[454]See Art. 126 of *CPL 2023*。见 2023 年《中华人民共和国民事诉讼法》第 126 条。

& Wales, where liberal pleadings are allowed to start a claim,[455] it is very different in PRC, where *specific-fact pleading* is required.[456]

而在中国则截然不同，中国要求提供具体事实的诉状。

In the third principle of civil procedure in *CPL*, the delicate balance between substantive and procedural justice is maintained by appropriate standards of proof and theory of evidence. This concept is founded on Soviet jurisprudence, whereby there is a need to find the *objective truth* is favoured. This may be because traditionally the populace has preferred substantive justice over procedural justice.[457] Scholars in the PRC from 1990 onwards have commented on the issue of lower standards of proof for civil litigation as compared to the higher standard of proof for criminal litigation.[458] The topic of standards of proof is analysed further in Chapter 7.[459]

在中国《民事诉讼法》民事诉讼程序的第三项原则中，通过适当的证据标准和证据理论来维持实体正义和程序正义之间的微妙平衡。这一概念建立在苏联法理学的基础上，即需要发现客观真相。这可能是因为传统上民众更倾向于实体正义而非程序正义。自 1990 年以来，中国的学者对民事诉讼的证明标准低于刑事诉讼的证明标准这一问题发表了评论。关于证明标准的问题，我们将在第七章进一步分析 。

Pursuant to *CPL*, PRC judges have to examine evidence '*comprehensively and objectively*'.[460] The standards of proof required in the PRC courts are higher than in common law courts, and maintain a delicate balance to satisfy scholars, who emphasise the need to find the '*objective truth*'. In order to balance the need for substantive justice with procedural justice, judges in the PRC have been given discretionary powers that are discussed in detail in the Chapter Six of this book.[461] An important issue in relation to this principle is that it has a huge effect on what can be considered appropriate training for judges.[462]

根据中国《民事诉讼法》，中国法官必须“全面客观”地审查证据，中国法院所要求的证据标准高于普通法法院，并保持着一种微妙的平衡，以满足学者们强调需要找到 "客观真相 "的要求。为了在实体正义与程序正义之间取得平衡，中国的法官被赋予了自由裁量权，本书第六章将对此进行详细讨论。与这一原则有关的一个重要问题是它对法官的适当培训产生巨大影响。

Additionally, the concept of adverse consequences for the party that was unable to adduce evidence was introduced through the

此外，最高法院的《意见》还引入了无法举证的一方当事人将承担不

[455]Scott Dodson, "The Challenge of Comparative Civil Procedure," *Ala. L. Rev.* 60, no. 1 (2008): 144.
[456]See Art. 122 of *CPL 2023*。见 2023 年《中华人民共和国民事诉讼法》第 122 条。
[457]Zhixiang Wang and Zengrun Wang, trans., *Soviet Civil Procedure* (Beijing: Law Press, 1957), 65 and they were cited and discussed in Huo, "Chinese Expression in CPL".
王志祥、王增润译，《苏联民事诉讼程序》，北京：法律出版社，1957 年，第 65 页。
[458]Huo, "Chinese Expression in CPL"。Huo，"民事诉讼法中的中文表达"。
[459]Refer, Chapter 7, §7.4。参见第 7 章第 7.4 节。
[460]See Art. 67 of *CPL 2023*。见 2023 年《中华人民共和国民事诉讼法》第 67 条。
[461]Refer, Chapter 6, §6.3。参见第 6 章第 6.3 节。
[462]Huo, "Chinese Expression in CPL"。Huo，"中华人民共和国民事诉讼法中的中文表达"。

Opinions of Supreme Court.[463] By adopting the German system, judges in the PRC have been given the authority to allocate the burden of proof based on principles of fairness and honesty.[464] Gradually, more rules are being developed within the field of evidence, for example, the adaptation of rules about the acknowledgment of facts in the statements of others which can assist judges in their judicial activities.[465] Huo has discussed, in his article, these aspects in the context of the new developments that have assisted judicial activities.[466]

利后果的概念 通过采用德国的 制度，中国的法官有权根据公平和诚实的原则分配举证责任 在证据领域，更多的规则正在逐步完善，例如，对他人陈述中的事实确认规则进行调整，以帮助法官开展司法活动。 霍建国在其文章中结合有助于司法活动的新发展对这些方面进行了论述。

As to the fourth principle, the PRC has modified a system where mediation was given prominence in *Civil Procedure Code (trial basis)*,[467] as compared to the contemporary view, where parties can opt for mediation based on legal principles and can voluntarily agree to go through mediation.[468] In the current scenario, the trial is at the core of the adjudication system. In 2010, *Supreme People's Court on Issuing Several Opinions on Further Implementing the Work Principle of "Giving Priority to Mediation and Combining Mediation with Judgment"* clearly highlighted the role of mediation in the adjudication system.[469]

至于第四项原则，中国修改了《民事诉讼法》（以审判为基础）中突出调解的制度， 而当代观点则认为，当事人可以根据法律原则选择调解，也可以自愿同意进行调解。 在当前情况下，审判是审判制度的核心。2010 年，《最高人民法院关于印发〈关于进一步贯彻"调解优先、调判结合"工作原则的若干意见〉的通知》明确强调了调解在审判制度中的作用。

The policy reasons that have been cited for the existence of such principles in the context of mediation are, first, that this is based on Chinese characteristics; and, second, to ensure that personal and business relationships will remain intact. In addition, there is an important need to maintain social harmony

在调解方面存在这些原则的政策理由是：第一，这是基于中国特色；第二，确保个人和企业关系保持不变。此外，在经济快速发展的同时，保持社会和谐也是一项重要需求 多年来，

[463]See, Art. 2 of *Some Provisions of Supreme People's Court on Evidence in Civil Procedures [No. 33 of 2001] (as revised in 2008)*. It provides: "Where any party cannot produce evidence or the evidences produced cannot support the facts on which the allegations are based, the party concerned that bears the burden of proof shall undertake unfavourable consequences."
见《最高人民法院关于民事诉讼证据的若干规定见《最高人民法院关于民事诉讼证据的若干规定》[2001 年第 33 号]（2008 年修订）第 2 条。该条规定"当事人不能提供证据或者提供的证据不能证明指控事实的，由负有举证责任的当事人承担不利后果"。
[464]See, Art. 7 of *Some Provisions of Supreme People's Court on Evidence in Civil Procedures [No. 33 of 2001] (as Revised in 2008).*
见《最高人民法院关于民事诉讼证据的若干规定参见《最高人民法院关于民事诉讼证据的若干规定》（2001 年第 33 号）（2008 年修订），第 7 条。
[465]See *Some Provisions of Supreme People's Court on Evidence in Civil Procedures [No. 33 of 2001] (as Revised in 2008).*
参见《最高人民法院关于民事诉讼证据的若干规定》[2001 年第 33 号]（2008 年修订）。
[466]See for further discussion Huo, "Chinese Expression in CPL."
进一步讨论见 Huo，"CPL 中的中文表达"。
[467]See Art. 6 of *Civil Procedure Law (Trial Implementation) 1982.*
见《1982 年民事诉讼法（审判执行）》第 6 条。
[468]See Art. 99 of *CPL 2023.* 见 2023 年《中华人民共和国民事诉讼法》第 99 条。
[469] *Supreme People's Court on Issuing Several Opinions on Further Implementing the Work Principle of "Giving Priority to Mediation and Combining Mediation with Judgment" (No.16 [2010] of Supreme People's Court).*
最高人民法院关于印发《关于进一步贯彻 "调解优先、调判结合 "工作原则的若干意见》的通知（法释〔2010〕16 号）。

despite rapid economic expansion.[470] Over the years, reforms have been made in this area, so that the separation of mediation and litigation within the court system has improved vastly. As a result of these reforms, litigants are given enhanced autonomy to resolve their disputes by mediation.[471]

在这方面进行了改革，使法院系统内的调解和诉讼分离得到了极大改善。由于这些改革，诉讼当事人通过调解解决纠纷的自主权得到加强。

The fifth principle of civil litigation is based on the process of trial supervision adopted from the Soviet Union's supervision procedure under their civil procedure law.[472] In countries practicing continental civil law system, the process of retrial is distinct from the 'retrial supervision procedure' that is available in the PRC. For example, according to section 578 of the *German Code of Civil Procedure*, retrial will be triggered when the judgment was based on false evidence, or if there were serious procedural violations. However, in the PRC, the motion for retrial supervision can be done *sua sponte* at the behest of the courts without it being triggered by the litigants.[473]

民事诉讼的第五项原则是以审判监督程序为基础，该程序借鉴了苏联民事诉讼法中的监督程序。在大陆法系国家，再审程序有别于中国的"再审监督程序"。例如根据《德国民事诉讼法》第 578 条规定，如果判决是基于虚假证据做出的，或者存在严重的程序违法行为，则会启动再审程序。但在中国，再审监督的动议可以由法院主动提出，而无需由诉讼当事人触发。

Finally, there is one more important principle that governs civil litigation in the PRC. Article 13 of *CPL 2023* provides:

最后，中国民事诉讼还有一项重要原则。2023 年《民事诉讼法》第 13 条规定：

Parties shall follow the principle of honesty and good faith.[474]

各方应遵循诚信原则。

4.2.2.1 Aims of PRC Procedural Code

《中华人民共和国程序法典》的宗旨

Article 2 of *CPL 2023* details its aims as follows:

…

- to protect the exercise of the litigation rights of the

2023 年《民事诉讼法》第 2 条对其宗旨作了如下详细规定：

…

[470] Ibid.

[471] Huo, "Chinese Expression in CPL"。Huo，"中华人民共和国民事诉讼法中的中文表达"。

[472] Ibid.

[473] See Art. 209 of *CPL 2023*。见 2023 年《中华人民共和国民事诉讼法》第 209 条。

[474] See Art. 13 of *CPL 2023*。 见 2023 年《中华人民共和国民事诉讼法》第 13 条。

parties;[475]

- to ensure the ascertaining of facts by the people's courts; distinguish right from wrong; apply the law correctly, try civil cases promptly;

- to affirm civil rights and obligations, impose sanctions for civil wrongs, protect the lawful rights and interests of the parties, educate citizens to voluntarily abide by the law;

- to maintain the social and economic order to guarantee the smooth progress of the socialist construction.

- 保护当事人行使诉讼权利，

- 保证人民法院查明事实，分清是非，正确适用法律，及时审理民事案件，

- 确认民事权利义务关系，制裁民事违法行为，保护当事人的合法权益，教育公民自觉遵守法律，

- 维护社会秩序、经济秩序，保障社会主义建设事业顺利进行。

These aims within *CPL 2023* are similar to overriding objectives of *CPR* in England & Wales. However, the aims as provided in *CPL 1991* are relatively less detailed in articles as compared with the English civil procedural Code. This may be due the fact that English courts have extensive experience of adversarial litigation. The above objectives in the PRC civil procedural system are supplemented as discussed earlier by important principles aimed at achieving the overriding objectives. In the authors' view, a few of these principles are as follows:

2023 年《民事诉讼法》的这些目标，与英格兰及威尔斯民事诉讼程序法的首要目标相若。然而，与英格兰的民事诉讼程序法典相比，2023 年中国《民事诉讼法》所订明的目标在条文上较为细致。这可能是由于英国法院在对抗式诉讼方面有着丰富的经验。如前文所述，中国民事诉讼制度的上述目标还辅以旨在实现首要目标的重要原则。笔者认为，其中的几项原则如下：

- In PRC, the principle of equal treatment and the principle of reciprocity are fundamental aims of *CPL*.[476] It is important to appreciate that the principle of equal treatment depends on the principles that are available in the foreign courts for assistance being applied in the PRC courts for foreign nationals. Similarly, the *principle of reciprocity*, which is called the *principle of retaliation* in *CPL*, ensures equality between countries.[477]

- 在中国，平等待遇原则和互惠原则是中国《民事诉讼法》的基本目标。重要的是要认识到，平等待遇原则取决于外国法院所提供的援助原则在中国法院是否适用于外国 。同様地，互惠原则，也即中国《民事诉讼法》中的平等原则，确保国家之间的平等。

[475]See also, Arts. 13 & 33 of *Constitution of PRC 1982.*
另见 1982 年《中华人民共和国宪法》第 13 和第 33 条。

[476]See Art. 5 of *CPL 2023.* See also, the discussion on Art. 5 in Weijian Tang, "The Evolution of Civil Procedure System of China," *Frontiers L. China* 7, no. 2 (2012): 205.
见 2023 年《中华人民共和国民事诉讼法》第 5 条。另见汤维建，"中国民事诉讼制度的演变"，《中国法学前沿》7，第 2 期（2012 年）205：关于第 5 条的讨论.

[477]See discussion on Art. 5 in Tang, "Evolution of CPL in PRC," 205. See also, *Civil Procedure Law 2023*, Art. 5.
参见 Tang，"中国民事诉讼法的演变"，第 205 页中关于第 5 条的讨论。另见 2023 年《中华人民共和国民事诉讼法》第 5 条。

- According to Tang, the *principle of equal litigation* in *CPL 1991* has two meanings – first, the parties to litigation enjoy equal rights and obligations according to *CPL 1991*; and second, in judicial practice, the courts must safeguard the parties' litigation rights, and accordingly must treat the parties equally when applying the articles of *CPL 1991*.[478] Similarly, the aim of providing *equal opportunity* to parties is enshrined in *CPL 1991* in order to enable them to argue their case in PRC courts. [479] This principle of providing equal opportunity is provided alongside the *principle of disposition* of *CPL 1991*;[480] it means that the parties can exercise their civil rights and litigation rights within the scope of the law.[481]

- 唐律师认为，1991年《民事诉讼法》中的平等诉讼原则有两层含义--第一，根据1991年《民事诉讼法》的规定，诉讼当事人享有平等的权利和义务；第二，在司法中，法院须保障当事人的诉讼权利，因此在适用1991年《民事诉讼法》的条款时必须平等对待当事人。同样，1991年《民事诉讼法》规定了为当事人提供平等机会的目标以使他们能够在中国法院进行辩论。提供平等机会的原则与1991年《民事诉讼法》的处分原则同时规定；这意味着当事人可在法律规定的范围内行使其民事权利和诉讼权利。

- Scholars in the PRC have acknowledged that even though these principles are enshrined in the law, there is a huge gap in the execution of such principles in the courts, pursuant to *CPL 1991*.[482] Scholars have recommended a separate legislation in order to fill this gap but it is a controversial topic and beyond the scope of the book.[483] This issue of a separate legislation has in fact raised demands for increased judicial supervision and separation of mediation under the civil procedure.[484]In the authors' view what is missing is consistency in both the application of the rules throughout the local courts in the PRC, and also in the training of judges. As Tang says in relation to the principles of *CPL 1991*:

- 中国学者们承认，尽管这些原则已载入法律，但根据1991年《民事诉讼法》，法院执行这些原则方面存在巨大差距。学者们建议单独立法以填补这一空白，但这是一个有争议的话题，超出了本书的范围。在笔者看来，中国地方法院在适用这些规则以及法官培训方面所缺乏的是一致性。正如 Tang 在谈到1991年《民事诉讼法》的原则时所说的那样：

[478]Tang, "Evolution of CPL in PRC," 205.
Tang, "《民事诉讼法》在中国的演变", 205。
[479]See Art. 12 of *CPL 1991* (as amended in 2023)。见1991年《民事诉讼法》第12条（2023年修订）。
[480]*Civil Procedure Law 1991 (as Amended in 2023)*。1991年《民事诉讼法》（2023 年修订）。
[481]See for discussion in detail on aims and principles, Tang, "Evolution of CPL in PRC," 204–5.
关于目的和原则的详细讨论，见 Tang, "中国民事诉讼的演变", 204-5。
[482]Tang, "Evolution of CPL in PRC," 207–8.
Tang, "《民事诉讼法》在中国的演变", 207-8。
[483]Ibid., 207.
[484]Ibid., 208.

In our view, there are two defining standards for the principles of the Civil Procedure Law: (a)implementing [these standards] throughout the [civil litigation] process; (b)serving the [purpose of providing] normative and guidance to the legislation, judicial and law obeying to the Civil Procedure Law.[485]

我认为，《民事诉讼法》的原则有两个界定标准：(a)在整个[民事诉讼]过程中贯彻[这些标准]；(b)服务于[为]遵守《民事诉讼法》的立法、司法和法律提供规范和指导的[目的]。

4.3 Historical Comparative Civil Procedure

历史上的民事诉讼比较

Before the authors start to compare different aspects of the civil procedure of the two jurisdictions, it is important to look at comparative civil procedure in a historical context. As far back as in 1889, the Japanese government adopted the *German Code of Civil Procedure of 1877*[486] because of their belief that Germany was a successful developed nation, without doing a thorough comparative analysis of the then-existing codes in Japan.[487] Another example of the adoption of the code of a different jurisdiction was the *Greek Civil Code of 1834*, which was a combination of the French and German codes, and came into existence without any comparative analysis.[488] However, there are instances where foreign influence upon the civil procedure systems was rejected, for example, in the USA, when it was suggested by a few US scholars that a few advantages of German civil procedure could be adopted in the US.

在作者开始比较两个司法管辖区民事诉讼程序的不同方面之前，有必要从历史背景来审视比较民事诉讼程序。早在 1889 年，日本政府就采用了德国 1877 年《民事诉讼法》。因为他们认为德国是一个成功的发达国家，而没有对日本当时已有的法典进行彻底的比较分析。另一个采用不同司法管辖区法典的例子是 1834 年《希腊民法典》，该法典综合了法国和德国的法典，在没有进行任何比较分析的情况下诞生。不过，也有拒绝接受外国对民事诉讼制度的影响的情况，例如在美国，当时有几位美国学者建议美国可以采纳德国民事诉讼程序的一些优点。

---

[485]Ibid., 206.

[486]Gottwald, “Comparative Civil Procedure,” 24–5.

Gottwald, "比较民事诉讼程序"，24-5。

[487]Gottwald, “Comparative Civil Procedure,” 24, where he discussed the historical context H. Nakamura’s 1971 article - “Die Rezeption Des Deutschen Rechts in Japan”.

Gottwald 著，"比较民事诉讼程序"，第 24 页，其中他讨论了 H. Nakamura 1971 年的文章 "Die Rezeption Des Deutschen Rechts in Japan "的历史背景。

[488]Gottwald, “Comparative Civil Procedure,” 24.

Gottwald, "比较民事诉讼程序"，24。

Gottwald's view is that even the German Civil procedure code is a mix of "German, Roman, Italian, French, Dutch, English and American influence".[489] Since the 1950, the World Congress of Procedural Law has been organised to study the comparative law process, with noble aims such as harmonisation and reforms of procedural systems. However, the research scholars that have attempted comparison of the civil procedures seem to have actually been comparing the legal systems in full, as the focus of early comparativists was only on comparisons of substantive laws in different jurisdictions.[490]

戈特瓦尔德认为，即使是德国的民事诉讼法也混合了 "德国、罗马、意大利、法国、荷兰、英国和美国的影响"。 自 1950 年以来，世界程序法大会一直在组织研究比较法程序，其崇高目标是协调和改革程序制度。然而，由于早期比较主义者的研究重点仅仅放在不同法域实体法的比较上，因此尝试对民事诉讼程序进行比较的研究学者似乎实际上是在对法律制度进行全面比较。

In the nineteenth century & immediately after the Second World War, civil procedure went through the stage of codification in many jurisdictions. However nowadays the focus of comparativists in this field has moved to transplantations of one procedural system into another jurisdiction's procedural system. It is only recently that attempts have been made by scholars to harmonise civil procedure laws, as can be seen in many research papers.[491]

在十九世纪和第二次世界大战后不久，许多司法管辖区的民事诉讼程序都经历了编纂阶段。然而，如今这一领域的比较学家关注的焦点已经转移到将一种程序制度移植到另一个司法管辖区的程序制度中。从许多研究论文中可以看出，学者们只是在最近才开始尝试协调民事诉讼法。

4.3.1 Unpopularity of Comparative Civil Procedure

比较民事诉讼程序不受欢迎

Scholars have cited various issues to suggest why comparativists have shown less interest in comparing civil procedure rather than other areas of laws from various jurisdictions. Gottwald, for e.g., has highlighted four reasons that the authors will discuss here, one by one:[492]

学者们列举了各种问题来说明为什么比较主义者对比较不同司法管辖区的民事诉讼程序而不是其他领域的法律兴趣不大。例如，戈特瓦尔德强调了四个原因，笔者将在此逐一讨论：

---

[489]Ibid., 25.
同上，第 25 页。
[490]James R. Maxeiner, "Legal Methods as a Point of Reference for Comparative Studies of Procedural Law," *XIIIth World Congress on Procedural Law, Salvador-Bahia, 16 to 22 September 2007* (2007): 1, http://ssrn.com/abstract=1232579.
[491]Ibid., 2。同上，第 2 页。
[492]Gottwald, "Comparative Civil Procedure," 26.
Gottwald, "比较民事诉讼程序"，第 26 页。

First, Gottwald discussed the issue of *Lex fori*, where if a civil dispute is to be litigated between two parties from two countries, then the most utilised concepts are the conflict of law rules, as at times a foreign substantive law can govern a dispute in another jurisdiction. However, whichever jurisdiction the civil disputes were to be litigated in, local civil procedural rules will be applied by the local courts. Often, in such cases, the local lawyers and judges in the local courts have no interest in knowing the foreign procedural rules. However, in the authors' view and experience where a party is dealing with the foreign country's civil procedural rules, those rules may or may not provide necessary comfort to the foreign litigants. For example, with the PRC's projects in Africa and SE Asia, the PRC companies and businessmen may have to litigate disputes in unfamiliar foreign jurisdictions.

首先，戈特瓦尔德讨论了诉讼地法的问题，即如果来自两个国家的双方当事人就民事纠纷提起诉讼，那么最常用的概念是法律冲突规则，因为有时外国实体法可以管辖另一司法管辖区的纠纷。然而，无论民事纠纷在哪个司法管辖区提起诉讼，当地法院都将适用当地的民事诉讼规则。在这种情况下，当地法院的当地律师和法官往往没有兴趣了解外国程序规则。然而，根据笔者的观点和经验，当一方当事人与外国民事诉讼规则打交道时，这些规则可能会也可能不会给外国诉讼当事人带来必要的安慰。例如，由于中国在非洲和东南亚的项目，中国的公司和商人可能不得不在陌生的外国司法管辖区进行诉讼。

With the increasingly globalised economy, more and more foreign litigants are experiencing commercial disputes and litigation in another country. There is no doubt that such litigants expect that the remedies available in the foreign jurisdiction pursuant to that system's rules will not be completely different from those of their own jurisdiction, and that the, foreign jurisdiction will be able to protect their interests. However, if the procedural rules in the foreign jurisdiction are not robust, then it can leave a bad taste in the mouths of foreign litigants, and consequently, can affect commercial trade and investments going forward. The only other area where comparative analysis in the field of civil procedure is usually pursued by research scholars is in the area of recognition and enforcement of foreign judgments and comparison of service rules, which allows them to obtain proofs using instruments of international judicial assistance.[493]

随着经济日益全球化，越来越多的外国诉讼当事人在另一个国家遭遇商业纠纷和诉讼。毫无疑问，这些诉讼当事人希望外国司法管辖区根据该系统的规则提供的救济不会与本国司法管辖区完全不同，并希望外国司法管辖区能够保护他们的利益。但是，如果外国司法管辖区的程序规则不健全，就会给外国诉讼当事人留下不好的印象，从而影响商业贸易和投资的发展。研究学者通常在民事诉讼程序领域进行比较分析的唯一其他领域是外国判决的承认与执行以及送达规则的比较，这使他们能够利用国际司法协助工具获得证据。

Another reason as to why comparative civil procedure has not

比较民事诉讼程序不受欢迎的另一个原因是法院的做法各不相同，而

[493]Ibid., 27。同上，第 27 页。

been so popular is due to *divergent court practices*,[494] and also due to difficulty in comparing civil procedures (rather than substantive law) between two jurisdictions. It will be difficult to measure and compare the exercise of discretion by judges (including availability of discretionary power to the judges) in the courts. In the authors' view, as discussed earlier, in a country such as the PRC, which is as big as a continent, the local courts' practices also differ from one province to another province. Court procedure in one court in one province of the PRC cannot be treated as representative procedure in all local courts of the PRC. A similar observation to this effect was made by Murray, who said that one local court in Freiberg was not representative of all the courts in Germany.[495]

且两个司法管辖区之间的民事诉讼程序（而不是实体法）也难以比较。很难衡量和比较法院中法官行使自由裁量权的情况（包括法官是否拥有自由裁量权）。笔者认为，如前所述，在中国这样一个幅员辽阔的国家，各省地方法院的做法也不尽相同。中国某省法院的诉讼程序不能代表中国所有地方法院的诉讼程序。穆雷也有类似的看法，他说弗莱贝格的一个地方法院不能代表德国的所有法院。

The courts are a symbol of constitution, where the relationships between the state and citizens are tested. The purpose of numerous courts in many jurisdictions is not only to render correct justice, but also to ensure the justice is delivered swiftly by making efficient utilisation of court resources,[496] to maintain the legitimacy of the courts and therefore, by extension the legitimacy of the state power.

法院是宪法的象征，是检验国家与公民之间关系的地方。在许多司法管辖区，众多法院的目的不仅是为了伸张正义，而且是为了通过有效利用法院资源来确保迅速伸张正义，以维护法院的合法性，进而维护国家权力的合法性。

In many jurisdictions, such as England & Wales, there is an application of human rights to the legal proceedings, and this can affect the proceedings and outcome. Clearly, any comparative analysis of civil procedure even within one jurisdiction is not a straightforward matter, but a product of many facts and influences. Due to these challenges, the field of comparative civil procedure has not been popular. Nevertheless, researchers (such as the authors) are coming into this area of law gradually to solve common problems that are

在许多司法管辖区，如英格兰和威尔士，人权适用于法律诉讼程序，这可能会影响诉讼程序和结果。显然，即使在一个司法管辖区内，民事诉讼程序的任何比较分析都不是一个简单的问题，而是许多事实和影响因素的产物。由于这些挑战，民事诉讼比较领域一直不受欢迎。然而，研究人员（如作者）正在逐步进入这一法律领

[494]The term 'divergent court practice' was coined in Gottwald, "Comparative Civil Procedure," 27. It was used in the context of highlighting why comparative civil procedure has not become popular as compared to many topics in substantive law that have been compared by comparativists.

分歧的法院实践 "一词源于 Gottwald, "比较民事诉讼程序", 第 27 页。该词的使用是为了强调，与比较主义者比较过的实体法中的许多主题相比，比较民事诉讼程序为何没有流行起来。

[495]Peter L. Murray, "A Morning at the Amtsgericht: German Civil Justice in Practice," in *Law and Justice in Multistate World: Essays in Honor of Arthur T. von Mehren*, James Nafziger and Symeon Symeonides (New York: Transnational Publishers, 2002), 779–92.

Peter L. Murray, "A Morning at the Amtsgericht: 德国民事司法实践》，载于《多州世界的法律与司法》: Essays in Honor of Arthur T. von Mehren, James Nafziger and Symeon Symeonides (New York: Transnational Publishers, 2002), 779-92.

[496]The concept of proportional use of court's resources as discussed in A. Zuckerman, *Civil Procedure: Principles of Practice*, 2nd Revised ed. (London: Sweet & Maxwell, 2006), 3, and cited in Gottwald, "Comparative Civil Procedure," 28.

A. Zuckerman 在《民事诉讼：实践原则》第 2 修订版（伦敦：Sweet & Maxwell 出版社，2006 年）第 3 版中讨论了法院资源比例使用的概念，引自 Gottwald，《比较民事诉讼》，第 28 页。

faced by litigants in almost all jurisdictions, especially in light of rapid globalisation.

域，以解决几乎所有司法管辖区的诉讼当事人所面临的共同问题，尤其是在全球化迅速发展的情况下。

Only in the last few years, due to the popularity of forum shopping, and the concept of *procedural advantages*,[497] have practising lawyers from one jurisdiction begun analysing key aspects of civil procedures from another jurisdiction, to be able to take advantage of a particular jurisdiction for their clients. However, as discussed above, there is a difference between knowing the procedural law in texts, and procedural law that is *actually experienced in practice* that a litigant might experience in a foreign jurisdiction.[498] The actual practice in the courts can make all the difference for litigants in civil disputes.

直到最近几年，由于择地诉讼的流行以及程序优势的概念，来自某一司法管辖区的执业律师才开始分析另一司法管辖区民事诉讼程序的关键方面，以便为其客户利用某一司法管辖区的优势。然而，如上所述，了解文本中的程序法与诉讼当事人在外国司法管辖区实际经历的程序法是不同的。对于民事纠纷中的诉讼当事人来说，法院的实际做法可能会带来很大的不同。

4.3.2 Purposes of Comparative Civil Procedure

比较民事诉讼程序的目的

Comparing the civil procedure of two jurisdictions can provide knowledge,[499] which can also be useful for practitioners in the area of *forum shopping*, or in cases where clients of a lawyer or businessmen have no choice, and therefore have to rely on civil

对两个法域的民事诉讼程序进行比较可提供相关知识，这些知识对于选择诉讼地领域的从业人员也很有用，或者在律师或商人的客户别无选

[497] See O. G. Chase, "American 'Exceptionalism' and Comparative Procedure," *Am. J. Comp. L.* 50, no. 2 (2002): 277, where issues such as pre-trial discovery and the possibility of liberal damages being awarded to the claimant were discussed to highlight the procedural advantages of US as a jurisdiction where disputes can be litigated. The US as a jurisdiction is usually selected by parties via the forum clause in their contracts.
参见 O. G. 查斯，《美国"例外论"与比较程序》，载《美国比较法杂志》第 50 卷第 2 期（2002 年）第 277 页，文中讨论了诸如庭前证据开示以及可能向原告判给高额损害赔偿金等问题，以突显美国作为诉讼地的程序优势。美国通常由当事人通过合同中的管辖权条款选定为诉讼地。

[498] Gottwald, "Comparative Civil Procedure," 27, where distinction between "law in the books" and "law in action" was described in the context of specific problems of comparative procedural law. See also, P. Gilles, "Eigenheiten der Prozessrechtsvergleichung" (1998), which was discussed by Gottwald in his paper.
Gottwald，"比较民事诉讼程序"，第 27 页，其中在比较程序法的具体问题的背景下描述了"书本上的法律"和"实践中的法律"之间的区别。参见 P. Gilles，"Eigenheiten der Prozessrechtsvergleichung"（1998），Gottwald 在他的论文中对此进行了讨论。

[499] Gottwald succinctly said "Comparative ...civil procedure in particular is working like a wonderful mirror: It opens your mind. The comparison increases your knowledge and wisdom." See also, Gottwald, "Comparative Civil Procedure," 35.
Gottwald 简明扼要地说道："比较……民事诉讼程序尤其像一面美妙的镜子：它开启了你的心智。比较增加了你的知识和智慧"。另见 Gottwald，"比较民事诉讼程序"，第 35 页。

procedural law in courts in another country's jurisdiction. A good comparative analysis can offer guidance about pitfalls and procedural advantages in another jurisdiction's civil procedures and rules to these practitioners. This will allow practitioners to assist their clients by being well-prepared, and thus avoiding nasty and costly surprises in that other jurisdiction.

择的情况下，不得不依赖另一国家管辖法院的民事诉讼法。良好的比较分析可为从业人员提供指导，使其了解另一司法管辖民事诉讼程序和规则中的陷阱和程序优势。这将使从业人员能够通过做好充分准备来帮助其客户，避免在其他司法管辖区出现令人讨厌和代价高昂的意外情况。

The comparative civil procedure is also utilised within the context of law reforms, possibilities of legal transplants, harmonisation, unification of laws such as in the European Union, drafting new regulations, and drafting model codes that can be adopted by other countries. One such example is *UNICTRAL Model Law on Arbitration of 1985*, which has been immensely successful and popular in most jurisdictions.

比较民事诉讼程序还在法律改革、法律移植的可能性、协调、统一法律（如欧盟）、起草新法规和可供其他国家采用的示范法等方面得到利用。其中一个例子是 1985 年《贸易法委员会仲裁示范法》，该示范法在大多数法域取得巨大成功并广受欢迎。

4.3.3 Methodology of Comparative Civil Procedural Law

民事诉讼法比较方法

The authors have discussed in Chapter 1 the functional approach that is becoming increasingly popular and is often adopted by comparativists.[500] However, such functional comparative methods are usually utilised by the comparativists in the context of comparison of substantive laws. This method of functionalism has been discussed in popular books on comparative law which compare German and US civil procedural rules. In order to compare civil procedure, one must find the *invisible factors* that influence the external law. The invisible factors are usually the factors that are taken for granted by lawyers in their home jurisdiction.[501] Once again, in

作者在第 1 章中讨论了功能比较法，这种方法越来越流行，也经常被比较主义者所采用。不过，比较主义者通常是在比较实体法时使用这种功能比较法。这种功能主义方法在比较法方面的流行书籍中有所论述，这些书籍对德国和美国的民事诉讼规则进行了比较。为了比较民事诉讼程序，我们必须找到影响外部法律的隐形因素。这些隐形因素通常是律师在其本国司法管辖认为理所当然的因素。作者再次认为，律师认为理所当然的因

[500]See Chapter 1, §1.4.3, Konrad and Hein Functionality Method; according to this method, the researcher should focus on the problem and it should be stated in functional terms.
参见第 1 章第 1.4.3 节，康拉德和海因功能性方法；根据该方法，研究人员应将重点放在问题上，并用功能性术语来表述问题。
[501]Refer, Chapter 1, §1.4.3 and invisible factors such as custom, sub-customs, history including legal history, religion, ethics, geography, language, philosophy, caste, creed, foreign invasion or interpretation or translation or foreign influence.

the authors' view, the factors that a lawyer takes for granted are more relevant to the context of the substantive law.

素与实体法的背景更为相关。

Comparativists have taken the above concepts further and have discussed the use of the above methodology within the context of civil procedural rules. Chase has described the court procedures as follows: "[C]ourt procedures reflect the fundamental values, sensibilities and beliefs (the 'culture') of the collectivity that employs them."[502] Maxeiner suggests that the two approaches of *functionalism* and *culturalism* represent the similarities and differences respectively among civil procedural systems.[503]This means that in order to analyse the similarities and differences between English civil procedural laws and PRC procedural law, the authors must first take a functional approach to find similarities and then look through the prism of culture and invisible factors to find differences. The second step is a difficult one for any researcher or foreign lawyer, and even at times for lawyers within the same jurisdiction.

比较主义者将上述概念进一步发扬光大，并在民事诉讼规则中讨论了上述方法的使用。柴斯对法院程序作了如下描述："法院程序反映了使用这些程序的集体的基本价值观、情感和信仰（'文化'）"。马克塞纳提出，功能主义和文化主义这两种方法分别代表了民事诉讼制度之间的相似性和差异性。这意味着，为了分析英国民事诉讼法与中华人民共和国诉讼法之间的相似性和差异性，笔者必须首先从功能主义的角度来寻找相似性，然后透过文化和隐形因素的棱镜来寻找差异性。第二步对于任何研究者或外国律师来说都是困难的，甚至有时对于同一司法管辖区的律师来说也是如此。

It is the amalgamation of jurists' opinions that form law and legal doctrines, and in the words of Maxeiner represent the "technical tool for organising society and those who see it as an historical development of the people's consciousness."[504]

它是法学家意见的综合，形成法律和法律学说，用马克塞纳的话说，它代表"组织社会和那些将社会视为人民意识历史发展的人的技术工具"。

In procedural law, it is very difficult to dissect varying functions in one element of procedural law,[505] and therefore, according to Maxeiner, various functions have to be analysed together. Maxeiner proposed a study of *legal methods* that govern how the procedural system will work in any

程序法中很难对程序法的一个要素的不同功能进行剖析，根据马克塞纳的观点，须对各种功能进行综合分析。马克塞纳提出一项关于法律方法的研究，这些方法制约着程序制度在任何司法管辖区的运作方式。然而，

参见第 1 章第 1.4.3 节，以及习俗、次习俗、历史（包括法律史）、宗教、伦理、地理、语言、哲学、种姓、信仰、外国入侵或解释或翻译或外国影响等隐形因素。

[502]O. G. Chase, "American Exceptionalism," 278, as quoted in Maxeiner, "Legal Methods in Comparative Procedural Law," 2. Maxeiner has described these as 'culturalism'.

O.O. G. Chase, "American Exceptionalism", 第 278 页，引自 Maxeiner, "Legal Methods in Comparative Procedural Law", 第 2 页。Maxeiner 将其称为 "文化主义"。

[503]Maxeiner, "Legal Methods in Comparative Procedural Law," 2. The discussion of 'culturalism' in context of comparative civil procedure is in many ways the same concept of analysing the invisible factors in general comparative law and as discussed earlier.

马克塞纳, "比较程序法中的法律方法", 第 2 页。 在比较民事诉讼程序中讨论"文化主义"在许多方面与分析一般比较法中的隐形因素的概念相同，如前文所述。

[504]Maxeiner, "Legal Methods in Comparative Procedural Law," 2.

[505]Ibid., 6.

同上，第 6 页。

jurisdiction. However, the purpose of civil procedure may differ in different jurisdictions, and highlights Fuller's question as whether the rules or the courts come first.[506]

民事诉讼程序的目的在不同的法域可能有所不同，这就突出了富勒的问题，即究竟是规则先行还是法院先行。

In the civil law system, such as in the PRC, the rules come first and the court has to apply the rules. In the common law system, where the courts will come first, procedures take the primacy and norms have to take the back seat. This is an important distinction one has to appreciate.

在大陆法系，例如在中国，规则是第一位的，法院必须适用规则。而在普通法系，法院先行，程序优先，规范次之。这是我们必须认识到的一个重要区别。

The starting point of any legal methodology will include the whole process of creation of the pertinent laws and rules in legislature, interpretation of statutes and case precedents, and subsequently applying the laws to the relevant problems. *Legal methodology* is therefore, the application of the laws, thereafter the facts are collated and analysis of facts is completed within the framework of law that has been legislated. Maxeiner highlighted the use of legal methodology by comparing the two legal systems of the US law (a common law system), and the German law (a civil law system). The US system is predominantly a common law system based on case precedents, while the German law is based upon the civil law system, where there is extensive codification that is usually fleshed-out in detail.

任何法律方法论的起点都包括立法机构制定相关法律和规则、解释法规和判例，以及随后将法律应用于相关问题的整个过程。因此，法律方法论就是法律的应用，然后在已立法的法律框架内整理事实并完成对事实的分析。马克塞纳通过比较美国法（普通法系）和德国法（大陆法系）这两种法律体系，强调了法律方法论的使用。美国的法律体系主要是以判例为基础的普通法体系，而德国的法律体系则是以大陆法系基础，其中有大量的法典，通常都有详细的内容。

In German courts, the legal rules are given prominence and facts of the cases are subsumed in the rules, whereas in the US courts, the norms are used, but they are not that prominent in deciding the issues between the parties. There is a maxim in German courts, famously called *lura novit curia,* which in English means 'the courts know the law.'[507] Most German law is drafted with precision, and excessive thought is given to ensuring proper quality control of the statutes during drafting stage. This is then followed by an attempt to find the most

在德国法院，法律规则被放在突出位置，案件事实也被纳入规则之中；而在美国法院，虽然也使用规范，但在裁决当事人之间的问题时，规范并不那么突出。德国法院有一句格言，著名的是 *lura novit curia*，意思是 "法院了解法律"。大多数德国法律在起草时都非常精确，在起草阶段也会过多考虑如何确保对法规进行适当的质量控制。然后再根据演绎推理找出最

[506]Ron Fuller, "The Forms and Limits of Adjudication," *Harv. L. Rev.* 92, no. 2 (1978): 353–409. This was discussed by Maxeiner in "Legal Methods in Comparative Procedural Law," 6.
Ron Fuller, "The Forms and Limits of Adjudication," Harv.92, no. 2 (1978)：353-409.Maxeiner 在 "比较程序法中的法律方法 "6 中对此进行了讨论。
[507]Maxeiner, "Legal Methods in Comparative Procedural Law," 5.

objective judgment based upon deductive reasoning.[508]

客观的判决。

On the other hand, Subrin was of the view that the highest goal for the US courts (a common-law system) appears to be that these courts will attempt not to apply the law to the facts of the disputes.[509] In addition, the US system seems to indicate a bit of indifference to the norms as compared with the German courts. Matters linked with the US procedural system are further complicated by vibrant democracy of the US, where legislation is drafted and agreed upon by competing lobbies. Solum state that there are two competing models in the US - the *accuracy model,*[510] and the *participation model.*

另一方面，苏布林认为美国法院（普通法系）的最高目标是这些法院试图不将法律适用于争议事实。与德国法院相比，美国法院似乎对规范有些漠不关心。美国充满活力的民主制度使与美国程序制度相关的问题变得更加复杂，在美国，立法是由相互竞争的游说团体起草并达成一致的。索卢姆指出，美国有两种相互竞争的模式——准确模式和参与模式。

In the traditional accuracy model, the aim of civil dispute resolution is to apply accurately the relevant laws to the facts, which in the authors' view is very similar to the German procedural law. However, the goal of the participation model, according to Solum, is that the correct outcome should be a function of a process that guarantees fair and equal participation. He further added that it is "…the process itself and not the outcome that defines **procedural justice** [emphasis added]."[511]

在传统的准确性模式中，民事纠纷解决的目的是将相关法律准确地适用于事实，这与德国的程序法非常相似。然而，索勒姆认为参与模式的目标是正确的结果应是一个保证公平和平等参与的过程的函数。他进一步补充，"...界定**程序正义**的是过程本身，而不是结果[着重部分由作者标明]。

As discussed earlier,[512] the functional comparative method has limitations in the context of civil procedures. To add to this complexity, in some procedural systems the purpose is to ensure that *'private rights'* are protected like in US,[513] whereas in many other civil jurisdictions, the *'public purpose'* is to

如前所述，功能比较法在民事诉讼程序中具有局限性。更为复杂的是，在某些程序制度中，目的是确保"私人权利"得到保护，如美国的，而在许多其他民事司法管辖区，"公共目的"是解决私人纠纷。因此，关于正义是指德国法院通过查明法律真相来维护法律

508Reinhard Zimmermann, "An Introduction to German Legal Culture," in *Introduction to German Law*, ed. Werner F. Ebke and Matthew W. Finkin (Hague, Boston: Kluwer Law International, 1996), 1,13.
509Stephen N. Subrin, "How Equity Conquered Common Law: The Federal Rules of Civil Procedure in Historical Perspective," *U. Pa. L. Rev.* 135, no. 4 (1987): 989.www.jstor.org/stable/3312053. It was further discussed in Maxeiner, "Legal Methods in Comparative Procedural Law," 5.
510Lawrence B. Solum, "Procedural Justice," *S. Cal. L. Rev.* 78, no. 1 (2004): 191. Solum's accuracy model was discussed in Maxeiner, "Legal Methods in Comparative Procedural Law," 6.
Lawrence B. Solum, "Procedural Justice," S. Cal.78, no. 1 (2004): 191。索勒姆的准确性模型在 Maxeiner, "Legal Methods in Comparative Procedural Law"第 6 页中进行了讨论。
511Solum, "Procedural Justice," 243. This was quoted in Maxeiner, "Legal Methods in Comparative Procedural Law," 6.
Solum, "Procedural Justice," 第 243 页。这句话引自 Maxeiner, "比较程序法中的法律方法", 第 6 页。
512Refer, Chapter 1, §1.4.3 on Konrad and Hein Functionality Method.
请参阅第 1 章第 1.4.3 节"康拉德和海因功能法"。
513P. L. Murray and Rolf H. Sturner, "German Civil Justice," in *German Civil Justice* (Durham, N.C.: Carolina Academic Press, 2004), 575. See also, the discussion on Murray and Sturner in Maxeiner, "Legal Methods in Comparative Procedural Law," 7.

resolve private disputes.[514] Therefore, there are arguments about whether justice is what happens in German Courts favouring the legal order by finding legal truth, or if it is the procedural justice of the US courts. In the US courts, the norms as derived from legal methods take a step back relatively to the procedural rules because the focus is on procedural justice. English courts, being common law courts, follow the US model to a great extent, while the PRC court follows the German courts but with Chinese characteristics.

秩序，还是指美国法院的程序正义，存在争议。在美国法院，从法律方法中衍生出来的规范相对于程序规则要退后一步，因为重点是程序正义。英国法院作为普通法法院，很大程度上沿袭了美国法院的模式，而中国法院则沿袭了德国法院的模式，但又具有中国特色。

4.3.4 Relevant Functions to Compare in Civil Procedural Systems

民事诉讼制度中需要比较的相关功能

The starting point of this discussion is Maxeiner's statement that "[p]rocedural law can only accomplish those tasks which the legal methods are capable."[515] However, in the authors' view, Maxeiner's statement and these concepts are more applicable in the context of substantive law. Whatever methods are available in substantive law will also be available for procedural law. There could be different causes of action in substantive law, but if there were to also be different requirements pertaining to procedural law for each of cause of action, then in the authors' view it would be an administrative nightmare. It could be argued that there could even be a possibility of the legal methods in a procedural system being incompatible with the legal methods of the substantive law in a few jurisdictions.

这一讨论的出发点是马克塞纳的声明，即"程序法只能完成法律方法所能完成的任务"。然而，作者认为，马克塞纳的声明和这些概念更适用于实体法。实体法中可用的方法同样适用于程序法。实体法中可以有不同的诉因，但如果对每种诉因的程序法也有不同的要求，那么笔者认为这将是一场行政噩梦。可以说，在少数司法管辖区，程序法体系的法律方法甚至有可能与实体法的法律方法相抵触。

In addition, there are models of procedural law as discussed above,[516] where procedural rules will be played out in the

此外，如上文所述，还有一些程序法模式，在这些模式中，程序规则将根据这些制度的哲学方法在法院中

[514]David J. Gerber, "Comparing Procedural Systems: Towards an Analytical Framework," in *Law and Justice in Multistate World: Essays in Honor of Arthur T. von. Mehren*, James A. R. Nafziger and Symeon C. Symeonides (2002), supra note 3, at 666, http://ssrn.com/abstract=12342579. The focus on procedural systems on private rights, as contrasted with Gerber's view of public purpose in resolving private disputes was discussed in Maxeiner, "Legal Methods in Comparative Procedural Law," 7.

[515]Maxeiner, "Legal Methods in Comparative Procedural Law," 6.

[516]Refer, discussion above in §4.3.3。参见上文第 4.3.3 节的讨论。

courts according to the philosophical approaches of the systems, i.e. having a public purpose or not having such public purpose when resolving private disputes in the courts. The PRC system does have the public purpose in mind even in private disputes as per their Civil Procedure Code as discussed earlier in Chapter 1, §1.2 and also §4.2.2.

实施，即在法院解决私人纠纷时具有公共目的或不具有这种公共目的。如前文第1章第1.2节和第4.2.2节所述，即使在私人纠纷中，《民事诉讼法》也会考虑公共目的。

The question arises as to the utility of comparative civil procedure: what can we compare in civil procedural laws or rules? The comparativists have tried to explain this, once more in functional terms, taking into account the philosophical approach of the US courts, where the courts come first. In this case, the norms of substantive law are inferior to those of procedures, but on the other hand, in the German courts, the norms are superior to the procedures before the courts.

比较民事诉讼程序的实用性问题由此产生：我们可比较民事诉讼法或规则中的哪些内容？比较主义者试图再次从功能的角度来解释这个问题，同时考虑到美国法院的哲学方法，即法院优先。在这种情况下，实体法规范低于程序法规范，但另一方面，在德国法院，实体法规范高于法院程序。

This point has been further explained in the terminology used by Maxeiner, who refers to *internal and external functions of the civil procedure*.[517] The internal function refers to the protection of the private rights of the parties, while external function of the civil procedure law in any jurisdiction refers to function of procedural law in resolving civil and commercial disputes within the context of whole legal system.

马克塞纳使用的术语进一步解释了这一点，他提到了民事诉讼程序的内部和外部功能。内部功能指的是保护当事人的私人权利，而民事诉讼法在任何司法管辖区的外部功能指的是程序法在整个法律体系范围内解决民商事纠纷的功能。

A very pertinent example is European Union project of harmonising provisional and interim measures; it has adopted the functional approach to these provisional remedies. The working paper provides that "The particular measure should be identified not by looking at the measures existing formally in the laws of different European states, but rather at the purposes/functions that they serve."[518] In this working paper, the EU working group analysed the various functions of interim remedies, and then for each function, they analysed various measures that could be taken to fulfil that function. Thereafter,

一个非常相关的例子是欧洲联盟统一临时措施的项目；该项目对这些临时补救措施采取了功能性办法。该工作文件规定："在确定具体措施时，不应着眼于不同欧洲国家法律中正式存在的措施，而应着眼于这些措施所服务的目的/功能。在这份工作文件中，欧盟工作组分析了临时救济的各种功能，然后针对每种功能分析了为实现该功能可以采取的各种措施。随

[517]Maxeiner, "Legal Methods in Comparative Procedural Law," 8.

[518]European Law Institute - Working Group on Provisional and Protective Measures, "First Report, November 2014," *Transnational Civil Procedure - Formulation of Regional Rules ELI - UNIDROIT Rules of Transnational Civil Procedure, Steering Committee and Working Groups Joint Meeting, Rome, 27–28 November 2014* UNIDROIT/ELI 2014, Study LXXVIA-Doc. 1 (2014): 5.

欧洲法律学会--临时措施和保护措施工作组，"第一次报告，2014 年 11 月"，跨国民事诉讼程序--制定区域规则 ELI--国际统一私法协会跨国民事诉讼程序规则，指导委员会和工作组联席会议，罗马，2014 年 11 月 27 日至 28 日 UNIDROIT/ELI 2014，Study LXXVIA-Doc.1 (2014):5.

they analysed different measures and the relevant terminology in each of the EU's contracting states.

后，他们分析了欧盟各缔约国的不同措施和相关术语。

4.3.4.1 External Function of Civil Procedural Rules

民事诉讼规则的外部功能

The authors will begin this section with Subrin's description of external functions of the civil procedural rules from the point of view of the US legal system. Subrin has listed these functions in the context of the US procedural system, as follows:[519]

笔者将从苏布林从美国法制度的角度对民事诉讼规则的外部功能进行描述作为本节的开头。苏布林结合美国的诉讼制度将这些功能列举如下:

- Resolving and ending disputes peacefully;
- Efficiency of the court system;
- Fulfilling societal norms through application of law
- Accurate ascertainment of facts;
- Predictability;
- Enhancing human dignity;
- Adding legitimacy and stability to government and society;
- Permitting citizens to partake in governance;
- Providing the growth and improvement of law;
- Restraining or enhancing power

-和平解决和结束争端;
-法院系统的效率;
-通过适用法律履行社会规范
-准确查明事实;
-可预测性;
-提升人类尊严;
-增加政府和社会合法与稳定性;
-允许公民参与治理;
-促进法律的发展和完善;
- 限制或加强权力

On the other hand, Murray and Sturner have listed the following external functions, taking a cue from transnational principles in the context of US procedural law:[520]

另一方面，穆雷和斯特纳根据美国程序法中的跨国原则，列出了以下外部功能:

[519]Stephen N. Subrin, "On Thinking about a Description of a Country's Civil Procedure," *Tul. J. Int'l & Comp. L.* 7 (1999): supra note 12,140. Subrin's view of internal functions was discussed in Maxeiner, "Legal Methods in Comparative Procedural Law," 9.
Stephen N. Subrin, "On Thinking about a Description of a Country's Civil Procedure," Tul.J. Int'l & Comp. L. 7 (1999): supra note 12,140.7 (1999): supra note 12,140.Subrin 对内部职能的看法在 Maxeiner 的 "比较程序法中的法律方法 "中进行了讨论。

[520]Murray and Sturner, "German Civil Justice," supra note 4, at 574. Also discussed in Maxeiner, "Legal Methods in Comparative Procedural Law," 9. These functions seem to have been derived from 31 principles from Transnational civil procedure.
Murray 和 Sturner, "德国民事司法", 前注 4, 第 574 页。Maxeiner 的"比较程序法中的法律方法"中也有讨论，第 9 页。这些职能似乎源自跨国民事诉讼程序的 31 项原则。

- Maintaining the independence and credibility of judicial institutions;	- 维护司法机构的独立性和公信力；
- Providing litigants with high-quality determinations of facts and law;	- 为诉讼当事人提供高质量的事实和法律裁定；
- Guaranteeing litigants procedural and systematic fairness;	- 保证诉讼当事人在程序上和制度上的公平；
- Producing final enforceable decisions without undue delay and at reasonable cost;	- 在不无故拖延的情况下，以合理的成本做出可执行的最终决定；
- Affording litigants reasonably free access to justice;	- 为诉讼当事人提供合理自由的司法途径；
- Contributing positively to the development and explication of the law;	-为法律的发展和阐释做出积极贡献；
- Generating among litigants and overall population confidence and satisfaction in civil justice and rule of law;	-使诉讼当事人和全体民众对民事司法和法治产生信心和满意度；
- Public regulation of economic and social actors (peculiar only to the US procedural system);	-对经济和社会行为者的公共监管（仅为美国程序制度所特有）；
- Public education (peculiar only to the US civil procedural system).	-公共教育（仅为美国民事诉讼制度所特有）。
The functions, therefore, can be grouped as:	因此，这些功能可分为以下几类：
- form-based functions such as method of finding facts and their accurate determination;	- 基于规范的功能，如发现事实的方法及其准确判定；
- Process-based functions such as systematic fairness;	-基于流程的功能，如系统公平性；
- Litigant-focused functions such as free justice, high-quality determination of dispute;	-以诉讼当事人为中心的职能，如免费司法、高质量的争议裁决；
- Legal system-focused functions such as development of law, independence of judiciary, etc.	-以法律制度为重点的职能，如法律发展、司法独立等。

4.3.4.2 Internal Function of Civil Procedural Rules

民事诉讼规则的内部功能

In the context of jurisdictions where there is a primacy of public purpose in resolving private disputes, Gerber's selection of	在以公共目的优先解决私人纠纷的司法管辖区，格伯对程序法功能的

functions of procedural law is as follows:[521]

选择如下：

- commencing litigation;
- acquiring data;
- shaping the facts;
- establishing the facts;
- law knowing: the background knowledge set;
- structuring law for the cases;
- law determination: deciding on law for the cases;
- decoding the outcome: fact-law interaction;
- dermination issues: appeals, etc.

- 开始诉讼；
- 获取数据；
- 塑造事实；
- 定事实；
- 法律知识：背景知识集；
- 为案件构建法律；
- 法律决定：决定案件的法律；
- 解码结果：事实与法律的互动；
- 决定问题：上诉等

It is important to note that the foregoing desired functions of procedural law are very norms-based, and it tend to relegate procedural justice to the margins. The above functions should be contrasted with the focus of the US system on finding the pertinent facts and allowing the litigants their "day-in-court."[522] Therefore, the focus of the PRC system would be less on procedural justice as compared to the common law system.

值得注意的是，程序法的上述预期功能是非常基于规范的，它倾向于将程序正义置于边缘地位。上述功能应与美国制度的重点——查明相关事实并允许诉讼当事人"出庭"——形成对比。因此，与普通法系相比，中国的制度对程序正义的关注较少。

If the authors were to analyse the internal functions suggested by Gerber in relation to German Civil Procedural System, it is clear the focus is clearly on norms in order to find the legal truth and accordingly decide the case. This aspect the author have discussed earlier in this chapter in relation to the legal philosophy of the civil jurisdictions. PRC would therefore focus on the finding the legal truth like any civil law system instead of focusing on prcedural justice in any common law system.

如果笔者要分析格伯就德国民事诉讼制度提出的内部功能，很明显，其重点显然是在规范上，以便找到法律真理，并据此对案件做出裁决。笔者在本章前半部分就民事司法管辖区的法律理念讨论过这方面的问题。因此，中国会像其他大陆法系国家一样注重寻找法律真理，而不是像其他普通法系国家一样注重程序正义。

[521]Gerber, "Comparing Procedural Systems," supra note 3, at 666, discussed in detail in Maxeiner, "Legal Methods in Comparative Procedural Law," 10.
[522]Maxeiner, "Legal Methods in Comparative Procedural Law," 10。Maxeiner, "比较程序法中的法律方法", 10。

4.3.4.3 Conclusions for Theoretical Comparative Civil Procedure

民事诉讼理论比较的结论

Many scholars have cited different functions within the context of the focus and priorities of different legal systems. The view of the authors based on the above findings, is that the functions need to be compared carefully in relation to civil procedure. It would therefore be a comparison of functions that are common between the jurisdictions.

许多学者根据不同法律制度的重点和优先事项列举了不同的职能。据上述研究结果，笔者认为需仔细比较民事诉讼程序方面的职能，需对各司法管辖区之间的共同职能进行比较。

However, there is a need to take into account factors that can be classed as *exceptions* within a particular jurisdiction, or cultural factors affecting those jurisdictions. **These exceptional factors can also be discussed in the context of invisible factors or cultural factors that are also not constant in any jurisdiction.** For example, Chase has identified four features that are very relevant to the US procedural law that he considers as 'American procedural exceptionalism':[523]

然而，有必要考虑到可归类为特定管辖范围内的例外因素或影响这些管辖范围的文化因素。**这些例外因素也可以在隐形因素或文化因素的背景下进行讨论**，这些因素在任何司法管辖区都不是一成不变的。例如蔡斯指出与美国程序法非常相关的四个特征，他认为这就是"美国程序例外论"：

- the civil jury;
- the use of party-controlled pre-trial investigation;
- the relatively passive role of the judge at the trials or hearings;
- the method of obtaining and using expert opinions on technical matters.

-民事陪审团

-使用由当事方控制的审前调查；

-法官在审判或听证中的角色相对被动；

-获取和使用技术专家意见的方法。

Even though culturalism or exceptionalism must be taken into account for the comparative project in the context of English and PRC civil procedure law, the initial research for the comparative exercise will have be on the common functions and how the civil procedure law differs in relation to those familiar functions. This is an appropriate time to bring in UNIDROIT Principles of Transnational Civil Procedure, prepared by a joint American Law Institute / UNIDROIT Study Group and adopted

尽管在英国和中国民事诉讼法的比较项目中必须考虑到文化主义或例外主义，但比较工作的初步研究必须是关于共同的功能以及民事诉讼法在这些熟悉的功能方面有何不同。现在是引入国际统一私法协会《跨国民事诉讼程序原则》的适当时机，该原则

[523] O. G. Chase, "American Exceptionalism," 287, Also discussed at great length in Maxeiner, "Legal Methods in Comparative Procedural Law," 11.

in 2004 by the Governing Council of UNIDROIT.

由美国法学会/国际统一私法协会联合研究小组制定，并于2004年由国际统一私法协会理事会通过。

The thirty-one principles/functions of transnational civil procedure of UNIDROIT[524] were adopted by the International Institute for the Unification of Private Law (UNIDROIT) in April 2004, and by the American Law Institute (ALI) in May 2004. The principles were adopted for the guidance of nations that were in the middle of drafting civil procedural codes for their own national systems. Many scholars within the field of comparative research in the context of civil procedural law regularly utilize these principles or functions to compare civil procedure systems or codes from different jurisdictions. The scholars find these more than thirty-one principles to be extremely useful.

国际统一私法协会（UNIDROIT）和美国法学会（ALI）分别于2004年4月和2004年5月通过了国际统一私法协会跨国民事诉讼程序的31项原则/功能。这些原则的通过是为了指导那些正在起草本国民事诉讼法的国家。民事诉讼法比较研究领域的许多学者经常利用这些原则或功能来比较不同司法管辖区的民事诉讼制度或法典。学者们认为这31多条原则非常有用。

Last but not least, the authors will be mindful of the fact that every jurisdiction has its own notion of civil justice with its own corresponding principles of civil justice. A few of the principles of civil justice are given prominence over other principles within a jurisdiction based on ideological or philosophical grounds or pursuant to the constitution governing that jurisdiction. Even though the principles are clear and might have been devised upon the basis of both common law and civil law, it is still useful to group them in such a way as to keep this issue clear-cut and plain. Prof. Andrews has noted this need, in relation to increasingly complicated sets of rules in each jurisdiction:

最后但并非不重要的是，作者注意到每一个司法管辖区都有自己的民事司法概念和相应的民事司法原则。在一个司法管辖区内，基于意识形态或哲学上的原因，或根据管辖该司法管辖区的宪法，一些民事司法原则被置于其他原则之上。尽管这些原则是明确的，而且可能是在普通法和民法的基础上制定的，但将其归类以保持这一问题的清晰明了仍是有益的。安德鲁斯教授在谈到各司法管辖区日益复杂的成套规则时指出了这一需要：

Another value of emphasising general principles is that they are an antidote to the numbing and bewildering complexity, detail, and technicality, which characterise many national procedural rule books. Finally, international scholarly discussion thrives on

强调一般原则的另一个价值在于，它们是许多国家程序规则书中令人麻木和困惑的复杂性、细节性和技术性的解毒剂。最后，国际学术讨论在基本原则的基础上蓬勃发展。

524 UNIDROIT (as adopted and promulgated by), “Principles of Transnational Civil Procedure.” www. Unidroit.org/instruments/transnational-civil-procedure.
国际统一私法协会（通过并颁布），"跨国民事诉讼原则"，www. Unidroit.org/instruments/transnational-civil-procedure。

the fundamental principle.[525]

Andrews, following the path of fundamental principles, has sub-grouped the principles of civil justice into four groups to avoid too much complexity. These four groups and key principles within these groups are as follows:[526]

安德鲁斯遵循基本原则的路径，将民事司法原则细分为四组，以避免过于复杂。这四组原则以及这四组原则中的主要原则如下：

- Regulating access to courts and justice —

  - ➢ Access to Justice;
  - ➢ Right to Choose a Lawyer;
  - ➢ Confidential Legal Consultation;
  - ➢ Protection against Spurious Claims and Defences;
  - ➢ Promoting Settlement and Facilitating Resort to Alternative Forms of Dispute Resolution, notably Mediation and Arbitration.

- 规范诉诸法院和司法的途径

  - ➢ 诉诸司法；
  - ➢ 选择律师的权利；
  - ➢ 保密法律咨询；
  - ➢ 防范虚假索赔和抗辩；
  - ➢ 促进和解并推动采用替代性争议解决方式，特别是调解和仲裁。

- Ensuring the fairness of the process —

  - ➢ Judicial Independence;
  - ➢ Judicial Impartiality;
  - ➢ Publicity or Open Justice;
  - ➢ Procedural Equality (equal respect for the parties);
  - ➢ Fair Play between the Parties;
  - ➢ Judicial Duty to Avoid Surprise: The Principle of Due Notice;
  - ➢ Equal Access to Information, including Disclosure of Information between Parties.

- 确保程序的公正性

  - ➢ 司法独立；
  - ➢ 司法公正；
  - ➢ 宣传或公开司法；
  - ➢ 程序平等（平等尊重各方）；
  - ➢ 双方公平竞争；
  - ➢ 避免意外的司法责任：适当通知原则》；
  - ➢ 平等获取信息，包括缔约方之间的信息披露。

---

[525]Andrews, "Fundamental Principles of CPR," 19. Andrews analysed the American Law Institute and UNIDROIT ('International Institute for Unification of Private law') common project started in 2004 called 'Principles and Rules of transnational civil procedure' that combined the best practices of common law and civil law. Andrew noted there were significant differences within the common law systems as well as differences between the civil law and common law systems.
Andrews, "Fundamental Principles of CPR," 19。安德鲁斯分析了美国法学会和国际统一私法协会于 2004 年启动的名为"跨国民事诉讼程序的原则和规则"的共同项目，该项目结合了普通法和大陆法的最佳实践。安德鲁指出，普通法系内部以及大陆法系和普通法系之间存在重大差异。

[526]Andrews, "Fundamental Principles of CPR," 33–34.
安德鲁斯，《心肺复苏术的基本原则》，33-34 页。

- Maintaining a speedy and efficient process —

- 保持快速高效的流程

➢ Judicial Control of the Civil Process to Ensure Focus and Proportionality (tempered, where appropriate, by principle of procedural equity; the process is not to be administered in an oppressive manner);
➢ Avoidance of Undue Delay.

➢ 对民事诉讼程序进行司法控制，以确保重点突出和比例适当（在适当的情况下，以程序公平原则作为调节；不得以压制性的方式管理诉讼程序）；
➢ 避免不当延误。

- Achieving just and effective outcomes —

-实现公正和有效的结果

➢ Judicial Duty to Give Reasons;
➢ Accuracy of Decision-making;
➢ Effectiveness (provision of protective relief and enforcement of judgments);
➢ Finality.

➢ 说明理由的司法责任；
➢ 决策的准确性；
➢ 有效性（提供保护性救济和执行判决）；
➢ 终结。

4.4 Comparison of Legal Philosophy of Civil Litigation

民事诉讼法律理念比较

The concept of procedural rights as *inherent in individuals* rather than *conferred* upon the litigants is an important feature in western civil procedures, in particular, common law systems. On the other hand, the PRC has adopted the *socialist* system where an individual is a member of a society, and all legal philosophies will rotate around the concept of society or public interests. PRC courts, as discussed, are required to maintain social and economic order and are in fact mandated to guarantee the smooth progress of the socialist construct.

诉讼权利是个人固有的而不是赋予诉讼当事人的这一概念，是西方民事诉讼程序，特别是普通法系的一个重要特征。另一方面，中华人民共和国采用的是社会主义制度，个人是社会的一员，所有的法律理念都将围绕社会或公共利益的概念而转动。如上文所述，中国法院需要维护社会和经济秩序，事实上，法院的任务是保障社会主义建设的顺利进行。

Issues of public interest could create concerns in commercial litigation, in particular where foreign corporations have reasonable commercial interests to protect in the PRC. Foreign lawyers acting for these foreign corporations may be in a bind as to how to advise their clients and what actually

公共利益问题可能会在商业诉讼中引起关注，特别是当外国公司在中国有合理的商业利益需要保护时。为这些外国公司代理的外国律师可能会陷入困境，不知道如何向其客户提供建议，以

are issues of public interest in the PRC. Any clear-cut guidance from the local PRC lawyer would probably not be clear with regard to these issues.

及在中国究竟哪些是公共利益问题。在这些问题上，中国本地律师的任何明确指导可能都不会很清楚。

In fact, in relation to commercial litigation, looking at profits or competition from the socialist angle can be quite contradictory in any market economy. Furthermore, the gradual transition of the PRC through the 1980s to a *socialist market economy* is not, in the authors' view, reflected in the PRC's civil procedure codes. For local businessmen and in particular foreign businessmen, when dealing with an economic powerhouse such as the world's second largest economy, there ought to be a reasonable expectation that other issues such as public interest can be filtered out of the pure business interests. Due to these arguments, many PRC scholars could critique the authors for apparently seeing the issues from the prism of capitalism. However, given that PRC international trade volumes are so huge and the level of commercial activities so gigantic, then it is difficult to accept such arguments.

事实上，就商事诉讼而言，从社会主义角度看待利润或竞争，在任何市场经济中都是相当矛盾的。此外，笔者认为，中国在 20 世纪 80 年代逐步向社会主义市场经济转型的过程并没有在中国的民事诉讼法中得到体现。对于本地商人，尤其是外国商人来说，在与世界第二大经济体这样的经济强国时，理应合理地期望其他问题（如公共利益）能够从纯粹的商业利益中过滤出来。基于这些论点，许多中国学者可能会批评作者显然是从资本主义的棱镜来看待问题。然而，鉴于中国的国际贸易量如此之大，商业活动水平如此之高，这种论点很难被接受。

In the English civil procedural system and in most continental civil procedural systems founded on western jurisprudence, there is an emphasis on ensuring *procedural rights*. But in the PRC system, there is an emphasis on securing *substantive justice*. This difference in philosophy has a considerable bearing upon the role of courts, and their respective approaches to civil litigation. In addition, in the PRC as well as in foreign civil law system, an inquisitorial system during civil trials is followed. Many aspects in continental civil law systems still have concepts such as adversarial debates (*principe de contradiction*) in civil trials, and there is no room for outside third-party interference, or any retrial without the request of the litigants. This is akin to the adversarial system as seen in common-law based civil procedure systems.

在英国民事诉讼制度和大多数建立在西方法学基础上的大陆民事诉讼制度中，强调的是确保程序权利。但在中国的制度中，强调的是确保实体正义。这种理念上的差异对法院的作用以及它们各自处理民事诉讼的方法有相当大的影响。此外，中国和外国大陆法系一样，在民事审判中遵循纠问式制度。大陆法系的许多方面在民事审判中仍有对抗辩论原则（*principe de contradiction*）等概念，不容许外部第三方干预，也不容许未经当事人请求的任何重审。这与普通法系民事诉讼制度中的对抗制相似。

The PRC seems to have been following continental civil traditions from the1990s onwards, but in the authors' view, it has only borrowed a few aspects of the continental system. In

从 1990 年代开始，中国似乎一直在追随大陆的民事传统，但在笔者看来，它只是借鉴了大陆制度的几个方面。事

fact, by adopting the concepts of re-trial and supervision, the PRC has adopted *democratic centralism* (*min zhu ji zhong zhi*) and *socialism*, and there is a subtle balance maintained between procedural justice, and substantive truth using theory of evidence. This balance between substantive and procedural rights is due to the influence of the Soviet Union's theory of *binary theory right of action*. The PRC has adopted the right to debate in *CPL*, thus bringing the system nearer to the continental civil procedural system.

实上，通过采用再审和监督的概念，中国采用了民主集中制和社会主义，并且在程序正义和使用证据理论的实体真理之间保持了微妙的平衡。这种实体权利与程序权利之间的平衡是由于受到苏联二元诉权理论的影响。中国在《民事诉讼法》中采纳了辩论权，从而使该制度更接近大陆民事诉讼制度。

Unlike in the English procedural system, the principle to debate as provided in the PRC's *CPL* is a *non-binding debate system*, as a result of which the PRC courts are not constrained by the facts presented by the parties. PRC courts are more likely to actively investigate the case themselves. This is also an example of the wide discretionary power given to judges, in particular, in relation to investigations.

与英国的程序制度不同，中国《民事诉讼法》规定的辩论原则是一种不具约束力的辩论制度，因此中国法院不受当事人陈述的事实的限制。中国法院更有可能自己积极调查案件。这也是赋予法官广泛酌处权的一个例子，特别是在调查方面。

The English civil procedural system promotes active case management and a process of disclosure, but the main obligation to present the case to the judge is on the parties. However, the PRC procedural system uses the '*discovery model led by the judges*'. From the time an application is submitted, the system requires a high standard of proof in relation to the evidence; this includes *specific-fact pleading*.[527]

英国民事诉讼制度提倡积极的案件管理和披露程序，但向法官陈述案情的主要义务在于当事人。然而，中国的诉讼制度采用的是"法官主导的证据开示模式"。从提交申请开始，该制度就要求对证据进行高标准的举证；这包括具体事实的抗辩。

In the PRC system, there are more formal requirements as to the form of evidence that is acceptable to the courts. In addition, at the level of practice of law in courts, requirements as to the evidence vary considerably in the local courts. In a way, the PRC's civil procedure system believes in the state's responsibility, carried out through the judges, to investigate what the parties have not even said in their

在中国的制度中，对法院可接受的证据形式有更正式的要求。此外，在法院的法律实践层面，各地法院对证据的要求也大不相同。在某种程度上，中国的民事诉讼制度认为国家有责任通过法官调查当事人甚至在诉状中都没有说过

[527]See *Provisions of the Supreme People's Court on Several Issues concerning the Registration-based Filing of Cases by People's Courts*, *Fa Shi* [2015] No. 8, effective from 1 May 2015. These provisions in a way attempt to improve the system but it is a relatively new system. However, the philosophical approach of the PRC civil procedure system is a major impediment, as higher standards of proof are usually required even at the time of filing of the cases.
参见《最高人民法院关于人民法院实行立案登记制若干问题的规定》，法释[2015]8号，自2015年5月1日起施行。这些规定在某种程度上试图完善这一制度，但这是一个相对较新的制度。然而，中华人民共和国民事诉讼制度的哲学方法是一个主要障碍，因为即使在立案时通常也要求更高的证明标准。

pleadings. This is an important difference between the two jurisdictions, and it has a profound effect on procedural justice and outcomes. How far English judges can investigate on their own is highly debated among academics and practicing lawyers.

的话。这是两个司法管辖区之间的一个重要区别，对程序正义和结果有着深远的影响。英国法官在多大程度上可自行调查，在学术界和执业律师中争论很大。

Any non-criminal matter, including commercial cases, can be brought to English civil courts, while in continental countries, it is usually the difference between public and private law that matters. On the other hand, in the PRC, there is a subtle distinction between commercial and civil cases, even though commercial cases can be brought in civil courts. In the PRC, there is no separate commercial code; rather, it seems to be scattered in various individual codes meant for different areas of law related to commerce such as partnership law, insurance law and so forth. In the PRC, the principle of civil law is absorbed in commercial law, but the key point to note that is even in commercial litigation, parties are supposed to be equal, and any litigation to be conducted in PRC courts will eventually follow the *concept of fairness*.

任何非刑事案件，包括商业案件，都可以提交英国民事法庭，而在欧洲大陆国家，公法和私法的区别通常才是最重要的。另一方面，在中国，商事案件和民事案件之间存在着微妙的区别，尽管商事案件可以提交民事法庭。在中国，没有单独的商法典；相反，商法典似乎散见于为与商业有关的不同法律领域（如合伙企业法、保险法等）制定的各种单行法典中。在中国，商法吸收了民法的原则，但需要注意的是，即使在商事诉讼中，当事人也应该是平等的，在中国法院进行的任何诉讼最终都将遵循公平的理念。

The concepts of *honesty* and *credibility* are brought into areas of commercial litigation. *General Principles of Civil Law 1986* acts likes an ethics clause, and it seems to impact commercial litigation, which was designed for common civil disputes and is clearly unsuitable for dealing with issues of commerce & trade, where there is already intense competition between the parties. However, in the authors' view, while the concept of socialist market economy pursuant to the 1993 amendment to the *Constitution of PRC 1982* is slowly impacting commercial litigation, in practice, there are divergences that have been observed in the local PRC courts due to the fact that there is no precise and straightforward distinction between civil and commercial litigation in PRC codes.

诚实信用的概念被引入商业诉讼领域。1986 年《民法通则》就像一个道德条款，它似乎对商事诉讼产生了影响，因为商事诉讼是为普通民事纠纷设计的，显然不适合处理当事人之间已经存在激烈竞争的商贸问题。然而，笔者认为，虽然根据 1993 年关 1982 年《中华人民共和国宪法》修正案提出的社会主义市场经济概念正在慢慢影响商事诉讼，但在实践中，由于中国法典中没有对民事诉讼和商事诉讼进行准确和直接的区分，因此在中国地方法院中观察到了一些分歧。

4.5 Comparison of Objectives in Civil Litigation

民事诉讼目标的比较

Prior to the advent of the new *CPR 1998* in England & Wales (even before the effects from continental jurisdictions), the concepts of a few statutes having an 'overriding' effect was known to legal stakeholders, but under this new approach, the meaning of the concept of overriding objective is much broader. *Overriding objective* encompasses the concept that lawyers and judges should also keep the overriding objectives in mind when analysing the other rules of the new *CPR 1998*. The *purposive construction* of *CPR 1998* was mooted to ensure the spirit of civil procedure is maintained within the courts, and it was the main reason for the advent of the new rules in 1998, replacing old rules. While discussing the overriding objectives, the *secondary objectives* such as ensuring that cases are dealt with justly and that costs are proportionate could also not be disregarded in this new spirit of *CPR 1998*.

在新的《1998年民事诉讼程序法》在英格兰和威尔士实施之前（甚至在受到大陆司法管辖区的影响之前），法律利益相关者都知道少数法规具有"优先"效力的概念，但在这种新方法下，优先目标这一概念的含义要广泛得多。凌驾性目标包含一个概念，即律师和法官在分析新的《1998年民事诉讼程序规则》的其他规则时，亦应紧记凌驾性目标。1998年《民事诉讼程序规则》的目的性解释是为了确保民事诉讼程序的精神在法院内得以保持，这也是1998年新规则取代旧规则的主要原因。在讨论首要目标的同时，1998年《民事诉讼程序规则》的新精神也不能忽视次要目标，如确保案件得到公正处理和费用相称。

Therefore, with increased efficiency due to proper case management, disputes are resolved between the parties, but the courts will always be mindful of the public interests in private disputes, although in western jurisprudence, the main reference point is individuals' rights and by extension the rights of businesses. In the authors' view, there is also no denying that there are public dimensions to civil litigation in England & Wales — firstly, due to the administrative burden of civil litigation and a need for the executive to manage it effectively; and secondly, because the stakeholder approach cannot be neglected by the courts in many cases. The second approach may be argued to some extent to be similar to the PRC's approach, even though this approach, in the context of taking into acccount public interest, is more visible in the PRC. The issue of public interest being taken into account is also likely to affect the outcome of any litigation in the PRC.

因此，由于适当的案件管理提高了效率，纠纷在当事人之间得以解决，但法院始终会注意私人纠纷中的公共利益，尽管在西方法学中，主要的参照点是个人权利，并延伸到企业权利。笔者认为，英格兰与威尔士的民事诉讼也不可否认存在公共性--首先，由于民事诉讼的行政负担，行政部门需要对其进行有效管理；其次，法院在许多情况下不能忽视利益相关者的方法。第二种方法在某种程度上可以说与中华人民共和国的方法相似，尽管在考虑公众利益的背景下，这种方法在中华人民共和国更为明显。考虑公众利益的问题也可能影响到在中国进行的任何诉讼的结果。

In the PRC, in *CPL* the principles and aims are mentioned at the beginning through its various articles detailing the *principles of equality, disposition, litigation rights of debate and argument, of mediation, of supervision and so forth.*[528] They are meant to be applicable throughout the civil process. According to PRC scholars, even the meaning of various articles needs be interpreted through the prism of the above principles. However, are these principles inherent in nature? If they are indeed inherent in nature, what was the need to list these principles out in the *CPL*? This again, in the authors' view, highlights where the theory diverges from the practice of law in the PRC. In defence of the PRC's civil procedural system and law, it is relatively new in comparison to *CPR 1998*.

在中国，《民事诉讼法》在开头就提到了这些原则和目标，并在各条款中详细说明了平等原则、处分原则、辩论和辩论的诉讼权利原则、调解原则、监督原则等 这些原则适用于整个民事诉讼过程。根据中国学者的观点，即使是各种条款的含义也需要通过上述原则的棱镜来解释。然而，这些原则是否是固有的？如果它们确实是固有的，又有什么必要在《民事诉讼法》中列出这些原则呢？笔者认为，这再次凸显了理论与中国法律实践的分歧。为中国的民事诉讼制度和法律辩护，与英格兰及威尔士 1998 年《民事诉讼程序规则》相比，中国的民事诉讼制度和法律相对较新。

In one way, because the *CPR 1998* in England & Wales has introduced case management powers for judges, it is now somewhat equivalent to the approach of judges in the PRC. However, *CPR 1998* also introduced in England & Wales the unique concept of overriding objective. This concept is unique to common law systems and brings elements of *procedural justice* into elements of *substantive justice*. This approach of the judges also serves the larger purpose within the English civil procedure system to ensure that stakeholders are aware of the need to act fairly to avoid using excessive judicial resources.

从某个角度来看，由于英格兰及威尔士《1998 年民事诉讼程序规则》引入了法官的案件管理权力，因此现时的做法在某程度上等同于中国法官的做法。然而，《1998 年民事诉讼程序法》还在英格兰和威尔士引入了"首要目标"这一独特概念。这一概念是普通法系所独有的，它将程序正义的要素融入实体正义的要素之中。法官的这一做法也符合英国民事诉讼制度的更大目的，即确保利益相关者意识到公平行事的必要性，以避免使用过多的司法资源。

The subtle difference between the PRC's aim to obtain substantive justice as compared to the English courts' focus to maintain the delicate balance between procedural and substantive justice,[529] is highlighted by Sorabjee's view on the overriding objectives in *CPR 1998,* which also highlights, in the authors' view, the contrast with the PRC

索拉布吉对 1998 年《民事诉讼程序规则》首要目标的看法突显了中国获得实体正义的目标与英国法院注重维持程序正义与实体正义之间微妙平衡的目标之间的微妙差异，在作者看来，这也突显了与中国民事诉讼程序制度的对比：

528Refer to Chapter 4, §4.2.2.1。参见第 4 章第 4.2.2.1 节。

529John Sorabji, Andenas Mads, et al., "The Road to New Street Station: Fact, Fiction and Overriding Objective," in *Legal Studies Research Paper Series: Paper No. 21/2011* (Cambridge, 2011), 18.
John Sorabji、Andenas Mads 等人, "通往新街车站之路：Fact, Fiction and Overriding Objective," in Legal Studies Research Paper Series: 第 21/2011 号论文，剑桥，2011 年，第 18 页。

civil procedural system:

(1) it does not contain a singular commitment to substantive justice's achievement; on the contrary it contains an equal commitment to both substantive and procedural justice [emphasis added];

(1) 它并不包含对实现实体公正的单一承诺；相反，它包含对实体公正和程序公正的同等承诺[着重部分由作者标明]；

(2) it does not treat economy and efficiency as means for securing substantive justice through the legal process; instead it regards economy and efficiency as principles which place a limit on the civil process' commitment to securing substantive justice; and

(2) 它不把节约和效率作为通过法律程序确保实质正义的手段；相反，它把节约和效率视为对民事程序致力于确保实质正义的承诺加以限制的原则；以及

(3) it requires a rigorous approach by courts to litigants who fail to comply with procedural obligations, and who thus fail to make proper use of a fair process provided so that they can pursue substantive justice.[530]

(3) 这就要求法院对不遵守程序性义务的诉讼当事人采取严格的处理办法，因为他们没有适当利用所提供的公平程序来追求实质性正义。

4.6 Comparison between Civil Litigation and Commercial Litigation

民事诉讼与商业诉讼的比较

In England & Wales, there is no difference between civil litigation and commercial litigation due to the adversarial nature of the system followed in litigation. However, in the PRC, first there is no separate commercial code, so civil law and commercial law would appear to be same. However, in practice, commercial litigation in the same civil justice system that also runs ordinary civil disputes would create hurdles as by operation of *General Principles of Civil Law 1986*, principles of honesty, fairness and public law enter the arena of commercial disputes and litigation by the backdoor. These principles operate in commercial law litigation even when these disputes are very private in nature and focus on earning profits.

在英格兰和威尔士，由于诉讼采用对抗制，民事诉讼和商业诉讼没有区别。然而，在中国，首先没有单独的商法典，因此民法和商法看似相同。然而，在实践中，在同样处理普通民事纠纷的民事司法系统中进行商事诉讼会造成障碍，因为根据 1986 年《民法通则》的规定，诚信、公平和公法原则通过后门进入商事纠纷和诉讼领域。这些原则适用于商业法诉讼，即使这些纠纷的性质是非常私人的，并且侧重于赚取利润。

[530]Ibid., 17。同上，第 17 页。

These principles will have a major impact on the course of any commercial litigation, as many cases find that public law and public interests affect the very private commercial disputes. The advent of the socialist market economy is a recent phenomenon dating from the 1990s it would appear that this aspect is not yet fully integrated in commercial litigation in PRC. This feature of PRC jurisdiction is very different from England & Wales, and it is a factor for the difference in how commercial litigation is run in the civil justice system in both jurisdictions.[531]

这些原则将对任何商业诉讼的进程产生重大影响，因为许多案件发现公法和公共利益影响到非常私人的商业纠纷。社会主义市场经济的出现是 20 世纪 90 年代以来的一个新现象，但在中国，这方面似乎尚未完全融入商业诉讼。中国司法的这一特点与英格兰和威尔士有很大的不同，这也是两个司法管辖区的民事司法系统中商业诉讼运作方式不同的一个因素。

[531]Refer, Chapter 4, §4.4, §4.5 & §4.6。参见第 4 章第 4.4、4.5 和 4.6 节。

CHAPTER FIVE — LAW IN ACTION— JUDGES' POWER AND REASONING —— COMMON LAW v. CHINESE LAW

第五章 诉讼中的法律——法官的权力与推论——普通法与中国法

5.1 Judges' Role in Accepting & Dealing with Case–England & Wales and PRC

法官在受理和处理案件中的角色——英格兰、威尔士和中国

In the previous Chapters, the authors have discussed issues from jurisprudence and philosophy, but in this Chapter, the authors will discuss their influence on *law in action* in courts. Very briefly, unlike in the PRC, where due to the inquisitorial system judges play an important role in whether to accept applications into the courts, English judges have no such role in the adversarial common law system. The differing role of the judge due to philosophical underpinnings has profound effects: due to their investigative powers in the inquisitorial system, judges in the PRC can even decline applications at an early stage. This issue is also discussed in Chapter Seven, when analysing issues from the perspective of standards of proof.[532] As discussed earlier, the claimants are required to adduce enough evidence even at the stage of submitting applications to the PRC courts to satisfy the judges manning the *case filing division*.

在前几章中，笔者已经讨论了法理学和哲学方面的问题，但在本章中，笔者将讨论它们在法庭诉讼中的影响。简而言之，与中国不同，在中国，由于调查制度，法官在是否接受法院的申请方面发挥着重要作用，而英国法官在对抗普通法制度中没有这样的作用。由于哲学基础的不同，法官的不同角色产生了深远的影响：由于他们在讯问制度中的调查权，中国的法官甚至可以在早期阶段拒绝申请。第七章从举证标准的角度分析了这一问题。参见第7章第7.4节。如前所述，即使在向中国法院提交申请的阶段，索赔人也须提出足够的证据，以满足负责案件归档部门的法官的要求。

[532] Refer, Chapter 7, §7.4。参见第 7 章第 7.4 节。

5.2 Judges – Common Law, Civil Law, PRC

法官——普通法系、大陆法系，中国

Judges are often seen as the representation of power within any state. However, in modern society, with the separation of power between executive, legislature and judiciary, judges are independent from intervention by the executive or legislative branch in democracies. However, the judges could, a long time ago, be dismissed at the whims of monarchs or the executive in most jurisdictions. Over the years, this arbitrary power of the monarchs and later the executive was curtailed and accordingly, the situation began to improve in England & Wales. The legislature started to legislate to ensure that judges could not be dismissed at the whims and fancies of executives and/or monarchs; however, judges can be dismissed under well-defined circumstances.

法官通常被视为国家权力的代表。然而，在现代社会，在行政、立法和司法三权分立的情况下，民主国家的法官是独立的，不受行政或立法部门的干预。然而，很久以前，在大多数司法管辖区，法官可以因君主或行政部门的一时兴起而被解雇。多年来，君主和后来的行政当局的专断权力被削弱，相应地，英格兰和威尔士的情况开始改善。立法机关开始立法，以确保法官不会因行政长官或君主的异想天开而被解雇；但是，在明确规定的情况下，法官可以被免职。

The above developments led to the concept of '*personal independence of a judge*' and was an important factor for ensuring '*judicial independence*'. It is important to note that in the PRC, the judiciary remains answerable to the National People's Congress ('NPC').[533] There is a case where a judge found one of the statutes of Local Congress at the provincial level not fit, and therefore declared that provincial legislation void. According to Wang, this judicial action led to the impeachment of that judge by the Local Congress.[534] The reporting structure of the judiciary to legislature, supervised by the Procuratorate System, is clearly a distinct system unique to the PRC.[535]

上述发展导致了“法官个人独立”的概念，是确保“司法独立”的重要因素。值得注意的是，在中国，司法机构仍然对全国人民代表大会负责。有一个案例，法官发现省级人民代表大会的一项法规不合适，因此宣布该立法无效。据王利明说，这一司法行动导致该法官被地方人民代表大会弹劾。司法机关向立法机关报告的结构，由检察院系统监督，显然是中华人民共和国特有的独特制度。

The judges work within the structure and organisation of the court system. The authors have briefly discussed the structure

法官在法院系统的结构和组织中工作。笔者在第四章中简要讨论了英格兰、

[533]See, Art. 67(6) of *Constitution of PRC 1982*, by which SPC is answerable to NPC. See also, Art. 104 of *Constitution of PRC 1982* pursuant to which People's Court is answerable to Local People's Congress at provincial level in PRC. Refer also to Figure 8 in Chapter 4 that highlights the reporting structure for the PRC courts.
参见1982年《中华人民共和国宪法》第67条第6款，最高人民法院对全国人民代表大会负责。另见1982年《中华人民共和国宪法》第104条，根据该条，人民法院对中国省级地方人民代表大会负责。另请参阅第4章图8，该图强调了中国法院的报告结构。

[534]Liming Wang, "The Achievements and Prospects of Court Reforms in China," *Frontiers L. China* 1, no. 1 (2006): 11.
王利明，“中国法院改革的成就与展望”，《中国司法前沿》第1卷，(2006): 11。

[535] Refer Chapter 4, Figure 8, 9 &10.
参见第 4 章，图 8、9 和 10。

and organisation of courts in both England & Wales and the PRC in Chapter Four.[536] Historically, in the later years, as the monarch was subject to the laws of England, this political feature ensured that the judges remained independent and were paid a salary. In one instance, between AD 1685-1688, a Monarch dismissed a few judges as they were not willing to grant that Monarch the requisite power to repeal Acts which were legislated in Parliament. Subsequently, in the eighteenth century, a piece of legislation called *Act of Settlement 1701*,[537] pursuant to which judges were appointed for life, helped to curtail the influence of monarchs on judges.[538]

威尔士和中国法院的结构和组织。从历史上看，在后来的岁月里，由于君主受制于英格兰的法律，这种政治特征确保了法官保持独立，并领取薪水。例如，在公元1685-1688年间，一位君主解雇了几名法官，因为他们不愿意授予君主废除国会立法的必要权力。随后，在18世纪，一项名为《王位继承法》的立法帮助削弱了君主对法官的影响。根据该法，法官是终身任命的。

The eligibility requirements to become judges are stated in *Tribunals, Courts and Enforcement Act 2007*.[539] This Act has vastly expanded the opportunity for people from a much larger section of society to become judges. Possible candidates are now not required to come from the exclusive club of barristers, but they can even be law scholars from the Universities. This has the effect of creating social mobility with regard to the selection of judges.

成为法官的资格要求见2007年《法庭、法院和执行法案》。该法案极大地扩大了社会上更多阶层的人成为法官的机会。现在，可能的候选人不需要来自大律师俱乐部，甚至可以是大学的法律学者。这在挑选法官方面产生了社会流动性的影响。

The ratio of judge to population in 2009 in a common law jurisdiction of England & Wales was around 1 to 39,506 inhabitants, whereas in the civil jurisdictions of Germany it was one judge per 4080 inhabitants in 2008, and one judge per 6368 in Sweden in the same period.[540] It seems there are more judges per inhabitants in the civil law jurisdictions in comparison to common law jurisdictions.

2009年，在英格兰和威尔士的普通法司法管辖区，法官与人口的比例约为1比39,506，而在德国的民事司法管辖区，2008年每4080名居民中有一名法官，同一时期瑞典每6368名居民中有一名法官。大陆法系司法管辖区的法官数量似乎比普通法司法管辖区多。

On the other hand, as discussed earlier, the legal system is relatively new in the PRC. *Law on Judges 1995* was introduced in the PRC to improve the quality of judges and thereby improve overall judicial activities within PRC courts. Following that, after years of flux in the legal system, 1999 heralded a massive attempt at reform, after which the

另一方面，如前所述，中国的法律体系相对较新。1995年中国颁布了《法官法》，旨在提高法官的素质，从而改善中国法院的整体司法活动。此后，经过多年的法律制度变动，1999年开始了大规模的改革尝试，随后公布了中央法

[536]Refer to the discussion of structure and organisation of the courts in England & Wales in Chapter 4, §4.1.1, and for the PRC in Chapter 4, §4.1.3.
参见第4章第4.1.1节中对英格兰和威尔士法院结构和组织的讨论，以及第4章第4.1.3节中对中国法院结构和组织的讨论。
[537]12 and 13 Will 3 c. 2.
[538]Thomas Lundmark, *Charting the Divide between Common and Civil Law* (New York; Oxford: Oxford University Press, 2012), 204.
托马斯·伦德马克：《划分普通法和大陆法》（纽约；牛津：牛津大学出版社，2012），第204页。
[539]2007, c 15.
[540]Lundmark, *Divide between Common and Civil Law*, 204–07.
伦德马克：《划分普通法和大陆法》，第204-207页。

centralised court reform blueprint was published.[541] In 2001, the NPC amended three laws — *The Law on Judges*, *The Law on Procurators* and *The Law on Lawyers*.[542] In 2001, the Supreme Court of the PRC issued guidelines on ethics to enable judges to implement both procedural and substantive justice.[543] Gradually, there was a focus on developing teams of judges, including assistants. There were plans put in place for their continuous training.

院改革蓝图。2001年，全国人大修改了法官法、检察法和律师法。2001年，中华人民共和国最高法院发布了道德准则，以使法官能够同时执行程序正义和实体正义。渐渐地，他们开始注重培养包括助理在内的法官团队。为他们的持续培训制定了计划。

Common-law judges depend on the advocates running the cases for their clients, while in civil law jurisdictions the focus is usually on one expert judge guiding everyone else in the panel. It would not be inaccurate to say that active judges in civil law jurisdictions also at times guide the parties' lawyers. It is important to note that the judge to population ratio is also higher in civil law jurisdictions in comparison to common law jurisdictions.

普通法法官依靠律师为其客户处理案件，而在民法司法管辖区，重点通常是由一位专家法官指导小组中的其他所有人。说大陆法系司法管辖区的在职法官有时也指导当事人的律师是不准确的。值得注意的是，与普通法司法管辖区相比，大陆法系司法管辖区的法官与人口比例也更高。

The authors wish to highlight the advances made in cognitive science that highlight "that patterns of acting and thinking [of any human] are not governed by reason, but rather are ingrained, unconscious, or triggered by our automatic nervous system."[544] The authors' view is that the effects of education, history, cultural values, predominant jurisprudence, and political philosophy are all bound to dominate thoughts and assumptions in all areas of the judicial process. These are exactly the invisible factors and contexts the authors have been speaking about from the start of the book.

笔者希望强调认知科学的进步，强调"任何人的行为和思维模式都不受理性的支配，而是根深蒂固的、无意识的，或者是由我们的自动神经系统触发的。"笔者的观点是，教育、历史、文化价值、主流法理学和政治哲学的影响都必然会主导司法过程各个领域的思想和假设。这些正是笔者从书的开头就一直在讲的看不见的因素和语境。这些因素甚至对法院内部的司法活动产生深远的

[541]See *Outline of Five-year Reform* (referred to here as *Five-year Outline),* Document Issued by the Supreme People's Court, No. [1999] 28, October, 20, 1999.
见《五年改革纲要》（以下简称《五年纲要》），最高人民法院发的文件，第 691 号。[1999] 1999 年 10 月 20 日。

[542]See *The Law on Judges*, passed through the 12th Convention of the Standing Committee of the 8th National People's Congress on Feb. 28, 1995, and amended by the 22nd Convention of the 9th National People's Congress on Jun. 30, 2001; *The Law on Procurators*, passed through the 12th Convention of the Standing Committee of the 8th National People's Congress on Feb. 28th, 1995, and amended by the 22nd Convention of the 9th National People's Congress on Jun. 30th, 2001; *The Law on Lawyers,* passed through the 19th Convention of the Standing Committee of the 8th National People's Congress on May.15th, 1996, and amended by the 25th Convention of the Standing Committee of the Ninth National People's Congress at its 25th Meeting on December 29, 2001, and revised at the 30th Meeting of the Standing Committee of the Tenth National People's Congress on October 28, 2007.
1995年2月28日第八届全国人民代表大会常务委员会第十二次会议通过并于2001年6月30日第九届全国人民代表大会第二十二次会议修正的《法官法》；1995年2月28日第八届全国人民代表大会常务委员会第十二次会议通过，2001年6月30日第九届全国人民代表大会第二十二次会议修正；《律师法》由1996年5月15日第八届全国人民代表大会常务委员会第十九次会议通过，2001年12月29日第九届全国人民代表大会常务委员会第二十五次会议修正，2007年10月28日第十届全国人民代表大会常务委员会第三十次会议修改。

[543]See *Basic Professional Ethics for Judges,* Document Issued by the Supreme People's Court of China, on October,18, 2001.
见2001年10月18日最高人民法院发布的《法官基本职业道德》。

[544]Nicole E. Negowetti, "Judicial Decisionmaking, Empathy, and the Limits of Perception," *Akron L. Rev.* 47, no. 3 (2015): 694.
妮可 E. 内格韦提，"司法决策、移情和感知的限制"，《亚克朗法律评论》，第47卷，第3期(2015): 第694页。

Such factors have a profound effect even on judicial activities within the courts. This dominance of assumptions and cultural habits in the minds of judges can lead them to take mental shortcuts called "'heuristics' or 'schemas' to make complex decisions."[545] All the above factors affecting the judges can lead them to have *cognitive illusions*.

影响。这种假设和文化习惯在法官头脑中的主导地位会导致他们采取被称为"启发式"或"图式"的心理捷径来做出复杂的决定。以上影响法官的因素都会导致法官产生认知错觉。

In western jurisprudence, there is a focus on emotional detachment from the cases so that judges can remain rational. However, the cognitive sciences seem to suggest it is impossible for any human being to have complete emotional detachment.[546] Accordingly, taking into account the fact that a complete emotional detachment is not possible for any judge, then it may be could be called as a realist version of jurisprudence that impinges on judicial decision making.

在西方法理学中，有一个重点是情感脱离案件，这样法官就可以保持理性。然而，认知科学似乎表明，任何人都不可能完全脱离情感。因此，考虑到完全的情感超然对任何法官来说都是不可能的，那么它可以被称为影响司法决策的法理学的现实主义版本。

5.2.1 Jurisprudence and Law in context of Judges in Adversarial System versus Inquisitorial System

抗辩制与讯问制下法官的法理学与法律

We have seen in Chapter Three that jurisprudents had various viewpoints in most jurisdictions. Nevertheless, whatever may be the schools of thought as to the concept of law, it ultimately boils down to the elementary fact that eventually the judges will have to adjudicate disputes in the courts through an interpretive process as to the function of practice of law.

我们在第三章中已经看到，在大多数司法管辖区，法理学家有不同的观点。然而，无论关于法律概念的思想流派是什么，它最终归结为一个基本事实，即法官最终将不得不通过对法律实践功能的解释过程来裁决法庭上的争端。

Comparativists, who prefer the continental system over the common law system, feel that the common-law judges' way of finding the appropriate law for the problem is unsystematic. It is even said that "continental lawyers think systematically; common lawyers think casuistically."[547] The mental process

比较主义者倾向于大陆法系而非普通法系，他们认为普通法系法官为问题寻找合适法律的方式是不系统的。甚至有人说，"大陆法学家有系统地思考；一般的律师都是诡辩的。"法官寻找相关法律的心理过程几乎在

[545] Ibid.

[546] Ibid., 698。同前注，第 698 页。

[547] Rene David and John E.C. Brierley, *Major Legal Systems in the World Today*, 3rd ed. (London: Sweet & Maxwell, 1985), 94. It was quoted in Lundmark, *Divide between Common and Civil Law*, 263.

that a judge goes through to find the relevant law is nearly the same in almost all jurisdictions. The attack on the incoherence of legal reasoning in common law, as discussed in Chapter Three, was accelerated in the USA by Legal realists.[548] The realists' argument was that there is incoherence not only because of inconsistent statutory interpretation, but also with reference to the legal reasoning emerging out of common law cases.[549] In fact, in the authors' experience, many Chinese students who go to the US , UK and other common law jurisdictions to study law, struggle to come to terms with the common law system.

所有司法管辖区都是一样的。正如第三章所讨论的，对普通法中法律推理不连贯的攻击在美国被法律现实主义者加速了。现实主义者的论点是，不连贯不仅是因为不一致的法定解释，而且还与普通法案例中出现的法律推理有关。事实上，根据笔者的经验，许多去美国、英国和其他普通法系国家学习法律的中国学生都很难适应普通法系。

The civil justice system comprises two kinds of systems — the adversarial system associated with common law systems such as in England & Wales, and the inquisitorial system such as in the PRC and continental Europe. Every system has its own set of procedures to ensure that justice is seen to be done and done eventually. The main difference between the two systems lies in which party is in control of the process; for example, in the inquisitorial system, the judges control the litigation process, whereas in the common law, the litigation is controlled by the parties to the dispute. The role of judges is more passive in the common law system, relative to the inquisitorial system.[550]

民事司法制度包括两种制度——与普通法系（如英格兰和威尔士）相关的对抗制度，以及与中国和欧洲大陆相关的讯问制度。每个制度都有自己的一套程序，以确保正义得到伸张，并最终得到伸张。这两种制度的主要区别在于哪一方在控制过程；例如，在讯问制中，法官控制诉讼过程，而在普通法中，诉讼由争议各方控制。与讯问制相比，普通法制度下法官的角色更为被动。

Hodgson has discussed the jurisprudential difference in the way the two systems work in practice. She was of the view that the inquisitorial system works on the concept that in litigation, it is the State's responsibility to "recreate what the parties do not say." The State's role, she notes, was also to balance any inequality between the parties. In the adversarial system available under the common law, it is assumed that all parties are equal and therefore, they must try their best to bring out the

霍奇森讨论了两种制度在实践中运作方式的法理差异。她认为，讯问制度的作用是基于这样一个概念，即在诉讼中，国家有责任"再现当事人没有说的话"。她指出，国家的作用还在于平衡各方之间的不平等。在普通法下的对抗制度中，假设所有当事人都是平等的，因此，他们须尽最大

Rene David, John E.C. Brierley，《当今世界的主要法律制度》，第3版（伦敦：Sweet & Maxwell出版社，1985），第94页。引自伦德马克，《划分普通法和大陆法》，第263页。

548Refer, Chapter 3, §3.2.4 in context of Legal Realism and Critical Legal Studies.
参见《法律现实主义和批判法律研究》第3章第3.2.4节。

549Hugh Collins, "Law as Politics: Progressive American Perspectives," in *Introduction to Jurisprudence and Legal Theory: Commentary and Materials*, Anne Barron, et al. (London: Butterworths, 2002), 287.
休·柯林斯，"作为政治的法律：进步的美国视角"，载《法理学和法律理论导论：评论和材料》，安妮·巴伦等人，伦敦：巴特沃斯出版社，2002），第287页。

550Fabien Gélinas, et al., *Foundations of Civil Justice: Toward a Value-Based Framework for Reform* (Heidelberg; New York; Dordrecht; London: Springer, 2015), 65. See also Antony Duff, et al., *The Trial on Trial: Volume I: Truth and Due Process* (Oxford: Hart Publishing, 2004), 223.
法比恩·格姆林纳斯等人，《民事司法基础：走向基于价值的改革框架》，海德堡；纽约；多德雷赫；伦敦：Sprinter，2015，第65页。另见安东尼·达夫等人，《审判中的审判：第一卷：真相与正当程序》（牛津：哈特出版社，2004年），第223页。

truth.[551] Shin, in the context of arbitrations, argued for the advantages of the adversarial system in finding the truth.[552]

努力说出真相。在仲裁背景下，申主张对抗制度在寻找真相方面的优势。

Over the years lot of research has been done by scholars on the advantages of one system over the other system. Block and his fellow scholars found that either of the two systems cannot assert their hold over the truth or efficiency. However, they found that efficiency, including hidden facts coming to the fore during litigation as well as accuracy of decision, depends "significantly upon the information structure of the case."[553] If there is no way any hidden information can be revealed, then it was found that inquisitorial system is better. However, if both the parties have access to the information, then Gélinas et al are of the view that the adversarial system is better for efficiency and accuracy of the decision.[554]

多年来，学者们对一种制度相对于另一种制度的优势进行了大量研究。布洛克和他的学者同事们发现，这两种体系中的任何一种都无法对真理或效率施加影响。然而，他们发现，效率，包括在诉讼过程中出现的隐藏事实以及判决的准确性，"在很大程度上取决于案件的信息结构"。如果没有办法揭露任何隐藏的信息，那么人们发现，讯问制度是更好的。然而，如果双方都能获得信息，那么格姆林纳斯等人认为对抗系统对于决策的效率和准确性更好。

However, there are scholars such as Shin, who have done research in the context of arbitration carried out in the common law tradition, have concluded that the common-law adversarial system is better than the inquisitorial system as burden of proof can be allocated more efficiently, and the common law system has more inherent ability to "extract maximal informational content from seemingly inconclusive results."[555] Shin states that this is due to "the <u>discretion</u> [emphasis added] of the arbitrator to exercise the appropriate degree of skepticism and to react in a sophisticated way to the self-interested reporting strategies of the two opposing parties."[556]

然而，也有像Shin这样的学者在普通法系仲裁的背景下进行了研究，他们得出结论，普通法系的对抗性制度比质询制度更好，因为它可以更有效地分配举证责任，而且普通法系更具有"从看似不确定的结果中提取最大信息内容"的内在能力。Shin表示，这是由于"仲裁者的<u>自由裁量权</u>（强调添加）行使适当程度的怀疑，并以一种复杂的方式对对立双方的自利报告策略做出反应。"

The authors' view is that though there is truth to the statement that there is an assumption in the common law system that

笔者认为，虽然普通法系存在着当事人平等的假设，但在当事人能否

[551] Jacqueline Hodgson, "Conceptions of the Trial in Inquisitorial and Adversarial Procedure," in *The Trial on Trial: Judgment and Calling to Account*, A. Duff, Farmer, S Marshall, and V. Tadros (Oxford; Portland; Or: Hart, 2004), 240n1. This was discussed and quoted in Gélinas et al., *Foundations of Civil Justice*, 66.
杰奎琳·霍奇森，"审讯和对抗性程序中审判的概念"，载于《对审判的审判：判决和问责》，A.达夫、法默、S.马歇尔和V.塔德罗斯(牛津；波特兰;或者：Hart，2004), 240n1。格姆林纳斯等人，《民事司法基础》，第66页对此进行了讨论和引用。
[552] H.S. Shin, "Adversarial and Inquisitorial Procedure in Arbitration," *Rand J. Economics* 29, no. 2 (1998): 378–405.
H.S. Shin，"仲裁中的对抗性和调查性程序"，《经济研究》第29期。2(1998): 378-405。
[553] M.K. Block, et al., "An Experimental Comparison of Adversarial Versus Inquisitorial Procedural Regimes," *AM. L. & Econ. Rev.* 2, no. 1 (2000): 170–94. This article was also discussed in Gélinas, et al., *Foundations of Civil Justice*, 66.
M.K. Block, et al.，"对抗性和调查性程序制度的实验比较"，*AM. L. & Econ. Rev* 第2卷，第1期。(2000)：第170-94页。这篇文章也在格姆林纳斯等人的《民事司法基础》（Foundations of Civil Justice）中讨论过。
[554] Gélinas, et al., *Foundations of Civil Justice*, 65–75.
格姆林纳斯等人，《民事司法基础》，第65-75页。
[555] Ibid., 66。同前注，第66页。
[556] Shin, "Adversarial or Inquisitorial," 395. This was also quoted in Gélinas, et al., *Foundations of Civil* Justice, 66.
Shin，《对抗或审讯》，第395页。格姆林纳斯等人，《民事司法基础》，第66页也引用了这一点。

every party is equal, the system is also aware of the reality of the matter in relation to the issue of whether a party can bear the legal costs. It is pertinent to note that in the most prominent common law jurisdictions such as England & Wales, there has been a system of disclosure of information by every party to the litigation to other parties. For example, CPR r. 31.6 in relation to *Standard disclosure* requires a party to disclose only –

承担诉讼费用的问题上，普通法系也意识到了现实情况。值得注意的是，在英格兰和威尔士等最突出的普通法司法管辖区，存在诉讼各方向其他各方披露信息的制度。例如，CPR第31.6条关于标准披露要求一方仅披露——

a. the documents on which he relies; and
b. the documents which –
c. adversely affect his own case [emphasis added];
d. adversely affect another party's case; or
e. support another party's case; and
f. the documents which he is required to disclose by a relevant practice direction.

a.他所依赖的文件；和
b.文件——
c.不利地影响他自己的情况；
d.对他人案件产生不利影响的；或
e.支持另一方的案件；和
f.有关执业指示要求他披露的文件。

It is noteworthy that a party is required to disclose even those documents that can adversely affect his own case as well, which is not usually the case in the inquisitorial system. In the inquisitorial system, it is incumbent upon the judges to find the relevant adverse facts.

值得注意的是，当事人甚至被要求披露那些可能对他自己的案件产生不利影响的文件，而在讯问制度中通常不是这样。在讯问制度下，找出相关的不利事实是法官的责任。

In the common law system, the arguments are usually presented in a partisan way, and the roles of the judges and advocates are clearly defined in this system. One key remark by Fuller was that the inquisitorial procedure has pre-trial efficiency but is in fact not prepared for unpredictable events during the trial. Fuller's view was that the early decision-making by a judge in the inquisitorial system was unsuitable to deal with the unpredictable events that can happen during the trial. Therefore, the civil system carries the risk of not having fully ascertained the weight of all the evidence. Pound also criticised the adversarial system as "contentious procedure, which turns litigation into a game" and "gives a false notion of the purpose and the end of law.[557]

在普通法系中，辩论通常以党派的方式进行，法官和辩护人的角色在普通法系中有明确的界定。富勒的一个关键评论是，讯问程序具有审前效率，但实际上并没有为审判期间不可预测的事件做好准备。富勒的观点是，在审讯制度下，法官的早期决策不适合处理审判过程中可能发生的不可预测的事件。因此，民事制度有可能没有充分确定所有证据的重要性。庞德还批评对抗性制度是“有争议的程序，它把诉讼变成了一种游戏”，并且“对法律的目的和目的给出了错误概念”。

In spite of the differences between the two systems, however, it

然而，尽管两种制度之间存在差

[557]R. Pound, "The Causes of Popular Dissatisfaction with the Administration of Justice," *Reports of the American Bar Association* 29 (1906): 395.
R.庞德：《大众对司法行政不满的原因》，《美国律师协会报告》，第29期，1906年，第395页。

is clear that both have the same objective. The underlying values or principles of the legal systems are, therefore, crucial to the discretionary power of any judge in either system.[558] A few of the examples of values or principles that are common to both the system are: "fairness, accuracy, humanity, and coherence with liberal-democratic values."[559]

异，但很明显，两者都具有相同的目标。因此，法律制度的基本价值或原则对两种制度中任何法官的自由裁量权至关重要。这两个系统共同的价值观或原则的几个例子是"公平、准确、人性和与自由民主价值观的一致性。"

5.2.1.1 Key Defining Characteristics of Adversarial and Inquisitorial Systems

抗辩制和问责制的关键定义特征

A few defining goals of the two systems are: finding the truth, discovery and disclosure to find the truth, cross-examination to find the truth, and economic equality in finding truth in the adjudication. The authors will discuss these goals later in this Chapter.

这两种制度的几个明确目标是：发现真相，发现和披露真相，质证发现真相，以及在裁决中发现真相的经济平等。笔者将在本章后面讨论这些目标。

5.2.1.1.1 Finding the truth

寻找真相

This aspect has been discussed in the preceding chapter under the section of Legal Philosophy.[560]

这方面已经在前一章的法哲学小节中讨论过了。

5.2.1.1.2 Discovery and Disclosure Process in Finding the Truth - England & Wales and PRC

寻找真相的发现与披露过程——英格兰、威尔士与中华人民共和国

Many movies show scenes where new evidence suddenly appears from one party in the middle of litigation. However, civil litigation does not work like this in the adversarial system. The approach of the lawyers to keep their cards close to the chest has been displaced by openness, with the onus now on parties to put their cards on the table, thus potentially encouraging settlement and saving ever-increasing litigation costs. This aspect of the common law system was discussed

很多电影都有在诉讼过程中突然出现新证据的场景。然而，民事诉讼在对抗性制度中并非如此。律师们守口如瓶的做法已经被公开所取代，当事人现在有责任把他们的牌放在桌子上，从而可能鼓励和解并节省不断增加的诉讼成本。在分析英格兰和威尔士CPR的首要目标时，讨论了普通法制度的这一方

[558]See § 5.3 of this Chapter。参见本章5.3节。

[559] Gélinas et al., *Foundations of Civil Justice*, 67.
格姆林纳斯等人，《民事司法基础》，第 67 页。

[560]Refer, Chapter 4, §4.2 & earlier §5.2.
参考第4章第4.2节和前面的第5.2节。

when analysing the overriding objective of CPR in the context of England & Wales. The authors have discussed earlier in this Chapter,[561] that pursuant to the obligations of *standard disclosure*, the parties to litigation need to disclose evidence even when such evidence would undermine their own case. This system works in the English courts, where the passive judge has no power to collate evidence, and each party is responsible for their own case.[562]

面。笔者在本章前文已经讨论过，根据标准披露义务，诉讼当事人即使在证据对自己的案件不利的情况下也需要披露证据。这一制度在英国法院有效，被动法官没有权力整理证据，每一方都要对自己的案件负责。

In the US, another prominent common law system, the process of discovery in its adversarial system is even more elaborate. In the discovery process, information is gathered formally from the parties through written questions by a process called '*interrogatories*'. In this process, requests for copies of documents and for admission, which the opponents are free to admit or deny, can be made. However, a special method by which civil litigation is carried out in the US is through the process of 'depositions.'[563] In this process, prior to the trial, witnesses are questioned under oath by the parties' attorneys, and the witnesses' answers are recorded by a court reporter; these recorded statements can be used in a future trial.

在另一个著名的普通法系国家美国，其对抗性制度的发现过程更为复杂。在证据开示过程中，信息是通过书面提问从当事人那里正式收集的，这一过程被称为"询问"。在这一过程中，可以要求提供文件副本和允许，对手可以自由地接受或拒绝。然而，在美国进行民事诉讼的一种特殊方法是通过"证词"程序。在这一程序中，在审判前，由当事人的律师对证人进行宣誓询问，证人的回答由法庭记录员记录；这些记录的陈述可以在将来的审判中使用。

However, in the inquisitorial system, most of the collection of evidence is left to the judges; to some extent the standard of proof to even commence a claim is higher, so considerable relevant evidence will have to be provided to the courts by the parties to the litigation.

然而，在讯问制度中，大部分证据的收集都留给了法官；在某种程度上，甚至提起诉讼的举证标准也更高，因此诉讼各方必须向法院提供相当多的相关证据。

In the PRC's *CPL 2023*, there is no separate law for any equivalent disclosure or discovery process. However, *CPL* regulates a system in relation to Chapter VI. CPL provides that the claimants have to provide evidence to prove their allegations. The courts will examine the evidence *comprehensively and objectively*.[564] In addition, in the PRC,

在中国2023年《民事诉讼法》中，没有单独的法律规定任何等效的披露或发现过程。但是，《民事诉讼法》规定了与第六章有关的制度，索赔人必须提供证据证明其索赔。法院将全面客观地审查证据。此外，在中国，原告的请求或被告的反诉必须附有证据。

[561] Refer, *CPR* r. 31.6 and its discussion in §5.2.1.
参考CPR第31.6条及其在§5.2.1中的讨论。

[562] Susan Blake, *A Practical Approach to Effective Litigation*, 7th ed. (Oxford: Oxford University Press, 2009), 378–9.
苏珊·布莱克：《有效诉讼的实践方法》，第7版，牛津：牛津大学出版社，2009年，第378-379页。

[563] See *Federal Rule of Civil Procedure 1938*, Rule 30.
参见《1938 年联邦民事诉讼规则》第 30 条。

[564] See Art. 67 of *CPL 2023*. See also Art. 105 of *Interpretations of the Supreme People's Court on Applicability of the Civil Procedure Law of the PRC, Zhu Shi [2015] No. 5* (*hereinafter* 'SPC's Interpretation of CPL 2015') that provides: "A people's court shall, under statutory procedures, conduct *comprehensive and objective examination* of evidence, and according to provisions of law, judge whether a piece of

evidence must be attached to the claimants' claims or defendants' counterclaims.[565]

The PRC courts will examine whether the evidence is relevant to the complaints alleged in the fact-specific pleadings.[566] A lawyer acting for a client has the right to investigate the claim.[567] The lawyer will investigate it by sending the questions to the other side. However, there is no obligation pursuant to *CPL 2023* to persuade the opponents to answer those questions, and in many cases, it is observed that the opponent simply ignores the requests. The relevant law for the lawyers also allows them to investigate materials held by others, provided the lawyer duly presents his professional qualification to the third parties.[568]

中国法院将审查证据是否与具体事实诉状中指称的申诉有关。代理委托人的律师有权调查该索赔。律师将通过将问题发送给另一方进行调查。但是，根据中国2023年《民事诉讼法》，没有义务说服对方回答这些问题，而且在许多情况下，可以观察到，对方完全无视这些要求。律师的相关法律还允许他们调查他人持有的材料，但律师必须向第三方正式出示其专业资格。

It is a common practice by PRC lawyers to question witnesses present at the relevant scene, or any witnesses who are relevant; thereafter, the lawyers can offer a notarized witness testimony record to the PRC courts.[569] It has been noted by many lawyers and scholars, that the PRC courts often prefer documentary evidence over other evidence.[570]

中国律师的惯例是询问在场的证人，或者任何与案件有关的证人；之后，律师可以向中国法院提供经过公证的证人证言笔录。许多律师和学者已经注意到，中国法院往往更倾向于书面证据而不是其他证据。

Lawyers can even utilise the notaries to record, photograph,

律师甚至可以利用公证人来记录、

evidence has probative force and the extent of its probative force, by *logical reasoning and daily life experience*, and then make public the reasons for, and the results of, such judgment. [emphasis added]".

见2023年《民事诉讼法》第67条。另见《最高人民法院关于适用<中华人民共和国民事诉讼法>的解释》注释[2015]第5号（以下简称《最高人民法院对民事诉讼法2015年解释》）第105条规定：人民法院应当依照法定程序，对证据进行全面、客观的审查，依照法律规定，根据逻辑推理和日常生活经验，判断一项证据是否具有证明力及其证明力的大小，并公布判断的理由和结果。（重点）"。

[565]See Art. 124 (4) of *CPL 2023*. 见2023年《中华人民共和国民事诉讼法》第124（4）条。

[566]See Art. 67 of *CPL 2023*. 见2023年《中华人民共和国民事诉讼法》第67条。

[567]See Art. 64 of *CPL 2023* which provides: "Lawyers who serve as litigation representatives or other litigation representatives shall have the right to investigate and collect evidence and may consult relevant materials to the case. The scopes and measures of consulting relevant materials to a case shall be regulated by the Supreme People's Court."

见2023年《中华人民共和国民事诉讼法》第64条规定："律师担任诉讼代理人或者其他诉讼代理人，有权调查收集证据，可以查阅与案件有关的材料。"查阅案件有关材料的范围和办法，由最高人民法院规定。"

[568]See *Lawyers Law of PRC 2008*, Art. 35, that provides: "When a lawyer investigates to collect evidence for a case on his own, he may, on the strength of his lawyer's practice certificate and the papers issued by his law firm, inquire of the unit or individual concerned about the legal matters which he has undertaken to handle."

见2008年《中华人民共和国律师法》第35条规定："律师自行调查收集案件证据时，可以持律师执业证书和律师事务所出具的文件，就其承办的法律事务向有关单位或者个人查询。"

[569]Elizabeth Fahey and Zhirong Tao, "The Pretrial Discovery Process in Civil Cases: A Comparison of Evidence Discovery between China and the United States," *B.C. Int'l & Comp. L. Rev.* 37, no. 2 (2014): 284.

Elizabeth Fahey and Zhirong Tao，《民事案件审前证据开示过程：中美两国证据开示的比较"，《B.C. 国际法和比较法评论》第37卷，第2期（2014）第284页。

[570]Richard W. Wigley and Jing Xu, "Evidence Collection and Alternatives to Discovery in PRC Litigation", www.chinalawinsight.com/2011/04/articles/dispute-resolution/evidence-collection-and-alternatives-to-discovery-in-prc-litigation.

Richard W. Wigley和Jing Xu，《中国诉讼中的证据收集和证据开示替代》，第1期www.chinalawinsight.com/2011/04/articles/dispute-resolution/evidence-collection-and-alternatives-to-discovery-in-prc-litigation。

and interview witnesses.[571] The authors' view, after discussions with other PRC lawyers, is that credibility of such evidence is relatively higher in the PRC courts. This utilisation of services of the notaries is very similar to the notary system found in other civil law systems. In the PRC there are strict formal requirements for any evidence to be accepted in the PRC courts, and many common lawyers find these requirements frustrating.

拍照和采访证人。在与其他中国律师讨论后，笔者认为这类证据在中国法院的可信度相对较高。公证人服务的这种利用与其他大陆法系的公证制度非常相似。在中国，任何证据要在中国法院被接受都有严格的正式要求，许多普通律师觉得这些要求令人沮丧。

Instead of the system of discovery or disclosure as seen in the adversarial system, in the PRC, there is a duty on the judges to investigate in any case before them, particularly when the evidence is not clear.[572] PRC judges can exercise the right of explanation and clarification, and therefore can urge the parties to improve their evidence in such cases.[573] Additionally, there is a positive duty on the PRC judges to investigate and collect evidence.[574] In practice, the parties can also petition the courts requesting to collate the evidence, especially if the evidence is in the possession of the third party.[575]

在中华人民共和国，法官有责任调查他们面前的任何案件，特别是在证据不明确的情况下，而不是在对抗制度中看到的发现或披露制度。中国法官可以行使解释权和澄清权，因此可以在此类案件中督促当事人改进证据。此外，中国法官有调查和收集证据的积极义务。在实践中，当事人也可以向法院提出请求，要求对证据进行整理，特别是在证据为第三方所有的情况下。

The PRC courts employ trial personnel to maintain written records of the inspection and examination, which leads to the production of transcripts of inspection and examination.[576] Such transcripts are acceptable by law and can be used as evidence. The trial personnel must conduct an examination on-site for facts and assist the courts, as some evidence is not easy to bring to the courts.[577] It is important to note that there is a provisio resembles the exchange of evidence in Art. 136 (4) of *CPL 2023*.[578] However, in practice, litigants in the PRC are not fully aware of it, and this provision is yet to be fully

中国法院由审判人员对检查、审查进行笔录，形成检查、审查笔录。这样的笔录是法律所接受的，可以作为证据使用。审判人员必须现场审查事实，协助法院，因为有些证据不容易带到法院。值得注意的是，中国2023年《民事诉讼法》中有一项条款类似于证据交换的规定。然而，在实践中，中国的当事人并不完全了解这一点，这一规定在实践中尚未得到充分实施。初审法院可以

---

571 See Art. 11 of *Notarization Law of PRC 2005.*
见《中华人民共和国公证法》2005年第11条。
572 The relevant part of Art. 67 of *CPL 2023* provides "...if the people's court considers the evidence necessary for the trial of the case, the People's Court *shall* [emphasis added] investigate and collect it."
2023年《中华人民共和国民事诉讼法》第67条的相关部分规定："...人民法院认为证据为审理案件所必需的，应当调查收集。"
573 Wigley and Xu, "Evidence Collection and Alternatives to Discovery in PRC Litigation."
Wigley and Xu, 《中华人民共和国诉讼中的证据收集与证据开示替代》
574 See Art. 68 of *CPL 2023*. 见2023年《中华人民共和国民事诉讼法》第68条。
575 Wigley and Xu, "Evidence Collection and Alternatives to Discovery in PRC Litigation," 288.
Wigley and Xu, 《中华人民共和国诉讼中的证据收集与证据开示替代》，第288页。
576 See Art. 66 (7) of *CPL 2023*. 见2023年《中华人民共和国民事诉讼法》第66(7)条。
577 See Art. 83 of *CPL 2023*. 见1991年《中华人民共和国民事诉讼法》第83条。
578 See Art. 136 (4) of *CPL 2023* which provides: "Where a court session is needed, the focus of the dispute may be clarified through requiring the parties concerned to swap evidence or by other means."
见2023年《民事诉讼法》第136 (4)条，该条规定："需要开庭审理的，通过要求当事人交换证据等方式，明确争议焦点。"

implemented in practice.[579] Trial courts can schedule the exchange of evidence by the parties.

安排双方交换证据。

Unlike the common law system where the discovery/disclosure is led by the parties and their lawyers, in the PRC system it is led by the judges and can therefore be called "discovery model led by judges."[580] One of the advantages of this model is that the discovery process is less time consuming, which is important as there are time limits for each process in the civil trial.[581] In the authors' view, it is relevant to practice in the PRC, and at the same time maintains balance in the context of the economic inequality prevailing within the society. It will also assist the PRC judges to avoid irrelevant evidence.

在普通法系中，发现/披露由当事人及其律师主导，而在中国法系中，发现/披露由法官主导，因此可以被称为“法官主导的发现模式”。这种模式的优点之一是发现过程较少耗时，这一点很重要，因为民事审判中每个过程都有时间限制。在笔者看来，它既与中国的实践相关，同时又在社会上普遍存在的经济不平等的背景下保持平衡。它还将帮助中国法官避免不相关的证据。

The authors' view is that the PRC judges do not spend too much time analysing the facts, but instead utilise their precious time in collecting the relevant evidence for the parties to the disputes. There is some question as to whether PRC judges can later rule on the evidence collected by them, if there were to be a rebuttal to the evidence from one of the parties to the dispute. The answer is not yet well-defined.

笔者认为，中国法官没有花太多时间分析事实，而是利用宝贵的时间为争议各方收集相关证据。有一些问题是关于中国法官是否可以在以后对他们收集的证据作出裁决，如果有来自争议一方的证据被反驳的话。答案尚不明确。

Although PRC lawyers have the right, enshrined in *CPL*, to collect evidence,[582] the process by which they can investigate and collect evidence is also not well-defined. This issue is of relevance, as in any inquisitorial system, any evidence so collected should be acceptable to the PRC courts even at the later stage of the civil trial. In practice, private investigators that

尽管中国的律师有收集证据的权利，但他们调查和收集证据的过程也没有明确规定。这个问题是相关的，因为在任何讯问制度中，任何这样收集的证据应该被中国法院接受，即使在民事审判的后期阶段。在实践中，

---

[579]Fahey and Tao, "The Pretrial Discovery Process in Civil Cases: A Comparison of Evidence Discovery Between China and the United States," 291–2. See also Peggy McInerny, "Modern Legal Profession in China Is Only 35 Years Old", UCLA Int'l Institute, http://web.international.ucla.edu/Institute/Article/136768, where McInerny in her article explored the evolution of legal awareness and implementation of laws for ordinary PRC residents.
Fahey and Tao，“民事案件审前证据开示：中美两国证据开示的比较”，第291-292页。另见Peggy McInerny，“现代法律职业在中国只有35年”，UCLA国际法研究所，http://web.international.ucla.edu/Institute/Article/136768，在她的文章中，McInerny探讨了中国普通居民法律意识和法律实施的演变。

[580]Fahey and Tao, "The Pretrial Discovery Process in Civil Cases: A Comparison of Evidence Discovery Between China and the United States," 292.
Fahey and Tao，“民事案件审前证据开示：中美两国证据开示的比较”，第292页。

[581]See Art. 152 & Art. 164 of *CPL 2023*. Art. 152 provides: "A People's Court shall complete the adjudication of a case to which ordinary procedure is applied *within six months* [emphasis added] after the case is accepted. Where an extension of the term is necessary for special circumstances, a six-month extension may be given upon the approval of the president of the court. Any further extension shall be reported to the People's Court at a higher level for approval." On the other hand, Art.161 provides: "The People's Court shall complete the adjudication of a case to which the summary procedure is applied within three months after the case is accepted."
参见 2023 年《中华人民共和国民事诉讼法》第 152 条和第 161 条。第 152 条规定：“人民法院对适用普通程序的案件，应当在受理之日起六个月内裁定完毕。有特殊情况需要延长的，经院长批准，可以延长六个月。延期的，报经上一级人民法院批准。”另一方面，第 164 条规定：“人民法院对适用简易程序的案件，应当在受理之日起三个月内裁定完毕。”

[582]See Arts. 52 and 64 of *CPL 2023*。见2023年《中华人民共和国民事诉讼法》第52和64条。

can assist the parties to collect evidence have increased in number, but the regulations are not clear-cut in relation to these private agencies.[583] There is no provision for third-party orders where the courts can compel the third parties to assist with ongoing litigation in PRC courts.

可以协助当事人收集证据的私家侦探数量有所增加，但有关这些私家侦探的规定并不明确。对于法院可以强制第三方协助在中国法院进行的诉讼的第三方命令，没有规定。

A similar situation exists in the context of investigation orders, where one party is refusing to provide the relevant evidence. In such circumstances, the judges take the investigative role upon themselves. The authors' view is that the ability of litigants to introduce new evidence at any time during the process of litigation, or to ask for an extension, is a major drawback in the PRC litigation system.[584] In practice, many litigants present new evidence on appeal, and in such cases, the PRC courts do not widely use the provision of fines in *CPL*.[585] There is no concept of perjury in cases of presenting wrong certificates or misrepresentation in the courts, including when contradicting testimonies are involved.[586]

在调查令方面也存在类似的情况，即一方拒绝提供有关证据。在这种情况下，法官自己承担调查的作用。笔者认为，诉讼当事人在诉讼过程中可以随时提出新的证据，或者要求延长诉讼期限，这是中国诉讼制度的一个重大缺陷。在实践中，许多诉讼当事人在上诉时提出了新的证据，在这种情况下，中国法院并没有广泛使用《民事诉讼法》中的罚款条款。在法庭上提供错误证明或虚假陈述的情况下，包括涉及相互矛盾的证词时，没有伪证的概念。

For the sake of completeness, it should be noted that there are other inquisitorial systems such as Germany and Japan that also have the parties-led discovery system.[587] On the other hand, as discussed above, the discovery model relevant to the PRC system is led by judges, and these judges are supervised by the Procuratorate system to maintain social harmony and public interests.

为了完整起见，需要指出的是，德国、日本等其他国家也有当事人主导的证据开示制度。另一方面，如前所述，与中华人民共和国制度相关的发现模式是由法官主导的，这些法官受到检察院系统的监督，以维护社会和谐和公共利益。

---

[583] Fahey and Tao, "The Pretrial Discovery Process in Civil Cases: A Comparison of Evidence Discovery between China and the United States," 299–300.
Fahey and Tao，“民事案件审前证据开示：中美两国证据开示的比较”，第299-300页。

[584] See Art. 68 of *CPL 2023*. In particular, it provides "...Where a party has difficulty in providing evidence within such time limit, *it may apply to the People's court for an extension of the time limit* [emphasis added] and the people's court may extend the time limit appropriately according to the application of the party..." See also *Art. 142 of CPL 2023* in the context of the parties' ability to present the evidence any time.
见2023年《中华人民共和国民事诉讼法》第68条。特别地规定"....当事人在限期内举证有困难的，可以向人民法院申请延长，人民法院可以根据当事人的申请适当延长...."另见2023年《民事诉讼法》第142条中关于当事人随时提供证据能力的规定。

[585] See Art. 658of *CPL 2023*. 见2023年《中华人民共和国民事诉讼法》第68条。

[586] See Art. 305 of the *Criminal Law of the People's Republic of China 1997*, which is not applicable to civil proceedings and only applicable to perjury committed during a criminal proceeding. It also does not seem to be included in Art.113 of *CPL 2023* which provides for criminal liabilities for disruptions, threats etc.
见1997年《中华人民共和国刑法》第305条，该规定不适用于民事诉讼，只适用于刑事诉讼中的伪证。它似乎也没有包括在2023年《中华人民共和国民事诉讼法》第113条中，该条款规定了破坏、威胁等的刑事责任。

[587] Fahey and Tao, "The Pretrial Discovery Process in Civil Cases: A Comparison of Evidence Discovery Between China and the United States," 299.
Fahey and Tao，“民事案件审前证据开示：中美两国证据开示的比较”，第299页。

5.2.1.1.3 Finding the Truth and Cross-examination

寻找真相和交叉盘问

In the PRC, the parties may cross-examine witnesses, expert witnesses, and inspectors with permission from the courts.[588] The authors' view is that permission will still be required to cross-examine; it appears that this is not available as a right. However, a party in England & Wales has the right to cross-examine all the witnesses presented through witness statements submitted by the opponents, to forward their own case. It is an important element of the trial process in the common law adversarial system. Lawyers are trained over many years in cross-examination skills.

在中国，经法院许可，当事人可以对证人、鉴定人、鉴定人进行质证。提交人的观点是，交叉询问仍然需要许可；这似乎不能作为一项权利。然而，英格兰和威尔士的一方当事人有权通过对方提交的证人陈述对所有证人进行交叉询问，以提出自己的案件。它是普通法系对抗制度中审判程序的重要组成部分。律师在盘问技巧方面接受了多年的训练。

The main purpose of cross-examining a witness is to put forward a case, to try to discredit witnesses and the related witness statements that have been exchanged with the opponents, and ultimately to undermine the strength of the evidence.[589] Nonetheless, the purpose is definitely not to trick or attack the witnesses. Cross-examination is an exercise in skill, and it assists in finding the truth, especially in the common law systems. Leading questions are put to the witnesses during the cross-examination, following the proper order of the questions according to the case theory.

证人质证的主要目的在于构建案件争点，力求削弱证人以及对方所交换的相关证人陈述的可信度，最终削弱证据的证明力。尽管如此，目的绝对不是为了欺骗或攻击证人。交叉询问是一种技巧练习，它有助于找到真相，在普通法体系中尤为如此。在质证过程中，对证人提出引导性问题，按照案件理论提出问题的顺序。

However, scholars have criticised the excessive focus on cross-examination in adversarial systems, as they are of the view that there is not enough time for any of the witnesses to reflect upon or deliberate, as compared to the ample time available to witnesses in the inquisitorial system. This lack of time, according to Kessler, may inhibit truth seeking.[590] Instead in the PRC, there is a system called *zhizheng* evidence, which examines all types of evidence that has been submitted on record in the PRC courts, and includes the process to confront

然而，学者们批评了对抗性制度中对交叉询问的过度关注，因为他们认为，与讯问制度中证人可以获得的充足时间相比，任何证人都没有足够的时间进行反思或审议。时间的匮乏可能会阻碍对案件事实真相的探寻。相反，在中国，有一种称为“质证”的制度，该制度审查在中国法院备案的所有类型的证据，并包括对抗证据的过程。这种中国式的证据对质过程

[588]Art. 142 of *CPL 2023*。见2023年《中华人民共和国民事诉讼法》第142条。

[589]Blake, *Practical Approach to Effective Litigation*, 602.
布莱克，《有效诉讼的实践方法》，第602页。

[590]A. D. Kessler, "Our Inquisitorial Tradition: Equity Procedure, Due Process, and the Search for an Alternative to the Adversarial," *Cornell L. Rev.* 90, no. 5 (2005): 1216. Kessler was also discussed in Gélinas, et al., *Foundations of Civil Justice*, 70.
A. D. Kessler，《我们的调查传统：公平程序、正当程序和对抗性替代方案的探索》，《康奈尔大学法律评论》，第90期，no.5(2005): 1216。Kessler也在Gélinas等人中讨论了，《民事司法基础》， 第70页。

it.[591] This process of Chinese style confrontation of evidence (*zhizheng*) appears to be much broader, and cross-examining witnesses is only part of that process.[592] The authors are not sure whether any hidden information can emerge from *zhizheng*.

似乎要广泛得多，而交叉询问证人只是这个过程的一部分。笔者不确定质证中是否有隐藏的信息。

5.2.1.1.4 Finding the Truth and Economic Equality

寻找真相和经济平等

It is no secret that the onus is on the parties to investigate and collate evidence, and cross-examine the opponents' witnesses, but this can be properly executed only by accomplished and experienced lawyers. Wealthy parties can afford good lawyers, and this can create inequality between the parties. Because of this, the system sometimes fails in achieving the primary goal of seeking the truth. In fact, in practice, in the authors' experience, the procedural rules have been used by well-off parties in the adversarial system to deny substantive justice. In the inquisitorial legal system, the judges' deep involvement in investigating the case may neutralise some of the negative effects of economic equality; however, the issue does still persist.

调查、整理证据以及盘问对方证人的责任在于诉讼各方，但只有技艺精湛且经验丰富的律师才能妥善完成这些工作。富有的当事人请得起优秀律师，这可能会在各方之间造成不公平。正因如此，该制度有时无法实现探寻真相这一首要目标。事实上，在实践中，以笔者的经验来看，在对抗制中，富裕的当事人会利用程序规则来阻碍实质正义的实现。在纠问式法律制度中，法官深度介入案件调查，这或许能抵消经济不平等带来的部分负面影响；然而，这一问题依然存在。

5.3 Judges and Legal Reasoning – Common Law and Inquisitorial, in particular, England & Wales and PRC

法官和法律推理：普通法和法庭，特别是英格兰、威尔士和中国

The authors will discuss now one by one the issue of the judges' legal reasoning in both jurisdictions. Even though England & Wales belong to the common law system and the PRC belongs

笔者现在将逐一讨论两个司法管辖区法官的法律推理问题。尽管英格兰和威尔士属于普通法体系，而中华

[591] Art. 49 of *Some Provisions of Supreme People's Court on Evidence in Civil Procedures [No.33 of 2001] (as revised in 2008)*, (hereinafter SPC Provisions on Evidence *2001*). Art. 49 provides "When documentary evidence, material evidence or audio-visual materials are cross-examined...." It appears from this section all types of evidence can be cross-examined.
《最高人民法院关于民事诉讼证据的若干规定》第49条（2008年修订），（以下简称《2001年最高人民法院证据规定》）。第49条规定："对书证、物证或者音像材料进行质证...."从这部分看来，所有类型的证据都可以被交叉询问。

[592] Paul J. Schmidt, "A Review of China's New Civil Evidence Law," *Pacific Rim L. & Pol. J.* 12, no. 2 (2003): 309.
Paul J. Schmidt, 《中国新民事证据法述评》, *Pacific Rim L. & Pol. J.*, no.(2003): 309。

to the civil law jurisdiction, it is quite possible that they may have a few unique features of their own, either due to overriding philosophy due to their constitution, or the underlying influence of jurisprudence. This aspect will be analysed as well in the forthcoming paragraphs.

人民共和国属于大陆法系，但它们很可能有一些自己的独特之处，要么是由于其宪法的压倒一切的哲学，要么是由于法理学的潜在影响。这方面也将在今后各段中加以分析。

5.3.1 Judges and Legal Reasoning – Common Law

法官和法律推理-普通法系

It is the authors' view, which is also acknowledged generally, that the legal reasons included in judgments by judges provide a legitimate motivation for the populace to follow the rules. However, in many empires and dynasties, there have been instances where giving reasons "would jeopardize rather than further the power and legitimacy of the courts."[593] The judges' reasons also ensure that individuals and society as a unit become more tolerant of contrary and dissimilar views within a society. It is, however, debatable whether common-law judges are under a duty to provide reasons,[594] unless it is expressly provided under the statutes, or it is imposed by procedural requirements. In contrast, it is common in inquisitorial systems that judges are under an obligation by statutes, often called affirmative duty,[595] to provide justifications in a particular format for decisions or judgments made in their courts.[596]

笔者认为，法官的判决中包含的法律理由为民众遵守规则提供了合法的动机，这也是普遍承认的。然而，在许多帝国和朝代中，也有这样的例子：给出理由“会损害而不是进一步加强法院的权力和合法性”。法官的理由也确保个人和社会作为一个整体变得更能容忍社会中相反和不同的观点。然而，普通法法官是否有义务提供理由是有争议的，除非成文法明文规定，或者是程序要求强加的。相比之下，在讯问制度中，法官通常有法律义务，通常称为肯定义务，以特定格式为法院作出的决定或判决提供理由。

[593]Mathilde Cohen, "When Judges Have Reasons not to Give Reasons: A Comparative Law Approach," *Wash. & Lee L. Rev.* 72, no. 2 (2015): 487. Cohen discussed jurisprudence, as discussed by Philippe Godding in the context of Italians in the twelfth and thirteenth centuries. Another reason cited was judicial secrecy.
玛蒂尔德·科恩，“当法官有理由不给出理由：比较法方法”，*Wash. & Lee L. Rev.* 72, no. 2 (2015): 487。科恩讨论了法理学，正如菲利普·戈丁在12世纪和13世纪意大利人的背景下所讨论的那样。另一个理由是司法保密。

[594]Cohen, "Judges' Reasons."
科恩，《法官的理由》。

[595]Ibid., 557–8.
同前注，第557-558页。

[596]In France, after the revolution of 1790, the reasons of judges in their judgment were monitored to prevent them from becoming corrupt, or to restrict their arbitrary/discretionary power. For further discussion on this aspect, see Cohen, "Judges' Reasons," 558. In France, it can be seen that though the courts have an obligation to give reasons, the judgments are in fact very brief. Further, though under an obligation to follow statutes, the courts have lately been involved in law-making of their own through very brief judgments. For details, see also, Cohen, "Judges' Reasons," 561.
在法国，1790年革命后，法官的判决理由受到监督，以防止他们腐败，或限制他们的任意/自由裁量权。关于这方面的进一步讨论，见科恩，《法官的理由》，第558页。在法国，可以看出，虽然法院有义务给出理由，但实际上判决非常简短。此外，尽管法院有义务遵守成文法，但法院最近通过非常简短的判决参与了自己的法律制定。详情请见科恩，《法官的理由》，第561页。

In spite of the fact that common law judges are under no obligation to provide reasons, it is a fact that common-law judgments are famous for including reasons in detail; therefore these judgments impart education to other judges and lawyers. In practice, reason-giving by judges is generally affected by the case-load of the courts and the judges in common law courts exercise their *discretion* to furnish either brief or detailed reasons.[597]

尽管普通法系法官没有义务提供理由，但事实是，普通法系的判决以详细列出理由而闻名；因此，这些判决对其他法官和律师具有教育意义。在实践中，法官的陈述理由一般受法院案件数量的影响，普通法法院的法官行使自由裁量权，提供简短或详细的理由。

According to Rawls' *jurisprudence of justice*, in a democratic liberal society, providing the public with detailed reasons for the opinion of the judges is their moral duty, and therefore, philosophically, it is very important for the judiciary's continued existence.[598] Another jurisprudent, Dworkin, viewed the necessity of judicial discourse in the courts as essential for enhancing the participation of the populace. Dworkin viewed the courts themselves as an important element in the integrity of the whole system, as they employ fair methods accepted by the populace. In Dworkin's school of thought, judges are constrained by their previous decisions.[599]

根据罗尔斯的正义法学，在一个民主自由的社会中，向公众提供法官意见的详细理由是他们的道德义务，因此，从哲学上讲，这对司法机构的继续存在非常重要。另一位法理学家德沃金认为，法庭中司法话语的必要性对于加强民众的参与至关重要。德沃金认为法院本身是整个系统完整性的一个重要因素，因为它们采用了民众接受的公平方法。在德沃金的思想流派中，法官受到他们之前的决定的约束。

Judicial reasoning encourages participation within the society, ensures losing parties in cases do not ruminate over loss due to any bias towards them, and lastly assists society to determine that judicial decisions were not arbitrary decisions. In addition, judicial decisions should take into account the facts and relevant law that the parties have put forward to the judges.[600] Cohen, while discussing social psychology, suggested that added participation in the form of arguments in front of judges also leads to consensus agreements.[601]

司法推理鼓励社会参与，确保案件中的败诉方不会因对他们的任何偏见而对损失进行反思，最后帮助社会确定司法裁决不是武断的决定。此外，司法判决应考虑到当事人向法官提出的事实和有关法律。科恩在讨论社会心理学时表示，在法官面前以辩论的形式增加参与也会导致达成共识。

---

[597]See "Judges' Reasons," 563 for a discussion in the context of judges in US, Cohen.
见科恩《法官的理由》，563页，关于美国法官的讨论。
[598]See *The Law of Peoples* (Cambridge, Mass.: Harvard University Press, 1999) for a discussion on legal reasoning by judges and issue of public reasons in John Rawls. See also, for further discussion about Rawls' jurisprudence, Cohen, "Judges' Reasons," 498–9.
见《万民法》（剑桥，马萨诸塞州）（哈佛大学出版社，1999年）的法官的法律推理和约翰罗尔斯的公共原因问题的讨论。关于罗尔斯法理学的进一步讨论，另见科恩《法官的理由》，第498-499页。
[599]See Ronald Dworkin, *Law's Empire (Legal Theory)*, New ed. (Oxford: Hart Publishing, 1998) for discussions on various aspects of law, institutions etc. See also, for further discussion on Dworkin's views, Cohen, "Judges' Reasons," 500–1.
参见罗纳德·德沃金，《法律的帝国（法律理论）》，新版（牛津：哈特出版社，1998），关于法律、制度等各个方面的讨论。另见关于德沃金观点的进一步讨论，科恩，"法官的理由"，第500-501页。
[600]Cohen, "Judges' Reasons," 504.
见科恩《法官的理由》，第504页。
[601]Ibid., 506.
同前注，第506页。

In addition, judgments containing detailed reasons ensure that the judges remain accountable, as their opinions can be read by the higher courts and the general public.[602] With fully reasoned opinions, any appeal or intervention by the higher courts will appear to be arbitrary. Thus the opinions of the judges will enhance rule of law by providing transparency in the whole process of adjudication for litigants and lawyers, other judges and above all the general public. Legal reasoning enhances accuracy by imposing self-discipline on the judges, by avoiding speculation, avoiding irrelevant information, and avoiding deficiency due to inadequate research, etc.[603]

此外，载有详细理由的判决书确保法官负责任，因为他们的意见可以被上级法院和公众阅读。有了充分的理由，高等法院的任何上诉或干预都将显得武断。因此，法官的意见将通过为诉讼当事人、律师、其他法官，尤其是公众提供整个审判过程的透明度，从而加强法治。法律推理通过对法官的自律、避免猜测、避免不相关的信息、避免由于研究不足而产生的缺陷等来提高准确性。

No doubt the populace living in any jurisdiction expects the judges to do their best in an honest way to adjudicate the issues before the courts. However, is it a valid expectation from the populace that all the judgments will be of high cognitive standard? This is also the question many jurisprudents have asked over the years when considering the role of judges.[604] Incoherence in legal reasoning in various judgments, and in statutory interpretation, has been observed quite frequently. However, as in any profession, some incoherence may be encountered from time to time and is part and parcel of any job. In the authors' view, it is to be expected that there will be mistakes. However, a system of appeal and checks and balances within the judicial system exists to provide legitimacy to the whole process.

毫无疑问，生活在任何司法管辖区的民众都希望法官以诚实的方式尽最大努力裁决法庭上的问题。然而，民众期望所有的判断都是高认知标准的，这是合理的吗？这也是许多法理学家多年来在考虑法官的角色时提出的问题。在各种判决书的法律推理和法律解释中，经常观察到不连贯的现象。然而，就像在任何职业中一样，有时会遇到一些不连贯的情况，这是任何工作的一部分。在笔者看来，错误在所难免。然而，司法系统内的上诉和制衡制度为整个过程提供了合法性。

However, there are jurisdictions where the political philosophy is *totalitarian*, where the political bosses insist on having very high expectations of the judges, and there is a reasonable expectation that these judges will conform to the major political philosophy.[605] Judicial systems that are not independent are definitely susceptible to demands from political bosses. Jurisprudents such as Dworkin were of the

然而，有些司法管辖区的政治哲学是极权主义的，政治老板坚持对法官抱有很高的期望，并且有一个合理的期望，这些法官将符合主要的政治哲学。不独立的司法系统肯定容易受到政治老板要求的影响。德沃金等法学家认为，正如政府官员受到压力，必须遵守

[602]Ibid., 507.
同前注，第507页。
[603]Ibid., 408.
同前注，第408页。
[604]James Penner, "Law and Adjudication: Dworkin's Critique of Positivism," in *Introduction to Jurisprudence and Legal Theory: Commentary and Materials*, by Anne Barron, et al. (London: Butterworths, 2002), 382.
詹姆斯·彭纳：《法律与裁决：德沃金对实证主义的批判》，载《法理学与法律理论导论：评论与材料》，安妮·巴伦等人著，伦敦：巴特沃斯出版社，2002年，第382页。
[605]Ibid., 377.
同前注，第377页。

view that just as government officials are subject to pressure to conform to the philosophy of their political bosses, in a similar way, judges are also subject to this doctrine of political responsibility. It is even said that the judges are like critiques in the newspapers in various subject areas and are trying to find the best law applicable in the circumstances. The moot question then is whether the issue of legal reasoning is that simple?

其政治老板的哲学一样，法官也以类似的方式受制于这种政治责任学说。甚至有人说，法官们就像各领域报纸上的评论员一样，试图找到适合具体情况的最佳法律。那么悬而未决的问题是，法律推理的问题是否那么简单？

In jurisprudential terms, legal reasoning refers to the arguments that judges give in their judgments/decisions on various cases in the courts. These arguments consist of the reasons behind their decisions, and these reasons are intended as *justifications* for the decisions.[606] The justifications can be through the exercise of precedents and/or through the interpretation of statutes. Legal reasoning in common law cases is in the form of *modus ponens*, which MacCormick has described as follows: "whenever certain *operative facts* [emphasis added] occur, a given legal consequences follows."[607] MacCormick further was of the view that this meant that all legal rules are only "*ordinarily necessary and presumptively sufficient*."[608]This will determine the legal rules to apply in any particular case. However, there may be exceptions within the judgments, which would mean that the result might not follow the facts governing the dispute. Gooden & Walton were of the view that because of this, the legal rules can be *undercut* or *undermined*.[609]

在法理学术语中，法律推理是指法官在法院对各种案件的判决/决定中给出的论点。这些论点由其决定背后的原因组成，这些原因旨在为这些决定提供理由。理由可以通过先例的运用和/或通过对成文法的解释。普通法案件中的法律推理采用的是现行方式（*modus ponens*），麦考密克将其描述如下："每当某些*有效事实*[着重号后加]发生时，就会产生给定的法律后果。"麦考密克进一步认为，这意味着所有法律规则只是"通常必要和假定充分的"。这将决定在任何特定情况下适用的法律规则。但是，判决中可能有例外，这意味着结果可能不符合支配争议的事实。古登和沃尔顿认为，正因为如此，法律规则可能会被削弱或破坏。

606David M. Gooden and Douglas Walton, "Defeasibility in Judicial Opinion - Logical or Procedural," *Informal Logic* 28, no. 1 (2008): 7n1. Gooden & Waldon discussed Golding's definition of legal reasoning in this paper.
大卫 M·古登和道格拉斯·沃尔顿，"司法意见的可否定性——逻辑的还是程序的"，《非正式逻辑》第28期， no. 1 (2008): 7n1。古登和 沃尔顿在本文中讨论了Golding对法律推理的定义。

607Neil MacCormick, *Legal Reasoning and Legal Theory*, Clarendon Law Series (Oxford: Clarendon Press, 1978), 67. MacCormick was discussed by Gooden & Waldon in Gooden and Walton, "Judicial Opinion -Logical or Procedural," 8. *Modus ponens* is the principle in the area of logic that whenever a conditional statement and its antecedent are given to be true its consequent may be validly inferred, for example, *if it is the author this must be Vivek*, and *it is Vivek, so this must be the author*. This principle is important in light of case precedents and statutes that are used as deductive reasoning as part of justifications.
Neil MacCormick, 《法律推理与法律理论》，克拉伦登法律丛书（牛津：克拉伦登出版社，1978年），第67页。古登和沃尔顿在《司法意见——逻辑的还是程序的》中讨论了麦考密克。命题法是逻辑领域的一个原则无论什么时候一个条件陈述和它的前因式被赋予为真它的后因式可以被有效地推断出来，例如，如果它是笔者这一定是Vivek，它是Vivek，所以这一定是笔者。这一原则是重要的，因为判例和法规被用作演绎推理作为辩护的一部分。

608Gooden and Walton, "Judicial Opinion — Logical or Procedural," 8. In this article they quoted from MacCormick, *Legal Reasoning and Legal Theory*, 103.
古登和沃尔顿，《司法意见——逻辑的还是程序的》，第8页，他们引用了麦考密克的《法律推理与法律理论》，第103页。

609Gooden and Walton, "Judicial Opinion — Logical or Procedural," 8.
古登和沃尔顿，《司法意见——逻辑的还是程序的》，第8页。

However, legal cases are not straight forward, and strait-jacket deductive reasoning cannot be applied universally, as it may lead to application of conflicting rules. In those scenarios, as discussed in Chapter Three,[610] and in this context, such conflicts are resolved by application of principles such as fairness, equality, justice, and so forth. It means that at times, legal arguments are overridden or rebutted by the stronger arguments of the judges.[611]

然而，法律案例并不是直截了当的，紧身衣式的演绎推理不能普遍适用，因为它可能导致相互冲突的规则的适用。在这些情况下，如第三章所讨论的，在这种情况下，这些冲突通过应用公平、平等、正义等原则来解决。这意味着有时，法律论点被法官更有力的论点所推翻或反驳。

It can by no means be said that all legal rules, such as case precedents or interpretations of statutes, or even statutes themselves, are perfect. Therefore, judges cannot just apply them in all factual scenarios; judges are supposed to be aware of all exclusions. At times, as common-law lawyers have found when looking for relevant legal rule(s) in a judgment, they cannot find the main operative fact(s) leading to that legal rule(s). Therefore, it is likely that such facts were omitted in the judgment. As said earlier, the concept of the legal rule in itself is far from being perfect. Additionally, such legal rules can be undermined by principles of natural justice, and/or can be outmaneuvered, undercut, overridden, or rebutted.

绝对不能说所有的法律规则，例如判例或成文法的解释，甚至成文法本身都是完美的。因此，法官不能将它们应用于所有的事实情景；法官应该知道所有的例外情况。有时，正如普通法律师在判决中寻找相关法律规则时发现的那样，他们找不到导致该法律规则的主要操作事实。因此，很可能在判决中遗漏了这些事实。如前所述，法律规则的概念本身远非完美。此外，这些法律规则可能会被自然正义原则所破坏，并且/或者可能被智取、削弱、推翻或反驳。

The judges operate in an environment of uncertainty. Hart said, "Fact situations do not await us neatly labeled, creased, and folded, nor is their legal classification written on them to be simply read off by the judge."[612] This succinctly emphasises that fact situations are not straightforward; therefore it can be said that MacCormick's *operative facts* are also not well-defined, and this could lead the judges to search for necessary legal rules to apply in new cases. From this analysis, it can be highlighted that the reasoning cannot be simply deductive. *Deductive reasoning* is where the reasoning moves from general premises to the particular and is circular

法官在不确定的环境中工作。哈特说："事实情况不会等待我们整齐地标记、折痕和折叠，它们的法律分类也不会写在上面，供法官简单地宣读。"这简洁地强调了事实情境并非直截了当；因此，可以说麦考密克的操作事实也没有明确界定，这可能导致法官寻找必要的法律规则来适用于新的案件。从这个分析中，可以突出指出，推理不能简单地演绎。演绎推理是从一般前提到特殊前提的推理，本质上是循环的。此外，

[610]Refer to Chapter 3, §3.2.3, where positivists such as Hart, though not agreeing that natural law concepts should be applied, acknowledged that in a few cases, to fill the gaps in law, principles of natural justice such as fairness and equality can be used by judges to provide justifications.
参考第3章第3.2.3节，像哈特这样的实证主义者，虽然不同意应该应用自然法概念，但承认在少数情况下，为了填补法律的空白，法官可以使用公平和平等等自然正义原则来提供理由。

[611]Gooden and Walton, "Judicial Opinion —Logical or Procedural," 8.
古登和沃尔顿，《司法意见——逻辑的还是程序的》，第8页。

[612]H.L.A Hart, "Positivism and Separation of Law and Morals," *Harvard L. Rev.* 71, no. 4 (1958): 607.
H.L.A .哈特，"实证主义与法律与道德的分离"，《哈佛法律评论》，第71期，4(1958): 607。

in nature. In addition, for the conclusion to be true, it is important that the premises (major or minor) are true.[613] This uncertainty leads to indeterminacy and the result is conceptual rule-indeterminacy.[614] MacCormick, on the other hand, considers this uncertainty as an issue of interpretation and not rule-indeterminacy.[615]

要使结论为真，前提（主要或次要）为真是很重要的。这种不确定性导致不确定性，其结果是概念规则不确定。另一方面，麦考密克认为这种不确定性是一个解释问题，而不是规则不确定性问题。

For judges equipped with many legal rules learned/obtained from cases, customs, and statutes, the main issue is whether modification as a result of new facts or information in a case from case precedents or previous interpretation of statute(s) can change the premises. This issue will have an impact on another issue, that is, whether the conclusions taken as legal rules from previous cases are applicable to the facts of the new case. These are a few scenarios that make the legal rules compelling but yet defeasible, as discussed by Gooden and Walton.[616]

对于那些从案例、习惯和成文法中学到/获得了许多法律规则的法官来说，主要问题是由于判例或以前对成文法的解释中出现了新的事实或信息而导致的修改是否会改变前提。这一问题会影响到另一个问题，即以往案件中作为法律规则的结论是否适用于新案件的事实。正如古登和沃尔顿所讨论的那样，这些都是使法律规则引人注目但又可行的一些情况。

In any event, most judgments can be appealed to the next stage, if the judges had failed to apply or had misapplied the legal rule; or used a legal rule other than the one which ought to have been applied; or failed to follow a correct procedure before the courts. Judges have to be careful when applying legal rules derived from the previous cases, where they might have been based on mistaken findings of operative fact(s) or missing or ignored evidence, or due to mistakes arising from faulty analysis of the link between premise and conclusion in judgments. The mistakes of the judges could include a scenario where they failed to give enough weight to the arguments of lawyers who were acting in the previous cases.

无论如何，如果法官未能适用或误用法律规则，大多数判决都可以上诉到下一阶段；或者不适用应当适用的法律规定的；或者在法庭上没有遵循正确的程序。法官在适用从以前的案件中得出的法律规则时必须谨慎，因为这些规则可能是基于对实际情况的错误发现或缺失或忽视的证据，或由于对判决中前提和结论之间的联系的错误分析而产生的错误。法官的错误可能包括他们没有给予在以前案件中代理律师的论点足够的重视。

In order to avoid the pitfalls of indeterminacy of legal reasoning, or excessive appeals, there are procedural requirements. Further, the judges themselves are aware of the

为了避免法律推理不明确或上诉过多的陷阱，有一些程序要求。此外，法官本身也意识到他们在法庭上面临的挑

613Lundmark, *Divide between Common and Civil Law*, 281.
伦德马克，《划分普通法和大陆法》，第281页。

614Gooden and Walton, "Judicial Opinion — Logical or Procedural," 10.
古登和沃尔顿，《司法意见——逻辑的还是程序的》，第10页。

615MacCormick, *Legal Reasoning and Legal Theory*, 65–68. MacCormick's theory was discussed in Gooden and Walton, "Judicial Opinion - Logical or Procedural," 10.
麦考密克，《法律推理与法律理论》，第65-68页。麦考密克的理论在古登和沃尔顿的《司法意见——逻辑的还是程序的》第10页中得到了讨论。

616Gooden and Walton, "Judicial Opinion — Logical or Procedural," 10.
古登和沃尔顿，《司法意见——逻辑的还是程序的》，第10页。

challenges they face in the courts and the associated risks in reaching conclusions in their judicial decisions. One such guideline for judges in the PRC is provided in Article 155 of *CPL 2023*; it provides features that are required in any judgment from the judges in the PRC:[617]

战以及在作出司法裁决时得出结论的相关风险。中国2023年《民事诉讼法》第155条规定了一项指导原则；它提供了中国法官作出任何判决所需的特征：

> A judgment shall state the outcome of the judgment and causes, and shall include the following content:
> (1) The cause of action, claims, and the facts and reasons of disputes;
> (2) The facts and causes affirmed by the judgment, applicable laws and causes.
> (3) The consequences of a judgment and the obligation of litigation costs; and
> (4) The time limit for filing an appeal and the appellate court with which the appeal shall be filed.
> The judgment shall be signed by the adjudicating personnel and the court clerk, and the seal of the people's court shall be affixed to it.

> 判决书应当载明判决结果和事由，并包括下列内容：
> （一）案由、请求和争议的事实、理由；
> （二）判决确认的事实和事由，适用的法律和事由。
> （三）判决的后果和诉讼费用的承担；和
> （四）提出上诉的期限和上诉的上诉法院。
> 判决书由审判人员和书记员签名，加盖人民法院印章。

In England and Wales, even though there are formal requirements in CPR 1998 r.40.2 for a judgment to be in a particular format, for example bearing date and seal of the courts, there are no requirements similar to those expressly stated in the PRC's Article 155 of CPL 2023. However, in most common law traditions, the cases will provide succinct, detailed reasons and justifications, which offer a great education to legal professionals.

在英格兰和威尔士，尽管1998年《民事诉讼法》第40.2条对判决书采用特定格式有正式要求，例如注明日期和法院盖章，但没有类似于中国2023年《民事诉讼法》第155条明确规定的要求。然而，在大多数普通法传统中，案件将提供简洁、详细的理由和理由，这对法律专业人士来说是一个很好的教育。

Generally speaking, on analysis, judgments provided in England & Wales are detailed, as they should be in the common law system. In the PRC, however, they are not so detailed as to include or consider each and every fact and every element of law that was applicable before the judgement was reached.

一般来说，在分析上，英格兰和威尔士提供的判决是详细的，因为他们应该在普通法系。然而，在中国，它们并没有详细到包括或考虑到判决达成前适用的每一个事实和每一个法律要素。

However, in common law itself, there is a school of thought that giving detailed judgments with reasons can itself cause disputes, reduce judicial efficiency, and create opportunities for divisions

然而，在普通法本身，有一种思想流派认为，给出带有理由的详细判决本身就会引起纠纷，降低司法效率，并为社会内部的分裂创造机会。科思

[617]Art. 155 of *CPL 2023*. 见2023年《中华人民共和国民事诉讼法》第155条。

within society.[618] Cohen even emphasised that having dissenting views from a multi-judge tribunal is frowned upon by this school of thought as such dissenting arguments have the potential to reduce the institutional legitimacy [of judiciary].[619] Another school of thought from psychology also is not in favor of excessive justifications for judgment as they are of the view either that reasoning is usually motivated to prove one side of the story based on cultural or subjective preference, or that justifications are provided in a strategic way, instead of these justifications being founded solely on evidence presented to the courts.[620] Cohen even said:

甚至强调，这个学派不赞成由多名法官组成的法庭持有不同意见，因为这种不同意见有可能降低[司法机构]的制度合法性。另一个来自心理学的思想流派也不赞成过多的判断理由，因为他们认为，推理通常是基于文化或主观偏好来证明故事的一方，或者是以一种战略方式提供的理由，而不是这些理由完全建立在提交给法院的证据之上。科恩甚至说:

> Imposing strict reason-giving requirements on judges may yield insincerity and artificiality in judicial discourse, rather than promoting accountability and transparency.[621]

> 对法官施加严格的理由要求可能会导致司法话语中的不真诚和不自然，且无法促进司法问责和透明度。

5.3.2 Judges in the Civil Law Tradition

大陆法系传统中的法官

As seen from the above analysis,[622] in the common law system the role or function of its judges is not to pro-actively seek the truth. In order to present a client's case to the judges, it is the duty of the lawyers, pursuant to Rules of Professional Conduct, that they cannot invent facts to assist their client's case.[623]

从上面的分析可以看出，在普通法系中，法官的角色或功能并不是主动寻求真相。为了向法官陈述委托人的案件，根据《职业行为规则》，律师有义务不得捏造事实来协助委托人的案件。

The above can be contrasted with the approach of the Court of Appeal in England and Wales, that has said that excessive

上述情况可以与英格兰和威尔士上诉法院的做法形成对比，该法院表

618Cohen, "Judges' Reasons," 515。 科恩，《法官的理由》，第515页。
619Ibid., 516–17。同前注，第516-17页。
620Cohen, "Judges' Reasons," 519, where Cohen discussed "motivated cognition "issues"".
科恩，《法官的理由》，第 515 页，科恩讨论了"动机认知"问题。
621Cohen, "Judges' Reasons," 522。 科恩，《法官的理由》，第522页。
622Chapter 5, §5.2.1.1。第5章，第5.2.1.1.1节。
623See *Medcalf v Mardell, Weatherill* [2002] UKHL 27, [2002] 3 All ER 731, [2003] 1 AC 120, [2002] NPC 89, [2002] PNLR 43, [2002] 3 WLR 172, [2002] CP Rep 70, [2002] CPLR 647, [2002] 3 Costs LR 428. In this case, judges were of the view that the conduct of lawyers who make allegations of dishonesty without adequate grounds would amount to improper conduct.
见Medcalf v Mardell, Weatherill [2002] UKHL 27, [2002] 3 All ER 731, [2003] 1 AC 120, [2002] NPC 89, [2002] PNLR 43, [2002] 3 WLR 172, [2002] CP Rep 70, [2002] CPLR 647, [2002] 3 Costs LR 428。在本案中，法官们认为，律师在没有充分理由的情况下提出不诚实指控的行为将构成不当行为。

intervention by trial judges during the course of a trial is prohibited, because it would be wrong for a judge to 'arrogate to himself a quasi-inquisitorial role,' this being something which is 'entirely at odds with the adversarial system'.[624] However for many years, the selection of judges in England and Wales was more like an election into an exclusive club. The current transparent process through application for the post of judge only started in 1997 for the High Court and in 1994 for sub-ordinate posts.

示，审判法官在审判过程中过度干预是被禁止的，因为法官"自封为准调查角色"是错误的，这是"与对抗制度完全不一致的"。然而，多年来，英格兰和威尔士的法官选拔更像是一个进入高级俱乐部的选举。目前通过申请法官职位的透明程序在1997年才开始适用于高等法院，在1994年才适用于下级职位。

These issues with selection of judges have been criticised by practitioners and social scientists alike in England & Wales as one of the hurdles to finding the truth in many cases. Therefore, the role of judges in the civil law system would likely not have been appreciated by common-law judges.

在英格兰和威尔士，法官遴选的这些问题受到了从业人员和社会科学家的批评，认为这是在许多案件中寻找真相的障碍之一。因此，大陆法系法官的作用可能不会得到普通法法官的认可。

5.3.2.1 In context of PRC Law (within civil law system)

在中华人民共和国法律背景下（大陆法系内）

Historically, judges in ancient China were famous for making judgments with the model of legal reasoning as seen in the eighteenth and nineteenth centuries in the Board of Punishments.[625] As discussed earlier,[626] in ancient sources such as *Kang kao and Lu hsing*, the procedure adopted was inquisitorial and no legal representation of any kind whatsoever was allowed by those judges.

从历史上看，中国古代的法官以运用法律推理的模式进行判决而闻名，这在18、19世纪的《刑板》中可见一见。如前所述，在《康诰》和《吕刑》等古代文献中，所采用的程序是审讯，这些法官不允许任何形式的法律代表。

Once the facts were ascertained, popularly called 'finding the truth', relevant rules from Codes were investigated and to them were applied the relevant facts that were ascertained in the

一旦事实被确定，通常被称为"发现真相"，就会调查法典的相关规则，并将在发现真相过程中确定的相关事

[624]See *Southwark LBC v Maamefowaa Koadu* [2006] EWCA Civ 281, [148]. See also the discussion on this case in Neil Andrews, "Fundamental Principles of Civil Procedure: Order out of Chaos," in *Civil Litigation in a Globalising World*, ed. X.E. Kramer and Rhee, H (The Hague: T.M.C. Asser Press, 2012), 29, 387.
见 Southwark LBC v Maamefowaa Koadu [2006] EWCA Civ 281, [148]。见Neil Andrews的《民事诉讼的基本原则：混沌中的秩序》，载于《全球化世界中的民事诉讼》，X.E. Kramer和Rhee主编，海牙：T.M.C. Asser出版社，2012，29，第387页。

[625]Geoffrey MacCormack, *The Spirit of Traditional Chinese Law*, The Spirit of the Laws (Athens: London: University of Georgia Press, 1996), 16.
杰弗里·麦考马克：《中国传统法律的精神》，《法律的精神》（雅典：伦敦：佐治亚大学出版社，1996），第16页。

[626]Refer, Chapter 2, §2.2.1。参见第2章第2.2.1节。

finding the truth process.

实应用于这些规则。

However, this procedure was limited to criminal procedure and to some civil issues that were made part of the Code. In the Tang Code, during the Tang Dynasty (AD 601-981), there was a possibility of scenarios where truth cannot be ascertained completely. To deal with this, a relatively small number of rules were drafted so that they could be used in combination, in different circumstances & for different scenarios and offences. To achieve this, a key term in a particular set of rules was utilised to prevent the creation of lengthy codes.[627]

但是，这一程序仅限于刑事程序和成为《治罪法》一部分的一些民事问题。在唐朝（公元601-981年）的《唐法典》中，有可能出现真相无法完全查明的情况。为了解决这个问题，起草了相对较少的规则，以便在不同的情况下，针对不同的情况和罪行，将它们组合起来使用。为了实现这一点，使用了一组特定规则中的关键术语来防止创建冗长的法典。

In later dynasties, torture was allowed to overcome the difficulty of excessive processes in the Codes; the priority was to extract quick confessions. This process of extraction of confessions by torture is deemed by western scholars as a failure of rationality.[628]

在后来的朝代，刑讯被允许克服法典中过度程序的困难；首要任务是迅速招供。这种刑讯逼供的过程被西方学者认为是理性的失败。

According to these scholars, the system ought to ascertain the facts clearly without legitimising torture, even in a milder form. Usually in ancient China, the Board of Punishments would discuss and analyse the procedure and findings and would sometimes send the case back to the magistrates.

根据这些学者的观点，司法系统应该在不使酷刑合法化的情况下，明确查明事实，即使酷刑的形式较为温和。通常在古代中国，刑罚委员会会讨论和分析程序和结果，有时会把案件发回地方长官。

The PRC still uses the inquisitorial system in its courts, where the judge's role is to find the truth, and the formal requirements and standards of proof are very high. However, in theory, the judges' power is limited, as will be discussed later in this Chapter.

中国仍然在法院使用讯问制度，法官的作用是发现真相，对证据的正式要求和标准非常高。然而，从理论上讲，法官的权力是有限的，这将在本章后面讨论。

[627] MacCormack, *The Spirit of Traditional Chinese Law*, 15。麦考马克：《中国传统法律的精神》，第15页。

[628] Ibid., 148。同前注，第148页。

5.4 Judges' Role in Accomplishing Various Functions in the Courts — Concept of Judge's Power

法官在法院履行各项职能中的作用——法官权力的概念

There are various functions that judges are asked to accomplish in relation to adjudication; some, as described by Katyal in the context of the US common law, are as follows:[629]

在审判方面，法官被要求履行各种职能；正如卡蒂亚尔在美国普通法背景下所描述的那样，其中一些如下：

- *Clarifications* of a statute or law;
  对成文法或法律的澄清；

- *Personification*, whereby they guide the role of government organs;
  拟人化，借此指导政府机关的作用；

- *Self-Alienation,* whereby the judiciary itself limits its role in a particular matter;
  自我疏离，即司法机构自身限制其在某一特定事务中的作用；

- *Exemplification*, whereby judges can strike down an act as unconstitutional;
  举例来说，法官可以以违宪为由驳回一项行为；

- *Demarcation*, whereby an act is deemed unconstitutional but with examples of similar unconstitutional ones;
  界定，据此一个行为被视为违宪，但有类似的违宪的例子；

- *Prescription*, whereby the judges give policy advice to the executive based on their experience;
  处方，即法官根据自己的经验向行政部门提出政策建议；

- *Penalization*, whereby the judges may ask the legislature to look at the acts as they are not serving the purpose.
  惩罚，法官可以要求立法机关审查这些行为，因为其未达到目的。

A lot of scholarly space has been devoted to *doctrines of separation* and *judicial independence*, which are important for ensuring judicial effectiveness. However, this concept of

分离主义和司法独立理论是保障司法实效的重要理论，学术界对此进行了大量的研究。然而，这种分离主义的

---

[629]Neal Kumar Katyal, "Judge as Advicegivers," *Stan. L. Rev.* 50, no. 6 (1998): 1722.
尼尔·库马尔·卡蒂亚尔，"作为顾问的法官"，斯坦福法律评论，第50卷，1998年第6期，第1722页。

doctrine of separation is very deeply rooted in western jurisprudence. Traditionally, in countries where the judiciary has not been independent, these concepts could be alien. However, in the authors' view, legal cultures can be different, and so this should not be treated as if it is an insurmountable obstacle.

概念却深深植根于西方法学。传统上，在司法不独立的国家，这些概念可能是陌生的。然而，在笔者看来，法律文化可以是不同的，所以这不应该被视为一个不可逾越的障碍。

Gillespie has discussed that there are no distinct economic benefits in copying western concepts in Far Eastern legal systems, and that therefore, the courts should be structured differently in these countries.[630] However, Gillespie's key finding was that *judicial effectiveness* is actually enhanced by judicial power much more than judicial independence, as in the early stages the judiciary itself needs protection.[631] Judicial power can be seen within the context of jurisdiction to handle disputes, and discretionary power to manage different types of disputes and to grant general and specific remedies. Judicial power can also be seen within the context of their ability to give binding judgments that can be enforced later by the same courts.

吉莱斯皮已经讨论过，在远东法律体系中复制西方概念并没有明显的经济利益，因此，这些国家的法院结构应该有所不同。然而，吉莱斯皮的关键发现是，司法效力实际上是由司法权力而不是司法独立来提高的，因为在早期阶段，司法本身需要保护。司法权可以在管辖权范围内处理纠纷，也可以在自由裁量权范围内管理不同类型的纠纷，并给予一般和具体救济。司法权也可以从他们作出有约束力的判决的能力来看，这些判决以后可以由同一法院执行。

Historically, the advent and evolution of legal judicial reasoning in the English courts ensured that the concept of judicial independence evolved to insulate the courts from external influences such as "clientelism, nepotism, hierarchical status and political cronyism."[632] In addition, legal reasoning that has emerged because of judges employing their discretionary power was used in England & Wales to find a way to resolve political interference before formal concepts of constitutional safeguards came into existence.[633]

从历史上看，英国法院中法律司法推理的出现和演变确保了司法独立概念的演变，使法院免受诸如"裙带关系、裙带关系、等级地位和政治任人唯亲"等外部影响。此外，由于法官运用其自由裁量权而出现的法律推理在英格兰和威尔士被用来寻找一种在宪法保障的正式概念存在之前解决政治干预的方法。

This ability of the courts proved very useful in resolving economic disputes, especially when England & Wales was an economic superpower in the nineteenth century. It is the authors' view that in legal systems where codes are new and still developing, such as in the PRC, judges need to have

事实证明，法院的这种能力在解决经济纠纷方面非常有用，尤其是在19世纪英格兰和威尔士成为经济超级大国的时候。笔者认为，在法典尚属新兴且仍在发展的法律体系中，例如在中国，

630 John Gillespie, "Rethinking the Role of Judicial Independence in Socialist-Transforming East Asia," *I.C.L.Q.* 56, no. 4 (2007): 840. 约翰·吉莱斯皮，《再思考司法独立在社会主义转型的东亚中的作用》，《美国法律与社会研究》第56期，4(2007): 840。

631 Gillespie, "Judicial Independence in East Asia.", where his main theme was that judicial power enhances judicial effectiveness. 吉莱斯皮，《东亚的司法独立》，他的主题是司法权提高司法效率。

632 Ibid., 848. 同前注，第 848 页。

633 Ibid., 849. 同前注，第849页。

discretionary power to apply such codes appropriately to the facts of the cases. However, while judges might have such discretionary power, the capability and desire of the judges to exercise them are an altogether different issue. This issue is only sparingly touched on in the PRC. Such discretionary power is also exercised by the judges in civil law countries such as France.[634]

法官需要有酌情权，以适当地将这些法典适用于案件的事实。然而，虽然法官可能有这种自由裁量权，但法官行使这种权力的能力和愿望是完全不同的问题。这个问题在中国很少被提及。这种自由裁量权在法国等大陆法系国家也由法官行使。

However, judicial discretion can be eroded easily, for example:[635]

然而，司法自由裁量权很容易受到侵蚀，例如：

- By guidance of senior courts' judges (outside of appeal process);
- By directive from a local or central leadership or ideology leadership;
- By formulating creative decision to protect interests of state;
- By relying heavily on state's organs for guidance on commercial cases.

-通过高级法院法官的指导（在上诉程序之外）；

-受地方或中央领导或意识形态领导的指示；

-通过制定创造性决策来保护国家利益；

-严重依赖国家机关对商事案件的指导。

At times, the judges' discretionary power is exhibited by employing sentiment, or local norms such as morality and sentimental value in the courts to gain legitimacy; this may itself lead to the erosion of the judges' discretionary power.[636] In many jurisdictions, discretion is employed so widely by the judges that any law, if it were to be an impediment to the state's interest, would be considered as irrelevant to the facts of the dispute. As a consequence, the textual narrative of codes or statutes is sometimes overlooked, eroding not only the discretionary power, but also the legitimacy of the courts.

有时，法官的自由裁量权通过在法庭上运用情感或当地规范（如道德和情感价值）来获得合法性；这本身可能会导致法官自由裁量权的削弱。在许多司法管辖区，自由裁量权被法官广泛使用，以至于任何法律，如果它阻碍了国家的利益，就会被认为与争议的事实无关。因此，法典或成文法的文本叙述有时被忽视，这不仅侵蚀了自由裁量权，也侵蚀了法院的合法性。

For discretionary power to be put into practice, judges in courts are usually encouraged to engage in legal discourse that assists in development of legal reasoning. Judges are further encouraged to exercise their discretionary power in a way that

为了将自由裁量权付诸实践，法院的法官通常被鼓励参与有助于发展法律推理的法律话语。进一步鼓励法官以一种有助于法官“将政治、道德和经济

[634]Ibid. 同前注。

[635]Ibid., 851–3. 同前注，第851-3页。

[636]Ibid., 855. 同前注，第855页。

can assist the judges "to transpose political, moral and economic precepts into legally judicable questions."[637]

戒律转化为法律上可审判的问题"的方式行使其自由裁量权。

5.5 Judicial Decision-making Process

司法决策程序

After the above discussion on judges' power, particularly in relation to discretionary power, it is important for the authors to discuss the whole process of decision-making by the judges in any jurisdiction. Whether it is the common law system or civil law inquisitorial system, the judges in their decision making are affected by "anchoring, hindsight bias, self-serving bias"[638] and that can have an effect on a final judgment in any case.

在对法官的权力，特别是自由裁量权进行了上述讨论之后，笔者有必要对任何一个司法管辖区的法官决策的全过程进行探讨。无论是普通法系还是大陆法系的审讯制度，法官在作出判决时都会受到"锚定、后见之明、自私自利"的影响，在任何情况下都会对最终判决产生影响。

The above factors affect the full judicial process, including the analysis of facts. The danger is even more pronounced when the judges are exercising their discretionary power. Therefore, any remedy that is dependent on the discretionary power of judges, for example interim applications, is affected by such factors.

上述因素影响了包括事实分析在内的整个司法过程。当法官行使他们的自由裁量权时，这种危险甚至更加明显。因此，任何依赖法官自由裁量权的补救办法，例如临时申请，都受到这些因素的影响。

Negowetti has said that ""Discretion-free" judging, bereft of the influence of one's own identity or experiences, is far-fetched in a profession populated by human beings, and not machines."[639] It is natural for judges to bring their assumptions, biases, intuitions, experience, religion, values, age, gender, political beliefs, sexual orientation and own sense of justice to bear. Complete emotional detachment of the judges from a case is impossible; they may well process only information that conforms to their world-view. Therefore, the theme of this book is that invisible factors do affect judges, and therefore law in action is affected by such invisible factors in various ways.

内格韦提曾说过，"在一个由人类而不是机器组成的职业中，失去了个人身份或经历影响的'自由裁量'判断是牵强的。"法官自然会运用他们的假设、偏见、直觉、经验、宗教、价值观、年龄、性别、政治信仰、性取向和自己的正义感。法官在情感上完全脱离案件是不可能的；他们很可能只处理符合他们世界观的信息。因此，本书主题是，看不见的因素确实影响着法官，因此，法律在行动中受到这些看不见的因素以各种方式的影响。

637Ibid., 864. 同前注，第864页。
638Negowetti, "Judicial Decisionmaking," 715. Negowetti，《司法决策》，第715页。
639Ibid., 717. 同前注，第717页。

Globally, judges have started to acknowledge the above vulnerability, and are sceptical about their own intuition because of this vulnerability. However, it is still a work in progress. This *unconscious influence* can be mitigated by the judges by acknowledging them and developing the skill of *empathy*, where the judges will start to take into account the perspective of every party in their courts.[640] Empathy is different from compassion and is the cognitive capacity to understand others' point of view. It is a skill that can be developed by acknowledging and then overpowering one's own biases, prejudices and loyalties.[641] Empathy assists judges to understand disputes better, including the motivations and intentions of the litigants before the courts.

在全球范围内，法官们已经开始承认上述脆弱性，并因为这种脆弱性而对自己的直觉持怀疑态度。然而，这项工作仍在进行中。法官可通过承认这种无意识的影响并培养移情技能来减轻这种影响，法官将开始考虑法庭上每一方的观点。同理心不同于同情心，它是一种理解他人观点的认知能力。这是一种可通过承认并克服自己的偏见、偏见和忠诚来培养的技能。同理心帮助法官更好地理解纠纷，包括法庭上诉讼当事人的动机和意图。

The role of empathy remains very important for handling applications in civil courts; as it is a fact that most of these applications require the judges to exercise their discretionary power. Many of the objective standards, test of reasonableness, and standards of proof in civil litigation can only succeed, if there is an impartial view of the facts. This is only possible if the litigators and judicial decision-makers are aware of their own personal biases.

在处理民事法庭的申请时，同理心作用仍非常重要；这是一个事实，大多数这些申请要求法官行使他们的自由裁量权。民事诉讼中的许多客观标准、合理性检验和证明标准只有在对事实有公正看法的情况下才能成功。只有当诉讼律师和司法决策者意识到自己的个人偏见时，这才有可能。

The above issue also exposes the issue of selection of judges in England & Wales from only a narrow section of the society, which in the practice of law could cloud social realities. This in turn could affect the outcome in any civil litigation. Similarly, in the PRC, the ideological training in the philosophy of communism, socialism, Marxism and various thoughts highlighted in *PRC Constitution 1982* (as amended) again could cloud the judges' views about disputes before them.

上述问题也暴露了英格兰和威尔士法官的遴选问题，其来源仅占社会的一小部分，这在法律实践中可能会对社会现实产生影响，进而影响民事诉讼的结果。同样，在中国，共产主义哲学、社会主义、马克思主义以及1982年《中华人民共和国宪法》（修订版）中所强调的各种思想的意识形态训练，可能会影响法官对他们所面对的争议的看法。

[640]Ibid., 724。同前注，第724页。
[641]Ibid., 727。同前注，第727页。

CHAPTER SIX — JUDGES' DISCRETIONARY POWER – COMMON LAW v. CHINESE LAW

第六章 -法官的自由裁量权-普通法与中国法

6.1 Judges' Discretionary Power

法官的自由裁量权

In the previous Chapter, the authors discussed jurisprudence of justice in the context of *law in action*, in particular judges' roles, their powers, biases, decision making processes, their role in relation to evidence and so forth. In the previous Chapter, the authors also touched upon the issue of judicial discretion and how it can be eroded due to interference from the executive and preservers of ideology. These issues were discussed from the point of view of both the common law system of England & Wales and PRC law. The authors will now analyse judges' discretionary power in the context of legal philosophy, traditions in the historical context, and most importantly the current practice in courts.

在前一章中，作者讨论了法律行动背景下的司法判例，特别是法官的角色、权力、偏见、决策过程、在证据方面的作用等。在上一章中，作者还谈到了司法自由裁量权的问题，以及它如何受到行政部门和意识形态维护者的干预。这些问题分别从英格兰和威尔士的普通法体系以及中国法律的角度进行了讨论。接下来，作者将从法律哲学、历史背景下的传统以及最重要的法院现行做法等方面分析法官的自由裁量权。

There is a need in any legal system to have certainty in the application of law and to curb the arbitrary power of judges. However, no statute or case law can be perfect or can imagine all scenarios that might emerge in the future, to which such statute or case law might be applied. There is a great deal of uncertainty surrounding facts, law, customs, procedures in court, issues related to third parties that can be affected by any judgment, issues of economic equality between the parties and policy and so forth. Faced with this uncertainty, learned judges in any jurisdiction will have to exercise their discretionary power. The main issues that

任何法律制度都需要法律适用的确定性，并遏制法官的专断权力。然而，任何法规或判例法都不可能尽善尽美，也无法想象未来可能出现的所有情况，而这些情况都可能适用于这些法规或判例法。围绕事实、法律、习俗、法庭程序、可能受任何判决影响的与第三方有关的问题、当事方之间的经济平等问题以及政策等等，存在着大量的不确定性。面对这种不确定性，任何司法管辖区的法官都必须行使其自由裁量权。在这两个司法管辖区出现的主要问题如下：

arise in both the jurisdictions are:

- Whether the judges in England & Wales and PRC jurisdiction are equipped with such power? and

-英格兰和威尔士以及中国司法管辖区的法官是否拥有这种权力？

- If they are equipped with such power, are the judges willing to exercise such discretionary power? and

- 若法官被赋予该项权力，他们是否愿意行使该项酌情权？

- If the judges are willing to exercise that power, are there any impediments in relation to such exercise of discretionary power?

- 若法官愿意行使该项权力，在行使酌情权方面有否任何障碍？

6.2 Principles and Philosophy in Current Legal System in English Law

英国法中现行法律制度的原则和理论

In traditional England, the concept of *rule of law* needs to be applied to all types of judicial activities. This strand of jurisprudence gained further popularity with Rawls' concept of *formal justice* where justice demands that there is impartial application of the rules.[642] In order to uniformly apply the rules, the judges will have to give up their 'personal' discretionary power that is available to all humans at the personal level, so that all trials, hearings, procedures in the courts and rules in relation to evidence are constant.[643] This uniform application of law will also be applicable to the executive and legislative branch in that society, and therefore, the rules will have primacy over all institutions, with the sole aim of curbing the arbitrary powers of officials. This leads to what Dicey has called

在传统的英国，法治的概念需要适用于所有类型的司法活动。罗尔斯的形式正义（*formal justice*）概念进一步普及了这一法学分支，形式正义要求公正地适用规则。为了统一适用法律规则，法官必须放弃其“个人”的自由裁量权，这是所有人在个人层面上都拥有的权力，这样所有的审判、听证、法庭程序以及与证据相关的规则都是不变的。这种法律的统一适用也将适用于该社会的行政和立法部门，因此，这些规则将优先于所有机构，其唯一目的就是遏制官员的专断权力。这就导致了迪西所说的“相对

[642]John Rawls, *A Theory of Justice*, 2nd ed. (Cambridge, Mass: Belknap Press of Harvard University Press, 1999), 235.
约翰-罗尔斯，《正义论》，第 2 版，马萨诸塞州剑桥：哈佛大学出版社贝尔纳普出版社，1999 年，第235页。
[643]Margaret Y.K. Woo, "Law and Discretion in the Contemporary Chinese Courts," *Pac. Rim L. and Pol'y J.* 8, no. 3 (1999): 583.
Margaret Y.K. Woo，《当代中国法院的法律与自由裁量权》，《环太平洋法学与政治学杂志》 (Pac. Rim L. and Pol'y J. 8, no. 3 (1999): 583.

"supremacy or predominance of regular law as opposed to influence of arbitrary power."[644]

于专断权力的影响而言，正规法律的至高无上或主导地位"。

However, there are scenarios where there is no consensus in a legislature to draft new law on a particular subject and therefore, there is no law on that subject. This results in a scenario where policy from the legislature is kept deliberately ambiguous and the only way for judges to resolve disputes in court is to employ their judicial resources. Hawkins argued that there are functional benefits to the judges having discretionary power, such as avoiding costly formalities, or filling gaps in law or policy.[645]

然而，在某些情况下，立法机构无法就某一特定主题起草新法律达成共识，因此也就没有关于该主题的法律。这就导致立法机构的政策故意保持模糊，法官在法庭上解决争议的唯一途径就是动用司法资源。霍金斯认为，法官拥有自由裁量权在功能上是有好处的，比如可以避免代价高昂的手续，或者填补法律或政策的空白。

On one hand, there is a need to enhance the legitimacy of the courts by providing certainty from the beginning; but on the other hand, there is also a need to do justice in the particular circumstances of a dispute. In ancient western jurisprudence, the Greek jurisprudent Aristotle was of the view that fair-minded judges could ensure justice was done for litigants in their courts.[646] In the historical English Legal system, as discussed earlier,[647] the role of certainty provided by formal rules in common law was balanced by courts of *equity* that granted discretionary power to provide justice to litigants. Now that both these courts are merged in the current legal system,[648] the judges' discretionary power is fully anchored in the system and is no longer considered an arbitrary power.

一方面，有必要通过从一开始就提供确定性来增强法院的合法性；但另一方面，也有必要在争端的特定情况下伸张正义。在古代西方法学中，希腊法学家亚里士多德认为，公正的法官可以确保诉讼当事人在法庭上得到公正的对待。在历史悠久的英国法律体系中，如前文所述，普通法中的正式规则提供了确定性，而衡平法法院则赋予自由裁量权，为诉讼当事人伸张正义。现在，这两种法院都已并入现行法律体系，法官的自由裁量权已完全固定在该体系中，不再被视为一种任意权力。

Dworkin has noted that the judges' power can be used in

德沃金指出，在普通法中，法官

---

[644]A.V. Dicey, *Introduction to the Study of the Law of Constitution* (London; New York: Macmillan, 1902), 202–3.
A.V. Dicey,《宪法法律研究导论》，伦敦；纽约：麦克米伦，1902年，第202-203页。

[645]Keith Hawkins, "Use of Legal Discretion: Perspectives from Law and Social Science" (1992), 37. Hawking is also discussed in Woo, "Discretion in Contemporary Chinese Courts," 584n16.
凯斯-霍金斯，《使用法律裁量权： 法律与社会科学的视角》，1992年，第37页。Woo, "当代中国法院的自由裁量权", 584n16 中也讨论了霍金。

[646]Aristotle and J. A. K. Thomson, trans., *The Ethics of Aristotle: The Nicomachean Ethics*, Reprinted ed. (London: Penguin, 1961), 146–47. Aristotle was discussed in relation to the concept of the fair-minded judge in Woo, "Discretion in Contemporary Chinese Courts," 584n12.
亚里士多德和 J. A. K.托马森译，《亚里士多德的伦理学》：尼各马可伦理学，重印版，伦敦：企鹅出版社，1961 年，第 146-147 页。亚里士多德曾在 Woo 的《当代中国法院的自由裁量权》一文中就公正法官的概念进行过讨论，584n12。

[647]Refer, Chapter 2, §2.1.1.2, where the role of the Courts of Equity was discussed.
参见第2章第2.1.1.2 节，其中讨论了衡平法院的作用。

[648]Refer, Chapter 2, §2.1.1.3 and the discussion of the merger of parallel court systems in England.
参见第2章第2.1.1.3 节以及关于英格兰平行法院系统合并的讨论。

various ways in the context of common law:[649]

的权力可以各种方式使用：

- Discretion is used in a weaker sense, meaning that judges cannot apply the rules or statutes mechanically, but will use their judgment based upon their training and experience;

-自由裁量权是在较弱的意义上使用的，这意味着法官不能机械地适用规则或法规，而是要根据自己的训练和经验做出判断；

- Another weaker sense in which discretionary power can be used is that the judges highest up in a hierarchy have the final say on the dispute, and their decisions cannot be reviewed or reversed;

- 自由裁量权的另一种较弱含义是，等级制度中最高级别的法官对争议拥有最终决定权，其裁决不得复审或者推翻；

- Discretion in the stronger sense (hereinafter '*third sense*' is most relevant in scenarios when the judges are not bound by the limits of law (statutes, case precedent, customary rules) but with exceptions. However, any discretion employed by the judges contains in it the principles of rationality, fairness, effectiveness, etc.

- 较强意义上的自由裁量权（下称"*第三种意义*"）最适用于法官不受法律限制（法规、判例、习惯规则）情况，但也有例外。然而，法官的任何自由裁量权都包含合理、公平、有效等原则。

Positivists like H L A Hart in England & Wales agree with the concept of discretionary power being employed by judges. According to Hart, employment of discretionary power is based on the 'court's principles.' However, one school of thought argues that the judges having such discretionary power itself means that the judges are disregarding the rules; having such discretion in itself also means that there are no limits on the power of the judges.[650] The usual circumstances in which judges exercise their discretionary power are in scenarios where a dispute is complex and there is no law or policy for them to consider. The judges' discretionary power can be also be seen in the context of obligation or duty: the judges are morally obliged, or the courts are institutionally obligated, or it is a part of the judges' work to apply such principles when adjudicating disputes in court.

英格兰和威尔士的ＨＬＡ哈特等实证主义者同意法官使用自由裁量权的概念。哈特认为，自由裁量权的使用是基于"法院原则"。然而，有一种观点认为，法官拥有这种自由裁量权本身就意味着法官无视规则；拥有这种自由裁量权本身也意味着法官的权力没有限制。法官行使自由裁量权的通常情况是在争议复杂，没有法律或政策供其考虑的情况下。法官的自由裁量权也可以从义务或责任的角度来看待：法官在道义上有义务，或者法院在制度上有义务，或者法官的工作之一就是在法院裁决争议时适用这些原则。

[649]Ronald Dworkin, *Taking Rights Seriously* (London: Duckworth, 1977), 29–36. Dworkin's views were also discussed in Penner, "Law and Adjudication" 342–43.
罗纳德-德沃金，《认真对待权利》，伦敦：达克沃斯，1977年，第29-36页。彭纳，《法律与裁决》342-343也讨论了德沃金的观点。
[650]Ronald Dworkin, *Taking Rights Seriously*, 29–36. See also, discussion on Dworkin in Penner, "Law and Adjudication" 344.
罗纳德-德沃金，《认真对待权利》，29-36。另见彭纳，《法律与裁决》344页中关于德沃金的讨论。

There is jurisprudential debate as to whether such *principles* are 'part of law' or, pursuant to Dworkin's argument, whether they play the role of extra-legal standards that the courts often employ in order to reach decisions.[651] However, in the positivists' view, it is very difficult to count the principles that the judges usually employ in their discretion as part of the law. However, careful reading and analysis show that Dworkin considers these principles as part of law. Therefore, when judges employ such principles when adjudicating disputes, it can be read as if they have no discretionary power, and/or may not actually be considered as their exercising discretionary power.

关于这些原则是否是"法律的一部分"，或者根据德沃金的论点，这些*原则*是否扮演了法院在作出判决时经常采用的法律外标准的角色，在法理学上存在争论。然而，在实证主义者看来，很难将法官在自由裁量时通常采用的原则算作法律的一部分。然而，通过仔细阅读和分析，德沃金认为这些原则是法律的一部分。因此，当法官在判决争议时使用这些原则时，可以解读为他们没有自由裁量权，和/或实际上可能不被视为他们行使了自由裁量权。

Raz explained in relation to Dworkin's view that when rules or law are read together with principles, there is no room for any vagueness. Therefore it seems clear to Raz that there is no need for the judges to have any discretionary power.[652] The only way to demonstrate that principles exist in the context of judges' discretionary powers is by appealing to 'community practices and understandings' along with the history of judicial practice, cases and legislations.[653] At the same time, however, Dworkin highlighted that the soundness of employment of discretionary power cannot be tested in exactly the same way, as the discretionary power of any other officials is incapable of being tested for soundness. Any other reasonable and educated person may very well disagree with the results after the exercise of discretionary power by the judges in courts.[654]

拉兹就德沃金的观点解释说，当规则或法律与原则放在一起解读时，就没有任何模糊的余地。因此，在拉兹看来，法官显然没有必要拥有任何自由裁量权。要证明原则存在于法官的自由裁量权中，唯一的方法就是诉诸"社会实践和理解"以及司法实践、案例和立法的历史。然而，德沃金同时强调，不能以完全相同的方式检验酌情权运用的合理性，正如任何其他官员的酌情权无法检验其合理性一样。任何其他有理智和受过教育的人都很可能不同意法官在法院行使自由裁量权后的结果。

Raz took the analysis and the debate further in the context of principles that judges often employ. He was of the view

拉兹结合法官常使用的原则进一

[651]Ronald Dworkin, *Taking Rights Seriously*, 29–36.
罗纳德-德沃金，《认真对待权利》，第29-36页。
[652]J. Raz, "Legal Principles and the Limits of Law," *Yale L.J.* 81, no. 5 (1972): 838–47. It was discussed in Penner, "Law and Adjudication" 357.
J. 拉兹，《法律原则与法律的局限性》，《耶鲁法学杂志》第 81 期，no. 5 (1972): 838–47。彭纳，《法律与裁决》357 中对此进行了讨论。
[653]Ronald Dworkin, *Taking Rights Seriously*, 36. See for further discussion Penner, "Law and Adjudication" 345.
罗纳德-德沃金，《认真对待权利》， 36。更多讨论见彭纳，《法律与裁决》，第345页。
[654]Ronald Dworkin, *Taking Rights Seriously*, 29–36. For further discussion on this aspect, see also Penner, "Law and Adjudication" 345.
罗纳德-德沃金，《认真对待权利》， 36。更多讨论见彭纳，《法律与裁决》，第345页。

that there was a difference between rules that are very specific in nature and could be found by judges in the law, in statutes or cases, and principles that are not specific enough, such as concept of justice or reasonableness or similar principles. In addition, the principles are relatively vague and less certain, but general goals and values can be reflected more patently by using such principles. These principles also provide relative flexibility to the judges.

步进行了分析和辩论。他认为，法官可在法律、法规或案例中找到性质非常具体的规则，而不够具体的原则，如正义的概念或合理性或类似原则，两者是有区别的。此外这些原则相对模糊，确定性较低，但使用这些原则可更明显地反映一般目标和价值。这些原则也为法官提供了相对灵活性。

However, Raz did mention that it is not easy to delineate rules from principles.[655] It is the authors' view that in legal systems where correctness of a judgment is crucial and judges go to great lengths to analyse and apply the rules, certainty or uniformity is given less precedence in the scheme of things. In such situations, principles will have a slightly larger role in a subtle way in their application to the facts in a dispute. The authors are of the school of thought that believes that in the application of principles, morality is in full force by the back door.[656] Raz is also of the same view, that morality prevails in such cases.[657]

不过，拉兹也提到，将规则与原则区分开来并非易事。笔者认为，在一些法律体系中，判决的正确性至关重要，法官会不遗余力地分析和应用规则，在这种情况下，确定性或统一性就不那么重要了。在这种情况下，原则在适用于争议事实时会以微妙的方式发挥稍大的作用。作者所属的学派认为，在适用原则时，道德会通过后门充分发挥作用。拉兹也持有同样的观点，即在这种情况下道德占上风。

Raz analysed the *principles* in detail in the context of the judges' power:

拉兹从法官权力的角度详细分析了原则：

- Principles as grounds for *interpreting laws,* whereby any interpretation by the judges should conform to the general principles of a legal system that decides the coherence of purpose amongst various laws;

- 原则是*解释法律*的依据，法官的任何解释都应符合法律制度的一般原则，这些原则决定了各种法律之间的目的一致性；

- Principles as grounds for *changing laws* where cases are modified using principles though the principles are used conservatively in this scenario;

- 将原则作为*修改法律*的依据，在这种情况下，虽然原则的使用是保守的，但案件的修改是以原则为依据的；

[655]Raz, "Legal Principles" On this aspect of the thin line between rules and principles and Raz's view see also Penner, "Law and Adjudication" 354.
拉兹，《法律原则》。关于规则与原则之间的界限以及拉兹的观点，另见彭纳，《法律与裁决》354。
[656]Refer to discussion on morality and natural Law in Chapter 3, §3.1.1.2.
参见第 3 章第 3.1.1.2 节中关于道德与自然法的讨论。
[657]Raz, "Legal Principles," 838–47. See also the discussion on this aspect and Raz's view in Penner, "Law and Adjudication" 354.
拉兹，《法律原则》838–47。另见彭纳，《法律与裁决》354 中关于这方面的讨论和拉兹的观点。

- Principles as grounds for a *particular exception to laws* — more often used in non-common-law countries, but in common law countries also have principles that have been developed in the courts of equity,[658] for example — one must come with clean hands to the courts; or, no one can profit from their own wrong; or, the claimants cannot unreasonably delay in enforcing his rights through the courts, etc.;

- 原则作为法律的*特定例外*的理由——在非普通法国家更常用，但在普通法国家也有在衡平法院中发展起来的原则，例如——一个人必须清白地来到法院；或者，任何人都不能从自己的错误中获利；或者，原告不能无理拖延通过法院行使他的权利，等等；

- Principles as grounds for *creating new rules* when in particular situations, the judges are unable to find a particular law in any forum. However, any new rules that judges may apply are formulated on the basis of established principles;

- 当法官在特定情况下无法在任何论坛找到特定法律时，可将原则作为制定新规则的依据。不过，法官可能适用的任何新规则都是根据既定原则制定的；

- Principles as the sole grounds for action in particular cases such as in administrative law; the *implementation* through discretionary power by officials is governed by these principles.[659]

- 在行政法等特定案件中，原则是采取行动的唯一依据；官员通过自由裁量权实施的行为受到这些原则的制约。

In order to understand the crucial differences between legal rules and principles, in the authors' view, it is important to know how they have evolved. A *legal rule* can be created by a single judgment or a single legislation, but the *principle(s)* are gathered over a period through the analysis of many such judgments.

作者认为，要理解法律规则与原则之间的关键区别，须了解它们是如何演变的。法律规则可由一个判决或一项立法创立，但原则是在一段时间内通过对许多此类判决的分析而成。

Raz said "...that legal principles do not exclude judicial discretion; they presuppose its existence and direct and guide it."[660] While the word 'discretion' leads many to believe it is arbitrary in nature, this is not the case in practice in common law systems. For example, even if there were no limits on discretionary power, the courts will still be "legally bound to act as they think is best according to their beliefs and values. If they do not, if they give arbitrary

拉兹说"...法律原则并不排除司法裁量权；*法律原则*预设了司法裁量权的存在，并对其进行指导和引导。"自由裁量权"一词让很多人认为它具有任意性，但在普通法系的实践中却并非如此。例如，即使对自由裁量权没有限制，法院仍将"受法律约束，按照他们的信仰和价值观行事，认为这样

[658]Refer, Chapter 2, §2.1.1.2参见第 2 章第 2.1.1.2 节。

[659]Raz, "Legal Principles," 838–47. See also. Penner, "Law and Adjudication" 355–57。 拉兹，《法律原则》838–847。另见彭纳，《法律与裁决》355–357。

[660]ibid, 358.

judgment by tossing a coin, for example, they violate a legal duty."[661] At a more concrete level, decisions/judgments made by the exercise of discretionary powers cannot be looked at in isolation, but has to be looked at through the prism of "some comprehensive theory or general principles and policies that is [sic] consistent with other decisions also thought right."[662]

做是最好的。如果他们不这样做，如果他们通过掷硬币等方式做出武断的判断，他们就违反了法律义务"。"在更具体层面上，不能孤立地看待通过行使自由裁量权做出的决定/判决，而须通过"与其他也认为正确的决定相一致的某种综合理论或一般原则和政策[原文如此]"的棱镜来看待。

6.2.1 Judges' Discretionary Power – in context of English law

法官的自由裁量权--以英国法律为背景

In England & Wales, there are two schools of thought in relation to principles and rules. According to one jurisprudential school of thought, such principles are there as part of law, and therefore, the judges employ no judicial discretion. On the other hand, in another jurisprudential school of thought, there is an acknowledgment of judicial discretion and the fact that principles play a big role in judicial activities. It is the authors' stance that no matter which school of thought we believe in, in legal practice or *law in action*, it is a fact, that judges do opt for principles, legal rules based on case laws, statutes, customs and policy reasons, and prioritise them.

在英格兰和威尔士，关于原则和规则有两种学派。一个法理学流派认为，这些原则是法律的一部分，因此法官没有司法裁量权。另一方面，在另一个法理学派别中，承认司法自由裁量权以及原则在司法活动中发挥重要作用的事实。笔者的立场是，无论我们信奉哪种学派，在法律实践或法律行动中，法官确实会选择基于判例法、成文法、习惯和政策原因的原则、法律规则，并将其置于优先地位，这是事实。

According to Raz, few legal systems expressly provide that if the judges are unable to find a rule in a case, then they will not be able to render judgment. Raz has discussed the issue of employment of discretionary power by the judges in the following instances:[663]

拉兹认为，很少有法律制度明确规定，如果法官无法在案件中找到规则，那么他们将无法做出判决。拉兹在以下例子中讨论了法官使用自由裁量权的问题：

[661]ibif, 358.
[662]ibid 358.
[663]Raz, "Legal Principles," 838–47. The various scenarios discussed by Raz were analysed in Penner, "Law and Adjudication" 357–58.
拉兹，《法律原则》838–47。彭纳，《法律与裁决》357-58 对拉兹讨论的各种情况进行了分析。

- No sentences constructed in any language can be devoid of *vagueness*. Nonetheless, the courts have built rules of interpretation and there are principles as discussed above to guide the courts. However, it is important to note that these principles are vague and are quite broad.

- 任何语言的句子都不可能没有含糊之处。尽管如此，法院还是制定了解释规则，并有上述原则为法院提供指导。但必须注意的是，这些原则是模糊的，而且相当宽泛。

- Judges are guided by the law as to what they need to consider when *applying the law*, but what weight the judges need to give in order to apply the rules (law of statute, customs or case law) or which rule will prevail or which rules need to be ignored is what judges have to consider. In other words, the judges have discretion to apply principles and to assess the relative importance of these principles.

- 法官在适用法律时需考虑哪些因素，这一点受法律的指导，但法官在适用规则（成文法、习惯法或判例法）时需给予多大的权重，或哪条规则优先，或者哪条规则需忽略，这些都是法官需要考虑的。换言之，法官拥有适用原则和评估这些原则相对重要性的自由裁量权。

- This special type of discretion is available to judges for them to apply *non- binding considerations*, but again this will be guided by principles.

-这种特殊类型的自由裁量权可供法官运用*不具约束力的考虑*因素，但这同样要以原则为指导。

The authors have discussed in Chapter 4 the concept of overriding objective in *CPR 1998*, which allows the courts to exercise their discretionary power. Therefore, it can be argued that the principles supplementing and complementing the law are expressly included in *CPR 1998*.[664]

笔者在第 4 章讨论了英国和威尔士《1998 年民事诉讼程序法》中压倒性目标的概念，该概念允许法院行使酌处权。因此，可以说《1998 年民事诉讼程序法》明确包含了补充和辅助法律的原则。

In many areas of both substantive and procedural law, common law sets its standards according to those of a 'reasonable person'. However, this community standard has been criticised, as they argue this is tantamount to the entry of judicial discretion by the back door. The criticism is due to the fact that there is a danger that judges can apply their own personal standards instead of the community standard in the 'reasonable person test'.[665]

在实体法和程序法的许多领域，普通法都是依"理性人"标准制定其标准。然而，这种社区标准受到批评，因为他们认为这等同于走后门进入司法裁量权。提出批评的原因是，在"理性人标准"中，法官有可能采用自己的个人标准，而不是社会标准。

---

[664] Anthony Clarke, "The Woolf Reforms: A Singular Event or an Ongoing Process," in *The Civil Procedure Ten Years On*, ed. Deirdre Dwyer (Oxford: Oxford University Press, 2009), 45. See also the discussion of overriding objectives and secondary objectives in Chapter 4, §4.2.1.1.
安东尼-克拉克，"伍尔夫改革： 一个独特的事件还是一个持续的过程" 见《十年后的民事诉讼》，Deirdre Dwyer编辑，牛津：牛津大学出版社，2009 年，第45页。另请参见第4章第4.2.1.1节中关于首要目标和次要目标的讨论。
[665] Negowetti, "Judicial Decisionmaking," 701.
内戈维蒂，"司法决策"，第701页。

In the current practice in England & Wales, in many areas of substantive law and procedural law, there is wide discretionary power that the judges in the English courts regularly employ in reaching their decisions. Numerous commentators who have analysed various judgments note that there were policy reasons behind these judgments, especially when there were no equivalent statutes and/or legislations to deal with those disputes.

在英格兰和威尔士的现行实践中，在实体法和程序法的许多领域，英国法院的法官在作出裁决时经常使用广泛的自由裁量权。许多评论家在分析了各种判决后指出，这些判决背后都有政策原因，尤其是在没有相应的法规和/或立法来处理这些争议的情况下。

6.3 Judges' Discretionary Power – in context of PRC Law

法官的自由裁量权——以中华人民共和国法律为背景

In order to analyse the issue of judges' discretionary power in the PRC, the authors will first discuss the pre-PRC era, and subsequently will discuss jurisprudential thinking in the current system. Finally, the authors will discuss current practice of law/law in this context, in the PRC courts.

为了分析中华人民共和国的法官自由裁量权问题，作者将首先讨论中华人民共和国成立前的时代，然后讨论现行制度下的法理学思想。最后，作者将讨论当前中国法院在此背景下的法律/法律实践。

6.3.1 Historical Analysis of Judges' Discretionary Power in Pre-PRC Era

中华人民共和国成立前法官自由裁量权的历史分析

We have discussed in Chapter 3 the various invisible factors in relation to jurisprudential thought[666] which have influenced Chinese law over the centuries, and the legal thought of *conservatism*, which links ancient traditions with current schools of thought as prevailing in PRC, both of which still influence modern law.

我们在第三章讨论了数百年来影响中国法律的与法学思想有关的各种无形因素，以及保守主义法律思想，它将古代传统与中国当前流行的思想流派联系在一起，这两种思想仍然影响着现代法律。

[666]Refer, Chapter 3 §3.2.2 -3.2.3, Chinese Legal history and jurisprudence.
参见第 3 章第 3.2.2 -3.2.3 节，中国法律史和法理学。

One jurisprudential thought in ancient China ensured that a ruler had all the legislative powers, and no officer could trespass upon this power. Legalism ensures that the officials' duties are thoroughly defined. Throughout legal history, Chinese judges had very limited discretionary powers, and in addition, they could even be held liable and could be punished for transgressing the limits of their power beyond the penal or administrative codes.[667] Therefore, in ancient Chinese legal practice, rulers insisted that officials have a thorough understanding of laws as compared to the general populace. Because of this, the codes were very detailed and well-defined.[668]

中国古代的一种法学思想确保统治者拥有所有立法权，任何官员都不得侵犯这一权力。法家思想确保彻底界定官员的职责。纵观法律史，中国法官的自由裁量权非常有限，此外，他们甚至可能因超越刑法或行政法规的权力范围而承担责任并受到惩罚。因此，在中国古代的法律实践中，统治者坚持要求官员比普通民众更深入地了解法律。正因为如此，法典非常详细和明确。

In ancient China, there were also the likes of Xunzi, as discussed in Chapter Three, who was of the view that when good, wise and capable men were selected for decision-making positions (such as judges of today), then it would not matter whether there were good laws. Xunzi was of the view that they would apply the external law in the textual form correctly by knowing the purpose of the law, and would thus do justice.[669] Was he, a few thousand years previously, alluding to the discretionary power of such wise men? It seems that such discretionary power could trump, if required, even the written law.

在中国古代，也有像荀子这样的人，正如第三章所讨论的那样，他认为，如果选拔优秀、贤明和有能力的人担任决策职位（如今天的法官），那么是否有好的法律并不重要。荀子认为，他们知道法律的目的，就会正确地应用文本形式的外部法律，从而主持正义。几千年前的荀子是否在暗指这些智者的自由裁量权？如果需要的话，这种自由裁量权似乎甚至可以超越成文法。

In the authors' view, Xunzi was more likely alluding to the discretionary power of the judges, which was and is important in dealing with cases. However, the authors feel that he was alluding to discretion in the weaker sense, rather than in the third sense as discussed above.[670] In the legal history of China, the discretionary powers of officials who sat as judges were curtailed by the drafting of Codes in detail, with strict directions not to 'invent' rules. One such

笔者认为，荀子更可能是在暗指法官的自由裁量权，这在过去和现在处理案件时都很重要。不过，笔者认为他所指的自由裁量权是较弱意义上的自由裁量权，而不是上文讨论的第三种意义上的自由裁量权。在中国的法律史上，担任法官的官员的自由裁量权通过详细制定法典而受到限制，

[667]MacCormack, *Spirit of Traditional Chinese Law*, 5.
麦考马克，《中国传统法律的精神》，第5页。
[668]MacCormack, *Spirit of Traditional Chinese Law*, 5–6. Cf, the approach in Tang Codes discussed in §5.3.2.1.
麦考马克，《中国传统法律的精神》，第5-6页。参见第 5.3.2.1 节中讨论的《唐氏密码》中的方法。
[669]Wejen Chang, "Classical Chinese Jurisprudence and Development of Chinese Legal System" (2009–10), 240.
张维仁，《中国古典法学与中国法律制度的发展》（2009-10 年），第 240 页。
[670]Ronald Dworkin, *Taking Rights Seriously*, 36.
罗纳德-德沃金，《认真对待权利》，36。

direction was to only apply the rules of the Emperor. It was a rule for judges that previous cases were not to be cited as a precedent; they had to strictly state the Code and sub codes used in any judgments.[671]

法典严格规定不得"发明"规则。其中一项指示是只适用皇帝的规则。法官的一项规则是不得引用以前的案例作为先例；他们必须在任何判决中严格说明所使用的法典和子法典。

The judges' capacity to even try using any residual discretionary power was curtailed by punishing them to ensure strict application of correct law. Any inadvertent, negligent or deliberate stepping out could result in punishment, thus discouraging judges from employing their residual discretionary power (even if there was any in the first place!). In addition, extensive supervisory rules also prevented the judges from stepping onto the path of equity by employing any discretionary power. This is in sharp contrast to developments in England & Wales, where many common law judges have assisted in development of laws in equity by developing new rules.[672]

法官甚至尝试使用任何剩余自由裁量权的能力都会受到惩罚，以确保严格执行正确的法律。任何不经意、疏忽或故意的越轨行为都可能导致惩罚，从而阻止法官使用其剩余的自由裁量权（即使本来就有！）。此外，广泛的监督规则也防止法官因行使任何自由裁量权而走上公平之路。这与英格兰和威尔士的发展形成鲜明对比，在那里，许多普通法法官通过制定新规则来协助衡平法的发展。

The only clear cut discretionary power available to ancient Chinese judges was to resort to *analogy* (*pi fu*), especially where it was difficult to find the exact rule to apply to the facts of a matter in front of them.[673] Analogy at times operated in situations where it was difficult for the judges to match the facts with the existing Code. In these scenarios, it was then possible for judges to decide based on the "spirit of the law, the meaning of the provisions, or the intention of the legislator [as] the basis of the analogy."[674] In the authors' view, it does seem that ancient PRC judges were adopting a technique similar to the modern English concept of the statutory interpretation, where the intent of legislators needs to be investigated. However, many judges, unlike in

中国古代法官唯一明确的自由裁量权是类推，尤其是在难以找到适用于所审理案件事实的确切规则时。类推有时适用于法官难以将事实与现行法典相匹配的情况。在这种情况下，法官可以根据"法律的精神、条款的含义或立法者的意图[作为]类推的基础"做出裁决。在笔者看来，古代中国法官似乎采用了一种类似于现代英国的成文法解释概念的技术，即需要调查立法者的意图。然而，与普通法系不同的是，许多法官并不准备扩大规则的含义，甚至在某种程度上不允

[671]MacCormack, *Spirit of Traditional Chinese Law*, 163.
麦考马克，《中国传统法律的精神》，163。
[672]Refer, Chapter 2, §2.1.1.2. 参见第 2 章第 2.1.1.2 节。
[673]MacCormack, *Spirit of Traditional Chinese Law*, 166.
麦考马克，《中国传统法律的精神》，第166页。
[674]Marinus Johan Meijer, "An Aspect of Traditional Chinese Law," *T'Oung Pao* 66 (1980): 348, as discussed in MacCormack, *Spirit of Traditional Chinese Law*, 170.
马里努斯-约翰-梅耶尔，《中国传统法律的一个方面》，大公报，第66期，1980年，第348页，见麦考马克，《中国传统法律的精神》，第170页。

the common law system, were not prepared to broaden the meaning of rules, and to a certain extent not even allowed to embark on this path. This seems to be the major difference between the historical common law and the historical Chinese legal system.[675]

许走上这条道路。这似乎是历史上的普通法与历史上的中国法律体系之间的主要区别。

As recently as the 18th and 19th centuries, *Qing Board of Punishments* in the context of criminal proceedings used to promote the 'value of consistency and certainty in the application of rules of penal code'.[676] This was another example of curtailing the discretionary power of the judges.

早在 18 世纪和 19 世纪，*清廷刑部*就在刑事诉讼中提倡“刑法规则适用的一致性和确定性价值”。这是限制法官自由裁量权的另一个例子。

6.3.2 Principles and Philosophy in Current Legal System in PRC

中国现行法律制度的原则和理念

We have seen in the previous Chapter[677] how principles govern the practice of law and rules in the courts. Most of the principles in relation to the PRC are relatively new and came to the forefront only after 1949. This is unlike the gradual development of such principles in the common law over centuries. In the PRC judicial organs are governed by following constitutional principles (that are further applicable to civil litigation):

我们在上一章中已看到原则是如何指导法律实践和法院规则的。与中国有关的大多数原则都是相对较新的，只是在 1949 年之后才开始受到重视。这与普通法中这些原则历经数百年的逐步发展不同。在中国，司法机关受以下宪法原则的制约（这些原则进一步适用于民事诉讼）：

- All citizens are equal before the law.[678]

- 公民在法律面前一律平等。

- In judicial proceedings, the laws are applied by judges equally to all citizens.[679]

- 在司法程序中，法官平等地对所有公民适用法律。

675 Supported in MacCormack, *Spirit of Traditional Chinese Law*, 173.
麦考马克，《中国传统法律的精神》，第173页中被支持。
676 MacCormack, *Spirit of Traditional Chinese Law*, 6.
麦考马克，《中国传统法律的精神》，第6页。
677 Refer to §5.3 and discussion of principles that are taken into account by the judges in the context of their employment of discretionary power in legal reasoning.
请参阅第 5.3 节，以及关于法官在法律推理中运用自由裁量权时所考虑的原则的讨论。
678 See Art. 33 of *Constitution of PRC 1982.*
见 1982 年《中华人民共和国宪法》第 33 条。
679 See Art. 5 of *Organic Law of People's Courts of People's Republic of China 1979.*

- The People's Courts exercise their judicial power independently, in accordance with the provisions of law, and are not subject to interference by any administrative organs, public organisations or individuals.[680]

- 人民法院依照法律规定独立行使审判权，不受任何行政机关、社会团体和个人的干涉。

- Citizens of all nationalities (in the PRC) have the right to use their own written and spoken language.[681]

- 中华人民共和国境内各民族公民都有使用本民族文字和语言的权利。

- Except in special circumstances, all hearings shall be public.[682]

- 除特殊情况外，庭审一律公开。

The Supreme Peoples' Court (hereinafter 'SPC'), the highest court in the PRC, has been given the power to interpret applications of law.[683] This power is also available with People's Procuratorates which have the power to exercise supervision over the judicial activities of the People's Courts to ensure they conform to the law.[684] In the context of differences in opinion, if any, between the Supreme Court and People's Procuratorates in relation to legal interpretation, then the National People's Congress Standing Committee (hereinafter 'NPCSC') has the power to decide on the final interpretation.[685] The SPC regularly publishes such interpretations of important laws for the benefit of all.

最高人民法院（下称 "最高法院"）是中华人民共和国的最高法院，有权解释法律的适用。人民检察院也拥有这一权力，有权对人民法院的司法活动进行监督，以确保其符合法律规定。如果最高法院和人民检察院在法律解释方面出现意见分歧，则全国人民代表大会常务委员会（以下简称 "全国人大常委会"）有权决定最终解释。最高法院定期公布此类重要法律的解释，并适用于所有人。

A factor that has significantly influenced the official ambivalence about the need to contain discretionary power is that the courts are often not seen as law-making

官方对限制自由裁量权的必要性态度暧昧，一个重要的影响因素是法院通常不被视为法律制定机构。一端

见 1979 年《中华人民共和国人民法院组织法》第 5 条。

680 See Art. 4 of *Organic Law of Peoples Courts of People's Republic of China 1979 (as amended in 1983)*. A similar article, Art. 126, can be found in *Constitution of PRC 1982*.

见 1979 年《中华人民共和国人民法院组织法》（1983 年修订）第 4 条。中华人民共和国宪法》1982 年第 126 条也有类似条款。

681 See Art. 8 of *Organic Law of People's Courts of People's Republic of China 1979 (as amended in 1983)*.

见 1979 年《中华人民共和国人民法院组织法》（1983 年修订）第 8 条。

682 See *Organic Law of Peoples Courts of People's Republic of China 1979 (as Amended in 1983)*, Art. 7.

见 1979 年《中华人民共和国人民法院组织法》（1983 年修订），第 7 条。

683 *Organic Law of Peoples Courts of People's Republic of China 1979 (as Amended in 1983)*.

1979 年《中华人民共和国人民法院组织法》（1983年修订）。

684 Ibid.同上。

685 See *Resolution on Strengthening the Work of Legal Interpretation*, para. 2, adopted on June 10, 1981 by the Standing Committee of the Fifth NPC at its 19th Session.

见1981年6月10日第五届全国人大常委会第十九次会议通过的《关于加强法律解释工作的决议》第2段。

institutions.[686] At one end of the spectrum is the anti-corruption drive and on the other end are the codified procedures for supervision of judges based on the ideology of *jiandu*.[687]

是反腐运动，另一端是基于简牍思想的成文法式的法官监督程序。

There is also the fact PRC courts are more concerned with the application of substantive law rather than uniformity in procedures; put simply, the outcomes of different adjudications are more important than the procedure. At the same time, PRC courts are extremely vigilant about situations where any infringement of the rights of the PRC could become an issue.[688] The dichotomy between maintaining legitimacy by applying the formal rules and thus maintaining *rule of law* (*fazhi*), and providing justice in specific circumstances using *rule by man* through judges *(renzhi)*, is also a constant here, as in any other legal system.[689]

此外，中国法院更关注实体法的适用而非程序的统一；简单地说，不同裁决的结果比程序更重要。同时，中国法院对任何侵犯中国权利的情况都保持高度警惕。与其他任何法律制度一样，通过适用正式规则来维护合法性，从而维持法治，以及通过法官在特定情况下实施枫桥经验，这两者之间的平衡也是这里的一个常态。

In relation to the debates discussed above, Yang has delineated *three schools* of thoughts:[690]

关于上述争论，阳玕桥划分了*三种学派*：

- The first school of thought does not reject *renzhi* but stresses the need to have qualified legal professionals. This school is realist and accepts the fact that any rule has to be applied by a man/woman. It seems this school of thought is receptive to the discretionary power of judges;

- 第一种学派并不反对"人治"，但强调需要有合格的法律专业人员。这一派是现实主义的，接受任何规则都必须由人来执行的事实。这一派似乎接受法官的自由裁量权；

- The second school of thought rejects *renzhi* in relation to officials who are seen to be abusing power but accepts renzhi in relation to revolutionary leaders and masses. The authors' view is that Yan is likely to include the abuse of discretionary power of the officials;

- 第二种学派认为，对于被认为滥用权力的官员，"人治"是不被接受的，但对于革命领袖和群众，人治是可以接受的。作者认为，"严"可能包括官员滥用自由裁量权；

686 Woo, "Discretion in Contemporary Chinese Courts," 581–2. Woo，《当代中国法院的自由裁量权》，第581-582页。
687 Ibid., 582. 同上，第582页。
688 Ibid. 同上。
689 Ibid., 585. 同上，第585页。
690 Ganqiao Yang, *New Thoughts of Chinese Jurisprudence (Zhonggguo Faxue Xin Siwei)* (Shanxi: Shanxi People's Publisher, 1989), 29–31. It was discussed in Woo, "Discretion in Contemporary Chinese Courts," 585.阳玕桥，《中国法学新思维》，山西：山西人民出版社，1989年，第29-31页。Woo，《当代中国法院的自由裁量权》，第585页。

- The third school of thought rejects the whole concept of *renzhi* and stresses ideological guidance based on CPC principles. This school of thought seems to suggest that such principles are part of the law, akin to Dworkin's debate in jurisprudence pertaining to law in action.

- 第三种学派反对整个“人治”概念，强调基于中国共产党原则的思想指导。这一派似乎认为这些原则是法律的一部分，类似于德沃金在法理学中关于法律在行动的辩论。

6.3.3 Current Thinking and Practice about Application of Discretionary Power in PRC Courts

当前中国法院适用自由裁量权的思考与实践

Woo has discussed three types of discretion that are available in the PRC in the context of legal philosophy – fact-based discretion, self-interested discretion and ideological discretion.[691]

Woo 从法律哲学的角度讨论了中国的三种自由裁量权——基于事实的自由裁量权、利己自由裁量权和意识形态自由裁量权。

In *fact-based discretion*, judges will adjudicate according to the facts about the dispute before them. They will take into account the need for harmony in society, rather than seeking the solution in terms of winners and losers.[692] The judges will attempt to extract the truth from the facts and even try to investigate and correct the parties' versions.

在以事实为基础的自由裁量权中，法官将根据其面前争议的事实作出裁决。他们会考虑到社会和谐的需要，而不是从赢家和输家的角度寻求解决办法。法官会试图从事实中提取真相，甚至试图调查和纠正当事人的说法。

In *fact-based discretion*, the focus of the judges on the facts of the disputes in the initial years of development of the legal system may be the result of lack of formal training of adjudication professionals. As per the Confucian model, the effects of morality and accordingly, the need to maintain social harmony, is always in the minds of the judges. This

在以事实为基础的裁量中，在法律制度发展的最初几年，法官对纠纷事实的关注可能是缺乏对裁判专业人员的正规培训的结果。按照儒家模式，道德的影响以及相应地维护社会和谐

[691]Woo, "Discretion in Contemporary Chinese Courts," 586.
吴，《当代中国法院的自由裁量权》，586。
[692]Ibid., 587. 同上，587。

mindset has become part of the legal system. Marxist philosophy also had its effects on the legal system, stating that the law should remain answerable to the populace.[693] Woo suggested that the role of judges is more as social crisis managers rather than as resolvers of the disputes of the parties.[694]

的需要始终存在于法官的头脑中。这种思想已成为法律制度的一部分。马克思主义哲学也对法律制度产生了影响，指出法律应始终对民众负责。吴提出，法官的角色更多是社会危机管理者，而非当事人纠纷的解决者。

In *self-interested discretion*, Woo has cited the use of discretion for the self-interest of the judges. Self-interest involves matters such as invitations to lavish parties for judges, or other forms of corruption, and takes the form of *renqing an* (where disputes are resolved using favours), or *guanxi an* (where disputes are resolved through personal relations or connections).[695] This problem is not only associated with a few judges, but is also is backed by litigants in the PRC.[696]

在自利裁量权中，吴列举了法官为自身利益而使用裁量权的情况。自利涉及诸如邀请法官参加奢华宴会或其他形式的腐败，其形式包括“人情案”（通过人情解决纠纷）或“关系案”(通过私人关系或关系解决纠纷)。在中国，这一问题不仅与少数法官有关，也受到一些当事人支持。

Another form of *self-interested discretion* seen in the PRC courts takes the form of *difang baohu zhuyi* (a form of local protectionism), where the local courts in a province will not accept a case from other provinces, because the local government is responsible for the budget of local judicial services. Judges tend to protect local litigants and commerce in their own provinces.[697] There is an attempt to curtail this discretionary power of the PRC judges through Codes.[698]

中国法院的另一种利己自由裁量权形式是地方保护主义，即一个省的地方法院不会受理来自其他省的案件，因为地方政府负责当地司法服务的预算。法官倾向于保护本省的本地诉讼当事人和商业。有人试图通过法典来限制中国法官的这种自由裁量权。

The scope for *ideological discretion* has been added explicitly in *CPL 2023*.[699] Woo has researched another form of judicial discretion in the PRC courts, famously called *ideological discretion*. The *Preamble of Constitution PRC 1982 as amended 2018* explicitly provides for the leadership of the Communist Party of China (‘CPC’), with guidance on

2023 年中国《民事诉讼法》明确增加了裁量权的范围。吴文俊研究了中国法院的另一种司法裁量权形式，即著名的意识形态裁量权。2018 年修订的 1982 年《中华人民共和国宪法》序言明确规定了中国共产党的领导，

[693]Woo, “Discretion in Contemporary Chinese Courts,” 588.
Woo, 《当代中国法院的自由裁量权》，588。
[694]Ibid. 同上。
[695]Ibid., 590. 同上，590。
[696]Ibid., 591. 同上，591。
[697]Ibid. 同上。
[698]See Art. 46 of *CPL 2023*, where power is curtailed in the Civil Procedure Code by prohibiting judges from accepting gifts, and there is the possibility of criminal prosecution if they do.
见2023年《中华人民共和国民事诉讼法》第46条，该法通过禁止法官收受礼物来限制法官的权力，如果法官收受礼物，有可能受到刑事起诉。
[699]See Art. 14 of *CPL 2023*, where State Procuratorates have been provided to supervise the trials.
见2023年《中华人民共和国民事诉讼法》第14条，其中规定由国家检察院监督审判。

the basis of *Marxism-Leninism, Mao Zedong's thoughts* and *Xi Jinping's thoughts*. This enables the judges faced with disputes in their courts to ensure that the results are compatible with ideological philosophy or any policy issued by CPC.[700]

并以马克思列宁主义、毛泽东思想和习近平思想为指导。这使得法官在法庭上面对纠纷时能够确保判决结果符合中国共产党的思想理念或政策。

In the early years of the PRC, there used to be a policy in relation to disputes in the courts that the cases were to be reviewed by the local CPC party secretary (*shuji pi'an*) through the local political affairs committee procedure *(zhengfa weiyuanhui)*. Now, the Procuratorate System supervises judges and ensures compatibility with ideological philosophy in the outcome and judgments. In the authors' view, this is a major issue when international commercial disputes are to be dealt with in PRC courts.

建国初期，法院对纠纷案件的处理政策是由当地党委书记书记批案通过当地政法委员会程序进行审查。现在，检察院系统对法官进行监督，并确保结果和判决符合意识形态理念。笔者认为，在中国法院处理国际商事纠纷时，这是一个重大问题。

CPL 2023 provides for supervisory procedures, where cases in the courts can be *re-opened* to check the unjust application of judicial discretion. This has the effect of limiting discretion, but also in a way increases judicial discretion at the same time.[701] Supervision of the justice system and system of procuratorates is even enshrined in the PRC constitution.[702] Protests against the judgment of the courts can be lodged according of *CPL 2023*.[703]

中国 2023 年《民事诉讼法规定了监督程序，法院可以再审案件，以检查司法裁量权的不公正应用。这起到了限制自由裁量权的作用，但同时也在某种程度上增加了司法自由裁量权。对司法系统和检察院系统的监督甚至写入了《中华人民共和国宪法》。根据 2023 年《民事诉讼法》，可以对法院的判决提出抗诉。

The system of Procuratorates has the power to interpret laws that are related to its own work, which is not considered to be within the realm of the judiciary. However, the system of procuratorates seems to intervene in civil cases only when the state's interests are affected.[704] There is a provision for supervision by the masses,[705] as part of the concept of democratic supervision (*mizhu jiandu*), and the NPC can seek a report on this aspect from the system of Procuratorates and courts. This system of supervision from multiple areas has led to a situation where PRC judges are

检察院系统有权解释与自身工作相关的法律，这不属于司法范畴。然而，检察院系统似乎只有在国家利益受到影响时才会介入民事案件。作为民主监督概念的一部分，有群众监督的规定，全国人大可以要求检察院和法院系统提供这方面的报告。这种多方监督的制度导致中华人民共和国法官乐于扮演行政角色，而将决策权交

[700] Woo, "Discretion in Contemporary Chinese Courts," 418.
Woo, 《当代中国法院的自由裁量权》，418。
[701] Ibid., 601. 同上，601。
[702] See Art. 129 of *Constitution of PRC 1982*. 见1982年《中华人民共和国宪法》第129条。
[703] See Art. 219 of *CPL 2023*. 见2023年中华人民共和国民事诉讼法第219条。
[704] Woo, "Discretion in Contemporary Chinese Courts," 607.
Woo, 《当代中国法院的自由裁量权》，607。
[705] See Art. 7(7) of *Judges Law 1995*. 见 1995 年《法官法》第 7(7)条。

happy to be in the administrative role and leave decision making to the adjudication committee.[706]

给审判委员会。

Ideological discretion is thus affected by supervision, as it is a tool to accomplish precisely that.[707] The principle of *democratic centralism*[708] ensures that all judges submit to the adjudication committees. These Committees in turn submit to Procuratorates. Procuratorates in turn should submit to the National People's Congress.[709]

因此，意识形态的自由裁量权受到监督的影响，因为监督正是实现这一目标的工具。民主集中制原则确保所有法官服从审判委员会。审判委员会又服从检察院。检察院则应服从全国人民代表大会。

In current legal practice in the PRC, the general view about the discretionary power of the judges is that it is a power conferred on the judges by law, in order to enable them to arrive at flexible decisions based on facts, evidence, legal principles and justice, especially when there is a gap in law or where the law is ambiguous.[710] Guo has stated that many in the PRC confuse *discretionary power* of the judges with arbitrariness, when actually it means *independence and freedom to decide* without taking help or advice from outside.[711]

在中国目前的法律实践中，对法官自由裁量权的一般看法是，它是法律赋予法官的一种权力，目的是使法官能够根据事实、证据、法律原则和正义作出灵活的裁决，特别是在法律存在空白或法律不明确的情况下。郭指出，在中国，许多人将法官的自由裁量权与任意性混为一谈，实际上，自由裁量权是指法官在不接受外界帮助或建议的情况下做出决定的独立性和自由性。

However, as the legal practice and system is still evolving in PRC, these practices are discouraged by the central CPC. At the same time, there are many examples from the news that concern judicial transfers or discharge of judges on socially sensitive cases. Such news is not uncommon in the PRC.[712]

然而，由于中国的法律实践和制度仍在发展中，中共中央不鼓励这些做法。与此同时，新闻中也有很多涉及法官因社会敏感案件而被调离或解职的例子。此类新闻在中国并不少见。

---

[706]Woo, "Discretion in Contemporary Chinese Courts," 609.
Woo，《当代中国法院的自由裁量权》，609。
[707]Ibid. 同上。
[708]See Art. 3 of *Constitution of PRC 1982 (as amended in 2018).*
见1982 年《中华人民共和国宪法》第3条（2018年修订）。
[709] Refer to Figure10 in Chapter 4. 参见第 4 章图 10。
[710]Zhenghua Li, "Theory of Discretionary Power," *Contemporary Law Review,* no. 4 (2000): 94, translated from quotation in Shandong Province People's Court Changle County, "The Application of Judges' Discretionary Power in China (Translated)." http://wfclfy.chinacourt.org/article/detail/2013/05/id/954542.shtml, accessed on July 16, 2016. Translated into English at the authors' request.
李正华，"自由裁量权理论"，《当代法律评论》，第 4 期（2000 年）：94，译自山东省昌乐县人民法院引文，"中国法官自由裁量权的适用"。
[711]Xiang Guo Hu and China Court Net Bozhou Qiaocheng Channel, "The Discretionary Power of Judge in Civil Proceedings and Its Improvements in China (Translated)." www.chinacourt.org/article/detail/2013/11/id/1122865.shtml, accessed on July 16, 2016. Translated into English at the authors' request.
胡祥国、中国法院网亳州侨乡频道：《中国民事诉讼中的法官自由裁量权及其完善（译）》。
[712]Woo, "Discretion in Contemporary Chinese Courts," 593.
吴，《当代中国法院的自由裁量权》，593。

In summary, in recent years, with the enactment of many procedural codes, *self-interest* discretion has been checked, to some extent, by good implementation of anti-corruption policies; however *ideological discretion* has, in fact, been codified.[713] *Fact-based discretion* has been adopted as part of the inquisitorial system, so it is present in the system. However, *minzhu jiandu* and *principle of democratic centralism* have the potential to create issues in the adjudication of commercial disputes.

总之，近年来，随着许多诉讼法的颁布，反腐政策的良好执行在一定程度上遏制了自利裁量权；然而，意识形态裁量权事实上已被法律化。以事实为依据的自由裁量权已被采纳为审问制度的一部分，因此它存在于审问制度中。然而，*民主监督*和*民主集中制原则*有可能在商事纠纷的裁决中产生问题。

6.3.3.1 Judicial Discretion in Day to Day Practice of PRC Courts

中国法院日常工作中的司法裁量权

The PRC courts are governed by the philosophy of *youji zhengti* in which the court is a single entity, and the judges are just part of the whole legal system. The judicial activities carried out by the judges are part of the legal system.[714] In the PRC today, looking at day to day work in the courts, discretionary power is exercised by the judge in lots of judicial activities in civil litigation.[715] For example:

中国法院遵循"法院是一个整体，法官只是整个法律体系的一部分"的有机整体哲学。法官开展的司法活动是法律体系的一部分。 在今天的中国，从法院的日常工作来看，法官在民事诉讼的许多司法活动中行使自由裁量权。 例如：

- In ascertaining evidence from cases, in particular, the materiality and authenticity of evidence. This discretionary power is relevant in the function of evidence for ascertaining the facts. The judges have wide discretion in such judicial activities, in particular, in criminal litigation.[716]

- 在查明案件证据，特别是证据的实质性和真实性方面。这种自由裁量权与证据查明事实的功能有关。法官在此类司法活动中拥有广泛的自由裁量权，尤其是在刑事诉讼中。

---

[713]Ibid., 594. 同上，594。

[714]Ibid., 604. 同上，604。

[715]Guodang Xu, *The Debate About the Trains of Thought for Drawing up a Chinese Civil Code,* (Beijing: Publishing House of CUPL, 2001) as cited in Hu and China Court Net Bozhou Qiaocheng Channel, "The Discretionary Power of Judge in Civil Proceedings and Its Improvements in China (Translated)," accessed on July16, 2016. Translated into English at the authors' request.
徐国党：《关于中国民法典制定思路的争论》，中国政法大学出版社，2001年，转引自胡和，中国法院网亳州侨乡频道，《民事诉讼中法官的自由裁量权及其在中国的完善》。

[716]Shu-Shan Guo, "The Discussion about Judges' Discretionary Power in Our Country." www.66law.cn/domianblog/20248.aspx, accessed on July 24, 2016. Translated into English at the authors' request.
郭书山：《关于我国法官自由裁量权的讨论》。

- The judges are equipped with wide discretionary power in relation to their ability to investigate, to decide on issues of admissibility for adducing evidence in their courts, to decide on the requirements for standards of proof, and similar issues throughout the adjudication process.

- 法官拥有广泛的自由裁量权，包括调查能力、决定在其法庭上举证的可采性问题、决定对证据标准的要求以及整个裁决过程中的类似问题。

- The judges are regarded as experts in finding the real facts, as sometimes even the parties to the dispute are unable to adduce the evidence, and judges are duty-bound to find the truth. In this context, the judges have discretionary power that has been provided by statutes.[717]

- 法官被视为查明真实情况的专家，因为有时甚至争议各方都无法举证，法官有责任查明真相。在这种情况下，法官拥有法规规定的自由裁量权。

- In the context of statutes general standards are mentioned such as in PRC criminal law, for example, including "serious nature" or "bad social impact." Those general standards can only be applied using the discretionary power of the judges.[718]

- 在成文法中提到了一般标准，例如在《中华人民共和国刑法》中，包括"性质严重"或"社会影响恶劣"。这些一般标准只能通过法官的自由裁量权来适用。

In addition to the above scenarios, PRC scholars, like their counterparts in western jurisprudence, also consider that the discretionary power of judges is necessary for the following reasons in legal practice:[719]

除上述情况外，中国学者与西方法学界一样，也认为法官自由裁量权在法律实践中是必要的，原因如下：

- New types of relationships are developing in contemporary PRC, especially in the commercial sector of its fast-moving economy. The need for frequent amendments to law cannot be a reasonable expectation, and therefore, there is a need for judges to exercise their discretionary power. This employment of discretionary power will ensure the certainty that people expect from the PRC courts, and will also increase the legitimacy of the civil justice system.

- 在当代中国，特别是在经济快速发展的商业领域，新型关系不断发展。因此，法官有必要行使其自由裁量权。这种自由裁量权的使用将确保人们对中华人民共和国法院的确定性的期望，同时也将增加民事司法制度的合法性。

---

717 See Arts. 66 & 67 of CPL 2023。见2023年《中华人民共和国民事诉讼法》第66和67条。

718 Guo, "The Discussion about Judges' Discretionary Power in Our Country."
郭，"关于我国法官自由裁量权的讨论"。

719 Jie Liu and China Court net Meishan City Dongpo channel, "Restriction and Guidance on Judges' Discretion (Translated)." www.chinacourt.org/article/detail/2013/05/id/959246.shtml, accessed on March 11, 2025. Translated into English at the authors' request.
刘杰，中国法院网眉山市东坡频道，《法官自由裁量权的限制与指导（译文）》。www.chinacourt.org/article/detail/2013/05/id/959246.shtml, 2025年3月11日访问。

- The judges' discretionary power is needed in any complex societies and relationships, to ensure all types of disputes can be resolved, in particular, in scenarios which the NPC could not anticipate in advance, or where judges could not wait for clarifications from the SPC, to resolve the disputes before them.

- 在任何复杂的社会和关系中都需要法官的自由裁量权，以确保各类纠纷都能得到解决，尤其是在全国人大无法提前预料的情况下，或者在法官无法等待最高人民法院的说明的情况下，更需要法官的自由裁量权来解决他们面前的纠纷。

- There is an inherent conflict between accuracy of judgments and the cognitive ability of judges. The judges are trained in the PRC's inquisitorial system to find out the facts of disputes. However, the judges' role in finding such facts only arises after the dispute has evolved. It is impossible for the judges to find all facts and the ultimate truth. Under modern evidence law, the approach that the judges take is the 'free evaluation of evidence', which, when the facts are not very clear, entitles the judges to take decisions based on their legal knowledge and experience. This approach cannot exist without the judges having discretionary power.

- 判决的准确性与法官的认知能力之间存在内在冲突。在中华人民共和国的审问制度中，法官接受了查明争议事实的培训。然而，法官在查明事实方面的作用只是在争议演变之后才会出现。法官不可能查明所有事实和最终真相。根据现代证据法，法官采取的方法是"自由评估证据"，当事实不十分清楚时，法官有权根据其法律知识和经验做出裁决。如果法官没有自由裁量权，这种方法就不可能存在。

- There is a tremendous case-load on the judges in the PRC, since it is the almost populous country in the world (India is the most populous country since April 2023). The exercise of discretionary power will enable the judges to consider the state of affairs, balance the interests of the stakeholders and render judgments in a timely manner, while ensuring that they have efficiently employed the judicial resources available in the PRC.

- 中国几乎是世界第一人口大国（自 2023 年 4 月起为印度为世界第一人口大国），因此法官的案件量非常大。行使自由裁量权将使法官能够考虑事态的发展，平衡利益相关者的利益，并及时做出判决，同时确保他们有效地利用了中国现有的司法资源。

- The judges are not machines or robots that can mechanically apply the law, and therefore, they "need to be positive and creative, rather than be in passive inaction, detached from the facts ...."[720]

- 法官不是可以机械地适用法律的机器或机器人，因此，他们"需要积极地、创造性地工作，而不是消极地无所作为，脱离事实...."。

[720]Hu He, China Court Net Bozhou Qiaocheng Channel, "The Discretionary Power of Judge in Civil Proceedings and Its Improvements in China (Translated)," http://qcqfy.ahcourt.gov.cn/article/detail/2013/11/id/1117694.shtml, accessed on 11 March, 2025. Translated into English at the authors' request.

However, scholars in the PRC have warned against the possible misuse of discretionary power by judges and have described it as a double-edged sword for the following reasons.[721]

然而，中国的学者对法官可能滥用自由裁量权提出了警告，并将其描述为一把双刃剑，原因如下。

- The exercise of discretionary power may lead to arbitrary decisions and abuse of power without proper training and strict rules of professional conduct.

- 如果没有适当的培训和严格的职业行为规则，行使自由裁量权可能会导致任意裁决和滥用权力。

- The judges who exercise discretionary power may hold different views about the same matter or persons, and these views are not even fixed. An individual judge's opinions about the same facts might differ at different times and places, or with their changed emotions. Therefore, there is an argument that the law conferring overly-wide discretionary power on the judges may bring in an element of arbitrariness, affecting the legitimacy of the courts.

- 行使自由裁量权的法官可能对同一件事或同一个人持有不同的看法，而这些看法甚至不是固定不变的。个别法官对同一事实的看法，可能在不同时间、不同地点或随着情绪的变化而有所不同。因此，有论点认为，法律赋予法官过大的酌情权，可能会带来任意性，影响法院的合法性。

- The misuse of discretionary power has the potential to greatly exacerbate issues of corruption within the judiciary.

- 自由裁量权的滥用有可能大大加剧司法机构内部的腐败问题。

The above observations in relation to exercise of discretion, a real need in a fast-developing economy, cannot be considered melodramatic. It must be appreciated that the PRC has in a very short span of time grown into a gigantic economy.

行使自由裁量权是经济快速发展的现实需要，上述有关行使自由裁量权的意见不能被视为夸张。我们必须认识到，中国在很短的时间内就发展成为一个巨大的经济体。

Scholars have cited two main problems with judges' discretionary power in the PRC— either *PRC judges exercise their discretionary power insufficiently, or the judges exercise their discretionary power excessively.*[722]

有学者指出，中国法官自由裁量权存在两大问题——要么中国法官行使自由裁量权不足，要么法官行使自由裁量权过度。笔者将对这两个问

胡和，中国法院网亳州侨乡频道，《论我国民事诉讼中法官的自由裁量权的现状与完善》，http://qcqfy.ahcourt.gov.cn/article/detail/2013/11/id/1117694.shtml, 2025年3月11日访问。

[721] Jie Liu and China Court net Meishan City Dongpo channel, "Restriction and Guidance on Judges' Discretion (Translated)," accessed on July 24, 2016. Translated into English at the authors' request.
刘杰，中国法院网眉山市东坡频道，《法官自由裁量权的限制与指导》。

[722] Hui Xing Liang, *Judging Methods* (Beijing: Beijing University Press, 2005), 76 as cited in Changle County, "The Application of Judges' Discretionary Power in China (Translated)," accessed on July 24, 2016. Translated into English at the author's request.

The authors will discuss these two problems as follows:

题讨论如下：

- The *first problem* is that the judges either do not know how to employ their discretionary power efficiently, or they do not know how to exercise this power. One of the reasons could be that PRC judges are habituated to hear cases totally in accordance with laws or rules, as *legalism* has strong roots in the PRC.[723] Therefore, when PRC judges encounter new circumstances or vague codes, they are not fully prepared or equipped to deal with those circumstances. The PRC is undergoing a social and economic transformation and such encounters with unique circumstances are becoming more common day by day.[724]

- 第一个问题是，法官要么不知道如何有效运用自由裁量权，要么不知道如何行使这一权力。原因之一可能是中国法官习惯于完全按照法律或规则审理案件，因为法律主义在中国根深蒂固。因此，当中国法官遇到新的情况或模糊的准则时，他们没有做好充分准备或装备来处理这些情况。中国正处于社会和经济转型期，这种特殊情况越来越常见。

- The *second problem* that has been observed is that the judges sometimes use excessive discretionary power, especially under the law of evidence. The judges exercise their excessive discretionary power in relation to fact-finding and evidence.[725]

- 观察到的第二个问题是，法官有时会过度使用自由裁量权，尤其是在证据法方面。法官在事实调查和证据方面过度行使自由裁量权。

From the above, it seems, while there is a concept of discretionary power for judges in the PRC, at the moment it is not well-developed. It is also unbalanced in a few aspects, such as in the area of the application of law to facts and ascertaining the facts themselves.[726] This problem is compounded due to the following:

由此看来，中国有法官自由裁量权的概念，但目前还不够完善。它在一些方面也是不平衡的，例如在对事实适用法律和查明事实本身方面。由于以下原因这一问题变得更加复杂：

- The current state of legislation and guidance are very general and not specific in nature, as a result of which PRC law can be ambiguous, and at times too flexible and vague. It can therefore be argued, in these

- 目前的立法和指导都非常笼统，没有具体的规定，因此中华人民共和国的法律可能含糊不清，有时过于灵活和模糊。因此可以说，在这种情况下，即使与

梁慧星：《审判方法》（北京：北京大学出版社，2005 年），第 76 页，转引自昌乐县：《中国法官自由裁量权的运用（译文）》，2025年3月11日访问。

723 Refer to Chapter 3, §3.2.1.3. 参见第 3 章第 3.2.1.3 节。

724 Guohua Sun, *Chinese Law Dictionary*, Jurisprudence Volume (Chinese Procuratorial Press, 1997), 542 It was cited in Changle County, "The Application of Judges' Discretionary Power in China (Translated)," accessed on July 24, 2016. Translated into English at the authors' request.
孙国华，《中国法律大辞典》，法理学卷（中国检察出版社，1997 年），542 引自昌乐县，"中国法官自由裁量权的适用"。

725 Ibid，见上引。

726 Ibid，见上引。

circumstances, that the discretionary power of the PRC judges is wider even compared to that of judges in the liberal and democratic western world.[727] This problem of excessive discretionary power is further compounded by a lack of proper procedural security and guidance.[728]

西方自由民主世界的法官相比，中国法官的自由裁量权也更为宽泛。缺乏适当的程序保障和指导，进一步加剧了自由裁量权过大的问题。

- Lack of training and guidance of the PRC judges in issues related to economic prosperity as the economy has developed too fast. Judges not only need laws, but also the ability to explain the law and its application.[729]

- 经济发展过快，中国法官在与经济繁荣相关的问题上需培训和指导。法官不仅需要法律，还需要解释法律及其应用的能力。

- PRC citizens and even external stakeholders in the PRC economy need more awareness about rights, in cases where discretionary power has been abused by judges.[730]

- 在法官滥用自由裁量权的情况下，中国公民甚至中国经济的外部利益相关者需更多权利意识。

- There is a fear of punishment among PRC judges, especially if a wrong decision were to be made, or if for some reason, the rendered judgment did not comply with guidelines from supervisors and committees further up in the hierarchy. This possibility makes PRC judges wary of exercising their discretionary power.

- 中国法官担心受到惩罚，尤其是在做出错误判决，或由于某种原因判决不符合上级领导和委员会的指导方针的情况下。这种可能性使得中国法官在行使自由裁量权时有所顾忌。

[727]Hu and China Court Net Bozhou Qiaocheng Channel, “The Discretionary Power of Judge in Civil Proceedings and Its Improvements in China (Translated),” http://qcqfy.ahcourt.gov.cn/article/detail/2013/11/id/1117694.shtml , accessed on March 11, 2025. Translated into English at the authors’ request.
胡和，中国法院网亳州侨乡频道：《论我国民事诉讼中法官自由裁量权的现状与完善》，http://qcqfy.ahcourt.gov.cn/article/detail/2013/11/id/1117694.shtml，2025年3月11日访问。

[728]Ibid. 同上。

[729]Ibid. 同上。

[730]Ibid. 同上。

CHAPTER SEVEN — IMPORTANT JUDICIAL ACTIVITIES – COMMON LAW v. CHINESE LAW

第七章 -重要的司法活动 —— 普通法与中国法

7.1 Introduction to Judicial Activities

司法活动简介

Having discussed the judges' power including discretionary power, the authors will now discuss three important concepts within the area of judicial activities, where such power is used. These selected judicial activities are:

在讨论了包括自由裁量权在内的法官权力之后，笔者现在将讨论司法活动领域中使用这种权力的三个重要概念。这些选定的司法活动是：

- Judicial Statutory Interpretation; and

-法定司法解释；以及

- Judicial use of Case Precedent; and

-案例先例的司法使用；以及

- Issues of Burden and Standards of Proof considered by judges;

-法官考虑的举证责任和标准问题；

7.2 Judicial Statutory Interpretation

法定司法解释

The issue of statutory interpretation arises in every legal system because of the following reasons, as discussed by

每个法律体系都会出现法律解释问题，原因如下，伊斯特布鲁克对此进行了讨论：

Easterbrook:[731]

- Legislatures lack time to look into all issues;

- 立法机构没有时间研究所有问题

- Legislative process is a process of compromises between legislators;

- 立法过程是立法者间妥协的过程；

- Legislative process is a complicated process comprising lobbying groups and multiple opinions. No draft legislation can imagine all the potential problems for which laws need to be legislated, or how the effects of such legislation will be experienced in society;

- 立法过程是一个由游说团体和多种意见组成的复杂过程。任何立法草案都无法想象需要立法解决的所有潜在问题，也无法想象这些立法的效果将如何影响社会；

- In the authors' view, statutes have sometimes been given a particular meaning or concept through the process of interpretation, and due to the doctrine of precedents in common law, subsequent judges are bound to follow that meaning.

- 作者认为，法规有时会通过解释过程被赋予特定的含义或概念，由于普通法中的先例理论，后来的法官必然会遵循这一含义。

For a century, there has been a debate between *rule-based* statutory interpretation and *rule-free* interpretation.[732] These debates have spawned many theories in relation to statutory interpretation:[733]

一个世纪以来，基于规则的成文法解释和无规则解释之间一直存在争论。这些争论催生了许多与成文法解释相关的理论：

- A few scholars give precedence to text in the statute (this is called *textualism*);

- 少数学者优先考虑成文法中的文本（这被称为文本主义）；

- Some focus on the structural argument, looking at the position of words within the statute;

- 一些学者关注结构论点，研究词语在法规中的位置；

- A few scholars give precedence to the judicial purpose behind the statute as a whole;

- 少数学者优先考虑法规整体背后的司法目的；

- A few scholars look at external sources to learn the history of legislative intent.

- 少数学者从外部来源了解立法意图的历史。

[731]Frank H. Easterbrook, "Legal Interpretation and Power of Judiciary," *Harv. J. L. & Pub. Pol'y* 7, no. 1 (1984): 88–90. 弗兰克-伊斯特布鲁克，"法律解释与司法权"，《哈佛法学评论和公共政治》，7, no. 1，1984年，第88–90页。

[732]Tina Hunter, "Interpretive Theories: Dworkin, Sunstein, and Ely," *Bond Law Review* 17, no. 2 (2005): 78. 蒂娜-亨特，解释性理论：德沃金、桑斯坦和伊利，债券法评论17，第二版（2005）：78。

[733]Ibid., 79–80. 同上，79-80。

The various philosophies pertaining to statutory interpretation can be distinguished by looking at different approaches. The approach that looks to the past in the form of tests, structure and legislative intent and is more akin to the *rule-based* approach and is referred to as '*originalism*' by scholars. This approach to judicial interpretation will result in reducing judicial discretion but will enhance judicial discipline. However, this approach fails to take into account the changing ethos of society and developments in law that can adapt to new circumstances, as it is too focused on wisdom from the past.[734]

可以通过研究不同的方法来区分与法律解释相关的各种理念。以检验、结构和立法意图的形式来审视过去的方法更类似于以规则为基础的方法，被学者们称为"原旨主义"。这种司法解释方法会减少司法裁量权，但会加强司法纪律。然而，这种方法由于过于注重过去的智慧，未能考虑到不断变化的社会情况和能够适应新情况的法律发展。

On the other hand, the philosophy of statutory interpretation that is more forward looking, argues on values, and seeks to fill gaps in legislations and find reasons behind the particular statute, is called '*non-originalism*'.[735] This approach is becoming popular in many jurisdictions as it takes on current values but also at the same time looks to the future.

另一方面，一种更具前瞻性、以价值观为论据、寻求填补立法空白并寻找特定法规背后原因的法规解释哲学被称为"非原旨主义"。这种方法在许多法域都很流行，因为它既考虑了当前的价值观，同时又着眼于未来。

The authors will do a comparative analysis by going deeper into the specific details of judicial statutory interpretation in the jurisdictions of England & Wales and the PRC.

作者将通过深入分析英格兰和威尔士以及中国司法管辖区司法法规解释的具体细节来进行比较分析。

7.2.1 Judicial Statutory Interpretation in England & Wales

英格兰和威尔士的法定司法解释

Lawyers in the seventeenth century were inclined towards reasoned judgments rather than legislation(s), due to legal reasoning contained in those judgments. The main reason for such preference was that scholars were against the idea of superiority of legislations over other matters. To these scholars, legislations seem to be above the will of the common man.[736]

十七世纪的法律人倾向于推理判决而不是立法，因为这些判决中包含法律推理。这种偏好的主要原因是学者们反对立法优于其他事项的观点。在这些学者看来，立法似乎凌驾于普通人的意愿之上。赫德利甚至认为，

[734]Ibid., 80–1. 同上，80-1。

[735]Ibid., 80–81. 同上，80-81。

[736]Gerald J. Postema, "Classical Common Law Jurisprudence (Part II)," *Oxford U. of Commw. L.J.* 3, no. 1 (2003): 18. According to Postema, jurisprudents such as Hedley and Blackstone were not in favour of legislation having priority over the case authority. Postema quoted Hedley

Hedley even was of the view that Parliament got its authority from common law and not the other way around.[737]

议会的权威来自普通法，而不是相反。

Coke stated that the judges at common law could invalidate even laws from Parliament if the legislated law was unreasonable. This view remained for a long time in England, though it was sometimes relegated to the background. In later years, scholars took the view that the process of integration of statutes and case law was similar in the common law. According to Hale, the process of integration involved regular use, interpretation (broad and narrow), exposition and extension.[738] A view also prevailed that it is quite possible that judges may not even consider a particular statute legislated by Parliament, thus not incorporating it into the practice.[739] However, the current status quo is as follows:

科克指出，如果立法不合理，普通法法官甚至可以宣布议会的法律无效。这一观点在英国保留了很长时间，尽管有时被置于次要地位。后来，学者们认为，成文法与判例法的整合过程与普通法类似。黑尔认为，整合过程包括常规使用、解释（广义和狭义）、阐述和延伸。还有一种普遍的观点认为，法官甚至有可能不考虑议会立法的某项法规，从而不将其纳入实践。然而，目前的现状如下：

- The judges in England & Wales are currently bound by the fundamental principle of the English Legal System, that the legislations originated in Parliament are supreme. This means that the Parliament can draft laws concerning anything. No Parliament can bind a future Parliament. In addition, a valid Act of Parliament cannot be questioned by the courts. Parliament is the supreme lawmaker in England & Wales.

- 目前，英格兰和威尔士的法官受英国法律制度基本原则的约束，即源自议会的立法具有至高无上的地位。这意味着议会可以起草任何法律。任何议会都不能约束未来的议会。此外，有效的议会法案提出质疑。议会是英格兰和威尔士的最高立法者。

- The judges are also bound by the common law doctrine of *stare decisis*, more commonly called the doctrine of precedents. This doctrine will be discussed later in this Chapter.

- 法官们还受普通法的"盯住决定"原则（通常称为先例原则）的约束。本章稍后将讨论这一原则。

- The third method through which the judges are bound is through various rules of judicial interpretation. There is

- 约束法官们的第三个方法是各种司法解释规则。此外，1978 年《解

---

who said in 1610, "...the parliament hath his power and authority from the common law, and not the common law from the parliament." Hedley also said, "the common law is of more force and strength than the parliament … The parliament may find some defects in the common law and amend them … But that the parliament may abrogate the whole law, I deny, for that were includedly to take away the power of the parliament itself, which power it hath by the common law."

杰拉尔德-J-波斯特马，"古典普通法法理学（第二部分）"，牛津大学英联邦法律杂志. L.J. 3, no. 1 (2003): 18. 波斯特马认为，赫德利和布莱克斯通等法学家不赞成立法优先于判例权威。波斯特马引用了赫德利在 1610 年所说的话："......议会的权力和权威来自普通法，而不是普通法来自议会。赫德利还说，"普通法比议会更有效力和力量......议会可以发现普通法中的一些缺陷并加以修改......但我否认议会可以废除整个法律，因为这等于剥夺了议会本身的权力，而议会的权力来自普通法"。

[737] Postema, "Classical Common Law Jurisprudence - II," 18.

波斯特马，"古典普通法法理学（第二部分）"，第18页。

[738] Ibid., 20. 同上，20。

[739] Ibid. 同上。

also the *Interpretation Act 1978*, which provides common definitions to assist the judges in their judicial activities. This is needed in practice because even though Parliamentary legislations are drafted with utmost care, no legislation can foresee all possible scenarios. Additionally, the words in the statutes themselves at times could be ambiguous and may need clarification, which can come from understanding the intent of the legislation.

释法》提供了通用定义，以协助法官开展司法活动。这在实践中是必要的，因为即使议会在起草立法时非常谨慎，但任何立法都不可能预见到所有可能出现的情况。此外，法规本身的用词有时可能模棱两可，需要加以澄清，这可以通过理解立法意图来实现。

The task of interpreting statutes is carried out by the judges. Historically, English statutes are *corrective* rather than *preventative*. They try to be as specific as possible. This is different from statutes in the civil jurisdiction, which are all-encompassing and very detailed.[740] Parliament through statutes can also override the case law, and this guidance is available to the judges.

解释法规的任务由法官们承担。从历史上看，英国法规是纠正性而非预防性的。它们尽量具体。这与民事司法管辖中的法规不同，后者包罗万象，非常详细。议会也可以通过成文法推翻判例法，法官们也可以利用这种指导。

One noticeable feature of statutory interpretation in England and Wales is that all stakeholders understand that the statutes are bringing about incremental change to the pre-existing common law. The law before the advent of common law also remains, though in the background.[741] Practitioners of law need to appreciate that the continuity of law in England & Wales is completely different from other continental systems such as Germany, which make complete changes in Codes every other century, completely discarding the previous laws. However, there is continuity in the evolution of the common law over the years and centuries.

英格兰和威尔士成文法解释的一个显著特点是，所有利益相关者都明白，成文法是对先前存在的普通法的渐进式变革。普通法出现之前的法律也依然存在，尽管处于背景之中。法律从业者需要认识到，英格兰和威尔士法律的连续性与德国等其他大陆体系完全不同，后者每隔一个世纪就会彻底改变法典，完全抛弃以前的法律。然而，普通法在数年或数百年间的演变具有连续性。

7.2.1.1 Presumptions

假设

Before the judges interpret any statute before them, there are a few presumptions that they will always keep in mind. These

法官在解释其面前的任何法规之前，会始终牢记一些推定。除非有充

[740]Lundmark, *Divide between Common and Civil Law*, 304.
伦德马克，《普通法与民法之分》，第304页。
[741]Ibid., 339. 同上，第339页。

presumptions will be taken to be true unless a good argument is provided to demonstrate that a particular presumption should not apply to the statutes. A few examples of these presumptions are as follows:

分的论据证明某项推定不应适用于法规，否则这些推定将被视为真实。这些推定的几个例子如下：

- It will be presumed by the judges that the existing law has not been changed, unless the Act containing statues shows a clear intention to change the existing law;

- 法官将推定现行法律未被改变，除非包含法规的法案显示出改变现行法律的明确意图；

- Each area of law has its unique points; for example, in the field of criminal law, it will be presumed that *mens rea* (criminal intent) is required in criminal cases;

- 每个法律领域都有其独特之处；例如，在刑法领域，将推定刑事案件中需要有犯罪意图；

- Presumption against interference with vested rights;

- 推定不干涉既得权利；

- Strict construction of penal laws in favor of the citizens;

- 严格解释有利于公民的刑法；

- Presumption against retrospective operation;

- 推定不溯及既往；

- Presumption that the statutes do not affect the Crown.

- 推定法规不影响王室。

7.2.1.2 Rules of Statutory Interpretation

法定解释规则

The authors will start with the dicta of Donaldson J.:[742]

笔者将从唐纳森大法官的判词入手：

> The duty of the Courts is to ascertain and give effect to the will of Parliament as expressed in its enactments. In the performance of this duty the Judges do not act as

> 法院的职责是确定并执行议会在其法令中表达的意愿。在履行这一职责时，法官并不像计算机一样，将法规和

742 See *Corocraft Ltd v Pan American Airways Inc* [1968] 3 WLR 714, 732. (Donaldson J).
见 Corocraft Ltd 诉 Pan American Airways Inc [1968] 3 WLR 714，732。(唐纳森法官）。

computers into which are fed the statutes and the rules for the construction of statutes and from whom issue forth the mathematically correct answer. The interpretation of statutes is a craft as much as a science and the judges, as craftsmen, select and apply the appropriate rules as the tools of their trade [emphasis added]. They are not legislators, but finishers, refiners and polishers of legislation which comes to them in a state that require varying degrees of further processing.

法规解释规则输入其中，并从中得出数学上正确的答案。对法规的解释既是一门技术，也是一门科学，而法官作为技术人员，会选择和应用适当的规则作为其工作的工具[着重部分由笔者标明]。他们不是立法者，而是立法的完成者、提炼者和抛光者，这些立法到了他们手里需要不同程度的进一步加工。

The authors will now consider the rules of statutory interpretation independently:

笔者现在将对法律解释的规则进行独立的思考：

- The *first rule* is the *literal rule* that means that as a starting point, judges must give all the words in a statute their ordinary and natural meaning. The literal rule is strict, and it ensures that the judges have to follow the rule, even if the meaning that comes out after such statutory interpretation is absurd. It was the dominant rule in the late nineteenth century. Scholars have argued that orthodox judges, who are cagey about creating law, tend to put too much faith in draftsmanship.[743] In *R. v The Judge of the City of London Court*,[744] Lord Esher MR was willing to follow the law even if the wording of the statute was absurd.

- 第一条规则是字面规则，即作为起点，法官必须赋予法规中的所有词语以普通和自然的含义。字面规则是严格的，它确保法官必须遵循该规则，即使这样的法律解释之后得出的含义是荒谬的。这是十九世纪末的主流规则。有学者认为，正统法官在创制法律时畏首畏尾，往往过于相信起草技巧。在 R. v The Judge of the City of London Court 一案中，埃舍尔勋爵愿意遵循法律，即使法规的措辞荒谬。

  Nevertheless, it will always be a starting point in most cases.However, senior judges have always shown resistance to departing from this rule, as can be seen in the dicta of Lord Simonds in *Magor and St Mellons Rural District*

  不过，在大多数情况下，这始终是一个起点。然而，资深法官总是对偏离这一规则表现出抵触情绪，西蒙兹勋爵在 Magor and St Mellons Rural District Council v

[743]See *The Law Commission Report on Interpretation of Statutes* 1969, LC021 where it was said the literal rule assumes an unattainable perfection in draftsmanship.
见《法律委员会关于成文法解释的报告》，1969年，LC021，其中指出，字面规则假定了起草技术中无法实现的完美。

[744][1892] 1 QB 273 (CA) (Lord Esher MR) said on p. 290 "the words of an Act are clear, you must follow them, even though they lead to a manifest absurdity [emphasis added]. The Court has nothing to do with the question whether the Legislature has committed an absurdity."
[1892]1QB273（CA）（埃舍尔勋爵）在第290页说："一项法案的措辞是明确的，你必须遵循它们，即使它们导致明显的荒谬[着重部分由笔者标明]。法院与立法机构是否犯下荒谬的问题无关"。

Council v Newport Corporation: in the context of statutory interpretation where a judge in the lower court attempted to openly espouse the cause of filling the gaps while embarking on an exercise of statutory interpretation, Simonds called the process "naked usurpation of legislative function under the thin disguise of interpretation". [745]

Newport Corporation 一案中的判词就说明了这一点：在法律解释的背景下，下级法院的一名法官在着手进行法律解释的同时，试图公开支持填补空白的事业，西蒙兹将这一过程称为 "在薄薄的解释伪装下赤裸裸地篡夺立法职能"。

However, there have been cases where absurdity has been observed; for example, see this case taken from the criminal law (cited in the footnotes).[746]

不过，也有出现荒谬的情况，例如，请参阅刑法中的这一案例（脚注中引用）。

- The *second rule* of statutory interpretation is commonly known as the '*golden rule*'. Under this rule, if the literal interpretation is going to result in an absurd result, which no Parliament would have intended at all, then the judges can substitute a reasonable meaning. The origins of this rule are in *Grey v Pearson* (1857) where Lord Wensleydale said:

> ...the grammatical and ordinary sense of the words is to be adhered to, unless that would lead to some absurdity, or some repugnance or inconsistency with the rest of the instrument [emphasis added], in which case the grammatical and ordinary sense of the words may be modified, so as to avoid that absurdity and inconsistency, but no further.[747]

- 法定解释的第二条规则通常被称为 "黄金规则"。根据这一规则，如果按字面解释会导致荒谬的结果，而这根本不是议会的本意，那么法官就可以用合理的含义来替代。该规则起源于 Grey 诉 Pearson 案（1857 年），温斯利戴尔勋爵在该案中说道：

> ...应遵守词语的语法和普通意义，除非这会导致某些荒谬，或与文书的其余部分相抵触或不一致[着重部分由笔者标明]，在这种情况下，可以修改词语的语法和普通意义，以避免荒谬和不一致，但不能再进一步。

[745] [1952]AC 189, 191 (Lords Simonds). [1952]AC189，191（西蒙兹勋爵）。

[746] See *R v Harris* (1836) 7 C & P 446. In this case, an Act existed that made it an offence to "stab, cut, or wound any person". Harris bit off his victim's nose. Did he commit the offence? The Court held that he would have required the use of an instrument/implement (e.g. a knife). Harris was found not guilty. If a word has a technical meaning, it should be given this technical meaning, according to the first rule of statutory interpretation.

见 R v Harris (1836) 7 C & P 446。在该案中，有一项法令规定 "刺伤、割伤或伤害任何人 "均属犯罪行为。哈里斯咬掉了受害人的鼻子。他犯法了吗？法院认为他需要使用工具/器具（如刀）。哈里斯被判无罪。根据法律解释的第一条规则，如果一个词具有技术含义，则应赋予其技术含义。

[747] 6 HL Cas 61,106 (Lord Wensleydale). 6 HL Cas 61,106（温斯莱代尔勋爵）。

There have been a few prominent cases in this field where golden rules were applied. In one particular case, for example, the judge clarified the meaning of a word in the statute (see footnote).[748] Such clarifications might *narrow* or *broaden* the meaning.

在这一领域，有几个著名的案例适用了黄金规则。例如，在一个特殊案件中，法官澄清了法规中一个词的含义（见脚注）。这种澄清可能会缩小或扩大含义。

The second rule allows the judges some leeway, but it still raises many interesting questions; for example, what level of absurdity is acceptable? This issue has gradually been analysed in the courts, for example, Lord Blackburn in *River Wear Commissioners v Adamson* said:

第二条规则允许法官有一定的回旋余地，但它仍提出了许多有趣的问题；例如，可接受的荒谬程度是什么？法院已逐渐对这一问题进行了分析，例如，布莱克本勋爵在River Wear Commissioners v Adamson 一案中说："我相信这一点是没有争议的：

> I believe that it is not disputed that what Lord Wensleydale used to call the golden rule is right, viz., that we are to take the whole statute together, and construe it all together, giving the words their ordinary signification, unless when so applied they produce an inconsistency, or an absurdity or inconvenience so great as to convince the Court [emphasis added] that the intention could not have been to use them in their ordinary signification, and to justify the Court in putting on them some other signification, which, though less proper, is one which the Court thinks the words will bear.[749]

> 我认为，温斯莱代尔勋爵所说的黄金法则是正确的，这一点没有争议，即我们应当把整部法规放在一起，一并加以解释，赋予这些词语普通的含义，除非这样应用这些词语会产生不一致之处，或者产生荒谬或不便之处，以至于使法院相信[着重部分由笔者标明]其意图不可能是使用这些词语的普通含义，并使法院有理由赋予这些词语以其他含义，尽管这些含义不太恰当，但法院认为这些词语可以承受。

[748]See, *Adler v George* [1964] 2QB 7. According to s 3 of the *Official Secrets Act 1920,* c 75 "no persons shall in the vicinity of any prohibited place obstruct any member of Her Majesty's forces". Defendant was actually on the airfield. The courts had to determine whether "in [the] vicinity of" includes on/in the premises. The court said that in the vicinity did include 'on or in' as well, as it would be absurd to define "in the vicinity' as a prohibited place, but to stop considering it prohibited when someone is actually on or in it.
见Adler 诉 George [1964] 2QB 7。根据《1920 年官方保密法》（1920 年，c 75）第3条，"任何人不得在任何违禁地点附近妨碍女王陛下部队的任何成员"。被告当时确实在机场上。法院必须确定"在[附近]"是否包括在房舍内。法院说，"附近"确实也包括"在或在"，因为将"附近"定义为违禁地点，但当有人实际在或在该地点时就不再将其视为违禁地点是荒谬的。

[749]See *River Wear Commissioners v Adamson* (1877) 2 App. Cas. 743,764-65. It was also quoted in The Law Commission *Report on Interpretation of Statutes* 1969, LC021.
见 River Wear Commissioners v Adamson (1877) 2 App. Cas. 743,764-65. 法律委员会 1969 年关于成文法解释的报告》（LC021）中也引用了该条款。

Even though the golden rule was a great improvement over the literal rule as it addresses the issues of absurdity, inconsistency or inconvenience for the first time, it still failed to provide a clear means to test the existence of absurdity or inconsistency, or how to measure it.[750]

尽管黄金规则与字面规则相比有了很大的改进，因为它首次解决了荒谬、不一致或不便的问题，但它仍然未能提供一个明确的方法来检验荒谬或不一致的存在，也没有提供如何衡量荒谬或不一致的方法。

- The *final rule* is called the '*mischief* approach'. This rule was developed during the time when fewer laws were legislated in Parliament and in fact, most laws were coming out of the common law courts. The starting point for this approach came from the Barons of the Court of Exchequer in *Heydon's Case* (1584),[751] where the judges met and considered all statutes of all kinds (may it be penal or beneficial, restrictive or enlarging the common law), and they decided that the following four points were to be considered by the judges under this rule:

  - What was the common law before the making of the Act?
  - What was the mischief and defect for which the common law did not provide?
  - What remedy had Parliament resolved, and what was appointed to cure the disease of the

- 第四条规则被称为“恶作剧方法”。这一规则是在议会立法较少，事实上大多数法律都是由普通法法院制定的时期形成的。这种方法的出发点来自于财政法院男爵们在海顿案（1584 年）中的观点，在该案中，法官们开会审议了所有各类成文法（可能是惩罚性的，也可能是有益的，可能是限制性的，也可能是扩大普通法的），他们决定根据这一规则，法官们应审议以下四点：

  - 在法案制定之前普通法是什么？
  - 普通法没有规定的问题和缺陷是什么？
  - 议会采取了什么补救措施，指定了什么来治疗联邦的疾病？

[750] The Law Commission *Report on Interpretation of Statutes* 1969, LC021, 19.
1969年法律委员会关于成文法解释的报告，LC021，19。

[751] 3 Co Rep 7a. See also *Magistrates and Town Council of Glasgow v Commissioners of Police of Hillhead* (1885) 12 R. 864, which said that "it is a settled principle that the court should so construe an Act of Parliament as to apply the statutory remedy to the evil or mischief which it is the intention of the statute to meet."
3 Co Rep 7a。另见 Magistrates and Town Council of Glasgow v Commissioners of Police of Hillhead (1885) 12 R. 864 一案，该案称“一项既定原则是，法院应如此解释一项议会法案，以便将法定补救措施适用于法规意图应对的邪恶或弊端”。

Commonwealth?

➢ The true reason for the remedy was also stated: and then the office of all the judges were always to make such construction as shall suppress the mischief, and advance the remedy, and to suppress subtle inventions and evasions for continuance of the mischief, and *pro privato commodo*, and to add force and life to the cure and remedy, according to the true intent of the makers of the Act, *pro bono publico*.

➢ 还说明了采取补救措施的真正原因：然后，所有法官的职责始终是根据该法案制定者的真正意图，为消除弊端和推进补救措施而进行解释，制止为延续弊端而进行的巧妙发明和规避行为，并为治疗和补救措施增添力量和活力，以利于公众。

However, the judges for many years were only willing to accept either the *literal rule* or the *golden rule*. In relation to this cautious approach, Lord Tenterden CJ in *Brandling v Barrington* said:

然而，多年来法官们只愿意接受字面规则或黄金规则。对于这种谨慎的做法，Tenterden 大法官在 Brandling 诉 Barrington 案中说：

...that . . . there is always danger in giving effect to what is called the equity of a statute, and that it is much better and safer to rely on and abide by the plain words [emphasis added], although the Legislature might possibly have provided for other cases had their attention been directed to them. [752]

....在实施所谓的成文法公平原则时总是存在危险，依靠和遵守明文规定要好得多，也安全得多[着重号后加]，尽管立法机构如果注意到其他情况，可能会对这些情况作出规定。

In addition to the undercurrents seen in the1950s and 1960s, the tide was slowly changing. Judges were more willing to be creative, with Lord Denning saying that “[the] judges are not the slaves of words but their masters.”[753] It was clear that the

除了 1950 年代和 1960 年代出现的暗流之外，潮流也在慢慢改变。丹宁勋爵说："法官不是文字的奴隶，而是文字的主人。很明显，第一条规则忽视了起草的局限性，即使是最高法院的法官也会对

[752](1827) 6 B & C 467, 475 (Lord Tenterden CJ).
(1827) 6 B & C 467, 475（坦特尔登 CJ 勋爵）。
[753]*Allen v Thorn Electrical Industries Ltd* (1968) 1 QB 481, 503 (CA) (Lord Denning MR).
见Allen v Thorn 电气工业有限公司 (1968) 1 QB 481, 503 (CA) (Lord Denning MR)。

first rule ignores the limitation of draftsmanship and even the judges in the highest courts can differ on the meaning of the same word. Therefore, this task of statutory interpretation is difficult. While the mischief rule seems to be satisfactory, however, the *Law Commission Report 1969* was of the view that:

同一个词的含义产生分歧。因此，这项法律解释的任务是困难的。虽然"恶作剧"规则似乎令人满意，但 1969 年法律委员会报告认为：

> Heydon's Case is also somewhat outdated in its approach, because it assumes that statute is subsidiary or supplemental to the common law [emphasis added], whereas in modern conditions many statutes mark a fresh point of departure rather than a mere addition to, and qualification of, common law principles.[754]

> 海登案例的方法也有些过时，因为它假定成文法是普通法的附属或补充[着重部分由笔者标明]，而在现代条件下，许多成文法标志着一个新的出发点，而不仅仅是对普通法原则的补充和限定。

Over the years, England & Wales has adopted the *purposive* approach. This purposive approach will always take into account the presumptions as discussed above. Lord Griffiths in a landmark case said:

多年来，英格兰和威尔士一直采用目的性方法。这种目的性方法始终会考虑到上文讨论的推定。格里菲斯勋爵在一个具有里程碑意义的案例中指出

> The days have long passed when the courts adopted a strict constructionist view of interpretation which required them to adopt the literal meaning of the language. The courts now adopt a purposive approach [emphasis added] which seeks to give effect to the true purpose of legislation and are prepared to look at much extraneous material that bears upon the background against which the legislation was enacted.[755]

> 法院采用严格的解释学观点，要求法院采用语言的字面含义的时代早已过去。法院现在采用的是目的论方法[着重部分由笔者标明]，旨在实现立法的真正目的，并准备研究与立法背景有关的许多外在材料。

The purposive approach was spreading in England & Wales, as can be seen in the

正如斯卡曼勋爵于 1980 年9月9日在莫纳什大学发表的第九次威尔弗雷德-富拉加纪念演讲中所述，目的论方法

[754]See *The Law Commission Report on Interpretation of Statutes* 1969, LC021, 20. Refer also, to views of Hedley and Coke as discussed earlier in Chapter 3, §3.2.1.
见 1969年法律委员会关于成文法解释的报告，LC021, 20。另参见第3章第3.2.1节中讨论的Hedley和Coke的观点。
[755]See *Pepper (Her Majesty's Inspector of Taxes) v Hart* [1993] AC 593, 617 (Lord Griffiths), [1992] UKHL 3.
见Pepper（英国税务督察）诉 Hart [1993] AC 593，617（格里菲斯勋爵）[1992] UKHL 3。

Ninth Wilfred Fullagar Memorial Lecture, delivered by Lord Scarman at Monash University on September 9, 1980:

在英格兰和威尔士得到了广泛传播:

> … when I, as an English judge, read some of the decisions of the High Court of Australia, I think they are more English than the English. In London no-one would now dare to choose the literal rather than a purposive construction of a statute: and 'legalism' is currently a term of abuse [emphasis added].[756]

> …当我作为一名英国法官阅读澳大利亚高等法院的一些判决时，我认为他们比英国人更英国。在伦敦，现在没有人敢选择按字面意思而不是按目的解释法规: '法律主义'目前是一个被滥用的术语[着重部分由笔者标明]。

It is interesting to note that within a few months of this lecture, the Australian Parliament enacted section 15AA of the *Interpretation Act 1901*[757] that empowered Australian judges and provides as follows:

值得注意的是，在这次演讲后的几个月内，澳大利亚议会颁布了《1901 年解释法》第 15AA 条，赋予澳大利亚法官如下权力:

> In the interpretation of a provision of an Act, a construction that would promote the purpose or object underlying the Act (whether that purpose or object is expressly stated in the Act or not) shall be preferred to a construction that would not promote that purpose or object.

> 在解释法案条款时，促进法案基本宗旨或目标（无论该宗旨或目标是否在法案中明确说明）的解释应优于不促进该宗旨或目标的解释。

In 2001, a senior judge, Spigelman CJ of the Supreme Court of New South Wales in Australia commented:

2001 年，澳大利亚新南威尔士州最高法院资深法官 Spigelman CJ 评论说

> The law of statutory interpretation has become the most important single aspect of legal practice [emphasis added]. Significant

> 法定解释法已成为法律实践中最重要的一个方面[着重部分由笔者标明]。法律的

[756]The Right Honourable Lord Scarman, (Ninth Wilfred Fullagar Memorial Lecture), "The Common Law Judge and the Twentieth Century - Happy Marriage or Irretrievable Breakdown?" *Monash L. Rev.* 7, no. 1 (1980): 6. Quoted in RR Geddes, "Purpose and Context in Statutory Interpretation," 129. www.judcom.nsw.gov.au/publications/education-monographs-1/monograph4/07_geddes.pdf.
尊敬的斯卡曼勋爵, (第九次威尔弗雷德-富拉加纪念讲座), "普通法法官与二十世纪--幸福的婚姻还是无法挽回的破裂？" 莫纳什法律评论 7, no. 1 (1980)： 6. 引自 RR Geddes, " 法律解释的目的和背景 ,"129. www.judcom.nsw.gov.au/publications/education-monographs-1/monograph4/07_geddes.pdf。

[757]Inserted into the principal Act by the *Statute Law Revision Act 1981*, s 115.
由《1981年成文法修订法》第115条插入主法。

areas of the law are determined entirely by statute. No area of the law has escaped statutory modification.[758]

重要领域完全由法规决定。没有一个领域的法律可以逃脱法规的修改。

In most common law jurisdictions, where the purposive approach is followed, judges will not embark upon literal statutory interpretation like robots, but in fact, will take into account the purpose of the statute, the historical view and even the policy considerations that led to the drafting of the statute. It is best to end this brief discussion on statutory interpretation with the words of Mason CJ:

在大多数遵循目的论的普通法司法管辖区，法官不会像机器人那样按照字面解释成文法，事实上，他们会考虑成文法的目的、历史观点，甚至导致起草成文法的政策考虑。在此，我们最好以大法官梅森的话来结束对法律解释的简短讨论：

> No one would suggest nowadays that statutory interpretation is merely an exercise in ascertaining the literal meaning of words. Statutory interpretation calls for reference not only to the context, scope and purpose of the statute but also to antecedent history and policy as well as community values [emphasis added].[759]

> 如今，没有人会认为法定解释仅仅是确定字面意思的工作。法定解释不仅需要参考法规的上下文、范围和目的，还需要参考先前的历史和政策以及社会价值观[着重部分由笔者标明]。

Presently, in order to follow the purposive approach, English judges may also use internal aids that are available with Parliamentary legislations, and external (outside the Act) aids.

目前，为了遵循目的明确的方法，英国法官还可以使用议会立法提供的内部辅助工具和外部（法案之外）辅助工具。

---

[758] JJ Spigelman, "The Poet's Rich Resource: Issues in Statutory Interpretation," *Australian Bar Rev.* 21, no. 3 (2001): 224. Quoted in Geddes, "Purpose and Context in Statutory Interpretation," 128.
JJ 斯皮格曼，"诗人的丰富资源： 澳大利亚律师评论》第21卷第3期（2001 年）："诗人的丰富资源： 法规解释问题,"澳大利亚律师协会修订. 21, no. 3 (2001): 224. 引自格德斯，"成文法解释中的目的和背景"，128。

[759] A. Mason, "Changing the Law in a Changing Society," *Commw. L. Bull.* 18, no. 3 (1992): 569.
A. 梅森，"在不断变化的社会中改变法律"，联邦法律公报18, no. 3 (1992): 569.

7.2.1.3 Internal and External Aids to Statutory Interpretation, Purposive Approach

法规解释的内部和外部辅助工具，目的明确的方法

A few examples of the Internal aids to Statutory Interpretation that can be utilised by judges in England & Wales are as follows:

- The long and short title of the Act;
- The Preamble of the Act;
- Section headings may be used if they do not contradict the rest of the statute;
- Schedules to the Act.

英格兰和威尔士的法官可使用的法定解释内部辅助工具的例子如下：

- 法令的长短标题；
- 法令的序言；
- 如与法规的其余部分不矛盾，可使用章节标题；
- 该法的附表。

A few examples of External aids to Statutory Interpretation in England & Wales are as follows:

- Dictionary;
- Historical Setting;
- Evidence of past customary practice;
- Related statutes or similar Acts;
- Law Commission Reports;
- Treaties and International Conventions;
- Hansards and Parliamentary Reports;[760]
- EU Community Law.

英格兰和威尔士的法定解释外部辅助工具举例如下：

- 词典；
- 历史背景；
- 过去习惯做法的证据；
- 相关法规或类似法案；
- 法律委员会报告；
- 条约和国际公约；
- 立法记录和议会报告；
- 欧盟共同体法。

[760] *Pepper v Hart [1991] AC 593*, the House of Lords significantly relaxed the general prohibition on using such materials for statutory interpretation. This was after years of prohibition in referring to the Hansard and other Parliamentary Reports due to primacy of parliamentary privilege.
在 Pepper 诉 Hart [1991] AC 593一案中，上议院大大放宽了禁止在法律解释中使用此类材料的一般规定。在此之前，由于议会特权的优先地位，多年来一直禁止引用《立法会议事录》和其他议会报告。

Once Parliamentary reports were allowed, it opened the route for the judges to use the '*purposive approach*'. Even though this rule is similar to the mischief rule, the focus in this rule is on Parliament's intention in drafting the legislation, and not the common law.

一旦允许使用议会报告，就为法官使用“目的性方法”开辟了道路。尽管该规则与“恶作剧规则”相似，但其重点在于议会起草立法的意图，而非普通法。

7.2.1.4 Rules of Language for Statutory Interpretation

法规解释的语言规则

There are also a few rules of language that judges take into account when embarking on the task of statutory interpretation, for example:

法官在进行法律解释时还会考虑一些语言规则，例如

- *Ejusdem generis* — general words following particular ones normally apply only to such persons or things that are of the same genus or class.[761]
- *Noscitur a sociis* — the meaning of a word can be ascertained from the other words used. For example, see an old case from 1875, in the footnotes.[762]
- *Expressio unius est exclusio alterius* —this means that the express member of one member within the class excludes other members from the class by implication, as

- 同类规则——特殊词语之后的一般词语通常只适用于同属或同类的人或事。
- 文理解释—— 一个词的含义可以从使用的其他词中确定。例如，参见脚注中 1875 年的一个旧案例。
- 明示其一排除其他原则——意思是类中一个成员的明示成员通过暗示将其他成员排除在类之外，脚注中的例子

[761]A word will take its meaning from the *foregoing* words. For example, if in any act it is stated “no tradesmen, artisan, workmen, labourer or other person whatsoever shall work on a Sunday” then it may mean “other person whatsoever” does not include occupations such as estate agents, barbers or farmers.
一个词的含义来自前面的词语。例如，如果任何法令规定“商人、工匠、工人、劳动者或其他人不得在星期日工作”，那么这可能意味着“其他人 ”不包括地产代理、理发师或农民等职业。

[762]See *Muir v Keay* (1875) LR QBD 594 where the court at that time considered the *Refreshment Houses Act 1860,* c27, and thereafter considered the meaning of 'entertainment'. This Act dealt with public refreshment, resorts and entertainment. The courts had to decide how to determine the meaning of entertainment. They looked at the other words and found it could not refer to theatrical or musical entertainment. The word referred to refreshment rooms, reception and accommodation of the public.
参见 Muir 诉 Keay (1875) LR QBD 594，当时的法院审议了《1860 年茶馆法》第27条，并随后审议了“娱乐”的含义。该法涉及公共茶点、度假村和娱乐。法院必须决定如何确定娱乐的含义。他们研究了其他词，发现它不能指戏剧或音乐娱乐。该词指的是茶点室、接待和公众住宿。

can be seen by the footnoted example.[763]

可以看出这一点。

7.2.1.5 Judicial Interpretation in context of Civil Procedure

民事诉讼程序中的司法解释

The concept of overriding objectives has been discussed previously:[764] overriding objectives are used in resolving conflicts between various rules of the CPR. It is a very useful tool especially when the wording of the CPR is silent or is not clear. For example, in one case (see footnotes),[765] the purposive approach to interpreting the civil procedural rules was used to lift a stay of procedure, because this stay was allowed only due to very technical application of rules. The overriding objective should have guided the conduct of the parties.

前面已经讨论过优先目标的概念：优先目标用于解决《民事诉讼程序法》各规则之间的冲突。这是一个非常有用的工具，尤其是在《民事诉讼程序法》的措辞没有规定或不明确的情况下。例如，在一个案件中（见脚注）使用了解释民事诉讼规则的目的性方法来取消程序的中止，因该中止只是由于规则的技术性应用而被允许。首要目标本应指导当事人的行为。

The CPR has been drafted with 'purposive approach to interpretation'.[766] It is particularly useful in the following scenarios:

《民事诉讼程序规则》是以"目的性解释方法"起草的。它在以下情况下尤其有用：

- Civil procedural rules are silent;
- Civil procedural rules are ambiguous;

- 民事诉讼程序规则未作规定；
- 民事诉讼程序规则含糊不清；

---

[763]See the case of *Tempest v Kilner* (1846) 3 CB 249. A contract for the sale of goods, wares, and merchandise for £10 or more had to be evidenced in writing. Applying this rule of language, it could be argued then, that the contract for sales of stocks and shares did not have to be evidenced in writing because they were not goods, wares or merchandise.
参见Tempest v Kilner (1846) 3 CB 249一案。10英镑或以上的货物、器皿和商品销售合同必须有书面证明。根据这一语言规则，可以说股票和股份的销售合同无需书面证明，因为它们不是货物、商品或货物。

[764]Refer, Chapter 4, §4.2.1. 参见第 4 章第 4.2.1 节。

[765]See *B v B [2005] EWCA Civ 237* In this case, the judgment clearly stated the duty imposed on the parties and their lawyers under CPR, r. 1.3 (to assist the courts to further the overriding objective). The Court was of the view that a lengthy and costly litigation could have been avoided if the lawyers had communicated with the defendant's solicitors shortly after the new proceedings commenced.
见 B v B [2005] EWCA Civ 237 在本案中，判决书明确指出了 CPR 第 1.3 条规定的当事人及其律师的责任（协助法院推进首要目标）。法院认为，如果律师在新的诉讼程序开始后不久与被告的律师进行沟通，就可以避免漫长而昂贵的诉讼。

[766]Deirdre Dwyer, "What is the Meaning of CPR r 1.1(1)," in *The Civil Procedure Rules Ten Years On*, Deirdre Dwyer (Oxford: Oxford University Press, 2009), 73.
迪尔德丽-德怀尔，"CPR r 1.1(1)的含义是什么？，" 在《民事诉讼程序规则》十年之后，迪尔德丽-德怀尔(牛津大学出版社, 2009), 73.

- Civil procedural rules are in conflict with old rules that led to the previous body of cases.

- 民事诉讼程序规则与导致先前案例的旧规则相冲突。

The above discussions lead us to the role of the authority of case precedents in analysing the Code. It is unthinkable that in the common law system, old cases are not considered relevant. However, there are relevant cases from the time of pre-*CPR 1998* rules. Cases before the new *CPR 1998* came into existence are not relevant, as can be seen from the case of *Biguzzi v Rank Leisure*.[767] The case of *Biguzzi* was tried before the court immediately after the new *CPR 1998* came into existence. However, in the later case of *Garratt v Saxby*,[768] it was said that previous cases could have some persuasive force. In particular, Dyson LJ said:

通过以上讨论，我们可以得出判例的权威性在分析法典中的作用。在普通法体系中，旧案例不被认为具有相关性是不可想象的。然而，在《1998年民事诉讼程序规则》之前的时期，却有相关的案例。从 Biguzzi v Rank Leisure 一案中可看出，新的《1998年民事诉讼程序法》出台之前的案例并不相关。Biguzzi 案是 1998 年新《民事诉讼程序法》生效后立即由法院审理的。不过，在后来的 Garratt v Saxby 案中，法院认为以前的案件可能具有一定的说服力。戴森大法官特别指出：

> Although it has been said on a number of occasions that decisions on pre-CPR procedural rules are not binding for the purpose of interpreting the CPR, *there are circumstances in which they may be of considerable persuasive force* [emphasis added]. In my view, this is a good example.[769]

> 虽然在很多场合都说过《民事诉讼程序法》之前的程序规则的判决对解释《民事诉讼程序法》没有约束力，*但在某些情况下，它们可能具有相当大的说服力*[着重部分由笔者标明]。我认为，这是一个很好的例子。

However, the circumstances where old cases could be binding are very limited and judges have shown caution in utilising pre-*CPR 1998* authorities. It is relevant at this point to bring in the dicta of Brooke LJ in a particular case:

然而，旧案例具有约束力的情况非常有限，法官在使用《1998年民事诉讼程序法》之前的权威案例时也表

767 See [1999] 1 WLR 1926 (CA). See also the discussion of the case in *Biguzzi v Rank Leisure [1999] 1 WLR 1926 (CA), [1999] 4 ALL ER 934, Biguzzi v Rank Leisure [1999] 1 WLR 1926 (CA), [1999] 4 ALL ER 934, Biguzzi v Rank Leisure [1999] 1 WLR 1926 (CA), [1999] 4 ALL ER 934.* See also, *Dwyer, "Overriding Objective," 67.*

见 [1999] 1 WLR 1926 (CA)。另见 Biguzzi v Rank Leisure [1999] 1 WLR 1926 (CA), [1999] 4 ALL ER 934, Biguzzi v Rank Leisure [1999] 1 WLR 1926 (CA), [1999] 4 ALL ER 934, Biguzzi v Rank Leisure [1999] 1 WLR 1926 (CA), [1999] 4 ALL ER 934 中对该案的讨论。另见德怀尔，"首要目标"，67。

768 [2004] EWCA Civ 341. *Garratt v Saxby [2004] EWCA Civ 341.*

[2004] EWCA Civ 341。Garratt 诉 Saxby [2004] EWCA Civ 341。

769 Ibid., [18]. *Garratt v Saxby [2004] EWCA Civ 341,* [18].

同上，[18]。Garratt 诉 Saxby [2004] EWCA Civ 341，[18]。

现得非常谨慎。在这一点上，布鲁克大法官在一个特定案件中的意见是有意义的：

> It is clear, in my view, that what Lord Woolf was saying was that reference to authorities under the former rules is generally no longer relevant. Rather it is necessary to concentrate on the intrinsic justice of a particular case in the light of the overriding objective.[770]

> 在我看来，伍尔夫勋爵的意思显然是，参照以前规则下的权威一般不再适用。相反，有必要根据压倒一切的目标，专注于特定案件的内在正义。

In the years following the advent of *CPR 1998*, there have been scholarly articles which submit that old cases can only be used in situations where difficulties arise.[771] However, it is clear that judges are adopting a cautious approach. Lord Woolf later released *Practice Direction on the Citation of Authorities, 2001*,[772] where he made an attempt to reduce reliance on case precedents in matters of civil procedural law. This *Practice Direction* advises users of *CPR 1998* that minor cases should not be cited, unless the judgment has established a new principle or extended the law.

在《1998年民事诉讼程序规则》问世后几年里，有学术文章认为只有在出现困难时才能使用旧案例。然而，法官显然采取了谨慎态度。伍尔夫勋爵后来发布了《2001年关于引用权威的实务指示》，试图在民事诉讼法事务中减少对先例的依赖。该《实务指示》建议《1998年民事诉讼法》的使用者，除非判决确立了新原则或扩展了法律，否则不应引用次要案例。

In summary, case precedents will only need to highlight the consistency of approach of the civil courts. However, most civil procedural lawyers will disagree with the above views, including the authors, as the relevant *White Book*[773] itself highlights many case precedents, and new cases are added every year to make the book even thicker.[774]

总之，先例只需突出民事法庭处理问题的一致性。不过，包括笔者在内的大多数民事诉讼律师都不会同意上述观点，因为相关的白皮书本身就强调了许多案例先例，而且每年都会增加新的案例，使白皮书更加厚实。

---

[770] *Walsh v Misseldine [2000] CP Rep 74*, [79], where he cited May LJ from the case of *Purdy v Cambran* [2000] CP Rep 67.
Walsh v Misseldine [2000] CP Rep 74, [79]，他引用了May LJ在Purdy v Cambran [2000] CP Rep 67一案中的观点。

[771] A. Zuckerman, *Zuckerman on Civil Procedure: Principles of Practice*, 2nd ed. (London: Sweet and Maxwell, 2006), [1.51] Zuckerman's views were discussed in Dwyer, "Overriding Objective," 67.
A. 祖克曼，祖克曼关于民事诉讼程序：实践原则，第二版，(伦敦: Sweet and Maxwell, 2006), [1.51] 德怀尔, "首要目标," 67中讨论了祖克曼的观点。

[772] See *Practice Direction (Citation of Authorities) [2001] 1 WLR 2001.*
见实践方向(引用文献) [2001] 1 WLR 2001。

[773] White Book is a famous text book for civil law practitioners, guiding them on civil procedural rules.
白皮书是民法从业人员的知名教科书，指导他们了解民事诉讼规则。

[774] The issue of *White Book* becoming thicker every year is discussed in Dwyer, "Overriding Objective," 68.
德怀尔, "首要目标," 68中讨论了白皮书逐年变厚的问题。

7.2.1.6 Human Rights Act 1998

1998 年人权法

After World War II, the *European Convention of Human Rights* (hereinafter '*ECHR*') entered into force on 3 September 1953. *The Human Rights Act 1998* (hereinafter '*HRA 1998*') is an Act of Parliament of the United Kingdom that came into force on 2 October 2000. It incorporated *EHCR* into the UK law and ensured that the remedies for breach of human rights pursuant to *ECHR* are available in local courts in the UK. There are different types of rights available in *HRA 1998*:

第二次世界大战后，《欧洲人权公约》（“《欧洲人权公约》”）于1953年9月3日生效。1998年《人权法》是英国议会的一项法案，2000年10月2日生效。该法案将《欧洲人权公约》纳入英国法律，并确保英国地方法院可根据《欧洲人权公约》对侵犯人权的行为进行补救。1998年《人权法》规定了不同类型的权利：

- A few of them ensure that all primary and subordinate legislations must be read and given effect according to *HRA 1998*;
- High Court or superior courts can declare the law invalid and incompatible with *HRA 1998,* and the courts can give notice to the relevant Ministry within the Executive;
- Jurisprudence of *ECHR* is taken into account by the English courts according to section 2 of *HRA 1998*.[775]
- All public bodies (including courts and tribunals)[776] are under the obligation to

- 其中几项权利确保所有主要立法和附属立法必须根据《1998年人权法》进行解读和生效；
- 高等法院或上级法院可宣布法律无效且不符合《1998年人权法》，法院可向行政部门的相关部委发出通知；
- 根据《1998年人权法》第2条，英国法院考虑《欧洲人权公约》的判例。
- 根据《1998年人权法》第6-8

[775] s 2 of *HRA 1998* Interpretation of Convention rights provides: (1) A court or tribunal determining a question which has arisen in connection with a Convention right must take into account any — (a) judgment, decision, declaration or advisory opinion of the European Court of Human Rights, (b) opinion of the Commission given in a report adopted under Article 31 of the Convention, (c) decision of the Commission in connection with Article 26 or 27(2) of the Convention, or (d) decision of the Committee of Ministers taken under Article 46 of the Convention.
《1998 年人权法》第2条对公约权利的解释规定：(1) 法院或法庭在裁定与《公约》权利有关的问题时，必须考虑到以下任何情况：(a) 欧洲人权法院的判决、裁决、声明或咨询意见；(b) 欧盟委员会在根据《公约》第 31 条通过的报告中提出的意见；(c) 欧盟委员会就《公约》第26条或第27(2)条作出的决定；或(d) 部长委员会根据《公约》第46条作出的决定。

[776] s 6 (3) of *HRA 1998* provides: … "public authority" includes —
(a) a court or tribunal, and (b) any person certain of whose functions are functions of a public nature.
1998年《人权法》第6(3)条规定：."公共当局 "包括 (a) 法院或审裁处；及(b)其某些职能属公共性质的任何人。

act in accordance with *HRA 1998* pursuant to sections 6-8 of *HRA 1998*.

条，所有公共机构（包括法院和法庭）都有义务按照《1998 年人权法》行事。

7.2.1.6.1 HRA's Effects on CPR

《人权法》对民事诉讼程序的影响

The foregoing discussion on the concept of overriding objective states that cases should be dealt with justly in the context of civil procedural rules. The philosophy of *overriding objective* also fits well with *HRA 1998*. It was even reported in the case of *Goode v Martin* (Times, January, 24, 2002): it was stated that *HRA 1998* functions as an extra tool in the interpretation of procedural rules.[777]

上文关于压倒一切的目标这一概念的讨论表明，在民事诉讼规则的范围内，案件应得到公正处理。这一理念也与 1998 年《人权法案》十分契合。在 Goode v Martin 案 (2002 年 1 月 24 日《泰晤士报》）中甚至有这样的报道：《1998 年人权法》是解释程序规则的一个额外工具。

Section 6(1) of *HRA 1998* brings into effect Article 6 of *ECHR* that provides:

1998 年《人权法》第 6(1)条使《欧洲人权公约》第 6 条生效，该条规定：

> In the determination of his civil rights and obligations or of any criminal charge against him, everyone is entitled to a fair and public hearing within a reasonable time by an independent and impartial tribunal established by law. Judgment shall be pronounced publicly [emphasis added] but the press and public may be excluded from all or part of the trial in the interest of morals, public order or national security in a democratic society, where the interests of juveniles or the protection of the private life of the parties so require, or the extent strictly necessary in the opinion of the court in special circumstances where publicity would prejudice the interests of justice.

> 在确定其公民权利和义务或对其提出的任何刑事指控时，人人有权在合理的时间内由一个依法设立的独立而无偏倚的法庭进行公正的和公开的审讯。判决应公开宣布[着重部分由笔者标明]，但为了民主社会的道德、公共秩序或国家安全，或为了青少年的利益或保护当事人的私生活而有此需要，或在公开审判会损害司法利益的特殊情况下，法院认为绝对必要的范围内，可以不让新闻界和公众旁听全部或部分审判。

Briefly, *HRA 1998* is applicable to the right to public hearing, the right to have access to the courts in litigation, the right to having unbiased judges with no conflict of interest, the right to

简言之，《1998 年人权法》适用于公开听证权、向法院提起诉讼的权利、由没有利益冲突的公正法官审理

[777] See for further discussion on *HRA 1998* and *CPR 1998*, Blake, *Practical Approach to Effective Litigation*, 57.
关于1998年《人权法案》和1998年《民事诉讼程序法》的进一步讨论，见布莱克，《有效诉讼的实用方法》，57。

adversarial procedure, equality of time and facilities, the right to hearing within a reasonable time, the right to receive reasons for a judgment and the right to fair proceedings.

的权利、抗辩程序权、时间和设施平等权、在合理时间内进行听证的权利、获得判决理由的权利及公平诉讼权。

In a case in the Court of Appeal, it was noted:

> … that a judgment should contain reasons that are sufficient to demonstrate that the essential issues that have been raised by the parties have been addressed by the domestic court and how those issues have been resolved. It does not seem … that the Strasbourg jurisprudence goes further and requires a judgment to explain why one contention, or piece of evidence, has been preferred to another [emphasis added].[778]

上诉法院在一案件中指出：

> …判决书应包含足够的理由，以表明国内法院已经处理了当事人提出的基本问题，以及如何解决这些问题。似乎……斯特拉斯堡的判例并没有进一步要求判决书解释为什么一个论点或证据比另一个论点或证据更受青睐[着重部分由笔者标明]。

7.2.2 Judicial Statutory Interpretation in PRC

中国的司法法规解释

Historically, the theory of statutory interpretation in PRC law is usually found in the PRC's civil law. Lately, there has been a trend within PRC legal studies to develop the study of statutory interpretation as an independent subject.

从历史上看，中国法中的法律解释理论通常见于中国民法。最近，在中国法学研究中出现了将成文法解释作为一门独立学科进行研究的趋势。

The right of interpretation of the statutes/codes is treated as an independent right. This right has been monopolized by the legislative authority and to a limited extent by the judicial authorities at the highest level within the hierarchy. The judges' right to interpret the law is not available in the PRC legal system. Because the PRC is in the midst of colossal economic and social change due to accelerated economic changes, there is a need to adapt the codes to these powerful changes within society.

成文法/法典的解释权被视为一项独立的权利。这一权利一直被立法机关垄断，并在一定程度上被最高级别的司法机关垄断。在中国法体系中，法官没有解释法律的权利。由于经济变革的加速，中国正处于巨大的经济和社会变革之中，因此有必要调整法典以适应社会中这些强大的变革。

[778]See *English v Emery Reimbold and Strick Ltd* [2002] EWCA Civ 605.
见 English v Emery Reimbold and Strick Ltd [2002] EWCA Civ 605。

7.2.2.1 Historical Judicial Interpretation

历史司法解释

For centuries, it was the Emperor of ancient China that was vested with most of the legislative authority, and the power associated with the application of those laws.[779] Therefore, ancient Chinese sovereign emperors were a major source of law. Moreover, all the judicial branches existed at the central level only and were relatively not very advanced.[780]

几个世纪以来，中国古代皇帝被赋予了大部分立法权以及与这些法律的实施相关的权力。因此，中国古代的君主是法律的主要来源。此外，所有的司法部门都只存在于中央一级，相对来说并不发达。

In relatively modern times, the Qing Dynasty in 1905 introduced fairly modern judicial reforms.[781] However, there is some evidence from Xunzi's writings that the *purposive interpretation* that is currently followed in the common law systems was in some form already thought of in ancient China. He appears to have suggested that the 'spirit of law' (*yi*) was more important than the law in texts (*shu*). Xunzi was of the view that if one did not know the *yi* but was only aware of *shu*, no matter how broad the judges' knowledge was of the relevant law (*shu*), according to him, there would still be some gaps when handling actual cases.[782] However, it is likely that Xunzi was alluding to the concept at the philosophical level.

在相对近代的 1905 年，清朝实行了相当现代的司法改革。不过，荀子著作中的一些证据表明，普通法系目前遵循的目的解释在某种形式上已经在中国古代出现。他似乎认为"法的精神"（"义"）比法律条文（"书"）更重要。荀子认为，如果不知"义"而只知"书"，那么无论法官对相关法律（"书"）的了解有多广泛，在处理实际案件时仍会存在一些漏洞。不过，荀子很可能是在哲学层面上暗指这一概念。

For the sake of completeness, and as discussed earlier,[783] there

为完整起见，如前文所述，中国

---

[779]Jinfan Zhang, *Tradition of Chinese Law and Its Transformation in Late Qing (Zhonggua Falu de Chuantong Yu Jindai Zhuanxing)* (Beijing: Beijing Law Press, 1997), 21–34. Zhang was discussed in Zhenbao Jin, "From a Supplementary Legislator to a Legitimate Judicial Lawmaker - on the Role of the Supreme People's Court in Developing the Law in Mainland China," in *Towards a Chinese Civil Code: Comparative and Historical Perspectives*, Lei Chen and C H van Rhee (Dordrecht: Martinus Nijhoff Publishers, 2012), 30.
张晋藩，《中国法律的传统与近代转型》（《中外法学》，北京：北京法律出版社，1997 年），21-34页。金振宝在《从辅助立法者到合法的司法立法者--论最高人民法院在中国大陆法律发展中的作用》一文中论述了张晋藩，收录于《走向中国民法典：比较与历史视角下》，陈雷和 C H van Rhee 著，（多德雷赫特：Martinus Nijhoff 出版社, 2012年），第30页。

[780]Ibid., 92–103 and as discussed in Zhenbao Jin, "Role of SPC," 29.
同上，第92-103页，以及金振宝的论述，"SPC 的作用"，第29页。

[781]Sheng Zhang, "Institutions and Practice of Independent Adjudication of Dali Yuan in the Early History of the Republic of China (*Minchu Daliyuan Shenpan Duli de Zhidu Yu Shijian*)," *Journal of China University of Political Science and Law (Zhengfa Luntan) 20* (2002): 146, as discussed in Zhenbao Jin, "Role of SPC," 30.
张胜，《民国初年大理院独立审判的制度与实践》，《中国政法大学学报》（政法论丛）2002年第20期：146, 如金振宝所述，"SPC 的作用"，第30页。

[782]Wejen Chang, "Classical Chinese Jurisprudence and Development of Chinese Legal System" (2009–10), 235.
张维仁，《中国古典法学与中国法律制度的发展》（2009-10 年），第235页。

[783]Refer, Chapter 3, §3.4.1.1 for discussion on Confucians and Neo-Confucians and their philosophy.
有关儒家和新儒家及其哲学的讨论，请参阅第3章第3.4.1.1节。

was a concept of benevolence and humanity *(ren)* that was applied in many ways in practice in ancient China. This concept was framed on the Confucian, especially Neo-Confucian, school of thought.

古代有一个“仁”和“人道”(ren)的概念，并以多种方式应用于实践。这一概念是以儒家，尤其是新儒家学派的思想为框架的。

However, this took time and it was only in 1912, when the Guoming-dang government came into existence, that *Dali Yuan* was established with independent power for carrying out statutory interpretation. *Dali Yuan* had exclusive jurisdiction over what appears to be points of law from Provincial High Courts that were tasked to bridge the gaps between the old and new China of the time.[784] However, the reign of *Dali Yuan* did not last very long after the arrival of the new government of the PRC in 1949.

然而，这需要时间，直到1912年国民政府成立时，大理院才建立起来，拥有独立的法律解释权。大理院对各省高等法院的法律要点拥有专属管辖权，而各省高等法院的任务是弥合当时新旧中国之间的差距。然而，1949年中华人民共和国新政府成立后，大理院的统治并没有持续太久。

The principle of checks and balances between the various organs of government under the concept of separation of powers, soon gave way to the principles of *democratic centralism*.[785] The concept of democratic centralism was borrowed from *Marxism* and *Leninism*, where there was absolute freedom for the party members to argue issues, but once the decision had been made by the central leadership using the majority decision, it was then expected to be followed by everyone.[786]

三权分立概念下各政府机关之间的制衡原则很快让位于民主集中制原则。民主集中制的概念借鉴了马克思主义和列宁主义，党员有争论问题的绝对自由，但一旦中央领导层以多数决定的方式做出决定，就必须得到所有人的遵守。

At the time of the formation of the PRC, the Communist Party of China ('CPC') instructed that all existing laws were to be abolished; this was in relation to the *Abolition of the Six Laws of the Kuomintang Regime and the Establishment of the Judicial Principle in the Liberated Areas* (*Feichu Guomindang*

中华人民共和国成立时，中国共产党指示废除一切现行法律，这与《废除国民党政权的六法全书与确立解放区的司法原则的指示》有关。在完整的法律体系形成之前，现有法院的审

[784]Yuansheng Huang, "Sources of Law in Civil Adjudication of the Dali Yuan in the Early Republic of China (Minch Dali Yuan Minshi Shenpan Fayuan)," in *100 Selected Precedents of the Dali Yuan (Dali Yuan Minshi Panli Baixuan)*, ed. Yuansheng Huang (Taibei: Wunan Book Co. Ltd., 2009), 60. It was further discussed in Sun Jin, "On the Practical Level of Judicial Interpretation of the Law - Reasoning Made by Judges in Judgments," 30. http://www.court.gmw.cn/html/article/201212/28/115659.shtml, accessed on July, 9, 2016. Translation done at the authors' request.
黄远生：《民国初年大理院民事裁判的法律渊源》，载《大理院判例选编100 种》，黄远生编（台北：五南图书有限公司，2009 年），第60页。孙进：《论司法解释的实践层面--法官在判决书中的说理》，30。

[785]Dingjina Cai, *History and Reforms: The Legal History of the New China (Lishiyu Biange: Xin Zhongguo Fazhi Jianshe de Licheng)* (Beijing: Press of China's University of Political Science and Law, 1999), 2., as discussed in Sun Jin, "On the Practical Level of Judicial Interpretation of the Law - Reasoning Made by Judges in Judgments," 30.
蔡定剑，《历史与改革：新中国法制建设的历程》（北京：中国政法大学出版社，1999），2，如孙进所述：《论司法释法的实践层面--法官在判决书中的说理》，第30页。

[786]The concept of democratic centralism is enshrined in Art. 3 of *Constitution of PRC 1982. Constitution of PRC 1982*, Art. 3.
民主集中制的概念载于1982年《中华人民共和国宪法》第3条。

de Liufa Quanshu yu Queli Jiefangqu de Sifa Yuanze de Zhishi).[787] The adjudicative works carried out by the existing courts had to follow and rely on the policies of the CPC in addition to following the guidelines, laws, regulations and resolutions promulgated by the People's government and the People's Liberation Army, before a complete legal system came into existence.

判工作除了遵循人民政府和人民解放军颁布的方针、法律、法规和决议之外，还必须遵循和依靠中国共产党的政策。

The above instructions led to the Supreme People's Court ('SPC') taking greater responsibility and gradually clarifying various policies. However, it was not until 1977, when economic development in the PRC accelerated, that the SPC began issuing more Opinions on many new economic and civil laws, coming into prominence as a result.

根据上述指示，最高人民法院承担了更大的责任，并逐步明确了各项政策。然而，直到 1977 年，中华人民共和国的经济发展加速，最高人民法院才开始就许多新的经济和民事法律发布更多意见，并因此崭露头角。

Under the *PRC Constitution of 1954*, the power of judicial interpretation was vested in the Standing Committee of National People's Congress (hereinafter 'NPCSC').[788] Even when the Constitution was altered in 1982, the power of judicial interpretation remained vested in NPCSC.[789]

根据 1954 年《中华人民共和国宪法》，司法解释权属于全国人民代表大会常务委员会（以下简称 "全国人大常委会"）。即使在 1982 年修改《宪法》时，司法解释权仍然属于全国人大常委会。

Pursuant to the Resolution of the NPCSC on *Statutory Interpretation of 1955*,[790] the SPC was conferred with the *delegated power* of statutory interpretation. This delegated power was later confirmed through another *Resolution of 1981*.[791] SPC has utilized this delegated power actively, and many scholars have commented that this was a significant contribution towards building a complete legal system in the modern PRC.[792] It is important to discuss the key points from

根据 1955 年《全国人大常委会关于法律解释的决议》，最高人民法院被授予法律解释权。这一授权后来通过 1981 年的另一项决议得到确认。最高人民法院积极利用这一授权，许多学者评论说，这是对现代中华人民共和国建立完整法律体系的重大贡献。我们有必要讨论一下 1981 年决议中的以下要点：

---

787 It was promulgated by the Central Committee of the CCP in February1949.
它由中共中央于 1949 年 2 月颁布。

788 See Art. 31 of *Constitution of PRC 1954.* 见1954年《中华人民共和国宪法》第31条。

789 See Art. 67 of *Constitution of PRC 1982.* 见1982年《中华人民共和国宪法》第67条。

790 See *Resolution of the NPCSC on Statutory Interpretations, 1955.*
见 1955 年全国人大常委会关于法定解释的决议。

791 See *Resolution of the NPCSC on Strengthening the Work of Statutory Interpretations, 1981*, adopted on June, 10, 1981.
参见1981年6月10日通过的《1981 年全国人大常委会关于加强法规解释工作的决议》。

792 National People's Congress, *Work Report of the 10th Standing Committee of the National People's Congress of 8 March 2008* (Beijing), where Banggu Wu while addressing the 2nd Plenary Session of the1st Conference of the 11th NPC C stressed the need for a complete socialist legal system with Chinese characteristics composed of the Constitution of the PRC, national laws, administrative regulations and local regulations.

this *Resolution of 1981,* which are as follows:

- ♦ All articles in laws requiring further definition or supplementary stipulations shall be interpreted or stipulated by NPC Standing Committee pursuant to the law;
- ♦ 凡法律中需要进一步界定或补充规定的条款，由全国人大常委会根据法律作出解释或规定；

- ♦ All questions arising from courts' civil trials concerning the specific application of laws and decrees shall be interpreted by SPC.
- ♦ 法院民事审判中涉及法律、法令具体应用的问题，由最高人民法院解释。

However, the SPC's power of statutory interpretation under their delegated power is not to be confused with power in relation to case precedent as seen in common law jurisdictions such as England & Wales.

然而，最高人民法院根据其授权进行法律解释的权力不能与英格兰和威尔士等普通法司法管辖区的判例解释权相混淆。

According to the authors, the SPC is now very similar to a legislative body, albeit supplementary. It is interesting to note the comments of Jin, who states:

笔者认为，最高人民法院现在与立法机构非常相似，尽管是补充机构。值得注意的是金振保的评论：

> Strictly speaking, this practice is indeed *de facto* law-making process and the SPC is playing the role of a supplementary legislative body, not subject to any substantive and procedural restriction stipulated in Law of Legislation of the People's Republic of China of 2000.[793]

> 严格说来，这种做法确实是事实上的立法过程，最高人民法院扮演的是补充立法机构的角色，不受 2000 年《中华人民共和国立法法》规定的任何实体和程序限制。

The delegated power of the SPC as a supplementary legislative body is, in practice, not even restricted by any substantive and procedural restrictions as prescribed in the *Law of Legislation 2000,*[794] in particular, section 4, Articles 39-42. This issue has been discussed by Jin.[795]

最高人民法院作为补充立法机关的授权，在实践中甚至不受 2000 年《立法法》，特别是第 4 部分第 39-42 条规定的任何实体和程序限制。金振保曾对这一问题进行过讨论。 除 1955 年和 1981 年的两项决议外，最高人民法院的

全国人民代表大会，2008年3月8日第十届全国人民代表大会常务委员会工作报告（北京）， 吴邦国在第十一届全国人民代表大会第一次会议第二次全体会议上的讲话中强调，要建立健全 由中华人民共和国宪法、国家法律、行政法规和地方性法规组成的中国特色社会主义法律体系。

793 Zhenbao Jin, "Role of SPC," 31. 金振保：《最高人民法院的作用》，第31页。

794 See *Law of Legislation of PRC 2000* (as revised in 2015).
参见2000年《中华人民共和国立法法》（2015年修订）。

795 Zhenbao Jin, "Role of SPC," 31. 金振保：《最高人民法院的作用》，31。

Apart from the two resolutions of 1955 and 1981, the delegated power of SPC is enhanced through another law that was promulgated in 1979, and then amended in 2006.[796] The SPC has also promulgated *Several Provisions on Judicial Interpretation Work (Guangyu Sifa Jieshi Gongzuo de Ruogan Guiding) in 1997 (as amended by '2007* Provisions'),[797] which itself enhanced the power of the SPC to carry out judicial statutory interpretation on various issues such as specific application of law for the People's Courts in their adjudicative work, the legal effect of the judicial interpretations promulgated by the SPC, and the procedure for enacting judicial interpretations.[798]

授权还通过1979年颁布的另一项法律得到加强，该法律随后于2006年进行修订。最高人民法院还于1997年颁布了《关于司法解释工作的若干规定》(经《2007 年规定》修订)，该规定本身加强了最高人民法院就人民法院审判工作中的具体法律适用、最高人民法院颁布的司法解释的法律效力以及司法解释的制定程序等问题进行司法解释的权力。

The *2007 provisions* introduced a few democratic norms in the judicial interpretations. According to these *Provisions, both 1997 and as amended in 2007*, the judicial interpretations of the SPC are expressly declared to have the force of law and shall take effect when they are promulgated. Thus this date is different from the date when the law was promulgated. Furthermore, if the statutory interpretation is not correct, the process by which the SPC can modify the incorrect version is very cumbersome. The authors find it chaotic and is supported in this opinion by Jin, who also feels that process needs improvement.[799]

2007年的规定在司法解释中引入了一些民主规范。根据1997年和2007年修订的这些规定，最高人民法院的司法解释被明确宣布为具有法律效力，并在颁布时生效。因此，这一日期不同于法律颁布的日期。此外，如果法律解释不正确，最高人民法院修改不正确版本的程序非常繁琐。提交人认为这一程序混乱不堪，金也支持提交人的观点，他也认为这一程序需要改进。

[796]See, Art. 33 of *Organic Law of People's Courts of People's Republic of China 1979 (as amended in 1983). Organic Law of Peoples Courts of People's Republic of China 1979 (as Amended in 1983).*
见1979年《中华人民共和国人民法院组织法》（1983年修订）第33条。1979年《中华人民共和国人民法院组织法》（1983年修订）。
[797]*Several Provisions on Judicial Interpretation Work (Guanyu Sifa Jieshi Gongzuo de Ruogan Guiding) 2007 Fa Fa [2007] No. 12.* This Provision repealed Rules of the *Supreme People's Court on the Work of Judicial Interpretation [1997], Fa Fa [1997] No. 15.*
《关于司法解释工作的若干规定》2007法发[2007]12号。该《规定》废止了《最高人民法院关于司法解释工作的规定》[1997]，法发[1997]15号。
[798]Jinfan Zhang, *Tradition of Chinese Law and Its Transformation in Late Qing (Zhonggua Falu de Chuantong Yu Jindai Zhuanxing)* (Beijing: Beijing Law Press, 1997), 39.
张晋藩：《中国法律的传统及其在晚清的转型》（《中外法学》，北京：北京法律出版社，1997年），第39页。
[799]Zhenbao Jin, "Role of SPC," 43. 金振保：《最高人民法院的作用》，43。

The SPC, according to the *Provisions 2007*, may promulgate four types of judicial interpretations, namely, *jieshi* (Interpretation), *guiding* (Provisions), *pifu* (Reply) and *jueding* (Decision), all of which have the effect of law and shall be published in the Gazette of the SPC. Briefly, each of the four types of judicial interpretations will be discussed below:[800]

根据2007年《规定》，最高人民法院可以颁布四类司法解释，即解释、规定、批复和决定，所有这些司法解释均具有法律效力，并应在最高人民法院公报上公布。下文将简要讨论这四种司法解释：

- *Jieshi* is the most important type of statutory interpretation. It refers to judicial interpretations of the specific statute, or interpretations that guide the application of law in special types of cases or issues. For example — *Opinions on Several Issues concerning the Implementation of General Principles of Civil Law of 1988,* the *Interpretation of Several Issues concerning the Implementation of Contract Law of 1999* and the *Interpretation of the Securities Law of 2001.*[801]

- 解释是最重要的法律解释类型。它是指对具体法规的司法解释，或指导特殊类型案件或问题的法律适用的解释。例如1988年《关于贯彻执行〈民法通则〉若干问题的意见》、1999年《关于执行〈合同法〉若干问题的解释》和2001年《证券法》解释。

- *Guiding* rules are enacted to regulate issues concerned mostly with non-substantive issues such as Procedural rules for the relevant substantive law, such as *2007 provisions.* However, the distinction between *guiding* and *jieshi* is not very clear.

- 制定指导性规则主要是为了规范非实体性问题，如2007年条款等相关实体法的程序规则。然而，指导性规则和碣石之间的区别并不十分明确。

- *Pifu* refers to judicial interpretations made in response to inquiries from the Higher People's Courts and Military courts of the People's Liberation Army concerning legal issues in pending cases.

- 批复指的是针对高级人民法院和中国人民解放军军事法院就未决案件中的法律问题提出的询问而作出的司法解释。

- *Jueding* is made for the purpose of modifying or nullifying the existing SPC's judicial interpretations.

- 决定的目的是修改或废止最高人民法院现有的司法解释。

---

[800] Ibid., 41. 同上，41。
[801] Ibid., 40. 同上，40。

The lower courts do not have any power of statutory interpretation; all the delegated power is limited completely to the SPC. The reason cited by PRC scholars for this lack of power in the lower courts is that it is "to secure uniform statutory interpretations among all the courts at different levels."[802]

下级法院没有任何法律解释权，所有授权完全限于最高人民法院。对于下级法院没有解释权，中国学者提出的理由是"为了保证各级法院对法律的统一解释"。

In this Chapter, it is important to consider the jurisprudential aspect of statutory interpretation in the PRC. The judiciary in the PRC is not a separate branch and there is no concept of separation of powers. However, the way the SPC carries out statutory interpretation, it is more like an extension of the NPC. PRC scholars have described the jurisprudence of judicial interpretation as being based on the Chinese socialist political system, where the "principle of '*democratic centralism*', or the principle of the unity of deliberation and execution"[803] prevails. This means that the SPC implements the decisions of the NPC, which are then supervised by the NPC.

在本章中，重要的是要考虑中国法律解释的法理方面。中国的司法机构不是一个独立的部门，也没有三权分立的概念。然而，从最高人民法院执行法律解释的方式来看，它更像是全国人大的延伸。中国学者将司法解释的法理描述为建立在中国社会主义政治制度的基础之上，即"'民主集中制'原则，即审议与执行相统一的原则"。这意味着最高人民法院执行全国人大的决定，然后由全国人大进行监督。

7.2.2.2 Current Practice of Judicial Statutory Interpretation in PRC

中国司法解释法规的现行做法

From the above discussion,[804] it is clear that the SPC has been delegated the responsibility for carrying out statutory interpretation for a great many legislations, resolutions, and customary practices. SPC \ actively utilizes this power to guide the lower courts. However, as discussed above, there is no power available to the lower courts with regards to statutory interpretation.

从上述讨论中可以看出，最高人民法院被赋予了对大量立法、决议和习惯做法进行法律解释的职责。最高人民法院积极利用这一权力来指导下级法院。然而，如上所述，下级法院在法律解释方面没有任何权力。

In order to resolve substantive disputes, PRC legal philosophers have divided the practice of statutory interpretation to two levels. First is the *narrow* level, limited to interpreting the legal terminology and sentences of the PRC code. On the other hand, at the *broader* level, statutory interpretation is done in the

为了解决实体争议，中国法律哲学家将法律解释实践分为两个层面。首先是狭义层面，仅限于解释中华人民共和国法典中的法律术语和句子。另一方面，在广义层面，则是在人、

[802]Ibid., 39. 同上，39。
[803]Ibid., 45. 同上，45。
[804]Refer Chapter 7, §7.2.2.1. 参见第7章第7.2.2.1节。

broader context of people, society, concepts, and so on.

社会、观念等更广泛的背景下进行法律解释。

The above is an example of dual centers of statutory interpretation, both with the NPC and SPC. While the SPC has been active in issuing guidelines, the same cannot be said of the NPC in relation to their task of issuing statutory interpretations. Therefore, the guidance given by SPC is very general in nature, while the judges in the lower courts in practice have to deal with the issue of statutory interpretation in a particular case with very specific facts. Therefore, whatever judicial interpretations are available from NPC or SPC provide only general guidance. In addition, these interpretations, in practice, ignore the judicial interpretations that may be required in specific cases in the lower courts.

以上是全国人大和最高人民法院法定解释双中心的例子。虽然最高人民法院一直积极发布指导意见，但全国人大在发布法律解释的任务方面却并非如此。因此，最高人民法院给出的指导意见非常笼统，而下级法院的法官在实践中必须根据非常具体的事实处理具体案件中的法律解释问题。因此，全国人大或最高人民法院的司法解释只能提供一般性指导。此外，这些解释实际上忽视了下级法院在具体案件中可能需要的司法解释。

The judge's role in dealing with cases in any jurisdiction is usually a three-step process, which is first to understand the facts of the commercial disputes, then apply the relevant law with proper interpretation applicable to material facts, and finally reach a conclusion in law.

在任何司法管辖区，法官处理案件的角色通常是三步曲，即首先了解商事纠纷的事实，然后适用相关法律并对重要事实作出适当解释，最后得出法律结论。

When judges deal with a legal case, they could either be looking for relevant facts from the points of law, or they could be looking at points of law to find material facts. A question arises: in a case before the lower courts in the PRC, is the application of law to the facts any different from the process of judicial interpretation?

法官在处理法律案件时，既可以从法律要点中寻找相关事实，也可以从法律要点中寻找重要事实。这就产生了一个问题：在中国下级法院审理的案件中，根据事实适用法律与司法解释的过程有什么不同吗?

As discussed above, the judges in the lower courts are not recognized in law as persons having any power to carry out statutory interpretation in the current PRC legal system. However, as also discussed above, statutory interpretation is inseparable from the application of law in the judges' work in the courts. At the same time, to assist the lower courts, there is a constitutional structure and the institution of '*replies*', which enables the lower courts to seek clarifications from the SPC.

如上所述，在中国现行法律制度中，下级法院的法官在法律上不被承认为有权进行法律解释的人。然而，正如上文所述，在法官的法院工作中，法律解释与法律适用密不可分。同时，为了协助下级法院，宪法结构和“答辩”制度使下级法院能够要求最高人民法院作出澄清。

In addition, as the limits of lower court judges in relation to

此外，由于下级法院法官在法定

statutory implementation is clear, there is also a provision of '*appeal on points of law*'. In the process of appeal on points of law, either party may have a chance to get a legal opinion from the Court of Appeal, or to have them checked by the Supreme Court.

执行方面的限制是明确的，因此还规定了“法律问题上诉”。在就法律问题提出上诉的过程中，任何一方都有机会获得上诉法院的法律意见，或由最高法院对其进行核查。

Due to this conflict in day-to-day work, there is a big difference in practice and theory of statutory interpretation. Is this a reason why many of the judgments in the PRC legal system are short on reasons, as compared to the English Legal system or even other civil jurisdictions? The paucity of reasons in the judgment can leave the litigants unsatisfied, and in the authors' view can even affect the legitimacy of the courts.

由于日常工作中的这种冲突，法律解释的实践和理论存在着差异。与英国法律制度甚至其他法域相比，中国法律制度中的许多判决缺乏理由，这是否是一个原因？判决书中理由的匮乏会让当事人不满意，笔者认为甚至会影响法院的合法性。

Another problem that has been on the rise in the PRC courts in recent years due to the above problem is something called *tong'an bu tong' pan* (similar cases, different rulings) .[805] It is very important to note what Jin has said about the current practice:

由于上述问题，近年来在中国法院出现的另一个问题是所谓的“同案不同判”。我们有必要了解一下金对当前做法的看法：

> It can be safely said that PRC courts, including the SPC, have not developed a consistent and predictable pattern or theory of legal interpretation. The most important reason might be that the judiciary in PRC is not an independent branch of state power.[806]

> 可以说，包括最高人民法院在内的中国法院尚未形成一致的、可预测的法律解释模式或理论。最重要的原因可能是中国的司法机构并非独立的国家权力机构。

Furthermore, the PRC courts are obliged to apply not only the laws and regulations, but also philosophies applicable at that particular time, or policies that have been adopted by NPC and/or CPC.[807] In a famous case in Shandong High Court,[808] a claimant was deprived of his constitutional right to education because a defendant went as an imposter in the Claimant's name. The judges, before they could receive clarification from the SPC, were of the view that civil law cannot be used to protect the claimant's constitutional rights. Scholars were of the

此外，中国法院不仅有义务适用法律和法规，还有义务适用当时适用的理念或全国人大和/或全国政协通过的政策。在山东高级法院审理的一起著名案件中，一名原告被剥夺了宪法赋予的受教育权，原因是一名被告冒用原告的名义。法官在得到最高人民法院的澄清之前，认为不能用民法来保护原告的宪法权利。学者们认为，

[805]Zhenbao Jin, "Role of SPC," 31. 金振保：《最高人民法院的作用》，31。

[806]Ibid., 34. 同上，34。

[807]Ibid. 同上。

[808]See a famous case of *Qi Yuling* of 2001 and its discussion in Zhenbao Jin, "Role of SPC," 34. 参见2001年齐玉苓的一个著名案例及其在金振保：《最高人民法院的作用》一文中的讨论，第34页。

view that there was an Article available in *General Principles of Civil law* 1986,[809] which could have been used by the judges to find a remedy in this case. The lack of discretionary power came to the forefront.

1986年《民法通则》中有一条规定，法官本可以利用这条规定找到本案的补救办法。缺乏自由裁量权的问题凸显出来。

In fact, none of the judges at any level mentioned that provision in their judgment.[810] Was it the judges' unwillingness to take the initiative? Was it the fear of punishment or the risk of appeal, or was it that the local committee had advised them to ignore the relevant article? In England & Wales, the active lawyers would have ensured that the judges take into consideration any relevant statutes or any principles that could be argued in the legal framework.

事实上，各级法官都没有在判决书中提及该条款。是法官们不愿意采取主动？是害怕惩罚或上诉风险，还是地方委员会建议他们忽略相关条款？在英格兰和威尔士，积极的律师会确保法官考虑到任何相关法规或任何可以在法律框架内论证的原则。

On the end of the spectrum is the accusation of judicial activism: by enacting *in abstracto* judicial interpretations, the SPC has been actually playing the role of legislator.[811] However, over the years, before issuing *Opinions*, the SPC has been seeking the views of the public. In the authors' view, it is difficult to comprehend and reconcile with the judges' role, where the judges themselves take public opinion as a benchmark to give their Opinion. In the authors' view, the SPC's role is rapidly moving into the area of legislature, and it is clearly an example of judicial activism. However, it seems this is not condemned by the NPC or other stakeholders, or even the public.

另一种指责则是司法能动主义：通过抽象地颁布司法解释，最高人民法院实际上扮演了立法者的角色。然而，多年来，最高人民法院在发布《意见》之前，一直在征求公众的意见。笔者认为，这与法官的角色难以理解和协调，法官本身就是以民意为基准来提出意见的。笔者认为，最高人民法院的角色正在迅速进入立法领域，这显然是司法能动主义的一个例子。然而，这似乎并没有受到全国人大或其他利益相关者甚至公众的谴责。

7.3 Doctrine of Precedents

先例原则

[809] See Art 106(2) of the *General Principles of Civil Law 1986*, Order No. 37 of the President of the People's Republic of China (and as revised by *Decision of the Standing Committee of the National People's Congress on Revising Certain Laws 2009*), which specifies: "Any citizen or legal person who, with fault attributable to them, infringes upon the property of the state or any collective, or upon the property, personal or family interest of other persons, shall bear civil liability."
参见1986年《民法通则》第106条第2款规定："公民、法人侵犯国家的、集体的财产，或者侵犯他人财产、人身、家庭利益，有过错的，应当承担民事责任"；"公民、法人因过错侵害国家的、集体的财产，侵害他人财产、人身、家庭利益的，应当承担民事责任"。

[810] See for discussion on the case in Zhenbao Jin, "Role of SPC," 35.
参见金振保：《最高人民法院的作用》，35中的案例讨论。

[811] Zhenbao Jin, "Role of SPC," 41. 金振保：《最高人民法院的作用》，第41页。

The role of case precedents is instrumental in the practice of law in most jurisdictions. The doctrine of *stare decisis* has been instrumental in the development of common law,[812] and in a way it also limits judicial discretion. The judges in later cases must follow the law developed in the previous cases. Judicial precedent promotes certainty, consistency; expectations of the litigants are managed, and, in a way, this assists in developing a rule of law.[813] Precedents are "prima facie commitments that future cases will be decided accordingly".[814]

判例在大多数司法管辖区的法律实践中都发挥着重要作用。判例原则在普通法的发展过程中发挥了重要作用，在某种程度上也限制了司法自由裁量权。法官在以后的案件中必须遵循以前案件中形成的法律。司法先例促进了确定性和一致性；诉讼当事人的期望得到了管理，这在某种程度上有助于法治的发展。先例是“对未来案件作出相应裁决的初步承诺”。

Case precedent ensures that the discretionary power of judges is curtailed, and at the same time it assists in the evolution of the law. Scholars have argued for a long time as to what comes first – legal reasoning or the application of case precedents. One school of thought argued that the common law developed as the judges in medieval England could not remember their reasons and had to cite cases, but another school of thought argued that it was the common law that demanded that reasons in the judgments develop.[815]

判例确保法官的自由裁量权受到限制，同时也有助于法律的演变。长期以来学者们一直在争论究竟是法律推理先行还是案例先例先行。一派认为，由于中世纪英国的法官记不住自己的理由，不得不引用案例，因此普通法得到了发展；但另一派则认为是普通法要求判决中的理由得到发展。

In simple words, it means that the judges in other courts, when deciding later cases, must enforce the rules established by the courts in earlier cases. This rule will be applied based upon the hierarchy of the courts in jurisdictions. The doctrine of precedents has been criticised because the judges seem to be making law through their judgments, which are then followed by the lower courts, when in fact, the judges should always be subordinate to the legislators. The legislators are the right people to balance different political-interest groups; only then can they formulate the policy reasons behind much legislation.

简言之，这意味着其他法院的法官在裁决以后的案件时，须执行法院在以前的案件中制定的规则。这一规则将根据司法管辖区法院的等级制度来适用。先例理论之所以受到批评，是因为法官似乎是在通过自己的判决来制定法律，然后由下级法院遵照执行，而事实上，法官应始终服从立法者。立法者是平衡不同政治利益集团

---

[812]Henry de Bracton in the thirteenth century published the rulings in over two thousand cases, which greatly assisted in rationalising the law of that time in England. The publication of a yearly book started from then. Slowly, more case reports were published with greater accuracy. With the advent of positivism, the idea that if there is no law by legislature, then the judgment must be taken as the law, also contributed to its development. For further discussion on this topic, see Lundmark, *Divide between Common and Civil Law*, 347–9.
13世纪，亨利-德-巴克顿出版了两千多个案例的判决书，极大地促进了当时英国法律的合理化。从那时起，每年出版一本书。慢慢地，更多更准确的案例报告得以出版。随着实证主义的出现，“如果立法机关没有法律，则必须将判决视为法律”的观点也促进了其发展。关于这一主题的进一步讨论，见伦德马克,《普通法与民法之分》，第347-349页。

[813]Cohen, "Judges' Reasons," 508. 科恩：《法官的理由》，第508页。

[814]Cohen, "Judges' Reasons," 509. Cohen discussed the view of Frederick Schauer about the importance of giving reasons.
科恩：《法官的理由》，第509页。科恩讨论了弗雷德里克-绍尔关于说明理由的重要性的观点。

[815]Cohen, "Judges' Reasons," 509. 科恩：《法官的理由》，第509页。

In addition, it has been argued that if a policy reason is introduced into a case by the judges, then it is arguable that a new policy reason cited in a case is actually a new law. Furthermore, it should be retroactively applicable to the facts that had happened before. [816]

的合适人选，只有这样，他们才能制定出许多立法背后的政策理由。此外，有观点认为，如法官在案件中引入政策理由，那么可以说案件中引用的新政策理由实际上就是新的法律。此外，它应追溯适用于以前发生的事实。

It is also very common that when the cases go to appeal, the judgments are written by many judges. Not infrequently, the judges differ and argue vehemently whether the principle at stake is actually a principle in law, and whether such a principle should even be considered by them. At stake might be the principle obtained from a previous case. These are all the challenges and criticisms that the doctrine of precedents must overcome. Nonetheless, even in the continental system, such criticisms are a part of the daily life of the courts at the level of adjudication.

案件上诉时，判决书由多名法官撰写的情况也很常见。法官们对所涉及的原则是否实际上是一项法律原则，甚至是否应由他们考虑这一原则，意见不一，争论激烈的情况并不少见。所涉及的可能是在以前的案件中获得的原则。这些都是先例理论必须克服的挑战和批评。然而，即使在大陆法系，这些批评也是法院在裁决层面日常生活的一部分。

7.3.1 Doctrine of Stare Decisis in England & Wales

英格兰和威尔士的遵循先例原则

For centuries in England, the binding value of a case was supposed to be limited to the parties only, and any case was at best the evidence of the law. Mansfield, a famous English jurist in the eighteenth century had said, "Precedent though it be evidence of law, is not the law itself, much less the whole of the law."[817] Postema defined the concept of common law as follows:

几个世纪以来，在英国，案件的约束力被认为只限于当事人，任何案件充其量只是法律的证据。十八世纪英国著名法学家曼斯菲尔德曾说过："先例虽然是法律的证据，但它本身并不是法律，更不是法律的全部"。波斯特马将普通法的概念定义为：

> The authority and force of any component of the common law depends on its integration into the framework of the whole and its satisfaction of a shared

> 普通法的任何组成部分的权威和效力都取决于其是否融入了整体框架，

[816]Penner, "Law and Adjudication," 364–8, where Dworkin's 'Right Thesis' was discussed and quoted. The quote is originally from R. Dworkin, "Hard Cases," *Harv. L. Rev.* 88, no. 6 (1975): 1057–1109.
彭纳，"法律与裁决"，364-8，其中讨论并引用了德沃金的 "权利论"。该引文最初出自 R. 德沃金，"疑难的案件，" 哈佛法律评论. 88, no.6 (1972)：1057-1109.

[817]Mansfield was quoted in Postema, "Classical Common Law Jurisprudence - II," 14.
曼斯菲尔德的话引自波斯特马：《古典普通法法理学 - II》，第14页。

sense of reasonableness rooted in this framework [emphasis added]. If a judicial ruling is entrenched and regarded to be peremptory, thereby blocking all subsequent assessment of its reasonableness and coherence with the whole …, Hedley argued, then the common law in general could no longer claim authority.[818]

是否满足了植根于这一框架的共同的合理性意识[着重部分由笔者标明]。赫德利认为，如果一项司法裁决根深蒂固并被视为强制性的，从而阻碍了随后对其合理性和与整体一致性的所有评估……，那么普通法总体上就不能再声称具有权威性。

Many jurisprudents have argued that the *principle of fairness* ensures that all cases should be treated in the same manner. This is the most important reason for the evolution of the doctrine of *stare decisis*. On the practical side, the publication from 1865 onwards of *Law Reports* supervised by the judges in the cases, a few private case reports such as All England Reports from 1936, and weekly law reports from 1953, also contributed in development of the common law. Since 2001, the judgments in the higher courts have been issued with neutral citations. However, there are many unreported cases. In the words of Park, CJ in *Mirehouse v Rennell* (1833) 1 Cl. & Fin. 527, "Precedent must be adhered to for the sake of developing the law as a science." This demonstrates the importance of case precedents in England & Wales.

许多法学家认为，公平原则确保所有案件都应以同样的方式处理。这也是"遵循先例"理论演变的最重要原因。在实践方面，自 1865 年起出版的由案件法官监督的《法律报告》、一些私人案件报告（如 1936 年的《全英格兰报告》）以及 1953 年的《每周法律报告》也为普通法的发展做出了贡献。自 2001 年起，高级法院的判决书都附有中性引文。然而，还有许多未报告的案例。用首席大法官帕克在 Mirehouse v Rennell (1833) 1 Cl. & Fin. 527 一案中的话，"为了将法律发展成为一门科学，必须遵守先例"。这表明了判例在英格兰和威尔士的重要性。

There is no statutory code/rule stating that the lower courts must follow the case law from the higher appellate court. However, there is only one statutory rule,[819] which is that the rulings from the Court of Justice of the European Union on the issue of Human rights will be binding on the courts in England & Wales. In addition, the highest court of England & Wales is the only court that was bound by its own courts' previous decisions unless the previous decision has been made *per incuriam*.[820] However, from 1966 onwards,[821] the House of

没有成文法典/规则规定下级法院必须遵循上级上诉法院的判例法。然而，只有一条法定规则，即欧盟法院就人权问题做出的裁决对英格兰和威尔士的法院具有约束力。此外，英格兰和威尔士的最高法院是唯一受本国法院先前裁决约束的法院，除非先前的裁决是根据"失察"（per incuriam）作出的。然而，从 1966 年起，上议院通过

[818]Postema, "Classical Common Law Jurisprudence - II," 14.
波斯特马：《古典普通法法理学 - II》，第14页。
[819]See sec. 3(1) *European Communities Act 1972*.
见1972年《欧洲共同体法》第3(1)条。
[820]See *London Street Tramways v London County Council* [1898] AC 375. The meaning of *per incuriam* is that the previous important case of statute was not brought to the notice of the House of Lords when the previous decision was made in the same court.
见 London Street Tramways v London County Council [1898] AC 375。per incuriam "的含义是，上议院在同一法院作出先前裁决时，并未注意到先前的重要成文法案例。
[821] See *Practice Statement (Judicial Precedent) (HL)* 1966, [1966] 3 All ER 77, [1966] 1 WLR 1234.
参见《惯例说明》（司法先例）(*HL*) 1966, [1966] 3 All ER 77, [1966] 1 WLR 1234.

Lords decided through this *Practice Statement* that they can overrule their previous decisions, if there was a mistake in previous decisions or if there are changes in the society, subject to their exercising caution by not disturbing retrospectively the basis of contracts, settlements of property, and fiscal arrangements.

《惯例说明》决定，如果以前的判决有误或社会发生变化，他们可以推翻以前的判决，但必须谨慎行事，不得追溯性地扰乱合同、财产清算和财政安排的基础。

Therefore in 1966, the House of Lords decided on their own to develop their own rule without waiting for the legislature to legislate on this aspect of judicial activities. The Court of Appeal, an appellate court lower than the House of Lords (currently Supreme Court), is bound to follow its own judgment with a few exceptions.

因此，在 1966 年，上议院自行决定制定自己的规则，而不等待立法机关就司法活动的这一方面进行立法。上诉法院是低于上议院的上诉法院（现为最高法院），除少数例外情况外，必须遵循自己的判决。

It is important to note that only the *ratio decidendi*, the legal reasoning aspect of the decision, is *binding* on the courts within this system of judicial precedents. Any observations made by the judges on any legal question or issue, but not arising in such a manner as requiring a decision, is known as *obiter dictum* (meaning 'by the way', an incidental remark). These observations are *persuasive in nature but are not binding* on the lower courts.

值得注意的是，在这一司法判例系统中，只有判决的法律推理部分对法院具有约束力。法官就任何法律问题或议题发表的任何意见，但并非以需要做出裁决的方式出现，均被称为"附带意见"（意为"顺便说一下"，一种附带评论）。这些意见具有说服力，但对下级法院没有约束力。

In practice, in order to apply a case precedent, similar facts in a decided case are first analysed with reference to the facts in the case before the judges, or it may involve distinguishing the facts between these two or more cases. There is no set methodology but will depend on the judges' understanding of law. The methodology to find an applicable relevant statute(s) for the particular circumstances of a case is not that different from this methodology of finding relevant cases.

在实践中，为适用案例先例，首先要参照法官审理的案件中的事实对已决案件中的类似事实进行分析，或者对这两个或更多案件中的事实进行区分。没有固定的方法，而是取决于法官对法律的理解。针对案件的特定情况寻找适用的相关法规的方法与寻找相关案例的方法并无太大区别。

It is important to appreciate that there has been a debate that by using this doctrine, the judges have been making law by back door and, as discussed in Chapter 3 §3.2.4, are in fact bringing their own world view into the reasoning. This is a critical issue in cases where the judges are not selected from every section of society or when some section of society is prevented, due to various reasons, from becoming judges. This is important as

重要的是要认识到，有一种争论认为，通过使用这一理论，法官一直在走后门制定法律，正如第 3 章第 3.2.4 节所讨论的那样，实际上是将自己的世界观带入了推理之中。在法官并非从社会

the judges are not elected by the populace. The judgments and legal reasoning in the cases are described in great detail and are accordingly a good source for the lawyers/academics to learn the legal reasons, including the facts of the case. The cases are also important for training of judges within the judicial system.

各阶层选出，或社会某些阶层因各种原因无法成为法官的情况下，这是一个关键问题。这一点非常重要，因为法官并非由民众选举产生。案例中的判决和法律推理描述得非常详细，因此是律师/学者了解法律原因（包括案件事实）的良好来源。这些案例对于司法系统内的法官培训也很重要。

7.3.2 Guiding Case System in China

中国的指导性案例制度

In this section, the authors will first analyse the history and tradition of a case guidance system in ancient China to decide the disputes. The author will then proceed to analyse the current guiding case system in the PRC.

在本节中，笔者将首先分析中国古代以案定纷的案例指导制度的历史和传统。然后，笔者将分析中国现行的案例指导制度。

7.3.2.1 History of Case Guidance (pre-PRC)

案例指导的历史(中华人民共和国成立前)

In ancient China, even though the feudal system and legislative activities were not fully established, there were still cases

在中国古代，尽管封建制度和立法活动尚未完全确立，但自西周以来，每

reported from every dynasty since the West Zhou dynasty.[822] These cases continue to have a general effect on other cases. One group of cases is from the era before the Qin Dynasty,[823] at which time not only were the Codes not fully shaped in the context of law, but the societal rules were also not fully fashioned.

个朝代都有案例报道。这些案例对其他案例仍有普遍影响。一类是秦朝以前的案例，在那个时代，不仅法典在法律方面没有完全成型，而且社会规则也没有完全形成。

On the other hand, there were cases that used to have a general effect only, and originated between the Qin to Qing Dynasties, when all the power was concentrated in the hands of the emperors. During that time, there were no clear concepts such as fairness, especially procedural fairness, and in fact the statutory system was just evolving with comprehensible and precise codes. However, the economy of ancient China was thriving. Legal philosophies and jurisprudential debates thrived, as discussed in Chapter 3, §3.4, §3.5, §3.6 & §3.7 affecting the ongoing codification and even affecting the issue of procedural fairness. For example, during the *Qing* dynasty, previous case references were required in specific cases due to nascent legal jurisprudence that was still developing at that time. In practice this resulted in increased complexity during application of statutes.[824]

另一方面，有些案例过去只具有普遍效力，起源于秦朝到清朝之间，当时所有权力都集中在皇帝手中。在那个时期，还没有明确的概念，如公平，特别是程序公平，事实上，成文法制度刚刚发展出可理解的精确法典。然而，古代中国的经济欣欣向荣。正如第3章第3.4节、第3.5节、第3.6节和第3.7节所讨论的那样，法律哲学和法学争论蓬勃发展，影响了正在进行的法典编纂工作，甚至影响了程序公正问题。例如，在清朝，由于当时的法律判例仍在发展之中，在具体案件中需要参考以前的案例。这在实践中增加了法规适用的复杂性。

The compilation of cases developed as a result of demands from Chinese society in between the Qin to Qing dynasties.[825] There was little compilation of cases before the Qin dynasty. In the Ming and Qing Dynasties, *lvli heyi* was applied to the cases. According to this principle, statutes and cases were compiled together.[826] In some ways, there was a similarity

案例汇编是在秦朝到清朝之间的中国社会需求下发展起来的。秦朝之前，几乎没有编纂过案例。到了明清时期，判例开始采用“律例合一”的原则。根据这一原则，成文法和案例被汇编在一起。在某些方面，适用以前的案例与

822Ducai Liu, “A Study of Judicial Precedent in Traditional China. (Zhongguo Gudai Panli Kaolun),” *Social Sciences in China (Zhonguo Shehui Kexue)*, no. 4 (2007): 150. Liu’s legal history was discussed in Jinting Deng, “The Guiding Case System in Mainland China,” *Frontiers of Law in China* 10, no. 3 (2015): 4.
刘笃才，《中国古代判例考论》，载《中国社会科学》2007年第四期，第150页；邓金廷，《中国大陆的指导性案例制度》，载《中国法学前沿》2015 年第3期第4页。

823The Qin dynasty was from 221-206 BC. Refer to Table of Dynasties of ancient China in Table 1.
秦朝为公元前 221-206 年。参见表 1 中的中国古代朝代表。

824Shirong Wang, “The Functions of Cases in Traditional Chinese Law. (Panli Zai Zhongguo Chuantongfa Zhong de Gongneng),” *Chinese Journal of Law (Faxue Yanjiu)*, no. 1 (2006): 125–34. Wang was discussed in Deng, “The Guiding Case System in PRC,” 4.
王世荣，“判例在中国传统法中的功能”，法学研究，2006年第1期，第125-134页；王世荣也在邓的《中国的指导性案例制度》第4页被讨论。

825Xingliang Chen, “The Jurisprudence of the Case Guidance System (Anli Zhidao Zhidu de Fali Kaocha),” *Law and Social Development (Fazhi Yu Shehui Fazhan)* 18, no. 3 (2012): 74–76. Chen’s findings were discussed in Deng, “The Guiding Case System in PRC,” 4.
陈兴良，“案例指导制度的法理考察”，《法制与社会发展》第18卷第3期（2012年）：74-76. 陈的发现也在邓的《中国的案例指导制度》第4页中被讨论。

826Sibin Yang, “On Basic Characteristics and Exchanges of Ancient China’s Case System. (Zhongguo Gudai Panli Zhidu de Yanbian Yu Jiben Tezheng),” *Law Science Magazine (Faxue Zazhi)*, no. 2 (2008): 121. Yang was cited in Deng, “The Guiding Case System in PRC,” 4.

between the application of previous cases and statutory interpretation by analogy as practised during the Qing Dynasty. The only difference was that it was compulsory for judges in ancient China to apply the correct statutes. However, unlike with the statutes, there was no punishment for not using a previous case or even using the previous case incorrectly.[827]

清朝实行的类比解释成文法有相似之处。唯一不同的是，中国古代法官必须适用正确的成文法。然而，与成文法不同的是，不使用以前的案例甚至错误使用以前的案例都不会受到惩罚。

In ancient China, guiding cases represented the will of the emperor and were also issued under the name of the emperor. The guiding cases were intended to be seen as if originating from the emperor (*fazi junchu*).[828] Most guiding cases were from the family and criminal branch of law as compared to commercial and civil litigation.[829] Most of the these deciding cases in ancient China were in fact used to supplement the existing statutes.[830] Scholarly articles note that these guiding cases did not restrict judicial discretion, which was already restricted to a considerable extent by the relevant statutes. In fact, these guiding cases were required due to the demands of society.[831] These guiding cases were very useful in meeting the needs of society, and they provided flexibility in relation to several issues during adjudication of disputes during those times.

在中国古代，指导性案例代表皇帝的旨意，也以皇帝的名义发布。指导性案例的目的是让人们认为其源于皇帝（法自君出）。 与商业和民事诉讼相比，大多数指导性案例来自家庭和刑事法律部门。中国古代的这些指导性案例实际上大多是用来补充现有法规的。学术文章指出，这些指导性案例并没有限制司法裁量权，因为相关法规已经在相当程度上限制了司法裁量权。事实上，这些指导性案例是因社会需求而产生的。这些指导性案例在满足社会需求方面非常有用，并且在当时的纠纷裁决中为若干问题提供了灵活性。

In the Song, Yuan, Ming and Qing Dynasties, the guiding cases even created exceptions that were to be given priority over the then-existing written codes.[832] These guiding ancient cases also served other purposes such as having educational

在宋、元、明、清时期，指导性案例甚至创造了一些例外情况，这些例外情况优先于当时已有的成文法典。这些古代的指导性案例还具有其他作用，例

杨思斌，《中国古代判例制度的演变与基本特征》，《法学杂志》，2008年第2期第121页。杨在邓的《中国的指导性案例制度》第4 页中被讨论。

[827]MacCormack, *Spirit of Traditional Chinese Law*, 186.
麦考马克，《中国传统法律的精神》，第186页。

[828]Xingliang Chen, "The Jurisprudence of Case Guidance System," n.20 at 74 and as discussed in Deng, "The Guiding Case System in PRC," 11.
陈兴良，"案例指导制度的法理考察"，第74页第20段，以及邓，"中国的案例指导制度"，第11页。

[829]Deng, "The Guiding Case System in PRC," 5.
邓，"中国的案例指导制度"，第5页。

[830]Shirong Wang, "The Functions of Cases in Traditional Chinese Law. (Panli Zai Zhongguo Chuantongfa Zhong de Gongneng)," n.18 at 130. See also Sibin Yang, "Basic China's Case System," 123n5. Both Wang and Yang were cited in Deng, "The Guiding Case System in PRC," 8.
王世荣，"判例在中国传统法中的功能"，第130页。另见杨思斌，《中国的基本案例制度》，第123页。邓在《中国的指导性案例制度》中引用了王和杨的观点。

[831]Deng, "The Guiding Case System in PRC," 8.
邓，"中国的案例指导制度"，第 8 页。

[832]Shirong Wang, "The Functions of Cases in Traditional Chinese Law. (Panli Zai Zhongguo Chuantongfa Zhong de Gongneng)," 134n18. Wang was discussed in Deng, "The Guiding Case System in PRC," 8.
王世荣，"判例在中国传统法中的功能"。邓在《中国的指导性案例制度》中引用了王的观点。

and declaratory functions for target audiences. However, unfortunately, the legal reasoning was not clearly postulated in those guiding cases.[833]

如对目标受众具有教育和宣示功能。但遗憾的是，这些指导性案例并没有明确阐述法理。

In ancient China, there was another institution, called *BiFu*, that was mostly utilised in criminal law. This institution would guide the lower courts to use the details provided in the guiding cases, to classify crimes which were based on a set of facts which were different from the guiding case. From this, a punishment appropriate to the facts could be delivered. This process was akin to matching of the crimes (*qingzui xiangfu*) of the guiding case(s) with the crime before the judges.[834]

在中国古代，还有一种被称为"比附"的制度，主要用于刑法。该制度指导下级法院利用指导性案例中提供的细节，对基于一系列与指导性案例不同的事实的犯罪进行分类。据此，可以做出与事实相适应的处罚。这一过程类似于将指导性案例中的罪行（情罪相符）与法官面前的罪行进行匹配。

Another reason for seeking the appropriate criminal code for the award of punishment was that all crimes had statutory penalties that could be found in the codes and were absolute in nature (*juedui queding fadingxing*).[835] Even if the cases had been decided by *BiFu*, those cases could also be re-issued as guiding cases.[836]

寻求适当的刑法典来量刑的另一个原因是，所有罪行都有法定刑，这些法定刑都可以在刑法典中找到，而且具有绝对确定法定性。即使是比附判决的案件，也可作为指导性案例重新发布。

Deng analysed thirty cases that were adjudicated in the lower courts, which were able to use *BiFu* to find similar cases with an "analogy of relationship, legal elements, or certain equitable feelings." This analogy was executed through the principle of *juzhong mingqin; juqing mingzhong* principle.[837]

邓分析了下级法院判决的 30 个案例，这些案例可以利用毕府找到"关系类推、法律要素类推或某种衡平情感类推"的类似案例。这种类比是通过"举重明轻；举轻明重"原则来实现的。

In ancient China, if the crime in front of the officials of the

在中国古代，如果下级法院官员面

---

833 Liu, "A Study of Judicial Precedent in Traditional China. (Zhongguo Gudai Panli Kaolun)," 148–15n16. Liu was cited in Deng, "The Guiding Case System in PRC," 8.
刘，"中国古代判例考论" 148–15n16. 邓在《中国的指导性案例制度》中引用了刘的观点。

834 Xinyu Chen, "Bifu and Leitui - Starts from Biyin Lvtiao. (Bifu Yu Leitui Zhibian - Cong 'Biyin Lvtiao' Chufa)," *Tribune of Political Science and Law (Zhengfa Luntan)* 29, no. 2 (2011): 118n2. Chen's analysis was discussed in Deng, "The Guiding Case System in PRC," 11.
陈新宇，"比附与类推之辨——从"比引律条"出发" 《政法论坛》第29期（2011年）118n2。邓在《中国的指导性案例制度》中引用了陈的观点。

835 Deng, "The Guiding Case System in PRC," 11.
邓，"中国的案例指导制度"，第11页。

836 Xinyu Chen, "Bifu and Leitui - Starts from Biyin Lvtiao. (Bifu Yu Leitui Zhibian - Cong 'Biyin Lvtiao' Chufa)," 114 It was discussed in Deng, "The Guiding Case System in PRC," 11. Deng cited Chen's discussion on cases that were decided according to *BiFu*, but were later reissued as guiding cases, such as the 30 cases compiled in Volume 47 of *Criminal Laws of Qing Dynasty.*
陈新宇，"比附与类推之辨——从'比引律条'出发"，第114页。邓在《中国的指导性案例制度》第11页中引用了陈的观点。邓引用了陈关于根据比附判决但后来作为指导性案例重新发布的案例的论述，如《大清刑律》卷47编纂的30个案例。

837 The analysis of the 30 cases was carried out by Xinyu Chen, "Bifu and Leitui - Starts from Biyin Lvtiao. (Bifu Yu Leitui Zhibian - Cong 'Biyin Lvtiao' Chufa)," 115n5, 116 –18. Chen's analysis and the principles were discussed in Deng, "The Guiding Case System in PRC," 11.
对这30个案例的分析由陈新宇进行，"比附与类推之辨——从'比引律条'出发" 115n5, 116 –18. 邓在《中华人民共和国的指导性案例制度》中讨论了陈的分析和原则。

lower courts was less severe than the available guiding case, that crime would be punished less severely. Similarly, if the crime were more severe than the available guiding case, then the crime would be punished more severely. *BiFu* is not allowed in the current PRC legal system, as *BiFu* goes against the Latin principle '*nulla poena sine lege*', which means that there cannot be any penalty without a law.[838]

前的罪行比现有的指导性案例轻，则该罪行会受到较轻的处罚。同样，如果罪行比现有的指导性案例严重，则会受到更严厉的惩罚。中国现行法律制度不允许"比附"，因为"比附"违背了拉丁语"法无明文者不罚"的原则，即没有法律就没有刑罚。

The case guiding system in ancient China needed a very detailed approval process, as it was necessary for the system to be seen as originating from the emperor. For example, in the Han Dynasty, *Tingwei*, the supreme judiciary of the time, was authorized to make guiding cases, called '*jueshibi'*, from reported cases that had been approved by the emperor.[839]

中国古代的案例指导制度需要非常详细的审批程序，因为必须让人们认为该制度源自皇帝。例如，在汉代，当时的最高司法机构廷尉有权根据经皇帝批准的上报案件制定指导性案例，称为 "决事比"。

Lastly, the authors would like the readers to ponder that thousands of years ago, Lord Lu, a high judicial officer of the Zhou dynasty, gave instructions to jurists, as recorded by Shang-shu:

最后，笔者希望读者思考一下，据《尚书》记载，几千年前，周朝的司法高官鲁公曾对法学家进行过指导：

> In a case of an offence less serious than one for which a heavy punishment is prescribed, a lighter punishment should be imposed; in a case of an offence more serious than one for which a light punishment is prescribed, a heavier punishment should be imposed.[840]

> 罪轻于重者，轻之；罪重于轻者，重之。

7.3.2.1 Case Guidance System (post-1985)

案例指导系统（1985 年后）

Lower courts in the PRC have been using the *Gazette* of

自 1985 年以来，中国的下级法院

[838]Deng, "The Guiding Case System in PRC," 12.
邓，"中国的案例指导制度"，第12页。
[839]Sibin Yang, "Basic China's Case System," as cited in Deng, "The Guiding Case System in PRC," 19.
杨思斌：《中国的基本案件制度》，转引自邓：《中国的指导性案例制度》，第19页。
[840]Wejen Chang, "Classical Chinese Jurisprudence and Development of Chinese Legal System" (2009–10), 235. The discussions and quote were from Qu Wanli, shi jing quan shi [ANNOTATION ON THE BOOK OF SONGS] 326, 347, 362, 372, 376, 395, 506, 527, 546 (1983) (Taiwan), 259.
张维仁，《中国古典法学与中国法律制度的发展》（2009-10），235。讨论和引文来自屈万里，《诗经诠释》326、347、362、372、376、395、506、527、546（1983年）（台湾），259。

published cases since 1985. The Gazette is published by the Supreme Peoples's Court ('SPC'). In recent years, the SPC has compiled *Cases of People's Courts* and *Guide Books of Judicial Cases in China*.[841] Over the years, many departments as well as the lower courts in various provinces have started publishing guide books of cases resulting in books, academic articles, and so forth.[842]

一直在使用已公布案件的《公报》。该公报由最高人民法院（"最高院"）出版。近年来，最高院编制了《中国人民法院案例》和《中国司法案例指南》。多年来，许多部门以及各省的基层法院都开始出版案例指导手册，并形成了书籍、学术文章等。

This formed the foundation upon which the guiding case system was formally established on November 26, 2010, when the SPCC issued the *Provisions on Case Guidance Work*,[843] announcing the establishment of the Guiding Case System in mainland China.[844] Later in the same year, the Supreme People's Procuratorate and the Public Security Ministry issued provisions on the case guidance system to guide work in their institutions, though this is more akin to 'administrative instructions' than judicial power, which is only vested in the SPC.[845]

在此基础上，2010 年 11 月 26 日，最高院发布《关于案例指导工作的规定》，宣布在中国大陆建立案例指导制度。同年晚些时候，最高人民检察院和公安部也相继发布了指导本单位工作的《案例指导制度规定》，但这更像是"行政指示"，而非司法权，因为司法权只属于最高人民法院。

In March 2011, during the fourth session of the eleventh NPC, the ex-chairman of the Standing Committee of the NPC, Mr. Wu Bangguo, declared that the statutory framework with Chinese characteristics has been fully established in the PRC as part of the socialist legal system. On May, 13, 2015, the SPC issued the *Detailed Rules of Implementation of the Provisions of the Supreme People's Court on Case Guidance Work* (hereinafter 'Detailed Rules').[846] Given that (based on the date of promulgation) the PRC legal system is so recent in origin, the level of expectation that anyone can have from the PRC legal

2011 年 3 月，在十一届全国人大四次会议期间，全国人大常委会前委员长吴邦国宣布，作为社会主义法律体系的一部分，中国特色社会主义法律体系框架已在中华人民共和国全面确立。2015 年 5 月 13 日，最高院发布了《最高人民法院关于案例指导工作的规定实施细则》（以下简称《细则》）。鉴于（以颁布时间为准）中华人民共和国法律制度的起源时间如此之短，任何人对中华人民共和国法

---

[841] *Guide Books of Judicial Cases* in China was compiled by the SPCC, the National Judges College and the Renmin University Law School together as discussed in Deng, "The Guiding Case System in PRC," 201.
《中国司法案例指导用书》由最高人民法院、国家法官学院和人民大学法学院共同编纂，详见Deng，《中国的指导性案例制度》，第201页。

[842] Deng, "The Guiding Case System in PRC," 2.
邓，"中国的案例指导制度"，第2页。

[843] *Fa Fa [2010]* No. 51 November 26, 2010. 法发[2010]51号2010年11月26日。

[844] For example, pursuant to *Provisions on guiding case system* of SPC, the SPC has issued *The Notice of the First Set of Guiding Cases* and published four guiding cases, then the second on April, 14, 2012, the third on September 18, 2012, the fourth on February 7, 2013, the fifth on November 15, 2013, the sixth on Jan. 29, 2014, and the seventh on July 8, 2014.
例如，根据《最高人民法院指导性案例制度规定》，最高人民法院发布了《关于公布第一批指导性案例的通知》，公布了四个指导性案例，之后于2012年4月14日公布了第二个指导性案例，2012年9月18日公布了第三个指导性案例，2013年2月7日公布了第四个指导性案例，2013年11月15日公布了第五个指导性案例，2014年1月29日公布了第六个指导性案例，2014年7月8日公布了第七个指导性案例。

[845] Deng, "The Guiding Case System in PRC," 2.
邓，"中国的案例指导制度"，第2页。

[846] *Fa Fa [2015] No. 130.* 法发[2015]130号。

system cannot be high.

律制度的期望值都不可能很高。

Scholars of PRC law assert that the next wave of reforms will be based on case guiding systems rather than on legislations and the SPC's opinions.[847] This view is also based on the fact that many of these scholars are dissatisfied with the vague codes and equally vague statutory interpretations provided by the SPC.[848]

研究中国法律的学者断言，下一波改革将以案例指导制度为基础，而不是以立法和最高院的意见为基础。这一观点也是基于许多学者对最高院提供的含糊不清的法典和同样含糊不清的法律解释感到不满这一事实。

It is important to highlight Deng's analysis of the guiding case management system:

有必要强调邓对指导性办案制度的分析：

> However, in both ancient and current China, statutes are primarily relied on to centralize power [emphasis added], and guiding cases are supplementary; while in early common law, cases are dominant and statutes are supplementary.[849]

> 然而，无论是古代中国还是现在的中国，都主要依靠成文法来集权[着重号后加]，指导性案例是辅助性的；而在早期的普通法中，案例是主导性的，成文法是辅助性的。

It is important to note that even in the common law systems, and in particular the *CPR 1998*, there is a growing reliance on the written laws/statutes/codes. Some scholars are of the view that statutes are growing more important even in prominent common law countries, such as England & Wales, the US and India.[850]

值得注意的是，即使在普通法系，尤其是 1998 年《民事诉讼程序法》中，对成文法/成文法典/法典的依赖也在不断增加。一些学者认为，即使在著名的普通法国家，如英格兰和威尔士、美国和印度，成文法也越来越重要。

It is believed that guiding cases can fill the gaps between the law as determined by the relevant codes in the area of substantive law, their interpretation by the judges, and the application of these laws to the specific set of facts.[851] This focus on interpretation and application is important, as the PRC

人们认为，指导性案例可以填补实体法领域相关法典所确定的法律、法官对这些法律的解释以及将这些法律适用于特定事实之间的空白。由于中国幅员辽阔、省份众多，许多学者

847Deng, "The Guiding Case System in PRC," 3.
邓，"中国的案例指导制度"，第3页。
848Refer above §7.2.2. 参见上文第 7.2.2节。
849Deng, "The Guiding Case System in PRC," 5.
邓，"中国的案例指导制度"，第5页。
850Melvin Aron Eisenberg, *The Nature of Common Law* (Cambridge: Harvard University Press, 1988), 1 Eisenberg was discussed in Deng, "The Guiding Case System in PRC," 6.
梅尔文-阿伦-艾森伯格，《普通法的性质》（剑桥：哈佛大学出版社，1988 年），第1页，艾森伯格在邓的《中国的指导性案例制度》一文中进行了讨论。
851Deng, "The Guiding Case System in PRC," 6.
邓，"中国的案例指导制度"，第6页。

is a vast land mass comprising many provinces, and the quality of the judges who interpret codes and apply laws in the lower courts has been questioned by many scholars. On the other hand, the increasing prosperity levels amongst the populace, achieved in just two decades, are also raising expectations in relation to judicial efficiency pertaining to PRC courts.

对基层法院解释法典和适用法律的法官的素质提出了质疑，因此这种对解释和适用的重视非常重要。另一方面，在短短二十年间，中国人民的生活日益富裕，这也提高了人们对中国法院司法效率的期望。

Another aim, it appears, of the guiding case system is to regulate the exercise of judicial discretion, and last but not least to resolve the longstanding issue of similar cases receiving different rulings in the PRC courts.[852] These guiding cases also have a political and declaratory function. Since these cases within the case guidance system are backed by reasons and methodologies, it can also be an important arena for training judges in the lower courts. Another objective of the case guidance system is to ensure that the lower courts rely less on the Reply system,[853] and to increase judicial efficiency in the PRC courts.[854]

看来，指导性案例制度的另一个目的是规范司法裁量权的行使，最后但并非最不重要的是解决长期以来类似案件在中国法院得到不同判决的问题。这些指导性案例还具有政治性和宣示性功能。由于案例指导制度中的这些案例都有理由和方法支持，因此也可以成为培训下级法院法官的重要舞台。案例指导制度的另一个目的是确保下级法院减少对答辩制度的依赖，提高中国法院的司法效率。

The SPC has been standardizing the format in which the cases selected for case guidance are written. The lower courts are motivated 'to cooperate in reporting, compiling and applying guiding cases, constructing relevant working and incentive mechanisms, and building case database.'[855] The SPC and High Court has recently organised meetings to fulfil this function. These meetings also clarified that the interpretations of the guiding cases lead the system towards uniformity in all the courts.

最高院一直在规范案例指导所选案例的撰写格式。激励下级法院配合做好指导性案例的申报、汇编和应用工作，构建相关工作机制和激励机制，建立案例库。最高院和高等法院最近组织召开了会议，以履行这一职能。这些会议还明确了指导性案例的解释将引导所有法院的制度走向统一。

The *Guiding cases* are published in SPC's *Gazette,* its web site, and People's Court Daily in both paper and electronic versions. Many PRC scholars have praised the new system, but others have criticised the lack of facts in the guided cases. These

指导性案例在最高院的公报、网站和《人民法院报》上以纸质和电子版本发布。许多中国学者对新制度表示赞赏，但也有学者批评指导性案例

---

[852]Zelin Su, "Fully Exploit the Function of the Guiding Case System with Chinese Characteristics; Courts, Positively Enforce Historical Missions of People's Application. (Chongfen Fahui Zhongguo Tese Anli Zhidao Zhidu Zuoyong Jiji Lvxing Renmin Fayuan Lishi Shiming)," *Journal of Law Application (Falv Shiyong)* 7 (2011): n. 12 at 5.
苏泽林，"充分发挥中国特色案例指导制度作用 积极履行人民法院历史使命。"（法律适用）7 (2011): n. 12 at 5.

[853] Refer §7.2.2.2. 参见第 7.2.2.2 节。

[854]Mingguo Chen and Weiming Zuo, "Practical Obstacles and Countermeasures of Guiding Cases. (Zhidaoxing Anli de Yingyong Zhangai Jiqi Kefu - Sichuan Fayuan Anli Yingyong Shidian Gongzuo de Chubu Fenxi)," *Journal of Law Application (Falv Shiyong)* 5 (2012): 69–70.
陈明国，左卫民：《指导性案例的应用障碍及其克服——四川法院案例应用试点工作的初步分析》，《法律适用》，2012年第5期第69–70页。

[855]Ibid., 10. 同上，10。

scholars have even questioned the criteria by which the cases are selected in the Case Guiding System.

缺乏事实依据。这些学者甚至质疑案例指导制度选择案例的标准。

In selecting cases for the Guiding Cases system, the SPC requires the selected cases should meet the following five conditions: [856]

最高院在遴选指导性案例时，要求入选案例应符合以下五个条件：

- The facts of the cases have aroused wide public concern;
- The cases involve circumstances, where relevant laws only stipulate principled provisions and the legal provisions are of relatively general nature;
- Cases are of a typical nature;
- Cases are difficult, complicated or are cases of new types within the PRC legal system;
- Other cases that can serve as guide.

- 社会广泛关注的；
- 法律规定比较原则的；
- 具有典型性的；
- 疑难复杂或者新类型的；
- 其他具有指导作用的案例。

Furthermore, Hu said, "A guiding case must be a just decision, a decision with its social effect and legal effect organically unified, and a model followed by judges."[857]

胡还说："指导性案例必须是公正的裁判，是社会效果和法律效果有机统一的裁判，是法官学习的榜样。"

Mr. Hu, Director of Research Office of SPC, has clarified that the lower courts must follow the guided cases.[858] Mr. Hu also stated that the guided cases were not a new type of statutory

最高院研究室主任胡先生明确指出，下级法院必须遵循指导性案例。胡还表示，指导性案例并不是一种新型的法律解释，并明确了其约束性。

[856]See Art. 2 of *Provisions of the Supreme People's Court Concerning Work on Guiding Cases, Fa Fa [2010]* No. 51 November 26, 2010.
《最高人民法院关于指导性案例工作的规定》第二条，法发[2010]51号，2010年11月26日。

[857]Comment by Hu Yunteng, Director of the Research Department of the Supreme People's Court, available at http://cgc.law.stanford.edu/why-guiding-cases-matter/#hyunteng (last viewed Mar. 11, 2025). It was cited in Jocelyn E.H. Limmer, "China's New 'Common Law' Using China's Guiding Cases to Understand How to Do Business in People's Republic of China," *Willamette J. Int'l L. & Dis. Resol.* 21, no. 2 (2013): 35. The authors have used the revised version of Limmer's paper available on ssrn.com.
最高人民法院研究室主任胡云腾的评论，http://cgc.law.stanford.edu/why-guiding-cases-matter/#hyunteng（最后浏览日期：2025年3月11日）。约瑟琳-利默, "中国的新 "普通法" 利用中国的指导性案例了解如何在中国经商" Willamette J. Int'l L. & Dis. Resol. 21, no. 2 (2013)：35. 笔者使用了利默论文的修订版，可在ssrn.com上查阅。

[858]Yunteng Hu, "The Constructing Cases Guidance System with Chinese Characteristics Exclusive Interview of Dr. Hu, Yunteng, Member of Judicial Committee and the Director of the Research Office in Supreme People's Court," *China L.*, no. 1 (2011): 4–6,58–60. It was cited in Deng, "The Guiding Case System in PRC," 20, see also Provisions of the Supreme People's Court Concerning Work on Guiding Cases, Article
胡云腾：《构建中国特色案例指导制度独家专访最高人民法院审判委员会委员、研究室主任胡云腾博士》，《中国法学》，第 1 期（2011 年）：4-6,58-60. 邓，《中国的指导性案例制度》，第 20 页，另见《最高人民法院关于指导性案例工作的规定》。

interpretation, and clarified their binding nature.[859]

It is not clear that "erroneous application of law" as grounds for appeal in Article 177 of *CPL 2023* includes 'erroneous application of guiding cases'.[860] Guiding cases are not grounds for such appeal, but it seems they are related to the correct position of law. However, the lower courts can depart from the guiding cases provided reasons are given.[861] In any event, the legislated Codes will prevail in the PRC; here, it diverges from common law's case precedent system, where the *ratio decidendi* even involving a statute will prevail. Therefore, it seems the SPC intentionally uses the word "guiding (*zhidaoxing*) *anli*" instead of "*panli*" to cautiously differentiate the guiding cases from normal cases and common law cases.[862]

2023 年《民事诉讼法》第 177 条中作为上诉理由的"法律适用错误"是否包括"指导性案例适用错误"并不明确。指导性案例并非此类上诉的理由，但似乎与法律的正确立场有关。但是，下级法院可偏离指导性案例，但须说明理由。无论如何，在中国，法典将以立法为准；这与普通法的案例先例制度不同，在普通法中，即使涉及成文法，也以判例为准。因此，最高院似乎有意使用"指导性案例"一词而非"判例"，以谨慎区分指导性案例与普通案例和普通法案例。

It appears from reading the translation of various scholars that even though guiding cases are not laws, and therefore should not be cited in the 'Judgment's Key Points' section of a statement of claim submitted to a Chinese court, they can nonetheless be cited in the reasoning section.[863] Further guidance on this issue has been given by Deng, but is beyond the scope of this book.[864]

从不同学者的译文来看，尽管指导性案例不是法律，因此不应在提交给中国法院的诉状的"判决要点"部分引用，但仍可在说理部分引用。邓就这一问题给出了进一步的指导，但不在本书的讨论范围之内。

In the authors' view, even though Deng has clarified the PRC law in relation to case guidance in a very succinct way. However, when comparing the system to the common-law system, he has failed to fully grasp what the common law is in terms of the judges' power to make law or whether they can

笔者认为，尽管邓以非常简洁的方式阐明了与案例指导有关的中国法律。但是，当他将这一制度与普通法系相比较时，却没有充分把握普通法系中法官制定法律的权力是什么，或

[859]Hu's statement was discussed in Deng, "The Guiding Case System in PRC," 21. Deng has disagreed with Hu. However, Hu's views will prevail over Deng's views, because Hu is from the SPC.
邓在《中华人民共和国的指导性案例制度》一文中讨论了胡的发言。邓不同意胡的观点。不过，胡的观点将优先于邓的观点，因为胡来自最高人民法院。
[860]Deng, "The Guiding Case System in PRC," 22.
邓，"中国的案例指导制度"，第 22 页。
[861]Hu's statement was discussed in this context in Deng, "The Guiding Case System in PRC," 22.
邓在《中华人民共和国的指导性案例制度》一文中就此对胡的陈述进行了讨论。
[862]Deng, "The Guiding Case System in PRC," 24.
邓，"中国的案例指导制度"，第 24 页。
[863]Limmer, "China's New 'Common Law' Using China's Guiding Cases to Understand How to Do Business in People's Republic of China," 36.
利默，"中国的新'普通法'--利用中国的指导性案例了解如何在中国经商"，36。
[864]Deng, "The Guiding Case System in PRC," 22, 27–28.
邓，"中国的案例指导制度"，第22、27-28页。

indeed make law in the common law system. The kind of training and autonomy the judges have in common law is unimaginable in the PRC system. The whole jurisprudence of the current common law revolves around this issue.

者在普通法系中法官是否真的可以制定法律。普通法系法官所受的训练和所有的自主权，在中国的制度下是不可想像的。现行普通法的整个法理学都是围绕这个问题展开的。

It is time to delineate the detailed rules as published by the SPC in *Detailed Rules of Implementation of the Provisions of the Supreme People's Court on Case Guidance Work* (hereinafter 'Detailed Rules'),[865] and analyse them. These rules have in fact been issued to prevent inconsistency in application. The key elements of these *Detailed Rules* are as follows:

现在是时候对最高院在《最高人民法院关于案例指导工作规定的实施细则》（下称《细则》）中公布的细则进行划分和分析了。这些细则的出台实际上是为了防止适用上的不统一。《细则》的主要内容如下：

- Article 7 – Where the Case Guidance Office deems it necessary to further study a potential case to be included as a guiding case, it may consult relevant State organs, departments and social organizations, members of the case guidance work expert committee, as well as experts and scholars. This is to ensure that the People's courts at all levels shall take them as a reference in future, when they try similar cases.

- 第七条——案例指导办公室认为有必要对可能列为指导性案例的案例作进一步研究的，可以征求有关国家机关、部门和社会团体、案例指导工作专家委员会成员以及专家学者的意见。这是为了保证各级人民法院今后在审理类似案件时可以作为参考。

- Article 9 –Where a case under adjudication by a People's court at any level is similar to a guiding case published by the Supreme People's Court in terms of basic facts and the application of law, then it is incumbent on the People's court to render a judgment/ruling by referencing the headnotes of the judgment/ruling on the guiding case. This means that the binding effect of a guiding case is limited by the law to a reference, rather than being a binding precedent that must be followed.

- 第九条——各级人民法院审理的案件，凡与最高人民法院公布的指导性案例在基本事实和法律适用方面相似的，人民法院应当参照指导性案例的判决/裁定要点作出判决/裁定。这意味着指导性案例的约束力被法律限定为参考，而不是必须遵循的具有约束力的先例。

- Article 10 –When a People's Court at any level refers to a guiding case in the adjudication of a similar case, it shall quote the guiding case as part of the reasons for

- 第十条--各级人民法院在审理类似案件时，引用指导性案例的，应当作为判决/裁定理由的一部分，但不得作为

[865]Fa Fa [2015] No. 130. 法发[2015]130号。

judgments/rulings; however, it shall not quote the same as a basis for judgment/ruling. Therefore, PRC judges are not allowed to use guiding cases as the legal basis for judgment. Instead, PRC judges can refer to a guiding case in the reasoning part of the judgments. If it were to be compared to the common law, then it would be as if common-law judges were to look for the reasons cited from another published decision as guidance only, to develop their legal reasoning in their case. However, these common-law judges cannot use such reasons from the other case as the basis of a decision in the present case. On proper analysis, it is the authors' view that the detailed rules, therefore, are an attempting to limit the judges' discretion in their ability to reference previous decisions.

判决/裁定的依据。因此，中国法官不得使用指导性案例作为判决的法律依据。相反，中国法官可在判决书的推理部分引用指导性案例。如果将其与普通法相比较，那么就好比普通法法官只能从另一个已公布的判决中寻找所引用的理由作为指导，以发展其案件的法律推理。然而，这些普通法法官却不能将其他案例中的理由作为本案判决的依据。经过适当分析，笔者认为，详细规则是试图限制法官参考先前裁决的自由裁量权。

◆ Article 11 –During the process of case handling, case handling officers must search relevant guiding cases. Having analyzed Article 11 the authors feel that now there is an obligation on the judges to actively participate in finding decisions from the case guiding system. However, the training aspect in relation to this article would be a big challenge throughout the PRC.

◆ 第十一条——办案人员在办案过程中必须查找相关指导性案例。通过对第十一条的分析，笔者认为现在法官有义务积极参与从案例指导系统中查找判决。然而，与该条款相关的培训工作在全中国都将是一个巨大的挑战。

7.4 Burden and Standards of Proof

举证责任和标准

In civil litigation, any party making allegations in a statement of case/claims must prove those allegations in order to win their case. The proof will be dependent on *weight and reliability* of

在民事诉讼中，在案件陈述/索赔中提出指控的任何一方都必须证明这些指控，才能赢得官司。举证取决于

the evidence. A party who has to prove the allegations, has the burden of proof in the civil litigation and that party has to provide enough evidence to satisfy the courts. An opponent, a Defendant, has to similarly prove his defence. This process is followed in most jurisdictions for trying civil litigation cases. However, the jurisprudential school of thoughts can influence the thinking of the judges and the legal system.

证据的重要性和可靠性。必须证明指控的一方在民事诉讼中负有举证责任，该方必须提供令法院满意的足够证据。对方（即被告）同样需要证明其辩护理由。大多数司法管辖区在审理民事诉讼案件时都遵循这一程序。然而，法理学派的思想会影响法官和法律制度的思维。

A good advocate or lawyer constantly reminds the courts as to which side has the requisite burden of proof, as sometimes it is not clear from the allegations in parties' statements of case. The most common example of such instances in England & Wales is where the judges are also in doubt in cases involving interpretation of contracts.[866] At times, the courts can decide based on the fact that a particular party is in the better position to adduce evidence in the dispute.[867]

好的辩护人或律师会不断提醒法庭哪一方负有必要的举证责任，因为有时从当事人的案情陈述中并不能清楚地看出。在英格兰和威尔士，此类情况最常见的例子就是法官在涉及合同解释的案件中也会产生疑问。 有时，法院会根据某一方在争议中更有优势举证这一事实做出判决。

However, the next question is how much evidence each party must submit to the courts to discharge the burden of proof. The answer can be found in the concept called *Standards of Proof*. Most civil cases are decided based on the *balance of probabilitie*s, except the Standards of proof will be higher in cases that have elements of a criminal nature such as contempt or fraud or deceit. Any lawyer in practice must analyse evidence objectively. For the sake of completeness, the test for Standard of Proof is 'beyond reasonable doubt' in criminal cases, and any jury should be left with no doubt before convicting anyone.

然而，接下来的问题是，各方必向法庭提交多少证据才能履行举证责任。答案可在"证明标准"这一概念中找到。大多数民事案件都是根据可能性的权衡来裁决的，但在具有刑事性质的案件中，如藐视法庭、欺诈或欺骗等，举证标准会更高。执业律师都须客观分析证据。为完整起见，在刑事案件中，证明标准的检验标准是"排除合理怀疑"，任何陪审团在给任何人定罪之前都不应有任何疑问。

---

[866]See *The Glandarroch* [1894] P 226, and *Hurst v Evans* [1917] 1 KB 352.
见 The Glandarroch [1894] P 226 和 Hurst v Evans [1917] 1 KB 352。
[867]See *Joseph Constantine Steamship Line Ltd v Imperial Smelting Corp Ltd* [1942] AC 154.
见Joseph Constantine Steamship Line Ltd v Imperial Smelting Corp Ltd [1942] AC 154.

7.4.1 Standards of Proof in context of England & Wales v Standards of Proof in Civil Law Jurisdictions

英格兰和威尔士的证明标准与大陆法系司法管辖区的证明标准

As discussed above, the balance of probabilities has been understood from various cases to mean that something is '*more probable than not*'.[868] In simple terms, this means that in order to win, any party must prove that at least fifty-one percent of the allegations in his civil case are true, or the defendant must prove that the allegations are fifty-one percent untrue. If either party can provide this level of proof, then that party will win the case. However, there is no mathematical formula for deciding the percentages, and that figure of fifty-one percent is used to provide a simple explanation. Every lawyer will try their best to ensure that they provide as much *relevant and admissible* evidence as necessary to prove his case at seventy percent or even more on the test of probability.

如上文所述，从不同的案例中，人们对"可能性的权衡"的理解是指某件事情"可能性大于不可能性"。简单地说，这意味着任何一方要想胜诉，必须证明其民事案件中至少有51%的指控属实，或者被告必须证明指控中有51%不属实。如果任何一方能够提供这种程度的证据，那么该方就会胜诉。然而，并没有数学公式来决定百分比，百分之五十一这个数字只是用来提供一个简单的解释。每位律师都会尽力确保提供尽可能多的相关可采纳证据，以证明其案件的可能性达到百分之七十甚至更高。

In a recent case, Lord Nicholls of Birkenhead succinctly explained the concept of standards of proof in the case *In Re H (Minors) (Sexual Abuse: Standard of Proof)*: [869]

在最近的一个案例中，伯肯黑德的尼克尔斯勋爵在 In Re H（未成年人）（性虐待：举证标准）一案中简明扼要地解释了举证标准的概念：

> The balance of probability standard means that a court is satisfied an event occurred if the court considers that, on the evidence, the occurrence of the event was more likely than not. When assessing the probabilities, the

> 概率权衡标准是指，如果法院认为，根据证据，事件发生的可能

[868] See Lord Denning's view in *Miller v Minister of Pensions* [1947] 2 All ER 372, 374. In another common law jurisdiction, Canada also has a similar test for Standards of Proof, which states that if there is a higher probability for this to happen than not, then in that case the burden of proof of such party shall thereby be released. In English Law, in the courts it would mean that either the burden has been discharged or it is not discharged at the end of the trial.
见 Lord Denning 在 Miller v Minister of Pensions [1947] 2 All ER 372, 374一案中的观点。在另一个普通法司法管辖区，加拿大也有一个类似的举证标准测试，其中规定，如果发生这种情况的可能性高于不发生的可能性，那么在这种情况下，该方的举证责任将因此而免除。在英国法中，在法庭上，这意味着要么举证责任已经解除，要么在审判结束时举证责任并未解除。

[869] See H and others (Minors) (A.P.) (Respondents) [1995] UKHL 16, [73] (Lord Nicholls). See also in the same case at [76] (Lord Nicholls) on further discussion of standards of proof to be applied in *Children Act 1989* cases, there is the balance of probabilities, which is same as in civil litigation. According to the judges, there are only two Standards of Proof and the test of balance of probabilities has in-built flexibility.
见 H 和其他人（未成年人）（A.P.）（答辩人）[1995] UKHL 16，[73]（尼科尔斯勋爵）。另见同案[76]（尼科尔斯勋爵）关于1989年《儿童法》案件中适用的举证标准的进一步讨论，即可能性的权衡，这与民事诉讼中的举证标准相同。法官认为，只有两种举证标准，而可能性权衡的检验标准具有内在灵活性。

court will have in mind as a factor, to whatever extent is appropriate in the particular case, that the more serious the allegation the less likely it is that the event occurred and, hence, the stronger should be the evidence before the court concludes that the allegation is established on the balance of probability [emphasis added]. Fraud is usually less likely than negligence. Deliberate physical injury is usually less likely than accidental physical injury. ...Built into the preponderance of probability standard is a generous degree of flexibility in respect of the seriousness of the allegation.

性大于不发生的可能性，则法院认为事件已经发生。在评估可能性时，法院会考虑到一个因素，即指控越严重，事件发生的可能性就越小，因此，在法院得出结论认为根据可能性的权衡，指控成立之前，证据应该越充分[着重部分由笔者标明]。欺诈的可能性通常低于过失。故意造成人身伤害的可能性通常低于意外造成人身伤害的可能性。……"……"可能性优势"标准在指控的严重性方面具有很大程度的灵活性。

The Standards of Proof is also called '*preponderance of evidence*'[870] in the United States. The test for Standards of proof in civil litigation is lower than in the criminal law, where the requirement for Standards of proof is 'beyond reasonable doubt'. In addition, it is an appropriate time to appreciate that the test for Standards of proof in the common law system are lower than in the continental civil tradition. In civil law jurisdictions, the test for Standard of proof is defined in terms of "*moral certainty* or as *intime conviction.*"[871]

在美国，证明标准也被称为"优势证据"。民事诉讼中的举证标准比刑法中的举证标准低，刑法中对举证标准的要求是"排除合理怀疑"。此外，现在也是了解普通法体系中的证明标准低于大陆民事传统的适当时机。在大陆法系的司法管辖区，证明标准的检验标准被定义为"*道德上的确信性或自由心证*"。

While the definition of Standards of Proof is easy, how the judges in the English courts go about deciding on the matter is quite complex. They will consider the following points very carefully:[872]

虽然"证明标准"的定义很简单，但英国法院的法官如何裁决却相当复杂。他们会仔细考虑以下几点：

---

[870]An American scholar has discussed the concept as follows: "the general standard of proof in civil action is Preponderance of Probability. That means the facts alleged will be deemed to be true when jury is convinced that the probability for its existence based on the evidence available, is higher." Quoted in Chen Chao-yang (Xiamen Intermediate People's Court), "Standards of Proof in Civil Proceedings: From the Perspective of Judicial Impartiality and Efficiency," *J. of Southwest U. P. Sc. & L.*, no. 1 (2002): 9–19.
一位美国学者对这一概念作了如下论述："民事诉讼的一般举证标准是优势概率。也就是说，当陪审团确信根据现有证据，指控的事实存在的可能性较大时，指控的事实将被认为是真实的"。引自陈朝阳（厦门市中级人民法院）："民事诉讼中的证明标准：从司法公正与效率的角度"，《西南政法大学学报》，第1期（2002 年），第9-19页。

[871]Dominique Demougin and Claude Fluet, "Deterrence Vs Judicial Error: A Comparative View of Standards of Proof," *J. of Inst. and Theoretical Econ.* 161, no. 2 (2004): 161.https://ssrn/abstract=585770. See also, *French Code de Procédure Pénale* (as on 5 June 2016), Art. 353; *German Zivilprozessordnung 2005 (as amended in 2013)*, § 286 (1); *German Strafprozessordnung 1987* (as amended in 2014), § 261.
多米尼克-德穆金和克劳德-弗卢埃，"威慑与司法错误：证据标准的比较观点"，J. of Inst. 161, no：161. https://ssrn/abstract=585770。另见《法国刑事诉讼法典》（2016 年 6 月 5 日），第 353 条；德国《民事诉讼法》2005.（修订于 2013），§286（1）；德国刑事诉讼法 1987（修订于 2014），§261。

[872]Susan Blake, *A Practical Approach to Effective Litigation*, 8th ed. (Oxford: Oxford University Press, 2015), 554.
苏珊-布莱克，《有效诉讼的实用方法》，第8版，津大学出版社，2015年，第554页。

- Quality of relevant evidence and not just quantity of evidence;

- The judges will repeat this exercise again and again against each cause of action stated in the Statements of Case of the parties.

- 相关证据的质量，而不仅仅是证据的数量；

- 法官将针对双方在案件陈述中陈述的每项诉讼理由反复进行这项工作。

Standards of proof in the common law system such as in England & Wales is an objective concept but in the continental tradition, it is a subjective concept. In spite of the difference, the goal of judiciary is the same in both systems. Both the common law and civil law jurisdictions operate within conditions of uncertainty.[873]

在英格兰和威尔士等地的普通法下，举证标准是一个客观概念，但在欧洲大陆的传统中它是一个主观概念。尽管存在差异，但两种体系中司法机构的目标是相同的。普通法和大陆法法域都在不确定的条件下应用。

Facts or allegations that are highly improbable will require stronger evidence. However, the probability of a fact happening does not alter the balance of probability test.[874]

极不可能发生的事实或指控需要更有力的证据。然而，事实发生的可能性并不会改变概率平衡测试。

The subjective aspect of the continental law tradition can be appreciated by analysing an example taken from the *German Code*, § 286 (1) of *Code of Civil Procedure* which provides:

分析《德国法典》中的一个例子，即《民事诉讼法》第 286(1)节的规定，可了解大陆法系传统的主观方面：

> Paying due regard to the entirety of the proceedings, including the evidence presented, if any, it is for the court to decide, based on its **personal** conviction [emphasis added], whether a factual claim is indeed true or not.

> 在适当考虑整个诉讼程序，包括所提供的证据（如果有）时，应由法院根据其个人信念[着重部分由笔者标明]决定事实主张是否属实。

It is clear from the above reading of § 286 (1) that in the German Code, '*personal convictions''* of the judges are very

从以上对 § 286(1)的解读可看出，在德国法典中，法官的“个人信念”

[873]James Brook, "Inevitable Errors: The Preponderance of Evidence Standard in Civil Litigation," *Tulsa L.J.* 18, no. 1 (1982): 79–109. Brook was discussed in the context of uncertainty of evidence in any civil litigation in Christoph Engel, "Preponderance of the Evidence Versus Intime Conviction: A Behavioural Perspective on Conflict between American and Continental European Law," *MPI Collective Goods Preprint No.2008/33* (2008): 2.
詹姆斯-布鲁克，“不可避免的错误： 民事诉讼中的优势证据标准” *Tulsa L.J.* 18, no. 1 (1982): 79–109. 克里斯托夫-恩格尔在“优势证据与即时定罪 ”一文中就任何民事诉讼中证据的不确定性对布鲁克进行了讨论： 从行为角度看美国法律与欧洲大陆法律之间的冲突", MPI Collective Goods Preprint No.2008/33 (2008)：2。
[874]See *Re H & others (A.P.) (Respondents)* [1995] UKHL 16, [76] (Lord Nicholls).
见Re H & others (A.P.) (Respondents) [1995] UKHL 16, [76] (Lord Nicholls)。

important.[875] The continental system relies upon the experience and convictions of the judges in deciding cases.[876] Kaplan, Mehren & Schaefer have discussed this in greater depth:

> What is the degree of conviction to which the civil court must be brought in ordinary situations before it is justified in holding that the burden of establishing a proposition has been met? [A German treatise says]: "The judge may and must always content himself with a degree of certainty that is appropriate for practical life, one which silences doubts without entirely excluding them." Evidently a rather high degree of probability is called for, and <u>there is a tendency toward at least verbal equation of the civil with the criminal standard</u> [emphasis added].[877]

However, scholars have argued that in jurisdictions where the concept of *objective* standards of proof is dominant, such as in the common law jurisdictions of the US and England & Wales, the evidence and arguments will still be processed by the judges' human minds. The human mind is always susceptible to bias, prejudices, and external influence, and the subjectivity of the judges cannot be avoided.[878] Thus common law decisions are still error prone due to the subjective element involved in processing the evidence.

The philosophy behind the concept of *balance of probabilities*

是非常重要的。大陆法系依靠法官的经验和信念来裁决案件。卡普兰，梅兰及谢弗对此进行了更深入的讨论：

> 在一般情况下，民事法庭必须达到何种程度的确信，才有理由认为已经履行了确立主张的责任？[德国的一篇论文说]“法官可以而且必须始终满足于与实际生活相适应的确定程度，这种确定程度既能消除疑虑，又不完全排除疑虑。显然，这需要相当高的概率，<u>而且有一种至少在口头上将民事标准等同于刑事标准的趋势</u>[着重部分由笔者标明]。

然而，有学者认为，在客观证明标准概念占主导地位的司法管辖区，如美国和英格兰及威尔士的普通法司法管辖区，证据和论据仍将由法官的人脑处理。人的思维总是容易受到偏见、成见和外界影响的影响，法官的主观性也无法避免。因此，普通法的判决仍然容易因证据处理过程中的主观因素而出错。

普通法中概率平衡概念背后的理

---

[875] Engel, "Preponderance of the Evidence versus Intime Conviction: A Behavioural Perspective on Conflict Between American and Continental European Law," 5.
恩格尔，优势证据与即时定罪：从行为角度看美国法律与欧洲大陆法律之间的冲突， 5.

[876] Engel, "Preponderance of the Evidence versus Intime Conviction: A Behavioural Perspective on Conflict Between American and Continental European Law," 5. Engel brings in other scholars, to discuss the issue of how a judge will decide in his mind as part of the continental jurisdiction such as Germany. For example, he discusses Schulz's view that the test is empirical, built on "ethos, experience and intuition", and "*the psychic state of taking a fact for true*".
恩格尔，“优势证据与即时定罪：从行为角度看美国法律与欧洲大陆法律之间的冲突”， 5. 恩格尔引入了其他学者，讨论作为德国等大陆司法管辖区的一部分，法官将如何在头脑中做出决定的问题。例如，他讨论了舒尔茨的观点，即检验是经验性的，建立在“精神、经验和直觉”以及“将事实视为真实的心理状态”之上。

[877] Benjamin Kaplan, Arthur T. von Mehren, and Rudolf Schaefer, "Phrases of German Civil Procedure (Pt.1)," *Harv. L. Rev.* 71, no. 7 (1958): 1242. This quotation was taken from E. Sherwin and K.M. Clermont, "A Comparative View of Standards of Proof," *Am. J. Comp. L.* 50, no. 2 (2002): 243. See also, Sherwin and Clermont, "Comparative Standard of Proof," 256, where the French legal system also seems to put lots of faith in judges' intuitive conviction. In the authors' view, if the judges are selected from a particular elite end of the society, then it could be dangerous.
本杰明-卡普兰、阿瑟-T-冯-梅伦和鲁道夫-谢弗，《德国民事诉讼程序用语（第一部分）》，哈佛法律评论71, no. 7 (1958): 1242. 另见E.谢尔文和 K.M. 克莱蒙特，《比较证明标准》 256, 法国的法律制度似乎也非常相信法官的直觉。笔者认为，如果法官是从社会的某一精英阶层中挑选出来的，那就会很危险。

[878] Refer, Chapter 5, §5.5. 参见第 5 章第 5.5 节。

in common law is that it minimises the frequency of errors by the judges, so that generally they are able to find the truth in the cases before them.[879] However, the question that could be asked is: why are the common law jurisdictions satisfied with finding the truth on a scale of averages, rather than adopting the more stringent concept of Standards of proof as in the Civil law jurisdiction? Does it really minimise the errors, as common law jurisdictions seek to find truth on the basis of the possibility of success in an average number of cases it handles? Sherwin and Clermont answered these questions within the context of civil law jurisdictions by explaining that there are many reasons why these civil jurisdictions have higher Standards of proof — such as settlement of disputes without having to worry over the quality of settlement, discouraging litigation to reduce costs, etc., but above all the reason is to enhance the legitimacy of judicial decisions.[880]

念是尽量减少法官出错的频率，使他们在审理案件时一般都能发现真相。然而，我们可以提出这样一个问题：为什么普通法司法管辖区只满足于根据平均值找出真相，而不像大陆法系司法管辖区那样采用更严格的证明标准概念？普通法司法管辖区根据所处理案件的平均胜诉可能性来寻求真相，这样做真的能将错误降到最低吗？谢尔文和克莱蒙特在大陆法系司法管辖区的背景下回答了这些问题，他们解释说，大陆法系司法管辖区采用较高的证明标准有很多原因——如解决纠纷而不必担心和解的质量、不鼓励诉讼以降低成本等，但最重要的原因是为了提高司法判决的合法性。

Based on the above analysis, the authors are going to discuss a few logical questions. Does it then mean that the decisions in civil-law countries are perfect? It could also mean that the burden is so high in civil law traditions, that the party which has the burden of proof might not be able to meet the Standards of proof required in the civil law courts, even though that party could have won the same case within a common law jurisdiction. As a result of these stringent requirements, the party might end up losing the case in the civil law jurisdiction. Does it then really help the civil law legal system to increase the legitimacy of the courts in civil law countries, if many Claimants will end up dejected because of the high burden of proof? Would this not affect the legitimacy of the courts?

基上，笔者将讨论几个逻辑问题。这是否意味着大陆法系国家的判决是完美无缺？这也可能意味着在大陆法系传统中举证责任过重，负有举证责任的一方可能无法达到大陆法系法院所要求的举证标准，即使该方在普通法系法域可打赢同样的官司。由于这些严格的要求，当事人最终可能会在大陆法系司法管辖区败诉。这样一来，如果许多索赔人因举证责任过重而垂头丧气，这对提高大陆法系国家法院的合法性真的有帮助吗？这难道不会影响法院的合法性吗？

Additionally, in many civil law jurisdictions as compared to common law jurisdictions, the exact details of these stringent requirements as to Standards of proof is not clear.[881] How much

此外，与普通法司法管辖区相比，在许多大陆法系司法管辖区，这些关

---

879 Demougin and Fluet, "Comparative Standards of Proof," 193.
德穆金和弗吕特，"比较证明标准"，第193页。

880 Sherwin and Clermont, "Comparative Standard of Proof," 252–54. Sherwin & Clermon' views were discussed in Demougin and Fluet, "Comparative Standards of Proof," 193.
E.谢尔文和 K.M. 克莱蒙特，《比较证明标准》252-54. 德穆金和弗吕特的《比较证明标准》中讨论了谢尔文和克莱蒙特的观点

881 Sherwin and Clermont, "Comparative Standard of Proof," 45.
E.谢尔文和 K.M. 克莱蒙特，《比较证明标准》45.

evidence will be sufficient for it to be classed as certain in the eyes of the judges, for the Standards of proof to be met in any civil law jurisdictions? Does it involve any exercise of discretion by the judges? It is said that civil law judges usually apply variable standards in this context.[882] Interventions from the civil law judges are very common, while, on the other hand, the judges in common law jurisdictions will let the parties' lawyers present the case to them.[883]

于举证标准的严格要求的具体细节并不明确。在任何大陆法系司法管辖区，多少证据才足以在法官眼中被归类为确定的证据，才符合举证标准？这是否涉及法官行使自由裁量权？据说，民法法官在这种情况下通常采用不同的标准。大陆法系法官的干预非常常见，而普通法系的法官则会让当事人的律师向其陈述案情。

Additionally, in the common law, there are lots of 'exclusionary principles'[884] that have the potential to exclude relevant evidence from being submitted to the judges. It is difficult to measure and thus confirm that errors are, in fact, minimized in the common law system as compared to the civil law system, based on the test of 'balance of probabilities'. In any event, the focus in the civil law system is on finding the ultimate truth. In addition, in the civil law jurisdiction there is a possibility of changing even the burden of proof midway due to judicial interventions. In contrast, in the civil law jurisdictions, there are fewer exclusionary principles in relation to what the courts may be willing to accept as evidence.

此外，在普通法中，有许多“排除原则”有可能排除向法官提交相关证据。与大陆法系相比，普通法系很难根据“可能性权衡”的检验标准来衡量和确认错误是否确实最小化。无论如何，大陆法系的重点在于找到最终的真相。此外，在大陆法系司法管辖区，由于司法干预，甚至有可能中途改变举证责任。相比之下，在大陆法系司法管辖区，有关法院可能愿意接受的证据的排除原则较少。

In the end, no system is perfect, and many scholars have written

归根结底，没有一种制度是完美

[882]Ibid., 47. 同上，47。

[883] Refer, Chapter 5, §5.2. 参见第 5 章第 5.2 节。

[884]Exclusionary principles were developed in the area of criminal legal systems in common law jurisdictions. These principles were developed in the context of law of evidence, where particular evidence can be excluded as its *prejudicial value exceeds the probative value* and thereby evidence such as confessions, improperly obtained evidence etc. can be excluded at the judge's discretion, some of which were codified later through legislations.

In the civil cases as well the judges have discretion as provided in *CPR 1998* r. 31.1 (2) that provides that the court can give directions on — (a) the issues on which it requires evidence; (b) the nature of the evidence which it requires to decide those issues; (c) the way in which the evidence is to be placed before the court. However, there is more flexibility in civil litigation on parties to present the cases, but common law has developed some exclusion principles such as in the case of *ITC Film Distributors v Video Exchange* [1982] 2 All ER 246, where the claimant was granted an injunction to prevent the use of evidence by the defendant. The said evidence was picked up by the defendant due to the claimant's error.

However, there are rules developed in common law on admissibility of evidence such as in the case of *First Subsea Ltd v Balltec Ltd* [2013] EWHC 1033, where it was decided that relevant evidence would be heard, best source evidence will be preferred, focus of the judges will be on relevance, weight and probative effect of evidence. Judges will exhibit a cautious approach where the evidence is second-hand and will exclude evidence that can be tampered with and will allow indirect evidence where direct evidence is not available. For further discussion on the above in detail, see Blake, *A Practical Approach to Effective Civil Litigation*, 547–49.

排除原则是在普通法司法管辖区的刑事法律制度领域发展起来的。这些原则是在证据法的背景下发展起来的，在证据法中，特定证据因其不利价值超过证明价值而可被排除，因此供词、不正当获取的证据等证据可由法官酌情排除。

在民事案件中，法官也有 CPR 1998 第 31.1(2)条规定的自由裁量权，该条规定法院可就以下事项作出指示：(a)它要求提供证据的问题；(b)它要求就这些问题作出裁决的证据的性质；(c)将证据提交法院的方式。不过，普通法中也有关于证据可采性的规则，例如在First Subsea Ltd诉Balltec Ltd [2013] EWHC 1033一案中，法官决定听取相关证据，优先考虑最佳来源证据，重点关注证据的相关性、重要性和证明效力。如果证据为二手证据，法官将采取谨慎态度，排除可能被篡改的证据，并在无法获得直接证据的情况下允许间接证据。有关上述细节的进一步讨论，见Blake, A Practical Approach to Effective Civil Litigation, 547-49。

on the debates between different types of legal systems. Many mathematical studies have also been carried out to find the answers to the above questions. For the sake of completeness, mathematical studies have shown that the common law test for Standards of proof is better at providing incentives to members of society to act correctly rather than minimising errors, but the civil law test of Standards of proof is more likely concerned with finding the truth.[885] Such questions are essential to be kept in mind while pursuing comparative study.

无缺的，许多学者都曾撰文讨论过不同类型法律制度之间的争论。为了找到上述问题的答案，还进行了许多数学研究。为完整起见，数学研究表明，普通法的证明标准测试更能激励社会成员正确行事，而不是尽量减少错误，但大陆法的证明标准测试更倾向于发现真相。在进行比较研究时，必须牢记这些问题。

In the authors' view, since there are so many variables such as exclusionary rules within the context of law of evidence in the common law, the unpredictability of judges' interventions in the civil jurisdictions (which could shift the burden of proof, or even make the causes of actions to be looked at differently) then it is likely that no firm conclusions from mathematical models can be drawn as to which of the two systems is better in minimising errors in courts.

笔者认为，由于存在诸多变数，如普通法证据法背景下的排除规则、民事司法管辖区法官干预的不可预测性（这可能转移举证责任，甚至使诉讼原因受到不同的看待），因此很可能无法通过数学模型得出两种制度哪种更能减少法庭错误的确切结论。

Lastly, due to the subjectivity of judges towards evidence being mandated in civil law jurisdictions, in the authors' view, the selection of judges is a crucial issue. It is important that the judges are selected from all sections of society.

最后，大陆法系司法管辖区的法官对证据的主观性是强制性的，笔者认为法官的选择是一个关键问题。重要的是法官应从社会各阶层中遴选。

7.4.1.1 Standards of Proof in Interim Hearings under CPR in England & Wales

英格兰和威尔士《民事诉讼程序法》规定的临时听证的举证标准

The above discussion was about Standards of Proof in general. However, when there are interim applications in courts, common-law judges in England & Wales have devised many tests pertaining to Standards of Proof. In a normal trial, as discussed earlier, if one of the parties proves the case as more

以上讨论的是一般的证据标准。但是，在法院进行临时申请时，英格兰和威尔士的普通法法官设计了许多与证明标准有关的检验标准。在正常审判中，如前所述，如果一方当事人

[885] Demougin and Fluet, "Comparative Standards of Proof," 205.
德穆金和弗吕特的《比较证明标准》，第205页。

probable than not, then that party will win the case in the courts.[886] The importance of burden of proof is that once the burden of proof is discharged by the appropriate test of Standards of proof, then the courts will consider the facts as having happened in a dispute.[887] However, interlocutory hearings are different.

证明案件的可能性大于不可能，那么该方当事人就会在法庭上胜诉。举证责任的重要性在于，一旦通过适当的“证明标准”测试履行了举证责任，法院就会认为争议中的事实已经发生。然而，非正审则不同。

In any interlocutory hearings, the purpose is not to resolve the disputes; rather the parties are trying to regulate their position until the trials are over, or to obtain case management directions, or other similar issues. It needs to be appreciated that fact-finding processes involving witnesses' credibility, demeanour and cross-examination are not usually available to English judges in such interim hearings.

在任何中间听证中，目的都不是为了解决争议；相反，当事方试图在审判结束前调整自己的立场，或获得案件管理指示，或其他类似问题。需要认识到的是，在此类临时听证中，英国法官通常无法利用涉及证人可信度、举止和交叉质证的事实调查程序。

In addition, reliance circumstantial or contemporaneous evidence is not an option for the judges. From the case of *Prince of Wales v Associated Newspapers Ltd*,[888] it is clear that judges will decide any interim application on the basis of written applications containing facts and any fact that is disputed by the Respondents' version of the story. Judges will not usually go into the merits of the cases unless there are applications, for example applications for summary judgements or security for costs.

此外，依赖间接证据或同期证据也不是法官的选择。从“威尔士亲王诉联合报业公司”一案中可以清楚地看出，法官会根据载有事实的书面申请以及答辩人的说法中存在争议的任何事实对任何临时申请作出裁决。除非提出申请，例如申请简易判决或费用担保，否则法官通常不会审理案件的实体问题。

In all such interim applications, the English judges have a duty to balance the aim of the interim applications along with the

在所有这类临时申请中，英国法官有责任平衡临时申请的目的和首要

---

[886]See *Miller v Minister of Pensions* [1947] 2 All ER 372.
见*Miller v Minister of Pensions* [1947] 2 All ER 372.

[887]Stuart Sime, "Disputes of Fact in Interim Applications," in *The Civil Procedure Rules Ten Years On*, ed. Deirdre Dwyer (Oxford; New York: Oxford University Press, 2009), 274 See also *Re B (children) (care proceedings: standard of proof)* [2008] UKHL 35, Judge Baroness Hale said at [32] that:
"In our legal system, if a judge finds it more likely than not that something did take place, then it is treated as having taken place. If he finds it more likely than not that it did not take place, then it is treated as not having taken place. He is not allowed to sit on the fence. He has to find for one side or the other. [emphasis added] Sometimes the burden of proof will come to his rescue: the party with the burden of showing that something took place will not have satisfied him that it did. But generally speaking a judge is able to make up his mind where the truth lies without needing to rely upon the burden of proof."
斯图尔特-西姆，在“临时申请中的事实争议”一文中，迪尔德丽-德怀尔编辑的《民事诉讼规则十年》（牛津；纽约：牛津大学出版社，2009 年），第274页。另见Re B（儿童）（护理程序：举证标准）[2008] UKHL 35，黑尔男爵夫人法官说到：“在我们的法律制度中，如果法官认为某件事情确实发生过的可能性大于没有发生过的可能性，那么它就被视为发生过。如果他认为某件事情很有可能没有发生，那么它就会被视为没有发生。他不能坐视不管。他必须找到支持的一方或另一方。[强调是后加的]有时举证责任会帮他一把：有责任证明某件事情发生过的一方并没有让他确信它确实发生过。但一般来说，法官无需依赖举证责任，就能确定事实真相”。

[888][2006] EWCA Civ 1776; [2008] Ch 57.

overriding objective.[889] The courts will try to avoid the interim hearings turning into mini-trials. In order to balance the interests of all parties in these applications, the courts have formulated various tests for Standards of proof.

目标。法院会尽量避免临时听证变成小型审判。为平衡这些申请中各方的利益，法院制定了各种举证标准测试。

In order to understand these tests, it is important to understand what needs to be proved in England & Wales:[890]

为了理解这些检验标准，有必要了解在英格兰和威尔士需证明什么：

- ♦ Law through statutes or case precedent may require that some facts need to be proved to establish legal right. These are called *facts in issue* that need to be proved on balance of probabilities by a party having the burden of proof;
- ♦ In any case, there are a few facts that are required to be proved in order to predict the occurence of material facts. These facts also need to be proved on balance of probabilities by a party having the burden of proof;
- ♦ Facts that are to become part of the foundation from which the fact of issue needs to be inferred, do not need to be proved to have happened.

- ◆ 法律通过法规或案例先例可能会要求证明某些事实以确立法律权利。这些事实被称为*争议事实*，需要由负有举证责任的一方在权衡各种可能性后加以证明；
- ◆ 在任何情况下，为了预测重要事实的发生，都需要证明一些事实。负有举证责任的一方也需要根据可能性的权衡来证明这些事实；
- ◆ 作为推断争议事实的基础的事实不需要证明已经发生。

The different types of tests for Standards of proof are applicable in the interlocutory or the interim hearings. In such interim hearings, the judges are not concerned with resolving the disputes or deciding the conflicting evidence presented to the courts. The default test for standards of proof in such interim hearings is that the applicants have a '*good arguable case*'. However, different Standards of proof have developed over the years for interim hearings, to ensure that the tests for Standards of proof are fit for the purpose.[891]

不同类型的举证标准测试适用于中间听证或临时听证。在此类临时听证中，法官并不关注解决争议或裁定向法庭提交的相互矛盾的证据。在此类临时听证中，默认的举证标准是申请人有“可论证的充分理由”。然而，多年来为临时听证制定了不同的举证标准，以确保举证标准测试符合目的。

[889] Sime, "Interim Application – Dispute of Facts," 271–74.
西姆，“临时申诉-事实争议”271–74。
[890] See *Re B (children) (care proceedings: standard of proof)* [2008] UKHL 35, [3]. (Lord Hoffmann)
见关于B（儿童）（照料程序：举证标准）[2008] UKHL 35，[3]。(霍夫曼勋爵）。
[891] Sime, "Interim Application - Dispute of Facts," 276–9.

The flexibility shown by tests is an example of common-law judges' discretionary power. More importantly, it also showcases the ability of the common law to adapt to different circumstances, or to the nature of applications, and to balance the interests of even other stakeholders not party to the disputes.

测试所显示的灵活性是普通法法官自由裁量权的一个例子。重要的是它还展示了普通法适应不同情况或申请性质的能力，以及平衡甚至非争议一方的其他利益相关者利益的能力。

A few of the tests for Standards of proof that have been developed over the years by the English courts for various types of interim applications in courts are as follows:

英国法院多年来针对各类型临时申请制定的一些举证标准测试如下：

- Test of 'Good arguable case' — In this test, a party needs to prove that the merits of the case have a few serious arguments. Sime is of the view this test is very similar to the usual *prima facie* test that the applicants have to satisfy in many different applications.[892] Cases have highlighted that this test can vary depending on the cases.[893]

- "有理有据"检验标准——在这一检验标准中，一方当事人需要证明的案件实体问题有几处需要认真论证。西姆认为，这一检验标准与通常的表面证据检验标准非常相似，申请人在许多不同的申请中都必须满足这一标准。一些案例表明，这一检验标准可能因案件而异。

- Test of 'better argument on the material available' — In this test, the applicants must prove their case a bit more on evidence as compared to the test of 'good arguable case'.

- "根据现有材料进行更好的论证"检验标准——与"良好的可论证案件"的检验标准相比，在这一检验标准中，申请人必须在更多的证据上证明自己的案件。

- Test of 'Serious cases on merits' — In the interim injunction applications, the applicants need to satisfy the courts that there is a *serious question that needs to be tried* in the dispute and accordingly, the

- "案情实质严重"检验标准——在临时禁令申请中，申请人需让法院确信在争议中存在需要审判的严重问题，因此，申请人需要根据证据

西姆，"临时申诉 - 事实争议"，第276–9页。

[892]Sime, "Interim Application - Dispute of Facts," 277.

西姆，"临时申诉 - 事实争议" 277。

[893]Sime, "Interim Application - Dispute of Facts," 277. See also, *WPP Holdings Italy SRL v Benatti* [2007] EWCA Civ 263; [2007] 1 WLR 2316.

西姆，"临时申诉 - 事实争议" 277。另见 WPP Holdings Italy SRL 诉 Benatti [2007] EWCA Civ 263; [2007] 1 WLR 2316。

applicants need to prove a prima facie case on merits on evidence. [894]

证明案情实质表面成立。

- Test of 'Real Prospect of success' — In these applications, the applicants have to prove that there is a '*realistic*' in contrast to a '*fanciful*' prospect of success in the main dispute.[895] From the recent case *ED & F Man Liquid Products Ltd v Patel*,[896] the test from dicta of Potter LJ must be as follows: "*case is better than merely arguable" and "must carry some degree of conviction."*

- "真实的胜诉前景"测试——在这些申请中，申请人须证明在主要争议中存在"现实的"而非"虚构的"成功前景。在最近的 ED & F Man Liquid Products Ltd v Patel 案中，波特大法官的判词规定了如下测试标准："*案件不仅仅是可争辩的*"，"*必须具有一定程度的说服力*"。

- Test of 'Equal prospect of success' — In applications for interim injunctions, in exceptional cases, the court had awarded a mandatory injunction on the basis of test of equal prospect of success with the opponent and accordingly the requirement of evidence will reflect that.[897]

- "胜诉机会均等"检验标准——在申请临时禁令时，在特殊情况下，法院会根据与对方胜诉机会均等的检验标准颁发强制禁令，因此证据要求也会反映这一点。

- Test of 'High degree of assurance' — As discussed earlier, the courts expect to be convinced that the merits of the case are *quite high*,[898] before they will grant the mandatory injunction. This means court would like to be satisfied a bit more on evidence.

- "高度确信"的检验标准——如前所述，法院在签发强制禁令之前，希望确信案件的案情相当重大。这意味着法院希望在证据方面更令人满意一些。

- Test of 'obvious case' — This test has been used by the courts before granting a

- "显而易见的案件"检验标准——法院在签发禁止令之前会使用该检验标准。

[894]See *American Cyanamid Co v Ethicon Ltd* (No 1) [1975] AC 396 (HL).
见 American Cyanamid Co v Ethicon Ltd (No 1) [1975] AC 396 (HL)。
[895]See *Swain v Hillman* [2001] 1 All ER 9.
见 Swain v Hillman [2001] 1 All ER 9。
[896][2003] CPLR 384, [8] (Potter LJ);[2003] EWCA Civ 472.
[897]See *Leisure Data v Bell* [1988] FSR 367 (CA). In this case, it appears that the mandatory injunction was granted as an exception because the applicant/claimant gave a wide-ranging undertaking to protect the defendant's position and on the facts of the case, only the claimant would have been able to commercially use the computer program.
见 Leisure Data v Bell [1988] FSR 367 (CA)。在本案中，强制禁令似乎是作为例外情况批准的，因为申请人/原告作出了广泛的承诺，以保护被告的地位，而且根据本案的事实，只有原告才能在商业上使用计算机程序。
[898]See *Chambers v British Olympic Association* (2008) LTL 18 July 2008; [2008] EWHC 2028 (QB).
见 Chambers 诉英国奥林匹克协会（2008 年）LTL 2008 年 7 月 18 日；[2008] EWHC 2028 (QB)。

prohibitory injunction.

- Test of 'No reasonable grounds' — This test is very similar to the test of Standards of proof, and it requires the party to show that there is no reasonable ground for the opponent to argue a particular cause of action.

- "无合理理由"检验标准——该检验标准与举证标准的检验标准非常相似，它要求当事人证明对方没有合理的理由提出特定的诉因。

- Test of 'Reasonable possibility' — It is granted to the applicants where there is a *reasonable possibility* that the applications for freezing injunction might be made in future.[899]

- "合理可能性"检验标准——如果申请人有合理的可能性在将来申请冻结令，则可获得冻结令。

- Test of 'real possibility' — In the applications for obtaining the search orders to preserve evidence, the applicants have to satisfy the courts with evidence that there is a *real possibility* that the material evidence will be destroyed.[900]

- "真实可能性"检验标准——在申请搜查令以保存证据时，申请人必须向法院提供证据，证明物证确实有可能被销毁。

- Test of 'extremely strong prima facie case' —In this test, the applicants' burden in relation to Standards of proof is *higher* as compared to just showing to the courts that they have a good arguable case. This test is used in obtaining search orders.

- "表面证据极其充分"检验标准——在这一标准下，申请人在举证标准方面的责任比仅仅向法院表明他们有一个很好的可论证的案件要高。该测试用于获得搜查令。

- Test of 'strong prima facie case' — This test is used by showing there is a *strong prima facie* case against respondents who included false information in the witness statement that was verified by a Statement of Truth.[901]

- "表面证据确凿"检验标准——该检验标准用于证明被申请人有确凿的表面证据，证明被申请人在证人陈述中提供了虚假信息，并经真实性声明核实。

[899]See *Lichter v Rubin* [2008] EWHC 450 (Ch); The Times, 18 April 2008.
见 Lichter 诉 Rubin [2008] EWHC 450 (Ch)；《泰晤士报》，2008 年 4 月 18 日。
[900]See *Anton Piller KG v Manufacturing Processes Ltd* [1976] Ch 55. See also CPR r. 25.1(1)(h).
见 Anton Piller KG 诉 Manufacturing Processes Ltd [1976] Ch 55。另见 CPR 第 25.1(1)(h)条。
[901]Sime, "Interim Application - Dispute of Facts," 277–8.
西姆，"临时申诉 - 事实争议" 277-8。

- Test of 'Solid Evidence' — In this test, the applicants must show clear evidence that the respondents have incriminating evidence against which an order of the court is requested.

- "确凿证据"检验标准——在此检验标准中，申请人必须出示明确的证据，证明被申请人拥有请求法院下达命令的有罪证据。

- Test of 'Overwhelming case' —The test is more stringent than that for a case that is merely a serious issue to be tried.[902] Accordingly, the judge needs to be satisfied a bit more on evidence.

- "压倒性案件"检验标准——该检验标准比仅仅是需要审判的严重问题的案件的检验标准更为严格。因此，法官需要更多的证据。

- Test of 'Reason to believe' — These tests are applied when the courts have to decide whether the claimants should provide security for costs to the defendants, in case the claimants were to lose the case in future trials.[903]

- "有理由相信"检验标准——这些检验标准适用于法院决定原告是否应向被告提供诉讼费用担保，以防原告在今后的审判中败诉。

7.4.2 Standards of Proof in context of PRC Procedural Law

《中华人民共和国诉讼法》中的证明标准

We have seen from the above discussion,[904] how the civil law tradition differs from the common law traditions, and even the philosophy behind approaches pertaining to Standards of Proof. The discussion on Standards of Proof in PRC law will be no different. Chen wrote as far back as in 2002, while working in Xiamen Intermediate People's Court, that the discussion on

从上述讨论中，我们看到了大陆法系传统与普通法系传统的不同之处，甚至是有关证明标准的方法背后的理念。关于中国法下的证明标准的讨论也不会有什么不同。早在 2002 年，陈朝阳写道："关于证明标准的讨论是

[902]See *Lansing Linde Ltd v Kerr* [1991] 1 WLR 251; [1991] 1 All ER 418. See also, *Phoenix Partners Group LLP v Asoyag* [2010] IRLR 594. See also, *Cayne v Global Natural Resources plc* [1984] 1 All ER 225.
见 Lansing Linde Ltd v Kerr [1991] 1 WLR 251; [1991] 1 All ER 418。另见 Phoenix Partners Group LLP 诉 Asoyag [2010] IRLR 594。另见，Cayne 诉 Global Natural Resources plc [1984] 1 All ER 225。

[903]See CPR r. 25.13(2) (c).
见 CPR 第 25.13(2)(c)条。

[904]Refer Chapter 7, §7.4.1. 参见第 7 章第 7.4.1 节。

Standards of proof is a matter of practice of law.[905]

一个法律实践问题。

In the civil law tradition or in the PRC, unlike with common law, the starting point for any discussion would be the relevant codes from *CPL*. The relevant codes from *CPL* are as follows:

在大陆法系或中国，与普通法不同，任何讨论的起点都是《民事诉讼法》等相关规则。相关规则如下：

- Article 66 of *CPL 2023* provides:

Evidence shall include as follows:
(1) Statements of parties concerned;
(2) documentary evidence;
(3) material evidence;
(4) audio-visual material;
(5) electronic data;
(6) testimony of witnesses;
(7) expert conclusions; and
(8) records of inspection.

<u>The evidence must be verified before it can be taken as a basis for ascertaining a fact</u> [emphasis added].

- 2023 年《民事诉讼法》第 66 条规定：

证据包括：
（一） 当事人的陈述；
（二） 书证；
（三） 物证；
（四） 视听资料；
（五） 电子数据；
（六） 证人证言；
（七） 鉴定结论；
（八） 勘验笔录。

<u>证据必须查证属实，才能作为认定事实的根据。</u>[着重部分由笔者标明]。

- Article 67 of *CPL 2023* provides:

If, for objective reasons, a party and his agent are unable to collect the evidence by themselves or if the people's court considers the evidence necessary for the trial of the case, <u>the People's court shall investigate and collect it</u> [emphasis added].
The People's court shall, in accordance with the procedure prescribed by the law, <u>examine and verify evidence **comprehensively and objectively**</u> [emphasis added].

- 2023 年《民事诉讼法》第 67 条规定：

当事人及其诉讼代理人因客观原因不能自行收集的证据，或者人民法院认为审理案件需要的证据，<u>人民法院应当调查收集</u>。[着重号后加]。

人民法院应当按照法定程序，<u>**全面地、客观地**审查核实证据</u>。[着重号后加]。

[905] Chen Chao-yang (Xiamen Intermediate People's Court), "Standards of Proof," 1.
陈朝阳（厦门市中级人民法院），《证明标准》，第1页。

- Article 96 of *CPL 2023* provides:

> In the trial of civil cases, the People's Court shall distinguish between right and wrong on the basis of the facts being clear [emphasis added] ....

- Article 177 of *CPL 2023* in the context of appeal in the second instance court provides:

> ... (3) if in the original judgment the basic facts were not clearly ascertained [emphasis added], the People's Court of second instance set aside the judgment and remand the case to the original people's court for retrial, or mend the judgment after investigating and clarifying the facts.

- 2023年《民事诉讼法》第96条规定：

> 人民法院审理民事案件，在事实清楚的基础上，分清是非，[着重号后加] ......

- 2023年《民事诉讼法》第177条在二审法院上诉时规定

> ...（三）原判决认定基本事实不清的[着重号后加]，裁定撤销原判决，发回原审人民法院重审，或者查清事实后改判。

Article 67 of *CPL 2023* clearly provides that the judges will examine the evidence '*comprehensively and objectively*'. In the authors' view, this test for standard of proof is a combination of the common law test and the civil law test. First, the Standards of proof are very comprehensive. They are similar to the continental European standards but again any *subjectivity of the judges* is ruled out by using the word '*objectively*'.

2023年《民事诉讼法》第67条明确规定，法官将"客观全面地"审查证据。这一证明标准是普通法检验标准和民法检验标准的结合。首先，证明标准非常全面。它们与欧洲大陆的标准相似，但同样通过使用"客观"一词排除了法官的主观性。

This objective test is similar to the common law test and can be differentiated from the civil law test for Standards of proof, for example as seen earlier from German Codes. The same article also allows the judges to investigate and collate the evidence. It seems to be the case that the focus in PRC courts is on finding the truth. It also means that the burden on the parties to prove their case in terms of Standards of proof is very high. In the authors' view, the claimants can win a case in the English jurisdiction but may end up losing the same case in the PRC courts because Standards of proof are set too high. It is also quite possible that case itself might not be accepted by the courts to be litigated as discussed earlier.[906]

这种客观检验标准与普通法检验标准类似，可以与大陆法系的证明标准检验标准区分开来，例如前面从《德国法典》中就可以看出这一点。同一条还允许法官调查和整理证据。看来，中国法院的重点是查明真相。这也意味着在举证标准方面，当事人的举证责任非常重。笔者认为，原告可以在英国司法管辖区打赢官司，但可能最终在中国法院输掉同样的官司，因为举证标准定得太高。如前所述，案件本身也很有可能不被法院受理。

[906] Refer §7.4.1 参见第7.4.1节。

From the various articles, the Standards of proof in criminal proceedings, administrative law proceedings or civil proceedings are nearly the same in the PRC legal system; namely that the evidence must be found 'objectively' by the judges. Nonetheless, as discussed in the context of the common law, even if the test is objective in terms of finding facts, the subjectivity of the judges' cognition is still involved in assessing this evidence. Cheng has also discussed this point in his book on evidence.[907] But then again, how high the Standards of proof actually are in the PRC courts is still debated even among academics and practising lawyers.

从不同的文章来看，在中国的法律制度中，刑事诉讼、行政法诉讼或民事诉讼的证明标准几乎是相同的，即证据必须由法官 "客观地" 认定。然而，正如在普通法中讨论的那样，即使在认定事实方面是客观的，但在评估这些证据时仍涉及法官认知的主观性。程在他的关于证据的著作中也讨论了这点。然而，中国法院的证据标准究竟有多高，即使在学术界和执业律师中也仍存在争议。

This debate swings between two poles. Chen and Wei suggest that it should be '*objectively true*' and it should mean that the judges must find as to what actually happened in the case.[908] However, other scholars have suggested the test for Standards of proof to be *'facts are clear and evidence is sufficient'* and are part of three-stage tests '*objectivity, legality and certainty*'.[909] A few PRC scholars have suggested the test for Standards of proof is to be '*legally true*' or '*relatively true*'.[910]

这一争论在两极之间摇摆。陈和韦认为，证据应该是 "客观真实的"，这意味着法官须查明案件中实际发生的情况。然而，其他学者则认为证明标准的检验标准应为 "事实清楚、证据充分"，并且是 "客观性、合法性和确定性" 三阶段检验标准的一部分。少数中国学者认为证明标准的检验标准是 "法律上真实" 或 "相对真实"。

In the authors' view, this excessive focus bordering on obsession to find the 'objective truth' in the PRC legal system

笔者认为，在中国的法律体系中，这种对 "客观真相" 的过度关注近乎

[907]Yiyun Cheng, *Science of Evidence* (Beijing: People's Public Security University of China Press, 1991), 114. Cheng's views on the issue of judges' role in relation to objective evidence in the context of the PRC was discussed in Chen Chao-yang (Xiamen Intermediate People's Court), "Standards of Proof.".
程逸云，《证据科学》（北京：中国人民公安大学出版社，1991年），第114页。程对中国法官在客观证据方面的作用问题的观点在陈朝阳（厦门市中级人民法院）的"证明标准"中有所论述。

[908]Chen Chao-yang (Xiamen Intermediate People's Court), "Standards of Proof." Chan and Wei's views were discussed in Chao-Yang's article. See also, Guangzhong Chen, Haiguang Chen, and Xiaona Wei, "The System of Criminal Evidence and Epistemology - Discussion between Legal Truth and Relative Truth," *China Legal Science*, no. 1 (2001): 37-52.
陈朝阳（厦门市中级人民法院），"证明标准"。陈、魏的观点在朝阳的文章中有所论述。参见陈光中、陈海光、魏晓娜："刑事证据制度与认识论--关于法律真实与相对真实的讨论"，《中国法律科学》，2001年第1期：37-52.

[909]Chen Chao-yang (Xiamen Intermediate People's Court), "Standards of Proof." Xiong's article was discussed in Chao-Yang. See also, Zhihai Xiong, "Objective and Subjective Norms of Procedural Testimony," *Modern Law Science* 22, no. 5 (2000): 75-80. 陈朝阳（厦门市中级人民法院），"证明标准"。朝阳对熊志海的文章进行了讨论。另见熊志海："程序性证言的客观规范与主观规范"，《现代法学》第22卷第5期（2000 年）："程序性证言的客观规范与主观规范"。5 (2000): 75-80。

[910]Chen Chao-yang (Xiamen Intermediate People's Court), "Standards of Proof." Fan's article was discussed in this comprehensive article. See also, Chongyi Fan, "Opinions on Objective Truth," *China Legal Science*, no. 1 (2000): 114-120.
陈朝阳（厦门市中级人民法院），"证明标准"。范崇义的文章在这篇综合文章中有所论述。另见范崇义，"关于客观真实的观点"，《中国法律科学》2000年第 1 期，第114-120页。

can cause delay and has the potential to waste judicial resources. PRC scholar Li's views on the risks of adopting high Standards of proof are as follows: [911]

- it can create inefficiency;
- it can scare the claimants due to the sheer burden of the high standards of proof;
- it can create possibilities for a retrial pursuant to Art 177 (3) of *CPL (as amended in 2021)* to fulfil the requirement of '*objective truth*'. This could affect finality of judgment; and
- it can necessitate the need to carry out further investigations

痴迷，可能会造成延误，并有可能浪费司法资源。中国学者李对采用高证明标准的风险有如下看法：

- 它可能造成效率低下；
- 高标准的举证责任可能会吓倒原告；
- 根据2023年《民事诉讼法》第177(3)条，为满足"客观真相"要求，可能会出现重审。这可能会影响判决终局性；
- 这可能导致有必要开展进一步调查。

In the authors' view, excessive judicial intervention in order to seek the comprehensive and objective truth is not beneficial to enhance the legitimacy of the legal system because these interventions have the potential to create a perception of bias against one of the parties. For the sake of completeness, Article 2 of *Some Provisions of the Supreme People's Court on Evidence in Civil Procedures (No. 33 of [2001], as amended in 2019*) provides that the PRC courts can participate in collecting evidence and will direct the parties in relation to it.[912]

笔者认为，为寻求全面客观的真相而进行过度的司法干预不利于提高法律制度的合法性，因为这些干预有可能造成对一方当事人有偏见的看法。为完整起见，《最高人民法院关于民事诉讼证据的若干规定》（法释[2001]33号，2019年修订）第二条规定，中华人民共和国法院可以参与收集证据，并指导当事人收集证据。

However, with the introduction of these latest Rules of Evidence, the litigants taking advantage of the philosophy of the PRC courts about seeking the '*objective truth*' cannot now force a retrial easily, as time limits are also set for the presentation of

然而，随着最新《证据规定》的出台，当事人利用中国法院追求"客观真实"的理念，现在已不能轻易强制重审，因为对当事人举证也有时间限制。

911Chen Chao-yang (Xiamen Intermediate People's Court), "Standards of Proof." See also, Guoguang Li, *Guidance and Reference on Economic Trail* (Beijing: Legal Press, 2001).
陈朝阳（厦门市中级人民法院），"证明标准"。另见李国光：《经济审判指导与参考》，北京：法律出版社，2001年。

912See Art. 2 *Some Provisions of the Supreme People's Court on Evidence in Civil Procedures (as amended in 2019*) provides: "The People's court shall inform the parties concerned of the requirements for producing evidences and the of the corresponding legal liabilities so that the parties concerned may produce evidence actively, completely, correctly and honestly within the reasonable time period. Any party who cannot independently collect evidences due to objective reasons may request the People's court to investigate and collect [emphasis added]."
见《最高人民法院关于民事诉讼证据的若干规定》(2019年修订）第2条规定"人民法院应当向当事人说明举证的要求及法律后果，促使当事人在合理期限内积极、全面、正确、诚实地完成举证。当事人因客观原因不能自行收集的证据，可申请人民法院调查收集[着重号后加]"。

evidence by the litigants.[913]

In the authors' view, there are so many uncertainties in any story having facts, human emotions, perceptions, prejudices, and biases; therefore, it is nearly impossible to find 'absolute truth', not just in the PRC but in any jurisdiction. Another factor, in the authors' view, is that focus on such high standards will definitely affect procedural justice. However, the authors have earlier discussed the issue of substantive and procedural justice in the PRC jurisdiction.[914]

笔者认为，任何故事都有许多不确定因素，包括事实、人的情感、认知、偏见和成见；因此要找到"绝对真理"几乎不可能，不仅在中国如此，在任何司法管辖区都是如此。笔者认为，另一个因素是对这种高标准的关注肯定会影响程序正义。然而，笔者早前已讨论过中国司法中的实体公正和程序公正问题。

It is a fact that in commercial and civil cases, the parties are not on equal footing. This focus on high Standards of proof needs to take this into account. The financially weaker parties are not fighting their case on an even footing as a financially stronger business entity. PRC scholars have recognised this dilemma and have therefore suggested a different version of Standard of proof that is '*legal truth*'.[915]

事实上，在商事和民事案件中，双方当事人的地位并不平等。对高标准举证的重视需考虑这一点。经济实力较弱的当事人与经济实力较强的商业实体在打官司时并不平等。中国学者已经认识到这一困境，因此提出了不同版本的证明标准，即"法律真实"。

As a comparativist, it appears to the authors that the PRC legal system, because it has such high Standard of proof requirements, is more concerned with substantive justice as compared to procedural justice.

作为一个比较主义者，笔者认为，中国法对举证标准要求如此之高，似乎更关注实体正义而非程序正义。

Standards of proof at the time of filing a case are also high and therefore, many cases do not even pass this initial high barrier pertaining to Standard of proof. This issue can even affect the litigation rights of parties, which are enshrined in the *PRC Constitution* and *CPL*.[916] Standards of proof at trial, as discussed above, seem to prefer substantive justice over procedural justice. However, the authors agree that a few causes of actions may demand higher Standards of proof such as cause

立案时的举证标准也很高，因此，许多案件甚至无法通过举证标准这一最初的高门槛。这个问题甚至会影响到《中华人民共和国宪法》和《民事诉讼法》所规定的当事人的诉讼权利。如上所述，审判中的证明标准似乎更倾向于实体正义而非程序正义。但笔者同意，少数诉因可能需要更高的举

[913]See *Rules on Civil Evidence, Interpretation of Laws issued by the Supreme People's Court, No. [2001]* 33, December 21, 2001, as amended in 2019.
《民事证据规则》，最高人民法院 2001 年 12 月 21 日法释[2001]33 号，2019 年修订。
[914] Refer, Chapter 4, §4.2.2 & §4.3.4.2. 参见第 4 章第 4.2.2 节和第 4.3.4.2 节。
[915]Chen Chao-yang (Xiamen Intermediate People's Court), "Standards of Proof."
陈朝阳（厦门市中级人民法院），"证明标准"。
[916]See Art. 2 of *CPL 12023.* 见2023年《中华人民共和国民事诉讼法》第2条。

of actions pertaining to commercial fraud, misrepresentation in contracts and so forth. However, the requirements for high Standards of proof cannot be taken as a requirement for all types of cases in civil and commercial litigations.

证标准，如与商业欺诈、合同虚假陈述等有关的诉因。但是，不能将高标准的举证要求作为民商事诉讼中所有类型案件的要求。

CHAPTER EIGHT — Can we understand China? Conclusions & Recommendations

第八章：我们能理解中国吗？结论与建议

8.1 Conclusions

结论

In this book, the authors have carried out a comparative analysis from various viewpoints and perspectives, for example, the effects of *invisible factors & contexts* in the civil justice system and how the two jurisdictions' legal systems have advanced on the recognised principles of civil and commercial litigations. The comparative analysis of individual invisible factors was carried out at the end of each chapter. In this section, the authors focuses on *an overview* of these analyses based on various practical aspects of economic development, augmented number of international projects originating in the PRC and further concluding remarks on the key findings.

在这本书中，笔者从不同的观点和角度进行了比较分析，例如，民事司法制度中无形因素和背景的影响，以及两个司法管辖区的法律制度如何推进公认的民商事诉讼原则。在每章的最后对各个无形因素进行对比分析。在本节中，笔者将根据经济发展的各个实际方面、源自中国的国际项目数量的增加以及对主要发现的进一步总结，重点概述这些分析。

The strengths and weaknesses of the law in both jurisdictions have been analysed through a comparative analysis of the invisible factors and contexts. Hopefully, the analysis carried out in the book will assist various stakeholders *to understand PRC a bit better*. The understanding of invisible factors and contexts is also required to understand one's own jurisdiction. This is in fact important for lawyers and judges, who usually originate from elite sections of society, particularly in many common law jurisdictions, and who may therefore assume, due to their elite background and education, that they know everything about the world or are aware of the aspirations and challenges of all segments of their own societies.

通过对无形因素和背景的比较分析，分析了两国法律的优势和劣势。希望本书中的分析能够帮助各利益相关者更好地了解中国。对看不见的因素和背景的理解也需要理解自己的管辖权。事实上，这对律师和法官来说很重要，他们通常来自社会的精英阶层，特别是在许多普通法司法管辖区，他们可能因此认为，由于他们的精英背景和教育，他们知道世界的一切，或者知道他们自己社会各阶层的愿望和挑战。

The *reason the authors selected* the jurisdictions of England & Wales and the PRC for the comparative study is that there are

笔者之所以选择英格兰和威尔士的司法管辖区和中国进行比较研究，

similarities between the two jurisdictions as both of these countries are leading trading and economic powers. On one hand, London (following the *common law system*) has been an international financial centre for over two centuries, while on the other hand, the PRC, following its own version of law ('PRC law') and influenced by many different schools of thought, has emerged as an economic superpower of the twenty-first century and is increasingly getting involved in international projects in many countries, for example through the Belt and Road Initiative.[917]

是因为这两个国家都是主要的贸易和经济大国，两者的司法管辖区有相似之处。一方面，伦敦（遵循普通法体系）两个多世纪以来一直是国际金融中心，而另一方面，中国遵循自己的法律（“中国法律”）并受到许多不同思想流派的影响，已成为二十一世纪的经济超级大国，并越来越多地参与许多国家的国际项目，例如通过“一带一路”倡议。

England & Wales, both being part of the United Kingdom, have a common substantive and procedural law within the unified and common civil justice system. As discussed in Chapter 1, the increase in international projects has meant that many PRC citizens involved in commerce now have to engage with foreign jurisdictions. The key findings in this book can help by acquainting them with invisible factors and contexts associated with other legal systems, helping them to protect their commercial interests.

英格兰和威尔士都是英国的一部分，在统一和共同的民事司法制度下有共同的实体法和程序法。正如第一章所讨论的，国际项目的增加意味着许多从事商业活动的中国公民现在不得不与外国司法管辖区打交道。本书的主要发现可以帮助他们了解与其他法律制度相关的无形因素和背景，帮助他们保护自己的商业利益。

Many of the International projects that originate in the PRC involve issues of Contract and Tort law, Investment law, Private International Law, Public International law, Banking Law, Environment Law, Maritime Law, Civil Procedural Law, and Alternative Dispute Resolution including Arbitration law and so forth. There is always an interaction of PRC law with the local law of the country where these international projects are carried out.

许多源自中国的国际项目涉及合同法和侵权法、投资法、国际私法、国际公法、银行法、环境法、海商法、民事诉讼法以及包括仲裁法在内的替代性争议解决等问题。中国法律与这些国际项目实施所在国的当地法律总是相互影响的。

The PRC is also involved in setting up Dispute resolution centres in many parts of world, for example in Hong Kong ("PRC") and Singapore. These dispute resolution centres are based on Chinese/PRC law characteristics and aim to resolve disputes arising in International projects. Additionally, many stakeholders can knock on the doors of PRC courts. Therefore, it is important for these stakeholders to understand the *invisible factors and contexts* that influence PRC law and also how the issues of *law in action* will pan out,[918] where PRC law or any

中国还参与在世界许多地方设立争议解决中心，例如在香港（“中华人民共和国”）和新加坡。这些争议解决中心以中国法为基础，旨在解决国际项目中产生的争议。此外，许多利益相关者可以敲开中国法院的大门。因此，对于这些利益相关者来说，了解影响中国法律的无形因素和背景，以及现行法律问题将如何产生，中国法或任何具有中

917 Refer, Chapter 1, §1.5.

918 Refer to Chapter 5. 参见第五章。

law with Chinese characteristics is applicable or even where it has an indirect influence through a back door channel.

国特色的法律在哪里适用，甚至在哪里通过渠道产生间接影响都很重要。

In order to understand the markedly unique PRC law, stakeholders from common law jurisdictions need a **benchmark** to comprehend the PRC legal system's strengths, weaknesses, opportunities and threats. In the authors' view, those benchmarks can be provided through a comparative analysis of invisible factors and contexts such as legal system, jurisprudence & philosophy, legal history, judges' powers including discretionary power and how the judicial activities are carried out pursuant to the PRC law as compared to the common law system. This book has attempted to fill this gap and be that initial benchmark study for such stakeholders, be they from the PRC or from countries outside the PRC.

为了理解明显独特的中国法律，来自普通法司法管辖区的利益相关者需要一个基准来理解中国法律制度的优势、劣势、机遇和威胁。笔者认为，这些**基准**可以通过对法律制度、法理学与哲学、法律史、法官的裁量权（包括自由裁量权）以及中国法律与普通法系的司法活动如何进行等无形因素和背景的比较分析来提供。本书试图填补这一空白，并成为这些利益相关者的初步基准研究，无论他们来自中国还是来自中国以外的国家。

In addition, economic growth in any nation, particularly with respect to trading powers, not only leads to increase of Gross Domestic Product in any country, but also steers the country towards am upsurge in export, import, buying & selling of goods and services, conceptualising & implementation of global projects and other market activities. The PRC's economy and its international projects are the perfect example of this phenomenon. The upswing in commerce & trade has piloted the country towards further investments (domestic & foreign direct investment), increased international and domestic trade, growth in both internal and external migration of people. Because of this, augmented transactions, both domestically and internationally, are carried out by that nation's own citizens and business organisations.

此外，任何国家的经济增长，特别是贸易大国的经济增长，不仅会导致任何国家国内生产总值的增加，而且还会使该国在出口、进口、商品和服务的买卖、全球项目的概念化和实施以及其他市场活动方面达到高潮。中国的经济及其国际项目就是这种现象的完美例子。商业和贸易的上升引导该国进一步投资（国内和外国直接投资），增加国际和国内贸易，国内和国外人口迁移的增长。正因为如此，无论是在国内还是在国际上，扩大的交易都是由本国公民和商业组织进行的。

The likelihood of *commercial disputes* arising during the upsurge of commercial activities, and possibly progressing to commercial litigation in the civil justice system or to arbitration, is a sizeable impediment to enhancing trade and enlarging the GDP of the country by increased trade and commerce. These potential commercial disputes could become even bigger stumbling blocks, if there were issues of trust in the civil justice system of the nation from which the business and projects originate. The benchmark study carried out in this book will assist stakeholders to avoid these potential disputes

在商业活动激增期间可能产生商业纠纷，并可能发展到民事司法系统的商业诉讼或仲裁，这对通过增加贸易和商业来促进贸易和扩大该国的国内生产总值是一个相当大的障碍。这些潜在的商业纠纷可能会成为更大的绊脚石，如果对商业和项目的发源地国家的民事司法制度存在信任问题的话。本书中进行的基准研究将帮助利益相关者避免这些潜在的争端转化为冲突，包括政

turning into conflicts, including political & military conflicts, in particular where there are big-ticket international projects between PRC organisations and organisations from other countries'.

治和军事冲突，特别是在中国组织与其他国家组织之间存在大型国际项目的情况下。

An important feature of this book has been the focus on the use of Maxeiner's distinction between *culturalism* and *functionalism.* This has allowed a comparison between the problems in a legal system or body of law from the *interior point of view* so that the readers can see how lawyers,[919] judges, arbitrators and other juridical stakeholders think of the legal process while using the *law in action* in both the PRC legal system and the common law of England & Wales. The authors have discussed in various chapters of this book how the thought process of the judges, [920]in particular, during the exercise of their discretionary power,[921] is affected by *contexts and invisible factors.*

这本书的一个重要特点是重点使用马克塞纳对文化主义和功能主义的区分。这允许从内部角度比较法律体系或法律体系中的问题，以便读者可以看到律师，法官，仲裁员和其他司法利益相关者在使用中国法律体系和英格兰和威尔士普通法中的现行法律时如何看待法律程序。笔者在本书的各个章节中讨论了法官的思维过程，特别是在行使其自由裁量权时，如何受到背景和无形因素的影响。

In addition, civil process in any jurisdiction is the mirror image of society and is affected by *contexts and invisible factors*. An understanding of the proper contexts and invisible factors through a comparative analysis will assist the readers to understand even the *external law* of both the common law system and the PRC system in the proper context.[922] To put it clearly, even the substantive law of codes, statutes, case precedents and so forth needs to be read and understood against the backdrop of contexts and invisible factors.

此外，任何司法管辖区的民事诉讼程序都是社会的镜像，受到语境和无形因素的影响。通过比较分析来理解适当的语境和无形的因素，将有助于读者在适当的语境中理解普通法系和中国法系的外部法。明确地说，即使是法典、成文法、判例等实体法，也需要在语境和无形因素的背景下进行阅读和理解。

The authors' advice to other researchers and stakeholders is to immerse themselves in the various aspects of PRC law and culture as part of the first step of comparative methodology, if they wish to take this benchmark study further. The contexts and invisible factors within a stakeholder's own jurisdictions are usually taken for granted, but in any comparative studies, it is crucial to understand the invisible factors and contexts within the PRC. It is hoped that the analysis in the book will assist PRC businessmen and corporations who have stakes outside the PRC, or who are arbitrating or litigating disputes in

笔者对其他研究人员和利益相关者的建议是，如果他们希望进一步开展这一基准研究，就应该将自己沉浸在中国法律和文化的各个方面，作为比较方法论的第一步。利益相关者自己管辖范围内的背景和无形因素通常被认为是理所当然的，但在任何比较研究中，了解中国境内的无形因素和背景至关重要。希望本书中的分析能够帮助在中国境外拥有股份的中国商人和公司，或者

919 Refer, Chapter 4, §4.3.3. 参见第 4 章，§4.3.3。
920 Refer to Chapter 5.参见第 5 章。
921 Refer to Chapter 6.参见第 6 章。
922 Refer Chapter 4, §4.3.3.参见第 4 章，第 4.3.3 节。

the common law system or even in other civil law based systems.

在普通法系甚至其他大陆法系进行仲裁或诉讼纠纷的商人和公司。

This book hopefully will assist the stakeholders and readers to avoid *assumptions* based on their own invisible factors and contexts, and/or the PRC's legal system. As a word of warning, the authors are not immune from the influence of invisible factors and biases; however, a great effort has been made to ensure that any discussion and analysis remain objective without any bias against either common law or PRC Law. Diversity of thought is what makes this world a beautiful place but there is also a need to avoid potential conflicts and disputes for the sake of the next generation.

本书希望能够帮助利益相关者和读者避免基于自身的无形因素和背景，以及/或中国法律制度的假设。需要提醒的是，笔者并非不受无形因素和偏见的影响；然而，我们已经做出了很大的努力，以确保任何讨论和分析都是客观的，没有任何对普通法或中国法的偏见。思想的多样性使这个世界变得美丽，但为了下一代，也需要避免潜在的冲突和争端。

It is believed that the findings in this book can also be useful in analysing the opportunities and threats that lie ahead for both jurisdictions, in particular, the effects of such threats and opportunities on sustaining and enhancing economic prosperity and commercial transactions, on enhancing the trust of stakeholders with commercial interests in both the legal systems, on reducing transaction costs by an effective civil justice system in the market economy, on initiating reforms in the respective jurisdictions, and so forth.

相信本书的研究结果也有助于分析两国司法管辖区面临的机遇和威胁，特别是这些威胁和机遇对维持和促进经济繁荣和商业交易的影响，对增强两国法律体系中具有商业利益的利益相关者的信任的影响，对通过有效的民事司法制度降低市场经济中的交易成本的影响。在各自的司法管辖区启动改革，等等。

It is noteworthy that in recent years there has been a surge in reforms carried out in Civil Procedure law in many countries such as England & Wales, Norway, Japan and so forth. As discussed above, the main reason for such a surge is globalization, which has led to increased business and commercial activities as a result of interaction between countries, their corporate businesses and also between citizens of these countries. Most reforms that were carried out in any jurisdiction were compelled to take into account the needs of stakeholders from outside that jurisdiction.

值得注意的是，近年来，英格兰和威尔士、挪威、日本等许多国家对民事诉讼法进行了大量改革。如上所述，这种激增的主要原因是全球化，由于国家之间、公司之间以及这些国家的公民之间的互动，全球化导致了商业和商业活动的增加。在任何司法管辖区进行的大多数改革都被迫考虑到该司法管辖区以外利益攸关方的需求。

As an example, reforms were carried out in Norway and have been in force from Jan. 1, 2008 due to the effects of globalisation. According to those reforms:

例如，由于全球化的影响，挪威进行了改革，并于2008年1月1日生效。根据这些改革：

> It is important that procedure be in principle familiar and understandable also for parties coming from

> 重要的是，程序原则上也要为来自国外的当事人所熟悉和理解。法院

abroad. The courts are increasingly dealing with cases originating in transnational activities which involve non Norwegian parties [emphasis added].[923]

越来越多地处理涉及非挪威当事方的跨国活动案件。

The above example from Norway is also relevant for the PRC.[924] The next logical step is for the authors to recommend the possible reforms that can be undertaken in both the jurisdictions based upon the key findings and discussion carried out in this book. One such area is effectiveness of the judges in both the systems, in particular in the PRC. In the authors' view, *judicial effectiveness* will be a significant factor in the PRC maintaining its status as an economic superpower, while it will also be important for London with its common law system to retain its position as the leading financial centre of the world.

上述挪威的例子也适用于中国。下一个合乎逻辑的步骤是笔者根据本书的主要发现和讨论，建议在这两个法域可能进行的改革。其中一个领域是两种制度中法官的效力，特别是在中国。在笔者看来，司法效力将是中国保持其经济超级大国地位的一个重要因素，而对于拥有普通法体系的伦敦来说，保持其作为世界主要金融中心的地位也很重要。

Even the perception among those involved in commerce of issues in the PRC – such as 'similar cases, different rulings' in different courts within PRC (*tong'an bu tong' pan*),[925] or local protection by the courts (*defang bao hu zhu yi*),[926] or misunderstandings in relation to discretionary power of judges in any civil law system, such as confusing it with arbitrariness – can be fatal to trade and commerce in the PRC in the long-term. In particular, it will deter stakeholders from resolving any disputes arising out of the PRC's big-ticket international projects such as the Belt and Road Initiative, in dispute resolution centres based on PRC law or in PRC courts.

即使涉及中国商业的人们对中国问题的看法——例如中国不同法院的“同案不同判”，或法院的地方保护主义，或对任何民法制度中法官的自由裁量权的误解，例如将其与任意性混为一谈——从长远来看，对中国的贸易和商业都是致命的。特别是，它会妨碍利益相关者在基于中国法律的争议解决中心或在中国法院解决因中国大型国际项目（如“一带一路”倡议）引起的任何争议。

Lastly, the understanding that judicial effectiveness during *law in action* is part of the *service* industry needs to gain traction within the PRC political and legal set-up, particularly for

最后，法律实施过程中的司法效力是服务业的一部分，这一认识需在中国的政治和法律体系中得到

[923]I.L. Backer, "The Norwegian Reform of Civil Procedure," *Scandinavian Studies in Law* 51 (2007): 41–76. It was Quoted in Oscar G. Chase and Vincenzo Varano, "Comparative Civil Justice," in *The Cambridge Companion to Comparative Law*, ed. M. Bussani and U. Mattei (Cambridge; New York: Cambridge University Press, 2012), 221.
贝克尔，《挪威民事诉讼制度改革》，《斯堪的纳维亚法学研究》，2007年第51期，第41-76页。引用于Oscar G. Chase和Vincenzo Varano, “比较民事司法”，《剑桥比较法指南》，M. Bussani和U. Mattei(剑桥；纽约：剑桥大学出版社，2012),221。

[924]The PRC is actively involved in many international projects and already is an economic superpower. This means that foreign interests are bound to increase in the PRC legal system. Most of the foreigners will not be interested in the PRC's Constitutional Law or Family law, but one area they will encounter regularly due to commercial interests is the Civil Procedural law and the invisible factors and contexts affecting the PRC law.
中国积极参与许多国际项目，已经是一个经济超级大国。这意味着外国利益在中国法律体系中必然会增加。大多数外国人不会对中国的宪法或家庭法感兴趣，但由于商业利益，他们会经常遇到的一个领域是民事诉讼法以及影响中国法律的无形因素和背景。

[925] Refer to, Chapter 7, §7.2.2. 参见第 7 章，第 7.2.2 节。

[926] Refer, Chapter 6, §6.3.3. 参见第 6 章，第 6.3.3 节。

resolving commercial disputes on international projects. However, this change in mind-set will require a fundamental change in selection, training, retention, and on-the-job training of the judges/arbitrators in the civil justice systems. This is relevant as these judges/arbitrators will ultimately decide on commercial disputes.

推动，特别是在解决国际项目的商业纠纷方面。然而，这种思维方式的转变需在民事司法系统中法官/仲裁员的选拔、培训、留用和在职培训方面发生根本性的变化。这是相关的，因为这些法官/仲裁员将最终决定商业纠纷。

The selection and training of judges and other employees in the legal system will be the key issue for administrators in the PRC. In addition, to maintain consistency in applying the law at all levels in all provinces of the PRC will not be easy because of its vast landmass. This issue is compounded by the fact that various judicial activities are still developing in the PRC,[927] and there is still a dearth of understanding of newly developed substantive laws and the issues surrounding them. For example, in English Courts, the judges have devised many interim remedies by taking into account the commercial needs of businesses. Any such exercise of judicial discretion is unthinkable in the PRC where judges are also supervised by the Procuratorate system.[928]

法官们和其他法律系统雇员的选拔和培训将是中国行政人员面临的关键问题。此外，由于幅员辽阔，要在中国所有省份的各级保持法律的一致性并不容易。中国的各种司法活动仍在发展，对新制定的实体法及其相关问题的理解仍然缺乏，这一事实使这一问题更加复杂。例如，在英国法院，法官们考虑到企业的商业需要，制定了许多临时补救办法。这种司法自由裁量权的行使在中国是不可想象的，因为中国的法官也受到检察制度的监督。

Therefore, as discussed above, the need to look at the civil justice system in the PRC in economic terms will definitely bring into focus the *software part of the legal system*; that is, the transforming role of judges in relation to commercial disputes, training of judges, independence of judges, supervision of judges and so forth. In order for judges to exercise discretionary power or be significantly more willing to exercise their discretionary power to grant appropriate remedies in commercial disputes, is where the greatest challenge lies in the PRC.

因此，如上所述，从经济角度看待中国民事司法制度的必要性肯定会使法律制度的软件部分成为焦点；即法官在商事纠纷中的角色转换、法官的培训、法官的独立性、法官的监督等。为了让法官行使自由裁量权或更愿意在商业纠纷中行使自由裁量权给予适当的救济，这是中国面临的最大挑战。

The effects of invisible factors such as historical jurisprudence, current legal system, origins of legal and civil procedure system are crucial in the software part of the legal system in the PRC. Stakeholders from the common law system will find this software aspect of the PRC legal system

历史法学、现行法律制度、法律渊源和民事诉讼制度等无形因素对中国法律制度软件部分的影响至关重要。来自普通法系的利益相关者会发现中国法律制度的软件方面

[927] Refer, Chapter 2, §2.2, Chapter 7, §7.2.2 & §7.3.2。
参第 2 章第 2.2 节，第 7 章第 7.2.2 和 7.3.2 节。
[928] Refer, Chapter 2, §2.2.1 and §2.4.
参考第 2 章第 2.2.1 节和第 2.4 节。

somewhat challenging, but the comparative analysis provided in this book, will help them to appreciate the reasons behind the differences that exist between the systems. However, to bring about reforms in this area in the PRC is an uphill task. Given the global undercurrents at play, it is uncertain, if it is conceivable, to bring about major reforms in the software part of the legal system.[929] The answer to the question is again beyond the scope of this book.

有些挑战性，但本书提供的比较分析将帮助他们了解系统之间存在差异背后的原因。然而，在中国推行这一领域的改革是一项艰巨的任务。考虑到全球暗流涌动，在法律体系的软件部分带来重大改革是不确定的，如可以想象的话。这个问题的答案同样超出了本书的范围。

In the authors' view, the *hardware of the legal system* in the form of laws, codes, procedures, and guidance is easily understood,[930] but the software part of the legal system, that is, issues pertaining to the judges, needs to be developed and nurtured constantly. The PRC has done well in the hardware part of the legal system, drafting a lot of substantive and even procedural law in the last decade. According to Gillespie, judicial effectiveness is actually enhanced by judicial power more than by judicial independence, as in the early stages of development, the judiciary itself needs protection.[931]

在笔者看来，法律体系的硬件部分，如法律、法典、程序和指南，很容易理解，但法律体系的软件部分，即与法官有关的问题，需要不断发展和培育。中国在法律体系的硬件部分做得很好，在过去十年中起草了许多实体法甚至程序法。吉莱斯皮认为，司法效能实际上更多的是通过司法权力而不是司法独立来提高的，因为在发展的早期阶段，司法本身需要保护。

The PRC's legal system is relatively new, in relation to its position as an economic superpower. It goes without saying that its legal system has only been evolving for the last three decades, as compared to a thousand years of development of the common law. These are a few of the substantial challenges that cannot be ignored by the PRC or stakeholders in the PRC's legal system.

与经济超级大国的地位相比，中国的法律体系相对较新。不用说，与普通法的千年发展相比，香港的法律制度只是在过去三十年才发展起来的。这些是中国或中国法律体系中的利益相关者不能忽视的一些重大挑战。

[929] Some of these global undercurrents include trade disputes originating within the World Trade Organisation ('WTO'), and doubts raised by a few countries as to the relevance of WTO given the huge trade deficit large economies like the US, EU, and India have with the PRC. In addition, the world order is currently in a state of flux with the emergence of the PRC as an economic superpower along with other BRICS economies such as India, Russia, Brazil and South Africa. For the PRC, to manage these changes may be a priority at this stage.
其中一些全球暗流包括源自世界贸易组织（WTO）内部的贸易争端，以及一些国家对 WTO 的相关性提出的质疑，因为美国、欧盟和印度等大型经济体与中国存在巨大贸易逆差。此外，随着中国与印度、俄罗斯、巴西和南非等其他金砖国家经济体一起成为经济超级大国，世界秩序目前正处于不断变化的状态。对于中国来说，管理这些变化可能是现阶段的首要任务。

[930] Refer, Chapter 1, §1.2, where Mr. Wu Bangguo, a senior PRC official, confirmed that the socialist legal system with Chinese characteristics was established in China in 2011 after promulgating many new substantive and procedural laws within a span of two decades.
参考第 1 章第 1.2 节，中国高级官员吴邦国先生确认，在 20 年的时间里颁布了许多新的实体法和程序法之后，中国于 2011 年建立了中国特色的社会主义法律体系。

[931] Refer, Chapter 5, §5.4. 参见第 5 章第 5.4 节。

8.2 Recommendation for Reforms in PRC

对中国改革的建议

As discussed in section §8.1, there are opportunities for both the jurisdictions to carry out meaningful reforms based on their experiences with one another. The comparative analysis carried out in the book can be utilised to carry out specific reforms in both jurisdictions.

如§8.1所述，两个司法管辖区都有机会根据彼此的经验进行有意义的改革。书中进行的比较分析可以用来在两个司法管辖区进行具体的改革。

A Chinese proverb says "stones from other mountains may help to polish a piece of local jade." This is true as a general statement in life; however, even for the authors as a comparativist to suggest recommendations for reforms in a country of size of PRC is a daunting task. As a first step, before the authors even attempts to recommend reforms arising out of this research, it is important to quote Sherwin and Clermont in relation to mistakes that a comparativist can make while giving recommendations:

中国有句谚语说："它山之石可以攻玉。"这是生活中的一个普遍命题；然而，即使作为一个比较主义者的笔者，为中国这样一个规模的国家提出改革建议也是一项艰巨的任务。作为第一步，在笔者试图建议这项研究产生的改革之前，重要的是要引用谢尔文和克莱蒙特关于比较主义者在提出建议时可能犯的错误：

> A comparativist should be sufficiently immersed in the different legal cultures to understand the context in which legal rules operate and the attitudes an insider might take toward the rules. To the extent the comparativist is not an insider, he or she should also approach the rules of a different system with modesty and respect. Then, in drawing lessons for home system, the comparativist should remain cautious. <u>He should be suspicious of drawing easy generalities or making confident calls for legal transplants</u> [emphasis added].[932]

> 比较主义者应该充分地沉浸在不同的法律文化中，以理解法律规则运作的背景以及内部人士可能对规则采取的态度。在某种程度上，比较主义者不是局内人，他或她也应该谦虚和尊重地对待不同系统的规则。那么，在为国内制度吸取教训时，比较主义者应该保持谨慎。他应该对轻易下结论或自信地呼吁法律移植持怀疑态度。

To introduce legal reforms in the PRC is an uphill task. In the authors' view, any scholar should ask two fundamental questions about the PRC that were also looked into by Chang, when introducing reforms through ideas that are borrowed

在中国推行法律改革是一项艰巨的任务。在笔者看来，任何学者在借鉴外国司法管辖区的思想进行改革时，都应该提出两个关于中国的基

[932]E. Sherwin and K.M. Clermont, "A Comparative View of Standards of Proof," *Am. J. Comp. L.* 50, no. 2 (2002): 244.
E. Sherwin和K.M. Clermont，"证据标准的比较观点"，第2期。J. Comp. L. 50, no。2(2002): 244。

from foreign jurisdictions: [933]

本问题，张也研究了这两个问题：

- What are the PRC's long-term goals in respect of its civil justice system or in respect of any one aspect of its civil justice system?

中国在民事司法制度或民事司法制度的任何一个方面的长期目标是什么？

- What will be the immediate tasks that need to be assigned to its new legal system after bringing in the requisite reforms?

在引入必要的改革后，新的法律体系需要分配的直接任务是什么？

From the comparative analysis, the authors recommend the following *specific* reforms in the PRC legal system:

通过比较分析，笔者提出了中国法律制度改革的具体建议：

- First, as discussed earlier, the software part of the PRC's legal system needs to be improved considerably. The focus on selection of judges, their training, and consistency within all courts should be the focus. The discretionary power of judges and their willingness to use it will also be for the evolution of any legal system. The administrative part of the courts also needs strengthening.

首先，如前所述，中国法律体系的软件部分需要大幅改进。重点应放在法官的选拔、培训和所有法院内部的一致性上。法官的自由裁量权及其使用这种权力的意愿也将有利于任何法律制度的发展。法院的行政部分也需要加强。

- Second, judicial efficiency can be enhanced and more clarity can be introduced by adopting tests of standards of proof from common law in commercial disputes, rather than the judges aiming for perfect substantive justice in PRC courts.[934] In addition, there could be different standards of proof at different stages of litigation, for example, at the time of submission of the claims, at the time of interim hearings, during the trials and so forth. The PRC courts expecting a very high standard of proof at the time of submission of claims is not

其次，在商事纠纷中采用普通法系的证明标准测试，而不是以中国法院的实体司法为目标，可以提高司法效率，并引入更多的明确性。此外，在诉讼的不同阶段可能有不同的证明标准，例如在提出索赔时、在临时听证时、在审判期间等等。中国法院在提出索赔时要求非常高的证明标准是不现实的。这一改革也将增强司法在商业利益相关者眼中的合法性。

[933]Weren Chang, "Classical Chinese Jurisprudence and Development of Chinese Legal System" (2009–10), 272.
张伟仁：《中国古典法学与中国法制的发展》（2009-10），第272页。

[934]See discussion on judicial efficiency in context of standards of proof in Chen Chao-yang (Xiamen Intermediate People's Court), "Standards of Proof in Civil Proceedings: From the Perspective of Judicial Impartiality and Efficiency," *J. of Southwest U. P. Sc. & L.*, no. 1 (2002): 9–19.
参见《从举证标准看司法效率的探讨》（厦门市中级人民法院，陈朝阳），"民事诉讼中的举证标准：司法公正与效率的视角"，《西南联合法学》，第2期，no.1 (2002): 9-19。

practical. This reform will also enhance judicial legitimacy in the eyes of stakeholders with commercial interests.

- Third, the next recommendation would be that the ideological supervision of judges should be removed in cases of commercial disputes, in contrast to the ordinary civil disputes litigated in the PRC courts. This step will ensure the enhanced trust of foreign stakeholders in the PRC legal system.

第三，下一个建议是在商事纠纷案件中取消法官的思想监督，这与中国法院审理的普通民事纠纷不同。这一步骤将确保提高外国利益相关者对中国法律制度的信任。

- Fourth, at this stage of legal development of the civil justice system, the laws, rules, Guidance from SPC and so on are all scattered in multiple locations, and the local courts in various provinces also have their own local guidance. All this adds greatly to the amount of rules and bye-rules that litigants need to look into in order to litigate commercial or civil disputes. Therefore, it may be worthwhile to carry out a major housekeeping exercise to collate all of these in one place and create a massive online guide, which can be updated regularly (even online).
The availability of an online guide in English can be useful for stakeholders who are not from the PRC, but who have a genuine interest in the PRC's legal system. It is the authors' view that for a large country like the PRC, this kind of house-keeping exercise is like a drop in the ocean. In the practice of law, an important concept is cross-referencing and, in particular, the availability of a means of cross-referencing information and rules. However, with the increase of laws in PRC, there is a requirement to maintain consistency in civil litigation. A very similar example of means of cross-reference (but at a different level) was available in the past, such as with the Tang Codes, which were divided into two sections –

第四，在民事司法制度的法律发展阶段，法律、法规、最高人民法院的指导意见等都分散在多个地方，各省的地方法院也有自己的地方指导意见。所有这些都大大增加了诉讼当事人为了提起商业或民事纠纷而需要研究的规则和附带规则的数量。因此，将所有这些整理到一个地方，并创建一个大型的在线指南，可以定期更新（甚至在线更新），这可能是值得的。对于那些不是来自中国，但对中国法律制度真正感兴趣的利益相关者来说，英文版的在线指南可能会很有用。笔者认为，对于像中国这样的大国来说，这种内务处理就像沧海一粟。在法律实践中，一个重要的概念是相互参照，特别是相互参照信息和规则的手段的可用性。然而，随着我国法律的不断增多，民事诉讼中需要保持一致性。在过去，有一个非常类似的交叉参考的例子（但在不同的层面上），比如唐代法典，它分为两个部分——一般原则和具体罪行（尽管是在刑法的背景下）。

general principles and specific offences (though in the context of criminal law).[935]

- Fifth, in order to increase consistency in practice before the PRC courts, there should be Practice Directions. The recommendation for Practice Directions for the PRC can be added to the authors' recommendations to collate *CPL*, other relevant laws, other civil procedure rules and directions from the SPC in one book. In the same book or as an annex to the book, there can be local court rules for the reference of the litigants.

第五，为了增加在中国法院实践中的一致性，应该有实践指引。《中国实务指导意见》的建议可以添加到笔者的建议中，将中国《民事诉讼法》、其他相关法律、其他民事诉讼规则和最高人民法院的指导意见整理成一本书。在同一本书中或作为本书的附件，可以有当地法院的规则供当事人参考。

These Practice Directions can even have draft standard orders, local court guides, details about the rules of practice of courts, relevant telephone numbers, guidance as to requirements of evidence in courts and so forth. This will be of immense assistance to foreign stakeholders in the PRC legal system. However, this adjective law needs to be flexible, so that it in itself does not become the means for procedural injustice at the level of local court officials.

这些实务指示甚至可以包括标准命令草案、地方法院指引、法院实务规则的详细内容、相关电话号码、法庭证据要求的指引等等。这将为中国法律体系中的外国利益相关者提供巨大的帮助。然而，这种程序法需要灵活，这样它本身就不会成为地方法院官员在程序上不公正的手段。

The above recommended undertaking appears to be daunting, but with the extraordinary resources that are available in the PRC, it is the authors' view that it can be completed in a few months. All the above can even be updated regularly every day for the benefit of the stakeholders.

上述所提建议中的任务看似令人望而却步，然而鉴于中国所坐拥的无与伦比的资源，笔者以为，假以时日，短短数月之内，便足以将其圆满完成。不仅如此，上述全部内容甚至能够做到每日定时更新，从而让利益相关方皆能从中受益，各得其所。

- Sixth, with many of the SPC's provisions/interpretations, there are very few days between the date of promulgation of any new Code and date at which they are

第六，由于最高人民法院的许多规定/解释，任何新法规颁布之日与它们在实践中适用和生效之日之间的时间非常短。笔者建议

[935] Geoffrey MacCormack, *The Spirit of Traditional Chinese Law*, The Spirit of the Laws (Athens; London: University of Georgia Press, 1996), 14–15. See also, Table 1 for Tang Dynasty.
杰弗里·麦考马克：《中国传统法律精神》，《法律精神》(雅典；伦敦：佐治亚大学出版社，1996),14-15。另见表1唐朝。

applicable and effective in practice.The authors recommend a gap of at least 3-4 months between these two dates. It will assist the commercial stakeholders to plan their businesses accordingly.

在这两个日期之间至少间隔3-4个月。它将协助商业利益相关者相应地规划其业务。

- Seventh, with the massive economic growth in the PRC, the number of stakeholders from abroad who have an interest in PRC laws will certainly grow. The procedures for commercial dispute resolution should become more friendly for foreign stakeholders, and there could even be a provision for separate commercial courts in the PRC for such cases. As discussed in the analysis, such practical measures are not just good from the point of view of procedural justice but can also ensure even stronger economic growth for the PRC by raising the trust of stakeholders in its civil justice system.

第七，随着中国经济的大幅增长，对中国法律感兴趣的外国利益相关者的数量肯定会增加。解决商事争议的程序应当对外国利益相关者更加友好，甚至可以规定在中国设立单独的商事法院审理此类案件。正如分析中所讨论的，这些切实可行的措施不仅从程序正义的角度来看是好的，而且还能通过提高利益相关者对中国民事司法制度的信任，确保中国经济更强劲地增长。

- Eighth, the requirements as to the pleadings in PRC courts should become more liberal: the prerequisite for any evidence to pass the hurdle of a very high standard of proof at the time of filing of claims should not be mandatory. The fear in the PRC legal system in relation to frivolous claims passing the net can be managed by imposing penalty in form of legal costs on claimants bringing these types of claims.

第八，中国法院对诉状的要求应该更加宽松：在提出索赔时，任何证据通过非常高的证明标准的先决条件不应该是强制性的。中国法律体系中对轻率索赔的担忧可以通过对提出此类索赔的索赔人施加法律费用形式的处罚来管理。

However, the above recommendations will avoid the scenario of genuine claimants being denied access to the PRC's civil justice system at this early stage of civil procedure. These recommendations will provide better access to justice for most claimants. In commercial litigation, it is essential that many of the stakeholders in the civil justice system are made aware of high standards of proof in relation to the evidence that is required of them even at the docking stage (the first stage in civil litigation, where

然而，上述建议将避免真正的索赔人在民事诉讼的早期阶段被拒绝进入中国民事司法系统的情况。这些建议将为大多数索赔人提供更好的诉诸司法的机会。在商业诉讼中，重要的是要使民事司法系统中的许多利益相关者意识到，即使在对接阶段（民事诉讼的第一阶段，索赔人向法院提交索赔表格），他们也需要高标准的证

claimants submit their claim forms in the courts).

据证明。

If foreign claimants' applications are rejected due to a lack of evidence based on the test of standards of proof, it can create a bad impression of the PRC's legal system. The PRC civil justice system can easily take steps to avoid this.

如果外国索赔人的申请因缺乏基于证明标准测试的证据而被拒绝，这可能会给中国的法律制度留下不好的印象。中国司法系统可以很容易地采取措施来避免这种情况。

In fact, foreign stakeholders who have not analysed the invisible factors and relevant contexts as discussed in this book will just end up assuming that these are akin to non-tarriff barriers for investment and trade in PRC.

事实上，外国利益相关者如果没有分析本书中讨论的无形因素和相关背景，最终只会假设这些因素类似于中国投资和贸易的非关税壁垒。

The issue of turning away cases at the docking stage due to legal technicalities, or due to lack of training of the judges who would rather reject and disallow any case instead of dealing with novel issues, is a major stumbling block in the PRC. In the authors' view, this serious gap should be remedied to maintain the universal principles of access to justice. The reason for the rejection of cases could also be due to the increasing workload of judges and increase in civil cases in the PRC courts.[936] The discretionary power of judges to reject cases is definitely not an asset to the PRC legal system.

在对接阶段，因法律技术问题，或因缺乏培训，他们宁愿拒绝和不允许案件，而不是处理新问题，而拒绝案件的问题是中国的一个主要障碍。发件人认为，应弥补这一严重差距，以维持诉诸司法的普遍原则。案件被拒的原因也可能是由于法官工作量的增加和中国法院民事案件的增加。法官驳回案件的自由裁量权绝对不是中国法律体系的资产。

Any requirement of filing of defence only arises pursuant to *CPL* after the case has been accepted at the docking stage. Even though after 1998, the case filing division was separated from the division responsible for adjudication within the court systems, the discretionary power exhibited by the rotational judges in the case filing division has been extraordinary, especially for rejecting cases rather than allowing them to be adjudicated in the courts on merits and evidence.

只有在案件在对接阶段被接受后，才会根据《民事诉讼法》提出任何提交辩护的要求。尽管1998年以后，立案部从法院系统内负责审判的部门中分离出来，但立案部轮换法官所表现出的自由裁量权是非同寻常的，特别是在驳回案件而不是让案件在法院根据案情和证据进行裁决方面。

This aspect of the legal system needs an overhaul, in particular, in relation to commercial disputes. To be fair

法律制度的这一方面需要彻底改革，特别是在商业纠纷方面。公平地

---

[936]Margaret Woo, Y.K., "Manning the Courthouse Gates: Pleadings, Jurisdictions, and the Nation-State," *Nev. L.J.* 15, no. 3 (2015): 1285. This article highlights that the number of civil cases that were filed at the first instance between 1991 – 2010 increased annually by more than 10%. According to the authors, it is a heavy workload and deserves immediate attention in terms of capacity building for the future.
Margaret Woo, y.k.，"曼宁法院大门：诉状、司法管辖区和民族国家"，内华达州。*L.J.* 15, no. 3 (2015): 1285。这篇文章强调，1991年至2010年间，一审民事案件的数量每年增长10%以上。笔者认为，这是一项繁重的工作，在未来的能力建设方面值得立即关注。

there has been an attempt to increase efficiency in this area. As a result, a full-fledged case registration system has been fully available from 2015.[937] There will be no use for any rules or laws or codes or procedures or any comparative analysis, if the cases of the claimants cannot even pass this initial docking stage.

说，一直在努力提高这一领域的效率。从2015年起，一个完整的案件登记系统已完全可用。如果索赔人的案件甚至不能通过这个最初的对接阶段，那么任何规则、法律、守则或程序或任何比较分析都将毫无用处。

Lastly, in the PRC, for a long time, the laws were seen as a means to sustain market economy, but the author recommends that with massive economic growth, there is a scope for role reversals. As a result, the requirements of the PRC's socialist market economy can instead act as a catalyst to bring in changes in the laws and or codes as required by stakeholders with commercial interests. These stakeholders could even be foreign. The need for legitimacy in the PRC's civil justice system is as strong today as it was in 1978, as stated by the then-President of the SPC, Mr. Jiang Hua.[938]

最后，在中国，长期以来，法律被视为维持市场经济的一种手段，但笔者建议，随着经济的大规模增长，存在角色转换的空间。因此，中国社会主义市场经济的要求可以作为一种催化剂，根据商业利益相关者的要求，对法律或法规进行修改。这些利益相关者甚至可能是外国人。正如时任最高人民法院院长的江华先生所言，中国民事司法制度对合法性的需求今天与1978年一样强烈。

The 2023 amendments to *CPL 1991* have given more case management power to the PRC's judges in respect of the litigants, and the author recommends that in commercial litigation, a move towards a really adversarial process can assist foreign stakeholders to appreciate the PRC's legal system, and therefore, can even lead to the making of an effective civil litigation system in the PRC. In this respect, experiences from the common law system can be borrowed for the PRC legal system.

2023年修订的中国《民事诉讼法》赋予了中国法官在诉讼当事人方面更多的案件管理权，在商事诉讼中，向真正的对抗性程序的转变可以帮助外国利益相关者了解中国的法律制度，因此，甚至可以在中国建立一个有效的民事诉讼制度。在这方面，普通法系的经验可为中国法系借鉴。

Any remedy, interim or permanent, invariably requires an exercise of discretion by the judges. In the authors' view, while legal reforms are a work in progress, a lot of work still needs to be done in the PRC to ensure good software in the legal system. Ensuring this will involve capacity building, training of judges, and continuous professional

任何救济，无论是临时的还是永久的，都必须由法官行使自由裁量权。在笔者看来，虽然法律改革正在进行中，但中国仍需要做很多工作来确保良好的软件在法律体系中。要做到这一点，就需要能力建设、法官培训以

[937]See *Opinion on the Implementation of the People's Courts Reform of the Case-filing Registration System*, promulgated by Supreme People's Court on April 1, 2015, effective May 1, 2015.
见最高人民法院2015年4月1日发布的《关于实施人民法院立案登记制度改革的意见》，自2015年5月1日起施行。
[938]See Minshi Shenpan Gongzuo Tongdeng Zhongyao (Civil Trial Is Equally Important), available at http://www.geilibook.com/book/2441/157831.html and http://www.geilibook.com/book/2441/157832.html. Quoted in Woo, "Manning the Courthouse Gates," 1274.
参见《民事审判同等重要》，网址为http://www.geilibook.com/book/2441/157831.html和http://www.geilibook.com/book/2441/157832.html。引用自吴，“看守法院大门”，第1274页。

development for the judges to ensure they are independent and fearless. The exercise of discretion in courts or an effective *law in action* is in fact dependent on judges and also on well-trained lawyers to argue cases in the courts.

及法官的持续专业发展，以确保他们的独立性和无所畏惧。在法庭上行使自由裁量权或有效的法律实际上取决于法官和训练有素的律师在法庭上辩论案件。

It is important for reformers to note that laws can be amended or new legislations introduced, but the customary practices and ethos of any group of people are difficult to change. Bearing this in mind, any reforms, including the author's recommendations, should be introduced with caution. In the author's experience, and in the opinion of many PRC scholars, any attempt at reform will need to balance two opposing views: on the one hand, one group of policy makers seem to highlight and even boast about the old civilisational virtues of the past while incorporating new ideas across-the-board regularly, and on the other hand, there is the group of policy makers who completely reject new ideas and border on being paranoid about safeguarding the ancient Chinese ethos or Chinese characteristics. It must be understood that a bridge between the old and new traditions is essential for many of PRC scholars and reformers.[939]

对于改革者来说，重要的是要注意法律可以修改或引入新的立法，但是任何一群人的习惯和精神是很难改变的。考虑到这一点，任何改革，包括笔者的建议，都应谨慎推行。根据笔者的经验，以及许多中国学者的观点，任何改革尝试都需要平衡两种对立的观点：一方面，一群政策制定者似乎在强调甚至吹嘘过去的旧文明美德，同时定期全面吸收新思想；另一方面，另一群政策制定者则完全拒绝新思想，近乎偏执地维护中国古老的民族精神或中国特色。必须理解的是，对于许多中国学者和改革者来说，新旧传统之间的桥梁是必不可少的。

The authors do not recommend letting go of the PRC's greatest asset, which is its *civilisational values*. However, modern ideas can be useful to improve the existing system in the PRC. The authors also fully recommend that many ancient jurisprudential aspects can be extracted from the current PRC's practice of conservatism, and can be incorporated into the local laws, rules and procedures. A few examples of relevant ancient concepts are: preservation of ancient moral traditions and humanity, great respect for the wisdom of ancestors, and concern for order and maintenance of social stability and the rejection of anarchy.[940]

笔者不建议放弃中国最大的资产，那就是它的文明价值。然而，现代思想可以用来改进中国现有的体制。笔者还充分建议，可以从当前中国的保守主义实践中提取许多古老的法学方面，并将其纳入当地的法律、法规和程序中。一些相关的古代概念的例子是：保存古代的道德传统和人性，非常尊重祖先的智慧，关心秩序和维持社会稳定以及拒绝无政府状态。

939 Refer, Chapter 3, §3.7. 参见第 3 章第 3.7 节。

940 See the key elements of conservatism as discussed by scholars in relation to the effect of *conservatism* in the context of the symbolic spirit of Law in China, MacCormack, *Spirit of Traditional Chinese Law*, 32.
参见学者们讨论的保守主义的关键要素，以及保守主义在中国法律象征精神背景下的影响，麦考马克，《中国传统法律精神》，第32页。

A word of caution: given the advent of globalisation, combined with unprecedented urbanisation, it is essential that policy makers appreciate that though it is good to have an element of conservatism, overdoing it in relation to the practice of law can have damaging effects on the aims of the PRC's system. Take, for example, the Confucian concept of managing the present using the past or respecting old institutions, as recommended by Ming Tai-Tsu, the founder of the Ming Dynasty;[941] he gave guidance in this respect to his successors. In the authors' view, this kind of practice may be troublesome in the current era, where the only constant is not just change, but rapid change. This phenomenon is experienced not only in the PRC, but across the entire digitally-connected, interdependent world.

提醒一句：考虑到全球化的到来，再加上前所未有的城市化，政策制定者必须认识到，尽管保守主义的元素是好的，但在法律实践中过度保守可能会对中国制度的目标产生破坏性影响。举个例子，明朝的缔造者明太祖所推崇的儒家的“用过去管理现在”或“尊重旧制度”的理念；他在这方面指导了他的继任者。在笔者看来，这种做法在当今时代可能会很麻烦，因为唯一不变的不仅仅是变化，而是快速的变化。这种现象不仅发生在中国，而且发生在整个数字互联、相互依存的世界。

There is a popular trend in the context of reforms in many countries which hold to different legal systems,[942] for example, the US, Australia, England, Germany, Austria, France, Spain, and Russia, in relation to civil procedural systems, to improve case management powers. Another trend has been to provide flexibility in the procedural steps that need to be taken in the civil justice system according to the complexity of the cases, to reduce delays and legal costs.[943]

在许多法系不同的国家，如美国、澳大利亚、英国、德国、奥地利、法国、西班牙和俄罗斯，在民事诉讼制度改革的背景下，提高案件管理权是一种流行的趋势。另一个趋势是，根据案件的复杂性，在民事司法制度中需要采取的程序步骤方面提供灵活性，以减少延误和法律费用。

There is another trend in civil justice systems, where preliminary matters related to evidence and plenary proceedings are arranged systematically to avoid delay and to ensure that the actual trial is more effective. Similarly, a popular trend in common law systems is the move towards summary procedures which rely less on oral evidence in proceedings.[944] In addition, there have been reforms, for example in England & Wales, where each party to litigation has to provide any evidence that goes

民事司法制度中还有另一种趋势，即有系统地安排与证据和全体诉讼有关的初步事项，以避免延误并确保实际审判更有效。同样，普通法系的一个流行趋势是趋向简易程序，在诉讼中较少依赖口头证据。此外，还进行了一些改革，例如在英格兰和威尔士，诉讼的每一方都必须提供不利于自己的证据，或者诉讼当事人可以向法院寻求协助以

[941]MacCormack, *Spirit of Traditional Chinese Law*, 41, says Confucius used to stress "on conserving and reestablishing the good customs of past." Another example he discussed was that Ming Tsai-Tsu ordered his descendants not to change the old institutions.
麦考马克在《中国传统法律精神》，41中说，孔子过去常常强调“保存和重建过去的好习俗”。他讨论的另一个例子是，明蔡祖命令他的后代不要改变旧的制度。

[942] Refer, Chapter 1, §1.4.3. 参考第 1 章第 1.4.3 节。

[943]MacCormack, *Spirit of Traditional Chinese Law*, 223.
麦考马克，《中国传统法律精神》，第223页。

[944]Ibid., 224. 同前注，第224页。

against them, or the litigants can seek assistance from the courts to obtain such evidence.[945]

获得此类证据。

Lastly, the PRC's current legal system can avoid the pitfalls of the more mature common law system. In spite of the reforms that have been carried out in England & Wales, there is still an urgent need for additional reforms to correct systemic issues. These are additional warning signs to the fast-evolving PRC legal system, in particular, the civil justice system. A few of the reforms that are needed in the common law jurisdiction of England & Wales are as follows:

最后，中国现行的法律制度可以避免更为成熟的普通法系的陷阱。尽管已经在英格兰和威尔士进行了改革，但仍然迫切需要进行额外的改革来纠正系统性问题。这些都是快速发展的中国法律体系，特别是民事司法体系的额外警告信号。在英格兰和威尔士的普通法管辖范围内，需要进行的一些改革如下：

- Costs to litigants to obtain remedies in the civil justice system are increasing by the day. The excessive cost of delivery of justice within the civil justice system has to be avoided, as it bars litigants from access to justice. During litigation the focus and discussion shifts at times to increasing legal costs rather than to obtaining justice or arguing substantive points. This recommendation from the authors is not new and was even provided by Anthony Clarke, Justice of the Supreme Court of the UK, when he referred to the 'holy trinity of complexity, costs and delay' as things to be avoided during reforms.[946]It is a fact that due to the multitude of variables in disputes, no civil procedure can be ever be perfect and there will always be complaints.[947]

- 诉讼当事人在民事司法制度中获得救济的费用日益增加。必须避免民事司法系统内司法执行费用过高，因为它妨碍诉讼当事人诉诸司法。在诉讼过程中，焦点和讨论有时会转移到增加法律费用上，而不是争取正义或争论实质性问题。笔者的这一建议并不新鲜，甚至是英国最高法院大法官安东尼·克拉克提出的，当时他将"复杂性、成本和延迟的神圣三位一体"称为改革期间要避免的事情。事实是，由于纠纷中的变量众多，民事诉讼程序不可能是完美的，总是会有投诉。

---

945 Ibid., 225. 同前注，第225页。

946 Anthony Clarke, "The Woolf Reforms: A Singular Event or an Ongoing Process," in *The Civil Procedure Ten Years On*, ed. Deirdre Dwyer (Oxford: Oxford University Press, 2009), 33. Justice Clarke was himself referring to the words of scholar Neil Andrews. Justice Clarke again in the same article on page 42 has advised that "... there are no short cuts where procedural reforms is concerned; there is no doing in haste and repenting at leisure."
安东尼·克拉克，《伍尔夫改革：一个单一事件还是一个持续的过程》，载于《十年后的民事诉讼》，迪尔德丽·德怀尔主编（牛津：牛津大学出版社，2009），第33页。克拉克法官自己引用了学者尼尔·安德鲁斯的话。克拉克法官再次在42页的同一篇文章中建议"……在程序改革方面没有捷径可走；做事不能操之过急，后悔莫及。"

947 Pound, "Dissatisfaction with Administration of Justice," 729 was cited in Clarke, "Woolf Reforms- Singular Event?" 34. Pound said '[D]issatisfaction with the administration of justice is as old as law.' The dissatisfaction with the civil justice system was seen as far back as the 13th century, in the Magna Carta in AD 1215, which said in Art. 40: 'To no one will we sell, to no one will we refuse or delay, right or justice.'
庞德，"对司法行政的不满"，第729页被克拉克引用，"伍尔夫改革——单一事件？"第34页。庞德说："对司法的不满和法律一样古老。"对民事司法体系的不满可以追溯到公元1215年的13世纪《大宪章》（Magna Carta），其中第40条规定："我们不向任何人出售权利或正义，我们不向任何人拒绝或拖延权利或正义。"

- The process of bringing reforms to the civil justice system is very delicate, and as a recommendation, any suggested reforms should not be implemented in haste. The elements of efficiency and right to justice are very important. However, Lord Justice Clarke has mentioned that there are no short-cuts to eliminating delay and excessive expense in civil litigation.[948] The failure of civil justice reforms in earlier decades was because the rules had become too technical, and in addition, the culture of litigation as practised by the judges and the lawyers was not changed.[949]

- 民事司法制度改革的过程是非常微妙的，作为一个建议，任何建议的改革都不应该匆忙实施。效率和正义的要素是非常重要的。然而，克拉克大法官曾提到，消除民事诉讼中的拖延和过度开支没有捷径。前几十年民事司法改革的失败是因为规则过于技术性，此外，法官和律师实践的诉讼文化没有改变。

- The authors recommend that that any further reforms even in England & Wales will require a change in culture as invisible factors influence every aspect of law, in particular law in action at the courts. This is relevant even for an established and mature legal system such as in England & Wales. Therefore, any reform in the civil justice system has to bring in a change of culture along with the procedural and structural reforms.

- 笔者建议，即使在英格兰和威尔士，任何进一步的改革都需要改变文化，因为无形的因素影响着法律的各个方面，特别是在法庭上执行的法律。这一点甚至适用于英格兰和威尔士等成熟的法律体系。因此，民事司法制度的任何改革都必须在程序和结构改革的同时带来文化的变革。

- According to the authors and many jurisprudents, lawyers and judges are the worst people to suggest and implement judicial reforms as they have deep vested financial interests in maintaining the status quo in terms of complexities and notions of law. The authors recommend that law, rules, adjective law and so forth should be made simple for laymen and commercial people. By reducing litigation costs, commerce will further improve in any jurisdiction.

- 根据笔者和许多法学家的观点，律师和法官是建议和实施司法改革的最差人选，因为他们在维持法律复杂性和概念方面的现状方面有着深厚的既得利益。笔者建议法律、规则、程序法等都应该对外行人和商业人士简单易懂。通过降低诉讼成本，商业将在任何法域得到进一步改善。

---

[948]Clarke, "Woolf Reforms- Singular Event?" 35. See also, Chapter 3 §3.2.5 for discussion on failure of civil justice reforms in the 18th and 19th century. This failure resulted in major reforms, particularly the Lord Woolf Reforms 1999. See also, Lord Woolf, *Access to Justice: Final Report to the Lord Chancellor on the Civil Justice System in England and Wales* (London: HMSO, 1996).
Clarke, 《伍尔夫改革——奇异事件？》"第35页。关于18世纪和19世纪民事司法改革失败的讨论，参见第3章第3.2.5节。这次失败导致了重大改革，特别是1999年伍尔夫勋爵改革。另见伍尔夫勋爵，《诉诸司法：向大法官提交的关于英格兰和威尔士民事司法制度的最后报告》（伦敦：英国皇家社会科学院，1996年）。

[949]Clarke, Woolf Reforms-Singular Event? 43. 《伍尔夫改革——奇异事件？》"第43页。

- The authors wish to highlight that in the context of reforms of the civil justice system in England & Wales, Lord Justice Anthony Clarke's was of the view that the following needs to be taken into an account:[950]

- 笔者希望强调，在英格兰和威尔士民事司法制度改革的背景下，大法官安东尼·克拉克认为需要考虑以下几点：

- Satellite litigation within the main litigation, where parties fight over smaller issues such as extension of time, should be avoided as much as possible as it uses a lot of the court's resources;

- 主诉讼中的附带诉讼，即当事人为延长时间等较小的问题而斗争，应尽可能避免，因为它占用了法院的大量资源；

- The carrot and stick approach, where the courts ensure parties reach consensual settlements through mediation, or via Part 36 offers from the parties to resolve the dispute (the carrots), while the stick of the court functions as a threat of punishment for any conduct of parties that is not in accordance with the overriding objectives of civil litigation;[951]

- 胡萝卜加大棒法，法院确保当事人通过调解达成共识，或通过当事人提出的第36部分来解决争议（胡萝卜），而法院的大棒则是对当事人的任何不符合民事诉讼首要目标的行为进行惩罚的威胁；

- Litigation costs should be within reasonable limits. The Woolf reforms had shortcomings in this area.

- 诉讼费用应控制在合理范围内。伍尔夫的改革在这方面有缺点。

- Reforms in relation to the rules should be to change the litigation culture, and it should be a continuous process.

- 与规则相关的改革应该是改变诉讼文化，并且应该是一个持续的过程。

- Reforms should set the agenda for today as well as for tomorrow.

- 改革应该为今天和明天设定议程。

- Lastly, Comparative law is popular in continental traditions such as in France & Germany; however common law systems such as England & Wales has been slow in the uptake of foreign ideas, and therefore a bit more needs to be done in this regard in practice. However, to be fair, the higher courts and above have been

- 最后，比较法在法国、德国等大陆传统国家盛行；然而，英格兰和威尔士等普通法体系在吸收外国思想方面进展缓慢，因此在实践中还需要做更多的工作。然而，公平地说，最近观察到高级法院及以上法院更愿意接受和吸收外国思想。

[950] Clarke, Woolf Reforms-Singular Event? 41-49. Clarke《伍尔夫改革——奇异事件？》，第41-49页。

[951] Refer, Chapter 4, §4.2.1 & §4.2.1.1.
参考第 4 章，第 4.2.1 节和 4.2.1.1 节。

observed lately to be more willing to accept and incorporate foreign ideas.[952]

8.3 CONCLUDING REMARKS

结语

The lawyer's role in providing relevant advice for commercial disputes with PRC connections, whether the lawyer is from the common law system or from the PRC jurisdiction, is dependent on their understanding the invisible factors and contexts surrounding the disputes. Disregarding the invisible factors and contexts or excessively focusing on the black letter law in the form of codes or statutes or case law and so on can prove to be quite costly for litigants involved in cross-border litigation, in particular when disputes have a PRC connection.

律师在为与中国有关的商事纠纷提供相关建议时所发挥的作用，取决于他们对围绕争议的无形因素和背景的理解，无论该律师来自普通法系还是中国司法管辖区。忽视无形的因素和背景，或过度关注法典、成文法或判例法等形式的重要法条，对于涉及跨境诉讼的诉讼当事人来说，代价可能相当高昂，特别是当争议与中国有关时。

The exercise of discretionary power of judges is needed in granting interim remedies, managing case-management power in courts and even to some extent in granting of the final remedies. Similarly, the role of judges' discretionary power in litigation is fundamentally decisive in most cases. In any jurisdiction, the discretionary power of judges,[953] their willingness to exercise this power during judicial activities,[954] and the limits of such power must be analysed in a cultural context; this cannot be disregarded by any litigants or their legal representatives.

法官的自由裁量权在给予临时救济、管理法院的案件管理权甚至在一定程度上给予最终救济都是需要的。同样，在大多数案件中，法官的自由裁量权在诉讼中的作用从根本上是决定性的。在任何法域，须在文化背景下分析法官的自由裁量权、他们在司法活动中行使这种权力的意愿以及这种权力的限制；诉讼当事人或其法律代表不应忽视这一点。

In section §8.2 of this book, the authors have been audacious enough to suggest a few reforms. Over the years, a lot of

在本书第8.2节中，笔者大胆地提出了一些改革建议。多年来，

---

[952] *See Fairchild v Glenhaven Funeral Services Ltd* & others [2002] UKHL 22, [32] (Lord Bingham).

[953] Refer, Chapter 6 with regard to the discussion on discretionary power of judges.
参见第六章关于法官自由裁量权的论述。

[954] Refer, Chapter 7 for a few examples of judges' role in judicial activities in courts.
有关法官在法院司法活动中的作用的几个例子，请参阅第 7 章。

reforms have been carried out in many jurisdictions using *legal transplants*, that is, borrowing law from another jurisdiction. Legal transplant is one of the many approaches available to administrators, and it remains a popular method.[955] Legal transplants are useful in areas where there are no laws or there are gaps, or even in order to arrive at a proved uniform outcome.[956] Even Lord Bingham said in relation to the utility of legal transplant in the context of England & Wales, the mother of the common law system:

许多司法管辖区通过法律移植进行了许多改革，即从另一个司法管辖区借用法律。法律移植是管理员可用的众多方法之一，它仍然是一种流行的方法。在没有相关法律或存在空白的地区，法律移植是有用的，甚至是为了达到一个被证明是统一的结果。甚至连宾厄姆勋爵在谈到法律移植在普通法之母英格兰和威尔士的应用时说：

> Development of the law in this country cannot of course depend on a head-count of decisions and codes adopted in other countries around the world, often against a background of different rules and traditions. The law must be developed coherently, in accordance with principle, so as to serve, even-handedly, the ends of justice. <u>If, however, a decision is given in this country which offends one's basic sense of justice, and if consideration of international sources suggests that a different and more acceptable decision would be given in most other jurisdictions, whatever their legal tradition, this must prompt anxious review of the decision in question. In a shrinking world... there must be some virtue in uniformity of outcome whatever the diversity of approach in reaching that outcome</u> [emphasis added].[957]

> 这个国家的法律演进，断不可邯郸学步，依赖于世界其他国家在截然不同的规则与传统背景下所通过的裁决和法典。法律必须按照原则有条理地发展，如此方能不偏不倚地实现正义之鹄的。<u>但是，如果在这个国家作出的决定触犯了一个人的基本正义感，如果对国际资料的考虑表明，在大多数其他司法管辖区，无论其法律传统如何，都会作出不同的和更可接受的决定，这就必须促使人们对有关决定进行急切的审查。在一个不断缩小的世界里……无论达到结果的方法如何多样化，结果的一致性必定有某种优点</u>[着重号后加]。

Even though there could be benefits in legal transplant to bring in legal reforms, it is important to appreciate the warnings of Chase in relation to the issue of legal transplants. Chase was of the view that even the most elegant foreign law will not have

尽管法律移植可以带来法律改革的好处，但重要的是要理解蔡斯在法律移植问题上的警告。蔡斯认为，即使是最优雅的外国法律，

[955]Chen Lei, "Contextualizing Legal Transplant: China and Hong Kong," in *Methods of Comparative Law*, ed. Pier G. Monateri (Cheltenham, U.K.; Northampton, MA: Edward Elgar Pub., 2012), 193.
陈磊，"法律移植的语境化：中国与香港"，载于《比较法方法》，Pier G. Monateri主编，英国切尔滕纳姆；北安普顿，马萨诸塞州：爱德华·埃尔加出版社。 2012)，第193页。

[956]Ibid.
同前注。

[957]See *Fairchild v Glenhaven Funeral Services Ltd* & others [2002] UKHL 22, [32] (Lord Bingham). Lord Bingham was also quoted in Lei, "Contexualizing Legal Transplant in PRC," 193.
参见Fairchild v Glenhaven Funeral Services Ltd & others [2002] UKHL 22， [32] （Lord Bingham）。宾厄姆勋爵的话也在《中华人民共和国法律移植的语境化》第193页被引用。

the desired effects in a completely different jurisdiction with a different culture; he was alluding to invisible factors and contexts, which have been discussed in this book.

也不会在一个完全不同的司法管辖区和不同的文化中产生预期的效果；他暗指的是书中讨论过的无形因素和背景。

In addition, any resultant conflict arising out of the borrowed ideas from a very different legal system or jurisdiction will affect the legitimacy of the legal system that has borrowed the ideas. Furthermore, it needs to be appreciated that any borrowed and incorporated procedural code or concepts from other jurisdictions can affect the society in which the code/idea was introduced.[958]

此外，从一个非常不同的法律制度或司法管辖区借来的思想所产生的任何冲突将影响到借用这些思想的法律制度的合法性。此外，需要认识到，任何从其他司法管辖区借用和合并的程序法典或概念都可能影响到引入该法典/想法的社会。

Any law reformers, before borrowing ideas or codes from another jurisdiction, should not ignore the fact that scholars drafting that code from that other jurisdiction could have analysed the issues from a completely different perspective. This is illustrated by an example from Ramseyer's study on Japan. Ramseyer initially concluded that the Japanese prefer mediation over litigation; however, further analysis showed that this preference for mediation only came about because in Japan, there were institutional barriers to pursuing litigation.[959] Haley traced this phenomenon to Japanese elites that had created those institutional barriers in order to maintain the status quo.[960] Therefore, it is important for reformers to understand the context behind the ideas or codes before robotically adopting foreign codes/ideas in their own jurisdiction.

任何法律改革者在借鉴其他司法管辖区的思想或法典之前，都不应忽视这样一个事实，即从其他司法管辖区起草法典的学者本可以从完全不同的角度分析问题。拉姆塞耶研究日本的一个例子说明了这一点。拉姆塞耶最初的结论是，日本人更喜欢调解，而不是诉讼；然而，进一步的分析表明，这种对调解的偏好只是因为在日本，在进行诉讼方面存在制度障碍。黑利将这种现象归因于日本精英阶层，他们为了维持现状而制造了这些制度障碍。因此，对于改革者来说，在机械地在自己的管辖范围内采用外国法规/理念之前，了解这些理念或法规背后的背景很重要。

In order for any civil justice system to command the respect and confidence of its stakeholders, there is a need for the *concept of proportionality* in the justice system. The issue of proportionality is important to the adjective law, which means

为了使任何民事司法制度得到其利益攸关方的尊重和信任，司法制度中需要有相称性的概念。比例性问题是程序法的一个重要问题，

[958]Oscar G. Chase, "Some Observations on the Cultural Dimension in Civil Procedure Reform," *Am. J. Comp. Law* 45, no. 4 (1997): 866.
Oscar G. Chase, "民事诉讼制度改革中的文化维度观察", 第3期。J. Comp. Law 45, no。4(1997): 866。
[959]See Oscar G. Chase, "Some Observations on the Cultural Dimension in Civil Procedure Reform," 869 for discussion on Ramseyer and Haley.
参见Oscar G. Chase:《论民事诉讼制度改革中的文化维度》，第869页。
[960] Ibid. 同前注。

"Procedural requirements should be proportionate to the subject matter of the litigation."[961] An understanding of how the justice system adapts to particular circumstances of commercial activities within the context of commercial litigation is vital for any civil justice system irrespective of the kind of legal system.

即"程序要求应当与诉讼标的成比例"。了解司法制度如何在商业诉讼的背景下适应商业活动的特殊情况，对于任何民事司法制度都是至关重要的，无论哪种法律制度。

The concept of *proportionality* is also relevant in terms of limits of the law to "intrude upon the private rights. The proportionality principle is one way of expressing those limits."[962] For example, to achieve the objectives of the pre-judgment remedies in a commercial dispute, the exercise of discretionary power of the judges should not exceed the required minimum to achieve those objectives. The judges' use of sanctions or adverse costs orders against the litigants are exceptions to the concept of proportionality.

比例概念也适用于法律对"侵犯私权"的限制。比例原则是表达这些限制的一种方式。"例如，为了在商业纠纷中实现判决前救济的目标，法官的自由裁量权的行使不应超过实现这些目标所需的最低限度。法官对诉讼当事人使用制裁或不利讼费令是相称性概念的例外。

The concept of proportionality requires the *optimum* exercise of discretionary power by the judges and more importantly, the willingness of the judges to exercise their discretionary power. In the end, in the words of Lord Woolf, the civil justice system needs to be just, fair, offer appropriate procedures at reasonable cost, deal with the issues at a reasonable speed, be understandable to those who need to use it (including foreign citizens), be responsive and provide certainty, be effective, and be adequately resourced and organised.[963] This is where the PRC legal system faces its biggest challenge as compared to other legal jurisdictions and legal systems, particularly for *law in action*.

比例原则要求法官对自由裁量权的最佳行使，更重要的是要求法官行使自由裁量权的意愿。最后，用伍尔夫勋爵的话来说，民事司法系统需要公正、公平，以合理的成本提供适当的程序，以合理的速度处理问题，对需要使用它的人（包括外国公民）来说是可以理解的，反应迅速，提供确定性，有效，资源充足，组织有序。与其他司法管辖区和法律体系相比，这是中国法律体系面临的最大挑战，特别是在现行法律方面。

The software part of the legal system of the PRC, or indeed any system, is where the real challenge lies; it does not matter whether the hardware of the legal system in the form of numerous drafted codes or rules or substantive law is perfect or not. In the end, what will matter the most is whether the

中国法律体系的软件部分，或者实际上是任何体系，才是真正的挑战所在；法律体系的硬件——以无数法典或规则草案或实体法的形式——是否完善并不重要。最后，

---

[961]Jackson, *The Reform of Civil Litigation*, 20.
杰克逊：《民事诉讼改革》，第20期。
[962]Ibid., 18.
同前注，第18页。
[963]Lord Woolf, *Access to Justice: Final Report to the Lord Chancellor on the Civil Justice System in England and Wales* (London: HMSO, 1996), section 1.
伍尔夫勋爵，《诉诸司法：向大法官提交的关于英格兰和威尔士民事司法制度的最后报告》（伦敦：HMSO，1996），第1节。

software part of the legal system, that is the judges, have the capacity to fulfil the following:

最重要的是法律系统的软件部分，即法官，是否有能力实现以下几点：

i. whether the judges can appreciate the changing business and commercial environment; and

ii. whether the judges can appreciate the need for an efficient relationship between the civil justice system and the local economy and, to some extent, the global economy; and

iii. the level of confidence and trust the stakeholders will have in the civil justice system to protect their commercial interests; and

iv. whether the judges are given discretionary power and, last but not least, whether the judges are willing to exercise this discretionary power without any fear or external influence.

i. 法官是否能体会到不断变化的商业和商业环境；和

ii. 法官是否认识到民事司法制度与本地经济，甚至在某种程度上与全球经济之间需要建立有效的关系；和

iii. 股东对保护其商业利益的民事司法制度的信心和信任度；和

iv. 法官是否被赋予自由裁量权，最后但并非最不重要的是，法官是否愿意在没有任何恐惧或外部影响的情况下行使这种自由裁量权。

The above issues are extremely relevant to the economic superpower of the day, the PRC. The PRC has been one of the success stories for creating wealth for its citizens and for being actively involved in international trade and commerce with its footprints expanding in all parts of the world through these trading activities and international projects like the Belt and Road Initiative ("BRI"). An efficient legal system is key to sustaining and enhancing the growth momentum of the PRC.

上述问题与当今作为经济超级大国的中国休戚相关。中国一直是为其公民创造财富和积极参与国际贸易和商业的成功案例之一，其足迹通过这些贸易活动和"一带一路"倡议等国际项目扩展到世界各地。行之有效的法律制度是维系并强化中国经济增长势头的中流砥柱。

A key test for ensuring that any legal system is efficient is the recognition by stakeholders of this fact, in particular the stakeholders from outside the jurisdiction. External stakeholders identifying the English legal system as an example of an efficient legal system with ethical, autonomous, empowered and well-trained judges is quintessential to the ability of London to remain a financial center of world. The PRC legal system would do well to emulate this, to enhance its own success.

确保任一法律制度切实有效的一项关键检验标准，便是利益相关者，尤其是来自管辖范围之外的利益相关者能够洞悉并认可这一实情。在外部利益相关者眼中，普通法体系是一个拥有道德、自主、授权和训练有素的法官的高效法律体系的典范，这对伦敦保持世界金融中心的能力至关重要。中国的法律体系借鉴可提高其自身的成功。

The intention of the PRC to move into the dispute resolution sector, at least for their international projects, will require the readers and legal students and practitioners to appreciate the

中国涉足争议解决领域的意图，至少是为了其国际项目，这将要求读者、法律学生和从业者领会

subtle comparative analysis accomplished in this book. A few of the issues will also remain relevant to the common law system, such as England & Wales, where one of the world's financial center is located, and which many commercial interests from around the world still use as the preferred choice of law in their contracts.

本书中微妙的比较分析。其中部分问题依旧会与诸如英格兰和威尔士这类普通法体系休戚相关。这些地区是世界的金融中心之一，世界各地诸多商业利益集团仍将其法律作为合同中的首选适用法律。

Bibliography

Books

Ruggero J. Aldisert, *The Judicial Process, Readings, Materials, and Cases*, American Casebook Series (St. Paul, Minn.: West Publishing Company, 1989).

ALI/UNIDROIT, *Principles of Transnational Civil Procedure*, rev. ed., Cambridge Books Online (Cambridge: Cambridge University Press, 2007).

Neil Andrews, *English Civil Procedure: Fundamentals of New Civil Justice System* (Oxford; New York: Oxford University Press, 2003).

Aristotle and J. A. K. Thomson, trans., *The Ethics of Aristotle: The Nicomachean Ethics*, Reprinted ed. (London: Penguin, 1961).

William Blake Odgers and Simon Goulding, eds., *Odgers on Civil Court Actions*, 24th ed. (London: Sweet & Maxwell, 1996).

Anne Barron, et al., *Introduction to Jurisprudence and Legal Theory: Commentary and Materials* (London: Butterworths, 2002).

Jeremy Bentham, *An Introduction to the Principles of Morals and Legislation* (New York: Dover Publications, 1996).

Berman, Harold J., ed., *Talks on American Law: A Series of Broadcasts to Foreign Audiences by Members of the Harvard Law School Faculty*, ed. Harold J. Berman (New York: Vintage Books, 1961).

Paul Schiff Berman, *Global Legal Pluralism: A Jurisprudence of Law beyond Borders* (Cambridge; New York: Cambridge University Press, 2012).

Kathryn Bernhardt and Philip Huang, *Civil Law in Qing and Republican China*, Law, Society, and Culture in China. (Stanford, Calif.: Stanford University Press, 1999).

William Blackstone, *Commentaries on the Laws of England* (Chicago: Chicago University Press, 1979).

Susan Blake, *A Practical Approach to Effective Litigation*, 7th ed. (Oxford: Oxford University Press, 2009).

Susan Blake, *A Practical Approach to Effective Litigation*, 8th ed. (Oxford: Oxford University Press, 2015).

Susan Blake, Julie Browne, and Stuart Sime, *A Practical Approach to Alternative Dispute Resolution*, 3rd ed., Practical Approach Series (Oxford: Oxford University Press, 2014).

Patricia Blazey and Kay-Wah Chan, *The Chinese Commercial Legal System* (Pyrmont, NSW, Australia: Lawbook Co., 2008).

M. H. Bond, *The Oxford Handbook of Chinese Psychology* (Hong Kong: Oxford University Press, 2010).

Yuanshi Bu, ed., *Chinese Business Law* (Oxford: Hart Publishing, 2010).

Yuanshi Bu, ed., *Chinese Civil Law* (Oxford: Hart Publishing, 2013).

Paul Burrows and Cento G. Veljanovski, eds., *The Economic Approaches to Law* (London; Boston; Sydney; Wellington; Durban; Toronto: Butterworths, 1981).

Mauro Bussani and Ugo Mattei, eds., *The Cambridge Companion to Comparative Law*, Cambridge Companions to Law (Cambridge: Cambridge University Press, 2012).

Dingjing Cai, *History and Reforms: The Legal History of the New China (Lishiyu Biange: Xin Zhongguo Fazhi Jianshe de Licheng)* (Beijing: Press of China's University of Political Science and Law, 1999).

David Campbell and Philip Thomas, *Fundamental Legal Conceptions as Applied in Judicial Reasoning; and Other Legal Essays*, Reprinted ed. (Oxford: Routledge, 2016).

T'ung-Tsu Ch'u, *Law and Society in Traditional China*, Selected Works of Modern Chinese Learning: English Version (Beijing: The Commercial Press, 2011).

Fabang Chai, *New Civil Procedure* (Beijing: Law Press, 1992).

Yi Chang, Chief Editor, *The Civil Procedure Law* (Beijing: China University of Law and Political Science and Law Press, 1996).

Chief editor Zexian Chen, *Contemporary Chinese Law* (Beijing: China Procuratorial Press, 2009).

Jianfu Chen, *Chinese Law: Context and Transformation*, Numen Book (Leiden; Boston: Martinus Nijhoff Publishers, 2008).

Lei Chen and C.H. (Remco) van Rhee, eds., *Towards a Chinese Civil Code: Comparative and Historical Perspectives* (Dordrecht: Martinus Nijhoff Publishers, 2012).

Yiyun Cheng, *Science of Evidence* (Beijing: People's Public Security University of China Press, 1991).

Hiram E. Chodosh, *Global Justice Reform: A Comparative Methodology* (New York: New York University Press, 2005).

J. Clore, *Civil Litigation*, 2nd ed., Legal Practice Course Companion (London: Routledge-Cavendish, 1998).

Jerome A. Cohen, ed., Chen, Fu-Mei Chang, *Essays on China's Legal Tradition*, Studies in East Asian Law (Princeton: Princeton University Press, 1981).

Danny Danziger and John Gillingham, *1215: The Year of Magna Carta* (New York: Simon & Schuster, 2004).

Rene David and John E.C. Brierley, *Major Legal Systems in the World Today*, 3rd ed. (London: Sweet & Maxwell, 1985).

A.V. Dicey, *Introduction to the Study of the Law of Constitution* (London; New York: Macmillan, 1902).

C. Dickens, *Bleak House* (Hammondsworth: Penguin, 1996).

Hao Dong, *On Judicial Interpretation* (Beijing: Press of China's University of Political Science and Law, 2007).

Antony Duff, et al., *The Trial on Trial: Volume I: Truth and Due Process* (Oxford: Hart Publishing, 2004).

Ronald Dworkin, *Law's Empire (Legal Theory)*, New ed. (Oxford: Hart Publishing, 1998).

Ronald Dworkin, *Taking Rights Seriously* (London: Duckworth, 1977).

Deirdre Dwyer, ed., *The Civil Procedure Rules Ten Years On* (Oxford; New York: Oxford University Press, 2009).

Deirdre Dwyer, *The Judicial Assessment of Expert Evidence* (Cambridge: Cambridge University Press, 2008).

Maurice Adams and Dirk Heirbaut, eds., *The Method and Culture of Comparative Law: Essays in Honour of Mark Van Hoecke* (Oxford: Hart Publishing, 2015).

Melvin Aron Eisenberg, *The Nature of Common Law* (Cambridge: Harvard University Press, 1988).

Joel Friedman and Michael Collins, *The Law of Civil Procedure: Cases and Materials*, 4th ed., American Case Book Series (St. Paul, Minn.: West Academic Publishing, 2013).

Lon L. Fuller, *The Law in Quest of Itself* (Boston, Mass.: Beacon Press, 1940).

Yu-Lan Fung and Derk Bodde, trans., *A History of Chinese Philosophy. Vol. 2, The Period of Classical Learning (from the Second Century B.C. to the Twentieth Century A.D.)*, 7th ed. (Princeton: Princeton (N.J.) Princeton University Press, 1983).

Yu-Lan Fung and Derk Bodde, trans., *A History of Chinese Philosophy. Vol. 1, The Period of the Philosophers (from the Beginnings to Circa 100 B.C.)* (Princeton: Princeton University Press, 1983).

Fabien Ge´linas, et al., *Foundations of Civil Justice: Toward a Value-Based Framework for Reform* (Heidelberg; New York; Dordrecht; London: Springer, 2015).

Gould J and Kolbe WL, *A Dictionary of the Social Sciences*, 1st ed. (London: Tavistock, 1964).

J.A.G. Griffith, *The Politics of the Judiciary*, 5th ed. (London: Harper Collins, 1997).

Hyman Gross and R. Harrison, eds., *Jurisprudence: Cambridge Essays*, ed. Hyman Gross and Ross Harrison (Oxford: Clarendon Press, 1992).

Gongyun Gu, *Tutorial of Commercial Law* (Shanghai: Shanghai People's House, 2001).

Wang Guiguo and John Mo, eds., *Chinese Law* (The Hague; London; Boston: Kluwer Law International, 1999).

Rongxing Guo, *An Introduction to the Chinese Economy: The Driving Forces Behind Modern Day China* (Singapore: John Wiley & Sons (Asia) Pte. Ltd., 2010).

Harold Cooke Gutteridge, *Comparative Law: An Introduction to the Comparative Method of Legal Study and Research* (Cambridge: Cambridge University Press, 2015).

H.L.A. Hart, *The Concept of Law*, 2nd ed. (Oxford: Oxford University Press, 1994).

H.L.A. Hart, *Essays on Bentham: Jurisprudence and Political Theory* (Oxford: Oxford University Press, 1982).

Keith Hawkins, ed., *The Uses of Discretion*, rev. ed. (Oxford: Clarendon Press, 1995).

John W. Head, *Great Legal Traditions: Civil Law, Common Law, and Chinese Law in Historical and Operational Perspective* (Durham, N.C.: Carolina Academic Press, 2011).

C. Stephen Hsu, ed., *Understanding China's Legal System: Essays in Honor of Jerome A. Cohen* (New York: NYU Press, 2003).

Philip C. C. Huang, *Chinese Civil Justice, Past and Present* (Lanham: Rowman & Littlefield, 2012).

Philip C.C. Huang and Kathryn Bernhardt, eds., *The History and Theory of Legal Practice in China: Toward a Historical-Social Jurisprudence*, The Social Sciences of Practice (Book 3) (Leiden: Brill Academic Publishing, 2014).

Lord Justice Jackson (Editor-in-chief), *Civil Procedure: Volume I & II*, general editors B. Fontaine and I.R. Scott. [Civil procedure 2015], The White Book Service 2015 (London: Sweet & Maxwell, 2015).

Lord Justice Jackson (Editor-in-chief), *Civil Procedure: Volume I & II*, general editors B. Fontaine and I.R. Scott. [Civil procedure 2016], The White Book Service 2016 (London: Sweet Maxwell, 2016).

The Rt. Hon. Lord Justice Jackson, *The Reform of Civil Litigation* (London: Sweet & Maxwell, 2016).

Jack I.H. Jacob, *The Fabric of English Justice*, Hamlyn Lecture Series (London: Sweet & Maxwell, 1987).

Michael James, *Litigation with a Foreign Aspect: A Practical Guide* (Oxford; New York: Oxford University Press, 2009), Http://ssrn.com/abstract=1113916.

P. Jessup, *Transnational Law* (New Haven: Yale University Press, 1956).

J.A. Jolowicz, *On Civil Procedure*, Cambridge Studies in International and Comparative Law (Book 13) (Cambridge; New York: Cambridge University Press, 2000).

Perry Keller, ed., *Chinese Law and Legal Theory*, The International Library of Essays in Law and Legal Theory (Second Series) (London: Routledge, 2001).

X.E. Kramer and C.H. van Rhee, eds., *Civil Litigation in a Globalising World* (Hague: T.M.C. Asser Press, 2012).

F. H. Lawson, *Selected Essays*, European Studies in Law (Amsterdam; New York: North-Holland Pub. Co., 1977).

Tahirih V. Lee, ed., *Basic Concepts of Chinese Law*, Chinese Law: Social, Political, Historical, and Economic Perspectives (London: Routledge, 1997).

James Legge, trans., *The Ch'un Ts'ew with the Tso Cheun in 5 the Chinese, Taiwan (1883)*, Taiwan (1883) (Oxford: Clarendon Press, 1971).

Buyun Li, *Constitutionalism and China* (Beijing: Law Press, 2006).

Guoguang Li, *Guidance and Reference on Economic Trail* (Beijing: Legal Press, 2001).

Qi Chao Liang, *The Collection of Yin Bing Shi, Vol. 5* (Shanghai: Shanghai Guangzhi Publishing House, 1936).

Shuwen Liang, ed., *Research for Problems in Implementation of Civil Procedure Law* (Beijing: People's Court Press, 2000).

K.N. Llewellyn, *The Common Law Tradition: Deciding Appeals* (New York: Aspen Law and Business, 1960).

Lord Mackay, *Halsbury's Laws of England, Volume 12: Civil Procedure* (London: LexisNexis, 2009).

Thomas Lundmark, *Charting the Divide Between Common and Civil Law* (New York; Oxford: Oxford University Press, 2012).

Wei Luo, *Chinese Law and Legal Research*, Chinese Law Series (Book 8) (Littleton, Colorado: Fred B. Rothman & Co, 2005).

Wei Luo, *The Civil Procedure Law and Court Rules of the People's Republic of China*, Chinese Law Series (Book 10) (Littleton, Colo.: Fred B Rothman and Co, 2006).

Geoffrey MacCormack, *The Spirit of Traditional Chinese Law*, The Spirit of the Laws (Athens; London: University of Georgia Press, 1996).

Geoffrey MacCormack, *Traditional Chinese Penal Law*, rev. ed., Law in East Asia Series. (London: Simmonds & Hill Publishing, 2013).

Neil MacCormick, *Legal Reasoning and Legal Theory*, Clarendon Law Series (Oxford: Clarendon Press, 1978).

Henry S. Maine, *Dissertations on Early Law and Custom* (Delhi: B. R. Pub Corporation, 1985).

F.W. Matiland, *Equity: A Course of Lectures*, Reissue ed. (Cambridge: Cambridge University Press, 2011).

Stephen McCaffrey and Thomas Main, *Transnational Litigation in Comparative Perspective: Theory and Application*, 1st ed. (New York; Oxford: Oxford University Press, 2009).

Sen Meng, *New Introduction to Jurisprudence* (Shanghai: Shanghai Commercial Press, 1911).

John Henry Merryman, trans, Peidong & Lu Gu, Zhengping, *The Civil Law Tradition*, 2nd ed. (Beijing: Beijing Law Press, 2004).

Catherine Mitchell, *Interpretation of Contracts (Current Controversies in Law)*, 1st ed., Current Controversies in Law (Book 2) (London: Routledge-Cavendish, 2007).

Charles A. Moore, ed., *The Chinese Mind: Essentials of Chinese Philosophy and Culture* (Honolulu: University of Hawaii Press, 1978).

P. L. Murray and Rolf H. Sturner, *German Civil Justice* (Durham, N.C.: Carolina Academic Press, 2004).

F. S. C. Northrop, *The Complexity of Legal and Ethical Experience: Studies in the Method of Normative Subjects*, 1st ed. (Boston: Little, Brown, 1959).

John O'Hare and Kevin D. Browne, *Civil Litigation*, 13th ed. (London: Sweet & Maxwell, 2007).

Hui Xing, Liang, *Judging Methods* (Beijing: Law Press, 2005).

W Blake Odgers and W. Blake Odgers, *The Common Law of England (V1)*, reproduction of 1920 book (Ithaca, New York: Cornell University Library, 2009).

W. B. Odgers, "Changes in Procedure and in the Law of Evidence," in *A Century of Law Reform: Twelve Lectures on the Changes in the Law of England During the Nineteenth Century* (London: The Macmillan Company, 1901).

Esin Örücü, *The Enigma of Comparative Law: Variations on a Theme for the Twenty-First Century* (Leiden; Boston: Martinus Nijhoff Publishers, 2004).

F. Pollock and F. Maitland, *The History of English Law Before the Time of Edward I, Volume 1 & 2* (Cambridge: Cambridge University Press, 1988).

Ernest Rabel, *Aufgabe und Notwendigkeit der Rechtsvergleichung*, in *Gesammelte Aufsatze III*, ed. Leser, 1967, Rabel (1925), 1.

Ernst Rabel, *The Conflict of Laws; a Comparative Study*, foreword by William Draper Lewis and Hessel E. Yntema, Michigan Legal Studies (Ann Arbor: University of Michigan Law School, 1958).

Gustav Radbruch, *Einführung in die Rechtswissenschaft* (Stuttgart: K. F. Koehler, 1969).

John Rawls, *The Law of Peoples* (Cambridge, Mass.: Harvard University Press, 1999).

John Rawls, *A Theory of Justice*, 2nd ed. (Cambridge, Mass: Belknap Press of Harvard University Press, 1999).

Mathias Reimann and Reinhard Zimmermann, eds., *The Oxford Handbook of Comparative Law*, 1st ed. (Oxford: Oxford University Press, 2008).

C.H. van Rhee, ed., *European Traditions in Civil Procedure*, Ius Commune Europaeum (Book 54) (Antwerp: Intersentia, 2005).

C.H. van Rhee and A. Uzelac, eds., *Truth and Efficiency in Civil Litigation: Fundamental Aspects of Fact-Finding and Evidence-Taking in a Comparative Context*, Ius Commune Europaeum (Book 111) (Cambridge: Intersentia, 2012).

C.H. van Rhee and A. Uzelac, eds, *Evidence in Contemporary Civil Procedure: Fundamental Issues in a Comparative Perspective*, Ius Commune Europaeum (Cambridge: Intersentia, 2015).

Norbert Rouland, *Legal Anthropology*, trans. Philippe G. Planel (California: Stanford University Press, 1994).

Zongling Shen, ed., *Jurisprudence (Fa Li Xue)*, 3rd ed. (Taipei: Beijing University Press, 2009).

Stuart Sime, *A Practical Approach to Civil Procedure*, 17th ed. (Oxford: Oxford University Press, 2014).

Stuart Sime, *A Practical Approach to Civil Procedure*, 5th ed. (Oxford: Oxford University Press, 2002).

Stuart Sime, *A Practical Approach to Civil Procedure*, 9th ed. (Oxford: Oxford University Press, 2016).

Stuart Sime, *A Practical Approach to Civil Procedure*, 14th ed., Practical Approach Series (Oxford: Oxford University Press, 2011).

Laura Slater, *Civil Litigation Practice: An Expert Guide* (London: Ark group, 2015).

Guohua Sun, *Chinese Law Dictionary*, Jurisprudence Volume (Chinese Procuratorial Press, 1997).

Lewis Talbot, Nadine H. Shelton, and Chief editor Mauro Cappelletti, eds., *International Encyclopedia of Comparative Law. Volume XVI: Civil Procedure.* (Tubingen: Mohr Sieback, 2014).

Karen G. Turner, James V. Feinerman, and R. Kent Guy, eds., *The Limits of the Rule of Law in China*, Asian Law Series (Seattle: University of Washington Press, 2015).

F. Venter, ed., et al, "Regsnavorsing - Metode en Publikasie, ('Legal Research - Method and Publication')," 1st ed. (Kaapstad: Juta, 1990).

Shizhou Wang, *Civil Procedure in China*, International Encyclopaedia of Laws (Alphen aan den Rijn: Wolters Kluwer Law & Business, 2014).

Zhixiang Wang and Zengrun Wang, trans., *Soviet Civil Procedure* (Beijing: Law Press, 1957).

Chen Weizuo, *Chinese Civil Procedure and the Conflict of Laws*, Tsinghua Chinese Law Series. (Beijing: Tsinghua University Press, 2011).

John Henry Wigmore, *A Treatise on the Anglo-American System of Evidence in Trials at Common Law -V3* (Whitefish: Literary Licensing, 2012).

Margaret Y.K. Woo and Mary E. Gallagher, eds., *Chinese Justice: Civil Dispute Resolution in Contemporary China* (Cambridge: Cambridge University Press, 2011).

Jialin Wu, *Xian Fa Xue ('Constitutional Law')* (Beijing: The Press of Central Radio and TV University, 1985).

Jing-Xiong Wu, *A Study of Legal Philosophy* (Shanghai: Shanghai Law Translation & Edition Press, 1933).

Guodang Xu, *The Debates about the Trains of Thought for Drawing up a Chinese Civil Code*, (Beijing: Publishing House of CUPL, 2001).

Ganqiao Yang, *New Thoughts of Chinese Jurisprudence (Zhonggguo Faxue Xin Siwei)* (Shanxi: Shanxi People's Publisher, 1989).

Jinfan Zhang, *Tradition of Chinese Law and Its Transformation in Late Qing (Zhonggua Falu de Chuantong Yu Jindai Zhuanxing)* (Beijing: Beijing Law Press, 1997).

Mingkai Zhang, *Criminal Law*, 4th ed. (Beijing: Law Press, 2011).

Bo Zhao, *Legal Principles and Chinese Law: A Philosophical Investigation*, CRBS-Dissertatiereeks (Hague: Boom Eleven International Publishing, 2009).

Yikun Zhu, *Concise Chinese Law* (Beijing: Law Press, 2007).

Yikun Zhu, *China's Procedural Law* (Beijing: Law Press China, 2003).

A. Zuckerman, *Civil Procedure: Principles of Practice*, 2nd Revised ed. (London: Sweet & Maxwell, 2006).

A.A.S. Zuckerman, *Civil Justice in Crisis: Comparative Perspectives of Civil Procedure* (Oxford: Oxford University Press, 2000).

Konrad Zweigert, Hein Kotz, and Tony Weir, trans., *An Introduction to Comparative Law: Volume I: The Framework*, 2nd Revised ed. (Oxford: Clarendon Press, 1987).

Konrad Zweigert and K. Kotz, trans., Tony Weir, *An Introduction to Comparative Law*, 3rd Revised ed. (Oxford: Clarendon Press, 1998).

Chapters in Books

Adam, "Ethonologische Rechtsforschung," in *Lehrbuch der Volkerkunde*, ed. Adam and Trimborn (1958), 189-n.a.

Neil Andrews, "Fundamental Principles of Civil Procedure: Order Out of Chaos," in *Civil Litigation in a Globalising World*, ed. X.E. Kramer and Rhee, H (The Hague: T.M.C. Asser Press, 2012), 19-38.

Paul Burrows and Cento G. Veljanovski, "Introduction to: Economic Approaches to Law," in *The Economic Approaches to Law*, ed. Paul Burrows and Cento G. Veljanovski (London; Boston; Sydney; Wellington; Durban; Toronto: Butterworths, 1981).

Oscar G. Chase and Vincenzo Varano, "Comparative Civil Justice," in *The Cambridge Companion to Comparative Law*, ed. M. Bussani and U. Mattei (Cambridge; New York: Cambridge University Press, 2012), 210-40.

J Church and A.B. Edwards, "Comparative Law/Comparative Method," in *Introduction to South African Law and Legal Theory*, WJ Hosten, et al. (Durban: Butterworths, 1995), 1261-70.

Anthony Clarke, "The Woolf Reforms: A Singular Event or an Ongoing Process," in *The Civil Procedure Ten Years On*, ed. Deirdre Dwyer (Oxford: Oxford University Press, 2009), 33-49.

Hugh Collins, "Law as Politics: Progressive American Perspectives," in *Introduction to Jurisprudence and Legal Theory: Commentary and Materials*, Anne Barron, et al. (London: Butterworths, 2002), 279-333.

Deirdre Dwyer, "What is the Meaning of CPR r 1.1(1)," in *The Civil Procedure Rules Ten Years On*, De'irdre Dwyer (Oxford: Oxford University Press, 2009), 65-73.

Lon L. Fuller, "The Adversary System," in *Talks on American law: A Series of Broadcasts to Foreign Audiences by Members of the Harvard Law School Faculty*, ed. Berman and Harold J. (New York: Vintage Books, 1961), 35-36.

David J. Gerber, "Comparing Procedural Systems: Towards an Analytical Framework," in *Law and Justice in Multistate World: Essays in Honor of Arther T. von. Mehren*, James A. R. Nafziger and Symeon C. Symeonides (2002), 665-74, Http://ssrn.com/abstract=12342579.

James Gordley, "The Functional Method," in *Methods of Comparative Law*, in *Methods of Comparative Law*, ed. Monateri. Pier G., Research Handbooks in Comparative Law. (Cheltenham, U.K.; Northampton, MA: Edward Elgar Pub., 2012), 107-19.

Wang Guiguo, "The Legal System of China," in *Chinese Law*, ed. Wang Guiguo and John Mo (The Hague; London; Boston: Kluwer Law International, 1999), 1-21.

Jacqueline Hodgson, "Conceptions of the Trial in Inquisitorial and Adversarial Procedure," in *The Trial on Trial: Volume 2: Judgment and Calling to Account*, ed. A. Duff, Farmer, S Marshall, and V. Tadros (Oxford; Portland; Or: Hart, 2004), 223-42.

D Howarth, "Making Sense Out of Nonsense," in *Jurisprudence: Cambridge Essays*, ed. Hyman Gross and Ross Harrison (Oxford: Clarendon Press, 1992), 29-53.

Huang Lie, "Rule of Law in China: Ideal and Reality," in *Constitutionalism and China*, in *Constitutionalism and China*, Buuyun Li (Beijing: Law Press, 2006), 175-90.

Yuansheng Huang, "Sources of Law in Civil Adjudication of the Dali Yuan in the Early Republic of China (Minch Dali Yuan Minshi Shenpan Fayuan)," in *100 Selected Precedents of the Dali Yuan (Dali Yuan Minshi Panli Baixuan), Ed. Yuansheng Huang*, ed. Yuansheng Huang (Taibei: Wunan Book Co. Ltd., 2009).

Zhenbao Jin, "From a Supplementary Legislator to a Legitimate Judicial Lawmaker- on the Role of the Supreme People's Court in Developing the Law in Mainland China," in *Towards a Chinese Civil Code: Comparative and Historical Perspectives*, Lei Chen and C H van Rhee (Dordrecht: Martinus Nijhoff Publishers, 2012), 29-60.

Junjian Jing, "Legislation Related to the Civil Economy in the Qing Dynasty," in *Civil Law in Qing and Republican China*, Kathryn Bernhardt, Philip C. Huang, and Mark A. Allee, Law, Society, and Culture in China. (Stanford, Calif.: Stanford University Press, 1994), 42-84.

J.A. Jolowicz, "On the Comparison of Procedures," in *Law and Justice in Multistate World: Essays in Honour of Arther T. Von Mehren*, ed. James Nafziger and Symeon Symeonides (New York: Transnational Publishers, 2002), 721-40.

J. A. Jolowicz, "Civil Litigation: What is It For?" in *The Civil Procedure Ten Years On*, ed. De'irdre Dwyer (Oxford: Oxford University Press, 2009), 51-63.

Zentaro Kitagawa, "The Development of Comparative Law in East Asia," in *The Oxford Handbook of Comparative Law*, ed. Mathias Reimann and Reinhard Zimmermann (Oxford: Oxford University Press, 2008), 237-60.

Nicola Lacey, "Modern Positivism: H L A Hart and Analytical Jurisprudence," in *Introduction to Jurisprudence and Legal Theory: Commentary and Materials*, by Anne Barron, et al. (London: Butterworths, 2002), 143-89.

Chen Lei, "Contextualizing Legal Transplant: China and Hong Kong," in *Methods of Comparative Law*, ed. Pier G. Monateri (Cheltenham, U.K.; Northampton, MA: Edward Elgar Pub., 2012), 192-209.

Sebastian McEvoy, "Descriptive and Purposive Categories of Comparative Law," in *Methods of Comparative Law*, ed. Pier G. Monateri (Cheltenham, U.K.; Northampton, MA: Edward Elgar Publishing, 2012), 144-61.

Chuncai Meng, "Civil Procedure Law," in *Chinese Law*, ed. Guiguo Wang and John Mo (The Hague, London, Boston: Kluwer Law International, 1999), 179-216.

Ralf Michaels, "The Functional Method of Comparative Law," in *The Oxford Handbook of Comparative Law*, ed. Mathias Reimann and Reinhard Zimmermann (Oxford: Oxford University Press, 2008), 339-82.

John Shijian Mo, "The General Principles of Civil Law," in *Chinese Law*, ed. Guiguo Wang and John Mo (The Hague, London, Boston: Kluwer Law International, 1999), 95-176.

John Shijian Mo, "Non-Judicial Means of Dispute Settlement," in *Chinese Law*, in *Chinese Law*, ed. Guiguo Wang and John Mo (The Hague, London, Boston: Kluwer Law International, 1999), 757-807.

Pier Giuseppe Monateri, "Methods in Comparative Law: An Intellectual Overview," in *Methods of Comparative Law* (Cheltenham, U.K.; Northampton, MA, USA: Edward Elgar Pub., 2012), 7-24.

Peter L. Murray, "A Morning at the Amtsgericht: German Civil Justice in Practice," in *Law and Justice in Multistate World: Essays in Honor of Arther T. von Mehren*, James Nafziger and Symeon Symeonides (New York: Transnational Publishers, 2002), 779-92.

Katerina Nilsson, Larry Lian, and Norla Gu, "People's Republic of China," in *Finding, Freezing and Attaching Assets*, ed. Jacob C. Jorgenson (Netherlands: Kluwer Law International, 2016).

Richards Nobles and David Schiff, "The Evolution of Natural Law," in *Introduction to Jurisprudence and Legal Theory: Commentary and Materials*, by Anne Barron, et al. (London: Butterworths, 2002), 35-90.

Richard Nobles and David Schiff, "Debating with Natural Law; the Emergence of the Legal Positivism," in *Introduction to Jurisprudence and Legal Theory: Commentary and Materials*, Anne Barron, et al. (London: Butterworths, 2002), 91-142.

Tim Parkes, "The Civil Procedure Rules Ten Years on: The Practitioners' Perspectives," in *The Civil Procedure Rules Ten Years On*, Deidre Dywer (Oxford: Oxford University Press, 2009), 435-51.

James Penner, "Law and Adjudication: Dworkin's Critique of Positivism," in *Introduction to Jurisprudence and Legal Theory: Commentary and Materials*, by Anne Barron, et al. (London: Butterworths, 2002), 334-426.

James Penner, David Schiff, and Richard Nobles, "Approaches to Jurisprudence, Legal Theory, and the Philosophy of Law," in *Introduction to Jurisprudence and Legal Theory: Commentary and Materials*, Anne Barron, et al. (London: Butterworths, 2002), 3-34.

Mathias Reimann, "Comparative Law and Neighbouring Disciplines," in *The Cambridge Companion to Comparative Law*, ed. Mauro Bussani and Ugo Mattei, Cambridge Companions to Law (Cambridge; New York: Cambridge University Press, 2012), 13-34.

Robert Reiner, "Classical Social Theory and Law," in *Introduction to Jurisprudence and Legal Theory: Commentary and Materials*, in *Jurisprudence and Legal Theory: Commentary and Materials*, Anne Barron, et al. (London: Butterworths, 2002), 230-78.

C.H.Van Rhee and R. Verkerk, "Civil Procedure," in *Elgar Encyclopedia of Comparative Law*, ed. J.M. Smits (Cheltenham: Edward Elgar Publishing, 2006), 120-34.

Max Rhenstein, "Comparative Law and Legal Systems," reprinted in 1 Max Rhenstein International Encyclopedia of the Social Sciences, 1 Gesammelte Schiriften (N.a.: MacMillan Publishers, 1968), 204-10.

Teemu Ruskola, "The East Asian Legal Tradition," in *The Cambridge Companion to Comparative Law*, in *The Cambridge Companion to Comparative Law*, ed. M. Bussani and U. Mattei (Cambridge; New York: Cambridge University Press, 2012), 257-77.

David Schiff, "Modern Positivism: Kelsen's Pure Theory of Law," in *Introduction to Jurisprudence and Legal Theory: Commentary and Materials*, Anne Barron, et al. (London: Butterworths, 2002), 190-229.

Carl E. Schneider, "Discretion and Rules: A Lawyers' View," in *The Uses of Discretion*, ed. Keith Hawkins (Oxford: Clarendon Press, 1992), 47-88.

Stuart Sime, "Disputes of Fact in Interim Applications," in *The Civil Procedure Rules Ten Years On*, ed. Deirdre Dwyer (Oxford; New York: Oxford University Press, 2009), 271-81.

G. Swanson, "Framework for Comparative Research: Anthropology and the Theory of Action," in *Comparative Methods in Sociology: Essays on Trends and Applications*, ed. Vallier Ivan and Aptter. David E. (Berkeley: University of California Press, 1971), 141-202.

Kristie Thomas, "Dynamism in China's Civil Procedure Law: Civil Justice with Chinese Characteristics," in *The Dynamism of Civil Procedure - Global Trends and Developments*, ed. C. Picker and G. Seidman (London: Springer, 2015), 119-39.

Joachim Zekoll, "Comparative Civil Procedure," in *The Oxford Handbook of Comparative Law*, ed. Mathias Reimann and Reinhard Zimmermann (Oxford: Oxford University Press, 2008), 1327-62.

Guobin Zhu, "Constitution Law and State Structure," in *Chinese Law*, ed. Wang Guiguo and John Mo (The Hague; London; Boston: Kluwer Law International, 1999), 23-61.

Reinhard Zimmermann, "An Introduction to German Legal Culture," in *Introduction to German Law*, ed. Werner F. Ebke and Matthew W. Finkin (Hague, Boston: Kluwer Law International, 1996), 1-n.a.

Articles in Journals or Periodicals

Janet E. Ainsworth, "Categories and Culture: On the 'Rectification of Names' in Comparative Law," *Cornell L. Rev.* 82, no. 1 (1996): 19-42. http://scholarship.law.cornell.edu/clr/vol82/iss1/3.

I.L. Backer, "The Norwegian Reform of Civil Procedure," *Scandinavian Studies in Law* 51 (2007): 41-76.

Benjamin J. Bai and Guoping Da, "Strategies for Trade Secrets Protection in China," *Northwestern J. Of Technology and Intellectual Property* 9, no. 7 (2011): 351-75. http://scholarlycommons.law.northwestern.edu/njtip/vol9/iss7/1.

M.K. Block, et al., "An Experimental Comparison of Adversarial Versus Inquisitorial Procedural Regimes," *Am. L. & Economics Rev.* 2, no. 1 (2000): 170-94.

Samuel L. Bray, "The System of Equitable Remedies," *UCLA L. Rev.* 63, no. 3 (2016): 530-93.

James Brook, "Inevitable Errors: The Preponderance of Evidence Standard in Civil Litigation," *Tulsa L.J.* 18, no. 1 (1982): 79-109.

Nicolas Browne-Wilkinson, "Territorial Jurisdiction and The New Technologies," *Israel L. Rev.* 25, no. 2 (1991): 145-55.

Ernest Caldwell, "Social, Change and Written Law in Early Chinese Legal Thought," *L. and History Rev.* 32, no. 1 (2014): 1-30.

Dennis Chang, "Towards a Jurisprudence of a Third Kind --One Country, Two Systems," *Case W. Res. J. Int'l L.* 20, no. 1 (1988): 99-125.

Wejen Chang, "Classical Chinese Jurisprudence and Development of Chinese Legal System," *Tsinghua China L. Rev.* 2, no. 2 (2010): 207-72.

O. G. Chase, "American 'Exceptionalism' and Comparative Procedure," *Am. J. Comp. L.* 50, no. 2 (2002): 277-301.

Oscar G. Chase, "Some Observations on the Cultural Dimension in Civil Procedure Reform," *Am. J. Comp. Law* 45, no. 4 (1997): 861-70.

Xingliang Chen, "The Jurisprudence of the Case Guidance System (Anli Zhidao Zhidu de Fali Kaocha)," *Law and Social Development (Fazhi Yu Shehui Fazhan)* 18, no. 3 (2012): 73-80.

Xinyu Chen, "Bifu and Leitui - Starts from Biyin Lvtiao. (Bifu Yu Leitui Zhibian - Cong 'Biyin Lvtiao' Chufa)," *Tribune of Political Science and Law (Zhengfa Luntan)* 29, no. 2 (2011): 113-21.

Albert H.Y. Chen, "The Developing Chinese Law and the Civil Law Tradition," *China Rev.* (1996): 29-59. http://www.jstor.org/stable/23453139.

Chao-yang (Xiamen Municipal Intermediate People's Court Chen, Xiamen), "Standards of Proof in Civil Proceedings: From the Perspective of Judicial Impartiality and Efficiency," *J. of Southwest U. P. Sc. & L.*, no. 1 (2002): 9-19.

Guangzhong Chen, Haiguang Chen, and Xiaona Wei, "The System of Criminal Evidence and Epistemology - Discussion between Legal Truth and Relative Truth," *China Legal Science*, no. 1 (2001): 37-52.

Mingguo Chen and Weiming Zuo, "Practical Obstacles and Countermeasures of Guiding Cases. (Zhidaoxing Anli de Yingyong Zhangai Jiqi Kefu - Sichuan Fayuan Anli Yingyong Shidian Gongzuo de Chubu Fenxi)," *Journal of Law Application (Falv Shiyong)* 5 (2012): 67-71.

H. Chodosh, "Comparing Comparisons: In Search of Methodology," *Iowa L. Rev.* 84, no. 5 (1999): 1025-1132.

Jerome A. Cohen, "China's Troubled Path to WTO," *Int'l Financial L. Rev.*, 1st September 2001, 71.

Mathilde Cohen, "When Judges Have Reasons not to Give Reasons: A Comparative Law Approach," *Wash. & Lee L. Rev.* 72, no. 2 (2015): 483-572.

E.J. Couture, "The Nature of Judicial Process," *Tul. L. Rev.* 25, no. 1 (1950-51): 1-28.

Vivian Grosswald Curran, "Cultural Immersion, Difference and Categories in U.S. Comparative Law," *Am. J. Comp. L.* 46, no. 1 (1998): 43-92. http://www.jstor.org/stable/841076.

Dominique Demougin and Claude Fluet, "Deterrence Vs Judicial Error: A Comparative View of Standards of Proof," *J. of Inst. and Theoretical Econ.* 161, no. 2 (2004): 193-206. https://ssrn/abstract=585770.

Jinting Deng, "The Guiding Case System in Mainland China," *Frontiers of Law in China* 10, no. 3 (2015): 449-74.

Yong Ding, "Research for Abusing Litigation of Blemish in Resolutions of Companies in Germany and Enlightenment," *Journal of Comparative Law*, no. 4 (2013): 35-48.

Scott Dodson, "The Challenge of Comparative Civil Procedure," *Ala. L. Rev.* 60, no. 1 (2008): 133-50.

R. Dworkin, "Hard Cases," *Harv. L. Rev.* 88, no. 6 (1975): 1057-1109.

Frank H. Easterbrook, "Legal Interpretation and Power of Judiciary," *Harv. J. L. & Pub. Pol'y* 7, no. 1 (1984): 87-100.

Edward J. Eberle, "The Method and Role of Comparative Law," *Wash. U. Global Stud. L. Rev.* 8, no. 3 (2009): 451-86.

Christoph Engel, "Preponderance of the Evidence versus Intime Conviction: A Behavioural Perspective on Conflict between American and Continental European Law," *MPI Collective Goods Preprint No.2008/33* (2008): 1-28.

William Ewald, "The Jurisprudential Approach in Comparative Law: A Field Guide to 'Rats'," *Am. J. Comp. L.* 46, no. 4: 701-7.

Elizabeth Fahey and Zhirong Tao, "The Pretrial Discovery Process in Civil Cases: A Comparison of Evidence Discovery between China and the United States," *B.C. Int'l & Comp. L. Rev.* 37, no. 2 (2014): 281-333.

Chongyi Fan, "Opinions on Objective Truth," *China Legal Science*, no. 1 (2000): 114-20.

Keith A Findley, "Innocents at Risk: Adversary Imbalance, Forensic Science, and the Search for Truth," *Seton Hall L. Rev.* 38, no. 3 (2008): 893-973.http://scholarship.shu.edu/shir/vol38/iss3/7.

R. Finkelstein, "The Adversarial System and the Search for the Truth," *Monash U. L. Rev.* 37, no. 1 (2011): 135-44.

Owen M. Fiss, "'Against Settlement'," *Yale L.J.* 93, no. 6 (1984): 1073-92.

Nicholas H. D. Foster, "Company Law Theory in Comparative Perspective: England and France," *Am. J. Comp. L.* 48, no. 4 (2000): 573-622.

Ron Fuller, "The Forms and Limits of Adjudication," *Harv. L. Rev.* 92, no. 2 (1978): 353-409.

E. Genzmer, "Zum Verhaltnis von Rechtsgeschichte und Rechtvergleichung ('In German')," *ARSP* 41 (1954/55): 326-47.

John Gillespie, "Rethinking the Role of Judicial Independence in Socialist-Transforming East Asia," *I.C.L.Q.* 56, no. 4 (2007): 837-70.

C. Glasser, "Solving the Litigation Crisis," *The Litigator* (1994): 14.

David M. Gooden and Douglas Walton, "Defeasibility in Judicial Opinion - Logical or Procedural," *Informal Logic* 28, no. 1 (2008): 6-19.

James Gordley, "Comparative Legal Research: Its Function in the Development of Harmonized Law," *Am. J. Comp. L.* 43, no. 4 (1995): 555-68.

Peter Gottwald, "Comparative Civil Procedure," *Ritsumeikan L. Rev.* 22 (2005): 23-35.

Gray S.J., "Towards a Theory of Cultural Influence on the Development of Accounting Systems Internationally," *ABACUS* 24 (1998): 1-16.

Bernard Grossfeld, "Global Accounting: Where Internet Meets Geography," *Am. J. Comp. L.* 48, no. 2 (2000): 261-306.

Bernhard Grossfeld and Edward J. Eberle, "Patterns of Order in Comparative Law: Discovering and Decoding Invisible Powers," *Tex. Int'l. L.J.* 38, no. 2 (2003): 291-316.

WJ Habscheid, "The Fundamental Principles of the Law of Civil Procedure," *Comp. & Int'l L.J. S. Afr.* 17, no. 1 (1984): 1-31.www.jstor.org/stable/23246919.

H.L.A Hart, "Positivism and Separation of Law and Morals," *Harvard L. Rev.* 71, no. 4 (1958): 593-629.

H L A Hart, "Definition and Theory in Jurisprudence," *L. Quarterly Rev.* 70 (1983): 37-60.

Qinhua He, "The Birth and Growth of Modern Jurisprudence in China," *Frontiers of Law in China* 1, no. 4 (2006): 486-513.

WJ Hosten, trans., Scott, "Romeinse Reg, Regsgeskiedenis en Regsvergelyking," *THRHR* 25 (1961): 16Pretoria: N.A., 1961.

Minjie Hu, "The Practical Obstacles and Road Selection of Administrative Guiding Case. (Xingzheng Zhidaoxing Anli de Shijian Kunjing Yu Lujing Xuanze)," *Law Science (Faxue)*, no. 1 (2012): 149-54.

Tina Hunter, "Interpretive Theories: Dworkin, Sunstein, and Ely," *Bond Law Review* 17, no. 2 (2005): 78-101.

Haihong Huo, "Chinese Expression or Theory of Civil Procedure Law," *Legal System and Social Development*, no. 4 (2013): 3-9.

Xin Hu, "Bifu in Criminal Law of Ancient China (Zhongguo Gudai Xingfa Zhong de Bifu)," *Law Review (Faxue Pinglun)*, no. 2 (1994): 84-87.

Yunteng Hu and Tongzhi Yu, "Research on Several Important Difficult Questions of the Guiding Case System. (Anli Zhidao Xhidu Ruogan Zhongda Yinan Zhengyi Wenti Yanjiu)," *Chinese Journal of Law (Faxue Yanjiu)*, no. 6 (2008): 3-24.

Ping Jiang and Jian Mi, "The Civil Law Tradition and Contemporary Chinese Law [Part II]. (Lun Minfa Chuantong Yu Dangdai Zhangguo Falii (Xia))," *The Tribune of Political Science and Law (Zhengfa Luntan)*, no. 3 (1993): 1-8.

Zhenbao Jin, "On the Power of the Supreme People's Court to Issue Judicial Intgerpretations in Abstracto (Lun Zuigao Renmin Fayuan de Chouxiang Sifa Jieshi Quan)," *Journal of Comparative Law (Bijiao Fa Yanjiu)*, no. 2 (2010): 55-66.

J.A. Jolowicz, "Adversarial and Inquisitorial Models of Civil Procedure," *I.C.L.Q.* 52, no. 2 (2003): 281-95.

J.A. Jolowicz, "Civil Litigation: What is it For?" *Camb. L.J.* 67, no. 3 (2008): 508-20.

Ann D. Jordan, "Lost in Translation: Two Legal Cultures, Common Law Judiciary and the Basic Law of Hong Kong Special Administrative Region," *Cornell Int'l L. J.* 30, no. 2 (1997): 335-80.

Benjamin Kaplan, Arther T. von Mehren, and Rudolf Schaefer, "Phrases of German Civil Procedure (Pt.1)," *Harv. L. Rev.* 71, no. 7 (1958): 1193-1268.

Neal Kumar Katyal, "Judge as Advicegivers," *Stan. L. Rev.* 50, no. 6 (1998): 1709-1824.

Kevin C. Kennedy, "Equitable Remedies and Principled Discretion: The Michigan Experience," *U. Det. Mercy L. Rev.* 74, no. 4 (1997): 609-56.

A. D. Kessler, "Our Inquisitorial Tradition: Equity Procedure, Due Process, and the Search for an Alternative to the Adversarial," *Cornell L. Rev.* 90, no. 5 (2005): 1181-1275.

Hein Kotz, "Comparative Law in Germany Today," *Revue Internationale de Droit Compare* 51, no. 4 (1999): 753-58.

Edouard M. Lambert, "Conception Generale et Definition de la Science due Droit Compare," *Procesverbaux Des Seances et Documents, Congres International de Droit Compare I* (1905): 26.

Zhiping Liang, "Explicating Law: A Comparative Perspective of Chinese and Western Legal Culture," *J. Chinese L.* 3, no. 1 (1989): 55-92.

Xiliang Li, "The Demarcation of 'Stakeholder' in Civil Procedure Law," *Science of Law (Journal of Northwest University of Political Science and Law)*, no. 1 (2012): 139-47.

Jocelyn E.H. Limmer, "China's New 'Common Law' Using China's Guiding Cases to Understand How to Do Business in People's Republic of China," *Willamette J. Int'l L. & Dis. Resol.* 21, no. 2 (2013): 96-133.

Shichun Li, "Studies on Basic Problems Concerning Procedures of Civil Preservation," *Peking U. L.J.*, no. 1 (2005): 43-74.

Ducai Liu, "A Study of Judicial Precedent in Traditional China. (Zhongguo Gudai Panli Kaolun)," *Social Sciences in China (Zhonguo Shehui Kexue)*, no. 4 (2007): 145-55, 207-8.

Kaixiang Liu, "About the Nature, Accordance and Features of Commercial Law," *Modern Law Science*, no. 5 (1997): 26-34.

Li Liu, "Discussion on Case Guiding System (Lun Woguo de Anli Zhidao Zhidu)," *Journal of Hubei University of Police (Hubei Jingguan Xueyuan Xuebao)*, no. 1 (2013): 132-34.

Nanping Liu and Michelle Liu, "Justice without Judges: The Filing Division in People's Republic of China," *U.C. Davis J. Int'l L. & Pol'y* 17, no. 2 (2011): 283-344.

Weimin Liu, "The Difference Between Thought of Civil Law and Thought of Commercial Law in Juridical Application," *Speed Reading (Published by Xihua University, Chengdu)*, no. 9 (2014): 256-57.

Yuwen Li, "Professional Ethics of Chinese Judges," *China Perspectives [Online Journal]* (2003), Http://chinaperspectives.revues.org/274, accesseed on 25 June 2016.

Zhenghua Li, "Theory of Discretionary Power," *Contemporary Law Review*, no. 4 (2000): 18-19, 66.

Karl Llewellyn, "Some Realism About Realism- Responding to Dean Pound," *Harv. L. Rev.* 44, no. 8 (1931): 1222-64.

Arabella Lyon, "Rhetorical Authority in Athenian Democracy and the Chinese Legalism of Han Fei," *Philosophy & Rhetoric* 41, no. 1 (2008): 51-71.

Geoffrey MacCormack, "Scandinavian Realism," *The Juridical Rev.* (1970): 33-55.

Thomas O. Main, "The Procedural Foundation of Substantive Law," *Wash. U. L. Rev.* 87, no. 4 (2009): 801-42. http://ssrn/abstract=1113916.

Thomas O. Main, "Traditional Equity and Contemporary Procedure," *Wash. L. Rev.* 78, no. 2 (2003): 429-514.

M. Martinek, "Rechtsverglechung Als Akademische Disziplin in Deutschland," *Ritsumeikan Law Review (International Edition)* 17 (2000): 79-117.

A. Mason, "Changing the Law in a Changing Society," *Commw. L. Bull.* 18, no. 3 (1992): 1166-72.

Ugo Mattei, "An Opportunity not to be Missed - A Future of Comparative Law In the United States," *Am. J. Comp. L.* 46, no. 4 (1998): 709-18.

Marinus Johan Meijer, "An Aspect of Traditional Chinese Law," *T'Oung Pao* 66 (1980): 199-216.

Nicole E. Negowetti, "Judicial Decisionmaking, Empathy, and the Limits of Perception," *Akron L. Rev.* 47, no. 3 (2015): 693-751.

Roderick O'Brien, "The Survival of Traditional Chinese Law in the People's Republic of China," *Hong Kong L. J.* 40, no. 1 (2010): 165-74.

V.V. Palmer, "From Lerotholi to Lando: Some Examples of Comparative Law Methodology," *Global Jurist Frontiers* 4, no. 2 (2004): 1-29.

Jianfeng Pan, "Scientific Reforms of Civil Trial Procedure System in China - Reflection on the Civil Procedure and its Relationship," *Tribune of Political Science and Law*, no. 5 (2012): 99-113.

Randall Peerenboom, "Judicial Accountability and Judicial Independence: An Empirical Study of Individual Case Supervision in the People's Republic of China," *The China Journal* 55 (2006): 67-92.

Anne Peters and Heiner Schewenke, "Comparative Law Beyond Post-Modernism," *I.C.L.Q.* 49, no. 4 (2000): 800-834.htttp://justor.org/stable/761761.

A. E. Plastas, "The Functional and the Dysfunctional in the Comparative Method of Law: Some Critical Remarks," *Electronic J. Comp. L.* 12, no. 3 (2008), Www.ejcl.org.http://www.ejcl.org/123/.

Gerald J. Postema, "Classical Common Law Jurisprudence (Part I)," *Oxford U. of Commw. L.J.* 2, no. 2 (2002): 155-80.

Gerald J. Postema, "Classical Common Law Jurisprudence (Part II)," *Oxford U. of Commw. L.J.* 3, no. 1 (2003): 1-28.

R. Pound, "The Causes of Popular Dissatisfaction with the Administration of Justice," *Reports of the American Bar Association* 29 (1906): 395-417.

J. Raz, "Legal Principles and the Limits of Law," *Yale L.J.* 81, no. 5 (1972): 823-54.

M. Reimann, "The Progress and Failure of Comparative Law in the Second Half of the Twentieth Century," *Am. J. Comp. L.* 50, no. 4 (2002): 671-700.http://www.justor.org/stable/41616734.

Mathias Reimann, "The Progress and Failure of Comparative Law in the Second Half of the Twentieth Century," *Am. J. Comp. J.* 50, no. 4 (2002): 671-700.http://www.jstor.org/stable/41616734.

John C. Reitz, "How to Do Comparative Law," *Am. J. Comp. L.* 46, no. 4 (1998): 617-36.

J. Resnik, "Managerial Judges," *Harv. L. Rev.* 96, no. 2 (1982): 374-448.

Michael D. Risinger, "'Substance' and 'Procedure' Revisited: With Some Afterthoughts on the Constitutional Problems of 'Irrebuttable Presumptions'," *UCLA L. Rev.* 30, no. 2 (1982): 189-216.

The Right Honourable Lord Scarman, (Ninth Wilfred Fullagar Memorial Lecture), "The Common Law Judge and the Twentieth Century - Happy Marriage or Irretrievable Breakdown?" *Monash L. Rev.* 7, no. 1 (1980): 1-15.

R.B. Schlesinger, "The Past and Future of Comparative Law," *Am. J. Comp. L.* 43, no. 3 (1995): 477-82.

Peter F. Schlosser, "Coordinated Transnational Interaction in Civil Litigation and Arbitration," *Mich. J. Int'l L.* 12, no. 1 (1990): 150-72.

Paul J. Schmidt, "A Review of China's New Civil Evidence Law," *Pacific Rim L. & Pol. J.* 12, no. 2 (2003): 291-313.

Ming Shao, "Abuse of Civil Litigation Law and Regulation," *Tribune of Political Science and Law*, no. 6 (2011): 175-80.

Ying Shao and Run Shao, "Commercial Law in Practice: Discuss Problems of Law Application in Our Commercial Trial," *Market Modernization*, no. 19 (2014): 40-41.

E. Sherwin and K.M. Clermont, "A Comparative View of Standards of Proof," *Am. J. Comp. L.* 50, no. 2 (2002): 243-76.

H.S. Shin, "Adversarial and Inquisitorial Procedure in Arbitration," *Rand J. Economics* 29, no. 2 (1998): 378-405.

Lawrence B. Solum, "Procedural Justice," *S. Cal. L. Rev.* 78, no. 1 (2004): 181-322.

John Sorabji, Andenas Mads, et al., "The Road to New Street Station: Fact, Fiction and Overriding Objective," in *Legal Studies Research Paper Series: Paper No. 21/2011* (Cambridge, 2011), 1-18.

Benjamin A. Spencer, "The Restrictive Ethos in Civil Procedure," *Geo. Wash. L. Rev.* 78, no. 2 (2010): 353-73.

J. Spigelman, "Judicial Accountability and Performance Indicators," *Civil Justice Quarterly* 21 (2002): 1-28.www.http://ssrn.com/abstract=1802176.

JJ Spigelman, "The Poet's Rich Resource: Issues in Statutory Interpretation," *Australian Bar Rev.* 21, no. 3 (2001): 224-34.

Zelin Su, "Fully Exploit the Function of the Guiding Case System with Chinese Characteristics; Courts, Positively Enforce Historical Missions of People's Application. (Chongfen Fahui Zhongguo Tese Anli Zhidao Zhidu Zuoyong Jiji Lvxing Renmin Fayuan Lishi Shiming)," *Journal of Law Application (Falv Shiyong)* 7 (2011): 3-6.

Stephen N. Subrin, "On Thinking about a Description of a Country's Civil Procedure," *Tul. J. Int'l & Comp. L.* 7 (1999): 139-52.

Stephen N. Subrin, "How Equity Conquered Common Law: The Federal Rules of Civil Procedure in Historical Perspective," *U. Pa. L. Rev.* 135, no. 4 (1987): 909-1002.www.jstor.org/stable/3312053.

Weijian Tang, "The Evolution of Civil Procedure System of China," *Frontiers L. China* 7, no. 2 (2012): 190-210.

Ching-I Tu, "Conservatism and Constructive Forum: The Case of Wang Kuowei (1877-1927)," *Monumenta Serica (Journal of Oriental Studies)* 28 (1969): 188-214.

Rui Wang, Feimin Wang, and Danning Li, "Comparative Research of Basic Principles between Civil Law and Commercial Law," *Journal of North China University of Technology* 20, no. 4 (2008): 26-32*Comparitive Research of Basic Principles Between Civil and Commercial Law.*

Shirong Wang, "The Functions of Cases in Traditional Chinese Law. (Panli Zai Zhongguo Chuantongfa Zhong de Gongneng)," *Chinese Journal of Law (Faxue Yanjiu)*, no. 1 (2006): 125-34.

Liming Wang, "The Achievements and Prospects of Court Reforms in China," *Frontiers L. China* 1, no. 1 (2006): 1-13.

Yanchuan Wang, "The Dual Development of Commercial Law and the Growing Logic of Modern Commercial Law," *Journal of Northwest University (Philosophy and Social Science Edition)* 45, no. 1 (2015): 58-65.

Margaret Woo, "Law and Discretion in Contemporary Chinese Courts," *Pacific Rim L. & Pol'y J.* 8, no. 3 (1999): 581-616.

Margaret Woo, Y.K., "Manning the Courthouse Gates: Pleadings, Jurisdictions, and the Nation-State," *Nev. L.J.* 15, no. 3 (2015): 1261-92

Zhihai Xiong, "Objective and Subjective Norms of Procedural Testimony," *Modern Law Science* 22, no. 5 (2000): 75-80.

Xuelu Xu and Peng Liang, "Research for the Principle of Honesty and Credibility in Commercial Law," *Law Review (Published by Wuhan University)*, no. 3 (2002): 32-41.

Sibin Yang, "On Basic Characteristics and Exchanges of Ancient China's Case System (Zhongguo Gudai Panli Zhidu de Yanbian Yu Jiben Tezheng)," *Law Science Magazine (Faxue Zazhi)*, no. 2 (2008): 121-24.

Liang Yue and Wei Han, "On the Thought of Commercial Law - Analysis with Comparison to Civil Law Thought," *Legal System and Society (Published by Yunan Provincial People's Association)*, no. 19 (2009): 6-7*On the Thought of Commercial Law- Analysis with Comparison to Civil Law Thought.*

Xianyi Zeng and Xiaohong Ma, "A Dialectic Study of the Structure and Basic Concept of Traditional Chinese Law and an Analysis of the Relationship Between Li (Ceremony) and Fa (Law)," *Frontiers of Law in China* 1, no. 1 (2006): 34-52.

Mo Zhang, "International Civil Litigation in China: A Practical Analysis of the Chinese Judicial System," *B.C. Int'l & Comp. L. Rev.* 25, no. 1 (2002): 59-96, http://lawdigitalcommons.bc.edu/iclr/vol25/iss1/3.

Sheng Zhang, "Institutions and Practice of Independent Adjudication of Dali Yuan in the Early History of the Republic of China (Minchu Daliyuan Shenpan Duli de Zhidu Yu Shijian)," *Tribune of Political Science & Law (Zhengfa Luntan)* 20, no. 4 (2002): 146-52.

Shiming Zhang, "Re-Examination of Abolishing Consular Jurisdiction," *Frontiers L. China* 10, no. 2 (2015): 343-64.

Weiping Zhang, "Restatement of China's Principle of Debate in Civil Litigation," *Legal Research (Cass J.L.)* 18, no. 6 (1996): 46-56.

Cui Zhou, "Research for Behaviour Preservation: Interpretation of Articles 100-105 in Civil Procedure Law," *Science of Law (Journal of Northwest University of Political Science and Law)* 33, no. 4 (2015): 92-106.

A.A. S. Zuckerman, "Quality and Economy in Civil Procedure - The Case for Commuting Correct Judgements for Timely Judgments," *Oxford J. of Legal Stud.* 14, no. 3 (1994): 353-88.

Monographs

Yunteng Hu, "The Constructing Cases Guidance System with Chinese Characteristics Exclusive Interview of Dr. Hu, Yunteng, Member of Judicial Committee and the Director of the Research Office in Supreme People's Court," *China L.*, no. 1 (2011): 4-6,58-60.

Linxia Liang, *Delievering Justice in Qing China: Civil Trials in Magistrate's Courts*, British Academy Post-Doctoral Fellowships Monograph (London: British Academy, 2008).

Papers presented at Conference

Jianfu Chen, "Civil Codification and Foreign Influence in China - Towards China's Own Civil Code," *Culture, Law and Order: Chinese and Western Traditions, Macao Ricci Institute* (2004).

Published Conference Proceedings

G. Jr. Hazard, "Civil Litigation without Frontiers- Harmonization and Unification of Civil Code," *World Congress on Procedural Law: Procedural Law on the Threshold of a New Milllenium* (2002), Walter Hans Rechberger and Thomas KlickaWien: Manzsche, 2002.

T. Kojima, "Legal Families in Procedural Law Revisited - Report to World Congress of Procedural Law," *World Conference on Procedural Law (10th) in Transnational Aspects of Procedural Law*, Italo Andolina (Taormina, Italy, 1998).

James R. Maxeiner, "Legal Methods as a Point of Reference for Comparative Studies of Procedural Law," *XIIIth World Congress on Procedural Law,* Salvador -Bahia, 16 to 22 September 2007 (Bahia, Brazil, 2007): 1-13, Http://ssrn.com/abstract=1232579.

Normand J. and K. Kerameus, "Provisional Remedies in Transnational Litigation," World Congress on Procedural Law (10th) in *Transnational Aspects of Procedural Law*, ed. Italo Andolina (Taormina, Italy, 1998).

E. Vescovi, "Improvement of Civil Litigation: Lessons from Administrative Procedures," in *Justice and Efficiency: General Reports and Discussions (Eight World Conference on Procedural Law, Utrecht, 1987)*, ed. W. Wedekind (Kluwer, 1989).

Technical Reports

Lord Chancellor, *Civil Procedure Rules: Practice Directions, Pre-Action Protocols and Forms* (London: HMSO, 2000).

Standing Committee, *Parliamentary Debates: House of Commons Official Report: Civil Procedure Bill* (London: HMSO, 1997).

First Standing Committee on Delegated Legislation. [Civil Procedure (Amendment no 2) Rules 2005.], *Parliamentary Debates: House of Commons Official Report: Civil Procedure (Amendment No 2) Rules 2005* (London: HMSO, 2005).

Third Standing Committee on Delegated Legislation, *Parliamentary Debates: House of Commons Official Report: Draft Civil Procedure (Modification of Enactments) Order 1998* (HMSO, 1998).

Fourth Standing Committee on Delegated Legislation, *Parliamentary Debates: House of Commons Official Report: Draft Civil Procedure (Modification of Crown Proceedings Act 1947) Order 2005* (London: HMSO, 2005).

Lord Evershed, *Committee on Supreme Court Practice and Procedure, Final Report*, Cmd 8878 (1953).

Civil Justice Reform (Hong Kong), *Final Report of the Working Party on Civil Justice Reform* (Hong Kong, 2004). http://www.civiljustice.gov.hk/eng/archives_fr.html>.

J. Hage, "Comparative Law as Method and the Method of Comparative Law," *Maastricht European Private Law Institute Working Paper No. 2014/11* (2014), Www.ssrn.com. www.ssrn.com.

Mark Van Hoecke, "Deep Level Comparative Law," *EUI Working Paper Law No. 2002/13* (2002). www.cadmus.eui.eu/bitstream/handle/1814/191/law02-13pdf?sequence=1.

Peter Middleton, *Review of Civil Justice and Legal Aid*, Report to the Lord Chancellor (London: Lord Chancellor's Department, 1997).

OECD, *What Makes Civil Justice Effective*, OECD Economic Department Policy Notes, No. 18 June 2013 (2013). www.oecd.org/eco/growth/civil%20Justice%20Policy%20note.pdf.

Lord Woolf, *Access to Justice: Final Report to the Lord Chancellor on the Civil Justice System in England and Wales* (London: HMSO, 1996).

Lord Woolf, *Access to Justice: Interim Report to the Lord Chancellor on the Civil Justice System in England and Wales* (London: HMSO, 1995).

Webpages and Blogs

Mark Cohen. "Case Filing" in China's Courts and their Impact on IP cases." Posted on March 24, 2012. Accessed on September 30, 2016. https://chinaipr.com/2012/03/24/case-filing-in-chinas-courts-and-their-impact-on-ip-cases/

Shandong People's Court. "The Application of Judges' Discretionary Power in China (Translated)." Changle County, Shandong Province People's Court. Posted on May 5, 2013. Accessed on July 16, 2015, http://wfclfy.chinacourt.org/article/detail/2013/05/id/954542.shtml

Xin Fu. "Try to Describe the Relation and Difference of Commercial Law, Economy Law and Civil Law." Posted on August 8, 2004. Accessed on June 15, 2016. http://www.law-lib.com/lw/lw_view.asp?no=3507.

RR Geddes. "Purpose and Context in Statutory Interpretation." Accessed on 28 May, 2015. www.judcom.nsw.gov.au/publications/education-monographs-1/monograph4/07_geddes.pdf.

Shu-Shan Guo. "The Discussion About Judges' Discretionary Power in Our Country." Posted on June 30, 2010. Accessed on July 24, 2016. www.66law.cn/domianblog/20248.aspx Dan Harris. "Where to Locate in China? or Why Weifang Isn't Suzhou." Posted on January 1, 2014. Accessed on September 30, 2016. http://chinalawblog.com/2014/01/where-to-locate-in-china-or-why-weifang-isnt-suzhou.html

Dan Harris. "China Litigation and Case Acceptance." Posted in March 24, 2013. Accessed on September 30, 2016. http://www.chinalawblog.com/2012/03/china-litigation-and-case-acceptance.html.

XiangGuo Hu. "The Discretionary Power of Judge in Civil Proceedings and Its Improvements in China (Translated)." China Court Net Bozhou Qiaocheng Channel. Posted on November 6, 2013. Accessed on July 16, 2015, http://www.chinacourt.org/article/detail/2013/11/id/1122865.shtml.

Sun Jin. "On the Practical Level of Judicial Interpretation of the Law - Reasoning Made by Judges in Judgments." Accessed on 22 December 2015. http://www.court.gmw.cn/html/article/201212/28/115659.shtml.

Jie Liu. "Restriction and Guidance on Judges' Discretion (Translated)." China Court net Meishan City Dongpo channel. Posted on May 16, 2013. Accessed on July 24, 2016, http://www.chinacourt.org/article/detail/2013/05/id/959246.shtml

Peggy McInerney. "Modern Legal in China is Only 35 Years Old." UCLA Int'l Institute. Posted on January 28, 2014. Accessed on April 12, 2016. http://web.international.ucla.edu/Institute/article/136768.

T.J. Scott. "The Comparative Method of Legal Research." Accessed on April 21, 2015. http://italeem.iium.edu.my/2014.

Richard W. Wigley and Xu Jing. "Evidence Collection and Alternatives to Discovery in PRC Litigation." Posted on April 15, 2011. Accessed on December 22, 2015, www.chinalawinsight.com/2011/04/articles/dispute-resolution/evidence-collection-and-alternatives-to-discovery-in-prc-litigation.

UNDROIT. "Principles of Transnational Civil Procedure." UNIDROIT (as adopted and promulgated by). Updated September 27, 2016, accessed on March 20, 2016 and October 30, 2016. http://www.unidroit.org/instruments/transnational-civil-procedure, accessed many times between April-November 2016.

Dissertations

Chen, Nanjun. "The Schism of the Legislation of Civil- Commercial Law: The Rational Choice of Legislation of Commercial Law in China," Ph.D. Thesis, Huaqiao University, Quanzhou, 2007.

Table I - Primary & Secondary Legislation of England & Wales

表 I - 英格兰和威尔士的一级和次级立法

Official Secrets Act 1920, c 75

《官方保密法》（1920 年），第 75 条

Access to Justice Act 1999, c 22

1999 年《诉诸司法法》，第 22 条

Bill of Rights 1689, 1 William & Mary Sess 2, c 2

1689 年《权利法案》，1 William & Mary Sess 2, c 2

Children Act 1989, c 41

1989 年《儿童法》，c 41

Civil Procedural Rules 1998, SI 1998/3132 (as amended Until August 2016), L.17

《1998 年民事诉讼程序规则》，SI 1998/3132（修订至 2016 年 8 月），L.17

Civil Procedure (Amendment No. 3) Rules 2016, No. 788, L.11

2016 年《民事诉讼程序（第 3 号修正案）规则》，第 788 号，L.11

Civil Procedure Act 1997, c 12

1997 年《民事诉讼法》，c 12

Civil Procedure Rules 1998, No. 3132, L.17

1998 年《民事诉讼程序规则》，第 3132 号，第 17L 条

Employment Act 1988, c 19

1988 年就业法》，第 19 条

Evidence (Proceedings in Other Jurisdictions) Act 1975, c 34

证据（其他司法管辖区的诉讼）法 1975，c 34

Habeas Corpus Act 1679, 31 Cha. 2. 2

1679 年人身保护法》，31 Cha. 2. 2

Human Rights Act 1998, c 42

1998 年《人权法》，第 42 条

Interpretation Act 1978, c 30

1978 年《解释法》，c 30

Judicature Act 1925, 15 & 16 Geo 5 c 49

1925 年《司法法》，15 和 16 Geo 5 c 49

Land Registration Act 1925, c 21, 15 and 16 Geo 5 (repealed)

1925 年土地注册法》，c 21，15 和 16 Geo 5（已废除）

Law Commission Report on Interpretation of Statutes 1969, LC 021

1969 年法律委员会关于成文法解释的报告，LC 021

Magna Carta (1215)

大宪章》（1215 年）

Official Secrets Act 1920, c 75

官方保密法》1920 年，第 75 条

Petition of Right 1628, 3 Car 1 c 1

权利请愿书 1628，3 Car 1 c 1

Refreshment Houses Act 1860, c27

1860 年《茶馆法》，c27

Rules of Supreme Court ("RSC") 1883

最高法院规则（"RSC"）1883

Supreme Court of Judicature Act 1873, 36 & 37 Vict, c 66

1873 年最高法院法》，36 & 37 Vict, c 66

Supreme Court of Judicature Act 1875, 38 & 39 Vict, c 77

1875 年《最高法院法》, 38 & 39 Vict, c 77

The Act of Settlement of 1701, 12 and 13 Will 3 c 2

Tribunals, Courts and Enforcement Act 2007, c 15

1701 年《和解法》，12 和 13 Will 3 c 2

2007 年法庭、法院和执行法》，c 15

Table II - International Legislations

表 II - 国际立法

UN Bodies

联合国机构

International Convention on Civil and Political rights of the United Nations 1966

联合国 1966 年《公民权利和政治权利国际公约》

Statute of International Court of Justice 1945

1945 年国际法院规约

UNICTRAL Model Law on International Commercial Arbitration 1985 (as amended in 2006)

1985 年《贸易法委员会国际商事仲裁示范法》(经 2006 年修订)

UNIDROIT/ALI Principles of Transnational Civil Procedure 2004

2004 年国际统一私法协会/法律协会跨国民事诉讼程序原则

United States

美国

7th Amendment to the US Constitution, as adopted in 1792

美国《宪法》第七修正案，1792 年通过

Bill of Rights 1791

1791 年《人权法案》

Federal Rules of Civil Procedure 1938

1938 年《联邦民事诉讼程序规则》

The United States Declaration of Independence 1776

1776 年美国独立宣言

The US Constitution 1789

1789 年美国宪法

Australia

澳大利亚

Interpretation Act 1901, a few insertions by the Statute Law Revision Act 1981

1901 年《解释法》，1981 年《成文法修订法》增加了一些内容

Statute Law Revision Act 1981

1981 年成文法修订法

Supreme Court Civil Rules 2006

最高法院民事规则 2006

Supreme Court Rules 1987 (superseded by 2006 Rules)

1987 年《最高法院规则》（被 2006 年规则取代）

European Union

欧盟

European Communities Act 1972

1972 年欧洲共同体法

European Convention of Human Rights 1950, effective from 1953

1950 年《欧洲人权公约》，1953 年生效

European Court of Human Rights 1998

1998 年欧洲人权法院

France

法国

Amendment to Code de procedure civile (France), Art 11 in 1972

1972 年《民事诉讼法》第 11 条修正案（法国）

Code of civil procedure was adopted in 1806. (France)

民事诉讼法》于 1806 年通过。法国

French Code de Procédure Pénale (as on 5 June 2016)

法国《刑事诉讼法典》（2016 年 6 月 5 日）

French Code of Civil Procedure 2007

2007 年法国民事诉讼法

Nouveau Code de procedure civile 1975 (France)

1975 年新《民事诉讼法》（法国）

Germany

德国

German Strafprozessordnung 1987 (as amended in 2014)

1987 年《德国刑事诉讼法》（2014 年修订）

German Zivilprozessordnung 1877

1877 年德国民事诉讼法

German Zivilprozessordnung 2005 (as amended in 2013)

2005 年《德国民事诉讼法》（2013 年修订）

Greek

希腊

Greek Civil Code 1834

希腊《民法典》1834 年

Norway

挪威

The Dispute Act 2005

2005 年《争议法

Table III – People's Republic of China ("PRC's") Primary Legislation (translated)

表 III - 中华人民共和国（"中国"）的主要立法（译文）

Abolition of the Six Laws of the Kuomintang Regime and the Establishment of the Judicial Principle in the Liberated Areas (Feichu Guomindang de Liufa Quanshu yu Queli Jiefangqu de Sifa Yuanze de Zhishi) 1949

废除国民党政权的"六法全书"和确立解放区的司法原则》1949 年

Administrative Litigation Law 1989

1989 年行政诉讼法

Arbitration Law 1995

1995 年仲裁法

Civil Procedure Law (Trial Basis) 1982

民事诉讼法（审判依据）1982

Civil Procedure Law 1991 Order No. 44

1991 年民事诉讼法》第 44 号命令

Civil Procedure Law 2012, Order No. 59 of the President of the PRC

2012 年民事诉讼法，中华人民共和国主席令第 59 号

Civil Procedure Law 2023, Order No. 44 of the President of the PRC

2023 年民事诉讼法，中华人民共和国主席令第 44 号

Constitution of PRC 1954

1954 年中华人民共和国宪法

Constitution of PRC 1975

1975 年中华人民共和国宪法

Constitution of PRC 1978

1978 年中华人民共和国宪法

Constitution of PRC 1982, as amended in 1987, 1993 and 1997, 2004 and 2018

1982 年《中华人民共和国宪法》，1987 年、1993 年、1997 年、2004 年和 2018 年修订

Contract Law, 1999

合同法，1999 年

Criminal Law of the People's Republic of China, 1997

中华人民共和国刑法，1997 年

Criminal Procedure Code 1979

1979 年刑事诉讼法

Decision of the Standing Committee of the National People's Congress on Revising the "Civil Procedure Law of the PRC", Order No. 59 of the President of the PRC promulgated on 31 August 2012, effective from 1 January 2013

全国人民代表大会常务委员会关于修改《中华人民共和国民事诉讼法》的决定，中华人民共和国主席令第 59 号，2012 年 8 月 31 日公布，自 2013 年 1 月 1 日起施行

Decree for Law Reform, 11 March 1902

法律改革法令，1902 年 3 月 11 日

First Amendments to Civil Procedure Law 1991, 28 October 2007

1991 年《民事诉讼法》第一修正案，2007 年 10 月 28 日

First Common Programme of the Chinese People's Political Consultative Congress 1949

中国人民政治协商会议第一届共同纲领 1949 年

First Constitution together with Organic Law of People's Courts 1954

1954 年第一部宪法和人民法院组织法

General Provision of Civil Law (*Minfa tongze*) in 1986 as revised by Decision of the Standing Committee of the National People's Congress on Revising Certain Laws 2009

根据 2009 年《全国人民代表大会常务委员会关于修改部分法律的决定》修订的 1986 年《民法通则

Imperial Constitution Outline (*Qinding Xianfa Dagang*) 1908

帝国宪法大纲》（清廷宪法大纲） 1908 年

Interim Organic Regulation of People's Courts 1953

1953 年人民法院暂行组织条例

Interim Organic Regulation of the Supreme People's Procuratorate 1953

1953 年最高人民检察院暂行组织条例

Law of Legislation of PRC 2000 (as revised in 2015)

2000 年《中华人民共和国立法法》（2015 年修订）

Law on Judges 1995, and amended by the 22nd Convention of the 9th National People's Congress on 30 June 2001

1995 年《法官法》，并经 2001 年 6 月 30 日第九届全国人民代表大会第 22 次会议修订

Law on the Application of Laws of Civil Relations with Foreign Aspects, 2010

涉外民事关系法律适用法，2010 年

Measures of Handling Disputes among People 1990

1990 年处理人民之间争端的措施

Notarization Law of PRC 2005

中华人民共和国公证法 2005

Organic General Principles of People's Procuratorates 1953

1953 年人民检察院组织通则

Organic Law of People's Courts of the PRC 1979 (as amended in 1983)

1979 年《中华人民共和国人民法院组织法》（1983 年修订）

Organic Law of People's Courts 1954

1954 年人民法院组织法

Organic Law of People's Procuratorates 1954

1954 年人民检察院组织法

Organic Law of the PRC 1979 (as amended in 1983)

1979 年《中华人民共和国组织法》（1983 年修订）

Organic Rules for People's Mediation Committees, 1989

人民调解委员会组织规则，1989 年

Property Law 2007

物权法 2007

Resolution of the NPCSC on Statutory Interpretations 1955

全国人大常委会关于 1955 年法定解释的决议

Resolution on Strengthening the Work of Legal Interpretation, para. 2, adopted on 10th June 1981 by the Standing Committee of the Fifth NPC at its 19th Session

1981 年 6 月 10 日第五届全国人大常委会第十九次会议通过的《关于加强法律解释工作的决议》第 2 段

Rules of Paying Litigation Costs (Order No. 481 of the State Council of the PRC 2007

诉讼费用交纳办法》（中华人民共和国国务院令 2007 年第 481 号

Second Amendments to Civil Procedure Law 1991, 31 August, 2012

1991 年民事诉讼法第二次修正案，2012 年 8 月 31 日

The Law on Lawyers 2008

2008 年律师法

The Law on Procurators, passed through the 12th Convention of the Standing Committee of the 8th National People's Congress on 28 February 1995 and amended by the 22nd Convention of the 9th National People's Congress on 30 June, 2001

1995 年 2 月 28 日第八届全国人民代表大会常务委员会第十二次会议通过、2001 年 6 月 30 日第九届全国人民代表大会常务委员会第二十二次会议修订的《检察官法》。

Treaty of Commerce and Navigation Renewed between China and Britain (also called Mackay Treaty), 5 September, 1902

中英续订通商航海条约》（又称《麦加条约》），1902 年 9 月 5 日

Work Report of the 10th Standing Committee of the National People's Congress of 8 March, 2008

2008 年 3 月 8 日第十届全国人民代表大会常务委员会工作报告

Table IV – PRC's Supreme People's Court – Provisions & Circulars, Interpretations, Replies & Opinions

表 IV - 中华人民共和国最高人民法院 - 规定与通知、解释、答复与意见

Provisions & Circulars

规定和通告

Basic Professional Ethics for Judges, Document Issued by the Supreme People's Court of China, on 18 October 2001

法官职业道德基本准则》, 中国最高人民法院 2001 年 10 月 18 日发布的文件

Decision of the Supreme People's Court on Adjusting Ordinal Numbers of Articles of the "Civil Procedure Law of the PRC" cited in Documents Including the Judicial Interpretation, *Fa Shi* [2008] No. 18

最高人民法院关于调整〈中华人民共和国民事诉讼法〉条文序号的决定》，转引自司法解释等文件, 法释[2008]18 号。

Detailed Rules of Implementation of the Provisions of the Supreme People's Court on Case Guidance Work, *Fa Fa* [2015] No. 130

最高人民法院关于案例指导工作的规定实施细则》，法发[2015]130 号

Outline of Five-year Reform (referred to here as Five-year Outline), Document Issued by the Supreme People's Court, [1999] No. 28, October 20, 1999

五年改革纲要》（以下简称《五年纲要》），最高人民法院发文[1999]28 号，1999 年 10 月 20 日

Promulgation of the Amended Regulations on Causes of Action in Civil Cases, *Fa* [2011] No. 42, February 18, 2011

民事案件诉讼理由规定（修订）》, 法[2011]42 号, 2011 年 2 月 18 日颁布

SPC's Regulation Regarding the Institution of the Procedure of Civil Cases 1979

1979 年最高人民法院关于民事案件诉讼程序的规定

SPC's Guidelines in relation to the application of Civil Procedure Act, *Fa Fa* [1992] No. 22

最高人民法院关于适用《民事诉讼法》的指导意见, 法发[1992]第 22 号

SPC's Summary of Experience of Civil Trial 1956

最高人民法院 1956 年民事审判经验总结

Certain Provisions of the Supreme People's Court on Issues Concerning the Application of Law in the Hearing of Patent Dispute Cases 2001, *Fa Shi* [2001] No. 20

最高人民法院关于审理专利纠纷案件适用法律问题的若干规定 2001》，法释[2001]20 号

Circular of the Supreme People's Court on the Issuance of the Document Samples for the Certain Rules for Evidence in Civil Procedures, *Fa Fa* [2003] No. 2, 1 September, 2003

最高人民法院关于印发《民事诉讼证据若干规定》文件样本的通知，法发[2003]2 号，2003 年 9 月 1 日

Several Provisions on Judicial Interpretation Work (*Guanyu Sifa Jieshi Gongzuo de Ruogan Guiding*) 2007, *Fa Fa* [2007] No. 12

关于司法解释工作的若干规定》，2007 年，法发[2007]12 号。

Some Provisions of Supreme People's Court on Evidence in Civil Procedures, [No. 33 of 2011] (as Revised)

最高人民法院关于民事诉讼证据的若干规定》[2011 年第 33 号]（修订本）

Some Provisions of the Supreme People's Court on Evidence in Civil Procedures] (promulgated by the Sup. People's Court, 21 December 2001, effective 1 April 2002) (as revised by the Decision of the Supreme People's Court on Adjusting Ordinal Numbers of Articles of the "Civil Procedure Law of the PRC", cited in documents including the Judicial Interpretation promulgated on 16 December, 2008

最高人民法院关于民事诉讼证据的若干规定]（2001 年 12 月 21 日最高人民法院公布，2002 年 4 月 1 日起施行 (最高人民法院关于民事诉讼证据的若干规定] (2001 年 12 月 21 日最高人民法院公布，2002 年 4 月 1 日起施行）（根据《最高人民法院关于调整〈中华人民共和国民事诉讼法〉条文序号的决定》修改，2008 年 12 月 16 日公布的司法解释等文件引用

Provisions of the Supreme People's Court on Evidence in Civil Procedures, promulgated, *Fa Shi* [2001] No. 33, adopted at the 1201st session of the Judicial Committee of the Supreme People's Court on 6 December 2001, and effective as of 1 April, 2002

最高人民法院关于民事诉讼证据的若干规定》，2001 年 12 月 6 日最高人民法院审判委员会第 1201 次会议通过，发布，法释[2001]33 号，自 2002 年 4 月 1 日起施行。

Provisions on Case Guidance 2010, *Fa Fa* [2010] No. 51.

2010 年案例指导规定，法发[2010]51 号。

Provisions of the Supreme People's Court on Several Issues concerning the Hearing of Cases by Circuit Courts, *Fa Shi* [2015] No. 3

最高人民法院关于巡回法庭审理案件若干问题的规定》，法释〔2015〕3 号

Provisions of the Supreme People's Court on Several Issues concerning the Registration-based Filing of Cases by People's Courts, *Fa Shi* [2015] No. 8, effective from 1 May 2015

最高人民法院关于人民法院实行立案登记制若干问题的规定》，法释〔2015〕8 号，自 2015 年 5 月 1 日起施行

Provisions on Several Issues concerning the Handling of Property Preservation Cases by the People's Courts, and it came into force on December 1, 2016, *Fa Shi* [2016] No. 22

关于人民法院办理财产保全案件若干问题的规定》，2016 年 12 月 1 日起施行，法释〔2016〕22 号

Interpretations

释义

Interpretation of Several Issues concerning the Implementation of Contract Law of 1999

关于执行《1999 年合同法》若干问题的解释

Interpretation of the Securities Law of 2001

2001 年《证券法》释义

Interpretation of the Supreme People's Court on the Applicability of the Civil Procedure Law of the PRC, 2015, Fa Shi [2015] No. 5, as adopted by the Judicial Committee of the Supreme People's Court at its 1636th session on December 18, 2014, and are hereby issued and shall come into force as from February 4, 2015

2015 年《最高人民法院关于适用〈中华人民共和国民事诉讼法〉的解释》（法释〔2015〕5 号）已由最高人民法院审判委员会 2014 年 12 月 18 日第 1636 次会议通过，现予发布，自 2015 年 2 月 4 日起施行

Interpretations of the Supreme People's Court on Several Issues concerning the Application of Law in the Trial of Criminal Cases of Refusing to Enforce Judgments or Rulings, *Fa Shi* [2015] No. 16 promulgated on 20 July, 2015 and effective from 22 July 2015

最高人民法院关于审理拒不执行判决、裁定刑事案件适用法律若干问题的解释》，法释〔2015〕16 号，2015年7月20日公布，自2015年7月22日起施行

Supreme People's Court on the Work of Judicial Interpretation [1997], *Fa Fa* [1997] No. 15

最高人民法院关于司法解释工作的意见[1997]，法释[1997]15 号

Replies

回复

Reply of the Supreme People's Court on How to Understand Paragraph 2 of Article 31 of the Opinions on Certain Issues Concerning the Application of the Civil Procedure Law of the People's Republic of China, *Fa Shi* [1998] No. 5

最高人民法院关于如何理解《关于适用〈中华人民共和国民事诉讼法〉若干问题的意见》第三十一条第二款的批复，法释[1998]5 号

Reply of the Supreme People's Court on How to Understand Paragraph 2 of Article 31 of the Opinions on Certain Issues Concerning the Application of the Civil Procedure Law of the PRC., Fa Shi [1998], No. 5, adopted at 2 April 1998 in a *Reply* to Shangxi People's Court

最高人民法院关于如何理解〈关于适用〈中华人民共和国民事诉讼法〉若干问题的意见〉第 31 条第 2 款的批复》，法释[1998]5 号，1998 年 4 月 2 日通过，批复商西人民法院

Opinions

意见

Guiding Opinions of the Supreme People's Court on Several Issues Concerning Trial of Cases on Disputes over Civil and Commercial Contracts in the Current Situation, *Fa Fa* [2009] No. 40

最高人民法院关于当前形势下审理民商事合同纠纷案件若干问题的指导意见》，法发[2009]40 号

Opinions of Supreme Court on Several Issues concerning the Implementation of the General Principle of the Civil Law of the PRC (For Trial Implementation), 1988

最高法院关于贯彻执行《中华人民共和国民法通则》若干问题的意见（试行），1988 年

Opinions of the Supreme People's Court on Some Issues Concerning the Application of the Civil Procedure Law of the People's Republic of China, 1992

最高人民法院关于适用《中华人民共和国民事诉讼法》若干问题的意见，1992 年

Opinions on Certain Issues Concerning the Application of the Civil Procedure Law by the Supreme People's Court, *Zhu Shi* [2015] No. 5, adopted by the Judicial Committee of the Supreme People's Court at its 1636th session on 18 December 2014

2014 年 12 月 18 日最高人民法院审判委员会第 1636 次会议通过的《关于最高人民法院适用〈民事诉讼法〉若干问题的意见》，法释[2015]5 号

Opinions on Several Issues concerning the Implementation of General Principals of Civil Law of 1988

关于贯彻执行 1988 年《民法通则》若干问题的意见

Opinions on the Implementation of the People's Courts of the Reform concerning the Case-filing Registration System (the "Opinions"), stipulating that regarding case filings, the current review system shall be changed to a registration system as of 1 May, 2015

关于人民法院推行立案登记制改革的实施意见》（以下简称《意见》），规定在立案方面，自 2015 年 5 月 1 日起，将现行的立案审查制改为立案登记制

Supreme People's Court on Issuing Several Opinions on Further Implementing the Work Principle of "Giving Priority to Mediation and Combining Mediation with Judgment", *Fa Fa* No. 16 [2010] of Supreme People's Court

最高人民法院关于印发进一步贯彻"调解优先、调判结合"工作原则的若干意见》，最高人民法院法发[2010]16 号

Opinions of the Supreme People's Court on Comprehensively Deepening the Reform of PRC, *Fa Fa* [2015] No. 3, effective from 2 April, 2015

最高人民法院关于全面深化改革若干问题的意见》，法发[2015]3 号，2015 年 4 月 2 日起施行

Table V – Table of Cases from England & Wales
表 V - 英格兰和威尔士案例表

Adler v George [1964] 2QB 7

Air Canada v Secretary of State for Trade (No 2) [1983] 2 AC 394

Allen v Thorn Electrical Industries Ltd (1968) 1 QB 481 (CA)

American Cyanamid Co v Ethicon Ltd No (1) [1975] AC 396; [1975] 2 WLR 316; [1975] 1 All ER 504; [1975] FSR 101; [1975] RPC 513; (1975) 119 SJ 136 (HL)

Anton Piller KG v Manufacturing Processes Ltd [1976] Ch 55; [1976] 2 WLR 162; [1976] 1 All ER 779; [1976] FSR 129; [1976] RPC 719; (1975) 120 SJ 63 CA (Civ Div)

B v B [2005] EWCA Civ 237

Biguzzi v Rank Leisure [1999] 1 WLR 1926 (CA)

Brandling v Barrington (1827) 6 B & C 467

Bromley LBC v Greater London Council [1983] 1 AC 768

Cayne v Global Natural Resource Plc [1984]1 All ER 225

Chambers v British Olympic Association (2008) LTL 18 July 2008; [2008] EWHC 2028

City and Country Properties Ltd v Kamali [2007] 1 WLR 1219

Clipper Maritime Co Ltd v Mineralimportexport [1981] 1 WLR 1262

Corocraft Ltd v Pan American Airways Inc [1968] 3 WLR714

Davies v Eli Lilly and Co [1987] 1 WLR 428

ED & F Man Liquid Products Ltd v Patel [2003] EWCA Civ 472; [2003] CPLR 384

English v Emery Reimbold and Strick Ltd [2002] EWCA Civ 605; [2002] 1 WLR 2409; [2002] CPLR 520; [2002] 3 All ER 385

First Subsea Ltd v Balltec Ltd [2013] EWHC 1033; [2013] All ER (D) 214 (Apr)

Garratt v Saxby [2004] EWCA Civ 341

The Glandarroch [1894] P266

Goode v Martin, Times, 24th January 2002

Grey v Pearson (1857) 6 HL Cas 61 106

ITC Film Distributors v Video Exchange [1982] 2 All ER 246

Jones v National Coal Board [1957] 2 QB 55

Joseph Constantine Steamship Line Ltd v Imperial Smelting Corp Ltd [1942] AC 154

Lansing Linde Ltd v Kerr [1991] 1 WLR 251; [1991] 1 All ER 418

Law v St Margarets Insurance Ltd [2001] EWCA Civ 30, 18th January 2001.

Leisure Data v Bell [1988] FSR 367 (CA)

Lichter v Rubin [2008] EWHC 450 (Ch), The Times, 18th April 2008

London Street Tramways v London County Council [1898] AC 375

Magistrates and Town Council of Glasgow v Commissioners of Police of Hillhead (1885) 12 R. 864

Magor and St Mellons Rural District Council v Newport Council [1952] AC 189; [1951] 2 All ER 839

Medcalf v Mardell Weatherill UKHL 27 [2002] 3 All ER 731; [2003] 1 AC 120; [2002] NPC 89; [2002] PNLR 43; [2002] 3 WLR 172; [2002] CP Rep 70; [2002] CPLR 647; [2002] 3 Costs LR 428

Miller v Minister of Pensions [1947] 2 All ER 372

Morris and Others v The Crown Office [1970] 2 QB 114

Muir v Keay LR 10 (1875) QBD 594

Pepper (Her Majesty's Inspector of Taxes) v Hart [1992] UKHL 3; [1993] AC 593

Phoenix Partners Group LLP v Asoyag [2010] IRLR 594

Practice Direction (Citation of Authorities) [2001] 1 WLR 2001

Practice Statement [1966] 3 All ER 77, [1966] 1WLR 1234

Prince of Wales v Associated Newspapers Ltd [2006] EWCA Civ 1776; [2008] Ch 57

Purdy v Cambran [2000] CP Rep 67

R v Harris (1836) 7 C & P 446

R v The Judge of the City of London Court [1892] 1 QB 273 (CA)

Re B (children) (care proceedings: standard of proof) [2008] UKHL 35; [2009] AC 11; [2008] 3 WLR 1; [2009] 1 AC 11; [2008] 4 All ER 1; [2008] 2 FLR 141; [2008] 2 FCR 339; [2008] Fam Law 619; [2008] UKHL 35; [2008] Fam Law 837

Re H and others (Minors) (A.P.) (Respondents) [1995] UK HL16

River Wear Commissioners v Adamson (1877) 2 App Cas 743

Southwark LBC v Maamefowaa Koadu [2006] EWCA Civ 281

Swain v Hillman [2001] 1 All ER 91

Tempest v Kilner (1846) 3 CB 249

Walsh v Misseldine [2000] CP Rep

Table VI – Abbreviations

表 VI - 缩写

Table VI-1 – Abbreviations of Journals

表 VI-1 - 期刊缩写

Journal	Abbreviation	Journal	Abbreviation
Akron Law Review 阿克伦法律评论	Akron L. Rev.	Harvard Journal of Law and Public Policy 哈佛法律与公共政策杂志	Harv. J. L. & Pub. Pol'y
Alabama Law Review 阿拉巴马法律评论	Ala. L. Rev.	Harvard Law Review 哈佛法律评论	Harv. L. Rev.
American Bar Association 美国律师协会	A.B.A.	Hong Kong Law Journal 香港法律杂志	Hong Kong L.J.
American Journal of Comparative Law 美国比较法杂志	Am. J. Comp. L.	Indiana Law Journal 印第安纳法律杂志	Ind. L. J.
American Law and Economic Review 美国法律与经济评论	Am. L. & Econ. Rev.	Informal Logic 非正式逻辑	Informal Logic
Archiv für rechts - und Sozialphilosophie 法律和社会哲学档案	ARSP	International & Comparative Law Quarterly 国际法与比较法季刊	I.C.L.Q.
Australian Bar Review 澳大利亚律师协会评论	Australian Bar Rev.	International Business Law 国际商业法	Int'l Bus. L.
Bond Law Review 债券法评论	Bond L. Rev.	International Business Lawyer 国际商务律师	Int'l Bus. Law.
Boston College International and Comparative Law Review 波士顿学院国际与比较法评论	B.C. Int'l & Comp. L. Rev.	Israel Law Review 以色列法律评论	Israel L. Rev.
Cambridge Law Review 剑桥法律评论	C.L.R.	Journal of Chinese University of Political Science 中国政法大学学报	J. of CUPL
Case Western Reserve Journal of International Law 凯斯西储国际法杂志	Case W. Res. J. Int'l L.	Journal of Comparative Law 比较法杂志	J. Comp. L.
Chengdu Speed Reading 成都速读	Chengdu Speed Reading	Journal of Institutional and Theoretical Economics 制度与理论经济学杂志	J. of Inst. And Theoretical Econ.
China Journal 中国日报	China J.	Journal of Law Application 法律应用期刊	J. L. App.
China Legal Science 中国法律科学	China Legal Science	Journal of Law 法律杂志	Falv Shiyong
China Review 中国评论	China Rev.	Journal of North China University of Technology 华北理工大学学报	Journal of N. China u. Tech

Chinese Journal of Law 中国法学杂志	Faxue Yanjiu	Journal of North Western University (Philosophy and Social Science Edition) 西北大学学报（哲学社会科学版）	J. No. West. U. (P. & So. Sc.)
Civil Justice Quarterly 民事司法季刊	C.J.Q.	Journal of Northwest University of Political Science and Law 西北政法大学学报	J. Of Northwest U of Pol. Sc. L.
Commonwealth Law Bulletin 英联邦法律公报	Comm. Legal Bulletin	Journal of Political Science and Law 政治学与法学杂志	J. Political Sc. L.
Comparative & International Law Journal of South Africa 南非比较与国际法期刊	Comp. & Int'l L.J. S.Afr.	Journal of South West University of Political Science and law 西南政法大学学报	J. South West U. of Pol. Sc. & L.
Cornell International Law Journal 康奈尔国际法杂志	Cornell Int'l L.J.	Law and History Law Review 法律与历史法律评论	Law & Hist. Rev.
Cornell Law Review 康奈尔法律评论	Cornell L. Rev.	Law and Social Development 法律与社会发展	Fazhi Yu Shehui Fazhan
Electronic Journal of Comparative Law 比较法电子期刊	Electronic J. Comp. L.	Law Review of Wuhan University 武汉大学法律评论	Law Review
Frontiers Laws of China 中国前沿法律	Frontiers. L. China	Legal System and Social Development 法律制度与社会发展	Legal Sys. & Soc. Dev.
Gansu Social Science 甘肃社会科学	Gansu. So. Sc.	Legal System and Society 法律制度与社会	Legal Sys. & Soc.
Global Jurist Frontiers 全球法学家前沿	GJF	Max Planck Institute for Research on Collective Goods 马克斯-普朗克集体财产研究所	MPI Collective Goods

Journal	Abbreviation	Journal	Abbreviation
Max Planck Institute for Research on Collective Goods 马克斯-普朗克集体财产研究所	MPI Collective Goods	The Litigator 诉讼律师	The Litigator
Michigan Journal of International Law 密歇根国际法杂志	Mich. J. Int'l L.	T'Oung Pao 通报	T'Oung Pao
Modern Law Science (Southwest University of Political Science) 现代法学（西南政法大学）	Modern L. Science	Tribune of Political Science 政治学论坛报	Zhengfa Luntan
Monash Law Review 莫纳什法律评论	Monash L. Rev.	Tsinghua China Law Review 清华中国法律评论	Tsinghua China L. Rev.

Monash University Law Review 莫纳什大学法律评论	Monash. U. L. Rev.	Tulane Journal of International and Comparative Law 杜兰国际法和比较法杂志	Tul. J. Int'l & Com. L.
Northwest Journal of Technology and Intellectual Property 西北技术与知识产权	Northwest J Tech. & Intellectual	Tulane Law Review 杜兰法律评论	Tul. L. Rev.
Oxford Journal of Legal Studies 牛津法律研究杂志	Oxford J. of Legal Stud.	Tulsa Law Journal 塔尔萨法律杂志	Tulsa L.J.
Oxford University Commonwealth Law Journal 牛津大学英联邦法律杂志	Oxf. U. Comm. L.J.	UC Davis Journal of International Law and Policy 加州大学戴维斯分校国际法与政策期刊	U.C. Davis J. Int'l L. & Pol'y
Pacific Rim Law & Policy Journal 环太平洋法律与政策期刊	Pacific Rim L. & Pol. J.	UCLA International Institute 加州大学洛杉矶分校国际学院	UCLA Int'l Inst.
Peking University Law Journal 北京大学法学院学报	Peking U. L.J.	UCLA Law Review 加州大学洛杉矶分校法律评论	UCLA L. Rev.
Philosophy and Rhetoric 哲学与修辞学	Phi. & Rh.	University of Detroit Mercy Law Review 底特律大学法律评论	U. Det. Mercy. L. Rev.
Rand Journal of Economics 兰德经济学杂志	Rand J. Economics	University of Pennsylvania Law Review 宾夕法尼亚大学法律评论	U.PA. L. Rev.
Ritsumeikan Law Review 立命馆法律评论	R.L.R.	Washington and Lee Law Review 华盛顿与李法律评论	Wash. & Lee L. Rev.
Scandinavian Law Review 北欧法律评论	Scandinavian L. Rev.	Washington University Global Studies Law Review 华盛顿大学全球研究法律评论	Wash. U. L. Rev.
Scandinavian Studies in Law 北欧法律研究	Scandinavian Studies L.	Washington University Law Review 华盛顿大学法律评论	Wash. U. L. Rev.
Seton Hall Law Review 塞顿霍尔法律评论	Seton Hall L. Rev.	Willamette Journal of International Law and Dispute Resolution 威拉米特国际法与争端解决期刊	Willeamete J. Int'l L. & Disp. Resol.
Social Sciences in China 中国的社会科学	Zhonguo Shehui Kexue	Yale Law Journal 耶鲁法学杂志	Yale L.J.
Southern Californian Law Review 南加州法律评论	S. Cal. L. Rev.	Yuenan: Legal System and Society 远安：法律制度与社会	Yuenan L. System Society
The Comparative and International Law Journal of Southern Africa 南部非洲比较法和国际法杂志	Comp. & Int'l L.J. S. Afr.	Zeitschrift fü r Zivilprozeß民事诉讼程序杂志	ZZP
The George Washington Law Review 乔治-华盛顿法律评论	Geo.Wash. L. Rev.		

Table VI-2 – Other Abbreviations

表 VI-2 - 其他缩略语

Abbreviation	Full Form	Abbreviation	Full Form
A-G	Attorney General 总检察长	Dept	Department 部门
AC	Appeal Cases 上诉案件	Dir	Directive 指导原则
Affd	Affirmed 维持原判	ECHR	European Court of Human Rights 欧洲人权法院
All ER	All England Reports 全英格兰报告	ER	English Reports 英文报告
ALL ER Rep	All England Law Reports Reprint 全英	EU	European Union 欧盟
Anon	Anonymous 匿名的	EWCA Civ	Neutral Citation Court of Appeal Civil Division 中立引证 上诉法院民事庭
Ann. Rep.	Annual Report 年报	EWHC (Comm)	Neutral Citation, High Court
App	Appendix 附录	EWHC (Admlty)	Neutral Citation High Court (Admiralty) 中立引用 高等法院（海事）
App Cas	Law Reports, Appeal Cases (UK) 法律报告，上诉案例（英国）	EWHC (Ch)	Neutral Citation High Court (Chancery Division) 中立引用 高等法院（大法官法庭）
Art. & Arts.	Article & Articles 文章	EWHC (QB)	Neutral Citation High Court (Queen's Bench Division) 中立引证 高等法院（王座庭）
BCE	Before Common Era 公元前	Fam	Law Reports, Family Division 法律报告，家事法庭
C	Chapter by which the Act is known in a year	FamD	Family Division 家事法庭
CA	Court of Appeal 上诉法院	FLR	Family Law Reports 家庭法报告
CC	County Council 县议会	Fn	Foot Note 脚注
CCR	County Court Rules 县法院规则	FSR	Fleet Street Reports 舰队街报道
CE	Common Era 公元	GB	Great Britain 大不列颠
cf.	Contrast to text 与文本形成对比	HL	House of Lords 上议院
Ch	Law reports of Chancery Division 大法官法庭法律报告	Inc	Incorporated 公司
ch/chs	Chapter/chapters 章节	Lloyd's Rep	Lloyd's Law Reports 劳埃德法律报告
ChD	Chancery Division 大法官法庭	Liq	Liquidation 清算
cl/cls	clause/clauses 条款/分句	LR Ch App	Law Reports, Chancery Appeals Cases 法律报告，大法官上诉案

CLR	Commonwealth Law Reports 英联邦法律报告	Ltd	Limited 有限公司
Co.	Company 公司	n.a.	Not Available 不详
Co-op	Co-operative 合作组织	n.d.	No date 未注明日期
col/cols	Column/columns 栏/列	n.p.	No Publisher 无出版商
Com. L	Commercial Law Reports 商业法报告	Ors	Others 其他
Comr/Comrs	Commissioner/Commissioners 专员/委	Para. & Paras.	Paragraph & Paragraphs 段落
Contra.	Direct Contrast 直接对比	PD	Practice Direction 实践方向
Corp	Corporation 企业	pt/pts	part/parts 部分
CPL	Civil Procedural Law 1991 of PRC (as amended) 中华人民共和国 1991 年民事诉讼法（修订本）	QB	Law Reports, Queen's Bench Division of High Court 高等法院后座法庭法律报告
CPR	Civil Procedural Rules 1998 (as amended), SI1998/3132 1998 年民事诉讼程序规则（修订版）, SI1998/3132	QBD	Queen's Bench Division 王座法庭
DC	District Council 区议会	R	Rex/Regina [The Queen (or King)] 雷克斯/雷吉娜 [王后（或国王）]

Table VI-2 – Other Abbreviations (continued 1)
表 VI-2 - 其他缩略语（续 1）

Abbreviation	Full Form	Abbreviation	Full Form
Reg. & regs.	Regulation & Regulations 规章制度	vol/vols	volume/volumes 容量/体积
RPC	Reports of Patent, Design and Trademark Cases 专利、外观设计和商标案件报告	LR Adm & Eccl	Llyords' Report Admiralty & Ecclesiastical Llyords'Report 海事和教会报告
RSC	Rules of the Supreme Court	DJ	District Judge 地区法官
S	Section 部分	MR	Master of The Rolls 卷轴大师
Sch.	Schedule 时间表	CJ	Lord Chief Justices, Chief Justice of Queen's Bench 首席法官、首席大法官
Sch.	Supreme Court 最高法院	LJ	Lord/Lady Justice of Appeal 上诉法官
sec.	Section 部分	V-C	Vice Chancellor 副校长
UKHL	Neutral Citation, House of Lords 中立引文，上议院	SCJ	Justice of Supreme Court of the United Kingdom 英国最高法院法官
UKPC	Neutral Citation, Privy Council 中性引文，枢密院	Lord	Lord of Appeal 上诉法院院长
WLR	Weekly Law Reports 法律周报	J	Justice of High Court 高等法院法官
		Judge	Circuit Judge 巡回法官

Table VII – PRC RELATED INFORMATION

表 VII - 中国相关信息

Table VII-1 – PRC Publishers

Beijing Law Press	北京法律出版社
China Procuratorate Press	中国检察出版社
Legal Press	法律出版社
Peking University Press	北京大学出版社
People's Court Press	人民法院出版社
People's Public Security University of China Press	中国人民公安大学出版社
Press of China's University of Political Science and Law	中国政法大学出版社
Shanghai Law Translation & Edition Press	上海法学编译出版社
Shanghai People's House	上海人民出版社
Shanxi People's Publisher	山西人民出版社
The Commercial Press	商务印书馆
The Press of Masses	人民出版社
Wunan Book Co. Ltd.	五南文化事业机构
Wunan Book Publisher	五南图书出版社

Table VII – 2 PRC Journals

China Law	中国法律
China Legal Science	中国法学
Chinese Journal of Law / Cass journal of law	法学研究
Frontiers of Law in China	中国法学前沿
Gansu Social Sciences	甘肃社会科学
Jiangsu Economic Weekly	江苏经济报
Journal of Comparative Law	比较法研究
Journal of Hubei University of Police	湖北警官学院学报
Journal of Law Application	法律适用
Journal of Northwest University	西北大学学报
Journal of Political Science and Law	政法学刊
Journal of Southwest University of Political Science and Law	西南政法大学学报
Law and Social Development	法制与社会发展
Law Review	法学评论
Law Science	法学
Law Science Magazine	法学杂志
Legal System and Social Development	法制与社会发展
Legal System and Society	法律制度与社会（云南)
Journal of North China University of Technology	北方工业大学学报
Market Modernization	商场现代化
Modern Law Science	现代法学
Peking University Law Journal	中外法学
Science of Law (Journal of Northwest University of Political Science and Law)	法律科学(西北政法大学学报)
Social Sciences in China	中国社会科学
Speed Reading	速读（成都)
Tribune of Political Science and Law	政法论坛
Tsinghua China Law Review	清华中国法学评论

C

D

E

J

N

O

P

R

S

C

D

E

F

G

H

I

J

K

L

M

N

O

P

www.ingramcontent.com/pod-product-compliance
Ingram Content Group UK Ltd.
Pitfield, Milton Keynes, MK11 3LW, UK
UKHW062002041026
15591UKWH00016B/1133